Sixth Edition

Counseling and Psychotherapy

Theories and Interventions

edited by
David Capuzzi and Mark D. Stauffer

American Counseling Association
6101 Stevenson Avenue, Suite 600
Alexandria, VA 22304
www.counseling.org

Sixth Edition

Counseling and Psychotherapy

Theories and Interventions

American Counseling Association
6101 Stevenson Avenue, Suite 600 ■ Alexandria, VA 22304

Associate Publisher ■ Carolyn C. Baker

Digital and Print Development Editor ■ Nancy Driver

Senior Production Manager ■ Bonny E. Gaston

Copy Editor ■ Beth Ciha

Cover and text design by Bonny E. Gaston.

Library of Congress Cataloging-in-Publication Data

Names: Capuzzi, David, editor. | Stauffer, Mark D., editor.
Title: Counseling and psychotherapy : theories and interventions/edited by David Capuzzi and Mark D. Stauffer.
Description: Sixth edition. | Alexandria, VA : American Counseling Association, [2016] | Includes bibliographical references and index.
Identifiers: LCCN 2015049585 | ISBN 9781556203541 (pbk. : alk. paper)
Subjects: LCSH: Counseling. | Psychotherapy. | Counseling—Case studies. | Psychotherapy—Case studies.
Classification: LCC BF636.6 .C6735 2016 | DDC 158.3—dc23 LC record available at http://lccn.loc.gov/2015049585

Table of Contents

Preface

This sixth edition of *Counseling and Psychotherapy: Theories and Interventions* presents a variety of theories and conceptual frameworks for understanding the parameters of the helping relationship. These parameters can include models for viewing personality development; explaining past behavior; predicting future behavior; understanding the current behavior of the client; diagnosing and planning treatment; assessing client motivations, needs, and unresolved issues; and identifying strategies and interventions for use during the counseling and psychotherapy process.

Theories help organize data and provide guidelines for the prevention and intervention efforts of counselors and therapists. They direct a professional helper's attention and observations and offer constructs, terminology, and viewpoints that can be understood by colleagues and used during supervision and consultation sessions. Theory directly influences the interventions used by counselors and therapists to promote a client's new insight, new behavior, and new approaches to relationships and problem solving. The greater a counselor or therapist's awareness of the strengths and possibilities inherent in numerous theoretical frames of reference, the greater the potential for understanding the uniqueness of a particular client and for developing the most effective treatment plan.

This book is unique in both format and content. All of the contributing authors are experts who provide state-of-the-art information about theories of counseling and psychotherapy (see the "Meet the Contributors" section for their backgrounds). In addition, each chapter discusses applications of theory as they relate to one particular case study: a hypothetical client named Maria to whom we are introduced in the introduction to Part 2. This book also includes information that is sometimes not addressed in other counseling and psychotherapy textbooks, such as the core dimensions of and brief and integrative approaches to the helping relationship, diversity and social justice issues in counseling, feminist theory, dialectical behavior theory, transpersonal theory, constructivist theories, and creative approaches in counseling and psychotherapy. The book's unique approach enhances its readability and should increase reader interest in the material.

FEATURES OF THE TEXT

This book is designed for students who are beginning their study of individual counseling and psychotherapy. It presents a comprehensive overview of each of the following: psychoanalytic, Jungian, Adlerian, existential, person-centered, Gestalt, cognitive behavior, dialectical behavior, and rational emotive behavior theories; reality therapy/choice theory; and family, feminist, transpersonal, constructivist, and creative approaches. Each theory is addressed from the perspective of background, human nature, major constructs, applications (which includes a discussion of the goals of counseling and psychotherapy, the process of change, traditional intervention strategies, and brief intervention strategies), clients with serious mental health issues, cross-cultural considerations, and evaluation (which evaluates both the supporting research and the limitations of the theory). Each discussion also includes a summary chart and a case study consistent with the theoretical model.

We know that one text cannot adequately address all of the factors connected with a given theory; entire texts have been written discussing each of the theories in this book. We have, however, attempted to provide readers with a consistent approach to analyzing and studying each theory and have included examples of how to apply the theory to a case study.

The format for this text is based on the contributions of the coeditors, who conceptualized the content and wrote the first chapter, as well as the contributions of 30 authors selected for their expertise in various theories. Each chapter contains theoretical and applied content. The text is divided into the following three parts: "Foundations for Individual Counseling and Psychotherapy," "Theories of Counseling and Psychotherapy," and "Constructivist Theories and Creative Approaches."

Part 1, "Foundations for Individual Counseling and Psychotherapy" (Chapters 1 and 2), begins by offering general information about the helping relationship and individual counseling as well as information on brief approaches to counseling and psychotherapy. This introductory information is followed by a chapter titled "Diversity and Social Justice Issues in Counseling and Psychotherapy," which sets the stage for developing awareness of the limitations of traditional Western theories and subsequent cross-cultural/diversity discussions.

Part 2, "Theories of Counseling and Psychotherapy" (Chapters 3–15), presents information on the 13 theories selected for inclusion in this portion of the text. Each of these chapters—"Psychoanalytic Theory," "Jungian Analytical Theory," "Adlerian Theory," "Existential Theory," "Person-Centered Theory," "Gestalt Theory," "Cognitive Behavior Theories," "Dialectical Behavior Theory," "Rational Emotive Behavior Therapy," "Reality Therapy/Choice Theory," "Family Theory," "Feminist Theory," and "Transpersonal Theory"—presents the theory and then applies the theory to the case study of Maria.

Part 3, "Constructivist Theories and Creative Approaches," is focused on the fourth force of counseling and psychotherapy and the use of creativity in counseling.

NEW TO THIS EDITION

This edition of our text includes some additional features that we think will be of great interest to readers. Chapter 1 has been updated and also includes a brief discussion on integrative counseling. An updated chapter on diversity and social justice issues in counseling and psychotherapy presents state-of-the-art information and perspectives to counselors who will be practicing with increasingly diverse client populations. Readers should really enjoy the new rendition of the psychoanalytic theory chapter, which now goes beyond a discussion of classical psychoanalysis and includes brief psychodynamic theory, psychodynamic interpersonal theory, and interpersonal psychotherapy. The cognitive–behavioral chapter provides the reader with general background about both behavioral and cognitive behavior theoretical views and discusses how the cognitive behavior approach developed from the behavioral point of view.

The updated chapter on family theory is included to sensitize the reader to the fact that counselors and therapists engaging clients in individual work must keep in mind the systemic variables influencing clients and the fact that some clients may need family counseling and psychotherapy as part of a comprehensive treatment plan.

Completely new to this sixth edition are chapters on constructivist theories and creative approaches to counseling and psychotherapy. Few counseling textbooks of this nature address these conceptual frameworks. We think readers will be stimulated by these features. Finally, professors adopting this text can request the PowerPoint slides and quiz items that have been developed for use with this text.

We, the coeditors, and the 30 other contributors have made every effort to give the reader current information and content focused on both theory and application. It is our hope that this sixth edition of *Counseling and Psychotherapy: Theories and Interventions* will provide the foundation that students need to make decisions about follow-up study of specific theories as well as the development of their own personal theory of counseling and psychotherapy.

Acknowledgments

We would like to thank the authors who contributed their time and expertise to the development of this book for professionals interested in individual counseling and psychotherapy. We also thank our families, who supported and encouraged our writing and editing efforts. Thanks go out to Carolyn Baker and other staff members of the Publications Department of the American Counseling Association for their collaborative and thorough approach to the editing and production of this book.

Special thanks go to Doug Gross, who so expertly and conscientiously served as coauthor and coeditor of the first five editions of this book, which could never have become a reality without his efforts.

Meet the Editors

David Capuzzi, PhD, NCC, LPC, is a counselor educator and member of the core faculty in clinical mental health counseling at Walden University and professor emeritus at Portland State University. Previously he served as an affiliate professor in the Department of Counselor Education, Counseling Psychology, and Rehabilitation Services at The Pennsylvania State University and scholar in residence in counselor education at Johns Hopkins University. He is past president of the American Counseling Association (ACA), formerly the American Association for Counseling and Development, and past chair of both the ACA Foundation and the ACA Insurance Trust.

From 1980 to 1984, Dr. Capuzzi was editor of *The School Counselor.* He has authored a number of textbook chapters and monographs on the topic of preventing adolescent suicide and is coeditor and coauthor with Dr. Larry Golden of *Helping Families Help Children: Family Interventions With School Related Problems* (1986) and *Preventing Adolescent Suicide* (1988). He coauthored and coedited with Douglas R. Gross *Youth at Risk: A Prevention Resource for Counselors, Teachers, and Parents* (1989, 1996, 2000, 2004, 2008, 2014), *Introduction to the Counseling Profession* (1991, 1997, 2001, 2005, 2009, 2013), *Introduction to Group Work* (1992, 1998, 2002, 2006; and with Mark Stauffer in 2010), and *Counseling and Psychotherapy: Theories and Interventions* (1995, 1999, 2003, 2007, 2011; coauthored and coedited with Mark Stauffer in 2016). Other texts are *Approaches to Group Work: A Handbook for Practitioners* (2003), *Suicide Across the Life Span* (2006), and *Sexuality Issues in Counseling* (2002), the last coauthored and coedited with Larry Burlew. He has also coauthored and coedited with Mark Stauffer *Career Counseling: Foundations, Perspectives, and Applications* (2008, 2012) and *Foundations of Addictions Counseling* (2008, 2012, 2016). He has authored or coauthored articles in a number of ACA journals.

A frequent speaker and keynoter at professional conferences and institutes, Dr. Capuzzi has also consulted with a variety of school districts and community agencies interested in initiating prevention and intervention strategies for adolescents at risk for suicide. He has facilitated the development of suicide prevention, crisis management, and postvention programs in communities throughout the United States; provides training on the topics of youth at risk and grief and loss; and serves as an invited adjunct faculty member at other universities as time permits.

An ACA Fellow, he is the first recipient of ACA's Kitty Cole Human Rights Award and is also a recipient of the Leona Tyler Award in Oregon. In 2010, he received ACA's Gilbert and Kathleen Wrenn Award for a Humanitarian and Caring Person. In 2011, he was named a distinguished alumni of the College of Education at Florida State University.

Mark D. Stauffer, PhD, NCC, is a core faculty member in the clinical mental health counseling program at Walden University. He specialized in couples, marriage, and family counseling during his graduate work in the Counselor Education Program at Portland State University, where he received his master's degree. He received his doctoral degree from Oregon State University, Department of Teacher and Counselor Education.

As a clinician, Dr. Stauffer has worked in the Portland Metro Area in Oregon at crisis centers and other nonprofit organizations working with low-income individuals, couples, and families. He has studied and trained in the Zen tradition and presents locally and nationally on meditation and mindfulness-based therapies in counseling. His research focus has centered on Eastern methods and East–West collaboration. In private practice, Dr. Stauffer has worked with couples and families from a family systems perspective.

Dr. Stauffer was a Chi Sigma Iota International Fellow and was awarded the American Counseling Association's Emerging Leaders Training Grant. He recently served as the cochair of the American Counseling Association International Committee.

In addition to this counseling textbook with Dr. David Capuzzi, Dr. Stauffer has coedited several textbooks in the counseling field: *Introduction to Group Work* (2010), *Career Counseling: Foundations, Perspectives, and Applications* (2006, 2012), *Foundations of Addictions Counseling* (2008, 2012, 2016), and *Foundations of Couples, Marriage and Family Counseling* (2015). Dr. Stauffer and Dr. Capuzzi are currently working on a new textbook on human growth and development across the life span to be published by Wiley for use in counselor education programs.

Meet the Contributors

Jonathan W. Carrier, MS, is the assistant director of the Center for Teaching and Learning and a psychology instructor at Laramie County Community College in Cheyenne and Laramie Wyoming. Mr. Carrier has been teaching psychology, statistics, and research methodology courses for the past 9 years and was previously a rehabilitation and mental health counselor for 4 years.

In addition to his roles as an assistant director and college educator, Mr. Carrier also spends time writing scholarly articles, book chapters, and giving presentations in the fields of counseling, psychology, and adult education. His published work focuses on suicide assessment, counseling theory, group work, classroom management skills, and best practices in adult education.

Thelma Duffey, PhD, president of the American Counseling Association (ACA), is a professor and department chair in the Department of Counseling at the University of Texas at San Antonio and owner of a multidisciplinary private practice. Dr. Duffey was the founding president of the Association for Creativity in Counseling, a division within the ACA, and she served two terms on the ACA Governing Council. Dr. Duffey is a past president of the Texas Association for Counselor Education and Supervision and served on the Executive Board of the Southern Association for Counselor Education and Supervision. Dr. Duffey is editor of the *Journal of Creativity in Mental Health* and served as guest coeditor for a *Journal of Counseling & Development* (*JCD*) special issue on counseling men. She is currently coediting a *JCD* special section on relational-cultural theory.

Dr. Duffey, an ACA Fellow, received the Association for Counselor Education and Supervision (ACES) Counseling Vision and Innovation Award, the ACES Distinguished Mentor Award, and the ACA Professional Development Award. Dr. Duffey is a licensed professional counselor, a licensed marriage and family therapist, and a clinical member of the American Association for Marriage and Family Therapy. She has more than 50 publications in the areas of creativity, innovations in grief and loss counseling, relational competencies (relational-cultural theory), and addictions. Her collaborative research project on relational competencies won the 2010 Texas Counseling Association Research Award, and her collaborative publication on assessment practices in counselor education programs received the 2014 American Association of Rehabilitation Counseling/Council of Rehabilitation Counseling Outstanding Outcome Research Award. Her edited book *Creative Interventions in Grief and Loss Therapy: When the Music Stops, a Dream Dies* (2007) was published by the Taylor & Francis Group, and she is coeditor of *A Counselor's Guide to Working With Men* (2014), published by the ACA.

Roxane L. Dufrene, PhD, LPC-S, LMFT, NCC, is an associate professor of counseling in the Department of Educational Leadership, Counseling, and Foundations at the University of New Orleans. She holds a doctorate in counselor education from Mississippi State University and a master's degree in counseling psychology from Nicholls State University. Dr. Dufrene has clinical experience in outpatient and inpatient state mental health treatment, college counseling, crisis intervention, training clinics, collaboration in schools, and private practice.

Dr. Dufrene is a Louisiana-licensed marriage and family therapist, a licensed professional counselor, a licensed professional counselor approved supervisor and a national certified counselor. Dr. Dufrene is also certified in critical incident stress management and psychological first aid, has Louisiana appraisal privilege, and is an American Red Cross mental health counselor. Her research and teaching interests include disaster mental health, crisis counseling, student remediation, counseling ethics, both qualitative and quantitative research in counseling, and supervision.

Cass Dykeman, PhD, is an associate professor of counselor education at Oregon State University. He earned his doctorate in counselor education from the University of Virginia and his master's degree in school counseling from the University of Washington. Before becoming a counselor educator, Dr. Dykeman served as a school counselor in Seattle, Washington.

Dr. Dykeman has served as the principal investigator for two federal grants and is the author of numerous books, book chapters, and scholarly articles in the area of counseling.

Emeline C. Eckart, MS, NCC, is the clinical coordinator for the University of New Orleans Counselor Education Department, in which she oversees the counseling lab and collaborates with the practicum and internship coordinator. She holds a master's degree in mental health counseling from Capella University and is currently a doctoral candidate in the University of New Orleans Counselor Education Program. Ms. Eckart also serves as a lieutenant commander in the U.S. Naval Reserves.

Ms. Eckart's clinical experience includes work in community mental health settings, addiction treatment, court-ordered child custody cases, and private practice. Her research interests include best practices for work with military clients, gender issues, supervision, and work–family conflict in women. She has taught at the University of New Orleans and was an international teaching assistant during the summer of 2015 at the University of Malta.

Abbé Finn, PhD, is the program coordinator for the Department of Counseling in the College of Health Professions and Social Work at Florida Gulf Coast University. She has worked extensively in the mental health field with individuals as well as groups in counseling. Before joining the university faculty full time, she was an employee assistance counselor with the U.S. Postal Service employee assistance program and worked at a residential treatment facility. Dr. Finn specialized in working with groups in crisis response, survivors of childhood sexual trauma, and clients in addiction recovery. Her areas of research include group counseling with people with addictions, suicide prevention, violence prevention, and addiction prevention.

Dr. Finn holds a doctorate in counselor education from the University of New Orleans; a master's degree in counseling from Loyola University, New Orleans; a master's degree in early childhood education from Tulane University; and a bachelor's degree in speech pathology and audiology.

Mary Lou Bryant Frank, PhD, currently serves as chief operating officer of the Southern Women's History Center and Fellow at the Institute for Higher Education at the University of Georgia, professor of psychology at Middle Georgia College, and an adjunct faculty member at Brenau University. Her doctorate in counseling psychology is from Colorado State University. She served as vice president for academic affairs at Middle Georgia College, associate vice president at Gainesville State College, dean of undergraduate and university studies at Kennesaw State University, and department head of psychology and sociology at North Georgia College and State University. She has served as a professor of psychology at Middle Georgia College, Gainesville State College, and Kennesaw State College and an associate professor at the University of Virginia at Wise.

Dr. Frank's research has focused on existential psychotherapy, academic success, as well as leadership. She received the Distinguished Provider Award in Counseling and has been the recipient of grants, national leadership awards, teaching and diversity leadership awards, and awards for community service. She has worked internationally on collaborations with universities in China, Morocco, Belize, and Dubai. Dr. Frank served as the president of the Georgia Association for Women in Higher Education and currently is the vice president and cofounder of the Georgia Women's Institute, vice chair of the Georgia Woman of the Year Committee, and secretary and cofounder of Possible Woman Foundation. As a mediator, she also serves on the International Association of Dispute Resolution Board of Directors.

Sarah H. Golden, MA, LPC, NCC, received her master's in counselor education from Western Michigan University and completed her undergraduate work at Hope College. She is currently working on her doctorate in counselor education and supervision with a concentration in consultation from Walden University. Sarah is a licensed professional counselor in Michigan, national certified counselor, and credentialed school counselor in California. Sarah is currently working in Los Angeles with diverse populations at USC Hybrid High School, an urban college preparatory charter high school that emphasizes positive multigenerational change. She is also the consulting counselor for an online/onsite blended learning charter school, where she saw a need for a counseling program and so developed and implemented counseling services. In addition to her school roles, Sarah is also a disaster mental health volunteer for the American Red Cross. Her other professional interests include working with marginalized populations, consultation, crisis intervention, program development, and multicultural counseling.

In addition to her career interests, Sarah is an enthusiast for volunteer work and giving back to the community. She is passionate about international work and has done short-term volunteering with youth in Rwanda, Africa. These projects included working with youth of preschool to high school age in various capacities. She is striving to develop counseling programs for youth through platforms of athletics or creative outlets in order to promote physical and mental health, positive personal growth, empowerment, and team building. Sarah is an avid runner and marathoner and has been a cross-country and track coach. She has also taught marathon classes. Sarah is passionate about utilizing her education, passions, and skills to create and promote change.

Douglas R. Gross, PhD, NCC, is a professor emeritus at Arizona State University, Tempe, where he served as a faculty member in counselor education for 29 years. His professional work history includes public school teaching, counseling, and administration. He is currently retired and living in Michigan. He has been president of the Arizona Counselors Association, president of the Western Association for Counselor Education and Supervision, chairperson of the Western Regional Branch Assembly of the American Counseling Association, president of the Association for Humanistic Education and Development, and treasurer and parliamentarian of the American Counseling Association.

Dr. Gross has contributed chapters to seven texts: *Counseling and Psychotherapy: Theories and Interventions* (1995, 1999, 2003, 2007, 2011, 2016), *Youth at Risk: A Resource Guide for Counselors, Teachers, and Parents* (1989, 1996, 2000, 2004, 2008, 2014), *Foundations of Mental Health Counseling* (1986, 1996), *Counseling: Theory, Process and Practice* (1977), *The Counselor's Handbook* (1974), *Introduction to the Counseling Profession* (1991, 1997, 2001, 2005, 2009), and *Introduction to Group Work* (1992, 1998, 2002, 2006, 2010). His research has appeared in the *Journal of Counseling Psychology; Journal of Counseling & Development; Counselor Education and Supervision; Journal of Educational Research, Counseling and Human Development; Arizona Counselors Journal; Texas Counseling Journal;* and the *Journal of Mental Health Counseling.*

Shane Haberstroh, EdD, is currently an associate professor and doctoral program director in the Department of Counseling at the University of Texas at San Antonio. He served on the founding board for the Association for Creativity in Counseling (ACC) and as the ACC president and treasurer. He is currently the Governing Council representative for the ACC and the Governing Council liaison for the Research and Knowledge Committee of the American Counseling Association (ACA). He was awarded the Professional Service Award from the ACC in 2006. He served as a delegate on the 20/20: A Vision for the Future of Counseling initiative for the ACA from its inception.

Dr. Haberstroh serves as the associate editor for the *Journal of Creativity in Mental Health.* He has published more than 30 articles and book chapters primarily focused on developmental relational counseling, online counseling, creativity in counseling, and addiction treatment and recovery. His collaborative research project on relational competencies won the 2010 Texas Counseling Association Research Award, and his collaborative publication on assessment practices in counselor education programs was recognized with the 2014 American Association of Rehabilitation Counseling/Council of Rehabilitation Counseling Outstanding Outcome Research Award. Dr. Haberstroh began his career in 1992 as a residential technician in a 28-day drug treatment program and worked for many years as a counselor and supervisor in addiction treatment centers, private practice, and criminal justice settings. He has been a counselor educator since 2003, and he joined the faculty of the University of Texas at San Antonio in 2004.

Laura R. Haddock, PhD, received her doctorate in counselor education from the University of Mississippi. She currently serves as the Counselor Education and Supervision PhD Program coordinator at Walden University. Dr. Haddock has been a counselor educator since 2001, supported by more than 2 decades of work as a mental health counselor. Her clinical practice includes work with a variety of populations, with a particular focus on trauma resolution. She is a licensed professional counselor, national certified counselor, and approved clinical supervisor.

Dr. Haddock is an active counseling professional and has served on the Mississippi Licensed Professional Counselors Board of Examiners and the executive boards for the Mississippi Counseling Association and Mississippi Licensed Professional Counselors Association. She routinely presents research at the state, national, and international levels and publishes scholarly writings for professional counseling journals and textbooks. She is a two-time winner of outstanding research awards by state counseling organizations and serves as a member of the editorial boards of the *Journal of Counseling Research and Practice; Journal of Social, Behavioral and Health Sciences;* and *Tennessee Counseling Association Journal.* Her research interests include counselor wellness and secondary trauma, spirituality, crisis response, cultural diversity, and supervision.

Melinda Haley, PhD, received her master's degree in counselor education at Portland State University (Oregon) and her doctorate in counseling psychology from New Mexico State University (Las Cruces) and was an assistant professor in the counseling and guidance program at the University of Texas, El Paso, for 5 years. Dr. Haley currently works as a core faculty member in the counselor education and supervision doctoral program at Walden University.

She has written numerous book chapters and journal articles on diverse topics related to counseling. She has extensive applied experience working with adults, adolescents, children, inmates, domestic violence offenders, and culturally diverse populations in the areas of assessment, diagnosis, treatment planning, crisis management, and intervention. Dr. Haley's research interests include multicultural issues in teaching and counseling, personality development over the life span, personality disorders, the psychology of criminal and serial offenders, trauma and posttraumatic stress disorder, bias and racism, and social justice issues.

Richard J. Hazler, PhD, is a professor of counselor education at The Pennsylvania State University. He is known for work in the areas of peer-on-peer abuse, youth violence, and humanistic approaches to counseling and counselor education. His professional work with youth began when he was an elementary school teacher and later a school counselor and counselor in a university, the Army, a prison, and private practice. During his 34 years as a counselor educator, Dr. Hazler's research and experience have resulted in a wealth of journal articles, book chapters, and books. Some recent books on counseling youth include *Breaking the Cycle of Violence: Interventions for Bullying and Victimization* (1996) and *Helping in the Hallways: Expanding Your Influence Potential* (2nd ed., 2008). A sample of other books for counseling students and professionals includes *The Therapeutic Environment* (2001), *The Emerging Professional Counselor: Student Dreams to Professional Realities* (2nd ed., 2005), and *What You Never Learned in Graduate School: A Survival Guide for Therapists* (1997).

Dr. Hazler also has a long history of serving the profession. He has been elected president of numerous national and state professional organizations, some of which include Chi Sigma Iota, the Association for Humanistic Education and Development, and the Kentucky and Ohio Counseling Associations.

He has been an editor and editorial board member of major national and international counseling journals. Counseling students have always been a focus of his work, including his inception and editing for 20 years of the Student Focus column in *Counseling Today*.

Kathryn L. Henderson, PhD, LPC, NCC, is an assistant professor of counselor education at Georgia Regents University in Augusta. She received her doctorate and master's degree in counselor education from the University of New Orleans (accredited by the Council for Accreditation of Counseling and Related Educational Programs). Dr. Henderson is a licensed professional counselor (Texas) and a national certified counselor. Dr. Henderson's clinical background includes working in a variety of settings, including public schools and community agencies. Her research interests include ethical and legal issues in counseling, trauma and crisis counseling, and working with children and adolescents. Dr. Henderson has published on student remediation and gatekeeping, child abuse and mandated reporting, and creative counseling practices. She is a member of the American Counseling Association, Association for Counselor Education and Supervision, Southern Association for Counselor Education and Supervision, and Chi Sigma Iota.

Barbara Herlihy, PhD, LPC-S, is a university research professor in the Counselor Education Program at the University of New Orleans. She is the coauthor of three current books and numerous book chapters and articles, primarily on the topics of ethics, feminist therapy, and diversity and social justice. Her recent work has focused on issues in the globalization of counseling.

Dr. Herlihy is a recipient of the Southern Association for Counselor Education and Supervision Courtland Lee Social Justice Award and the Association for Counselor Education and Supervision Outstanding Mentor Award. She is a past chair of the American Counseling Association (ACA) Ethics Committee and served on the ACA Code of Ethics Revision Taskforce in 2005. She chaired the ACA International Committee in 2011–2012. She has presented seminars and workshops across the country and internationally, most recently in Malta.

Adrianne L. Johnson, PhD, is an assistant professor in the clinical mental health counseling program at Wright State University. She earned her doctorate in counselor education from the University of Arkansas in 2007 and holds a professional clinical counseling license in Ohio.

Dr. Johnson is active in various organizations committed to mental health advocacy and strongly promotes excellence in counselor education through teaching, research and publication, and international presentation. Dr. Johnson's research interests and professional experience include higher education leadership, community mental health counseling, multicultural counseling, and chemical dependency counseling.

Cynthia R. Kalodner, PhD, is a professor of psychology at Towson University. She received her doctoral degree in counseling psychology from The Pennsylvania State University in 1988. She has been employed in academic positions at The University of Akron and West Virginia University and also maintains a limited private practice focusing on adults with mood and anxiety disorders using a cognitive–behavioral focus.

Dr. Kalodner's current research focus is the effects of international service-learning on the personal and professional development of students.

Julian Rafferty (Rafe) McCullough, MS, is currently a doctoral student in the counselor education and practice program at Georgia State University. He holds a master's degree in education in school counseling from Seattle University. He served on the Professional Education Advisory Board for school counseling at Seattle University from 2008 to 2013 and on the American Counseling Association Council for Accreditation of Counseling and Related Educational Programs Revisions Committee in 2013. He was an adjunct instructor in the counseling program at Seattle University from 2010 to 2013.

Mr. McCullough was one of the founding members of Seattle University Counselors for Social Justice, one of whose goals was to increase awareness and support of lesbian, gay, bisexual, transgender, and queer (LGBTQ) students in kindergarten–Grade 12 settings and on college campuses. He was a professional school counselor for 5 years in an urban Seattle middle school. He currently serves on the Multicultural Competency Revision Committee for the Association for Multicultural Counseling and Development. His writing and research interests are centered on advocacy, social justice, and LGBTQ issues in counseling.

Nathanael G. Mitchell, PhD, is an assistant professor at Spalding University School of Professional Psychology, a doctoral program in clinical psychology located in Louisville, Kentucky. He serves as the director of the Health Psychology Emphasis Area, training doctoral psychology students in health promotion, behavioral medicine, and integrated care. His research expertise includes the areas of health disparities, the promotion of health behaviors in underserved and marginalized populations, psychosocial correlates of obesity, and provider bias toward patients.

In addition, Dr. Mitchell works part time as a psychotherapist focusing on treating anxiety, depression, and grief and coping with chronic illness. He incorporates the transpersonal components of mindfulness and spirituality in psychotherapy when appropriate to meet client needs.

Rebecca D. Nate, MS, is a doctoral student in the counselor education and supervision program at Walden University. She received her master's degree in mental health counseling from Walden University and her bachelor's degree in psychology from the University of Texas at San Antonio. Ms. Nate has worked in behavioral health for the U.S. Air Force; as a children's therapist at Family Violence Prevention Services in San Antonio, Texas; and as an adjunct professor at San Antonio College.

Ms. Nate has also contributed to newsletters, presented at the Air Force Diabetes Champion Course at Lackland Air Force Base, and served the counseling profession as a bylaws committee member for the Association for Humanistic Counseling. Ms. Nate has published in the American Counseling Association's VISTAS on counselor supervisor requirements and has a dissertation focus on professional advocacy in counselor educators. Ms. Nate's research interests include behavioral health, professional advocacy, and supervision.

Kimberly Nelson, PhD, is a core faculty member in the Clinical Mental Health Counseling Program at Walden University. She received her master's degree in psychology from Eastern Washington University and her doctorate in counselor education and supervision from the University of Northern Colorado.

Dr. Nelson is a licensed professional counselor, approved clinical supervisor, and chartered psychologist in Alberta, Canada. Her nearly 20 years of higher education experiences are varied, including several years of teaching at traditional universities and colleges, with the past 10 years spent teaching exclusively online in counseling graduate programs. Her clinical work is diverse and includes community mental health work, private practice, as well as assessment and counseling in kindergarten–Grade 12 schools.

Candace N. Park, PhD, obtained her doctoral degree in counselor education from the University of New Orleans. She is a licensed professional counselor supervisor in the state of Louisiana and a national certified counselor. Her research is primarily in the area of sexual assault and the reporting process for college women, and her publications have included topics such as ethics, theories, and sexual assault.

She has presented nationally on topics related to feminist theory, multicultural counseling, ethics, and supervision and contributed to the *ACA Ethical Standards Casebook* (7th ed., 2014). She has taught feminist therapy as a special topics course and served as a guest lecturer for theories courses to speak on her experience and knowledge in feminist theory. She is a clinical manager for Magnolia Family Services, LLC, in Thibodaux, Louisiana, where she also teaches as an adjunct faculty member at Nicholls State University.

Yurandol O. Powers, PhD, received a master's degree in professional counseling from Argosy University and a doctorate in counselor education and supervision from Walden University. She is a nationally certified counselor as well as a licensed professional counselor, a certified school counselor, and a certified professional counselor supervisor in the state of Georgia. Dr. Powers is the owner of Powerful Alternatives Counseling & Consulting, LLC, in Atlanta, Georgia, serving children, adolescents, adults, and families. In addition to working in her private practice, she teaches part time and supervises doctoral students and individuals seeking licensure.

Dr. Powers has presented at the local, state, regional, and national levels on multicultural supervision, counselor education, and counseling military families. Dr. Powers's professional research interests include diversity issues, multicultural supervision, and the use of creative and innovative techniques in working with members of the military and their families.

Manivong J. Ratts, PhD, is an associate professor of counseling at Seattle University. He has three major lines of research: (a) lesbian, gay, bisexual, transgender, intersex, and questioning status and minority health disparities (e.g., the impact of oppression on psychological health and well-being); (b) the psychological impact privilege has on privileged groups; and (c) multicultural and social justice competent care (e.g., balancing culturally relevant individual counseling with systems-level advocacy). He has published in various peer-reviewed counseling journals and is lead author of the book *Counseling for Multiculturalism and Social Justice: Integration, Theory, and Application* (2014) with Dr. Paul B. Pedersen. He is also the lead coeditor of the book *ACA Advocacy Competencies: A Social Justice Framework for Counselors* (2010) with Dr. Judy Lewis and Dr. Rebecca Toporek. He has produced two videos through Alexander Street Press, titled *Four Approaches to Counseling One Client: Medical, Intrapsychic, Multicultural, and Social Justice Counseling Paradigms* (2011) and *Five Forces of Counseling and Psychotherapy: Psychoanalytic, Cognitive-Behavioral, Existential-Humanistic, Multicultural, and Social Justice* (2013).

In addition, he is past president of Counselors for Social Justice, a division of the American Counseling Association, and founder of Seattle University Counselors for Social Justice, an advocacy organization that addresses issues of equity impacting individuals, communities, and schools. Dr. Ratts has also served on the editorial boards of the *Journal of Counseling & Development* and *Journal for Social Action in Counseling and Psychology*. Dr. Ratts received his doctorate in counseling from Oregon State University (OSU). He also holds an associate's degree from Yakima Valley Community College, a bachelor's degree in psychology from Western Washington University, and a master's degree in counseling from OSU.

Deborah J. Rubel, PhD, was raised in a bicultural household in Salcha, Alaska. She trained as a food scientist at Utah State University and worked in the field of food research and development for 10 years before deciding to become a counselor. Deborah received her master's degree in mental health counseling and doctorate in counselor education and supervision from Idaho State University. After finishing her doctorate, she began working at Oregon State University. Her areas of specialization are diversity issues, qualitative research methods, group work, and pedagogy.

Marilyn Rush-Ossenbeck, MA, graduated from Miami University in Oxford, Ohio, in 2012 with a bachelor's degree in psychology and family studies. During her undergraduate career, she fell in love with family counseling, especially research about families. She then attended the University of Cincinnati, where she earned a master's degree in clinical mental health counseling in 2015 and continued her research on military veterans and their families.

Currently, she is employed full time as a mental health and substance abuse counselor at an inpatient drug rehabilitation facility. She hopes to pursue a doctoral degree in counseling in the future and further her research on both substance abuse and military veteran populations and their families.

Heather Trepal, PhD, LPC-S, is an associate professor in the Department of Counseling at the University of Texas at San Antonio. She is a licensed professional counselor and board-approved supervisor in the state of Texas. Dr. Trepal's counseling experience includes working in rape crisis, college counseling centers, and private practice. Her research focuses on self-harm (nonsuicidal self-injury and eating disorders), relational-cultural Theory, gender issues, and counselor education and supervision. She has more than 30 publications in the areas of creativity, innovations in grief and loss counseling, relational competencies (relational-cultural theory), and addictions. Her collaborative research project on relational competencies won the 2010 Texas Counseling Association Research Award, and she was the recipient of the Association for Counselor Education and Supervision Research Award.

Dr. Trepal has served in a number of national, regional, and state professional service roles, including president of the Association for Creativity in Counseling, a division of the American Counseling Association (ACA); chair of the ACA graduate student committee; president of the Southern Association for Counselor Education and Supervision; and president of the Texas Association for Counselor Education and Supervision.

Ann Vernon, PhD, is a professor emerita at the University of Northern Iowa, where she served as coordinator of the school and mental health counseling programs for many years. In addition, she had a large private practice. Dr. Vernon has published more than 20 books, as well as numerous chapters and articles, most of which focus on effective counseling strategies with children and adolescents. Dr. Vernon is president of the Albert Ellis Institute and is considered to be a leading expert on applications of rational emotive behavior theory with children and adolescents. She is an international consultant and does rational emotive and cognitive behavior therapy training in various parts of the world, including Greece, Romania, Australia, and South America. She also provides pro bono counseling services to low-income clients at a clinic in Tucson, Arizona.

Cirecie A. West-Olatunji, PhD, is an associate professor of counseling at Xavier University in New Orleans. Prior to moving to New Orleans she served as associate professor and director of the Center for Traumatic Stress Research at the University of Cincinnati. She is also a past president of the American Counseling Association (ACA). At the national level, Dr. West-Olatunji has initiated several clinical research projects that focus on culture-centered community collaborations designed to address issues rooted in systemic oppression, such as transgenerational trauma and traumatic stress. Dr. West-Olatunji has conducted commissioned research under the auspices of the National Science Foundation, ACA, Kellogg Foundation, federal Witness Assistance Program, Spencer Foundation, American Educational Research Association, and African-American Success Foundation.

Dr. West-Olatunji's publications include two coauthored books, numerous book chapters, and more than 40 articles in peer-reviewed journals. In addition to national presentations, Dr. West-Olatunji has delivered research papers in the Americas, in West and southern Africa, in Eastern and Western Europe, and throughout the Pacific Rim. In addition, she provided consultation to a Public Broadcasting Service initiative to create a children's television show focusing on diversity through KCET-TV in Los Angeles, California (*Puzzle Place*). Dr. West-Olatunji has also provided consultation to the Center for American Education in Singapore and to the Buraku Liberation Organization in Japan to enhance their early childhood and counseling initiatives. Over the past decade, she has coordinated disaster mental health outreach projects in post-Katrina New Orleans, southern Africa (Botswana and South Africa), and Haiti. Dr. West-Olatunji is a graduate of Dartmouth College (New Hampshire) and received her master's degree and doctorate in counselor education from the University of New Orleans (Louisiana).

Robert E. Wubbolding, EdD, clinical counselor, psychologist, board-certified coach, is the director of the Center for Reality Therapy in Cincinnati, Ohio; past director of training for the William Glasser Institute (1988–2011); a professor emeritus of counseling at Xavier University; and the author of 13 books on reality therapy, including *Reality Therapy for the 21st Century* (2000), *Counselling With Reality Therapy* (1999), *A Set of Directions for Putting and Keeping Yourself Together* (2001), and *Reality Therapy: Theories of Psychotherapy Series* (2010).

Dr. Wubbolding has taught choice theory/reality therapy in North America, Asia, Australia, Europe, the Middle East, and North Africa. His work has focused on making reality therapy a cross-cultural approach with extended applications to education, management, addictions, and corrections. He has also developed the central procedure of self-evaluation to include 22 interventions based on choice theory. His current interest is reviewing research studies validating the use of reality therapy, thereby rendering reality therapy respected as a freestanding and validated system of counseling. In the past, he was an elementary and high school counselor, high school teacher, private practitioner, administrator of adult basic education, and correctional counselor. In 2014, he received recognition as a living legend of counseling at the American Counseling Association conference in Honolulu.

Part 1

Foundations for Individual Counseling and Psychotherapy

CHAPTERS

Counseling and psychotherapy encompass a number of relationship and personal and professional modalities in which the counselor or therapist needs to be proficient. These modalities include the creation of essential core conditions that are both foundational to the establishment of a helping relationship and prerequisite to change on the part of the client. In addition, because brief approaches to counseling and psychotherapy are a rapidly developing area and their development has been encouraged by managed care, and because counselor awareness of diversity and social justice issues is so important in the context of the counseling and psychotherapy process, these areas, along with the possibility of taking an integrative approach to working with clients, are also addressed in Part 1 of our text.

The helping relationship is the foundation on which the process of counseling and psychotherapy is based. It is not possible to use the concepts and associated interventions of a specific theory unless such applications are made in the context of a relationship that promotes trust, insight, and behavior change. Chapter 1, "The Helping Relationship: From Core Dimensions to Brief and Integrative Possibilities," is designed to aid students in both the development and delivery of the helping relationship. To achieve this purpose, we present the helping relationship in terms of definitions and descriptions, stages, core conditions and personal characteristics, and helping strategies and their application with diverse populations. **Chapter 1** also introduces the reader to the importance of considering brief approaches to counseling and psychotherapy and how traditional theories can be adapted for briefer, more focused work in the counseling and psychotherapy process. Because so many counselors combine elements of different theories as they work with clients, an introduction to integrative counseling is also provided. Authors of Chapters 3 through 17 provide follow-up information by discussing both traditional and brief interventions in the applications sections of their chapters.

To address the limitations of traditional counseling theories and practices, **Chapter 2**, "Diversity and Social Justice Issues in Counseling and Psychotherapy," enhances counselor awareness of the variety of diversity and social justice issues that need to be addressed in the context of the counseling and psychotherapy process. The chapter provides this context by clarifying key concepts and reviewing the history of diversity and social justice issues in counseling; increasing reader understanding of how diversity influences individual and group functioning; increasing reader awareness of how diversity may influence the counseling and psychotherapy process; providing several perspectives on diversity-appropriate interventions; and making suggestions for how counselors and therapists can develop their self-awareness, knowledge of diverse populations, and counseling skills relevant to diversity and social justice.

As these chapters indicate, practitioners must achieve high levels of competence, effectiveness, and expertise to create a helping relationship beneficial to clients. They must also become sensitive to diversity and social justice issues as they affect their work with clients. We have made every attempt to introduce readers to these topics in the chapters included in this section of the text. Readers are encouraged to do additional reading and follow-up coursework and to commit to personal counseling or therapy to achieve the purposes we have outlined in these chapters.

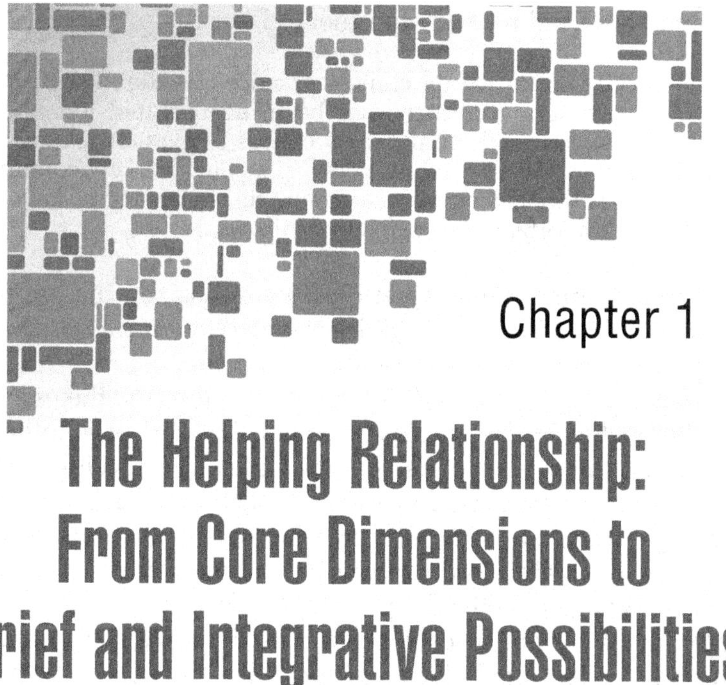

Chapter 1

The Helping Relationship: From Core Dimensions to Brief and Integrative Possibilities

David Capuzzi, Mark D. Stauffer, and Douglas R. Gross

The helping relationship is the cornerstone on which all effective helping rests (Bertolino & O'Hanlon, 2002; Seligman, 2001; Skovholt, 2005; Sommers-Flanagan, 2007, 2015). Words such as *integral, necessary,* and *mandatory* are used to describe this relationship and its importance in the ultimate effectiveness of the helping process. Even though different theoretical systems and approaches use different words to describe this relationship (see Chapters 3–17), each addresses the significance of the helping relationship in facilitating client change. Kottler and Brown (1992), in their *Introduction to Therapeutic Counseling,* made the following comments regarding the significance of this relationship:

> Regardless of the setting in which you practice counseling, whether in a school, agency, hospital, or private practice, the relationships you develop with your clients are crucial to any progress you might make together. For without a high degree of intimacy and trust between two people, very little can be accomplished. (p. 64)

In further support of the significance of the helping relationship, Brammer and MacDonald (1996) noted,

> The helping relationship is dynamic, meaning that it is constantly changing at verbal and nonverbal levels. The relationship is the principal process vehicle for both helper and helpee to express and fulfill their needs, as well as to mesh helpee problems with helper expertise. Relationship emphasizes the affective mode, because relationship is commonly defined as the inferred emotional quality of the interaction. (p. 52)

Barry Farber and Erin Doolin (2011) commented,

> While the Rogerian influence on clinical practice has diminished in the last three decades—or, more accurately, has been incorporated into the psychotherapeutic mainstream with minimal awareness or explicit acknowledgment (Farber, 2007)—therapists of varying persuasions, even those from theoretical camps that had traditionally emphasized more technical factors, have begun to acknowledge the importance of the relationship. (p. 58)

Most recently, John Sommers-Flanagan (2015) emphasized the importance of the helping relationship by using a relationally oriented evidence-based practice model to achieve competence as a mental health counselor.

The ideas expressed by these and other authors describe the essential value of the helping relationship in the process of counseling and psychotherapy and the significant role that the counselor or therapist plays in developing this relationship. Through the counseling relationship and the therapeutic alliance that develops, client change occurs. Although the creation of this relationship is not the end goal of the process, it certainly is the means by which goals are met. It serves as the framework within which effective helping takes place.

This chapter has three purposes. First, it aids the reader in understanding the various factors that affect the helping relationship: definitions and descriptions, stages, core dimensions, strategies, and issues of diversity. Second, because we have asked each of our theory authors to discuss brief approaches as applied to the theory under consideration, we provide our readers with an overview of selected brief approaches, because these approaches, plus the impact of managed care, have precipitated an emphasis on using traditional theories in shorter term counseling. Third, because we know that, after reading this book, readers will have questions about whether to be a purist, in the literal sense of the term, and base all of their work with clients on a single theoretical set or somehow integrate the possibilities for working with clients into a more flexible way of helping, we also provide an overview of integrative counseling. We hope that the information presented in this chapter will not only help readers to understand the dynamics of the helping relationship and their application in both theory-specific and brief approaches but also aid them in incorporating these dynamics into an integrative theoretical approach.

DEFINITIONS AND DESCRIPTIONS

Although agreed-on definitions and descriptions of the helping relationship should be easy to find, this is not the case. Despite the importance of this relationship in the overall helping process, a perusal of textbooks and articles dealing with counseling and psychotherapy shows the lack of a common definition. Rogers (1961), for example, defined a helping relationship as one "in which at least one of the parties has the intent of promoting the growth, development, maturity, improved functioning and improved coping with life of the other" (p. 39). Okun (1992) stated that "the development of a warm, trustful relationship between the helper and helpee underlies any strategy or approach to the helping process and, therefore, is a basic condition for the success of any helping process" (p. 14). According to Miars and Halverson (2001), "The ultimate goal of a professional helping relationship should be to promote the development of more effective and adaptive behavior in the clients" (p. 51). Skovholt (2005) provided an overview of the evidence-based research on counseling outcomes and overwhelmingly concluded that the counseling relationship is key to successful client outcomes. Sommers-Flanagan (2015) noted that "each mental health counselor will inevitably display therapeutic relational factors in unique ways that may be difficult for other practitioners to replicate, because anything relational or interpersonal is alive, automatically unique, and therefore resists sterile descriptive language" (p. 100). Sommers-Flanagan then went on to recommend that counselors implement core relational attitudes and behaviors based on evidence-based practice principles (see Sidebar 1.1).

It is easy to see the difficulty in categorically stating an accepted definition or description of the helping relationship, regardless of which of the aforementioned statements one chooses to embrace. However, despite the differences, each carries with it directions and directives aimed at a single goal: the enhancement and encouragement of client change. The following definitive characteristics of the helping relationship embrace this goal and describe our conceptualization of this relationship:

- A relationship initially structured by the counselor or therapist but open to cooperative restructuring based on the needs of the client
- A relationship that begins with the initial meeting and continues through termination
- A relationship in which all persons involved perceive the existence of trust, caring, concern, and commitment and act accordingly
- A relationship in which the needs of the client are given priority over the needs of the counselor or therapist
- A relationship that provides for the personal growth of all persons involved
- A relationship that provides the safety needed for self-exploration for all persons involved
- A relationship that promotes the potential of all persons involved

The major responsibility in creating this relationship rests initially with the counselor or therapist, with increasing demands for client involvement and commitment over time. It is a shared process, and only through such shared efforts will this relationship develop and flourish. This development evolves in stages that take the relationship from initiation to closure. The stages in this evolving process are the subject of the following section.

Sidebar 1.1. The Importance of a Constructive Therapeutic Alliance

One of the most important things a counselor (beginning or experienced) must provide to all clients is a safe and constructive therapeutic alliance. Whether the counselor follows the constructs of a specific theory or develops an integrative approach, the helping relationship must be established in a way that encourages client self-disclosure and motivation to establish and work toward the attainment of goals. No matter how much expertise a counselor or therapist has to contribute to the counseling process, the helping relationship must be established in a way that provides a safe and affirming holding environment so that the client can move toward greater self-acceptance and decision making.

HELPING RELATIONSHIPS: STAGES

The helping relationship is a constant throughout the counseling or psychotherapeutic process. The definitive characteristics we have already presented indicate that the relationship must be present from the initial meeting between the client and the counselor or therapist and continue through closure. Viewing the helping relationship as a constant throughout the helping process leads to visualizing this process from a developmental perspective. This development can best be viewed in terms of a narrow path whose limits are established by the client's fear, anxiety, and resistance. Such client reactions should not be seen as lack of commitment to change; rather, they need to be understood in terms of the unknown nature of this developing alliance and the fact that this may be the first time the client has experienced this type of interaction. These reactions are often shared by the counselor or therapist based on his or her level of experience. The path broadens through the development of trust, safety, and understanding as this relationship develops. The once narrow path becomes a boulevard along which two persons move courageously toward their final destination—change. The movement along this broadening path is described by various authors in terms of stages or phases. Osipow, Walsh, and Tosi (1980), in discussing the stages of the helping relationship, stated:

> Persons who experience the process of personal counseling seem to progress through several stages. First, there is an increased awareness of self and others. Second, there is an expanded exploration of self and environment (positive and negative behavioral tendencies). Third, there is increased commitment to self-enhancing behavior and its implementation. Fourth, there is an internalization of new and more productive thoughts and actions. Fifth, there is a stabilization of new behavior. (p. 73)

Brammer (1985) divided this developmental process into two phases, each with four distinctive stages. Phase 1, Building Relationships, includes preparing the client and opening the relationship, clarifying the problem or concern of the client, structuring the process, and building a relationship. Phase 2, Facilitating Positive Action, involves exploration, consolidation, planning, and termination.

Purkey and Schmidt (1987) set forth three stages in building the helping relationship, each containing four steps. Stage 1, Preparation, includes having the desire for a relationship, expecting good things, preparing the setting, and reading the situation. Stage 2, Initiating Responding, includes choosing caringly, acting appropriately, honoring the client, and ensuring reception. Stage 3, Follow-Up, includes interpreting responses, negotiating positions, evaluating the process, and developing trust.

Egan (2013) stated that the helping relationship can be broken down into a minimum of three phases—building the relationship, challenging the client to find ways to change, and facilitating positive client action. The goal in the first phase is to build a foundation of mutual trust and client understanding. In the second phase, the counselor challenges the client to try on new ways of thinking, feeling, and behaving. In the third phase, the counselor aids the client in facilitating actions that lead to change and growth in the client's life outside the counseling relationship.

Authors such as Corey and Corey (2015), Gladding (2012), and Egan (2013) have provided other models of the developmental nature of the stages of the helping relationship. Although the terms used to describe these stages may differ, there seems to be a consistency across these models: The stages move from initiation of the relationship through a clinically based working stage to a termination stage. The following developmental stages show our conceptualization of this relationship-building process and are based on the consistency found in our research and our clinical experience:

- *Stage 1: Relationship development.* This stage includes the initial meeting of the client and counselor or therapist, rapport building, information gathering, goal determination, and informing the client about the conditions under which counseling will take place (e.g., confidentiality, taping, counselor/therapist–client roles; see Sidebar 1.2).
- *Stage 2: Extended exploration.* This stage builds on the foundation established in the first stage. Through selected techniques, theoretical approaches, and strategies, the counselor or therapist explores in depth the emotional and cognitive dynamics of the client, problem parameters, previously tried solutions, and decision-making capabilities of the client. There is also a reevaluation of the goals determined in Stage 1.
- *Stage 3: Problem resolution.* This stage, which depends on information gained during the previous two stages, is characterized by increased activity for all parties involved. The counselor or therapist's activities include facilitating, demonstrating, instructing, and providing a safe environment for the development of change. The client's activities focus on reevaluation, emotional and cognitive dynamics, trying out new behaviors (both inside and outside of the sessions), and discarding those behaviors that do not meet goals.
- *Stage 4: Termination and follow-up.* This stage is the closing stage of the helping relationship and is cooperatively determined by all persons involved. Methods and procedures for follow-up are determined prior to the last meeting.

It is important to keep in mind that people do not automatically move through these identified stages in a lockstep manner. The relationship may end at any one of these stages based on decisions made by the client, the counselor or therapist, or both; nor is it possible to identify the amount of time that should be devoted to any particular stage. With certain clients, much more time will need to be devoted to specific stages. D. Brown and Srebalus (1988), in addressing the tentative nature of these relationship stages, had the following caution for their readers:

> Before we describe a common sequence of events in counseling, it is important to note that many clients, for one reason or another, will not complete all the

Sidebar 1.2. Client Transparency

In the first stage of a helping relationship, the client may not be entirely forthcoming about what he or she really wants to address. Often this is because the client needs time to feel safe and comfortable with the counselor. However, many times some clients will move very quickly to the core of the issue or concern. Neither possibility should be a surprise to the counselor.

> stages of counseling. The process will be abandoned prematurely, not because something went wrong, but because of factors external to the counselor-client relationship. For example, the school year may end for a student client, or a client or counselor may move away to accept a new job. When counseling is in process and must abruptly end, the participants will feel the incompleteness and loss. (p. 69)

Viewing the helping relationship as an ongoing process that is composed of developmental stages provides counselors and therapists with a structural framework within which they can function effectively. Inside this framework fit the core conditions and strategies that serve the goals of movement through the relationship process and enhancement and encouragement of client change. We discuss these core conditions and strategies in the following two sections.

HELPING RELATIONSHIPS: CORE CONDITIONS

The concept of basic or core conditions related to the helping relationship has its basis in the early work of Rogers (1957) and the continued work of such authors as Carkhuff and Barenson (1967), Combs (1986), Egan (2013), Ivey (1998), and Truax and Carkhuff (1967). More recent studies (Coutinho, Silva, & Decety, 2014) connecting the neurobiological correlates of a wide range of human behaviors, including those connected with core conditions of the helping relationship, have piqued the interest of counselors and therapists and point to some interesting ways this line of research can be applied to enhance the helping relationship. Ivey, Ivey, and Zalaquett (2013), for example, expressed the idea that counseling can change the brains of both the counselor and the client and promote healthier interpersonal relationships. This concept incorporates a set of conditions that, when present, enhance the effectiveness of the helping relationship. The terminology for these conditions varies from author to author but generally includes the following: *empathic understanding, respect and positive regard, genuineness and congruence, concreteness, warmth,* and *immediacy.*

It should be obvious in reviewing this listing that the concept of core or basic conditions relates directly to various personal characteristics or behaviors that the counselor or therapist brings to and incorporates into the helping relationship. It is difficult to pinpoint with any exactness how such characteristics or behaviors develop. Are they the result of life experiences, classroom instruction, or some combination of both? Our experience in education favors the last explanation. The ability to provide clients with core conditions in the context of a helping relationship must already be present to some degree in graduate students for supervision, instruction, and mentoring to enhance or expand the ability to cocreate core conditions (see Sidebar 1.3).

The remainder of this section deals with the core conditions and relates these directly to personal characteristics or behaviors of counselors or therapists that should enhance their ability to effectively utilize these conditions in the process of helping. Although definitions, emphases, and applications of these conditions differ across theoretical systems, there appears to be agreement about their effectiveness in facilitating change in the overall helping relationships (Brammer, Abrego, & Shostrom, 1993; Brems, 2000; Clark, 2010; Farber & Doolin, 2011; Freedberg, 2007; Gatongi, 2008; Gladding, 2012; Prochaska & Norcross, 2013).

Sidebar 1.3. Supervision Responsibility and the Counselor Educator

The idea that graduate students must already be able to provide clients with core conditions in a helping relationship for supervision, instruction, and mentoring to enhance or expand this ability raises some interesting questions about the role of the counselor educator in the process of working with a graduate student enrolled in a counselor education program. Is the role of the counselor educator to help raise awareness on the part of a beginning counselor with respect to inherent traits and ways of relating to others that automatically contribute to the provision of therapeutic core conditions that can be enhanced and strengthened, or is it possible for the counselor educator to help a mentee develop such traits if they are not already present? What is the responsibility of the counselor educator if an individual who wants to be a licensed, professional counselor cannot seem to provide the core conditions needed to establish a safe working alliance with clients?

Empathic Understanding

Empathic understanding is the ability to feel with clients as opposed to feeling for clients. It is the ability to understand feelings, thoughts, ideas, and experiences by viewing them from the client's frame of reference. The counselor or therapist must be able to enter the client's world, understand the myriad aspects that make up that world, and communicate this understanding so that the client perceives that he or she has been heard accurately (Coutinho et al., 2014; Freedberg, 2007; Gatongi, 2008; Singer, Critchley, & Preuschoff, 2009).

Egan (2013) identified both primary and advanced levels of empathic understanding. At the primary level, it is the ability to understand, identify, and communicate feelings and meanings that are at the surface level of the client's disclosures. At the advanced level, it is the ability to understand, identify, and communicate feelings and meanings that are buried, hidden, or beyond the immediate reach of a client. Such feelings and meanings are more often covert rather than overt client expressions.

Personal characteristics or behaviors that enhance a counselor or therapist's ability to provide empathic understanding include, but are not limited to, the following:

- The knowledge and awareness of one's own values, attitudes, and beliefs and the emotional and behavioral impact they have on one's own life
- The knowledge and awareness of one's own feelings and emotional response patterns and how they manifest themselves in interactive patterns
- The knowledge and awareness of one's own life experiences and one's personal reactions to those experiences
- The capacity and willingness to communicate these personal reactions to one's clients

Respect and Positive Regard

Respect and *positive regard* are defined as a belief in each client's innate worth and potential and the ability to communicate this belief in the helping relationship. This belief, once communicated, provides clients with positive reinforcement relative to their innate ability to take responsibility for their own growth, change, goal determination, decision making, and eventual problem solution. It is an empowering process that delivers a message to clients that they are able to take control of their lives and, with facilitative assistance from the counselor or therapist, foster change. Communicating and demonstrating this respect for clients takes many forms. According to Baruth and Robinson (1987), it "is often communicated by what the counselor does not do or say. In other words, by not offering to intervene for someone, one is communicating a belief in the individual's ability to 'do' for himself or herself" (p. 85).

Personal characteristics or behaviors that enhance a counselor or therapist's ability to provide respect and positive regard include, but are not limited to, the following:

- The capacity to respect oneself
- The capacity to view oneself as having worth and potential
- The capacity to model and communicate this positive self-image to clients
- The capacity to recognize one's own control needs and the ability to use this recognition in a manner that allows clients to direct their own lives

We think it is worth noting, however, that in no type of counseling is it possible for the counselor, a conditioned cultural product, to provide unconditional positive regard unless he or she is sensitive to the cultural norms of the client (Ibrahim & Dykeman, 2011).

Genuineness and Congruence

Congruence or genuineness is a relational quality that has received renewed interest in recent years (Klein, Michels, Kolden, & Chisolm-Stockard, 2001). *Genuineness* and *congruence* describe the ability to be authentic in the helping relationship (D. W. Sue & Sue, 2013). The ability to be real as opposed to artificial, to behave as one feels as opposed to playing the role of the helper, and to be congruent in terms of actions and words are further descriptors of this core condition (Kolden, Klein, Wang & Austin, 2011). According to Schnellbacher and Leijssen (2009),

> The findings underline the significance and value of genuineness in communication with the client. Indeed, the results indicate that therapist genuineness can be a crucial process for healing and personality change and that self-disclosure can be [a] powerful and directional [intervention]. (pp. 222–223)

Implicit in this statement is the idea of the counselor's ability to communicate and demonstrate this genuineness, not only for relationship enhancement but also to model this core condition so that clients can develop greater authenticity in their interactions with others.

Personal characteristics or behaviors that enhance a counselor or therapist's ability to prove genuineness and congruence include, but are not limited to, the following:

- The capacity for self-awareness and the ability to demonstrate this capacity through words and actions
- The understanding of one's own motivational patterns and the ability to use them productively in the helping relationship
- The ability to present one's thoughts, feelings, and actions in a consistent, unified, and honest manner

- The capacity for self-confidence and the ability to communicate this capacity in a facilitative way in the helping relationship

Concreteness

Concreteness is the ability not only to see the incomplete picture that clients paint with their words but also to communicate to clients the figures, images, and structures that will complete the picture. In the process of exploring problems or issues, clients often present a somewhat distorted view of the actual situation. Concreteness enables the counselor or therapist to help clients identify the distortions in the situation and fit them together in such a way that they are able to view the situation in a more realistic fashion. The concreteness helps clients clarify vague issues, focus on specific topics, reduce degrees of ambiguity, and channel their energies into more productive avenues of problem solution.

Personal characteristics and behaviors that enhance a counselor or therapist's ability to provide degrees of concreteness include, but are not limited to, the following:

- The capacity for abstract thinking and the ability to read between the lines
- The willingness to risk being incorrect as one attempts to fill in the empty spaces
- The belief in one's own competence in analyzing and sorting through the truths and partial truths in clients' statements
- The ability to be objective while working with clients in arriving at the reality of clients' situations

Warmth

Warmth is the ability to communicate and demonstrate genuine caring and concern for clients (Skovholt, 2005). Using this ability, counselors and therapists convey their acceptance of clients, their desire for clients' well-being, and their sincere interest in finding workable solutions to the problems that clients present. The demeanor of the counselor or therapist is often the main avenue for communicating and demonstrating warmth, for it is often through nonverbal behaviors—a smile, a touch, tone of voice, a facial expression—that genuine caring and concern are communicated. The counselor or therapist's capacity for transmitting concerns and caring to clients, either verbally or nonverbally, enables clients to experience, often for the first time, a truly accepting relationship.

Personal characteristics or behaviors that enhance a counselor or therapist's ability to demonstrate warmth include, but are not limited to, the following:

- The capacity for self-care, and the ability to demonstrate this capacity in both actions and words
- The capacity for self-acceptance, basing this acceptance on one's assets and liabilities
- The desire for one's own well-being, and the ability to demonstrate this desire through both words and actions
- The desire to find, and successful personal experience in finding, workable solutions to one's own problems, and the ability to communicate this desire through words and actions

Immediacy

Immediacy is the ability to deal with the here-and-now factors that operate within the helping relationship (Clemence et al., 2012). These factors are described as overt and covert interactions that take place between the client and the counselor or therapist. A client's anger at a counselor or therapist, the latter's frustration with a client, and the feelings of the client and counselor for each other are all examples of factors that need to be addressed as they occur and develop (Mayotte-Blum et al., 2012). Addressing such issues in the safety of the helping relationship should help participants in two ways: Participants can (a) gain insight into personal behavioral patterns that may be conducive and not conducive to growth and (b) use this insight in relationships outside the helping relationship. As an example, a counselor might ask, "How is sharing with me right now given our cultural difference and the mistrust you feel?" or "How is our work together going?" when a client has mentioned that it is hard to share.

Dealing with these factors can be threatening, as it is often easier to deal with relationships in the abstract and avoid personal encounters. A counselor or therapist needs to be able to use this factor of immediacy to show clients the benefits that can be gained by dealing with issues at they arise. According to Egan (2013), immediacy not only clears the air but also is a valuable learning experience (see Sidebar 1.4).

Personal characteristics or behaviors that enhance a counselor or therapist's ability to use immediacy effectively include, but are not limited to, the following:

- The capacity for perceptive accuracy in interpreting one's own feelings for, thoughts about, and behaviors toward clients
- The capacity for perceptive accuracy in interpreting clients' feelings for, thoughts about, and behaviors toward the counselor or therapist
- The capacity for and willingness to deal with one's own issues related to clients on a personal as opposed to an abstract level
- The willingness to confront both oneself and clients with what one observes to be happening in the helping relationship

HELPING RELATIONSHIPS: STRATEGIES

The previous section identified the core conditions that need to be present for the effective development of the helping relationship. The difference between these core conditions and strategies is the subject of this section.

The core conditions relate to specific dynamics present in the personality and behavioral makeup of counselors or therapists that enable them to communicate to clients. The term *strategies* refers to skills gained through education and experience that define and direct what counselors or therapists do within the relation-

Sidebar 1.4. Personal Characteristics of the Counselor Candidate

In conjunction with each of the core conditions described in this chapter (empathic understanding, respect and positive regard, genuineness and congruence, concreteness, warmth, and immediacy), there is a list of personal characteristics the counselor should have to draw on. Do you think you are a person with such attributes? If not, do you view this as a dilemma given your choice to become a counselor?

ship to obtain specific results and to move the helping relationship from problem identification to problem resolution.

Various terms have been used to address this aspect of the helping relationship Some authors prefer the term *strategies* (Combs & Avila, 1985; Cormier, Nurius, & Osborn, 2013; Gilliland, James, & Bowman, 1989), others prefer *skills* (Halverson & Miars, 2005; Ivey, 1998), and still others prefer the term *techniques* (Belkin, 1980; J. A. Brown & Pate, 1983; Osipow et al., 1980). The terms, however, are interchangeable.

We decided to use the term *strategies*, which denotes not only deliberative planning but also action processes that make the planning operational. We feel that both factors are necessary. For the purpose of the following discussion, we have grouped the strategies into the following categories: (a) strategies that build rapport and encourage client dialogue, (b) strategies that aid in data gathering, and (c) strategies that add depth and enhance the relationship.

Note that specific strategies, such as those stemming from various theoretical systems, are not included in this section. They are presented in Chapters 3 through 17, which deal with specific theories. It is also important to understand that there is much overlap between these arbitrary divisions. Strategies designed to build rapport and encourage client dialogue may also be used to gather data and enhance relationships. With this caveat in mind, we present the following strategies.

Strategies That Build Rapport and Encourage Client Dialogue

This group of strategies includes the active listening strategies that enhance the listening capabilities of counselors and therapists. When used effectively, these strategies should provide an environment in which clients have the opportunity to talk and to share their feelings and thoughts with the assurance that they will be heard. By using such strategies, counselors and therapists enhance their chances of providing such an environment.

This set of strategies includes attending and encouraging, restating and paraphrasing, reflecting content and reflecting feeling, clarifying and perception checking, and summarizing. The following paragraphs present explanations and examples of these strategies.

Attending and Encouraging

These strategies use the counselor or therapist's posture, eye contact, gestures, facial expressions, and words to indicate to clients not only that they are being heard but also that the counselor or therapist wants them to continue sharing information.

Example

Encouraging

Counselor/Therapist: (smiling) Please tell me what brought you in today.

Client: I'm having a hard time trying to put my life in order. I'm very lonely and bored, and I can't seem to maintain a lasting relationship.

Attending/Encouraging

Counselor/Therapist: (leaning forward) Please tell me more.

Client: Every time I think I have a chance of developing a relationship, I screw it up by saying or doing something dumb.

Encouraging

Counselor/Therapist: (nodding) This is helpful, please go on.

Restating and Paraphrasing

These strategies enable a counselor or therapist to serve as a sounding board for the client by feeding back thoughts and feelings that the client verbalizes. Restating involves repeating the exact words used by the client. Paraphrasing is repeating the thoughts and feelings of the client but in the words of the counselor or therapist.

Example

Client: I don't know why I do these dumb things. It's almost as if I did not want a relationship.

Restating

Counselor/Therapist: You don't know why you do dumb things. It may be that you don't want a relationship.

Client: I do want a relationship, but each time I get close I seem to do everything in my power to destroy it.

Paraphrasing

Counselor/Therapist: You are very sure that you want a relationship, but each time you have the opportunity you sabotage your chances.

Reflecting Content and Reflecting Feeling

These strategies enable the counselor or therapist to provide feedback to the client regarding both the ideas (content) and the emotions (feelings) that the client is expressing. By reflecting content, the counselor or therapist shares his or her perceptions of the thoughts that the client is expressing. This can be done either by using the client's words or by changing the words to better reflect the counselor or therapist's perceptions. By reflecting feelings, a counselor or therapist goes beyond the ideas and thoughts expressed by the client and responds to the feelings or emotions behind those words.

Example

Client: "Sabotage" is a good word. It's like I see what I want, but instead of moving toward it, I take a different path that leads nowhere.

Reflecting Content

Counselor/Therapist: You have a good idea of what you want, but when you see it developing, you turn and walk the other way.

Client: I am not sure "walk" is the right word. "Run" is more descriptive of what I do, and all the time I'm looking back to see if anyone is following.

Reflecting Feeling

Counselor/Therapist: You're afraid of getting close to someone, so you put as much distance between the other person and yourself as possible. I also hear that you're hoping that someone cares enough about you to run after you and stop you from running away.

Clarifying and Perception Checking

These strategies enable a counselor or therapist either to ask the client to define or explain words, thoughts, or feelings (clarifying) or to request confirmation or correction of perceptions he or she has drawn regarding these words, thoughts, or feelings (perception checking).

Example

Client: If what you say is true, I'm a real jerk. What chance do I have to be happy if I run away every time I get close to someone else?

Clarifying

Counselor/Therapist: You say you want to be happy. What does "happy" mean to you?

Client: (long pause) I would be happy if I could let someone care for me, get to know me, want to spend time with me, and allow me to just be me and stop pretending.

Perception Checking

Counselor/Therapist: Let me see if I'm understanding you. Your view of happiness is having someone who cares enough about you to spend time with you and to allow you to be yourself. Am I correct?

Summarizing

This strategy enables the counselor or therapist to do several things: first, to verbally review various types of information that have been presented in the session; second, to highlight what the counselor or therapist sees as significant information based on everything that has been discussed; and third, to provide the client with an opportunity to hear the various issues that he or she has presented. Therefore, summarizing provides both the client and the counselor or therapist with the opportunity not only to review and determine the significance of information presented but also to use this review to establish priorities.

Example

Client: Yes, I think that's what I'd like to have happen. That would make me happy. I would be in a relationship, feel cared about, and yet be able to be myself without having to either run or pretend.

Summarizing

Counselor/Therapist: We've talked about many things today. I'd like to review some of this and make plans for our next meeting. The parts that stick out in my mind are your loneliness, boredom, and desire to have a lasting relationship; your behaviors that drive you away from building such a relationship; and your need for caring and the freedom to be yourself. Am I missing anything?

Client: Only that I want someone who wants to spend time with me. I think that's important.

Summarizing

Counselor/Therapist: So now we have a more complete picture that includes loneliness, boredom, desire for a relationship, desire for someone to spend time with, desire for someone who cares, and the need to be yourself. On the other side of the picture, we have your behaviors that keep this from happening. Where do you think we should begin next week?

Strategies That Aid in Data Gathering

This group of strategies includes all of the active listening strategies plus three strategies designed to extract specific information and gain a greater depth of information in areas that are significant in the client's statements. As with active listening strategies, a counselor or therapist who uses the following strategies enhances his or her chances of gaining significant information. This set of strategies includes questioning, probing, and leading. The following paragraphs present explanations and examples of these strategies.

Questioning

This strategy, when done in an open manner, enables the counselor or therapist to gain important information and allows the client to remain in control of the information presented. Using open questioning, the counselor or therapist designs questions to encourage the broadest client responses. Open questions, as opposed to closed questions, generally cannot be completely answered by either yes or no, nor can they be answered nonverbally by shaking the head. This type of questioning places responsibility with clients and allows them a degree of control over what information will be shared.

Example

Client: I've thought a lot about what we talked about last week, and I feel I have to work on changing my behavior.

Open Questioning

Counselor/Therapist: Would you tell me what you think needs to be done to change your behavior?

Client: (short pause) I need to stop screwing up my chances for a relationship. I need to face what it is that makes me run away.

Open Questioning

Counselor/Therapist: Would you please talk more about the "it" that makes you run away?

Client: I can't tell you what it is. All I know is that I hear this voice saying, "Run, run."

Probing and Leading

These strategies enable a counselor or therapist to gather information in a specific area related to the client's presented concerns (probing) or to encourage the client to respond to specific topic areas (leading). Each of these strategies enables the counselor or therapist to explore in greater depth areas that are seen as important to progress within the session.

Example

Probing

Counselor/Therapist: I want you to be more specific about this "voice." Whose voice is it? What does it say to you?

Client: (very long pause) I guess it's my voice. It sounds like something I would do. I'm such a jerk.

Leading

Counselor/Therapist: You told me whose voice it is, but you didn't tell me what the voice says. Would you talk about this?

Client: (raising his voice) It says, "Get out or you're going to get hurt. She doesn't like you and she'll use you and drop you just like the rest."

Strategies That Add Depth and Enhance the Relationship

This group of strategies is used to enhance and expand the communicative and relationship patterns that are established early in the counseling or therapeutic process. When used effectively, these strategies should open up deeper levels of communication and strengthen the relationship patterns that have already been established. Counselors or therapists using these strategies model types of behaviors that they want their clients to emulate. Such behaviors include, but are not limited to, risk taking, sharing of self, demonstrating trust, and honest interaction. This set of strategies includes self-disclosure, confrontation, and responding to nonverbal cues. The following paragraphs present explanations and examples of these strategies.

Self-Disclosure

This strategy has implications for both clients and counselors or therapists. In self-disclosing, the counselor or therapist shares with the client his or her feelings, thoughts, and experiences that are relevant to the situation presented by the client. The counselor or therapist draws on situations from his or her own life experiences and selectively shares these personal reactions with the client. It is important to note that self-disclosure could have both a positive and a negative impact on the helping relationship, and care must be taken in measuring the impact it may have. From a positive perspective, it carries with it the possibility of modeling self-disclosure for the client or helping the client gain a different perspective on the presenting problems. From a negative perspective, self-disclosure might place the focus on the counselor or therapist's issues rather than on those of the client. When self-disclosure is used appropriately, gains are made by all persons involved, and the relationship moves to deeper levels of understanding and sharing.

Example

Self-Disclosure

Counselor/Therapist: (aware of the client's agitation) The anger I hear in your voice and words triggers anger in me as I think of my own lost relationships.

Client: (smiling) I am angry. I'm also glad you said that. Sometimes I feel like I'm the only one who ever felt this way.

Self-Disclosure

Counselor/Therapist: (smiling) I am very pleased with what you just said. At this moment, I also do not feel alone with my anger.

Confrontation

This strategy enables the counselor or therapist to provide the client with feedback in which discrepancies are presented in an honest and matter-of-fact manner. A counselor or therapist uses this strategy to indicate his or her reaction to the client, to identify differences between the client's words and behaviors, and to challenge the client to put words and ideas into action. This type of direct and honest feedback should provide the client with insight into how he or she is perceived as well as indicate the degree of counselor or therapist caring.

Example

Client: (smiling) I feel angry at myself a great deal. I want so much to find a person and develop a relationship that lasts.

Confrontation

Counselor/Therapist: You've said this several times in our sessions, but I'm not sure I believe you, based on what you do to keep it from happening. Make me believe you really want this to happen.

Client: What do you mean, you don't believe me? I just told you, didn't I? What more do you want?

Confrontation

Counselor/Therapist: Yes, I've heard your words, but you haven't convinced me. I don't think you've convinced yourself, either. Say something that will convince both of us.

Responding to Nonverbal Cues

This strategy enables a counselor or therapist to go beyond a client's words and respond to the messages that are being communicated by the client's physical actions. Care must be taken not to overgeneralize regarding every subtle body movement. The counselor or therapist is looking for patterns that either confirm or deny the truth in the words the client uses to express himself or herself. When such patterns become apparent, it is the responsibility of the counselor or therapist to share these patterns with the client. It becomes the client's responsibility to confirm or deny the credibility of the perception.

Example

Client: (turning away) Yes, you're right. I'm not convinced this is what I want. (smiling) Maybe I was never meant to be happy.

Responding to Nonverbal Cues

Counselor/Therapist: What I said made you angry and, I would suspect, hurt a little. Did you notice you turned away before you began to speak? What were you telling me when you turned away?

Client: (smiling) What you said did hurt me. I was angry, but I'm also embarrassed not to be able to handle this part of my life. I don't like you seeing me this way.

Responding to Nonverbal Cues

Counselor/Therapist: I've noticed that on several occasions when you talk about your feelings of anger, embarrassment, or hopelessness, you smile. What does the smile mean?

Client: (long pause) I guess I want you to believe that it isn't as bad as it sounds or that I'm not as hopeless as I think I am.

Counselor/Therapist: It is bad, or you wouldn't be here, and "hopeless" is your word, not mine. Our time is up for today. Between now and next week, I want you to think about what we've discussed. See you next week?

The strategies we have outlined in this section enable a counselor or therapist to achieve more effectively both the process and outcome goals related to counseling or therapy. Choosing which strategy to use, when to use it, and what its impact will be in the helping relationship is based on the education, experience, and personal dynamics that a counselor or therapist brings to the helping relationship (see Sidebar 1.5).

The Helping Relationship and Diversity

A final factor that affects the helping relationship is diversity. An awareness of diversity addresses the counselor or therapist's openness and motivation to understand more about his or her own diversity as well as the cultural differences that clients bring to the helping relationship (Collins & Arthur, 2010; Montgomery & Kottler, 2005; D. W. Sue & Sue, 2013; S. Sue, Zane, Hall, & Berger, 2009). Such understanding is often characterized as the cornerstone on which the helping relationship rests. The American Counseling Association has reinforced the importance of being sensitive to the various worldviews clients bring to their work with counselors by including the following competencies needed for counseling diverse groups on its website at www.counseling.org/knowledge-center/competencies:

- Advocacy Competencies (March 2003)
- Competencies for Counseling With Lesbian, Gay, Bisexual, Queer, Questioning, Intersex, and Ally Individuals (June 2012)
- Competencies for Addressing Spiritual and Religious Issues in Counseling (May 2009)
- Competencies for Counseling the Multiracial Population (March 2015)
- Multicultural and Social Justice Counseling Competencies (July 2015)
- Multicultural Career Counseling Competencies (August 2009)

In addition, diversity encompasses differences connected with age, disability, religion, gender, geographical location, socioeconomic status, trauma, and a myriad of other defining variables. This understanding, based on both education and life experience, should enable counselors and therapists to increase their sensitivity to the issues that confront clients; should enable them to develop insight into the many variables that affect clients; and should enable them to place clients' issues, problems, and concerns in their proper perspective. The key word in this last statement is *should*. Experience indicates that the key factor in the development of the counselor or therapist's awareness of diversity and its impact on the helping relationship is the counselor's receptiveness, openness, and motivation to gain such awareness. Without these three characteristics, education and experience will have little value. The combination of these characteristics with both education and experience enhances the chances of changing the *should* to *will*.

It is interesting that during the past 15 years, both the American Counseling Association and the National Board for Certified Counselors have been sponsoring and promoting efforts to provide counselor education opportunities to individu-

Sidebar 1.5. Strategy Challenges

This section of the chapter described three sets of strategies (for building rapport, for aiding in data gathering, and for adding depth and enhancement to the relationship). Which of the three sets did you find the most challenging as you read the descriptions and examples? What were the reasons you found them challenging? What could you do to meet the challenges you think those skill sets present?

als residing in other countries. Because interest in providing such opportunities has resulted in a crescendo of international counselor education and supervision programs and platforms, members of the counseling profession have put even more emphasis on the fact that, although counselor receptiveness, awareness, and motivation to become more and more sensitive to the needs of diverse clients are paramount, having an open mindset is only one step in the process of creating a therapeutic helping relationship with diverse clients. Counselors and therapists must be adept at altering their use of basic and advanced counseling skills so that they do not attempt to use interventions connected with Western theories of counseling and psychotherapy with clients with differing worldviews residing in the United States or other countries. What might be readily accepted by a client raised in an individualist family of origin culture can be quite uncomfortable and unacceptable for a client raised in a collectivist family of origin culture. Use of the skill sets, assessment instruments, diagnostic criteria, and approaches to case conceptualization connected with the way counselors work with clients in the United States, for example, would need to be modified. It is important for readers of this book to keep the foregoing discussion in mind as they read Chapter 2, "Diversity and Social Justice Issues in Counseling and Psychotherapy," and are introduced to the theories in Chapters 3 to 17.

The Helping Relationship: Some Final Notes

The helping relationship is the foundation on which the process of counseling or psychotherapy rests. It is best viewed in terms of developmental stages, the first of which begins with the initial meeting of the client and the counselor or therapist and is characterized by rapport building, information gathering, goal determination, and information sharing. Building on the foundation established in the first stage, later stages address extended exploration and problem resolution and then lead to the final stage in this process: termination and follow-up.

The helping relationship, when viewed from this developmental perspective, progresses from stage to stage through the presence of certain components that the counselor or therapist brings to the relationship. The first of these are the core conditions of empathic understanding, respect and positive regard, genuineness and congruence, concreteness, warmth, and immediacy. The provision of these conditions is very much aligned with the personality characteristics of the counselor or therapist that he or she is able to incorporate into the helping relationship.

The second component is a set of strategies aimed at building rapport and encouraging client dialogue, gathering data, and enhancing the relationship. These strategies are skills and techniques that a counselor or therapist gains through education and experience and is able to use effectively within the helping relationship.

The third component centers on issues of cultural diversity and the counselor or therapist's motivation and willingness to develop awareness, understanding, acceptance, and appreciation of client diversity along with his or her capacity to modify the use of skills and techniques that are not congruent with the worldview of a particular client. These factors, when communicated effectively, often are viewed as the cornerstone on which the helping relationship is based.

In combination, the developmental nature of the helping relationship, the presence of the core conditions, the implementation of various strategies, and attention paid to issues of diversity create a facilitative environment in which both the client and the counselor or therapist have the strong potential for positive growth. The potential exists, but guarantees do not. Achieving the true potential of the helping relationship depends on what the client and counselor or therapist bring to the relationship and what each takes from it.

BRIEF APPROACHES: AN OVERVIEW

Tracing the exact beginnings of brief approaches to counseling and therapy is not an easy task. Did they become part of the therapeutic world during World War II, as suggested by Herman (1995), when he stated that military clinicians devised a "menu of creative psychotherapeutic alternatives and shortcuts" (p. 112) to ensure that the maximum number of soldiers could be returned to active duty in the minimum amount of time? Was it the pioneering work at the Mental Research Institute, in the 1950s and 1960s, under the direction of Don Jackson and Gregory Bateson, with consultation and collaboration with Richard Fisch, John Weakland, Jay Haly, William Fry, Jr., Virginia Satir, and Milton Erickson, that provided the real thrust in the development of brief approaches to counseling and psychotherapy? Regardless of where one places the responsibility, brief approaches are today a major part of the therapeutic picture.

According to R. Lewis (2005), approximately 50 brief approaches exist in the literature. Many of these are tied into existing theoretical systems (e.g., rational emotive behavior therapy, reality therapy, psychodrama, Adlerian therapy), and a few stand alone as developing theoretical and therapeutic approaches (e.g., problem-focused brief therapy, solution-focused brief therapy, and solution-oriented and possibility therapy; Palmatier, 1996; Shulman, 1989). Brief approaches are a rapidly developing area, and this development has been encouraged by the response from managed care and its attraction to brief approaches because of their focus on symptom relief and increased functioning as pragmatic and cost effective (Battino, 2007; Hoyt, 1995; Seidel & Hedley, 2008).

R. Lewis (2005) stated that "the overemphasis on length of treatment may take those interested in brief counseling approaches down the wrong path" (p. 176). When discussing brief approaches to counseling and psychotherapy, the emphasis should not be on "brief" but on the concepts of counseling and therapy. Mahoney (1997) stated that "indeed, the actual number of hours logged in psychotherapy is much less important . . . than is the significance of the experiences that transpire during that time" (p. 141). There appears to be no hard and fast rule regarding how long brief counseling and psychotherapy should take. Sharf (1996) stated that three to 40 sessions could be the range. This, of course, is debatable, and generally brief counseling and therapy ranges from one to 25 sessions, with 25 generally considered the maximum number of sessions. Hoyt (1995) perhaps best captured the essence of this number debate when he stated that brief counseling and psychotherapy are not defined by "a particular number of sessions but rather the intention of helping clients make changes in thoughts, feelings, actions in order to move toward or reach a particular goal as time-efficiently as possible" (p. 1).

Given the existence of many different brief approaches, it is important to look at certain factors that seem to be common across these approaches. Cooper (1995) offered the following eight recommendations found in various forms of brief counseling:

- Keep a clear and specific treatment focus.
- Use time conscientiously.

- Limit goals and clearly define outcomes.
- Place an emphasis on the present and the here and now.
- Assess rapidly and integrate this into treatment.
- Review progress frequently and discard ineffective interventions.
- Maintain a high level of therapist–client collaboration.
- Be pragmatic and flexible in technique use.

Addressing this issue further, Fisch (1994) provided counselors or therapists with the following four suggestions common across brief approaches: (a) Narrow the data base regarding counselor–client focus, (b) use interactional rather than intrapsychic concepts, (c) develop a task orientation rather than an insight orientation, and (d) define goals in order to know when to stop therapy.

These common factors were further supported by Bertolino and O'Hanlon (2002) and Hoyt (2000) when they suggested that brief counselors or therapists (a) embrace pragmatism and parsimony, (b) see human change as inevitable, (c) build on client resources and competence, (d) focus on work outside of counseling and psychotherapy, (e) recognize that sometimes counseling and therapy do not help, and (f) view counseling and psychotherapy as more effective when based on specific contexts and problem areas. R. Lewis (2005) further stated that brief counselors or therapists shift their efforts from concentrating on deficits to looking for strengths, from exploring problems to creating solutions, and from a fixation on the past to active construction of a preferred future.

Building on these common factors, the following paragraphs provide brief comparative discussions of the three brief approaches mentioned previously; namely, (a) problem-focused brief therapy, (b) solution-focused brief therapy, and (c) solution-oriented and possibility therapy. These three brief approaches have developed from a common theme rooted in client competence and strengths (DeJong & Berg, 2012; Fisch, 1994) and represent constructivist theoretical approaches to counseling covered in Chapter 16. We cover several interventions here rather than in that chapter, though this section should be revisited when reading Chapter 16. Each of these brief approaches draws on client strengths in solving problems, finding solutions, or discovering possibilities. According to R. Lewis (2005), these

> strength based approaches do not embrace a normative model that prescribes which is normal and healthy or abnormal and deviant, the approaches move away from viewing the client as pathological and resistant, and concentrate on working with clients to find out what works in their own lives. (p. 178)

These approaches were selected as they seem to be representative of the current brief counseling and psychotherapy movement.

Problem-Focused Brief Therapy

Problem-focused brief therapy had its beginnings at the Mental Research Institute in Palo Alto, California. In 1966, Richard Fisch opened the Brief Therapy Center with the express purpose of finding what therapeutic results could occur in a maximum of 10 one-hour sessions. These sessions focused on the main presenting problem, used active techniques to promote change, and searched for the minimum change required to resolve the problem (R. Lewis, 2005). The therapeutic goal was to resolve the presenting problem as it occurs between people with emphasis placed on change and outcomes, not knowledge, insight, or other such concerns. It was assumed that change would be easier if people did something differently (see Sidebar 1.6).

According to Fisch, Weakland, and Segal (1982), clients come to therapy for the following reasons: (a) Clients are concerned about the behavior, actions, thoughts, or feelings of themselves or someone with whom they are involved; (b) clients describe the problem as deviant in the sense of being unusual or inappropriate; (c) clients' efforts to stop or change the behavior have been unsuccessful; and (d) clients seek professional help, as they have not been able to make changes on their own. Clients want change, but the problem formation and problem maintenance form a vicious circle, leaving clients stuck. In fact, the clients' misinterpretation of ordinary life difficulties and their unsuccessful attempts at a solution often aggravate the problem. Given these assumptions, the therapeutic goals for the problem-focused brief therapy approach are to interrupt this vicious circle and initiate resolution of the problem by assessing where clients are stuck, assessing what they are doing to get unstuck, and stopping them from doing what they see as logical or necessary (Fisch, 1990). Reframing, or infusing new meaning into a situation, is a technique often used in this initial process.

During the initial stages of treatment, assessment, via data gathering, is very important. The counselor or therapist, being persistent, firm, and polite and working within clients' position, language, and values, attempts to answer the following questions:

- What is the essential complaint, to whom does it belong, who is doing what that presents a problem to whom, and why does such behavior constitute a problem?
- What solutions have been attempted to solve the problem?
- What are the clients' minimal goals, and how will clients evaluate the achievement of these goals?
- Who is most invested in change?

According to Fisch et al. (1982), it is important that counselors or therapists keep their options open and avoid taking positions prematurely. It is important to take time and encourage clients to be specific in committing to a position. Counselors or therapists need to take a one-down position and put clients at ease by asking for their assistance. It is also important to determine who is most discomforted by the problem: the clients or other persons.

Based on the fact that the solutions attempted by clients maintain and perpetuate the problem, interventions are directed toward helping clients depart from these solutions by either stopping the problem-maintaining behavior or altering the clients' view of the problem so that it is no longer viewed as a problem. Counselors or therapists, using this approach, view problems as arising from the fol-

Sidebar 1.6. The Role of Knowledge or Insight

Do you think a person can solve a problem without knowledge or insight? Why or why not?

lowing five basic solutions that clients tend to maintain: (a) attempting to force something that can occur spontaneously, (b) attempting to master a feared event by postponing it, (c) attempting to reach accord through opposition, (d) attempting to attain compliance through volunteerism, and (e) confirming the accuser's suspicions by defending self.

Other interventions include (a) going slow, directed at clients whose main solution is trying too hard; (b) recognizing the dangers in resolving the problem too quickly; (c) making a U-turn or going in an opposite direction because the strategy being used is not working; and (d) continuing the ineffective approach at arriving at solutions. This is used with clients who are having difficulty changing what they are doing (Fisch et al., 1982). Termination occurs without fanfare and includes assessing goals in a cautionary way.

Solution-Focused Brief Therapy

Solution-focused brief therapy was developed by Steve de Shazer and Insoo Kim Berg at the Brief Family Therapy Center in Milwaukee, Wisconsin. It has its foundation in the theoretical ideas of Bateson and the clinical work of Erickson and the pioneering work conducted at the Mental Research Institute. According to Lipchik (2002), solution-focused brief therapy looks closely at the pattern of interaction surrounding a problem, approaches for changing the pattern, and the creation of outcomes. Its focus, however, shifts from a concentration on problems to a concentration on solutions, drawing on client strengths as well as using all that the client brings that can promote change. For solution-focused counselors or therapists, the solution-finding process holds therapeutic promise and helps clients develop expectations of change and solutions.

Little attention is paid to the details of the problem. More attention is directed at highlighting how the client will know when the problem is solved. The key to this approach is using what clients have, in terms of strengths and resources, that will meet their needs in such a way that they will be able to find satisfactory solutions to problems. This approach emphasizes that counselors or therapists must do more than assess how problems are maintained or how to solve them. Solutions come when people involved in problematic situations are required to do something different, even if it seems irrational, irrelevant, bizarre, or humorous. No one problem or group of problems occurs all the time. A goal of this approach involves getting clients to envision their future without the presenting problem. When this happens, the problem is diminished (de Shazer, 1991; Lipchik, 2002; Walter & Peller, 2000).

According to Miller (2001), solution-focused brief therapy is based on the assumption that solutions are constructed rather than the assumption that problems are solved. This implies that knowing a lot about the problem may not be necessary to formulating a solution. In fact, problems may be unconnected and even irrelevant to the change process (T. F. Lewis & Osborn, 2004). This approach assumes that a small change in one area can lead to greater changes in other areas. This is often referred to as the *ripple effect*, whereby problem irregularities, or times when the problem is not a problem, are identified (Berg & Miller, 1992).

Solution-focused brief therapy assumes that clients want to change and client resistance is not an issue. Counselors or therapists compliment clients on positive steps they have taken; suggest things for them to do that might be good for them; and often assume the role of a student, placing clients in the role of teacher. Clients are encouraged and trusted to know and make decisions regarding what is best for them.

de Shazer (1985) provided a listing of categories (building blocks) under which client complaints could be grouped together with basic assumptions to help counselors and therapists understand these complaints and construct solutions. The building blocks are as follows:

- A bit or sequence of behavior
- The meanings ascribed to the situation
- The frequency and location in which the complaint happens
- The degree to which the complaint is involuntary
- Significant others involved in the complaint
- The question of who or what is to blame
- Environmental factors
- The psychological or feeling state involved
- The past
- Dire predictions of the future
- Utopian expectations (p. 27)

The assumptions include the following:

- Recognize that clients' complaints are brought on by their worldview.
- Realize that complaints are maintained based on the clients' belief that the original decision was the only thing that could have been done. They remain trapped because they keep doing the same thing.
- Initiate minimal change, and once this process begins, clients will provide additional changes for resolving the complaint.
- Focus on clients' view of what reality would look like without the complaint, and use this viewpoint to generate ideas for change.
- Promote problem resolution by suggesting new frames of reference and new behaviors based on clients' view of reality.
- View change holistically; a change in one part of the system will bring about changes in other parts of the system.

Intervention in solution-focused brief therapy takes many forms. Given the nature of the counselor–client or therapist–client relationship, establishing rapport and promoting cooperation are crucial. Based on the interactional process of change and the belief that clients can solve their own problems, counselors or therapists must fit into the worldview of clients. When this is achieved, counselors or therapists begin a change question technique that involves seeking exceptions to the problem or exploring the solutions that clients have attempted. Questions such as, "Since the last time we met, have you been noticing some changes in yourself or discovering a new way of looking at the problem?" "When did you manage this problem in the past?" "What did you do differently?" and "When were things just a little bit better?" all serve to create an expectation for change, emphasize clients' role in this change, and stress the fact that change occurs outside of the counselor or therapist's office.

The miracle question is another intervention that aids clients in clarifying goals and identifying exceptions to the problem by encouraging them to imagine a solution and remove constraints to solving the problem and by building hope for change. Clients are asked, "Suppose that one night, while you were asleep, there was a miracle and this problem was solved. How would you know? What would be different?" (de Shazer, 1991, p. 113). This type of question allows clients to visualize their life without the problem.

The use of scaling questions is another intervention designed to make the abstract concrete by quantifying intangibles, placing power with clients, and demonstrating change (R. Lewis, 2005). In this intervention, clients are asked, "On a scale from 1 to 10, where 1 means you have no influence over your problem, and 10 means you have total influence, where would you place yourself today?" This is often followed by such questions as, "Where would others place you on this scale?" and "What do you need to move a fraction of a point up the scale?"

These examples highlight interventions that attempt to induce doubt regarding the severity and dominance of the problem and aid clients in both finding exceptions to the problem and defining goals that concentrate on constructing solutions. Solution-focused brief therapy concentrates its techniques and interventions on creating the expectation that solutions exist or are imminent.

Solution-Oriented and Possibility Therapy

Solution-oriented and possibility therapy was developed by Bill O'Hanlon and Michele Weiner-Davis and was influenced not only by the work of the Mental Research Institute and the Brief Family Therapy Center but also by that of Milton Erikson and narrative therapists such as White and Epston. The term *possibility* was coined by O'Hanlon to reduce the confusion that often exists between solution-focused and solution-oriented approaches. Solution-oriented and possibility therapy emphasizes clients' competence with counselors or therapists cocreating solvable problems. It has a future goal orientation and focuses on bringing about small but positive outcomes for clients. It emphasizes the clients' internal experiences and stresses that clients must be heard and understood if change is to occur.

Solution-oriented and possibility counselors or therapists view clients as being stuck not only by how they are doing the problem but also by how they are viewing the problem. Therefore, views, actions, and context become crucial, and practitioners are encouraged to attempt the following actions (O'Hanlon & Weiner-Davis, 1989): (a) Change what clients are doing, as this relates to the situation seen as problematic; (b) change the clients' frame of reference and their view of the problem; and (c) bring resources, solutions, and strengths to bear on the problematic situation.

The solution-oriented and possibility approach begins the process by looking at clients' strengths, solutions, and competence and moves the process away from purist thinking toward diverse ideas found in literature using such terms as *constructivist, narrative, postmodern, collaborative, competency-based, interactional,* and more (Bertolino, 1999; Bertolino & O'Hanlon, 2002; DeJong & Berg, 2012). Solution-oriented and possibility therapy validates clients' emotional experiences; is flexible rather than formulaic; and takes into consideration the political, historical, and gender influences that impinge on the clients' problems. It is heuristic in nature and is open to using ideas and perspectives from differing approaches. O'Hanlon (1999) offered the following three principles to guide the work of the solution-oriented and possibility counselor or therapist: (a) Acknowledge and validate clients' perceptions and experiences; (b) facilitate clients in changing how they view things and/or do things; and (c) acknowledge client resources, expertise, and experiences and collaborate with them about the direction counseling is going.

In solution-oriented and possibility therapy, assessment and intervention are not separated into distinct steps. Often, the initial interviewing process is seen as an intervention because, through the use of solution-oriented and possibility techniques (i.e., presuppositional questioning), clients come to view their situations differently. In place of asking, "Did anything good come from the relationship?" one might ask, "What were the good things that came from the relationship?" This type of approach focuses on the way clients perceive and talk about their problems and aids the counselor or therapist in looking for exceptions to the problem in an attempt to normalize the problem, making it simply a natural response to life events. O'Hanlon and Weiner-Davis (1989) offered the following eight techniques for changing patterns of doing or viewing problems:

- Change the frequency or rate of occurrence of the problem.
- Change the time when the problem occurs.
- Change the length of time the problem occurs.
- Change where the problem takes place.
- Change the pattern of the problem by adding something to it.
- Change the sequence of events in the problem pattern.
- Change the problem pattern by breaking it down into smaller parts or elements.
- Change the problem pattern by linking it with some burdensome task.

In each of these change processes, interventions are negotiated collaboratively with clients in a relationship in which change is expected. The goal is to help clients identify possibilities rather than problems and involves using what is going right rather than focusing on what is going wrong. Solution-oriented and possibility counselors and therapists use stories, anecdotes, parables, and humor to help clients change. This is similar to what narrative therapists do in aiding clients to move from problem-saturated stories to more hope-filled alternative stories. Narrative therapists also believe that the client is never the problem—the problem is the problem. This problem externalization has been embraced by solution-oriented and possibility counselors and therapists and has been refined in such a way that the problem is placed outside the clients. For example, if the client's presenting problem is feelings of inferiority, then the counselor or therapist might ask, "How long has this inferiority been controlling your life?" Thus, the presenting problem becomes a controllable entity outside of the client as opposed to an internalized entity within the client. Solutions and possibilities are sought to work effectively with this external visualization (see Sidebar 1.7).

Brief Approaches: Some Final Notes

Brief therapies, regardless of their name, their emphasis, or the techniques and interventions utilized, are major players in today's counseling and therapy marketplace. Spurred on by not only third-party payers but also research regarding the effectiveness of brief approaches, and a client population wanting to be helped as quickly as possible, brief approaches to counseling and psychotherapy have challenged professionals to evolve. This evolution is not one of instant cures but one of timely and efficient provision of service to clients.

MOVING TOWARD AN INTEGRATIVE APPROACH TO COUNSELING AND PSYCHOTHERAPY

Even though this book provides the reader with introductions to a number of theories of counseling and psychotherapy, it is important to realize that few counselors are purists in their practice. In other words, only a small percentage of practitioners (5% or less) describe themselves as maintaining allegiance to only one theoretical set to guide their work with clients (McClure, Livingston, Livingston, & Gage, 2005; Norcross & Beutler, 2011). In the past, many counselors described themselves as eclectic, but the term *integration* is currently being used in the profession because it is a more accurate description of correct practices. Lazarus (2005), in a short history of eclecticism in counseling and psychotherapy, explained that eclecticism has been supplanted by integrationism because of the negative connotation ascribed to the term eclectic because some counselors who called themselves eclectic never developed a theoretical underpinning or rationale for the use of techniques borrowed somewhat haphazardly from various theories. In comparison, integration suggests a merging that may be more reflective of what is happening with the skilled practitioner. Norcross and Beutler (2011) described the four most common types of integration of theories of counseling and psychotherapy: technical integration, theoretical integration, assimilative integration, and common factors integration.

Technical integration is focused on selecting the best treatment option for the individual and the diagnosis and is, as far as possible, evidence based. This type of integrationism uses techniques connected with various theories rather than techniques connected with a single theory or conceptual frame of reference. Arnold Lazarus is one of the pioneers of technical integration, and he called his approach multimodal behavior therapy (Lazarus, 1997). A number of resources available to practitioners connect diagnoses and treatment plans based on what the research shows to be the most efficacious. Barlow and colleagues' (2011) *The Unified Protocol for Transdiagnostic Treatment of Emotional Disorders: Therapist Guide* is an excellent example of this type of integration.

Theoretical integration is based on the idea of blending the best components of two or more theories and assuming that the outcomes of counseling or psychotherapy will be better than the result of using either theory by itself. An excellent example of this kind of an integrative approach can be found in Chapter 10, "Dialectical Behavior Theory."

Assimilative integration is focused on a single theoretical orientation but incorporates, on a very selective basis, techniques from other therapeutic paradigms.

Sidebar 1.7. The Use of Brief Approaches

Which of these three brief approaches do you think you could apply to your life? To the client you are counseling? What is your rationale?

The advantage of working this way is that the counselor bases the case conceptualization and accompanying treatment plan on a single theory. Although the major constructs and goals remain consistent, the transpersonal counselor draws from both Eastern and Western traditions, in selecting the interventions that best address the client's concerns. An example of assimilative integration can be found in Chapter 15, "Transpersonal Theory."

Finally, the common factors integrative approach emphasizes common practices connected with a variety of theories of counseling and psychotherapy. Many of the core dimensions of the helping relationship discussed in this chapter (e.g., empathic understanding, stages, strategies, brief approaches) and common to many theoretical practice sets are drawn on by counselors who see themselves as adhering to a common factors integrative philosophy of counseling.

We want to emphasize the fact that it takes considerable time as well as years of supervised practice to become familiar with the myriad of theories that could be used to guide the process of counseling and psychotherapy. We are not suggesting that by the time they finish this book readers will be able to move toward an integrative approach, but we want them to be thinking about this topic as they read and study each of the chapters in this book.

SUMMARY

This chapter addressed three main themes. First, it provided the reader with information about the factors that affect the helping relationship: definitions and descriptions, stages, core dimensions, strategies, and issues of diversity. Second, it provided an overview of selected brief approaches to counseling, because these approaches, plus the impact of managed care, have precipitated an emphasis on using traditional theories in shorter term counseling. Third, it provided an overview of integrative counseling because it is very likely that, after reading this book, readers will have questions about whether to be a purist in their work or somehow integrate the possibilities for working with clients into a more flexible way of helping. We hope that the information presented in this chapter will not only help readers to understand the dynamics of the helping relationship and their application in both theory-specific and brief approaches but also aid them in incorporating these dynamics into an integrative theoretical approach.

REFERENCES

Barlow, D. H., Farchione, T. J., Fairholme, C. P., Ellard, K. K., Boisseau, C. L., Allen, L. B., & Ehrenreich-May, J. (2011). *The unified protocol for transdiagnostic treatment of emotional disorders: Therapist guide*. New York, NY: Oxford University Press.

Baruth, L. G., & Robinson, E. H. (1987). *An introduction to the counseling profession*. Upper Saddle River, NJ: Prentice Hall.

Battino, R. (2007). Expectation: Principles and practice of very brief therapy. *Contemporary Hypnosis, 24*(1), 19–29.

Belkin, G. S. (1980). *An introduction to counseling*. Dubuque, IA: Brown.

Berg, I. K., & Miller, S. D. (1992). *Working with the problem drinker: A solution-focused approach*. New York, NY: Norton.

Bertolino, B. (1999). *Therapy with troubled teenagers: Rewriting young lives in progress*. New York, NY: Wiley.

Bertolino, B., & O'Hanlon, B. (2002). *Collaborative, competency-based counseling and therapy*. Boston, MA: Allyn & Bacon.

Brammer, L. M. (1985). *The helping relationship: Process and skills* (3rd ed.). Upper Saddle River, NJ: Prentice Hall.

Brammer, L. M., Abrego, P., & Shostrom, E. (1993). *Therapeutic counseling and psychotherapy* (6th ed.). Upper Saddle River, NJ: Prentice Hall.

Brammer, L. M., & MacDonald, G. (1996). *The helping relationship: Process and skills* (6th ed.). Needham Heights, MA: Allyn & Bacon.

Brems, C. (2000). *Dealing with challenges in psychotherapy and counseling*. Belmont, CA: Brooks/Cole.

Brown, D., & Srebalus, D. J. (1988). *An introduction to the counseling profession*. Upper Saddle River, NJ: Prentice Hall.

Brown, J. A., & Pate, R. H. (1983). *Being a counselor: Direction and challenges*. Monterey, CA: Brooks/Cole.

Carkhuff, R. R., & Barenson, B. G. (1967). *Beyond counseling and psychotherapy*. New York, NY: Holt, Rinehart & Winston.

Clark, A. J. (2010). Empathy: An integral model in the counseling process. *Journal of Counseling & Development, 88,* 348–356.

Clemence, A. J., Fowler, J. C., Gottdiener, W. H., Krikorian, S., Charles, M., Damsky, L., & Johnson, B. (2012). Microprocess examination of therapeutic immediacy during a dynamic research interview. *Psychotherapy, 49*(3), 317–329. doi:10.1037/a0026090

Collins, S., & Arthur, N. (2010). Culture-infused counselling: A model for developing multicultural competence. *Counselling Psychology Quarterly, 23*(2), 217–233. doi:10.1080/09515071003798212

Combs, A. W. (1986). What makes a good helper? A person-centered approach. *Person-Centered Review, 1,* 51–61.

Combs, A. W., & Avila, D. (1985). *Helping relationships: Basic concepts for the helping professions*. Boston, MA: Allyn & Bacon.

Cooper, J. F. (1995). *A primer of brief psychotherapy*. New York, NY: Norton.

Corey, M. S., & Corey, G. (2015). *Becoming a helper* (7th ed.). Pacific Grove, CA: Brooks/Cole.

Cormier, W. H., Nurius, P. S., & Osborn, C. J. (2013). *Interviewing and change strategies for helpers* (7th ed.). Pacific Grove, CA: Brooks/Cole.

Coutinho, J. F., Silva, P. O., & Decety, J. (2014). Neurosciences, empathy, and healthy interpersonal relationships: Recent findings and implications for counseling psychology. *Journal of Counseling Psychology, 61,* 541–548. doi:10.1037/cou0000021

de Shazer, S. (1985). *Keys to solution in brief therapy*. New York, NY: Norton.

de Shazer, S. (1991). *Putting difference to work*. New York, NY: Norton.

DeJong, P., & Berg, I. K. (2012). *Interviewing for solutions* (4th ed.). Pacific Grove, CA: Brooks/Cole.

Egan, G. (2013). *The skilled helper* (10th ed.). Pacific Grove, CA: Brooks/Cole.

Farber, B. A., & Doolin, E. M. (2011). Positive regard. *Psychotherapy, 48*(1), 58–64. doi:10.1037/a0022141

Fisch, R. (1990). Problem-solving psychotherapy. In J. K. Zeig & W. M. Munion (Eds.), *What is psychotherapy? Contemporary perspectives* (pp. 269–273). San Francisco, CA: Jossey-Bass.

Fisch, R. (1994). Basic elements in the brief therapies. In M. F. Hoyt (Ed.), *Constructive therapies* (pp. 126–139). New York, NY: Guilford Press.

Fisch, R., Weakland, J. H., & Segal, L. (1982). *Tactics of change: Doing therapy briefly.* San Francisco, CA: Jossey-Bass.

Freedberg, S. (2007). Re-examining empathy: A relational-feminist point of view. *Social Work, 52*(1), 251–259.

Gatongi, F. (2008). Person-centred approach in schools: Is it the answer to disruptive behaviour in our classrooms? *Counseling Psychology Quarterly, 20,* 205–211.

Gilliland, B. E., James, R. K., & Bowman, J. T. (1989). Theories and strategies in counseling and psychotherapy (2nd ed.). Upper Saddle River, NJ: Prentice Hall.

Gladding, S. (2012). *Counseling: A comprehensive profession* (7th ed.). Englewood Cliffs, NJ: Prentice Hall.

Halverson, S., & Miars, R. (2005). The helping relationship. In D. Capuzzi & D. Gross (Eds.), *Introduction to the counseling profession* (4th ed., pp. 56–74). Boston, MA: Allyn & Bacon.

Herman, E. (1995). *The romance of American psychology: Political culture in the age of experts.* Berkeley, CA: University of California Press.

Hoyt, M. F. (1995). *Brief therapy and managed care: Readings for contemporary practice.* San Francisco, CA: Jossey-Bass.

Hoyt, M. F. (2000). *Some stories are better than others: Doing what works in brief therapy and managed care.* Philadelphia, PA: Brunner/Mazel.

Ibrahim, F. A., & Dykeman, C. (2011). Counseling Muslim Americans: Cultural and spiritual assessments. *Journal of Counseling & Development, 89,* 387–396. doi:10.1002/j.1556-6676.2011.tb02835.x

Ivey, A. E. (1998). *Intentional interviewing and counseling: Facilitating client development in a multicultural society.* Pacific Grove, CA: Brooks/Cole.

Ivey, A., Ivey, M., & Zalaquett, C. (2013). *Intentional interviewing and counseling: Facilitating client development in a multicultural world* (8th ed.). Belmont, CA: Brooks/Cole.

Klein, M. H., Michels, J. L., Kolden, G. G., & Chisolm-Stockard, S. (2001). Congruence or genuineness. *Psychotherapy: Theory, Research, Practice, Training, 38,* 396–400. doi:10.1037/0033-3204.38.4.396

Kolden, G. G., Klein, M. H., Wang, C., & Austin, S. B. (2011). Congruence/genuineness. *Psychotherapy, 48*(1), 65–71. doi:10.1037/a0022064

Kottler, J., & Brown, R. (1992). *Introduction to therapeutic counseling* (2nd ed.). Pacific Grove, CA: Brooks/Cole.

Lazarus, A. (1997). *Brief but comprehensive psychotherapy: The multimodal way.* New York, NY: Springer.

Lazarus, A. (2005). Is there still a need for psychotherapy integration? *Current Psychology, 24*(3), 149–152. doi:10.1007/s12144-005-1018-5

Lewis, R. (2005). Individual counseling: Brief approaches. In D. Capuzzi & D. Gross (Eds.), *Introduction to the counseling profession* (4th ed., pp. 173–193). Boston, MA: Allyn & Bacon.

Lewis, T. F., & Osborn, C. J. (2004). Solution-focused counseling and motivational interviewing: A consideration of confluence. *Journal of Counseling & Development, 82,* 38–48.

Lipchik, E. (2002). *Beyond technique in solution-focused therapy: Working with emotions and the therapeutic relationship.* New York, NY: Guilford Press.

Mahoney, M. J. (1997). Brief moments and enduring effects: Reflections on time and timing in psychotherapy. In W. J. Mathews & J. H. Edgette (Eds.), *Current thinking and research in brief therapy: Solutions, strategies, narratives* (pp. 123–142). New York, NY: Brunner/Mazel.

Mayotte-Blum, J., Slavin-Mulford, J., Lehmann, M., Pesale, F., Becker-Matero, N., & Hilsenroth, M. (2012). Therapeutic immediacy across long-term psychodynamic psychotherapy: An evidence-based case study. *Journal of Counseling Psychology, 59*(1), 27–40. doi:10.1037/a0026087

McClure, R., Livingston, R., Livingston, K., & Gage, R. (2005). A survey of practicing psychotherapists. *Journal of Professional Counseling: Practice, Theory, & Research, 33*(1), 35–46.

Miars, B. D., & Halverson, S. (2001). The helping relationship. In D. Capuzzi & D. Gross (Eds.), *Introduction to the counseling profession* (3rd ed., pp. 50–68). Needham Heights, MA: Allyn & Bacon.

Miller, G. (2001). Changing the subject: Self-construction in brief therapy. In J. F. Gubrium & J. A. Holstein (Eds.), *Institutional selves: Troubled identities in a postmodern world* (pp. 64–83). New York, NY: Oxford University Press.

Montgomery, M., & Kottler, J. (2005). The developing counselor. In D. Comstock (Ed.), *Diversity and development: Critical contexts that shape our lives and relationships* (pp. 91–110). Belmont, CA: Brooks/Cole.

Norcross, J. C., & Beutler, L. E. (2011). Integrative psychotherapies. In R. J. Corsini & D. Wedding (Eds.), *Current psychotherapies* (9th ed., pp. 502–535). Belmont, CA: Brooks/Cole.

O'Hanlon, W. H. (1999). *Do one thing different: And other uncommonly sensible solutions to life's persistent problems.* New York, NY: Morrow.

O'Hanlon, W. H., & Weiner-Davis, M. (1989). *In search of solutions: A new direction in psychotherapy.* New York, NY: Norton.

Okun, B. (1992). *Effective helping: Interviews and counseling techniques* (4th ed.). Pacific Grove, CA: Brooks/Cole.

Osipow, S. H., Walsh, W. B., & Tosi, D. J. (1980). *A survey of counseling methods.* Homewood, IL: Dorsey.

Palmatier, L. L. (1996). Freud defrauded while Glasser defreuded: From pathologizing to talking solutions. *Journal of Reality Therapy, 16,* 75–94.

Prochaska, J. O., & Norcross, J. C. (2013). *Systems of psychotherapy: A transtheoretical analysis* (8th ed.). Pacific Grove, CA: Brooks/Cole.

Purkey, W. W., & Schmidt, J. J. (1987). *The inviting relationship: An expanded perspective for professional counseling.* Upper Saddle River, NJ: Prentice Hall.

Rogers, C. R. (1957). The necessary and sufficient conditions of therapeutic personality change. *Journal of Consulting Psychology, 21,* 95–103.

Rogers, C. R. (1961). *On becoming a person: A therapist's view of psychotherapy.* Boston, MA: Houghton Mifflin.

Schnellbacher, J., & Leijssen, M. (2009). The significance of therapist genuineness from the client's perspective. *Journal of Humanistic Psychology, 49,* 207–228.

Seidel, A., & Hedley, D. (2008). The use of solution-focused therapy with older adults in Mexico: A preliminary study. *American Journal of Family Therapy, 46,* 242–252.

Seligman, L. (2001). *Systems, strategies, and skills of counseling and psychotherapy.* Upper Saddle River, NJ: Prentice Hall.

Sharf, R. S. (1996). *Theories of psychotherapy and counseling: Concepts and cases.* Pacific Grove, CA: Brooks/Cole.

Shulman, B. H. (1989). Some remarks on brief therapy. *Individual Psychology: The Journal of Adlerian Therapy, Research & Practice, 45*(1–2), 34–37.

Singer, T., Critchley, H. D., & Preuschoff, K. (2009). A common role of insula in feelings, empathy and uncertainty. *Trends in Cognitive Sciences, 13,* 334–340. doi:10.1016/j.tics.2009.05.001

Skovholt, T. M. (2005). The cycle of caring: A model of expertise in the helping professions. *Journal of Mental Health Counseling, 27,* 82–93.

Sommers-Flanagan, J. (2007). The development and evolution of person-centered expressive art therapy: A conversation with Natalie Rogers. *Journal of Counseling & Development, 85,* 120–125.

Sommers-Flanagan, J. (2015). Evidence-based relationship practice: Enhancing counselor competence. *Journal of Mental Health Counseling, 37,* 95–108.

Sue, D. W., & Sue, D. (2013). *Counseling the culturally diverse: Theory and practice* (6th ed.). Hoboken, NJ: Wiley.

Sue, S., Zane, N., Hall, N., & Berger, L. (2009). The case of cultural competency in psychotherapeutic interventions. *Annual Reviews: Psychology, 60,* 525–548.

Truax, C. B., & Carkhuff, R. R. (1967). *Towards effective counseling and psychotherapy: Training and practice.* Chicago, IL: Aldine.

Walter, J. L., & Peller, J. F. (2000). *Recreating brief therapy: Preferences and possibilities.* New York, NY: Norton.

Chapter 2

Diversity and Social Justice Issues in Counseling and Psychotherapy

Manivong J. Ratts, Julian Rafferty McCullough, and Deborah J. Rubel

Issues of diversity and social justice have been brought to the forefront of discussion among educators and counselors as the racial and cultural diversification of the United States have underscored an increased commitment to providing multicultural and advocacy-competent counseling to diverse populations (Johnson & Jackson Williams, 2014; Sue & Sue, 2013; Zalaquett, Foley, Tillotson, Dinsmore, & Hof, 2008). Although there is widespread acceptance that counselors must provide competent services to diverse clients, those within the helping professions continue to more clearly define what competency means and how best to deliver these services to clients who encompass uniquely diverse populations. Often, traditional theories of counseling seem to fall short of addressing the needs of diverse clients and have been criticized for their limitations for this purpose.

To challenge the limitations of traditional counseling theories and practices, a variety of models, theories, and concepts have been created to address the needs of diverse clients during the counseling process. These theories are not meant to replace existing theories but to add to the ways in which counselors understand themselves and diverse clients, broaden their view of the counseling process, and add to their repertoire of techniques and strategies. Most important, they are meant to assist counselors in seeing themselves, their clients, and the practice of counseling within a broad cultural context (Sue & Sue, 2013).

This chapter provides a context for diversity and social justice issues in counseling by (a) clarifying key concepts and reviewing the history of diversity and social justice issues in counseling; (b) increasing understanding of how diversity and social justice issues influence individual and group functioning; (c) increasing awareness of how diversity and social justice may influence the counseling process; (d) presenting several perspectives on diversity and social-justice-oriented interventions; and (e) suggesting ways to develop self-awareness, knowledge of diverse populations, and counseling skills relevant to diversity and social justice.

DEFINITIONS

Though they are deeply connected, multiculturalism and social justice are often confusing and difficult to discuss because of the lack of clear, common language and meanings with which to communicate these important ideas. In this chapter, we provide definitions for key concepts as they are discussed. First, however, we define several key terms.

Within the counseling profession, the term *multicultural* encompasses individual and group cultural differences. Multicultural counseling not only incorporates racial and ethnic differences but includes other dimensions of diversity, such as socioeconomic status, ability/disability status, gender, gender identity, sexual orientation, immigration status, age, religion, and spirituality. Although the term *multicultural* has become more comprehensive of these dimensions, more inclusive definitions of multiculturalism have been criticized for diverting discussion away from issues related to race and ethnicity to other issues when discussion becomes uncomfortable (Helms & Cook, 1999; Sue & Sue, 2013; see Sidebar 2.1).

Discussions about multicultural counseling often refer to cultural differences. *Culture* is the "characteristic values, behaviors, products, and worldviews of a group of people with a distinct sociohistorical context" (T. Smith & Kehe, 2004, p. 329). Cultural differences may be readily observable as differences in clothing, foods, customs or traditions, and languages or as more subtle but crucial differences in parenting beliefs, family structure, social hierarchy, gender-role expectations, communication style, and relationship to time and space.

Diverse groups, such as women, individuals with disabilities, or lesbian, gay, bisexual, and transgender (LGBT) persons, may also encompass distinct group cultures, and their unique experiences are significant to the counseling process. Moreover, within LGBT group identities, for instance, there are many additional intersections of identity, such as age, class, race, or ethnicity, that contribute to the complexity and diversity of individuals who identify as members of LGBT groups (McCullough & Winninghoff, 2014). It is important for counselors to understand this interplay of multiple identities when they are present in clients.

Sidebar 2.1. Race and Ethnicity

What is the difference between race and ethnicity? Many people use the terms *race* and *ethnicity* interchangeably, but how do these terms differ? *Race* is a categorization of individuals based on skin color and other physical attributes, historical geographic origin, and the perceptions of the dominant group. *Ethnicity* is an individual's identification with a group based on culture; nationalism; citizenship; or interactions of race, religion, and sociopolitical history (T. Smith & Kehe, 2004).

When discussing diversity, it is important to understand terms that describe social or cultural groups that are numerically superior to or hold more power and status than groups that have fewer numbers or less power and status. The terms *majority, dominant culture,* and *agent* refer to groups and members of groups who are more numerous or hold more power. The terms *minority, nondominant culture, underrepresented, marginalized,* and *target* refer to groups and individuals who have fewer numbers and/or less power. In this chapter, all terms used reflect the literature from which the information was drawn. However, the term *diverse clients* is used to indicate clients who differ significantly in experiences, culture, or social identity from the counselor and/or who identify predominantly with minority, nondominant cultural, underrepresented, or target groups.

It is difficult to work with diverse clients without an understanding of social justice, oppression, and what it means to be a change agent (Ratts, 2009b). The social justice counseling perspective has at its core the goal of full and equal participation of all groups in society (Bell, 2007). D. J. Goodman (2011) further described social justice as a process of seeking dignity, self-determination, and safety for all people by addressing issues of equity, power, and oppression. Thus, counselors working from a social justice perspective facilitate client well-being by seeking to establish a more equal distribution of power and resources in society through macrolevel interventions, such as advocacy with and on behalf of a group, or microlevel interventions that occur while working with a client, addressing issues in session (L. A. Goodman et al., 2004; Lewis, Arnold, House, & Toporek, 2002).

The premise behind the social justice counseling perspective is the belief that oppression is the root of many client problems. According to Hardiman and Jackson (1982), *oppression* is

> simply not an ideology or set of beliefs that asserts one group's superiority over another. Nor is it random acts of discrimination or harassment toward members of the subordinate group. It is a system of domination with many interlocking parts. (p. 2)

A *change agent* is "someone who strives to move against the status quo when [he or she] feels that it is hurting those individuals whom [he or she] is trying to help" (Baker & Cramer, 1972, p. 661). Both multicultural and social justice counseling perspectives responded to a growing awareness of the effects of cultural oppression on the counseling relationship and the changing demographics of the U.S. population (Ratts & Pedersen, 2014).

CHANGING DEMOGRAPHICS IN U.S. SOCIETY

The increasing diversity of the U.S. population is often mentioned in the rationale for increased attention to the impact of social and cultural differences on the counseling process (Johnson & Jackson Williams, 2014; Zalaquett et al., 2008). According to the most current population projections, by the year 2044, there will be a minority–majority crossover. More than half of Americans will identify as a member of a racial or ethnic minority group; individuals identifying as two or more races will be the fastest growing group, followed by Asian Americans and then Hispanic and Latino Americans (Colby & Ortman, 2015). Considering the current population of individuals younger than the age of 18, the country has already become a majority–minority crossover nation in terms of age.

The same census projection estimates that persons older than the age of 65 will account for nearly 20% of the population, and 20% of the population will identify as having a disability (Colby & Ortman, 2015). Although the 2010 U.S. Census reported same-sex households, it did not track sexual orientation. According to Gates (2011) and Gates and Newport (2012), adults who identify as LGBT make up between 3.4% and 3.8% of the U.S. population, yet the estimated number of LGBT people living in the United States could be higher, considering the social stigma that accompanies these identities. When self-reporting, adults may not disclose their LGBT identities out of fear (Gates & Newport, 2012). The census estimates that approximately 1% of U.S. households identified as same sex but that the numbers vary greatly by region, with 0.29% for Wyoming and 4.01% for the District of Columbia (Lofquist, 2011). These numbers, coupled with the relatively low status and power of the aforementioned marginalized groups and women in U.S. society (Sue & Sue, 2013), indicate that understanding diversity and working toward social justice are major issues facing U.S. society.

Diversity has the potential to strengthen society, but it may also contribute to misunderstanding, conflict, and oppression (Bell, 2007). The counseling profession is often cited for promoting the well-being of diverse people; however, it has often failed in this capacity (Prilleltensky, 1994; Sue & Sue, 2013). More specifically, it has been cited that racial/ethnic minority populations underutilize counseling services, terminate services prematurely, and suffer psychological harm when treated according to traditional models (Berger, Zane, & Hwang, 2014). It has also been asserted that when counseling does not acknowledge cultural issues and societal power dynamics, it may promote an unjust status quo (J. H. Katz, 1985).

These criticisms are generally linked to cultural bias in counseling practice. Issues contributing to cultural bias include such counselor issues as adhering to culturally determined definitions of normal behavior, language, and other differences that impede counselor–client communication; minimizing or ignoring the impact of client group sociopolitical history; and underutilizing client support systems and systemic interventions. A. D. Katz and Hoyt (2014) contended that counselor automatic prejudice was a significant predictor of racial bias toward clients. Furthermore, counselors often seemed unaware of personal biased attitudes toward clients; even if their behaviors displayed otherwise, and even if they were aware of the biases, they were not always honest when solicited. Addressing these limitations to provide competent counseling to diverse clients continues to be the focus of both multicultural and social justice counseling perspectives (Ratts, D'Andrea, & Arredondo, 2004).

MULTICULTURAL AND SOCIAL JUSTICE COUNSELING PERSPECTIVES

The need to address issues of diversity in counseling has given rise to two emerging but complementary perspectives. The multicultural counseling perspective has been predominantly represented in professional literature and organizations. As this perspective has developed and matured, critics have noted its limitations, and the social justice counseling perspective has gained credibility as a complement that answers the limitations (Vera & Speight, 2003). Although the two perspectives differ to some degree, they share many foundational values, concepts, and skills. For readers to more fully understand both perspectives, it is useful to review their history, similarities, and differences.

Multicultural Counseling

Many scholars have attempted to define multicultural counseling during its evolution. Vontress (1988) defined *multicultural counseling* as "counseling in which the counselor and the client are culturally different because of socialization acquired in distinct cultural, subcultural, racioethnic, or socioeconomic environments" (p. 74). More recently, Sue and Sue (2013) described multicultural counseling as a helping process that relies on both universal and culture-specific techniques to meet goals that are consistent with client values; recognizes individual, group, and universal dimensions of client identity; and integrates client worldview into the assessment, diagnosis, and treatment of clients and client systems.

These definitions share the assumptions that counseling professionals should recognize the impact of cultural differences on client life experiences, client–counselor relationships, and the counseling process. Prior to the development of a multicultural counseling perspective, counseling was often viewed as a culture-free process in which cultural differences between the client and counselor were largely ignored (Ivey, D'Andrea, & Ivey, 2012).

The multicultural counseling movement originated in the 1950s (Jackson, 1995) in response to recognition that the United States had become increasingly diverse in terms of race, culture, and language. Racial segregation, systematic discrimination, and prejudice were widespread during this era, and as an extension to societal inequality, counseling with clients of color during this time focused primarily on assimilation into the White dominant culture. Although the professional literature at the time had begun to address these issues, people of color were underrepresented as counselors, counseling scholars, and members and leaders of counseling-related professional organizations (Jackson, 1995). The inequalities served as painful motivation for society and the profession to change as they entered the 1960s.

The 1960s were a time of social and political unrest, and open challenge of the White establishment and racist institutions became commonplace. During this time, mental health scholars and practitioners began to question the racist counseling practices that were prevalent in the field (Pope-Davis, Coleman, Liu, & Toporek, 2003; Sue & Sue, 2013). This questioning led to positive changes in the profession, such as increased numbers of publications and studies dedicated to issues of race and professional groups to raise awareness (Jackson, 1995).

The end of the 1960s marked the formation of the Association of Non-White Concerns (ANWC), which consisted mainly of African American members of the American Personnel and Guidance Association, the predecessor of the American Counseling Association (ACA). Initially, the American Personnel and Guidance Association refused to recognize ANWC as an official division, and it was not until 1972 that official divisional status was granted (McFadden & Lipscomb, 1985). This led to the creation of the ANWC journal, the *Journal of Non-White Concerns.* Also, the 1970s began to bring a broader focus to counseling that included other racial and ethnic groups as well as women and people with disabilities.

In the 1980s and 1990s, multicultural issues became a priority in the counseling profession, with unprecedented numbers of publications devoted to the subject (Jackson, 1995). During this era, ANWC changed its name to the Association for Multicultural Counseling and Development (AMCD; Parker, 1991), which reflected a desire to widen the focus from primarily African American concerns to include the concerns of Latino/Latina Americans, Asian Americans, and Native Americans (Lee, 1999).

The 1990s and the new millennium brought legitimacy to multicultural counseling (Sue & Sue, 2013). Part of this legitimacy can be attributed to AMCD's 1991 approval of the Multicultural Counseling Competencies (MCC) as standards for counselor training and practice (Sue, Arredondo, & McDavis, 1992). The original MCC contained 31 competencies, organized by attitudes and beliefs, knowledge, and skills, that emphasize counselors' actively seeking understanding of themselves, their clients, and their clients' environments and providing services that fully respect, embrace, and utilize diverse clients' unique life experiences (see Sidebar 2.2).

In addition to increased credibility, debate regarding the scope of multicultural counseling as well as its limitations has emerged (Pope, 1995). The most prominent criticisms are that the multicultural counseling movement has emphasized cultural awareness within counseling sessions but has placed less emphasis on systemic social change strategies and social justice (Vera & Speight, 2003) and that the movement has emphasized issues of race and ethnicity over other social identity variables such as gender, sexual orientation, religion, class, and disability status (Carroll, Gilroy, & Ryan, 2002; Fukuyama, 1990; Pope, 1995). These limitations have led to increased calls for the inclusion of a social justice perspective in counseling (L. A. Goodman et al., 2004; Vera & Speight, 2003).

In the summer of 2015, AMCD and the ACA both endorsed a more contemporary version of the MCC. The MCC were updated to reflect the multiple intersections of identities and their complexities within the counseling context. The competencies have been renamed the Multicultural and Social Justice Counseling Competencies and include a social justice advocacy framework to address the increasing need for counselors to advocate for clients not only on an individual level but also within a more institutional context (Ratts, Singh, Nassar-McMillan, Butler, & McCullough, 2015).

Social Justice Counseling

Although emphasis on social justice counseling as a paradigm unto itself is recent, the origins of social justice within the counseling profession are much deeper. According

Sidebar 2.2. The Evolution of Multicultural Counseling

1950s: The multicultural counseling movement originates amid a climate of social inequality in the United States.

1960s: The questioning of racist counseling practices by practitioners leads to the formation of the ANWC.

1970s: Official divisional status is granted to ANWC, and the division begins to widen its focus to include women and individuals with disabilities.

1980s: Multicultural issues are prioritized in counseling, as evidenced by increased publications dedicated to the subject. ANWC becomes the AMCD.

1990s: AMCD approves the MCC, setting standards for counselor training and practice.

2000s: The field of multicultural counseling continues to broaden its focus to include other social identity variables, such as gender, gender identity, sexual orientation, religion, social class, ability/disability status, and immigration status, leading many to look to more of a social justice perspective in counseling.

to Kiselica and Robinson (2001), social justice has been an integral part of the counseling profession since the early 1900s, when counseling pioneers Frank Parsons and Clifford Beers responded to the exploitation of immigrants to the United States and the inhumane treatment of people with mental illness, respectively. Though they were not counselors, their work affected the counseling profession in profound ways. Both believed that counseling should address larger social, political, and economic issues that contribute to clients' problems.

Despite these deep roots, social justice concepts made few appearances in the counseling literature until the 1970s. Articles published during this time addressed such topics as systemic barriers to client well-being (Dahl, 1971) and advocacy for marginalized groups (Gardner, 1971; Killinger, 1971; Ream, 1971; P. M. Smith, 1971). Psychological problems, which had been viewed as originating inside the client, were now linked with factors outside the client (Jackson, 1995).

Calls for the adoption of a social justice counseling perspective continued in the 1980s. J. H. Katz (1985) argued that all counseling theories and practices emerge from limited cultural contexts and thus are not value neutral. Moreover, she claimed that adhering to traditional counseling paradigms promoted a White, middle-class status quo and that counselor denial of the value-laden nature of the helping process was a significant barrier to understanding diverse client concerns.

Several key events occurred during the 1990s that advanced the social justice counseling perspective. In 1999, Loretta Bradley was elected ACA president, and during her tenure she selected "Advocacy: A Voice for Our Clients and Communities" as the theme of her presidential address. That same year, the formation of Counselors for Social Justice, a division of the ACA, served to legitimize the social justice counseling perspective (Ratts, 2009a).

During the new millennium, the social justice counseling perspective has continued to gain support. Since 2000, Division 17 of the American Psychological Association has published two special issues of *The Counseling Psychologist* dedicated to social justice issues in counseling. In addition, the ACA Advocacy Competencies, which serve as a how-to manual for addressing issues of social justice and oppression in counseling, were finalized in 2003 by a task force of Counselors for Social Justice leaders (Toporek, Lewis, & Crethar, 2009).

Ratts and Pedersen's (2014) book *Counseling for Multiculturalism and Social Justice* merged the two movements. In this book, they provided a practical framework to help counselors balance individual counseling with social justice advocacy using the counselor–advocate–scholar model. Moreover, Steele, Bischof, and Craig (2014) conducted a study of 214 members of the ACA to determine perceptions of social justice advocacy. The findings indicated a gap between theory and practice associated with social justice advocacy. Although participants emphasized the importance of social justice advocacy, they indicated that they did not often participate in activities to promote social justice advocacy. Indeed, this is an area for greater development in counselor training for the future. In their recent book, R. D. Goodman and Gorski (2015) illustrated the need to infuse both multicultural and social justice counseling. They urged counselors to consider "a transformative multiculturalism grounded in ideals of equity and social justice" (p. 2).

In summary, both multicultural and social justice counseling perspectives share at their core assumptions that counselors must consider clients' social and cultural contexts during the counseling process, that oppression significantly affects the lives of many diverse clients, and that counselors must go outside the boundaries of traditional counseling theory and technique to serve these clients (Constantine & Sue, 2005; Parham, Ajamu, & White, 2011). Given the historical, philosophical, and practical connections that exist, counselors should understand that both perspectives are needed to adequately address the impact of social and cultural differences and oppression on diverse clients (Ratts et al., 2004). Accordingly, in this chapter, we address diversity in a broad sense and discuss both macrolevel and microlevel conceptualizations of and interventions for diverse clients and their environments.

COUNSELING WITH DIVERSE CLIENTS

Becoming a counselor who is competent in diversity and social justice means learning to view oneself, others, and the world in new ways. The process of stepping outside one's life experience to understand and interact differently with others is inherently difficult. Counseling theories assist counselors in this process by providing a framework for understanding clients and their concerns, defining the counseling relationship, suggesting the goals and overall process of counseling, and describing interventions and strategies to achieve these goals. Although no comprehensive counseling theories exist that address all aspects of diversity, we review in this section a range of useful theories, concepts, and suggestions for understanding and working with diverse clients.

Berger et al. (2014) found that mental health care providers who understand the communities, individuals, and cultural factors inhibiting or increasing well-being are more likely to provide culturally competent care, potentially increasing satisfaction and reducing the dropout rates of ethnic and cultural minority groups. Moreover, according to Constantine (2001), counselors need to be able to understand diverse clients and their concerns in terms of sociocultural and systemic factors to adequately treat them. However, most traditional counseling theories do not account for these factors and contain culturally determined assumptions about behavior that tend to skew judgments of abnormality toward diverse clients (Sue & Sue, 2013).

Fortunately, the diversity, multicultural, and social justice counseling literatures provide theories and concepts that help integrate sociocultural and systemic factors into the understanding of diverse clients and their concerns. The following sections describe three such concepts: the oppression model, social identity development, and worldview.

Understanding Diverse Clients Through the Oppression Model

Both multicultural and social justice counseling perspectives stress the importance of understanding clients and their concerns in terms of the systems in which they develop and live. This type of understanding allows counselors to see themselves, their clients, and the counseling relationship as part of societal systems; envision external barriers to client well-being; and implement systemic interventions, such as advocacy. One way to conceptualize societal systems is through the oppression model (Bell, 2007).

Social identity groups are collections of people who share physical, cultural, or social characteristics within one of the categories of social identity. The common social identity group categories included in discussions of diversity are race, ethnicity, gender, sexual orientation, class, disability, age, and religion (Hardiman & Jackson, 2007). According to the oppression model, within each identity group category, specific identity groups are valued more highly and consequently have more power than other groups. Social identity groups with more power are known as *dominant* or *agent groups*.

Currently in the United States, agent groups include Whites, heterosexuals, males, the able bodied, the upper class, and young or middle-aged adults (Hardiman & Jackson, 2007). Social identity groups that have less power are known as *target groups* and include, but are not limited to, people of color, LGBT people, females, people with disabilities, people who are undocumented immigrants, the working class or poor, and older adults or children (Hardiman & Jackson, 2007).

Young (2011) described the process of cultural oppression as "the universalization of a dominant group's experience and culture, and its establishment as the norm" (p. 59). Oppression begins with agent groups systematically devaluing the values, beliefs, and experiences of target groups. A multileveled socialization process that occurs both overtly and covertly perpetuates this devaluation. Many social and psychological processes contribute to the devaluation process, but the basic dynamics can be understood through examining the roles of stereotypes, prejudice, discrimination, and privilege.

Stereotypes are negative generalizations about social identity groups and group members. Stereotypes allow people to selectively attend to negative group attributes that may or may not exist and form simplistic, negative views that dehumanize and deny the complexity of human identity. Consequently, many prejudices are based on stereotypes. Prejudices are judgments of social identity groups or group members made without adequate information or contact (T. Smith & Kehe, 2004). Prejudices serve individuals and groups by contrasting their group with another and then by justifying the unequal treatment of the other group. This, the active form of prejudice, is called *discrimination*.

Discrimination is behavior by one social identity group that causes harm to members of other social identity groups (T. Smith & Kehe, 2004). Discrimination can take several forms. Individual and institutional discrimination result from the actions of individuals and institutions that discriminate against target social identity groups and individuals. Structural discrimination results from policies and practices that unintentionally discriminate against target social identity groups.

Related to structural discrimination is *privilege*, which is defined as unearned access to resources that is readily available to members of agent groups (T. Smith & Kehe, 2004). Because of their access to resources and power, members of agent groups can function without understanding the needs of target individuals and group members; consequently, they are blind to their own privilege and to the experiences of target groups and group members. Thus, privilege is much more difficult to identify and eradicate than overt discrimination.

Unfortunately, privilege allows for the creation of policies, laws, organizations, and institutions that are discriminatory because of its association with agents in decision-making positions, its ability to blind agents to the needs and experiences of target groups and group members, and its invisibility. These structures continue to socialize generations of agents to privilege while socializing targets to oppression, powerlessness, and discrimination.

The material, emotional, and relational results of oppression are very relevant to the counseling process. Clients may lack access to resources such as basic human needs and education and suffer discriminatory treatment by banks, law enforcement, and employers. The experience of being oppressed profoundly affects how target groups and individuals view themselves and others. The emotional results of oppression include internalized oppression, learned helplessness, and functional paranoia (Sue & Sue, 2013). In addition, the relational results of oppression may manifest in the therapeutic relationship as mistrust and anger (Helms & Cook, 1999).

The oppression model gives counselors a basic framework for understanding the large and small systems in which counselors and clients function, understanding agent and target client experiences, and understanding themselves as people who have also developed within these systems. The oppression model also reminds practitioners to be vigilant for oppression, discrimination, and privilege and to assume that all dominant cultural systems encompass some oppressive aspects.

Understanding Diverse Clients Through Social Identity Development

Counselors have traditionally understood client identity through human theories such as Erik Erikson's psychosocial theory and Sigmund Freud's psychoanalytic theory (Qin & Comstock, 2005). However, these theories do not adequately assist counselors in understanding how social, political, and cultural contexts influence diverse client identity. Social identity development models have emerged in part to answer this need. According to Sue and Sue (2013), racial/cultural identity models, a form of social identity development model, represent some of the most useful frameworks for better understanding and treating clients with diverse identities. This section describes a process of social identity development, identifies prominent social identity models, and discusses the utility of these models.

Identity is profoundly affected by the socially assigned designations of culture, race, ethnicity, gender, religion, sexual orientation, gender identity, ability/disability, and class, among others. Identity, or sense of self, begins with the individual characteristics and social identity group memberships with which a person is born (Tatum, 2000). Throughout life, one's identity is influenced by family; institutions such as schools, churches, and legal systems; and the cultural environments of communities, regions, and nations.

Bronfenbrenner (1981) referred to this as the *ecological environment* and described these distinct settings as similar to Russian nesting dolls, with one layer inside of the other and the innermost layer containing the developing person. Within these contexts, social identity group memberships are valued differently. For instance, within one family, males may be valued more highly than females, or within a community, being heterosexual may be valued more highly than being gay, lesbian, or bisexual. Each valuation may be internalized by the person to some degree as part of his or her identity. In this way, social identity development affects how people view and feel about themselves, members of their identity groups, and those in other groups (Helms & Cook, 1999).

Social identity development models emerged for the purpose of simplifying the complexities of identity development. Most social identity development models characterize individuals as having varying degrees of awareness and acceptance of their social identities. These models describe individuals' level of identification with social identity groups through the behaviors and attitudes they display (Helms & Cook, 1999). This variability validates that members of a social identity group may share characteristics and experiences but also may vary significantly in their identification with that group, which allows counselors to conceptualize diverse clients without stereotyping (Sue & Sue, 2013).

The predominant social identity development models describe minority racial, ethnic, and cultural group members' experiences as they develop within the dominant White culture. Examples of these models are Atkinson, Morten, and Sue's racial/cultural identity development model (Sue & Sue, 2013) and the people of color racial identity model (Helms, 1995; see Sidebar 2.3). These models and others share a progression of statuses from dominant culture acceptance to minority culture acceptance and, finally, to a complex state of minority culture acceptance that allows connection to and valuing of other cultures, including the dominant culture.

The stages of the racial/cultural identity development model (Sue & Sue, 2013) provide an example of this progression. In the initial stage, conformity, minority-group individuals prefer dominant cultural values over those of their own groups. In the dissonance stage, these individuals become increasingly aware of racism and discrimination and experience conflict as dominant cultural values are challenged. Individuals in the resistance and immersion stage may strongly ascribe to minority values and beliefs, reject the dominant culture, and become passionate about combating discrimination against their own group. Individuals in the introspection stage may experience discomfort with the rigid views they held before, reevaluate the dominant culture, and struggle with how to integrate these values and beliefs with the minority culture. During the final stage, integrative awareness, individuals develop an appreciation of their own culture and the dominant culture, critically evaluate all cultures, and commit to ending all forms of oppression.

Models have also been developed to describe the social identity development of dominant-group individuals. Helms's White racial identity development model is an example of this type of model (Helms & Cook, 1999). The assumption that healthy identity development for dominant-group members involves becoming aware of privilege and its effect on other groups forms the basis of this model. Seven stages describe White individuals as they move from ignorance of and con-

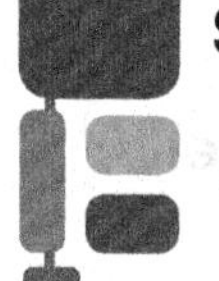

Sidebar 2.3. Atkinson, Morten, and Sue's Racial/Cultural Identity Development Model

Conformity: Individuals show a preference for the dominant culture rather than their own culture.

Dissonance: Individuals are presented with new information that is in opposition to their previously held cultural beliefs and values.

Resistance and Immersion: Individuals become aware of racism and injustice and embrace their own culture while rejecting the beliefs and values of the dominant culture.

Introspection: Individuals reevaluate their beliefs and values about the dominant culture and begin to integrate these values into their minority cultural identity.

Integrative Awareness: Individuals are able to evaluate and identify both positive and negative aspects of the dominant culture and develop an appreciation of both cultures.

tentment with the racist status quo (contact stage) through stages of increasing awareness, varying attitudes toward group identity, and increasing personal responsibility (disintegration, reintegration, pseudoindependence, immersion/emersion stages). By the final stage (autonomy), White individuals have developed a positive, White, nonracist identity; value diversity; and take an active stance toward combating racism (autonomy stage; see Sidebar 2.4).

Although many social identity models are structured around race and ethnicity, other models describe the identity development processes of other social identity group categories. An example is Cass's (1979) model of gay, lesbian, and bisexual sexual identity formation. Hardiman and Jackson (2007) described a generic model of social identity development that includes all target and agent groups within society. This model, like the aforementioned racial/ethnic models, moves from target and agent individuals having little or no consciousness of their group identity to acceptance, resistance, and redefinition, and finally to a stage called *internalization.*

Understanding clients through social identity development is complicated by the reality that each person has multiple social group memberships spanning many dimensions of diversity (Jones & McEwen, 2000). For example, a person may identify as lesbian, female, Asian American, and working class. Reynolds and Pope (1991) suggested that people experience several stages of social identity development simultaneously and thereby live a blend of social identities that results in a complex experiencing of themselves and the world. Thus, the person described here may experience varying levels of identity development with respect to each of her identities and have disparate feelings about each aspect. The notion that a person only identifies with one group creates false binaries whereby individuals are forced to choose whether they are members of an oppressed group or a dominant group (Hahn Tapper, 2013).

Social identity development models offer counselors several benefits. Foremost among these is that these models allow practitioners to better understand clients' experiences, issues, and needs. Each phase of development is associated with different behavior and feelings, which may influence the process of counseling. For instance, African American clients in the conformity and immersion stages described by the racial/cultural identity development model (Sue & Sue, 2013) will likely have different feelings toward the dominant culture and dissimilar views about the role of racism. They will have different levels of comfort with discussing issues of race

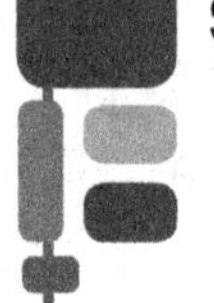

Sidebar 2.4. Helms's White Racial Identity Development Model

Contact: Individuals are unaware of their own racial identity and often hold the belief that everyone is the same.

Disintegration: Individuals come into contact with people of color, which challenges their previously held beliefs.

Reintegration: Individuals attempt to resolve feelings of discomfort by retreating into the comfort of their own group.

Pseudoindependence: Individuals may intellectually acknowledge the existence of racism but may see it as a problem for people of color to resolve.

Immersion/Emersion: Individuals explore their own culture, understand what it means to be White, and more honestly evaluate racism and their role in it.

Autonomy: Individuals experience more positive feelings about their own culture, equally value other cultures, and adopt an antiracist identity.

and may express differing levels of comfort and trust with a White therapist or an African American therapist. All of these factors influence the process of counseling.

Social identity development models also allow counselors to better understand themselves. Whether counselors have agent or target identities—or more likely, a combination of both—their relationships with these identities will affect how they view and interact with clients during the counseling process (Helms & Cook, 1999). Self-assessment of social identity development enables counselors to better identify their own vulnerabilities with regard to diversity and target knowledge and experiences, including counseling, which may assist them in better serving diverse client populations.

Although social identity development models can be great tools for counselors, they have limitations. Reynolds and Pope (1991) cautioned against oversimplifying the use of identity development models and suggested that rigidly ascribing one identity to a client may result in an inaccurate view of the client's experience. Others (e.g., Kwong-Liem, 2001; Sue & Sue, 2013) have cautioned that social identity theories should not be used to stereotype clients but should be used to help understand clients in their current context.

Understanding Diverse Clients Through Worldview

In addition to understanding diverse clients' systems and social identities, counselors should also understand clients as individuals with their own unique experience of the world (Ibrahim, 1991). The concept of worldview is useful for this purpose (Ibrahim, 1991; Sue & Sue, 2013). van Beek (2015) defined *worldview* as "views or opinions in process of how life was, is, will be, or should be organized" (p. 124). Worldview is related to social identity but includes individual, group, and universal dimensions; both cultural upbringing and individual life experiences; and all client conceptions that guide clients' meaning making, decisions, and behavior (Ibrahim, 1991; Sue & Sue, 2013). Worldview encompasses clients' individual, social, and universal contexts, including dimensions of family; social identity; history; language; and biological, ecological, or environmental factors (T. Smith & Kehe, 2004).

Although worldview is complex, models such as Kluckhohn and Strodtbeck's (1961) value orientation model may simplify understanding of its important dimensions. This model highlights four dimensions in which counselor and client worldviews may differ significantly: experiencing and valuing time, attitudes toward activity, views of social relationship, and beliefs regarding the essential nature of people. Ibrahim (1991) expanded Kluckhohn and Strodtbeck's work into a theory; developed a measurement instrument called the Scale to Assess Worldviews (Ibrahim, 1991); and described the categories, listed below, to more specifically express a wide range of worldviews:

- View of human nature: good, bad, and a combination of good and bad
- View of social relationships: lineal–hierarchical, collateral–mutual, and individualistic
- View of nature: subjugate and control nature, live in harmony with nature, and accept the power and control of nature over people
- Time orientation: past, present, and future
- Activity orientation: being, being-in-becoming, and doing

Ibrahim (1991) also suggested that orientations within this framework must be understood in the context of the history of the client's identified group(s), language(s), gender, religion, family history as well as current family life (from both ethnic/cultural and majority culture perspectives), and neighborhood in which the client grew up.

Other authors have focused on three other dimensions of worldview: locus of control, locus of responsibility, and collectivism–individualism (Oyserman, Coon, & Kemmelmeier, 2002; Sue & Sue, 2013). *Locus of control* refers to beliefs about the degree to which a person can influence his or her own life and ranges from internal, in which the person can exert control, to external, in which external factors control the individual. *Locus of responsibility*, conversely, describes beliefs about where responsibility for a problem lies, generally in terms of attributing responsibility to either the individual or the system (Sue & Sue, 2013). Most counseling theories that emphasize intrapsychic phenomena demonstrate an individual locus of responsibility, whereas theories that emphasize family, organizational, or societal dynamics demonstrate a systemic locus of responsibility.

In addition to locus of control and locus of responsibility, worldview can be characterized in terms of individualism–collectivism. An individualist worldview places the individual and his or her goals, uniqueness, and power at the center of importance, whereas a collectivist worldview places the social (family, community, nation) at the center (Oyserman et al., 2002). A primary concern for autonomy of the individual demonstrates a high level of individualism, whereas attention to the influence of choices on family and community demonstrates a high level of collectivism. Clients whose orientation is primarily collectivist will have very different priorities and choices during therapy compared with clients who are more individualist.

Counselors who gain knowledge of their own and their clients' worldviews will more accurately understand diverse clients' experiences, issues, goals, and way of being during the counseling process. Because worldview allows counselors to understand clients in terms of their universal, group, and individual identities (Sue & Sue, 2013), counselors can be both culturally sensitive and client specific, thereby avoiding stereotypic understanding and treatment of clients that may be damaging (Ibrahim, 1991).

DIVERSITY AND THE COUNSELING PROCESS

Adequate understanding is only part of providing competent counseling to diverse clients. Differences between counselor and client affect the counseling process from relationship formation to goal setting and implementation of strategies and techniques. van Beek (2015) posited that worldview issues can be contentious and cause discord within the therapeutic relationship, so they require considerate and careful handling. Counselors must be aware of and manage the influence of diversity on the counseling relationship, collaborate with diverse clients to form appropriate goals, and then implement socially and culturally sensitive interventions and strategies to meet those goals. The following sections discuss the implications of diversity on the counseling relationship, goals, and diversity-appropriate counseling interventions.

The Counseling Relationship

A strong relationship is necessary for effective counseling to take place. The qualities of such relationships were summarized in the first chapter as empathic understanding, respect and positive regard, genuineness and congruence, concreteness, warmth, and immediacy. Strong counseling relationships become even more important when one is working with diverse clients; however, forming a strong relationship may be challenging. Issues that deserve particular attention during the formation and maintenance of the counseling relationship are developing cultural empathy (Chung & Bemak, 2002) and trust (Helms & Cook, 1999; Slattery, 2004; Sue & Sue, 2013) and striving for an egalitarian relationship when appropriate (McWhirter, 1991; Slattery, 2004).

Cultural Empathy

Empathy is accepted as one of the core conditions in the counseling relationship and has been described as the counselor's ability to view and experience the world cognitively and emotionally as the client does (Chung & Bemak, 2002). Attaining and communicating this level of understanding when counseling diverse clients is a different experience and requires special consideration. The term *cultural empathy* is used to describe this experience and process. Ridley and Lingle (1996) defined *cultural empathy* as a counselor's learned ability to both understand and communicate understanding of the culturally diverse client's experience as well as to experience and communicate concern for the culturally diverse client. Cultural knowledge is a prerequisite; however, cultural empathy moves a step beyond cognitive understanding to include emotional understanding, concern, and especially communication.

Several authors have discussed concrete ways to establish cultural empathy. The following list summarizes the suggestions of Chung and Bemak (2002) and Ridley and Lingle (1996). To establish cultural empathy, the counselor should communicate the following in clear but culturally appropriate ways during the counseling process:

- His or her understanding of the client's experience for clarification
- A humble but realistic sense of how well the counselor may or may not understand the client's cultural background and experience
- A sincere interest in learning more about the client's cultural background and experience
- Openness to clarifying verbal and nonverbal communication, checking out assumptions, and adapting the counseling process and techniques to be more culturally appropriate
- Affirmation of the client's cultural experience, as well as cultural differences between the counselor and client

Trust

Trust is an important component of effective counseling relationships, whereas cultural mistrust can be a barrier to effective counseling relationships and may be based on personal experience, group history, association of counseling with the establishment, or therapist behavior (Slattery, 2004). Kocet and Herlihy (2014) recommended the use of ethical bracketing, which requires the counselor to separate his or her personal and professional views in order to provide more ethical and culturally respectful counseling. Ethical bracketing can be especially beneficial in situations in which worldview issues may affect trust in the counseling relationship. This may be especially true when clients have predominantly target group identities and counselors have predominantly agent identities. Because of experiences with institutional discrimination, clients from target groups may tend to view mental health professionals as representatives of the dominant establishment and as not to be trusted unless there is evidence to the contrary.

Sue and Sue (2013) reported that therapists and school counselors who are perceived as trustworthy by clients have more influence and potential effectiveness during the counseling process. Responsibility for developing trust in the diverse counseling relationship rests on the counselor. Counselors should not immediately assume mistrust on the part of the client. Diverse clients may test dominant-culture counselors for sincerity and openness. Even subtle verbal or nonverbal behavior by the counselor that indicates prejudice will lower levels of trust, whereas responses that are honest, are genuine, include some self-disclosure, and acknowledge obvious differences will more likely be perceived as trustworthy (Sue & Sue, 2013).

Creating Egalitarian Relationships

Egalitarian relationships, when consistent with client expectations and needs, are ideal for work with diverse populations, especially those who have been disempowered by chronic oppression (Cheatham et al., 2006; Slattery, 2004). Many of the ideas regarding egalitarian counseling relationships are derived from feminist therapy and are counter to some traditional counseling theories that place the bulk of power in the counseling relationship with the counselor. Egalitarian counseling relationships occur when the client's and counselor's balance of power is somewhat equalized. McWhirter (1991) suggested the following for developing egalitarian relationships:

- Counselors should not use psychological jargon, blame the client for lack of improvement, or refuse to share knowledge or educate the client. These acts mystify the process.
- Counselors should collaborate with clients on problem definition and identification of goals.
- Counselors should present themselves realistically, as fallible humans with specialized knowledge and skills that may be helpful.
- Clients should be presented as experts on themselves and their environments.
- Counselors should educate clients so that they may participate in an informed manner as well as increase their power to deal with issues on their own.

In light of the fact that many diverse clients, because of their presenting issues, stage of development, and worldview, may require a more direct or authoritarian style (Sue & Sue, 2013), counselors must be sensitive to cues that indicate that a client may need a more direct style. Such cues may include the client frequently requesting and accepting feedback, verbally or nonverbally expressing displeasure with a lack of direction or authority, and needing prompting before expressing opinions (Slattery, 2004).

Counseling Goals

Previous sections have described some ways in which clients' experiences of oppression, social identity and level of development, and worldviews may influence the formation and prioritization of counseling goals. Above all, counseling goals that are inconsistent with a diverse client's values, beliefs, and current environment are to be avoided (Helms & Cook, 1999). For example, a common counseling goal is autonomy or independence, which may not be an appropriate goal for a client who is deeply socialized in a collectivist culture or a culture in which families are viewed as very central. To avoid this kind of mismatch, counselors should construct the goals of counseling with the client and should reflect the client's worldview and cultural orientation, as well as the client's current environment (Slattery, 2004).

In addition to these cautions, various authors have discussed general counseling goals for diverse clients. Helms and Cook (1999) described symptom remission, social identity development, bicultural identity development, and cultural congruence as potentially appropriate counseling goals for many diverse clients. From a social justice perspective, an important goal of counseling is the removal of exterior barriers, such as discriminatory policies and practices, that impede client well-being (Chung & Bemak, 2011).

Empowerment is a commonly mentioned goal of both multicultural and social justice counseling (McWhirter, 1991; Slattery, 2004). According to McWhirter (1991),

> empowerment within the context of counseling is the process by which people, organizations, or groups who are powerless (a) become aware of the power dynamics at work in their life context, (b) develop the skills and capacity for gaining some reasonable control over their lives, (c) exercise this control without infringing upon the rights of others, and (d) support the empowerment of others in their community. (p. 224)

Empowerment may be an especially appropriate goal for those whose self-determination is limited, who are members of stigmatized or oppressed social identity groups, and who are distressed by their own dependency and sense of powerlessness (McWhirter, 1991).

Appropriate Counseling Interventions With Diverse Clients

Providing socially and culturally appropriate interventions is the end result of counselor awareness and knowledge of self and diverse clients. Culturally appropriate interventions are interventions that take into account clients' communication styles, values and beliefs, and life experiences such that functional counseling relationships are formed and appropriate goals are attained. These interventions can range from the skills and strategies of traditional counseling approaches to indigenous or folk healing methods, or a synthesis of both.

The form of the intervention may be conventional, delivered one on one in a mental health setting, or may be delivered within the context of group, family, community, or other systems. Following is a list of recommendations adapted from Sue and Sue (2013) and Arredondo et al. (1996). Counselors who want to use socially and culturally appropriate intervention skills should adopt the following recommendations:

- Become familiar with a variety of theoretical orientations and approaches, because a flexible counseling approach is necessary to meet the needs of diverse clients.
- Be open to interventions that are outside the scope of traditional counseling, such as systemic interventions and indigenous or folk healing methods.
- Become knowledgeable about the effects of all dimensions of diversity on communication style.
- Become aware of your own communication style. Feedback from varied sources that are knowledgeable about diversity is especially useful.
- Assess all counseling interventions for strengths and weaknesses with respect to clients' social, cultural, spiritual, and political dimensions.
- Focus on actual skill building.
- Be mindful of the goals of interventions.

Successful adaptation of skills is more likely if client needs are clear and interventions are designed to meet those needs.

In the following sections, we discuss adapting traditional counseling interventions, incorporating indigenous or folk healing methods, communication issues with diverse clients, skills and interventions for empowerment, and advocacy skills and interventions.

Adapting Traditional Counseling Interventions

Adapting traditional skills and interventions for diverse clients can range from using the skills as is to providing context to clients about the purpose of the skill or intervention, to incorporating cultural variations. Working with diverse clients does not mean throwing out all traditional counseling skills (Sue & Sue, 2013); however, these skills will be much more useful if counselors orient clients to the counseling process and explain the purpose of specific skills and interventions (Arredondo et al., 1996). Diverse clients may become comfortable with skills and interventions once they understand their purpose. Providing this type of context may also be helpful if the counselor and client decide to brainstorm alternative interventions and will also assist the counselor in finding appropriate cultural adaptations.

The range of adaptation can be demonstrated using as an example the common counseling skill of reflection of feeling. The counselor may choose to use reflection of feeling with a diverse client without much explanation or adaptation if the client is verbally expressive of feelings; seems comfortable with the counselor commenting on feelings; and responds to the reflection by agreeing, correcting, or expanding.

The counselor may also choose to explain the purpose of reflecting feelings. The explanation may take a form similar to this:

> I will say what I believe you are feeling because it is important for me to understand what you are feeling and for you to know that I understand. I would like to know if you feel differently or if my words make you uncomfortable.

Because some diverse clients may not be comfortable challenging the counselor, the counselor should monitor client verbal and nonverbal behavior for signs of shutting down or discomfort with feeling reflections. If the client does not respond well to reflection of feeling or if the counselor anticipates a poor response, the counselor may choose to adapt the skill to meet the client's needs. The counselor should consider, and possibly explore with the client, whether verbal expression of feeling is discouraged by the client's cultural group or whether the client is uncomfortable discussing feelings in an individualist context versus a family or community context. In the first instance, the counselor and client can collaborate to find a suitable option, perhaps nonverbal techniques for expression (Arredondo et al., 1996). Cheatham et al. (2006) suggested that, in the second instance, feeling reflections can be reworded to include relationship and context; for example, "You feel anxious in relationships with your family." If the use or adaptation of a customary skill or intervention does not seem to meet the diverse client's needs, then using indigenous or culturally based interventions is another alternative.

Incorporating Indigenous or Folk Healing Methods

Many authors consider the incorporation of indigenous and folk healing into counseling to be a potentially effective treatment option for culturally diverse clients (Koss-Chioino, 2000; Sue & Sue, 2013; Yeh, Hunter, Madan-Bahel, Chiang, & Arora, 2004). Incorporating these methods may be particularly useful if clients are deeply involved in their culture and request or mention these methods (Koss-Chioino, 2000). In addition, Sue and Sue (2013) contended that becoming familiar with indigenous healing practices may help counselors better understand the worldview of diverse clients and assist counselors in anticipating potential conflicts in belief systems that may affect the therapeutic process.

Every society and culture has its own versions of healing and healers that address physical and psychological disturbances (Sue & Sue, 2013). According to Koss-Chioino (2000), alternative healing methods are not only a part of communities of underrepresented groups but also a part of dominant groups. Examples of indigenous or folk healing include Asian culture practices such as Reiki, qigong, and pranic healing (Yeh et al., 2004); the use by some Mexican Americans of a *curandero* or spiritual advisor; and Native American healing traditions such as those of the Native American church, as well as more regional tribal traditions (Koss-Chioino, 2000).

The following is a summary of suggestions by Koss-Chioino (2000), Sue and Sue (2013), and Yeh et al. (2004) for counselors who are considering incorporating indigenous or folk methods or consulting with or referring to indigenous or folk healers:

- Become aware of your attitudes toward indigenous healing practices. Clients may hesitate to disclose interest in these methods if they sense negative attitudes.
- Become familiar with the beliefs and healing practices of different cultures.
- Extend knowledge of these practices by engaging in different communities and personalizing the information.
- Be willing to form respectful relationships with indigenous and folk healers. These relationships may provide useful information, build counselor credibility within the community, and facilitate future referral and consultation.
- Recognize the importance of spirituality in the lives of many diverse clients. Know your clients' views on indigenous healing.

- Be aware of the ethical and practical challenges of consulting with indigenous healers or incorporating their healing methods into treatment.
- Become aware of new practices that synthesize indigenous methods with traditional counseling.

Communication Issues With Diverse Clients

Therapy is a process of interpersonal interaction and social influence that relies on effective communication (Sue & Sue, 2013). Both counselor and client must communicate adequately, in both verbal and nonverbal realms, for effective therapy to take place. In particular, the counselor's communication should be both accurate and appropriate. Sue and Sue (2013) discussed several aspects of communication style that may affect the counseling intervention. Differences in counselor and client proxemics, kinesics, and paralanguage may all contribute to miscommunication during counseling. Proxemics describes individuals' culturally influenced sense of personal space, whereas kinesics describes the use of movement such as facial expressions, posture, gestures, and eye contact to communicate. Paralanguage describes the use of voice loudness, pauses, silences, speech rate, and inflection to express differences in meaning.

Counselors should also consider whether the client's cultural communication style is low context or high context. Low-context communication relies largely on the message relayed by verbal communication, whereas high-context communication relies less on the verbal communication and more on additional shared understanding, nonverbals, and paralanguage to convey the full meaning of the message. Counseling interventions for diverse clients should take into consideration all of these dimensions (Sue & Sue, 2013).

Skills and Interventions for Empowerment

Empowerment is a commonly mentioned goal of counseling, particularly with diverse clients who may have experienced oppression (Lee, 1999; McWhirter, 1991; Slattery, 2004). For empowerment to occur, counselors should use empowering interventions throughout the counseling process. According to McWhirter (1991), empowering interventions start with the attitudes, beliefs, and person of the counselor or therapist. To be empowering, counselors should believe in the client's ability to make positive changes. Thus, empowering interventions should give no more help than is required.

Empowering interventions may be used early in counseling. Slattery (2004) suggested that the counseling process will be most empowering if clients are offered the least restrictive effective treatment possible and are given choices about receiving treatment. Clients should be educated about the rationale for treatment and interventions during informed consent, and they should be aware that counseling is as much about learning to solve problems as it is about solving problems. In addition, the therapeutic relationship should be egalitarian and collaborative within culturally appropriate boundaries.

Empowerment should also continue through the problem identification phase (McWhirter, 1991; Slattery, 2004). To maximize empowerment during this phase, counselors should listen to and respect clients' views of problems and desired outcomes (Slattery, 2004). Empowering conceptualizations take into account the social, political, and economic context; resist blaming the client for things beyond his or her control; and clearly differentiate between responsibility for the problem, which may be environmental, and responsibility for coping with the problem, which is the client's (Chung & Bemak, 2011; McWhirter, 1991). Ineffective or problem behavior should be viewed as best attempts to cope with the situation (Slattery, 2004).

Helping clients become aware of personal resources is also critical to empowerment. Identification of problem-free times and areas of life is essential to empowerment. Counselors should recognize and validate client strengths, including support networks. Clients' attempts at solutions should be acknowledged and potentially used as building blocks for further problem solving (Slattery, 2004).

Education is one of the most empowering interventions and can be used throughout the counseling process. Educating clients to the power dynamics that surround them empowers them by making overt the external influences that have hindered them, helping clients see themselves as less damaged, and encouraging more active and effective problem solving. Within the session, clients should be educated and encouraged to identify their own patterns and environmental barriers rather than relying on the counselor. Helping clients gain necessary skills, such as decision-making, assertiveness, and social skills, is also empowering, although it is always important to consider the impact of these skills on other parts of the clients' system (Slattery, 2004).

Advocacy Skills and Interventions

Both the multicultural and social justice counseling literatures have called on counselors to include advocacy within the scope of their practice (Chung & Bemak, 2011; Sue & Sue, 2013; Vera & Speight, 2003). However, counselor education or training programs have not focused on advocacy as an intervention, which may explain why counselors are hesitant to implement advocacy strategies. In this section, we define advocacy and its forms and identify advocacy skills and their use with diverse clients.

McAuliffe, Grothaus, Pare, and Wininger (2008) defined *advocacy* as "the act of empowering individuals or groups through actions that increase self-efficacy, remove barriers to needed services, and promote systemic change" (p. 613). Thus, advocacy is distinct from traditional counseling interventions in that its focus is ultimately the system and not the client. Ezell (2001) suggested that advocacy, in some form, is appropriate for clients who have little power and may not be able to advocate for themselves within the necessary systems without assistance.

Increasing acceptance of advocacy as a counseling intervention has increased discussion of its scope and targets. Ezell (2001) noted that advocacy may be undertaken for a specific client (case advocacy) or for a group of clients with similar issues or identity (class advocacy). Targets of advocacy may also vary. The ACA Advocacy Competencies describe advocacy as occurring at the microlevel, mesolevel, and macrolevels, which include the client/student level, school/community level, and the public information/social/political levels (Lewis et al., 2002).

- At the client/student level, counselors identify and facilitate client understanding of social, political, economic, and cultural barriers to client well-being and advocate with or on behalf of clients to respond to these barriers.

- At the school/community level, counselors advocate for clients within the clients' communities and relevant institutions using nontraditional interventions to change attitudes, policies, rules, and structures that are detrimental to client well-being.
- At the public arena level, counselors intervene on a larger scale to raise awareness of broad societal issues, change attitudes and beliefs of the general public, and change public policy and laws that are harmful to groups of clients.

To make the variety of advocacy targets and interventions more concrete, we present several examples adapted from Ezell (2001) that represent different advocacy types and targets:

- Teaching a client advocacy skills so she can advocate for fair work conditions for herself (client level, case advocacy)
- Representing a student/client at an administrative hearing to decide whether he will be reinstated to school (school/community level, case advocacy)
- Presenting a rationale to the board of directors of a private, nonprofit counseling center for providing translators and bilingual counselors for non-English-speaking clients (school/community level, class advocacy)
- Gathering data about disparities in mental health services for immigrants to the United States (social/political level, class advocacy)

According to Kiselica and Robinson (2001), advocacy requires special skills and attributes, including verbal and nonverbal communication skills, an understanding of how systems work, an awareness of group dynamics, technology and research skills, and a commitment to human rights issues. Ezell (2001) suggested that counselors who undertake advocacy must be persistent, persuasive, collaborative, assertive, and resourceful.

Because many counselors are relatively unfamiliar with advocacy, they should be vigilant of ethical issues (Ezell, 2001). Counselors should make every attempt to receive informed consent from clients or client groups before undertaking advocacy activities. Similarly, clients should have the right to refuse advocacy. Counselors should also evaluate whether advocacy for one client or client group will harm another client or client group. Also, because advocacy is often meant to help clients from diverse groups, the methods and outcomes of the advocacy should be carefully evaluated for consistency with clients' values and beliefs (Ezell, 2001).

BECOMING A DIVERSITY- AND SOCIAL-JUSTICE–COMPETENT COUNSELOR

Becoming a Diversity-Competent Counselor

Sue and Sue (2013) contended that, in the changing world of counseling, there is no clinical competence without multicultural competence. In the MCC, Sue et al. (1992) described three necessary characteristics of culturally competent counselors: (a) an awareness of one's own assumptions, values, and biases; (b) an understanding of the worldview of the culturally different client; and (c) the ability to develop appropriate intervention strategies and techniques. The preceding sections have discussed various ways to understand and work with diverse clients. However, acquiring the awareness, knowledge, and skills necessary for diversity-competent counseling must extend far past reading this chapter. Therefore, in this section, we discuss gaining self-awareness and gaining additional knowledge and skills (see Sidebar 2.5).

Gaining Self-Awareness

As the MCC have outlined, counselors' awareness of self is critical to providing competent services to diverse clients (Sue et al., 1992). Counselors' views of themselves and others are shaped by their experiences as members of multiple social identity groups. Without an awareness of stereotypes, biases, and culturally based reactions, counselors will unwittingly view diverse clients' experiences, issues, goals, and interactions in counseling from their own perspective, which may be inaccurate or harmful to the client. This phenomenon is called *cultural encapsulation* (Sue & Sue, 2013).

To minimize cultural encapsulation, counselors should develop a clear sense of their place within society, their cultural background and influences, their beliefs and values, and their interpersonal impact on others. Counselors should know their cultural background and how it has influenced attitudes, values, and biases that affect how they view normal and abnormal behaviors. They also are able to recognize the limits of their competence, recognize the sources of their discomfort with diverse clients, and understand how the dynamics of oppression affect them personally and in their interactions with others (Arredondo et al., 1996).

To achieve this, counselors are encouraged to attend to their personal growth, seek out opportunities for professional development, actively seek a nonracist identity, maintain personal and professional relationships with individuals different from themselves, and seek feedback regarding behavior (Arredondo et al., 1996). Counselors can also become more aware of their socialization through a variety of learning activities, such as completing a social group membership profile (Bell, 2007) or analyzing their own social identity development level using a relevant model (Cheatham et al., 2006; see Sidebar 2.6).

Gaining Additional Knowledge and Skills

As has been outlined in the preceding sections, knowledge of clients' worldviews is critical for counselors to understand clients' experiences, issues, and goals and the best path to healing and functioning. However, the complexity of worldview and the breadth of diversity make this a monumental task. Counselors should begin by collecting knowledge about their own social and cultural background. Exploration and gathering of knowledge should then extend

Sidebar 2.5. Multicultural Counseling Competencies

The original MCC (Sue et al., 1992) transformed the field of counseling and helped counselors to understand the importance of the cultural values and bias and their impacts on the counseling relationship. As the field of professional counseling continues to evolve, the AMCD has recently commissioned a committee to revise and contemporize the competencies. The new competencies address the importance of both multicultural and social justice elements within the counseling context.

Sidebar 2.6. Exploring Your Assumptions (Helms & Cook, 1999)

- What do you consider to be normal therapist and client behavior during therapy?
- If group goals are in conflict with a client's individual needs or desires, how do you resolve the conflict?
- At what age do you believe a child should leave his or her parents and make a life independent of them?
- What strategies do you use to include a client's support systems as allies?
- Can you describe an instance in which you intervened to change a system to fit a client's need rather than requiring him or her to change to fit the system?

to populations or cultural groups with whom counselors will commonly work and those about whom they have little knowledge. Counselors should explore the group's history within the society, including the impact of oppression, and knowledge of the group's culture, including common beliefs and values regarding parenting, family, spirituality, social hierarchy, gender roles, communication styles, and relationship to time and space. Knowledge of a cultural group's areas of strength, resistance, and resilience is also critical (Arredondo et al., 1996; Slattery, 2004).

In addition, Hanna, Bemak, and Chung (1999) indicated that gaining book knowledge is not sufficient for developing adequate knowledge and skills. Receiving supervision from clinicians who are knowledgeable about diversity or who differ in social identity has the potential to increase awareness, knowledge, and skills related to counseling diverse clients (Lum, 2010). Lum (2010) suggested making book knowledge and skills come alive by becoming familiar with community demographics, reading local alternative news sources, and interviewing community leaders. He also suggested spending time in diverse communities, observing, patronizing businesses, attending social functions, talking with community members, and shadowing helping professionals who have developed effective relationships within the community.

Becoming a Social-Justice–Competent Counselor

According to Vera and Speight (2003), multicultural competence is limiting if it is not combined with a commitment to social justice and advocacy. Lewis and Arnold (1998) added that counselors who develop a sense of multicultural competence often find that client problems are rooted in larger social, political, and economic conditions. However, they are ill equipped to help clients who present issues that are systemically based. The inability to address systemic issues may stem from the lack of social justice training efforts in counselor education programs (L. A. Goodman et al., 2004). Chung and Bemak (2011) suggested that counselors can incorporate social justice into their work, helping clients to address the systemic issues that affect their health and wellness by focusing on social, economic, historical, political, and ecological concerns within the therapeutic relationship.

In their critical analysis of the social justice counseling movement, S. D. Smith, Reynolds, and Rovnak (2009) suggested that it is important to articulate a set of social justice awareness, knowledge, and skills. We attempt to articulate this awareness, knowledge, and skills in the following section.

Gaining Self-Awareness

Being a social justice change agent requires that counselors develop an awareness of themselves as change agents and advocates. More specifically, counselors with a commitment to social justice need to understand the strengths and challenges to being an advocate for their clients. This can be accomplished through professional development opportunities and through the use of assessment instruments. For example, Chen-Hayes (2001) developed the Social Justice Advocacy Readiness Questionnaire, a 188-item instrument that measures respondents' awareness, knowledge, and skills around diversity and social justice issues. Hays, Chang, and Decker (2007) developed the Privilege and Oppression Inventory, an 82-item instrument that assesses counselors' awareness of privilege and oppression along the dimensions of race, sexual orientation, religion, and gender. Similarly, Rubin and Peplau (1975) developed the 20-item Belief in a Just World Scale, which measures an individual's attitudes and beliefs toward acceptance of a just world.

The Social Justice Advocacy Scale was also created to measure respondents' advocacy behaviors on behalf of individuals from oppressed populations (van Soest, 1996). Ratts and Ford (2010) developed the Advocacy Competencies Self-Assessment Survey. This survey provides counselors with a means of determining their level of competence around the three levels and six domains of the ACA Advocacy Competencies. Collectively, these instruments serve as a tool for the helping professional who seeks to gain an awareness of what it means to be a change agent and advocate for social justice.

Sue and Sue (2013) noted that counselors are often hesitant to implement social justice advocacy strategies. Much of this may be due to a lack of knowledge and skills around social justice. Helping professionals can gain more knowledge of social justice by familiarizing themselves with community action theories and concepts, such as Moyer, McAllister, Finley, and Soifer's (2001) movement action plan framework for organizing social movements. Rogers's (2003) theory of diffusion of innovation can also be useful when considering how to diffuse anxieties and fears that come with introducing new social justice ideas into an organization.

SUMMARY

The counseling profession is committed to providing competent treatment to diverse clients; however, traditional approaches are limited in their usefulness for this purpose. The multicultural and social justice counseling perspectives share the assumptions that counselors must integrate diverse clients' social and cultural contexts and experiences of oppression during the counseling process and that counselors must go outside the boundaries of traditional counseling approaches to adequately serve these clients. These perspectives highlight the importance of using broad definitions of diversity in counseling as well as a dual focus on both microlevel and macrolevel counseling interventions.

Human diversity affects nearly every aspect of the counseling process, and thus counselors use new lenses to understand themselves and diverse clients and to guide them in the counseling process. This chapter introduced the oppression model, social identity development, and the concept of worldview as frameworks for integrating sociocultural and systemic factors into counselors' understanding of diverse clients. Counselors who can view themselves and their clients through these lenses will better understand the experiences and concerns of diverse clients and have a solid foundation for understanding the influence of diversity on the rest of the counseling process.

The counseling process is affected by diversity through the counseling relationship, counseling goals, and the appropriateness of interventions and strategies for clients. Developing trust and empathy may be challenging; however, initial challenges can be overcome with sufficient knowledge of client worldview and appropriate communication. Egalitarian counseling relationships may be beneficial for diverse clients, though client needs and expectations for structure should be considered. Counselors should collaborate with diverse clients to set counseling goals because worldview and environment may influence desired outcomes.

One of the most important ways that diversity affects the counseling process is through skills and interventions. The skills and interventions used should reflect diverse clients' communication styles, values and beliefs, and life experiences. Although traditional techniques and strategies may be effective with diverse clients, adaptation or incorporation of culturally based methods may be necessary. In addition, the use of systemic interventions such as advocacy may be necessary to fully address the issues of diverse clients.

Finally, continuing counselor development is an absolute must for attaining competence in matters relating to diversity. Attaining the necessary self-awareness, knowledge, skills, and actions goes far beyond reading. Counselors will be unable to work adequately with diverse clients until they fully understand themselves as social, historical, cultural, and political beings. Their knowledge and skill acquisition should extend beyond book learning to actual experiencing of differences and personal change.

REFERENCES

Arredondo, P., Toporek, R., Brown, S., Jones, J., Locke, D. C., Sanchez, J., & Stadler, H. (1996). Operationalization of the Multicultural Counseling Competencies. *Journal of Multicultural Counseling and Development, 24,* 42–78.

Baker, S. B., & Cramer, S. H. (1972). Counselor or change agent: Support from the profession. *Personnel and Guidance Journal, 50,* 661–665.

Bell, L. (2007). Theoretical foundations for social justice education. In M. Adams, L. Bell, & P. Griffin (Eds.), *Teaching for diversity and social justice* (2nd ed., pp. 1–14). New York, NY: Routledge.

Berger, L. K., Zane, N., & Hwang, W. C. (2014). Therapist ethnicity and treatment orientation differences in multicultural counseling competencies. *Asian American Journal of Psychology, 5*(1), 53–65.

Bronfenbrenner, U. (1981). *The ecology of human development: Experiments by nature and design.* Cambridge, MA: Harvard University Press.

Carroll, L., Gilroy, P. J., & Ryan, I. (2002). Counseling transgendered, transsexual, and gender-variant clients. *Journal of Counseling & Development, 80,* 131–139.

Cass, V. C. (1979). Homosexual identity formation: A theoretical model. *Journal of Homosexuality, 4,* 219–235.

Cheatham, H., D'Andrea, M., Ivey, A., Ivey, M. B., Pedersen, P., Rigazio-DiGilio, S., . . . Sue, D. W. (2006). Multicultural counseling and therapy. In A. Ivey, M. D'Andrea, M. Ivey, & L. Simek-Morgan (Eds.), *Theories of counseling and psychotherapy: A multicultural perspective* (5th ed., pp. 329–362). Boston, MA: Allyn & Bacon.

Chen-Hayes, S. (2001). Social justice advocacy readiness questionnaire. *Journal of Gay and Lesbian Social Services, 13,* 191–203.

Chung, R., & Bemak, F. (2002). The relationship of culture and empathy in cross-cultural counseling. *Journal of Counseling & Development, 80,* 154–160.

Chung, R. C. Y., & Bemak, F. P. (2011). *Social justice counseling: The next steps beyond multiculturalism.* Thousand Oaks, CA: Sage.

Colby, S. L., & Ortman, J. M. (2015). *Projections of the size and composition of the U.S. population: 2014 to 2060: Population estimates and projections.* Retrieved from https://www.census.gov/content/dam/Census/library/publications/2015/demo/p25-1143.pdf

Constantine, M. (2001). Multicultural training, theoretical orientation, empathy, and multicultural case conceptualization ability in counselors. *Journal of Mental Health Counseling, 23,* 357–372.

Constantine, M. G., & Sue, D. W. (Eds.). (2005). *Strategies for building multicultural competence in mental health and educational settings.* New York, NY: Wiley.

Dahl, S. (1971). Who is building the bridges? *Personnel and Guidance Journal, 49,* 693–697.

Ezell, M. (2001). *Advocacy in the human services.* Belmont, CA: Brooks/Cole.

Fukuyama, M. A. (1990). Taking a universal approach to multicultural counseling. *Counselor Education and Supervision, 30,* 6–17.

Gardner, J. (1971). Sexist counseling. *Personnel and Guidance Journal, 49,* 705–714.

Gates, G. J. (2011). *How many people are lesbian, gay, bisexual and transgender?* Retrieved from http://williamsinstitute.law.ucla.edu/wp-content/uploads/Gates-How-Many-People-LGBT-Apr-2011.pdf

Gates, G. J., & Newport, F. (2012). *Special report: 3.4% of US adults identify as LGBT.* Retrieved from http://www.odec.umd.edu/CD/LGBT/Special%20Report%203.4%25%20of%20U.S.%20Adults%20Identify%20as%20LGBT.pdf

Goodman, D. J. (2011). *Promoting diversity and social justice: Educating people from privileged groups* (2nd ed.). New York, NY: Routledge.

Goodman, L. A., Liang, B., Helms, J. E., Latta, R. E., Sparks, E., & Weintrab, S. R. (2004). Training counseling psychologists as social justice agents: Feminist and multicultural principles in action. *Counseling Psychologist, 32,* 793–837.

Goodman, R. D., & Gorski, P. C. (Eds.). (2015). *Decolonizing "multicultural" counseling through social justice.* New York, NY: Springer.

Hahn Tapper, A. J. (2013). A pedagogy of social justice education: Social identity theory, intersectionality, and empowerment. *Conflict Resolution Quarterly, 30,* 411–445.

Hanna, F., Bemak, F., & Chung, R. (1999). Toward a new paradigm for multicultural counseling. *Journal of Counseling & Development, 77,* 125–134.

Hardiman, R., & Jackson, B. (1982). Oppression: Conceptual and developmental analysis. In M. Adams, P. Brigham, P. Dalpes, & L. Marchesani (Eds.), *Social diversity and social justice—Diversity and oppression: Conceptual frameworks* (pp. 1–6). Dubuque, IA: Kendall/Hunt.

Hardiman, R., & Jackson, B. (2007). Conceptual foundations for social justice courses. In M. Adams, L. Bell, & P. Griffin (Eds.), *Teaching for diversity and social justice* (pp. 35–66). New York, NY: Routledge.

Hays, D. G., Chang, C. Y., & Decker, S. L. (2007). Initial development and psychometric data for the Privilege and Oppression Inventory. *Measurement and Evaluation in Counseling and Development, 40,* 66–79.

Helms, J. E. (1995). An update of Helms's White and people of color racial identity models. In J. G. Ponterotto, J. M. Casas, L. A. Suzuki, & C. M. Alexander (Eds.), *Handbook of multicultural counseling* (pp. 181–191). Thousand Oaks, CA: Sage.

Helms, J. E., & Cook, D. A. (1999). *Using race and culture in counseling and psychotherapy.* Needham Heights, MA: Allyn & Bacon.

Ibrahim, F. (1991). Contribution of cultural worldview to generic counseling and development. *Journal of Counseling & Development, 70,* 13–19.

Ivey, A. E., D'Andrea, M., & Ivey, M. B. (2012). *Theories of counseling and psychotherapy: A multicultural perspective* (7th ed.). Thousand Oaks, CA: Sage.

Jackson, M. L. (1995). Multicultural counseling: Historical perspectives. In J. G. Ponterotto, J. M. Casas, L. Suzuki, & C. M. Alexander (Eds.), *Handbook of multicultural counseling* (pp. 3–16). Thousand Oaks, CA: Sage.

Johnson, A., & Jackson Williams, D. (2014). White racial identity, color-blind racial attitudes, and multicultural counseling competence. *Cultural Diversity and Ethnic Minority Psychology, 20*(4), 1–10.

Jones, S. R., & McEwen, M. K. (2000). A conceptual model of multiple dimensions of identity. *Journal of College Student Development, 41,* 405–414.

Katz, A. D., & Hoyt, W. T. (2014). The influence of multicultural counseling competence and anti-Black prejudice on therapists' outcome expectancies. *Journal of Counseling Psychology, 61*(2), 299–305.

Katz, J. H. (1985). The sociopolitical nature of counseling. *Counseling Psychologist, 13,* 615–624.

Killinger, R. R. (1971). The counselor and gay liberation. *Personnel and Guidance Journal, 49,* 715–719.

Kiselica, M. S., & Robinson, M. (2001). Bringing advocacy counseling to life: The history, issues, and human dramas of social justice work in counseling. *Journal of Counseling & Development, 79,* 387–398.

Kluckhohn, F., & Strodtbeck, F. (1961). *Variations in value orientation.* Evanston, IL: Row, Peterson.

Kocet, M. M., & Herlihy, B. J. (2014). Addressing value-based conflicts within the counseling relationship: A decision-making model. *Journal of Counseling & Development, 92,* 180–186.

Koss-Chioino, J. (2000). Traditional and folk approaches among ethnic minorities. In J. Aponte & J. Wold (Eds.), *Psychological intervention and cultural diversity* (2nd ed., pp. 149–166). Needham Heights, MA: Allyn & Bacon.

Kwong-Liem, K. (2001). Models of racial and ethnic identity development: Delineation of practice implications. *Journal of Mental Health Counseling, 23,* 269–277.

Lee, W. M. L. (1999). *An introduction to multicultural counseling.* Philadelphia, PA: Accelerated Development.

Lewis, J., & Arnold, M. S. (1998). From multiculturalism to social action. In C. C. Lee & G. R. Walz (Eds.), *Social action: A mandate for counselors* (pp. 51–65). Alexandria, VA: American Counseling Association.

Lewis, J., Arnold, M. S., House, R., & Toporek, R. (2002). *Advocacy competencies.* Retrieved from https://www.counseling.org/Resources/Competencies/Advocacy_Competencies.pdf

Lofquist, D. (2011). *Same-sex couple households: American Community Survey briefs.* Retrieved from http://www.census.gov/prod/2011pubs/acsbr10-03.pdf

Lum, D. (Ed.). (2010). *Culturally competent practice: A framework for understanding diverse groups and justice issues* (4th ed.). Belmont, CA: Brooks/Cole.

McAuliffe, G., Grothaus, T., Pare, D., & Wininger, A. (2008). The practice of culturally alert counseling. In G. McAuliffe & Associates (Ed.), *Culturally alert counseling: A comprehensive introduction* (pp. 570–631). Thousand Oaks, CA: Sage.

McCullough, J. R., & Winninghoff, A. C. (2014). Social justice counseling practices: Affirming queer pluralism with LGBQ clients. In M. J. Ratts & P. B. Pedersen, *Counseling for multiculturalism and social justice: Integration, theory, and application* (4th ed., pp. 211–228). Alexandria, VA: American Counseling Association.

McFadden, J., & Lipscomb, W. D. (1985). History of the association for non-White concerns in personnel and guidance. *Journal of Counseling & Development, 63,* 444–447.

McWhirter, E. H. (1991). Empowerment in counseling. *Journal of Counseling & Development, 69,* 222–227.

Moyer, B., McAllister, J., Finley, M. L., & Soifer, S. (2001). *Doing democracy: The MAP model for organizing social movements.* Gabriola Island, British Columbia, Canada: New Society.

Oyserman, D., Coon, H., & Kemmelmeier, M. (2002). Rethinking individualism and collectivism: Evaluation of theoretical assumptions and meta-analyses. *Psychological Bulletin, 128,* 3–72.

Parham, T. A., Ajamu, A., & White, J. L. (2011). *The psychology of Blacks: Centering our perspectives in the African consciousness.* New York, NY: Prentice Hall.

Parker, W. M. (1991). From ANWC to AMCD. *Journal of Multicultural Counseling and Development, 19,* 52–65.

Pope, M. (1995). The "salad bowl" is big enough for us all: An argument for the inclusion of lesbians and gay men in any definition of multiculturalism. *Journal of Counseling & Development, 73,* 301–304.

Pope-Davis, D. B., Coleman, H. L. K., Liu, W. M., & Toporek, R. L. (Eds.). (2003). *Handbook of multicultural competencies in counseling and psychology.* Thousand Oaks, CA: Sage.

Prilleltensky, I. (1994). *The morals and politics of psychology: Psychological discourse and the status quo.* Albany, NY: State University of New York Press.

Qin, D., & Comstock, D. (2005). Traditional models of development: Appreciating context and relationship. In D. Comstock (Ed.), *Diversity and development: Critical contexts that shape our lives and relationships* (pp. 1–20). Belmont, CA: Brooks/Cole.

Ratts, M. J. (2009a). Counselors for social justice. In American Counseling Association (Ed.), *The ACA encyclopedia of counseling* (pp. 129–130). Alexandria, VA: American Counseling Association.

Ratts, M. J. (2009b). Social justice counseling: Toward the development of a "fifth force" among counseling paradigms. *Journal of Humanistic Counseling, Education and Development, 48,* 160–172.

Ratts, M., D'Andrea, M., & Arredondo, P. (2004). Social justice counseling: A "fifth force" in the field. *Counseling Today, 47,* 28–30.

Ratts, M. J., & Ford, A. E. (2010). Advocacy Competencies Self-Assessment Survey. In M. J. Ratts, R. L. Toporek, & J. A. Lewis (Eds.), *ACA advocacy competencies: A social justice framework for counselors* (pp. 21–26). Alexandria, VA: American Counseling Association.

Ratts, M. J., & Pedersen, P. B. (2014). *Counseling for multiculturalism and social justice: Integration, theory, and application* (4th ed.). Alexandria, VA: American Counseling Association.

Ratts, M., Singh, A. A., Nassar-McMillan, S., Butler, S. K., & McCullough, J. R. (2015). *Multicultural and social justice counseling competencies.* Retrieved from http://www.counseling.org/knowledge-center/competencies

Ream, C. (1971). Youth culture: Humanity's last chance. *Personnel and Guidance Journal, 49,* 699–704.

Reynolds, A. L., & Pope, R. L. (1991). The complexities of diversity: Exploring multiple oppressions. *Journal of Counseling & Development, 70,* 174–180.

Ridley, C., & Lingle, D. (1996). Cultural empathy in multicultural counseling: A multidimensional process model. In P. Pedersen, J. Draguns, W. Lonner, & J. Trimble (Eds.), *Counseling across cultures* (4th ed., pp. 21–46). Thousand Oaks, CA: Sage.

Rogers, E. M. (2003). *Diffusion of innovations* (5th ed.). New York, NY: Free Press.

Rubin, Z., & Peplau, L. A. (1975). Who believes in a just world? *Journal of Social Issues, 31*(2), 65–89.

Slattery, J. (2004). *Counseling diverse clients: Bringing context into therapy.* Belmont, CA: Brooks/Cole.

Smith, P. M., Jr. (1971). Black activists for liberation, not guidance. *Personnel and Guidance Journal, 49,* 721–726.

Smith, S. D., Reynolds, C. A., & Rovnak, A. (2009). A critical analysis of the social advocacy movement in counseling. *Journal of Counseling & Development, 87,* 483–491.

Smith, T., & Kehe, J. (2004). Glossary. In T. Smith (Ed.), *Practicing multiculturalism: Affirming diversity in counseling and psychology* (pp. 325–337). Boston, MA: Pearson Education.

Steele, J. M., Bischof, G. H., & Craig, S. E. (2014). Political ideology and perceptions of social justice advocacy among members of the American Counseling Association. *International Journal for the Advancement of Counselling, 36,* 450–467.

Sue, D. W., Arredondo, P., & McDavis, R. J. (1992). Multicultural competencies and standards: A call to the profession. *Journal of Counseling & Development, 70,* 477–486.

Sue, D. W., & Sue, D. (2013). *Counseling the culturally diverse: Theory and practice* (6th ed.). New York, NY: Wiley.

Tatum, B. (2000). The complexity of identity: Who am I? In M. Adams, W. Blumenfeld, R. Castaneda, H. Hackman, M. Peters, & X. Zuniga (Eds.), *Readings for diversity and social justice: An anthology on racism, antisemitism, sexism, heterosexism, ableism, and classism* (pp. 9–14). New York, NY: Routledge.

Toporek, R., Lewis, J., & Crethar, H. (2009). Promoting systemic change through the advocacy competencies. *Journal of Counseling & Development, 87,* 260–268.

van Beek, A. M. (2015). Developing a diagnostic filter for cross-cultural counseling: Five cases involving Asian Americans examined from a worldview perspective. *Pastoral Psychology, 64,* 123–134.

van Soest, D. (1996). Impact of social work education on student attitudes and behavior concerning oppression. *Journal of Social Work Education, 32,* 191–202.

Vera, E. M., & Speight, S. L. (2003). Multicultural competence, social justice, and counseling psychology: Expanding our roles. *Counseling Psychologist, 31,* 253–272.

Vontress, C. E. (1988). An existential approach to cross-cultural counseling. *Journal of Multicultural Counseling and Development, 16,* 73–83.

Yeh, C., Hunter, C., Madan-Bahel, A., Chiang, L., & Arora, A. (2004). Indigenous and interdependent perspectives of healing: Implications for counseling and research. *Journal of Counseling & Development, 82,* 410–419.

Young, I. M. (2011). *Justice and the politics of difference.* Princeton, NJ: Princeton University Press.

Zalaquett, C. P., Foley, P. F., Tillotson, K., Dinsmore, J. A., & Hof, D. (2008). Multicultural and social justice training for counselor education programs and colleges of education: Rewards and challenges. *Journal of Counseling & Development, 86,* 323–329.

Part 2

Theories of Counseling and Psychotherapy

CHAPTERS

Part 2 contains 13 chapters, each of which addresses a selected theoretical system that has direct application to the counseling or therapy process. We selected the theoretical systems based on their current use in the field of counseling and therapy, and we chose the chapter authors based on their expertise and their current application of the theoretical system in their work with clients. To provide the reader with a consistent format, each chapter contains information dealing with the following areas:

- **Background:** Historical information related to the development of the theoretical system and the individual(s) responsible for its development is presented.
- **Human Nature: A Developmental Perspective:** The process of individual development over time, as defined by the theoretical system, is discussed in this section.
- **Major Constructs:** The structural components that constitute the theoretical system are described.
- **Applications:** This section includes the following areas:
  Overview: An introduction to the six areas that follow
  Goals of Counseling and Psychotherapy: A description of desired client outcomes based on the tenets of the theory
  The Process of Change: The factors within the theory that address what brings about change in the individual
  Traditional Intervention Strategies: Techniques for implementing the process of change
  Brief Intervention Strategies and Current Practices: Techniques for implementing the process of change using a brief approach
  Clients With Serious Mental Health Issues: A discussion of how each theory can be used with clients with serious mental health issues
- **Evaluation:** This section includes the following areas:
  Overview: An introduction to the three areas that follow
  Supporting Research: Current research studies that form the basis for continued use of this theoretical system
  Limitations: A description of the factors that limit the use of this theoretical system
  Summary Chart: A summary of the material presented
- **Case Study:** A case analysis and treatment is provided based on the theory.

The first three chapters in Part 2 deal with the theoretical systems, often classified as *analytical,* that were developed by Sigmund Freud, Carl Jung, and Alfred Adler. **Chapter 3**, "Psychoanalytic Theory," provides background information relative to counseling and therapy within a psychoanalytic framework and emphasizes current use of this framework for individual counseling and therapy. **Chapter 4**, "Jungian Analytical Theory," takes the reader from the development and definition of the major constructs of Jungian psychology to their application in the case of Maria, the subject of our hypothetical case study. We think readers will find this journey both intriguing and enlightening. **Chapter 5**, "Adlerian Theory," highlights the contributions of Alfred Adler and demonstrates the application of his major constructs in current approaches to counseling and psychotherapy.

The next three chapters in Part 2 deal with the theoretical systems often classified as *humanistic.* **Chapter 6**, "Existential Theory," sets forth the philosophical underpinnings of existential counseling and psychotherapy and demonstrates how this philosophy translates into approaches that can be used by the counselor or therapist in working with clients. **Chapter 7**, "Person-Centered Theory," deals specifically with the work of Carl Rogers and highlights the continual development of this theoretical system from Rogers's work in the early 1940s to the last years of his life, when he traveled to the most troubled places in the world and used his person-centered approach to promote peace among warring groups. **Chapter 8**, "Gestalt Theory," emphasizes the pioneering work of Frederick Perls and his development of Gestalt counseling and psychotherapy. Major concepts and interventions are presented in combination with their current use in counseling and therapy.

The next four chapters in Part 2 deal with the theoretical systems, often classified as *behavioral,* that were developed by theorists such as Aaron Beck, Donald Meichenbaum, Marsha Linehan, William Glasser, and Albert Ellis. **Chapter 9**, "Cognitive Behavior Theories," provides the reader with a general background about both the behavioral and cognitive–behavioral theoretical views and discusses how the cognitive–behavioral approach developed from the behavioral point of view. **Chapter 10**, "Dialectical Behavior Theory," is a therapeutic methodology initially developed by Marsha M. Linehan in the late 1970s to treat individuals with borderline personality disorder. Dialectical behavior therapy combines customary cognitive–behavioral techniques for emotional regulation and reality testing with concepts of mindful awareness, distress tolerance, and acceptance predominantly derived from Buddhist meditative practice. **Chapter 11**, "Rational Emotive Behavior Therapy," emphasizes the work of Albert Ellis, with special attention directed to the ABCDE model for understanding how thoughts and behaviors are related. Contributions to counseling and therapy made by Ellis and his colleagues are stressed. **Chapter 12**, "Reality Therapy/Choice Theory," highlights the work of William Glasser and places special emphasis on a system he developed to provide reality therapy to help others remediate deficiencies, make better choices, and become more fully self-actualized.

Chapter 13, "Family Theory," provides the reader with ideas for working with families, because it is important to understand that individual approaches do not adequately address the patterns of communicating and relating that connect individuals to one another in families. The purpose of the chapter is to help the reader find ways to add systems-level interventions to the individualist approaches studied in previous chapters. We think readers will find this chapter both interesting and informative.

Chapter 14 on "Feminist Theory," which has evolved gradually over time as a response to women's rejection of traditional psychotherapies, addresses some of the sexist, oppressive aspects of many of the currently used theories of counseling and psychotherapy and encourages counselors and therapists not to apply theories based on male developmental models to women.

Generally known in the literature as transpersonal psychology, "Transpersonal Theory" is the subject of **Chapter 15**. This chapter discusses transpersonal theories as they apply to not only the diagnosis and treatment of psychological problems associated with normal human development but also the difficulties associated with developmental stages beyond that of the adult ego. The practices of transpersonal theory can include discussions and interventions pertaining to spiritual experiences; mystical states of consciousness; mindfulness and meditative practices; shamanic states; ritual; the overlap of spiritual experiences with disturbed mental states such as psychosis, depression, and other psychopathologies; and the transpersonal dimensions of interpersonal relationships, service, and encounters with the natural world. We think the readers of our text will appreciate the inclusion of this material in the sixth edition of the book.

The theoretical systems included in Part 2 provide the reader with a comprehensive and current review of major counseling and psychotherapy approaches to working with individuals. Our conviction is strengthened by our selection of authors, who not only have expertise in the specific theoretical systems but also practice these approaches in working with clients.

We asked each author or set of authors in Part 2 of this text to address the following case study information in the development of a treatment or counseling plan that is consistent with the specific theoretical system presented. This approach gives readers the opportunity to view the theoretical systems from a comparative perspective as they search for the theoretical system that is most appropriate for their future work as counselors or therapists.

THE CASE OF MARIA

Client Demographics

The client, Maria, is a 32-year-old Latina female. She is the oldest of five children and was raised in a culturally encapsulated Latino neighborhood in a large metropolitan area in the Southwest. She attended Catholic schools, and her religion remains a very significant part of her life. She is a single parent raising two children, a 6-year-old son and an 8-year-old daughter. She is bilingual, graduated from college with honors, has a degree in education, and for the past 4 years has taught middle school math and science. She and her husband of 5 years divorced 3 years ago. She receives no financial assistance from her former husband, and the only knowledge the children have of their father is through communication with their paternal grandparents.

Presenting Problems

Maria arrived 15 minutes early for her initial appointment. She related easily and expressed herself well, but her body appeared tense and her voice was strained. She expressed appreciation for getting an early appointment because she felt that she could not have waited much longer. She had been referred to the mental health agency by her physician because of insomnia and frequent unexplained crying spells. During the intake process, she stated that she is depressed, unable to sleep because of reoccurring nightmares, not eating, losing control of her two children, and having difficulty dealing with family members. She said that she has thought about suicide but stops because of the guilt she feels about abandoning her children and the tenets of her religion. She has difficulty concentrating, and this is affecting her teaching. She has been absent frequently from work, and her principal is recommending that she take a leave of absence. This decision is causing her great stress, as she needs the income to support her children. If she leaves her teaching position, she would be forced to move back with her family. She is unable to maintain meaningful relationships with various men she has been dating and views her future as very negative. When asked what words she would use to describe herself, she used terms such as *insecure, frightened, distrustful of self and others, lonely,* and *lacking hope.*

Family Background

Based on information gathered during the intake process, Maria describes her family of origin as very close knit, held together by both cultural and religious values. She was raised to be proud of her Latino heritage, her language, and her culture's traditions. She has three younger brothers and one younger sister, all of whom look to her for advice and support. Education was stressed in her home, and her academic success was the center of much family pride. She was touted as a model to her siblings and was expected to perform in an exemplary way, not only in school but also in other aspects of her life.

Maria's parents were self-educated and operated a small business near their home. Because of the fact that the business demanded a large time commitment from both parents, Maria often found herself, during adolescence, taking care of both the house and her younger siblings. Most of the family activities centered on their local parish and the activities generated in the community. Maria's social life was very much tied to her immediate family and contacts she made at either the Catholic school or church youth groups. She was encouraged to bring her friends to her home and to date young men within the community. Cultural pride, religion, and the parameters of the local Hispanic community affected much of her formative development.

Early Adult Years

Maria's first true exposure to other cultures came on her leaving home to attend a state university. She had received scholarships from two of the state's three universities, and even though her parents wanted her to stay at home and attend the local university, she decided to attend a university approximately 200 miles from her home. Her decision caused conflict within her family, and she reported that it placed a good deal of strain on her relationships with both parents. Her sister supported her actions, but her brothers felt that she was abandoning the family.

She was very successful at the university, and it was here that she met and later married the first person she had dated outside of her religion and culture. Mark was a Euro-American student in the College of Engineering and seemed to have no specific religious affiliation. It was not until their graduation that Maria introduced Mark to her family and, at the same time, announced their plans to be married.

Maria's family, with the exception of her sister, were very opposed to the marriage and made their opposition known not only to Maria but also to Mark. Maria and Mark also faced opposition from his parents. In order to avoid further confrontations, Maria and Mark eloped and were married by a justice of the peace in a nearby state.

After their marriage, they returned to their home area, secured jobs, and began to build a life together. It was not until after their first child was born that contact with both families was renewed. By the time their second child was born, both families were much more involved with both their children and grandchildren.

The second child put a strain on the marriage, and within 2 years, Maria and Mark separated and were later divorced. Mark left the state and has had no contact with Maria or his children in 2 years. The paternal grandparents do, however, continue to have contact with their grandchildren.

Postdivorce Years

Since the divorce 3 years ago, Maria has been able to discuss the physical and psychological abuse that she received from Mark. He became physically abusive when drinking and constantly demeaned her profession, culture, and religion. He drew away from both Maria and the children and spent more and more time away from the home. Turning to her family for support, Maria was confronted with indifference and reminders of their opposition to the marriage. Her sister, once supportive, now blames Maria for a great deal of the disunity within the family. The children's paternal grandparents refuse to believe that their son was abusive and are very critical of the manner in which Maria is raising their grandchildren.

With the lack of support coming from family, Maria turned to friends for help. One friend suggested that Maria needed to date and get back into "circulation." She found that she had difficulty relating to men, was afraid to trust, and felt that all they wanted was sex. She felt that when they found out she had two children, the relationships cooled down rapidly.

She turned next to her work and poured all of her energy into her students. This left very little for her own children, and the mother–child relationship grew very strained. It was at this time that she began to have disturbing dreams that kept her from sleeping. The dreams, according to Maria, generally entail the following:

> I am always running and there are shadowy figures behind me. I am in a large warehouse-type structure with lots of boxes and crates. The boxes and crates are all marked with arrows reading "Exit." The only problem is that the arrows are all going in different directions. Therefore, I never find the exit, and the figures keep getting closer and closer. I wake up in a cold sweat, breathing rapidly, heart pounding, and a scream struck in my throat. I lie there trying to calm down, knowing that I am too afraid to go back to sleep. In a little while I get up and spend the rest of the long night sitting at the kitchen table drinking coffee.

The more often the dreams occurred, the more depressed Maria became. She fought sleep because of her fear of dreaming, and at times she found herself crying uncontrollably. Her eating habits have also changed drastically, and she finds herself buying fast food for the children so that she does not have to cook. She seldom eats and has lost 15 pounds, weight she really cannot afford to lose.

The depression kept her away from work and away from people. She began spending more and more time alone. In Maria's words, "I have nothing to live for. No one cares about me. I have ruined my life and the lives of two families and I am currently hurting my children." On the advice of her priest, she sought the help of her physician, who recommended that she seek psychological help.

Chapter 3

Psychoanalytic Theory

Adrianne L. Johnson

The concepts of psychoanalysis have become interwoven into the fabric of U.S. culture, with terms such as *Freudian slip, repression,* and *denial* appearing regularly in everyday language. Psychoanalytic theory is based on the concept that individuals are unaware of the many factors that cause their maladaptive behaviors and discomforting emotions. Psychoanalytic treatment is highly individualized, is lengthy in duration, and seeks to show how early childhood experiences have affected the formative aspects of one's personality development.

Psychoanalysis in its classical form is limited in empirical support across contexts and populations and has evolved since its beginnings to meet the changing needs of managed care and community-based programs that emphasize productivity led by evidence-based practices. Traditional techniques have changed to accommodate brief settings, meet the unique needs of diverse client populations, and foster client self-awareness through modified techniques and strategies. This evolution in approach is now conceptualized as psychodynamic therapy and fluidly relates to other rapidly emerging approaches such as psychodynamic interpersonal therapy, object relations theory, and interpersonal psychotherapy. All of these approaches echo the original psychoanalytic theme of unconscious thoughts, instinctual drives, and psychological defenses formed early in life. However, each approach features uniquely identifying techniques that distinguish each in general approach and problem resolution.

The aim of this chapter is to help counselors gain a broad understanding of classical psychoanalytic theory and its current practices and applications in contemporary mental health treatment. The goals of this chapter are to help counselors meet the following objectives: (a) to gain a basic understanding of the foundation, history, and development of psychoanalytic theory; (b) to gain a basic understanding of the implications of psychoanalytic theory across populations and contexts;

and (c) to gain a basic understanding how to apply psychoanalytic and psychodynamic techniques in counseling practice for the most effective outcome.

BACKGROUND

Psychoanalytic theory was an enormously influential force during the first half of the 20th century. The theory first emerged with the pioneering efforts of neuroscientists Josef Breuer and Jean-Martin Charcot, and the primary components of the theory were later adapted, refined, and popularized by Sigmund Freud. Throughout Freud's professional career, his articulated ideas regarding unconscious motivations and psychosexual development and his dynamic insights about coping mechanisms greatly influenced psychological and medical explanations of how the human mind works.

Jean-Martin Charcot and Josef Breuer

French neurologist Jean-Martin Charcot made significant neuroscientific discoveries while teaching at the University of Paris in France during the 1860s. These discoveries led to the eventual diagnostic conceptualization of Lou Gehrig's disease, multiple sclerosis, Parkinson's disease, and Tourette's syndrome. However, Charcot's primary focus of research was the concept of hysteria, which was believed at the time to be a physical manifestation of a weak hereditary neurological system. He suggested that if an individual, male or female, were exposed to a trauma or physical accident, the condition would present itself as partial paralysis, hallucinations, and nervousness and would worsen with time. Charcot believed that individuals did not suffer from the trauma itself but from the ideas they developed in relation to it. He promoted hypnosis as a verifiable method of studying and identifying the true cause of hysteria, which would lead to the prevention of its troubling symptoms (Poirier, Clarac, Barbara, & Broussolle, 2012).

Josef Breuer, an Austrian physician and physiologist, is known as the founder of psychoanalysis based on his theory of unconscious processes and his assertion that the neurotic symptoms of hysteria could disappear when these underlying causes became part of the conscious mind. Like Charcot and many medical practitioners of the era, Breuer was a strong proponent of hypnosis. Using hypnosis, Breuer found that the severity of hysterical symptoms presented in one of this patients, "Anna O." (later identified as 21-year-old Bertha Pappenheim, 1859–1936), was dramatically reduced. During daily hypnosis sessions throughout the early 1880s, Breuer encouraged her to describe her fantasies and hallucinations with no self-censorship, which led to the identification of traumatic memories. Breuer referred to this process as *catharsis* and noticed that her symptoms disappeared shortly thereafter (Kaplan, 2004).

Sigmund Freud

Sigmund Freud diligently studied medicine at the University of Vienna and in 1882 began practicing medicine and researching medical pathology at Vienna General Hospital. In 1885, he was appointed as a university lecturer and discovered an increased interest in the clinical presentation of aphasia and neuropathy in asylum patients. During the early years of his career, he developed an interest in neurology. He engaged in research with Jean-Martin Charcot and was greatly influenced by the potential of hypnosis in the treatment of both hysteria and aphasia (Gay, 2006). Freud also conducted research with Josef Breuer and was intrigued by the case of Anna O. and the application of hypnosis to cure her symptoms. He noted that talking about her life appeared to greatly relieve her "hysteric" symptoms and further suggested that many psychological conditions were found to greatly improve once repressed trauma and their related emotions were expressed by talking rather than by using hypnosis. He coauthored "Studies on Hysteria" with Josef Breuer, published in 1895, but then shortly thereafter abandoned hypnosis altogether.

These experiences led Freud to popularize the concept of the talking cure, or the free-flowing catharsis of symptoms and their possible origins (Swartz, 2014). During the following years in private practice, he utilized free association and dream analysis as cures for a constellation of unusual symptoms he observed, including anxiety, amnesia, unexplained paralysis, and psychosomatic complaints, primarily observed in his female patients. Freud found that patients' dreams could be fruitfully analyzed to reveal the complex structuring of unconscious material and to demonstrate the psychic action of repression that underlay symptom formation. By 1896, Freud had redefined hysteria in the psychological community and popularized the term *psychoanalysis* to refer to his new clinical method and the theories on which it was based (Gay, 2006).

HUMAN NATURE: A DEVELOPMENTAL PERSPECTIVE

Psychoanalytic theory suggests that early life experiences shape one's social interactions and relationships in adulthood. Humans across cultures are conceptualized largely in terms of biological instincts and psychological drives, and maladaptive behaviors are symptomatic of a subconscious response to social interactions that the mind interprets as unsafe, thereby threatening the stability of the human personality structure. Within a psychoanalytic framework, culture is viewed as having defensive hierarchies that result in cultural patterns and ethnic characters. There is a commonality of defenses and conflicts that are both provided and facilitated by a particular culture, and concepts such as anxiety, depression, defense mechanisms, and dreams are present in people of all cultures. An assumption of this theory is that the modes of expression of these concepts may differ in diverse cultures (Lijtmaer, 2006; see Sidebar 3.1).

Sidebar 3.1. Culture and Hysteria

The evolution of the definition of hysteria led to the clinical conceptualization of somatoform, conversion, dissociative identity, and amnestic disorders. The diagnosis of these disorders is culture bound, and the *Diagnostic and Statistical Manual of Mental Disorders*, Fifth Edition, addresses this directly in a distinct section, "Culture-Related Diagnostic Issues," which helps counselors diagnose syndromes in an appropriate cultural context (American Psychiatric Association, 2013, pp. 211–212). For example, *ataque de nervios* comprises a constellation of symptoms that would have been analogous to a diagnosis of hysteria in 1890. In Hispanic culture, this is interpreted as an "intense emotional upset, including acute anxiety, anger, or grief; screaming and shouting uncontrollably; attacks of crying; trembling; heat in the chest rising into the head; and becoming verbally and physically aggressive" or otherwise feeling out of control (p. 833).

MAJOR CONSTRUCTS

Psychoanalysis

One of the most well-known constructs of psychoanalytic theory is that of an interactive system constituting the human personality. The instinctual and biological drives of the psyche are referred to as the *id;* the critical, moralizing function is the *superego;* and the organized, realistic part that mediates and seeks a balance between the former two is known as the *ego.* The id, the ego, and the superego are used to describe the structural model of the personality that drives and guides one's functions and behavior. This concept is also the foundation for many other major constructs in psychoanalysis (Pigman, 2014).

Id, Ego, and Superego

The id constitutes the unorganized part of the personality structure that contains the basic drives, and it is the only component of personality that is present from birth. This aspect of personality is entirely unconscious and includes the individual's instinctive drives and primitive behaviors. The id is the source of all psychic energy, making it the primary component of personality. The id functions on the pleasure principle, which emphasizes wants and desires and instant self-gratification, and if not satisfied immediately, the result is a state of anxiety or tension (Pigman, 2014). For example, should an infant be hungry or uncomfortable, he or she will cry until the demands of the id are met.

The superego strives to act in a moral, socially appropriate manner and directly contradicts the instant self-gratification desire of the id. This component of personality consists of one's internalized ideals, morals, and ethics acquired from one's parents and from society (Cherry, 2010). This helps an individual conform to societal norms by encouraging him or her to behave in socially constructed moral and civilized ways. The superego is present in the conscious, preconscious, and unconscious. This is the last component of personality to develop, emerging around age 5. There are two parts to the superego: The first is the *ego-ideal,* which includes the rules and standards for good behaviors. These behaviors include those that are approved of by parental and other authority figures. Obeying these rules leads to feelings of pride, value, and accomplishment. The second part is the *conscience,* which includes information about things that are viewed as bad by parents and society. These behaviors are often forbidden and lead to bad consequences, punishments, or feelings of guilt and remorse (Cherry, 2010).

The ego is the largely unconscious part of the personality that mediates the demands of the id and the superego. The ego prevents individuals from acting on their basic urges (created by the id) but also works to achieve a balance with their moral and idealistic standards (created by the superego). The ego is the component of personality that is responsible for helping an individual cope with reality. According to Freud, the ego develops from the id and ensures that the impulses of the id can be expressed in a manner acceptable in the real world. Like the superego, the ego functions in the conscious, preconscious, and unconscious mind. The ego functions on the reality principle, which strives to satisfy the id's desires in realistic and socially appropriate ways (Cherry, 2010). The reality principle weighs the costs and benefits of an action before deciding to act on or abandon impulses.

In many cases, the id's impulses can be satisfied through a process of delayed gratification, in which the ego will eventually allow the behavior but only in the appropriate time and place.

Psychosexual Development

Psychoanalysis assumes that personality develops through a series of childhood stages during which the pleasure-seeking energies of the id become focused on certain erogenous areas. Psychosexual energy, or *libido,* is suggested to be the driving force behind behavior. At particular points in the developmental process, a single body part is particularly sensitive to sexual, erotic stimulation (Zepf, 2010). These *erogenous zones* are the mouth, the anus, and the genital region. A child at a given stage of development has certain needs and demands, and if these psychosexual stages are completed successfully, the result is a healthy functioning personality. However, frustration occurs when these needs are not met, and if these frustrations are not resolved in the associated psychosexual stage, the individual will become fixated and will exhibit dysfunctional symptomatology until this early conflict is resolved.

Psychoanalytic theory proposes five psychosexual stages that incorporate a specific erogenous zone in each corresponding stage. The first stage is the *oral stage,* experienced during the first year of life. During the oral stage, the infant's primary source of interaction occurs through the mouth, so the rooting and sucking reflexes are especially important (Knight, 2014). The mouth is vital for eating, and the infant derives pleasure from oral stimulation through gratifying activities such as tasting and sucking. Because the infant is entirely dependent on caregivers to satiate these needs, the infant also develops a sense of trust and comfort through this oral stimulation. The primary conflict at the oral stage is the weaning process: The infant must become less dependent on caregivers and more self-reliant to meet his or her own needs. If fixation occurs at this stage, the individual will have issues with dependency or aggression later in life, which will result in problems with an emphasis on oral stimulation, such as drinking, eating, smoking, or nail biting (Nevid, 2009).

The second stage is the *anal stage,* occurring between 1 and 3 years of age. The focus of this stage is on controlling bladder and bowel movements. The major conflict at this stage is toilet training: The child has to learn to control his or her bodily needs. Success at this stage is dependent on toilet training, and if the child develops a sense of control over bodily expulsions during this stage, the result is a feeling of accomplishment and independence as an adult (Juni, 2009). Positive experiences and accomplishments during this stage serve as the basis for adults to become competent, productive, and creative. Punitive caregiver responses to behavior problems during toilet training result in two primary negative outcomes. If caregivers lack diligence in toilet training, the child develops an anal-expulsive personality as an adult and has a messy, wasteful, or destructive personality. And if caregivers are too strict during training or begin training prematurely, an anal-retentive personality develops, and the individual is stringent, orderly, rigid, and obsessive (Knight, 2014).

The third stage is the *phallic stage,* in which the libido is primarily focused on the genitals between ages 3 and 6. Children discover the differences between males and females at this stage, and boys begin to view their fathers as rivals for their mothers' affections (Berberovic, 2012). The *Oedipus complex* describes these feelings of wanting to possess the mother and the desire to replace the father. However, the child also fears that he will be punished by the father for these feelings, resulting in *castration anxiety.* The term *Electra complex* has been used to describe a similar set of feelings experienced by young girls but is derived from penis envy, or the effort to possess the opposite-sex parent by identifying with the parent of the same sex. Unlike boys, for whom the Oedipus complex is resolved before adolescence, girls experience penis envy into adulthood, and women never resolve this conflict (Levy-Warren, 2008).

Between ages 6 and 12 children experience the *latency stage,* during which the id, the ego, and the superego develop the foundation for the adult's instinctual drives and behavioral responses. This fourth stage is a time of exploration in which sexual energy is still present but is directed into age-appropriate areas, such as academic pursuits and peer interactions. The stage begins around the time that children enter school and places increasing importance on developing social relationships, extracurricular activities, and personal interests. The development of the ego and superego contribute to this period of calm as the id and libido are suppressed (Knight, 2014).

The fifth and final stage, the *genital stage,* begins after age 12 and continues through adulthood. During this stage, the individual develops strong sexual interests, drives, and desires. An interest in the welfare of others supersedes the concentration on individual needs from earlier stages. If the other stages have been completed successfully, the individual should now be well balanced, warm, and caring. The goal of this stage is to establish a balance between the various life areas. In a sense, this is the stage in which the ego fully emerges to mediate the conflict between the id and superego with regard to one's social and sexual interactions with others (Carducci, 2009).

Life and Death Instincts

During Freud's self-analysis later in life, he explored the purpose and motivations of human existence. Toward the turn of the century, psychoanalysis expanded to include a new class of drives in addition to those mentioned earlier. These drives, the life instincts, are classified into two categories: life instincts and death instincts. Life instincts are those that deal with basic survival, pleasure, and reproduction, and behaviors commonly associated with the life instinct include love, cooperation, and other prosocial actions. These instincts are important for sustaining the life of the individual as well as continuing the species. These are often called *sexual instincts* because the energy created by the life instincts is the psychosexual energy conceptualized as libido, but they also include such constructs as thirst, hunger, and pain avoidance. Conversely, death instincts emerge as self-destructive behavior, self-harm, and self-sabotage. Death instincts are often expressed as aggression or violence and are tempered by the life instincts (Georgescu, 2011).

Defense Mechanisms

The concept of the defense mechanism can be observed daily across cultures and contexts, even among those who are not familiar with Freud or psychoanalytic theory. These mechanisms are a function of the ego, which develops coping strategies to protect the individual from experiencing anxiety and guilt provoked by the discord between the id and superego. These mechanisms shield the mind against feelings and thoughts that are interpreted by the mind as inappropriate, unwanted, or uncomfortable. Psychoanalysis theory proposes several defense mechanisms (Corey, 2012):

- *Compartmentalization* is a process of separating parts of the self from awareness of other parts and behaving as if one had separate sets of values.
- *Compensation* is a process of psychologically counterbalancing perceived weaknesses by emphasizing strength in other areas.
- *Denial* is refusing to accept reality and acting as if a painful event, thought, or feeling did not exist. It is considered one of the most primitive of the defense mechanisms because it is characteristic of very early childhood development.
- *Displacement* is the redirecting of thoughts, feelings, and impulses from an object that gives rise to anxiety to a safer, more acceptable one.
- *Intellectualization* is the use of a cognitive approach without the attendant emotions to suppress and attempt to gain mastery over the perceived disorderly and potentially overwhelming impulses.
- *Projection* is the attribution of one's undesired impulses to another.
- *Rationalization* is the cognitive reframing of one's perceptions to protect the ego in the face of changing realities.
- *Reaction formation* is the converting of wishes or impulses that are perceived to be dangerous into their opposites.
- *Regression* is the reversion to an earlier stage of development in the face of unacceptable impulses.
- *Repression* is the blocking of unacceptable impulses from consciousness.
- *Sublimation* is the channeling of unacceptable impulses into more acceptable outlets.

A client may use any combination of these coping strategies at any one time. It is when these mechanisms fail to protect the individual at a certain point, however, that the individual will unconsciously experience an overwhelming sense of emotional discord, and it will most likely be at this time that he or she seeks counseling.

Transference and Countertransference

One of the most important concepts associated with psychoanalysis and still referred to today is the idea of transference, or the process of attributing one's feelings to another. Transference during a counseling session can be observed in many forms, including sexual attraction, rage, hatred, dependence, or mistrust (Etchegoyen, 2005). This concept is discernable from displacement or projection because the feelings are attributed primarily to the counselor. Once the transference is identified, the counselor assumes a *blank screen* position, engaging the client in exposing the unconscious motivation behind the individual's defense mechanisms by welcoming all transferred attitudes, feelings, impulses, and desires that were generated in early life by important figures in the client's life. It is assumed that the motivations will appear on their own during this process, and they may then be examined and redirected by the conscious.

Countertransference is also used in counseling, especially when addressing issues of ethics and practice. Countertransference is the emotional reaction to a client based on the counselor's own unconscious conflicts that have been triggered by the client's dialogue. As a counseling tool, this concept can have both positive and negative effects on treatment. Awareness of this process by the counselor can provide important insight into the client's inner world and into the emotions and reactions the client often tends to induce in others. However, the counselor must be able to recognize these feelings and address his or her own fears and distortions to use countertransference as an effective counseling tool (Thomas, 2008), or damaging enactments and impaired judgment may occur.

Object Relations and Attachment

Object relations psychology was first articulated in the 1940s by several British analysts, including Melanie Klein, W. R. D. Fairbairn, D. W. Winnicott, and Harry Guntrip. This approach is derived from psychoanalytic concepts but specifically emphasizes interpersonal relations and attachment, especially primarily in the family and between mother and child. It focuses on the development of the self in relation to the continuing influence of early social environments and internalization of early experiences in relationships and proposes that clients experience pain and dysfunction arising from the struggle between relating to others while differentiating the self (Charuvastra & Cloitre, 2008).

At its core, object relations theory suggests that internal representations of the self and others acquired in childhood are later replicated in adult relations, and in order to establish a healthy relationship with the self and the other, the client must examine how self-esteem, self-concept, and unhealthy attachments are impeding healthy social support. Psychologist John Bowlby developed this concept further with his attachment theory, which suggests that relationships with primary caregivers during early development influence emotional and behavioral responses across the life span through a behavioral system that influences expectations of both self and others in close relationships (Bowlby, 1969; see Sidebar 3.2).

Sidebar 3.2. Psychodynamic Theory and Neuroscience

A strong trend in counseling is a growing interest in the relationship between personality disorders, attachment theory, and links to neuroscience. This relationship is being explored by using neuroimaging techniques, which are now discerning the difference between psychodynamics (or the motivational influences that are actively blocked from awareness) and etiology (or causes of pathological behaviors). Counselors may use this information to understand how different brain structures react with incredible precision to a variety of stimuli, whether they are cognitive, pharmacological, or emotional. For example, data acquired from neuroimaging techniques show that explicit memory is defined as conscious memory, whereas implicit memory is unconscious. The hippocampus, which is responsible for coding memory, is directly affected by the amygdala, the emotion center of the brain. Thus, when a client experiences an emotional trauma, the perception of the trauma is coded into memory as conscious, or unconscious, content (Barry, 2014).

Self Psychology

Self psychology was founded by Heinz Kohut, MD, in Chicago during the 1970s. Kohut observed that the self refers to a person's perception of his or her experience of his or her self, including the presence or lack of a sense of self-esteem. The self is perceived in relation to the establishment of boundaries and the differentiations of self from others (Banai, Mikulincer, & Shaver, 2005). This approach suggests that the self is the essence of a person's being and consists of sensations, feelings, and self-image. This is similar to Freud's conceptualization of the self as a three-part dynamic; however, Kohut viewed the self as a force that explains the development of personality rather than a system of drives and motivations (Riker, 2013).

This approach suggests that the quality of the relationship between a child and a caregiver has a significant role in the development of a healthy and cohesive personality structure. When a child does not have an appropriate self–object differentiation, and is exposed to a trauma, the child is unable to separate the self from the object (in this case, the traumatic experience). The trauma then remains unprocessed and stays in the unconscious as a core negative experience, which derails normal development into adulthood. This would be expressed in the adult client as preoccupations with negative thinking, depression, suicidal thinking, attention deficits, hyperactivity, self-mutilation, and eating disorders (Rowe, 2013).

In terms of psychosis, a client strives to exist in an alternative reality that is preferable over the feelings of powerlessness and vulnerability that have evolved from this lack of differentiation. When antipsychotic medications are administered, depression results. This depression is a representation of the transition into actual reality from a grandiose state, and this is the point at which counselors may actively intervene with techniques aimed at integrating the self and the trauma stored in the unconscious. This integration allows the client to remain safely in reality without the dependence on escape (Potik, 2014).

APPLICATIONS

Overview

The process of change emerges from the use of traditional and modified techniques to bring awareness to the client and frame current maladaptive behaviors in the context of prior experiences contributing to current circumstances in the client's life. Recently, the use of psychoanalytic techniques has expanded to include an emphasis on the treatment of serious mental health issues, cross-cultural considerations, and brief applications across contexts.

Goals of Counseling and Psychotherapy

Psychoanalytic theory focuses on unconscious processes as they are manifested in the client's present behavior. The general goals of psychodynamic counseling are client self-awareness and understanding of the influence of the past on present behavior, and the correction of the client's distortions is often the primary focus of therapeutic treatment (Thomas, 2008). The primary goal of psychoanalysis is to bring the drives of the id into consciousness, allowing them to be understood and addressed directly, thus reducing the client's reliance on defense mechanisms to function in social contexts (Levenson, 2007). When symptoms are elucidated to bring the unconscious into consciousness or awareness, the ego is strengthened and the client learns to express his or her needs and wants within a realistic paradigm, resulting in a greater balance between the id and superego.

The Process of Change

The primary method of psychoanalysis is the identification, analysis, and interpretation of the unconscious conflicts that interfere with the client's daily functioning. This is done using a variety of traditional strategies and techniques, such as the analysis of dreams, transference, resistance, and defenses, which encourage the client to increase his or her awareness of the etiology and manifestation of symptoms and how to cope with new experiences in a more healthful, productive manner based on this new awareness. In its brief form, a psychodynamic approach uses direct dialogue and interpretation to examine unresolved conflicts and symptoms that arise from past dysfunctional relationships and manifest themselves in maladaptive symptoms and behaviors.

Traditional Intervention Strategies

Analysis of Transference

One of the most important tools of change for the counselor is the concept of transference. Assuming the position of a blank screen allows the counselor maintain a neutral position in the therapeutic relationship. This encourages the client to transfer unconscious feelings onto the counselor. Within a psychoanalytic framework, the client experiencing the transference is unconsciously searching for a transformational meeting with another person, and in the case of a counseling relationship, the counselor becomes that person (Binder, 2004). The counselor, as the object of transference, assumes the position of an anonymous tool for the client to expose the unconscious issues driving the maladaptive behaviors and maintains an obscure presence during the process of transference with the goal of analyzing the transferred material later (see Sidebar 3.3).

Analysis of Resistances

In addition to analyzing transference, the counselor also analyzes the resistances observed from the client during sessions with the intent to expose, or bring into consciousness, the underlying causes for those resistances. One of the most important tasks of the counselor–client alliance is to overcome resistance through

> **Sidebar 3.3. Transference-Focused Psychotherapy**
>
> Transference-focused psychotherapy is a developing approach that researchers suggest as an evidence-based treatment for narcissistic personality disorder. This approach integrates contemporary object relations theory and attachment theory and focuses on the interpretation of devalued and idealized representations of self and others. These are key components of this approach, and the aim is to expose the underlying reasons for the profound sense of vulnerability and imperfection that results in the hallmark compensatory grandiosity associated with narcissistic personality disorder. Randomized clinical trials suggest that this is a promising innovative combination of psychoanalysis and object relations for improving symptomatic functioning in clients with identified attachment disruptions stemming from trauma (Diamond & Meehan, 2013).

remembering, reenacting events, and working through negative feelings. Resistance is interpreted as an instinctual reaction to uncomfortable situations in which the client attempts to keep hidden from himself or herself and the counselor. It is a way of avoiding the expression of feelings, fantasies, and drives that the client's subconscious has learned over time to repress and defend. Psychoanalysis classifies client resistance into five categories, all emanating from the ego, the id, and the superego. All of the categories serve the explicit purpose of defending the ego against feelings of discomfort and require an immersion in analysis using various psychoanalytic techniques.

The first category, *repression resistance*, emerges from the ego and includes various defenses and symptoms such as reaction formation, obsession, anxiety, and phobias. This is the result of the unconscious struggle of the psyche to repress painful material and keep it from reaching exposure during sessions. The second category is *transference resistance*, which also emerges from the ego and presents as projection. The third resistance, and the last to originate within the ego, is *ego resistance* and is framed as a secondary gain or a gain from illness or dysfunction. The fourth category, *working through*, arises from the id and presents as a compulsion to repeat maladaptive behaviors. Even after the ego releases its resistances, it still has difficulty undoing existing repressions. Working through addresses this concept and aims to reinforce the ego's successful transcendence (Weiss, 2014). The fifth resistance, *self-sabotage*, stems from the superego and appears as a sense of guilt or need for punishment. It opposes every move toward success, including the client's own progress in counseling.

Posthypnotic Suggestions

Hypnosis is a mental state or set of attitudes usually induced by a procedure known as a *hypnotic induction*, which is commonly composed of a series of preliminary instructions and suggestions. The use of hypnotism for therapeutic purposes is referred to as *hypnotherapy* and features one or more suggestions made to a hypnotized client that specifies an action to be performed after awakening, often in response to a cue, with the aim of unconsciously redirecting the behavior. Suggestions that are embedded in the induction procedure and expectancies derived from cultural beliefs can clearly influence an individual's experience of hypnosis (Oakley & Halligan, 2013). Hypnosis produces a highly focused, absorbed attentional state that minimizes competing thoughts and sensations. It typically involves two processes: induction and suggestion. Induction comprises a series of instructions that cause the participant to voluntarily adopt a particular mental behavior. Hypnotic suggestions consist of factual statements describing changes in experience or behavior that do not require an individual's voluntary engagement.

Free Association

In free association, psychoanalytic clients are invited to relate whatever comes into their minds during the session without self-censorship. The counselor uses clarification and confrontation to help the client analyze unconscious or latent content in dreams, fantasies, or enactments that appear in the expressed content (Lothane, 2009). This technique is intended to help the client learn more about what he or she thinks and feels in a nonjudgmental, accepting atmosphere. Psychoanalysis assumes that people are often conflicted between their need to learn about themselves and their conscious or unconscious fears of and defenses against change and self-exposure. The method of free association is dynamic and unplanned; the client reveals intuitive links between thoughts and patterns that identify new personal insights and meanings. The goal of this technique is not to unearth specific answers or memories but to instigate a journey of codiscovery that can enhance the client's integration of thought, feeling, agency, and selfhood.

Dream Analysis

Traditional psychoanalysis places a strong emphasis on dreams as keys to the unconscious and wish fulfillments shown in the mind as symbols. The manifest content of the dream is the dream as it is recalled by the client, and the latent content is the actual meaning of the dream once analyzed. In practice, this consists of analyzing four aspects of dreams: In *condensation*, one dream object stands for several associations and ideas; in *displacement*, a dream object's emotional significance is separated from its real object or content and attached to an entirely different one; *representation* is a thought that is translated to visual images; and meaningful *symbols* replace an action, person, or idea (Diena, 2014). These associations point to the inner conflicts and repressed drives of the client and are analyzed throughout the course of treatment.

Brief Intervention Strategies and Current Practices

In brief counseling, the central focus is developed during the initial evaluation process, occurring during the first two sessions. This focus must be agreed on by the client and counselor, and free association is not utilized to generate further topics for exploration. The central focus singles out the most important issues and thus creates a structure and identifies a goal for the treatment. The counselor is expected to be fairly active in keeping the session focused on the main issue. Having a clear focus makes it possible to do interpretive work in a relatively short time because the counselor only addresses the circumscribed problem area. When using a brief psychoanalytic approach, the counselor has an orientation toward the future, but both client and counselor remain focused on the present with the goal of reducing anxiety and framing positive goals for the future (Macdonald, 2007).

Brief Psychodynamic Theory

In its brief form, a psychodynamic approach enables the client to examine unresolved conflicts and symptoms that arise from past dysfunctional relationships and manifest themselves in maladaptive needs and desires. The primary goal is to estimate what may have happened in the past that created a current issue. There is generally one major focus in the sessions, and although free association is not utilized so that the generation of additional topics is avoided, clients are still encouraged to explore issues that have tangential relation to the primary problem (Haggerty, 2013).

The two primary aims of this approach are (a) to help the client understand the connection between his or her presenting symptoms and what is happening in his or her relationships through identifying a core, unconscious, repetitive pattern of relating that becomes the focus of the therapy; and (b) to encourage the patient's capacity to reflect on his or her own states of mind and so enhance his or her ability to manage interpersonal difficulties. It is assumed by the counselor that changes will happen rapidly and that a short intervention will begin a long change process that extends beyond the duration of counseling. The number of sessions varies from one approach to another, but brief psychodynamic counseling relies on the estimated time that is needed to achieve the counseling goals as determined at the beginning of counseling and generally does not extend beyond 16 sessions (Lemma, Target, & Fonagy, 2011).

The brief psychodynamic approach is conceptualized in three phases. In the initial phase, the client is engaged in the counseling process, and by providing structure, direction, and confrontation, the counselor engages the client in assessing current difficulties and defenses. In the middle phase, the counselor focuses on one problem or pattern, and, using a variety of interpretation methods, such as dynamic interpretation, resistance interpretation, transference interpretation, or dream interpretation, the client builds awareness of the presentation of symptoms related to the identified problem. In the ending phase, the counselor and client cooperatively review material, evaluate progress, and transition toward the end of treatment by focusing on the conscious and unconscious meaning of separation from the counselor following termination (Lemma et al., 2011).

Psychodynamic counseling generally involves developing a therapeutic alliance and addressing defense mechanisms and intrapsychic conflicts in an attempt to show the multiple conscious and unconscious factors that influence a client's symptoms and behaviors. A current example of recent psychoanalytic evolution is the introduction of psychodynamic interpersonal therapy and interpersonal psychotherapy. Each approach has a basis in classical psychoanalysis but can be applied in a brief context and has a specific set of techniques that uniquely define it.

Psychodynamic Interpersonal Therapy

Psychodynamic interpersonal therapy was developed in 1983 by psychiatrist Robert Hobson, who believed that many psychoanalytic techniques were effective in treatment and should be teachable, researchable, and evidence based. This approach integrates psychodynamic, humanistic, and interpersonal concepts. The emphasis of the sessions is on the counselor and client collaborating to develop a feeling of partnership through a mutual understanding of language and communication, resulting in a conversational style of insight-driven dialogue. The counselor focuses on the use of metaphor, staying in the present and focusing on hidden affect.

This approach helps clients understand feelings in interpersonal encounters and process them as signals or cues to unconscious content that, if addressed directly, may become a tool for adjusting current behaviors. The counselor and client share the goal of examining the problems in the client's interpersonal relationships and developing an understanding of how new language and communication styles can redefine relationships for more satisfying outcomes. Within eight sessions, the client examines negative patterns between childhood and adult relationships, identifies current symptomatology that results from these repeated maladaptive patterns, develops working hypotheses about relational behaviors, and relearns verbal and nonverbal cues during feeling analysis (Guthrie & Moghavemi, 2013). The focus on immediacy is an important aspect of this approach as clients learn to recognize their symptoms as manageable in current circumstances and feel empowered as a result of experiencing short-term change.

The efficacy of psychodynamic interpersonal therapy has been studied in depth in randomized trials and through linguistic analysis methods. These studies suggest that language is a large determinant of a client's level of functionality, and the structure, grammar, and content used during a session reflects whether the client is experiencing dissociation and to what degree (Butt, Moore, Henderson-Brooks, Meares, & Haliburn, 2010). As the counselor makes this determination, the counselor and client simultaneously experience a unique discourse that contributes to understanding, validation, and rapport.

During this process, it is especially important that the counselor remain neutral and nonjudgmental. The counselor's role is to help the client to consolidate his or her own identity and to exhibit total acceptance of the client by engaging in an ongoing, self-reflective awareness of bias leading to therapeutic ineptitude and impairment. Attention to cultural dynamics is important here; psychodynamic techniques may reveal the influences of trauma that were caused or shaped by diversity inequities (see Sidebar 3.4).

Interpersonal Psychotherapy

Interpersonal psychotherapy is a time-limited treatment that encourages the client to engage in active mood regulation and awareness of functional levels within approximately 12 weeks. It is an evidence-based practice that is delivered in three phases. The counselor identifies the diagnosis and the interpersonal contexts in which it presents. The counselor then links the diagnosis to an interpersonal focus and brings the client into the second phase of treatment, in which the counselor uses specific strategies to help the client identify and resolve clear interpersonal problem areas. The final phase consists of the counselor and client discussing role transition and rebuilding interpersonal deficits with a focus on termination and maintenance beyond counseling (Markowitz & Weissman, 2004).

Narration

One specific strategy the counselor may use is a narrative approach; this approach in a current psychoanalytic practice would intertwine free association with storytelling to gather a comprehensive look at the client's history and ideology based on how the client experienced traumatic events. Leffert (2010) suggested that nar-

Sidebar 3.4. Psychodynamic Interpersonal Therapy and Major Depressive Disorder (MDD)

Psychodynamic interpersonal therapy is often used to treat MDD. This approach assumes that symptoms reflect a treatable illness that is not the client's fault and that symptoms arise in an interpersonal context. When treating MDD, counselors frame the disorder in one of four interpersonal contexts: (a) grief (complicated bereavement), (b) a role dispute (struggle with a significant other that the patient is invariably losing), (c) a role transition (any life change, such as a geographical move, the onset of medical illness, a marriage or divorce, starting or losing a job), or (d) interpersonal deficits (social isolation). The overall goal in treating MDD within this framework is to resolve the life crisis, helping patients to build social skills, communicate their emotions more effectively, and mobilize protective social supports. Randomized controlled trials have provided evidence-based support for this method (Markowitz, Lipsitz, & Milrod, 2014).

rative change occurs through the analysis of transference. For example, as clients tell their story, their cognition changes while they process their affect in response to the recalled event. The clients then will transfer their affect onto the counselor, who will then help them build insight regarding how their articulation of the event has provided an opportunity for reinterpretation.

Examining Life and Death Instincts

In his book *Beyond the Pleasure Principle,* Freud (1920/1955) stated that "the goal of all life is death" (p. 38). He noted that, after people experience a traumatic event, they often reenact the experience, and these reenactments contradict the presentation of the life instincts. He concluded that people hold an unconscious desire to die but that this wish is largely tempered by the life instincts. Within a psychodynamic view, self-destructive behavior is an expression of the energy created by the death instincts. When this energy is directed inward, it appears as masochism and self-loathing. If directed outward onto others, it is expressed as aggression and violence. Understanding this concept helps the client illuminate the relationship between life, death, and meaning (Georgescu, 2011).

Expressive Psychotherapy

Expressive psychotherapy utilizes similar techniques to those used in psychoanalysis although there is more focus on the client's problems and external life. The counselor's neutrality may need to be suspended when the client enters a crisis, but the counselor reassumes neutrality as soon as the crisis has been appropriately addressed. Clients are usually seen face to face instead of in the traditional anonymous couch/chair context and are seen far less frequently than in classical analysis (weekly or bimonthly rather than biweekly). Although the results of expressive therapy are expected to be less extensive than the results of psychoanalysis, both forms of treatment are assumed to be capable of producing structural personality change (Bush & Meehan, 2011).

Supportive Techniques

Supportive techniques are hypothesized to operate through different change mechanisms. They are intended to bolster the functioning of clients with permanently or temporarily weakened egos. Supportive techniques counteract regression, strengthen adaptive defenses, and provide a positive interpersonal relationship in which the therapist is interactive, offers practical help and guidance, and provides emotional reassurance and support (Bush & Meehan, 2011; see Sidebar 3.5).

Sidebar 3.5. Psychoanalytic Psychotherapy and Eating Disorders

In Denmark and other European countries, psychoanalytic psychotherapy and associated techniques have been widely practiced as a treatment for eating disorders. In a 2014 randomized controlled trial comparing the efficacy of cognitive behavior therapy and interpersonal psychotherapy, researchers found that interpersonal psychotherapy is as effective as cognitive behavior therapy in reducing bingeing and purging through the facilitation of heightened affect tolerance and insight into the psychological function of the symptoms (Poulsen et al., 2014).

Clients With Serious Mental Health Issues

Psychoanalytic theory in its traditional and current forms suggests that psychological disorders are the result of unconscious conflicts becoming extreme or unbalanced. It is assumed that serious mental illness consists of a constellation of symptoms that are caused by intrusions of hidden drives into voluntary behavior when defense mechanisms fail. All presenting symptoms are meaningful and relevant to the client's subjective experience and are therefore useful in treatment. For example, hallucinations are understood and interpreted like dreams, and delusions are understood primarily as transference to the world at large.

Several different approaches to brief psychoanalytic practice have evolved from traditional psychoanalytic theory and are now clinically applied to a wide range of serious mental health disorders with positive outcomes. Concurrent with a new focus in counseling on the incorporation of neuroscience and techniques, many diagnoses, including chronic depression, borderline personality disorder, and posttraumatic stress disorder, range in length and depth and are often combined with pharmacotherapy. The emphasis on insight varies by client functionality, and the focus remains on transference and countertransference with consideration placed on the event, neuropsychological function, and current circumstances (Bond, 2006).

Current psychodynamic approaches that emphasize time limit, therapeutic focus, and the counselor's activity are particularly relevant for addressing disorders that require intensive intervention. The degree to which structure and support is generally provided by the counselor depends on the functional level of the client. Experienced counselors who have incorporated psychodynamic techniques into their practice with clients with serious mental illness suggest taking the following steps during interventions (Lemma et al., 2011, pp. 67–68):

1. Identify an attachment-related problem with a specific relational emotional focus that the client feels is causing the diagnostic symptoms.
2. Collaborate with the client to create a concrete conceptualization of interpersonal issues raised by the problem.
3. Attend to the structure of the dialogue between counselor and client and examine transference as a relational theme to generate alternative ways of thinking and feeling.
4. Attend to the therapeutic process, and invite the client to evaluate the process of change as it is happening.
5. Provide the client with a written summary of the collaboratively created view of the client's area of unconscious conflict. This serves as a tangible reference for the client in moments of relapse.

Conscious insight is helpful but is only effective in a strong, stable, and safe therapeutic relationship. For many clients with serious mental illness, client symptoms and concerns need to be addressed early and proactively, and counselors need to be acutely aware of their own feelings during these interactions. Seligman and Reichenberg (2014) noted that countertransference may be useful in understanding these clients, as reactions may enhance understanding of reinforcing social interactions beyond the session. Countertransference reactions should be examined using psychoanalytic techniques in a supportive, empathetic manner. The counselor is responsible for modeling a healthy ego, and the relationship with the counselor is internalized as what a human relationship might be like. The client is encouraged to keep the internalizations that are useful, and as the client gets healthier, he or she takes a more active role than the counselor in the therapeutic relationship.

Past experiences provide valuable insight into the client's current functioning and object relations themes and may be included in a dialogue with the client to meaningfully frame current difficulties in the context of contributed experiences. However, this is not a major focus of a psychodynamic approach for clients with serious mental illness, and the counselor instead focuses on a core segment of the client's interpersonal functioning that is closely connected with the presenting symptoms causing functional impairment. The unconscious remains the primary focus of treatment, and in the treatment of serious mental illness, the aim is to trace the overt symptoms of the diagnosis back to their unconscious origins and analyze them through the use of rational thought and processing. This is an active and directive process for the counselor, and the goal is to develop a sense of stability in the client by creating a conscious link between historical processing and current circumstances, thereby synthesizing personality components into one functional unit.

EVALUATION

Overview

Psychoanalytic theory has been both acclaimed for its effectiveness and highly criticized for its limitations. Traditional psychoanalysis used structural, developmental, and motivational constructs to describe the complexity of human personality functioning. Many theorists and practitioners focus their criticisms on the lack of specific attention to the present and future, and in particular the lack of attention to cross-cultural applications and the potential for bias toward specific client populations. Other theorists favor the theory because of the dynamic foundation of development and structural components used to explain personality development and its contemporary applications to present maladaptive functioning (Petrocelli, Glaser, Calhoun, & Campbell, 2001).

Supporting Research

Although the limitations of psychoanalytic theory may challenge counselors in unique ways, numerous outcome studies have shown that, in its brief form, the efficacy of its techniques is equal to that of other mainstream counseling modalities, such as a cognitive–behavioral approach (Horvath, 2005). Derived from these techniques, psychodynamic psychotherapy has much emerging evidence-based support and is noted for its effectiveness with many diagnoses and populations (Shedler, 2010). Meta-analytic reviews of treatment outcome studies and randomized controlled trials support its efficacy for treating mood and anxiety disorders, somatoform disorders, and schizophrenia. This approach has also been compared to dialectical behavior therapy in its effectiveness and quality of treatment for borderline personality disorder (Seligman & Reichenberg, 2014). In the area of psychoanalytic and psychodynamic research, the trend toward evidence-based support has encouraged practitioners to examine traditional techniques and randomized controlled trials; brain scans; and the effects of talk therapies on behavior, brain activity, and brain function. These methods are now emerging forms of strong clinical research conducted by both psychoanalytic and psychodynamic investigators (Sonnenberg, 2011).

Originally intended as a theory to explain psychological concepts, psychoanalysis has evolved to include explanations of personality development and aberrant behaviors resulting from disturbances in that development. Many counselors suggest that psychoanalysis can also be used to describe or explain a vast array of other concepts outside the realm of the psychological field and is a powerful model for understanding the role and impact of early childhood conflicts in clients' lives. One of the greatest strengths of psychoanalytic theory is the breadth and depth of the explorations into personality development and coping skills, making this a comprehensive theory with much versatility in practical use.

This theory is especially useful in understanding the basis for resistances that may present as missing appointments, refusing to engage in introspection, and being reluctant to examine the use of defenses (Corey, 2012). From a psychoanalytic viewpoint, the client will bring to the session a consistent set of themes, rich with content accumulated over his or her lifetime. Individually or in combination with other theories, psychoanalysis is a valuable tool that counselors may use to develop an effective treatment plan based on the symptoms and patterns of behaviors initially observed within a psychoanalytic framework. Katz-Bearnot (2009) suggested that the psychoanalytic orientation offers the most comprehensive approach to counseling because the theory considers unconscious factors, including transference, enactments, and aspects of the client's personal relationships.

Limitations

A primary limitation of traditional psychoanalysis is the lack of empirical research and evidence-based support for the efficacy of its techniques. Psychoanalysis has historically relied on the applications of case studies to demonstrate its usefulness, and this has limited its broad external validity. Traditional psychoanalysis is known to be a lengthy and costly therapeutic method. The treatment is prolonged and expensive, and an analysis, or course of counseling, is estimated to require 5 years or more, with four or five sessions per week. The time and expense involved with psychoanalysis makes it prohibitive to many, and the number of practitioners of traditional psychoanalysis is few. This is because of the intensive training required and the limitations of coverage by health insurance and managed care.

Another strong criticism of psychoanalytic theory is an oversimplification of cultural paradigms due to its strong focus on sexual development without consideration of the important contributions of class, race, sexuality, gender, and disability across all aspects of development. Psychodynamic approaches are now considering the influence of culture in personality development and sociocultural implications in the formation of trauma, but literature addressing this area and direct practical applications are lacking (Layton, 2007; see Sidebar 3.6).

Summary Chart: Psychoanalytic Theory

Human Nature

Psychoanalytic theory suggests that behavior is largely determined by irrational forces, unconscious motivations, and biological or instinctual drives. Humans are conceptualized largely in terms of biology, and maladaptive behaviors are symptomatic of a subconscious response to social interactions that is shaped mostly by early life experiences.

Major Constructs

The instinctual and biological drives of the psyche are referred to as the *id;* the critical, moralizing function is the *superego;* and the organized, realistic part that mediates and seeks a balance between the former two is known as the *ego.* These drives guide one's functioning and behaviors. Personality develops through a series of childhood stages during which the pleasure-seeking energies of the id become focused on certain erogenous areas. Psychosexual energy, or libido, is suggested to be the driving force behind behavior. Life instincts are those that deal with basic survival, pleasure, and reproduction. Death instincts explain the unconscious desire to die. Defense mechanisms are a function of the ego, which strives to protect the individual from experiencing anxiety and guilt, provoked by the discord between the id and superego. This coping strategy safeguards the mind against unwanted thoughts and impulses. Transference is the process of attributing one's feelings to another. Countertransference is a redirection of a counselor's feelings toward a client.

Goals

Psychoanalysis aims to bring unconscious processes into the conscious, thereby exposing the cause of dysfunctional behaviors, a retroactive reaction to earlier life experiences, thereby resolving anxious or neurotic conflicts that lead to maladaptive behaviors in daily functioning.

Change Process

The basic method of traditional psychoanalysis is the analysis and interpretation of the client's unconscious conflicts that are interfering with daily functioning. This is done using a variety of traditional strategies and techniques to encourage the client to increase his or her awareness of how the processes and behaviors have manifested. Brief psychodynamic therapy accomplishes this in fewer sessions and utilizes similar techniques but disregards the use of free association.

Interventions

Analyzing transference and resistance makes obvious the unconscious drives of the client. The use of hypnotism for therapeutic purposes is referred to as *hypnotherapy*

Sidebar 3.6. Association for the Psychoanalysis of Culture and Society

The Association for the Psychoanalysis of Culture and Society was established in 1994 to promote a greater understanding of how cultural and social phenomena affect human subjectivity in ways that are socially significant and to promote new, more socially beneficial ways of applying psychoanalysis to social problems. Association members support the assertion that psychoanalysis is the most useful model for understanding how the basic phenomena of subjectivity, such as love, hate, desire, and anxiety, are affected by culture. By enabling mental health counselors to understand the motivations underlying serious social problems, psychoanalysis can help counselors articulate the broad psychological and social benefits that culture offers (Charles & O'Loughlin, 2013).

and features one or more suggestions made to a hypnotized client that specifies an action to be performed after awakening. In free association, psychoanalytic clients are invited to relate whatever comes into their minds during the session without self-censorship. Dream analysis frames dream content as exposed symbols of repressed drives. Brief interventions utilize similar techniques but reduce the frequency of sessions and scope of treatment. The interventions are utilized with the goal of immediate symptom reduction and elevated client functioning.

Limitations

A major criticism of psychoanalytic theory is the idea that humans are driven by sexuality without regard for other cultural dynamics. Some practitioners suggest that psychoanalysis is entirely inappropriate for use with certain cultures because of a lack of structure, lack of direct problem solving, and consistent emphasis on the reflection of childhood experience. Traditional psychoanalysis is known to be a lengthy and costly therapeutic method and is used primarily with adults, limiting its external validity.

THE CASE OF MARIA: A PSYCHOANALYTIC APPROACH

Maria arrives for her appointment 15 minutes early and appears motivated to reduce her troublesome symptoms. Her anxiety is evident, and from the standpoint of psychoanalytic theory, it could be assumed that her symptoms are a result of a conflict between her id (or her basic drives) and her superego (the moral and ethically responsible component of her personality). From a psychoanalytic perspective, Maria appears to be experiencing anxiety and depression as a result of unconscious conflicts originating from early childhood experiences. Although Maria is aware of her depressive symptoms and is able to articulate her history and the current circumstances that are contributing to her mental state, she is mostly unaware of the primary origin of her unconscious conflicts and how her early life has shaped her adult experiences and contributed to her current presentation.

In addition, she is experiencing an elevated level of guilt, indicating the strong presence of the ego (or the mediator between the id and superego). The counselor, practicing from a psychoanalytic perspective, may assume that Maria is experiencing unconscious psychological conflicts between her personal need to gain autonomy and be independent and her need to remain loyal to her cultural traditions and family expectations. The ego is being challenged because Maria is using strong defense mechanisms, including repression (or the blocking of unconscious conflicts from awareness) and compensation (or her attempt to cope with the discomforting feelings by immersing herself in her work).

Maria mentions that she has considered suicide. On a superficial level, this is associated with her depressive symptoms. However, the psychoanalytic practitioner would apply Freud's concept of death instincts and examine Maria's recent experiences in an abusive relationship. These experiences may have led Maria to unconsciously contradict her life instincts and gravitate toward a natural impulsive desire to die. The psychoanalytic practitioner understands that the energy created by the life instincts is known as the *libido* and is exemplified in love, cooperation, and other prosocial actions. Maria details her negative relationship experiences and thereby illustrates the dramatic imbalance between the love she needs and the lack of love she received.

Maria also mentions that she is unable to maintain meaningful relationships with various men, and though she has been dating, she views her future as negative. This would indicate an arrest at an earlier stage of life, during which her tasks were left unaccomplished. She appears to be developmentally arrested at the fourth psychosexual stage, the latency stage, during which the development of the ego and superego contribute to a period of calm in personality development as the id and libido are suppressed. This stage occurs between ages 6 and 12, and Maria states that, during this time of her life, she spent most of her time taking care of both the house and her younger siblings. Therefore, it may be assumed that she did not involve herself in developmental tasks appropriate to this stage, including intellectual pursuits, social interactions with both genders, and personal interests. Unable to resolve this stage before now, she seems to be struggling with these areas in her life as a result.

Maria also seems to be struggling with these issues in her dreams, which present as recurring nightmares with saturated psychoanalytic themes. The first poignant theme is that of Maria running from shadowy figures. In psychoanalytic theory, this would represent the parts of herself that she is struggling to repress, or her id impulses and desires intruding on her carefully articulated reality. This aspect of her dream also indicates the rapidity of her unconscious struggle, which indicates a strong desire to merge her unconscious with her conscious. As she runs from the figures, she is faced with boxes and crates with arrows pointing in all directions. This would indicate options and opportunities with multiple choices, but the contents of the containers still remain hidden.

The primary goal of the psychoanalytic counselor would be to help Maria bring her unconscious processes into consciousness and alert her to how her mind is hiding past experiences to help her cope with current experiences. The counselor may begin with dream analysis, exploring the symbols in the dream and engaging Maria in connecting those symbols to themes in her life. For example, the counselor may illustrate how the shadowy figures represent the repressed, unconscious drives that Maria is feeling increased pressure to acknowledge and confront and then address the boxes and arrows as symbolic of a needed change in her life.

The counselor may also use free association to encourage Maria to recognize her own unconscious processes as they become evident to her through this exercise. As the counselor helps Maria to analyze her dreams and fantasies, identifiable themes and patterns will become evident and will provide Maria and her counselor with a great deal of material to examine. The counselor will most likely explore with Maria the implications and consequences of her psychosexual development and elucidate how any unaccomplished tasks at these levels have greatly contributed to her relationship issues and the manifestation of her anxious and depressive symptoms. For example, because Maria was immersed in family responsibilities during her adolescence, she was unable to engage in her own self-development. Consequently, she is now struggling to maintain a healthy balance between all aspects of her life. Maria and her counselor will likely meet weekly or biweekly for months, or even years, until both Maria and the counselor are satisfied that her unconscious processes are now fully in her awareness. She may recognize how the manifestation of maladaptive behaviors and symptoms indicates a psychic struggle that she must fully contemplate in terms of mental and personality processes.

REFERENCES

American Psychiatric Association. (2013). *Diagnostic and statistical manual of mental disorders* (5th ed.). Arlington, VA: Author.

Banai, E., Mikulincer, M., & Shaver, P. R. (2005). "Self object" needs in Kohut's self psychology. *Psychoanalytic Psychology, 22*(2), 224–260.

Barry, V. (2014). Research on the relation of psychoanalysis and neuroscience: Clinical meaning and empirical science. *Journal of the American Psychoanalytic Association, 62*, 1087–1096.

Berberovic, J. I. (2012). Sexual compulsivity, promiscuity and phallic stage of psychosexual development fixation. *HealthMed, 6*, 1875–1884.

Binder, J. L. (2004). *Key competencies in brief dynamic psychotherapy: Clinical practice beyond the manual.* New York, NY: Guilford Press.

Bond, M. (2006). Psychodynamic psychotherapy in the treatment of mood disorders. *Current Opinion in Psychiatry, 19*, 40–43.

Bowlby, J. (1969). *Attachment* (Vol. 1). New York, NY: Hogarth.

Bush, M., & Meehan, W. (2011). Should supportive measures and relational variables be considered a part of psychoanalytic technique? Some empirical considerations. *International Journal of Psychoanalysis, 92*, 377–399.

Butt, D., Moore, A., Henderson-Brooks, C., Meares, R., & Haliburn, J. (2010). Dissociation, relatedness, and "cohesive harmony": A linguistic measure of degrees of "fragmentation"? *Linguistics and the Human Sciences, 3*, 263–293.

Carducci, B. J. (2009). *The psychology of personality: Viewpoints, research, and applications* (2nd ed.). Hoboken, NJ: Wiley-Blackwell.

Charles, M., & O'Loughlin, M. (2013). *Association for the Psychoanalysis of Culture and Society.* Retrieved from http://apcsweb.net/index.html

Charuvastra, A., & Cloitre, M. (2008). Social bonds and posttraumatic stress disorder. *Annual Review of Psychology, 59*, 301–328.

Cherry, K. (2010). *The everything psychology book* (2nd ed.). Avon, MA: Adams Media.

Corey, G. (2012). *Theory and practice of counseling and psychotherapy* (6th ed.). Pacific Grove, CA: Brooks/Cole.

Diamond, D., & Meehan, K. B. (2013). Attachment and object relations in patients with narcissistic personality disorder: Implications for therapeutic process and outcome. *Journal of Clinical Psychology, 69*, 1148–1159.

Diena, S. (2014). Workshop on dream interpretation. *Romanian Journal of Psychoanalysis, 7*(1), 67–78.

Etchegoyen, H. R. (2005). *The fundamentals of psychoanalytic technique.* London, England: Karnac Books.

Freud, S. (1955). Beyond the pleasure principle. In J. Strachey (Ed. & Trans.), *The standard edition of the complete psychological works of Sigmund Freud (1920–1922): Vol. XVIII. Beyond the pleasure principle, group psychology and other works* (pp. 1–64). London, England: Hogarth Press. (Original work published 1920)

Gay, P. (2006). *Freud: A life for our time.* London, England: Norton.

Georgescu, M. (2011). The duality between life and death instincts in Freud. *Contemporary Readings in Law and Social Justice, 3*(1), 134–139.

Guthrie, E., & Moghavemi, A. (2013). Psychodynamic-interpersonal therapy: An overview of the treatment approach and evidence base. *Psychodynamic Psychiatry, 41*, 619–635.

Haggerty, J. (2013). *Psychodynamic therapy.* Retrieved from http://psychcentral.com/lib/psychodynamic-therapy/000119

Horvath, A. O. (2005). The therapeutic relationship: Research and theory. *Psychotherapy Research, 15*(1), 3–7.

Juni, S. (2009). Conceptualization of hostile psychopathy and sadism: Drive theory and object relations perspectives. *International Forum of Psychoanalysis, 18,* 11–22.

Kaplan, R. (2004). O Anna: Being Bertha Pappenheim—historiography and biography. *Bulletin of the Royal Australian and New Zealand College of Psychiatrists, 12*(1), 62–68.

Katz-Bearnot, S. (2009). Combined psychotherapies: Searching for an order of operations in a disordered world. *Journal of the American Academy of Psychoanalysis and Dynamic Psychiatry, 37,* 299–313.

Knight, R. (2014). A hundred years of latency: From Freudian psychosexual theory to dynamic systems nonlinear development in middle childhood. *Journal of the American Psychoanalytic Association, 62*(2), 203–235.

Layton, L. (2007). What psychoanalysis, culture and society mean to me. *Psychoanalysis, Culture and Society, 5,* 146–157.

Leffert, M. (2010). *Contemporary psychoanalytic foundations: Postmodernism, complexity, and neuroscience.* New York, NY: Routledge.

Lemma, A., Target, M., & Fonagy, P. (2011). *Brief dynamic interpersonal therapy: A clinician's guide.* Cambridge, England: Oxford University Press.

Levenson, L. N. (2007). Paul Gray's innovations in psychoanalytic technique. *Psychoanalytic Quarterly, 76,* 257–273.

Levy-Warren, M. H. (2008). Wherefore the Oedipus complex in adolescence? Its relevance, evolution, and appearance in treatment. *Studies in Gender & Sexuality, 9*(4), 328–348.

Lijtmaer, R. (2006). Black, White, Hispanic and both: Issues in bi-racial identity and its effects in the transference-countertransference. In R. Moodley & S. Palmer (Eds.), *Race, culture and psychotherapy: Critical perspectives in multicultural practice* (pp. 130–138). London, England: Brunner-Routledge.

Lothane, Z. (2009). Dramatology in life, disorder, and psychoanalytic therapy: A further contribution to interpersonal psychoanalysis. *International Forum of Psychoanalysis, 18,* 135–148.

Macdonald, A. (2007). *Solution-focused therapy: Theory, research and practice.* London, England: Sage.

Markowitz, J. C., Lipsitz, J., & Milrod, B. L. (2014). Critical review of outcome research on interpersonal psychotherapy for anxiety disorders. *Depression & Anxiety, 31*(4), 316–325.

Markowitz, J. C., & Weissman, M. M. (2004). Interpersonal psychotherapy: Principles and applications. *World Psychiatry, 3*(3), 136–139.

Nevid, J. S. (2009). *Essentials of psychology: Concepts and applications* (2nd ed.). Belmont, CA: Wadsworth.

Oakley, D. A., & Halligan, P. W. (2013). Hypnotic suggestion: Opportunities for cognitive neuroscience. *Nature Reviews Neuroscience, 14,* 565–576.

Petrocelli, J. V., Glaser, B. A., Calhoun, G. B., & Campbell, L. F. (2001). Early maladaptive schemas of personality disorder subtypes. *Journal of Personality Disorders, 15,* 546–559.

Pigman, G. W., III. (2014). Freud and his manuscripts: A critical edition of beyond the pleasure principle. *American Imago, 71*(1), 85–88.

Poirier, J., Clarac, F., Barbara, J. G., & Broussolle, E. (2012). Figures and institutions of the neurological sciences in Paris from 1800 to 1950. *Revue Neurologique, 168*(5), 389–402.

Potik, D. (2014). Self psychology conceptualization of post psychotic depression and recover among paranoid schizophrenic patients. *Bulletin of the Menninger Clinic, 78*(1), 70–86.

Poulsen, S., Lunn, S., Daniel, S. I. F., Folke, S., Mathiesen, B. B., Katznelson, H., & Fairburn, C. G. (2014). A randomized controlled trial of psychoanalytic psychotherapy or cognitive-behavioral therapy for bulimia nervosa. *American Journal of Psychiatry, 171*(1), 109–116.

Riker, J. H. (2013). The philosophical importance of Kohut's notion of the self. *International Journal of Psychoanalytic Self Psychology, 8*, 495–504.

Rowe, C. (2013). Extending Kohut's concept of self-object: The undifferentiated self-object. *Clinical Social Work Journal, 41*(1), 26–33.

Seligman, L., & Reichenberg, L. W. (2014). *Selecting effective treatments: A comprehensive systematic guide to treatment mental disorders.* Hoboken, NJ: Wiley.

Shedler, J. (2010). The efficacy of psychodynamic psychotherapy. *American Psychologist, 65*, 98–109.

Sonnenberg, S. M. (2011). Psychoanalysis and the United States research university: Current trends. *International Journal of Psychoanalysis, 92*, 641–659.

Swartz, S. (2014). Words, interpretation and setting: Changing forms of the talking cure. *Psycho-Analytic Psychotherapy in South Africa, 22*(1), 1–25.

Thomas, B. (2008). Seeing and being seen: Courage and the therapist in cross-racial treatment. *Psychoanalytic Social Work, 15*, 60–68.

Weiss, H. (2014). Projective identification and working through of the countertransference: A multiphase model. *International Journal of Psychoanalysis, 95*, 739–756.

Zepf, S. (2010). Libido and psychic energy—Freud's concepts reconsidered. *International Forum of Psychoanalysis, 19*(1), 3–14.

Chapter 4

Jungian Analytical Theory

Kimberly Nelson and Abbé Finn

Jungian analytical psychology, developed by Swiss psychiatrist Carl Gustav Jung (1875–1961), is an approach that looks at the total person: mind, body, and soul (Jung, 1928/1954). The approach links the conscious and unconscious aspects of the individual in a search for life's meaning and also takes into account collective influences. A basic assumption of the theory is that within each person are competing forces that must be balanced. These forces reveal people's true selves through a process Jung referred to as *individuation,* and this often occurs after middle age (Corbett, 2014; Schultz & Schultz, 2013). *Individuation* is the Jungian term for self-actualization and is the process of becoming one's true self (Wakefield, 2014).

Jung developed his theory as a reflection of his personal experiences and dreams and refined it through the years using data from his clinical work. As a child, he often spent his time alone trying to understand his own dreams and analyzing his experience and thoughts. His tendency to isolate stemmed from a belief that others would not understand him, and it kept him removed from his parents' tumultuous marriage. His desire to understand personality led him to the up-and-coming field of psychiatry. Jung was well read, and in addition to having a medical degree, he took interest in religion, psychology, parapsychology, anthropology, philosophy, classical languages, mythology, alchemy, and the occult. His desire to learn and diverse interests became evident is his clinical work. Cultural sensitivity is a hallmark of Jungian counseling, and he was the first to integrate all of these disciplines to aid in understanding human behavior (Casement, 1996). He was also the first to explore commonality and symbolism shared by all humanity (Cochrane, Flower, MacKenna, & Morgan, 2014).

Jung was already making a name for himself when he met Sigmund Freud and was drawn to him because they both had an interest in the influence of the unconscious in personality development and life choices. Jung was considered a protégé of Freud and was recommended by Freud to be the first president of the International Psychoanalytic Association. However, through a series of circumstances, dreams, and interactions with Freud, Jung resigned his presidency and parted ways with Freud in 1913 because of fundamental differences in regard to personality development.

Jung believed the libido to be a life energy, unlike Freud, who presented the libido as a sexual energy (Schultz & Schultz, 2013). Jung also believed people are influenced by their pasts, through archetypes. However, he had a more optimistic outlook on personality development than Freud and believed personality develops throughout one's life, particularly in middle age. Another point of contention with Freud was in regard to the influence of the unconscious, as Jung made it a key feature in one's personality development.

The separation from Freud was very difficult for Jung, and for 6 years, he withdrew and became introspective and isolated. During this time, he was heavily involved in his private practice and his personal analytic work. It is believed that Jung had his own neurotic episode lasting close to 3 years, which led him to do his own introspective work. His self-analysis included journaling; dream analysis; expression through art; and exploration of culture, myth, and Eastern religions (Schwartz, 2007). During this time, Jung developed what he later called the process of individuation; he believed it to be an inevitable process as one ages and becomes more introspective and reflective on life (Corbett, 2014).

BACKGROUND

Carl Jung was born in 1875 in Kesswil, Switzerland. His father was an impoverished but genteel country minister in the Swiss Reformed Church. Although Jung did not come from wealth, the men in his extended family were highly educated and respected clergy and physicians, and his father was an Oriental and classics scholar (Casement, 2001). During his developing years, Jung was immersed in religion and the classics, and his mother exposed him to mysticism and spiritualism.

His mother was the more dominant parent but often struggled with emotional instability. She reportedly had melancholy and frequently isolated herself from her family and general society. She was hospitalized intermittently and became increasingly remote from Jung and his father. Jung recalled his mother often complying with social expectations and then contradicting them privately with her personal beliefs and opinions. It is believed that Jung used this as the basis for his theoretical distinction of personal unconscious and collective unconscious (Schwartz, 2007). In general, he was emotionally distant from his parents (see Sidebar 4.1).

Jung devoted himself to his studies and became an accomplished student. He studied Latin and Greek, ancient history, and mythology, and at the turn of the

Sidebar 4.1. Jung's Childhood Friend

Jung reportedly had a very challenging and unhappy childhood. To escape his parents' arguing, he would often isolate himself and escape into his own dreams and fantasies. At age 10, Jung carved a wooden figure resembling a man, and his doll became his constant companion. He believed his doll was the only one he could confide in and the only one who truly understood him.

century, Jung graduated from the medical school at the University of Basel. In addition to medicine, he studied anthropology, philosophy, and archeology. He was influenced by the writings of Immanuel Kant, Carl Gustov Carus, Eduard von Hartmann, Gottfried Leibniz, Johann Bachofen, and Arthur Schopenhauer. He continued his interest in philosophy and the occult, completing his dissertation, *On Psychology and Pathology of So-Called Occult Phenomenon,* in 1902 (Jung, 1902/1978).

From 1907 to 1913, Freud and Jung maintained a close personal and professional relationship. However, the collegial relationship ended over theoretical differences when Jung published *Symbols of Transformation* in 1911, putting an emphasis on the collective unconscious rather than the sexual drives, which were the essence of Freud's theory (Jung, 1911/1956). Jung's view of personality development was not as deterministic as Freud's and left room for development throughout one's life (Corbett, 2014; Schultz & Schultz, 2009), unlike Freud's focus on early development and experiences. After Jung broke off his relationship with Freud, he underwent 6 years of intensive psychoanalysis, which was considered an integral part of his psychoanalytic training. This period coincided with the outbreak of World War I, and although Switzerland was neutral, Jung was drafted into the army and made the commandant of an internment camp for British soldiers (see Sidebar 4.2).

Following the end of World War I, Jung reemerged and was once again prolific in his research and publications. In search of information on the collective unconscious, he traveled to various parts of the world studying primitive cultures. During these travels, he studied religions, myths, occult, folklore, and mysticism. He developed a theory that there are universal archetypes represented in all cultures and that individuals express these characteristics symbolically in their dreams, creative works, and relationships.

HUMAN NATURE: A DEVELOPMENTAL PERSPECTIVE

In contrast to Freud's five psychosexual stages (with a focus on early childhood) and Erik Erikson's psychosocial stages across all aspects of one's life span, Jung believed that there are four basic stages of development: childhood, adolescence, middle age, and old age. Jung placed more importance on middle age than the other stages, and coincidentally, middle age is the stage of life Jung was in when he became deeply reflective and reinvented himself (Jung, 1928/1954).

Childhood

Childhood is the first stage, and in Jung's view, children are ruled by primitive urges and desires. He believed it is the parent's role to discipline children and to help them individuate and develop their personality. Although he believed child-

> **Sidebar 4.2. Jung's Collective Unconscious**
>
> A key distinction between Freud and Jung was Jung's emphasis on the collective unconscious instead of the sexual drives of an individual. Freud believed sex played a central role in one's development and was a cause of many issues, and he often denied his own sexual urges and suffered from the consequences of this denial. Ironically, it was Jung who minimized the role of sex in personality development but who had several extramarital affairs and often slept with his patients and disciples.

hood experiences are influential, he did not believe that they shape personality at such a young age like Freud did (Schultz & Schultz, 2013). He took a family perspective when it came to problems in childhood and believed people develop complexes in response to problems in the family. Rather than treat a child, he would treat the entire family (Jung, 1928/1954). Although Jung believed that children are unique individuals who enter the world with their own unique inherited, collective unconscious, he also recognized that some children are more impressionable than others and are more affected by the character of their parents, the culture, and environmental influences (Frankel, 1998).

Adolescence

Adolescence ranges from childhood to early adulthood and reflects the time in which young people are making educational plans, creating intimate relationships, and choosing careers. This time of life is often believed to be the most confusing developmental period marked by distinct physical changes, changing thoughts and feelings, and often unpredictable behavior (Prout, 2005). Jung believed each person has ways of dealing with the outside world that are indicative of a personality preference. For example, how one relates to oneself and others has to do with where one falls on the introversion–extraversion continuum. Adolescence is a period when individuals are discovering their personality characteristics and personae and reconciling them with parental and societal expectations.

Wickes (1927) interpreted this behavior as the parents' unconscious impinging on the child's developing psyche. This is evidenced when parents impose their fears and phobias on their children. Likewise, they may superimpose their hopes and dreams on their children and live vicariously through their children's achievements. For example, American parents attend sporting events wearing their child athlete's jersey number and drive home in cars displaying bumper stickers touting pride in their child's athletic and academic accomplishments.

Some parents welcome the changes that come to the family when children enter adolescence. Others deny the changes and restrict their children as if they were toddlers. Children in these families may complain that their parents don't want them to grow up. Other parents join in their children's youthful energy and are their children's best friend, competing with them for attention and becoming overly involved with their children's friends (Frankel, 1998). Regardless of the parental approach, adolescence is a time of distinct change for all individuals.

Middle Age

In contrast with Freud, who focused on early childhood, and Erikson, who put equal emphasis on development across the entire life span, Jung focused on experiences and development in middle age in what he referred to as the *second half of life* (Corbett, 2014). He believed personality changes are inevitable and universal during this time because most adults have met the goals and challenges of the first half of their lives and need to redirect their interest and energies (Schultz & Schultz, 2013).

This developmental stage marked the point in Jung's life when he himself went through a period of self-examination and in-depth psychoanalysis. Jung believed middle age is the stage when people naturally reexamine their lives, goals, and accomplishments, often looking for deeper spirituality and meaning in life (Corbett, 2014). He believed the attitude of one's personality shifts from extraversion to introversion to start facing one's subjective inner world, which is often neglected in the first half of life (Schultz & Schultz, 2009). Middle age is the time to integrate the unconscious with the conscious and move toward individuation, which Jung described as becoming more who you are (Cochrane et al., 2014). He believed individuals need to follow their unconscious creativity and dreams and not be as guided by rational thinking and that middle age is the time in many people's lives when they can explore other interests. Jung was particularly interested in the problems encountered by middle-aged adults.

Old Age

Jung believed that when people enter old age, they become more reflective of their life experiences and in touch with their unconscious (Corbett, 2014). He thought this is the time for examining end-of-life issues such as mortality and the legacy left behind. Jung believed that the search for meaning in one's life makes acceptance of death more tolerable. He also suggested that the aspects of personality that are often denied are more likely to emerge in later life as a resolution of opposing forces coming together. He believed that people continue to develop across their life span and was one of the few theorists who looked at development across the life span as well as the influence of culture on one's development (Heyer, 2012).

MAJOR CONSTRUCTS

Personality Theory

The psyche represents the integration of the personal conscious, the personal unconscious, the collective unconscious, and the ego. The personal conscious includes the individual's spirit as well as his or her spirituality, orientation to the outer world (optimism vs. pessimism, introversion vs. extraversion), beliefs, emotions, thoughts, feelings, and behaviors. The personal unconscious includes thoughts and memories that can be recalled. The collective unconscious is derived from the universal thoughts, emotions, fears, dreams, and mythical themes symbolically represented by archetypes. The ego perceives, thinks, and feels and is the center of the consciousness. Jung believed all components of the personality influence one another.

The Personal Conscious

The *personal conscious* begins at birth and continues to develop across the life span. It is the only part of the person that is fully revealed to that person. These conscious thoughts consist of easily retrieved memories and current and recalled feelings and emotions. As the personality develops, the personal conscious becomes more and more unique. This process allows the person to become more self-aware and is known as *individuation* (Jung, 1936/1959).

The Ego

The *ego* is the center of personal consciousness and has the executive function of organizing thoughts, feelings, perceptions, and emotions. The ego provides the foundation, stability, and organization for the personality by selecting which thoughts, emotions, and memories are recalled or experienced (Jung, 1936/1959). The personal conscious and personal unconscious balance each other and are in a constant state of flux, with content flowing back and forth (Cochrane et al., 2014). There is a self-regulatory function of the psyche that leads to psychic health (Bishop, 1999; Casement, 2001).

The Personal Unconscious

Jung's concept of the *personal unconscious* is similar to the psychoanalytical concept of the unconscious (Schultz & Schultz, 2013). The personal unconscious contains all thoughts and experiences that are accessible to the conscious as well as impulses and repressed memories that are buried in the unconscious. The thoughts, feelings, memories, experiences, and emotions that are not permitted by the ego are maintained in the unconscious. These may range from inconsequential experiences to traumatic events or thoughts. The personal unconscious may also be composed of behaviors that are suppressed because of emotions such as fear or shame or because they are inconsistent with the imagined self.

Jung believed the material in the personal unconscious to be emotionally loaded and valuable and not content to stay buried. He believed that aspects of the repressed material emerge in dreams, fantasies, or themes for artistic expressions such as visual art, poetry, and music. When the unconscious material emerges and pairs with charged emotions, it results in a complex. There are many different types of complexes, for example, the *puer aeternus* (the eternal child), the father complex, the mother complex, the Cassandra complex, the God complex, the martyr complex, the Napoleon complex, and the superiority complex. Jung believed a complex has a disproportionate influence on one's behavior and choices and continues to resurface in one's life.

An example of a common complex is the father complex. A person with such a complex typically relates to the world by protecting, managing, and controlling others. In women, the father complex is manifest as hero worship. In contrast, the mother complex is characterized by nurturing. It has as its core the personal experience with one's own mother but also the archetype of the earth mother. In a female, it is demonstrated through apparent self-sacrifice, caregiving, loyalty, and nurturing. Jung hypothesized that, in men, the mother complex could lead to a variety of behaviors, from homosexuality to Don Juan–type serial romances and flirtations with women. Men and women with the mother complex appear to be devoted to their mother, often sacrificing for her. Jung hypothesized that each personal complex also contains elements of the collective unconscious.

The Collective Unconscious

The Jungian concept of the *collective unconscious* is a feature that most distinguishes Jung's theory from others (Sharf, 2008). Before Freud, the prevailing theories for human development perceived children as emerging as a blank slate (the *tabula rasa*). Freud introduced the revolutionary concept of infant biological and sexual drives. Jung was a disciple of Freud but separated from Freudian theory by introducing the concept that humans inherit unconscious memories from their ancestors' experiences. Jung believed that people's collective unconscious represents collective symbols and instinctual commonality that are universal to mankind (Cochrane et al., 2014). It is "an inherited tendency of the human mind to form representations of mythological motifs—representations that vary a great deal without losing their basic pattern" (Jung, 1959/1970, p. 228). Jung likened the collective unconscious to animal instincts that cause species to respond in prescribed ways when presented with triggering "sign stimuli" (Stevens, 1990).

For example, this would explain how weaverbirds know how to build their nests (Evans, 1976) or how a first-time mother dog knows to lick her newborn puppy, open the amniotic sac, and chew through the umbilical cord without harming the slippery and squirming puppy. Although people react to the environment in many unique ways, they are evolved from similar roots and share the experience of the world, culture, and environment.

As Jung explained, the collective unconscious is an inherited way (scheme) of functioning; people carry tendencies to respond to and experience life situations in typical ways or behavioral patterns (Cochrane et al., 2014; Evans, 1976). He believed that the archetypal experiences are engraved on the psyche from the experiences of ancestors over the previous millennia. Because of evolution, people are predisposed to interpreting experiences according to archetypes. Although the archetypes represent typical ways of interacting with the world, they are not prescriptive. This is because there are numerous archetypes influencing behavior (Stevens, 1990).

Archetypes

The collective unconscious is universal, is made of images and symbols that occur in a variety of cultures and religions, and represents people's ancestral past (Sharf, 2014). Jung referred to these images as *archetypes* and believed that people have tendencies to respond to universal situations in predetermined ways inherited from their ancestors (Cochrane et al., 2014). He perceived an archetype as a force that could overcome a person, like experiencing a seizure. Archetypes are instinctual and often lay dormant until activated by a life event (Wakefield, 2014). He used the example of love at first sight. He explained that people have an image in their mind of their perfect partner, and when they see someone who reminds them of that idealized partner (the archetype), they are immediately attracted, even against their better judgment (Evans, 1976).

Four basic archetypes manifest themselves within each person's personality at different times and in different ways. These archetypes are the *shadow, anima, animus*, and *self*. The shadow is the part of a person that tends toward chaos. It may consist of parts of a person's personality that he or she wants to suppress and deny, but it still exists. It is often referred to as the *dark side* of the personality. Sometimes, in one's attempts to deny one's shadow, one projects it onto others. This may explain how the things that a person notices about another person are commonly his or her own failings. This may also explain how a person erroneously attributes negative motivations, leading to the misinterpretation of behaviors (see Sidebar 4.3).

Sidebar 4.3. Inherited Attraction

Jung belleved that attraction is inherited from people's ancestral past and is reflected through their anima and animus projections on potential partners. He believed all people hold an unconscious image of their ideal mate and that when they meet someone who matches their projected standards, they are more likely to engage in a relationship with that person.

The shadow reveals itself in dreams, nightmares, artistic work, paranoid delusions, religion, and hallucinations. In extreme cases, it may lead to violence when nonviolent behavior is misinterpreted as threatening, thereby triggering a preemptive defensive assault. To a Jungian, this would explain how a person who is typically peaceful becomes violent when in a state of intoxication or under the influence of drugs (Jung, 1968).

The anima and animus represent a person's true self, as opposed to the masks the person wears every day, and are the source of creativity. The anima is predominant in females, and the animus is predominant in males. However, men have aspects of the female anima in their personality, and women have aspects of the male animus in their personality. In contemporary American culture, it is accepted that men have a feminine side (romantic, nurturing, playful) and women likewise have a masculine side (protective, aggressive, ambitious). In myths, they are represented by the heroes and heroines. The animus is particularly evident in children's relationship to their parents and their belief that their parents are all powerful and have omnipotence when it comes to protecting them. It is also apparent in children's fascination with superheroes (Jung, 1968). When 4-year-olds don a cape, they are not just dressed as Superman; they *are* Superman.

The archetype of the self is the most important archetype. It is the center between the conscious and the unconscious self. The symbolic self is the perfect balance of all of the various parts of the personality. Jung used the balance of the solar system to help explain this concept. He described this as *syzygy*, an astronomical term for the perfect balance between planets creating equal gravitational pull. The self is exemplified by the perfect, proportional balance between the anima and animus.

Syzygy can exist in a single person, but it can also be present in a well-matched couple or a balanced team. The confluence of anima and animus brings great power and can be found in mythological and religious combinations such as the Christian Holy Trinity (Father, Son, and Holy Ghost). A perfect partnership between individuals can occur when they are well matched physically as well as balanced with anima and animus (Jung, 1968).

APPLICATIONS

Overview

The following sections highlight the goals, process of change, and key intervention strategies used in Jungian therapy. The intent of Jungian therapy is to obtain a state of individuation in which one's conscious and unconscious facets of personality are integrated. Jung believed that the desire for individuation is innate and inevitable and that the process of change is unique to each individual. Jung traveled widely, was well versed in many disciplines, and was fascinated by different cultures (Casement, 2001) and, because of his experiences, believed that before analyzing a person, the psychotherapist must be familiar with the person's culture, religion, social relationships, language, ethnicity, and gender belief systems (Samuels, 1991). Without this knowledge, the therapist cannot understand the client's transference, dreams, and personal and collective unconscious (Eleftheriadou, 2003).

Goals of Counseling and Psychotherapy

The goals of Jungian analysis vary depending on the developmental stage of the person. In general, the primary goals are individuation and the integration of the personal conscious with the personal unconscious. Individuation occurs when a person becomes aware of his or her unique self by coming to terms with his or her own strengths and weaknesses and by bringing the unconscious to conscious awareness while living in the here and now. According to Jung,

> But the great thing is the here and now, this is the eternal moment, and if you do not realize it, you have missed the best part of your life; you will have missed the realization that you are the carrier of a life contained between the poles of an unimaginable future and an unimaginably remote past. Millions of years of untold millions of ancestors have worked up to this moment. Anything that is past is no longer reality, anything that is ahead is not yet reality, reality is now. (Jung, as cited in Wilmer, 1987, p. 3)

Jung believed that the splitting off of two powerful complexes is at the root of neurosis and mental illness. The dissociation is a defense against the unbearable psychic pain and emotional suffering that usually stems from traumatic experiences. Jung was intrigued by the opposites and polarities he observed in the complexes exhibited by his psychiatric patients. In today's psychiatric jargon, many of his patients would be diagnosed with borderline personality disorder. Jung believed that everyone splits his or her personality to a degree. It is when the splitting cuts too deep and interferes with activities of daily living that it becomes pathological. What differentiates Jungian psychotherapy from other theories is the collective unconscious: Jung believed that some of the complexes originate in the collective unconscious as archetypal images rather than life experiences or biological urges. Jung viewed the symptoms of his patients as opportunities for wholeness (Sander & Beebe, 1995).

Jung described patients whose complexes have taken over their lives, resulting in serious personality and psychiatric disorders, as being possessed *by* the complex. Jung wrote, "Everyone knows nowadays that people 'have complexes', what is not so well known, though far more important theoretically, is that complexes can have us" (Jung, 1934, p. 96). This interpretation shows the influence of Jung's interest in the paranormal, with the primitive belief that possession causes mental illness. He believed that complexes can wage a coup d'état and take over. Under these conditions, the ego-projected archetypes take over the personality and are fraught with emotions, instability, labile mood, and being out of touch with reality (see Sidebar 4.4).

Sidebar 4.4. Complexes

People often hear of guilt complexes or mother/father complexes, and this is Jung's influence on current vocabulary. A complex involves emotions, images, ideas, memories, perceptions, and behaviors around a common theme. The complex often becomes a driving force in one's life, and the person with the complex is generally not aware of the complex, even though others can easily see its impact.

The Process of Change

The goal of Jungian psychotherapy is to achieve an actualized life, in which the person is integrated and living a balanced life, with congruence of body and mind (Casement, 1996). There are four nonsequential phases of Jungian analytical psychology. The first phase, *catharsis,* is the stage in which the client shares feelings and expresses emotions. In the second phase, the *analytical stage,* the therapist analyzes dreams; transference and countertransference; and other assessments, such as word association tests, projective tests, or type indicators. In the third phase, the *insight stage,* the client and the therapist draw on information from the client's history, life experience, and emotional goals to bring the unconscious to the conscious. In the fourth phase, the *transformational* or *individuation stage,* the client utilizes insight to understand his or her complexes and to integrate the dissociated parts of his or her personality (Sharf, 2008).

Traditional Intervention Strategies

Dream Analysis

Jung viewed dream analysis as the primary means to the client's unconscious, creativity, and psyche. He believed dreams represent suppressed conflicts and often represent a person in the client's life or part of the client's psyche (Wongpakaran, Elsegood, Wongpakaran, Wannarit, & Promkumtan, 2014). Jungian clients are instructed to record their dreams as soon as they awaken so that they can remember important details. Jung was most interested in the important dreams, which are representative of repressed material, are symbolic representations of traumatic experiences, or contain upsetting memories. Instead of analyzing a single dream, like Freud did, he liked to work with a series of dreams and look for recurring themes, problems, and issues that were present in the patient's unconscious and explore the client's feelings regarding the dreams as well as the cultural context of the dreams (Schultz & Schultz, 2009; see Sidebar 4.5).

There are four phases to dream narratives. In the first phase, the client tells the who, what, when, and where of the dream. In the second phase, the complexes are exposed and explored, and feelings associated with the dream are discussed. In the third phase, the turning point within the dream is identified. The fourth and final phase includes the conclusion of the dream. The goal of the Jungian therapist in dream analysis is to recognize the symbolic elements from the personal and collective unconscious and link them with the client's conscious experiences (Jung, 1945/1960).

Sharf (2008) wrote that most dreams relate to the client's past or current life (subjective), and some reflect archetypes and are significant because they reveal

Sidebar 4.5. Dream Analysis

Dreams have been regarded as glimpses into one's truth across all times and cultures. Jung believed recurring dreams, nightmares, and childhood dreams are all significant and a means for one's unconscious to communicate suppressed material to free complexes. Nothing was considered absolute in dream analysis, and he believed dreams are self-regulating and reflect the progression and regression of one's psyche.

the collective unconscious and can be analyzed to expose symbolic meaning (objective). In other circumstances, dreams function to compensate for "one-sided conscious attitudes toward life situations" (Wyly, 1995, p. 108). To draw meaning from dreams, the analyst needs contextual information about the client, the client's experiences, and the client's personality. The analyst relies on other assessment techniques to gain additional information and interpret dreams. Jung usually elicited information regarding the client's association with elements of the dreams. Clients are asked to say the first thoughts that come to their heads when they think about their dream. In another technique, known as *amplification,* clients are asked to expand on their dream images. Hall (1977) stated,

> Amplification can take place on different levels. The most immediate level produces material from the personal unconscious of the analysand, from his own memories and feeling. The second level is of cultural material assimilated to the image. The third and most abstract level consists of archetypal; it brings in associations from folklore, mythology, religious traditions, and other systems of imagery that may not be known consistently to the dreamer. (p. 130)

Word Association

The word association test has its origins in Jung's early work with severely disturbed schizophrenic and hysterical patients. He reported that he often felt overwhelmed and did not know how to break into their private worlds. He believed that there are four main ways to understand clients: through word association, case studies, exploration of the unconscious, and analysis of symptoms and dreams. Jung, in conjunction with Eugen Bleuler, Europe's leading psychiatrist, invented the word association test as a vehicle to tap into the unconscious and reveal the patient's complexes (Sander & Beebe, 1995). He stated that when he was young he was

> completely disoriented with patients. I didn't know where to begin or what to say; and the association experiment has given me access to their unconscious. I learned about the things they did not tell me, and I got a deep insight into things of which they were not aware. (Jung, as cited in Evans, 1976, pp. 119–120)

The word association test developed by Jung consisted of a combination of 100 neutral and emotionally laden words. He administered the test to hospitalized psychiatric patients and to a control group. He noted the patterns of responses, including the word associations; the response ties; and other variables, such as resistance. He found that unique responses, slow reaction time, perseveration, and refusal to respond indicated the presence of complexes (Jung, 1905/1973a, 1905/1973b; Sander & Beebe, 1995).

When Jung published his findings on the use of word association tests to tap into clients' emotions, he achieved worldwide recognition. Jung integrated these findings with dream analysis for further illumination of complexes plaguing his clients. This was groundbreaking, because Jung presented a means of understanding and interacting with patients who were, up to that point, unreachable. He was able to demonstrate that the psyche is constructed of complexes that are measurable and observable (Sander & Beebe, 1995).

Psychological Attitudes and Types

In 1913, Jung presented his paper on typology (Jung, 1923/1971), presenting his concept of two psychological attitudes: introversion and extraversion. Neither of these attitudes is healthy or unhealthy, or positive or negative, and the intensity of the attitudes falls along a continuum with each person having a dominant function. In addition, Jung postulated that these polarities describe four psychological function types explaining how a person sees the world and processes information and experiences (Spoto, 1995).

Jung stated that the energy and attention of the extravert is directed outward (toward the object), resulting in gregariousness, volubility, and social relationships. In contrast, persons with an introverted attitude perceive energy as constantly flowing toward them, and they are always defending themselves from the almost overwhelming onslaught. The introvert may appear to be a deep thinker, shy, or timid (von Franz & Hillman, 1998). Jung, as quoted in Storr (1983), explained the extravert personality as

> having an interest in the external object, responsiveness, and a ready acceptance of external happenings, a desire to influence and be influenced by events, a need to join in and get "with it," the capacity to endure bustle and noise of every kind, and actually find them enjoyable, constant attention to the surrounding world, the cultivation of friends and acquaintances, none too carefully selected, and finally by the great importance attached to the figure one cuts, and hence by a strong tendency to make a show of oneself. Accordingly, the extravert's philosophy of life and his ethics are as a rule of a highly collective nature with a strong streak of altruism, and his conscience is in a large measure dependent on public opinion. (pp. 140–141)

Jung differentiated introversion from extraversion as follows:

> [B]eing directed not by the object but to the subject, and not be oriented by the object, is not so easy to put into perspective. The introvert is not forthcoming; he is though in continual retreat before the object. He holds aloof from external happenings, does not join in, has a distinct dislike of society as soon as he finds himself among too many people. In a large gathering he feels lonely and lost. The more crowded it is, the greater becomes his resistance. . . . He is not a good mixer. . . . Under normal conditions, he is pessimistic and worried. . . . His own company is the best. He feels at home in his own world. . . . Crowds, majority views, public opinion, popular enthusiasm never convince him of anything. (pp. 142–143)

In addition to the introversion–extraversion attitudinal polarities, there are four functions: thinking versus feeling and intuiting versus sensing (von Franz & Hillman, 1998). According to Evans (1976), Jung explained that sensing communicates that there is something there, thinking lets a person know what that something means, feeling communicates whether that something is agreeable or disagreeable, and intuition communicates that hunch or gut feeling that is known but unexplainable. Thinking and feeling are considered polar opposites, just as sensing and intuiting are polar opposites. As Jung (1968) said, "When you think you must exclude feeling, just as when you feel you must exclude thinking" (p. 16).

People who are intuitive are more strongly influenced by their unconscious, as intuition involves a prediction without factual context (Evans, 1976). The functions of sensing and intuition were identified by Jung as irrational functions because they do not rely on the process of reason and they both occur without the thought process. These functions accept experiences without evaluating them. In contrast, Jung considered thinking and feeling to be rational, as both functions are focused on organizing and categorizing experiences (Storr, 1983).

By combining the two attitudes (introversion and extraversion) and four functions (thinking, feeling, sensing, and intuition) Jung identified eight psychological types. Ideally, the attitudes and functions would be equally developed and would be balanced; however, that is rarely the reality. Usually one attitude and one function become dominant, with the other attitude and functions remaining dormant or sometimes unconscious. Jung believed the underdeveloped attitude and functions often surface through dreams, in fantasies, and in other unexpected ways. The eight personality types follow with a brief description:

- *Thinking extraverts* follow the rules and expect others to do the same. They tend to repress feelings and emotions and rely on intellectual analysis of their experiences. They are often perceived as cold, rigid and uncaring. Jung believed many scientists are thinking extraverts.
- *Feeling extraverts* make friends easily and tend to conform to the social norms and expectations of others. They tend to repress thinking, sensing, and intuiting and respond and adjust to the demands of a situation by often doing what is expected instead of what is personally preferred. This approach is more typical of women than men.
- *Sensing extraverts* seek new adventures, pleasure, and happiness. They tend to repress thinking, intuiting, and feeling. Without a reliance on introspection or analysis, they tend to be adaptable, to be outgoing, and enjoy what life throws at them.
- *Intuiting extraverts* tend to seek new experiences and be creative. Sensing, thinking, and feeling are repressed, and they are often drawn to business and politics for the ability to exploit opportunities. There is often little concern for others, so this type is sometimes viewed as unscrupulous or immoral.
- *Thinking introverts* do not get along well with others and have difficulty communicating ideas. For these people, the subjective truth is all that matters, regardless of the impact on others. Logical thought is only used to support their skewed subjective perspective, and they are more concerned with ideas than people. They are often viewed as stubborn, arrogant, inconsiderate, and aloof. Jung described himself as a thinking introvert.
- *Feeling introverts* tend to repress rational thought and, although capable of feeling deep emotion, often suppress emotion. They appear to be unavailable to others and are often seen as quiet, unsympathetic, and indifferent. They have little interest in others' perceptions and prefer to keep to themselves.
- *Sensing introverts* focus on the subjective experiences in life and tend to repress intuition. They tend to be creative and often express themselves through art and music and seek aesthetic interests.
- *Intuiting introverts* are the most misunderstood type and are often viewed as odd and eccentric. They tend to be visionaries and daydreamers so out of touch with reality that they tend to struggle with day-to-day life and planning for the future. Of all of the types, this one is the most aloof and is often considered the eccentric genius.

Analysis of Transference and Countertransference

Transference refers to an ego defense whereby the client unconsciously projects his or her own thoughts and fears onto the therapist. When the therapist reacts to the client with projections of his or her own thoughts and feelings, this is *countertransference.* Addressing transference and countertransference is an integral component of Jungian therapy.

Personal experiences, current issues, dreams, relationships, as well as archetypal projections from the collective unconscious can become part of the transference. The transference material can also be unconscious and symbolic and is reflective of the multicultural influence in Jung's theory (Heyer, 2012). It is the role of the therapist to analyze personal and archetypal elements of transference and countertransference and integrate information from the client's ego, neurosis, and complexes (Wyly, 1995).

Outside of the session, the client is required to journal thoughts, feelings, and emotions and engage in creative activities to make the unconscious conscious. Analysis of transference and countertransference brings attitudes and patterns of behavior that interfere with functioning and full psychological development to conscious awareness and will allow the client to understand his or her own psyche (Kirsch, 1995). The process requires active engagement and presence from both the client and therapist. Because of the personal nature of the therapeutic relationship, a Jungian therapist must complete his or her own psychological work prior to being able to facilitate the process with others. Jung believed that therapists cannot take their clients further than they have gone themselves (Hollis, 2013).

Brief Intervention Strategies and Current Practices

Jungian Therapy With Children and Adolescents

Jungian psychotherapy is an in-depth approach to life situations and stresses the process of personality unity, individuation, and transcendence. The length of the process always depends on how extensively the individual wants to become involved. The interventions mentioned previously can all be applied to brief therapeutic work (Schwartz, 2007). The following discussion of play therapy and sandplay therapy highlights Jungian techniques that are brief intervention strategies.

Play Therapy

Adolescents are paradoxically both egocentric and idealistic. They view themselves as young gods, at the center of the universe, while at the same time they are capable of great self-sacrifice, willing to give their life for a cause. Contemporary Jungian therapists utilize art, play, drama, dance, and visualization as interventions and assessments with adolescents. Serial drawing is a technique in which children draw pictures each time they come to therapy. As the child feels more secure and safe, he or she more freely projects his or her unconscious onto the paper, bringing his or her unconscious to consciousness. Jung utilized serial drawings on himself when he was emerging from his period of introspection after World War I (Allan, 1988).

After traumatic events, children will often draw the images they witnessed. Given the opportunity, they will attempt to repair the damage by placing at the scene something that would have mitigated the harm. For example, immediately following the World Trade Center disaster, schoolchildren who had witnessed the death and destruction quietly took out paper and began to draw. Many drew sad buildings or the Statue of Liberty in mourning. Parents expressed concern because their children drew machine guns on the roofs of buildings near the World Trade Center. The parents were relieved when the artwork was interpreted as an attempt by the children to make the situation right. In the children's unconscious (expressed in their artwork), they were self-soothing by rewriting history and making it possible to protect the buildings and the inhabitants and bring the events to a more satisfactory conclusion.

Sandplay is another play therapy technique that is often used with young children who are more likely to show a therapist their thoughts and feelings than use words to tell them. Sandplay is unique, because it allows the client a space to create a world in the sand representative of his or her thoughts and feelings. It also offers a unique kinesthetic experience and often produces a calming effect in anxious children. This technique is particularly useful with children experiencing bereavement and loss (Green & Connolly, 2009) and in brief therapy (Taylor, 2009).

Clients With Serious Mental Health Issues

Jung began his practice working with seriously mentally ill psychiatric inpatients. Therefore, his theory and the interventions are designed to work well with them. Word association tests, the Rorschach Inkblot Test, and the Thematic Apperception Test (TAT) are projective tests that are frequently used by psychotherapists as part of their assessment and treatment of clients.

Jung believed that major psychiatric disorders have their roots in brain-based biochemical disorders (Jung, 1909), and he believed that psychoanalysis is ineffective without medical intervention. His beliefs were confirmed in the 1950s when Swiss physicians stumbled onto the use of monoamine oxidase inhibitors (MAOIs) as a treatment for depression (Satinover, 1995). More severe issues like personality disorders, borderline personalities, schizoid diagnoses, and narcissism tend to respond to a Jungian approach because of the in-depth analysis of the psyche (Schwartz, 2007).

Borderline Personality Disorder

People with borderline personality disorder have many characteristics in common. They tend to be emotionally labile, with wide swings of emotions from feeling joyous to feeling intense anxiety and anger. They also show high degrees of impulsivity with potential self-injurious behavior and a strong potential for substance abuse. They have distorted thinking that, in extreme cases, may be to the point of delusions. This highly unstable pattern of behavior is marked by mercurial shifts in attachments and relationships and changes in career paths, with a negative impact on their financial situations and most areas of their lives (American Psychiatric Association, 2013).

With clients exhibiting these problems, the Jungian analyst would interpret these thoughts, feelings, and behaviors as occurring as a result of dissociation of the clients' conscious and collective unconscious. Some of these characteristics would be interpreted in relation to archetypes that are clamoring to be expressed but are instead repressed. The goal of therapy would be to reintegrate the disowned parts into one functioning personality. The therapist would use case history, word association, analysis of transference and countertransference, assessment of types and attitudes, analysis of dreams, and talk therapy (Sander & Beebe, 1995). Psychiatrists would recommend medication in situations in which medication would relieve some of the problematic behaviors associated with borderline personality disorder (i.e., impulsivity, unstable mood, and/or delusional thoughts; Satinover, 1995).

Psychosis

Clients who are psychotic manifest a lost touch with reality, often experiencing delusions and hallucinations. Jung (1909) believed psychosis is a biochemical brain disorder. From a Jungian perspective, the therapist would explore the client's belief systems, case history, and conscious and unconscious, as well as the transference and countertransference that occurs in therapy. The therapist would analyze the symbolic meaning of delusions, hallucinations, fears, and anxieties, and assessments such as the word association test and the TAT would be interpreted to uncover pervasive complexes. Dream analysis would be utilized to understand what the client is experiencing, and psychotropic medications would be recommended, when appropriate, for the alleviation of psychotic symptoms (Satinover, 1995).

Major Depression

Jungian therapists believe that depression is most likely to occur with perfectionist clients. Therefore, they would investigate complexes relating to inferiority, as well as archetypes that are perfect and heroic beyond mortal capacity. People with depression are also likely to be weighed down. Therefore, special attention would be paid to symbols and metaphors related to weight and mass. People who are depressed also trap their energy and sometimes turn it on themselves. Therefore, the role of the therapist is to discover where this energy is trapped and then release it so that it is directed away from the individual (Samuels, 1991). Because of the increased risk of suicidal behavior, the therapist must be sensitive to self-injurious threats and communication of symbols of death. Jungians also advocate for the use of psychotropic medications for the treatment of endogenous major depression. When Swiss physicians discovered that MAOIs treat depression in the 1950s, Jung's belief in the brain-based roots of psychiatric disorders was confirmed (Jung, 1909; Satinover, 1995).

EVALUATION

Overview

Jungian psychotherapists use a number of assessments and utilize objective and subjective instruments and techniques. Jungian theories have had an impact on the development of subjective techniques such as word association, projective tests such as the Rorschach Inkblot Test (Ellenberger, 1970) and the TAT (Groth-Marnat, 2009), and objective instruments such as the Myers–Briggs Type Indicator (MBTI). The goal is to determine the client's psychological attitudes and types, unconscious thoughts and feelings, and complexes. By becoming aware of their attitudes and personality types, clients can understand their primary way of interacting with the world and gain better self-understanding. These assessments are used in individual counseling, career counseling, scholastic advising, psychological evaluations, workplace conflict resolution, family counseling, and couples counseling.

Word Association

When Jung was a novice psychiatrist, he invented the word association test as a means of entering the world of his severely impaired patients at the psychiatric hospital. With the word association test, clients are presented with a series of words and are asked to reply with the first thought that enters their mind. He regularly used the word association test to uncover complexes in his patients. Response time, physiological responses, repeated responses, slips of the tongue, made-up responses, stammering, the use of more than a one-word response, and failure to respond were all believed to be indicative of a complex (Schultz & Schultz, 2009).

Rorschach Inkblot Test

The Rorschach Inkblot Test is the test that most people think of when they think of traditional projective psychological evaluations (Erford, 2007). Hermann Rorschach was inspired by Jung's introversion and extraversion attitudes when he developed the inkblot test (Ellenberger, 1970). This is a subjective test in which clients are asked to look at bilaterally symmetrical shapes and report what they see. In this way, they project their thoughts about the drawing and give information about their unconscious thoughts and feelings, needs, motivations, and conflicts. The overarching construct behind this instrument is this: Responses to the ambiguous inkblot stimuli indicate how individuals respond to other ambiguous situations in their lives. Responses are scored along three general categories: (a) the location on the inkblot that the respondent focuses on; (b) the properties, such as color and shape, of the inkblot that the respondent focuses on; and (c) the category (e.g., human, animal, architecture, anatomy) that the response fits into (Groth-Marnat, 2009).

TAT

The TAT is another projective instrument that was developed based on Jungian theoretical constructs. When Henry Murray developed the TAT with Christina Morgan in 1935, he was one of Jung's protégés (Sharf, 2008). This instrument consists of a series of 20 pictures of ambiguous scenes. A children's edition, which includes 16 cards, has been developed using children or animals in the pictures, and the majority of the pictures can be matched to the child's gender.

With any of the apperception instruments, the examinee is asked to tell the story in each picture. The examiner asks the examinee to give details regarding the events leading up to the picture and also to tell the outcome. The responses are rated quantitatively and qualitatively along a continuum in terms of the sophistication of the responses, detail, and personal information that is revealed.

There is not a specific scoring guide for the instruments; instead, the interpretation rests with the therapist's clinical judgment. Although the TAT is the sixth most commonly used instrument for psychological assessment (Camara, Nathan, & Puente, 2000), it is recommended that it be used with a battery of other instruments because the TAT is open to subjective analysis (Groth-Marnat, 2009).

MBTI

In 1933, Katharine Cook Briggs and her daughter, Isabel Briggs Myers, developed an instrument to assist in the placement of women at work. During World War II, when most of the men were deployed in the various branches of military service, women were encouraged to enter the workforce to fill the needs of the war effort. Briggs and Myers developed an instrument known as the MBTI that differentiated 16 personality types and characteristics. The section on MBTI characteristics associated with types (Sharf, 2010) describes the attitudes, dispositions, and characteristics associated with each personality type. Examples of these include, but are not limited to, (a) ISTJ—the introverted, sensing, thinking, judging type, with characteristics such as quiet, serious, successful, dependable, and so on; and (b) ESFP—the extraverted, sensing, feeling, perceiving type, with characteristics such as extraverted, friendly, the life of the party, hedonistic, and so on.

The results of the MBTI are combined with other skills, aptitude, and interest inventories to acquire the most information to assist clients in career exploration. The MBTI is used beyond helping clients choose careers. Information regarding types is used in personal counseling to help clients gain insight into the ways in which they interact with the world. It is also used in couples counseling so that clients can better understand their partner's personality and typical ways of interacting (Erford, 2007). In addition, the MBTI is used by managers to understand their employees' personalities so that they may create more compatible and better functioning work groups, and it is often used as an assessment tool for career advancement (Myers, McCauley, Quenk, & Hammer, 1998; Sharf, 2010). The MBTI is considered the best known assessment from Jung's work (see Sidebar 4.6).

Supporting Research

Jung's introversion–extraversion concept inspired several other personality theorists, and the introversion–extraversion scale was a key personality dimension measured by the Minnesota Multiphasic Personality Inventory. Modern therapists continue to incorporate Jungian therapeutic techniques and assessments. For example, the majority of therapists use the TAT as part of their assessment (Camara et al., 2000), and most psychoanalysts incorporate dream analysis as a component of most of their analytic sessions (Hill, Schottenbauer, Liu, Spangler, & Sim, 2008). A Jungian approach is effective in helping clients address psychological and spiritual growth in their later years, which Jung believed to be some of the most important years of one's life (Corbett, 2014). Jung's work is also influential in cultural awareness (Heyer, 2012).

Jungian theory has been successful in helping women with sexual individuation (Wakefield, 2014). Dream analysis continues to produce promising results in work with traumatized children and adults (Cochrane et al., 2014: Najam, Mansoor, Kanwal, & Naz, 2006), adults and children experiencing end-of-life issues (Goelitz, 2007; Lempen & Midgley, 2006), and those with nightmare disorder (Wongpakaran et al., 2014) and is often used in long-term Jungian analysis (Cochrane et al.,

Sidebar 4.6. The Myers–Briggs Assessment

What has since become an instrumental tool for helping place men and women in the workforce started as a means for Katharine Briggs to understand the distinct personality differences between her daughter, Isabel, and her future son-in-law, Clarence Myers. Katharine and her daughter were daring, imaginative, and intuitive, whereas Clarence was detail oriented, logical, and very pragmatic; she just did not see how the two could be a good match. She was so intrigued by the differences that she read Jung's book *Psychological Types* and discovered a way to categorize people based on Jung's explanations of personalities. With her daughter's help, they developed the MBTI without any university affiliation, research grant money, or graduate students. The MBTI is considered one of the most practical and visible results of Jung's work on personality.

2014). Jung's theory continues to be used for play therapy (Green & Myrick, 2014), grief and bereavement (Green & Connolly, 2009), and treating child sexual assault survivors (Green, 2008).

Summary Chart: Jungian Analytical Theory

Human Nature

People desire to be whole, and they strive for an awareness of their conscious and unconscious selves. Spirituality and the collective unconscious play a major role in the motivation of emotions and behaviors, and all people share a universal past. Personalities can be categorized along the continuum of the attitudes of introversion and extraversion and along the polarity of four functions: thinking versus feeling and intuiting versus sensing. Individual personalities fall on various points along the continuum and affect people's relationships with their internal, personal experiences as well as their interaction with the external world.

Major Constructs

Personality consists of the psyche, which includes all conscious and unconscious thoughts. The unconscious consists of the personal and the collective unconscious. The collective unconscious stems from the genetic experiences of one's ancestors as well as from one's culture, religion, society, and ethnic background. Integration and unity are the goals of the developed personality. Within the conscious and unconscious are attitudes, feelings, behaviors, motivations for behaviors, and spirituality. Personality can be analyzed through an examination of case history, transference, and countertransference; dream analysis; and projective tests such as the TAT and Rorschach Inkblot Test.

Goals

The goals of therapy are to help clients become aware of their conscious and unconscious thoughts and become fully integrated. Jungians believe that it is beneficial for people to become aware of their personal and collective unconscious. The relationship between the Jungian analyst and the client is unique for each of them, and the goals of therapy are specific to each individual. The immediate goal of therapy is to alleviate intense emotional suffering, with the long-term goal of integrating the unconscious and conscious into one (Stein, 1995). Jung believed that healing the mind is like curing the soul and that the relationship between the therapist and the client is similar to the relationship between a minister and his or her congregation (Jung, 1928).

Interventions

A strong client–therapist relationship is essential for any change to occur and requires an active commitment from both participants. The majority of the work will take place through talk therapy, in which the client will be encouraged to share his or her thoughts, feelings, dreams, and desires (Stein, 1995). A Jungian therapist may use projective assessments such as word association tests, the TAT, the MBTI, and the Rorschach Inkblot Test and will rely on dream analysis throughout therapy to gain an understanding of the client's personal and collective unconscious. The transference and countertransference occurring between the analyst and the client is also a key component in Jungian therapy.

Limitations

The Jungian psychological approach has some key limitations worth noting. Appropriate application of the techniques and interventions requires that the therapist undergo advanced training as well as complete his or her own personal psychoanalysis. For the client, it requires a high degree of abstract thinking, intelligence, and an acceptance of ambiguity. It is often a lengthy process that requires a commitment of money, emotion, and time from the client. The client must be willing to engage in in-depth analysis of dreams; engage in the analysis of transference and countertransference; and examine the symbolism of unconscious thoughts, images, and feelings. Although there is a great deal of research on the assessment instruments developed from Jungian theory, there is a startling lack of empirical data to support the efficacy of the Jungian psychoanalytical approach (Hill et al., 2008; Sharf, 2008).

THE CASE OF MARIA: A JUNGIAN APPROACH

The Jungian psychotherapist welcomes Maria and listens carefully to her life story. Because Jungian psychotherapists believe that the analysis of dreams is an opportunity to uncover unconscious thoughts and feelings, the therapist focuses on the detailed content of the dreams. It is essential to learn about Maria's dreams and to understand the personal, as well as transpersonal, material from the collective unconscious (Wyly, 1995). Several elements of the dreams are analyzed in the context of Maria's life story. Maria and her therapist also search for the meaning of the archetypal characters that play major roles in her dreams and the emotional conflicts within the dreams.

Attention is given to Maria's reactions to the characters in her dreams. How does she feel? How does she react to the characters in the dreams? How does she react to the events of the dreams? What do the events of the dreams mean to Maria? Has she ever had a life experience similar to the events of the dreams? The therapist then analyzes the meaning of the events of the dreams. For example, the therapist analyzes the meaning of being pursued, the feelings associated with the dream environment, the images generated by the dreams, and the relevance of previously omitted details of the dreams (repressed material).

The therapist is also interested in the impact of the dream ego on the functioning of the waking ego. In Maria's case, the dream ego has a great impact on her waking ego. Because of her fear of dreaming, she is avoiding sleep and is suffering the consequences of chronic sleep deprivation. It is affecting her mood, her work, and her relationship with her children.

In reviewing Maria's childhood and adolescence, the therapist interprets her animus (soul) as the Madonna archetype. With a maturity beyond her years, Maria serenely became the mother to her younger siblings and ran the household while her parents managed their family business. She also was a leader and inspiration to her religious community. To accomplish this, she had to surrender her own natural anima.

After high school, Maria broke with her family and her religious community, and she was accused of abandoning them. Although her parents wanted her to stay home, she went to college 200 miles away. While there, she met and married a man who personified the child archetype. For a while, they were compatible because her husband fulfilled her desire to mother someone, and he wanted to be mothered. However, after their children were born, he felt jealous of the attention Maria paid to the children and was upset because he had adult responsibilities. When he became unhappy, he had adult-size temper tantrums that turned into physical and emotional abuse. No matter how hard she tried, Maria could not be the perfect wife and mother and satisfy his need to be the child. Eventually he abandoned Maria and their children, leaving her to raise the children on her own, which increased her sense of failure.

Maria feels conflicted because she has disowned many parts of herself in an effort to satisfy her husband, family, church, and work. The first of her many conflicts occurred when she disowned many parts of herself when she was an adolescent and took up the archetype of the Madonna. To play that role, she had to deny her natural sensuality and her inner child to take up adult roles, and she sacrificed spontaneity to be the dutiful daughter. Later, she believed that she abandoned her family and siblings to attend college. This placed a strain on her family because she could no longer take care of her home and her younger siblings. Because she was accustomed to taking on the role of mother, she was attracted to a man/child.

Her second abandonment occurred when she married her husband and became estranged from her parents and siblings. The third abandonment occurred when she was abandoned by her husband and was left alone to raise her children. Finally, to divorce her husband, she had to abandon her religion's commandments against divorce. As a result of decisions she has made, she is now abandoned by the family of origin that she raised and supported during her childhood and adolescence. In an attempt to reintegrate and find meaning, she is attempting to find a new partner but is discouraged by their other-than-Madonna expectations. To tap into the subconscious and understand Maria's complexes, the therapist does a word association test.

The therapist analyzes Maria's dreams in the following way: There is a central theme of abandonment. In her dreams, Maria is being pursued by something. Maria is advised to replay the dreams in her mind and narrate the dreams to aid in the interpretation. She describes the boxes scattered throughout the warehouse. Her soul (animus) is chasing her through an abandoned warehouse, and she is running because she feels pursued by the competing demands of her family in contrast to her personal goals and is frightened by the person she has become. However, this time, she is encouraged to imagine that she stops and looks inside the boxes. She is surprised to discover objects symbolizing parts of her personality that she has disowned (abandoned) in her attempt to please others.

The arrows point in different directions, indicating the maturity or immaturity of the disowned parts. When she opens the boxes, she is instructed to converse with her split-off personality parts and to ask them to join her and help her reintegrate her personality. For example, in one box, she discovers a miniature copy of the Pietà, Michelangelo's masterpiece of the Virgin Mary holding the dead body of Jesus on her lap. When she looks on Mary as she supports her dead son, Maria is filled with a sense of calm, majesty, and inner strength. She realizes that she has abandoned that strength in response to her husband's and her family's demand for attention.

Maria is able to own her various archetypes and personas and becomes aware of her conscious and unconscious thoughts and feelings. As a result, she is able to sleep without further nightmares. She is also able to face down the various competing demands of her family members and prioritize their needs with her own. She is able to live a more congruent and actualized life.

REFERENCES

Allan, J. (1988). *Inscapes of the child's world: Jungian counseling in schools and clinics.* Dallas, TX: Spring.

American Psychiatric Association. (2013). *Diagnostic and statistical manual of mental disorders* (5th ed.). Arlington, VA: Author.

Bishop, P. (1999). Introduction. In P. Bishop (Ed.), *Jung in contexts: A reader* (pp. 1–30). New York, NY: Routledge.

Camara, W., Nathan, J., & Puente, A. (2000). Psychological test usage: Implications in professional psychology. *Professional Psychology: Research and Practice, 31,* 141–154.

Casement, A. (1996). Psychodynamic therapy: The Jungian approach. In W. Dryden (Ed.), *Handbook of individual therapy* (pp. 77–102). Thousand Oaks, CA: Sage.

Casement, A. (2001). *Carl Gustav Jung.* Thousand Oaks, CA: Sage.

Cochrane, M., Flower, S., MacKenna, C., & Morgan, H. (2014). A Jungian approach to analytic work in the twenty-first century. *British Journal of Psychotherapy, 30,* 33–50.

Corbett, L. (2014). Successful aging: Jungian contributions to development in later life. *Psychological Perspectives, 56,* 149–167.

Eleftheriadou, Z. (2003). Cross-cultural counseling psychology. In R. Woolfe, W. Dryden, & S. Strawbridge (Eds.), *Handbook of counseling psychology* (2nd ed., pp. 500–517). Thousand Oaks, CA: Sage.

Ellenberger, H. F. (1970). *The discovery of the unconscious: The history and evolution of dynamic psychiatry.* New York, NY: Basic Books.

Erford, B. (2007). *Personality assessment: Assessment for counselors.* New York, NY: Houghton Mifflin.

Evans, R. (1976). *Jung on elementary psychology: A discussion between C.G. Jung and Richard I. Evans.* New York, NY: Dutton.

Frankel, R. (1998). *The adolescent Psyche: Jungian and Winnicottian perspectives.* New York, NY: Routledge.

Goelitz, A. (2007). Exploring dream work at end of life. *Dreaming, 17,* 159–171.

Green, E. (2008). Reenvisioning Jungian analytic play therapy with child sexual assault survivors. *International Journal of Play Therapy, 17*(2), 102–121.

Green, E., & Connolly, M. (2009). Jungian family sandplay with bereaved children: Implications for play therapists. *International Journal of Play Therapy, 18*(2), 84–98.

Green, E., & Myrick, A. (2014). Treating complex trauma in adolescents: A phase-based integrative approach for play therapists. *International Journal of Play Therapy, 29*(1), 31–41.

Groth-Marnat, G. (2009). *Handbook of psychological assessment* (5th ed.). Hoboken, NJ: Wiley.

Hall, J. (1977). *Clinical uses of dreams: Jungian interpretations and enactments.* New York, NY: Grune & Stratton.

Heyer, G. (2012). Caught between cultures: Cultural norms in Jungian psychodynamic process. *Journal of Psychoanalytic Psychology, 57,* 629–644.

Hill, C., Schottenbauer, M., Liu, J., Spangler, P., & Sim, W. (2008). Working with dreams in psychotherapy: What do psychoanalytic therapists report that they do? *Psychoanalytic Psychology, 25,* 565–573.

Hollis, J. (2013). Theogonies and therapy: A Jungian perspective on humanity's dark side. In A. C. Bohart, B. S. Held, E. Mendelowitz, & K. J. Schneider (Eds.), *Humanity's dark side: Evil, destructive experience and psychotherapy* (pp. 83–97). Washington, DC: American Psychological Association.

Jung, C. (1909). Psychology of dementia praecox. In *Collected works* (Vol. 3, pp. 36–37). Princeton, NJ: Princeton University Press.

Jung, C. (1928). Psychoanalysis and the cure of souls. In *Collected works* (2nd ed., Vol. 11, pp. 348–354). Princeton, NJ: Princeton University Press.

Jung, C. (1934). A review of the complex theory. In *Collected works* (Vol. 3, pp. 1–151). Princeton, NJ: Princeton University Press.

Jung, C. (1954). Child development and education. In *Collected works: The development of personality* (Vol. 17, pp. 47–62). Princeton, NJ: Princeton University Press. (Original work published 1928)

Jung, C. (1956). *Collected works: Symbols of transformation* (2nd ed., Vol. 5). Princeton, NJ: Princeton University Press. (Original work published 1911)

Jung, C. (1959). Conscious, unconscious, and individuation. In *Collected works: The archetypes and the collective unconscious* (Vol. 9, Part 1, pp. 42–53). Princeton, NJ: Princeton University Press. (Original work published 1936)

Jung, C. (1960). On the nature of dreams. In *Collected works: The structure and dynamics of the psyche* (Vol. 8, pp. 281–297). Princeton, NJ: Princeton University Press. (Original work published 1945)

Jung, C. (1968). *Collected works of C. G. Jung* (2nd ed., Vol. 9, Part 1). Princeton, NJ: Princeton University Press.

Jung, C. (1970). Symbols and the interpretation of dreams. In *Collected works: The symbolic life* (Vol. 18, pp. 185–266). Princeton, NJ: Princeton University Press. (Original work published 1959)

Jung, C. (1971). *Collected works: Psychological types* (Vol. 6). Princeton, NJ: Princeton University Press. (Original work published 1923)

Jung, C. (1973a). Experimental observation on the faculty of memory. In *Collected works* (Vol. 2, pp. 272–287). Princeton, NJ: Princeton University Press. (Original work published 1905)

Jung, C. (1973b). The reaction-time ratio in the association experiment. In *Collected works* (Vol. 2, pp. 221–271). Princeton, NJ: Princeton University Press. (Original work published 1905)

Jung, C. (1978). On psychology and pathology of so-called occult phenomena. In *Collected works: Psychology and the occult* (Vols. 1, 8, and 18, pp. 3–88). Princeton, NJ: Princeton University Press. (Original work published 1902)

Kirsch, J. (1995). Transference. In M. Stein (Ed.), *Jungian analysis* (2nd ed., pp. 170–209). Chicago, IL: Open Court.

Lempen, O., & Midgley, N. (2006). Exploring the role of children's dreams in psychoanalytic practice today: A pilot study. *Psychoanalytic Study of the Child, 61,* 228–253.

Myers, J., McCauley, M., Quenk, N., & Hammer, A. (1998). *MBTI manual: A guide to the development and use of the Myers–Briggs Type Indicator* (3rd ed.). Palo Alto, CA: Consulting Psychologists Press.

Najam, N., Mansoor, A., Kanwal, R., & Naz, S. (2006). Dream content: Reflections of the emotional and psychological states of earthquake survivors. *Dreaming, 16,* 237–245.

Prout, H. T. (2005). Counseling and psychotherapy with children and adolescents: An overview. In D. Prout & D. Brown (Eds.), *Child and adolescent counseling* (pp. 1–25). Danvers, MA: Wiley.

Samuels, A. (1991). *Psychopathology: Contemporary Jungian perspectives.* New York, NY: Guilford Press.

Sander, D., & Beebe, J. (1995). Psychopathology and analysis. In M. Stein (Ed.), *Jungian analysis* (2nd ed., pp. 297–348). Chicago, IL: Open Court.

Satinover, J. (1995). Psychopharmacology in Jungian practice. In M. Stein (Ed.), *Jungian analysis* (2nd ed., pp. 349–371). Chicago, IL: Open Court.

Schultz, D. P., & Schultz, S. E. (2009). *Theories of personality* (9th ed.). Belmont, CA: Wadsworth.

Schultz, D. P., & Schultz, S. E. (2013). *Theories of personality* (10th ed.). Belmont, CA: Wadsworth.

Schwartz, S. (2007). Jungian analytical theory. In D. Capuzzi & D. Gross (Eds.), *Counseling and psychotherapy: Theories and interventions* (4th ed., pp. 98–122). Upper Saddle River, NJ: Pearson.

Sharf, R. S. (2008). *Theories of psychotherapy and counseling: Concepts and cases* (4th ed.). Belmont, CA: Brooks/Cole.

Sharf, R. S. (2010). *Applying career development theory to counseling.* Belmont, CA: Brooks/Cole.

Sharf, R. S. (2014). *Theories of psychotherapy and counseling: Concepts and cases* (5th ed.). Boston, MA: Cengage Learning.

Spoto, A. (1995). *Jung's typology in perspective* (Rev. ed.). Wilmette, IL: Chiron.

Stein, M. (Ed.). (1995). The aims and goals of Jungian analysis. In *Jungian analysis* (2nd ed., pp. 29–49). Chicago, IL: Open Court.

Stevens, A. (1990). *On Jung.* New York, NY: Routledge.

Storr, A. (1983). *The essential Jung.* Princeton, NJ: Princeton University Press.

Taylor, E. (2009). Sand-tray and solution focused therapy. *International Journal of Play Therapy, 18,* 56–68.

von Franz, M., & Hillman, J. (1998). *Lectures on Jung's typology.* Woodstock, CT: Spring.

Wakefield, C. (2014). In search of Aphrodite: Working with archetypes and an inner cast of characters in women with low sex drive. *Sexual and Relationship Therapy, 29*(1), 31–41.

Wickes, F. (1927). *The inner world of childhood.* New York, NY: Signet.

Wilmer, H. (1987). *Practical Jung: Nuts and bolts of Jungian psychotherapy.* Wilmette, IL: Chiron.

Wongpakaran, T., Elsegood, K. J., Wongpakaran, N., Wannarit, K., & Promkumtan, P. (2014). Using control-mastery and Jungian theories to treat nightmare disorder: A case in Thailand. *Journal of Mental Health Counseling, 36,* 189–207.

Wyly, J. (1995). Dreams and Jungian analysis. In M. Stein (Ed.), *Jungian analysis* (2nd ed., pp. 105–136). Chicago, IL: Open Court.

Chapter 5

Adlerian Theory

Roxane L. Dufrene, Kathryn L. Henderson, and Emeline C. Eckart

Alfred Adler founded individual psychology, a social theory widely applied by counselors and educators. His theory provides a framework for understanding a person within his or her environment, thus providing guidance for improving both the individual's psychological state and his or her connectedness to the social environment (Ellenberger, 1970). This understanding occurs within the context of an instinctive social interest (*Gemeinschaftsgefühl*) characterized by cooperation and contribution to the social good. Adler's theory is designed to provide opportunity for a person's psychological health to flourish where social equality prevails. It introduces the possibility of a society in which psychopathology is not only treatable but also preventable.

Individual psychology is based on three major constructs that Adler and his associates have refined over the past century (Ellenberger, 1970; Uytman, 1967). First, human behavior is goal oriented (purposeful). Behaviors are stimulated by an instinctive, creative aptitude in a manner to fit in. Second, humans have a drive that is directed toward living cooperatively and contributing to social interest. Third, the general evaluative attitude that affects choices occurs within the whole person (is holistic), not a sublevel of the person. Adler's aim was a philosophy of living that would produce a democratic family structure and a healthy social interest resulting in an ideal culture for child development. Adler's theory is reflected in common terms used in counseling today, such as *birth order* and *social interest,* and the impressive list of people he influenced, such as Albert Ellis, Victor Frankl, Abraham Maslow, and Rollo May.

BACKGROUND

Adler was an Austrian physician and psychiatrist born in Vienna on February 7, 1870 (Ellenberger, 1970). He was the second son of six children of a Jewish grain merchant. Childhood illnesses of rickets and pneumonia left him weak and sickly as a child. Adler was an average student, was very socially outgoing, and made friends easily. During his college years, his peer group was made up of socialist students, including Raissa Epstein, a social activist (Hoffman, 1996; Uytman, 1967). They married in 1897 and had four children: Valentine, Alexandra, Kurt, and Nelly. Alexandra and Kurt became psychiatrists in the United States and promoters of Adler's theory. After receiving his medical degree from the University of Vienna in 1895, Adler practiced medicine for a while and then specialized in psychiatry (Hoffman, 1996). In 1898, at 28, he wrote one of his first works on the medical conditions of tailors, within their unique environment, describing one of the main ideas in his theory: the individual as part of an integrated whole within the environment. In 1902, Sigmund Freud invited Adler to join a weekly group to discuss the characteristics of psychopathology and to join the Viennese Psychoanalytic Society, and Adler became the editor of the organization's newsletter (Milliren, Evans, & Newbauer, 2007).

Adler published several works that featured a form of social theory counter to Freud's deterministic theory. A rivalry began to develop between the friends, and eventually, Adler's direction toward a more social theory of development caused a rift with Freud. Contrary to popular belief, although Adler was a contemporary and professional associate of Freud, he was not a student of Freud (Milliren et al., 2007). He never accepted Freud's theory that mental difficulties were caused primarily by sexual trauma or that dreams should be interpreted as attempts at sexual fulfillment. Adler began to view Freud as inflexible in his ideas and obsessed with sex and death. In 1907, Adler published *Study of Organ Inferiority and Its Psychical Compensation* (Adler, 1907/1917), which detailed the focus of his early work on organ disabilities and the compensatory responses of individuals. In 1911, his rift with Freud led to his resignation from the Viennese Psychoanalytic Society and the formation of his own group, the Society for Individual Psychology.

In 1912, he published *The Neurotic Constitution* (Adler, 1912/1926), in which he discussed the main constructs of his theory (Uytman, 1967). The Vienna College of Professors rejected his work as more similar to philosophy than medicine. Eventually, Adler turned to bringing his theory to the public through an educational model, not a medical model. His next book, *Understanding Human Nature* (Adler, 1927/1946), contained many of his lectures given at the Viennese Institute for Adult Education. He was influenced by philosophers such as Immanuel Kant and Friedrich Nietzsche. He believed that the drives for power and superiority contribute to human behavior by compensating for a sense of inferiority, or *inferiority complex.* Adler traveled and lectured for nearly 25 years presenting his ideas on socially oriented psychology. He sought to overcome the superiority dynamic of a therapist, moving the theater of analysis from the couch to two chairs, promoting the idea of equality between the patient and counselor.

In 1914, Adler started the journal *The Individual Psychologist.* That same year, he edited a book, *Healing and Education: Medical-Educational Papers of the Society for Individual Psychology* (Adler & Furtmüller, 1914), moving more into the field of education (Hoffman, 1996). Adler's work was interrupted by World War I, when he served as a physician. He noted the war's destructive power on Vienna society. His views began to incorporate the concept of social interest as an approach to larger societal problems such as education (specifically, adult education), teacher training, and child guidance. In 1918 and 1919, after the war, he founded several child guidance clinics in Vienna and educational clinics in Austria, where he pioneered group therapy.

From 1921 forward, Adler was a frequent lecturer in Europe and the United States (Ellenberger, 1970). His approach was popular worldwide, with many associations of individual psychology in several countries. In 1934, when Hitler came to power, the child guidance clinics were closed as fostering democracy. In 1937 Adler began a series of lectures in several European countries. He published *Understanding Human Nature* (Adler, 1927/1946), which presented his idea of social interest (King & Shelley, 2007). In 1937, during his lecture tour, Adler died of a heart attack. His daughter, Dr. Alexandra Adler, completed the series. After Adler's death, his theory continued to flourish and evolved through the further work of Rudolf Dreikurs and many other enthusiasts worldwide. One of Dreikurs's major contributions was the continuation of Adler's child guidance clinics in the United States in the form of family education centers. Individual psychology remains strong today as a psychological theory even after Adler's death, with an enormous effect on the counseling profession (Ellenberger, 1970).

HUMAN NATURE: A DEVELOPMENTAL PERSPECTIVE

In this section, important characteristics of Adler's approach to human development are discussed, exploring lifestyle, birth order, family constellation, and early recollections.

Adler (1927/1946, 1924/1959) considered the developmental process as the formation of an individual's lifestyle. A lifestyle is unique and composed of a person's relationships with the self, others, and the universe. Like Freud, Adler saw the lifestyle or personality as established early in life and usually fixed at around age 5 or 6. At that point, new experiences tend to be interpreted within the terms of the established lifestyle rather than causing further adjustment to the fixed lifestyle. From the moment of birth, a child begins to construct a lifestyle out of experiences that occur in the environment. As the child develops a particular style of fitting in, perceptions become increasingly selective, and actions and reactions become habitual. Within a lifestyle, values are learned from family and become set.

Adler (1927/1946, 1924/1959) believed that humans have attributes that are purposeful, social, subjective, and interpretive. A child interacts and, in turn, becomes a shaping force in defining and redefining the family system. Reactions are on the basis of subjective perspectives, and those subjective interpretations may or may not match the actual facts of the environment. Many beliefs and perceptions are based on mistaken interpretations of the environment. Thus, an Adlerian counselor views lifestyle formation as an attempt to reach agreement with thoughts, feelings, and actions in the social environment.

Early Development

Adler introduced three concepts as guides to interpreting the patterns of behavior a child uses to give action to his or her lifestyle: birth order, family constellation, and early recollections. These concepts assist counselors in understanding the factors that affect a child's development.

Birth order is one concept for which Adler is best known (Adler, 1927/1946). Birth order is an important factor in a child's developmental process because it provides a template around which thoughts and behaviors are understood. Adler constructed a framework of birth order characteristics based on the natural hierarchy created within a family. A child's parents are older, more experienced, and mandated by society on how to rear a child; therefore, parents are the natural leaders and role models who influence the child's development. Adler also proposed that a child or a sibling has as much or even more of an impact on the interactions of the family than the parents alone. In most situations, a child's needs and behaviors affect the family interactions, with the resulting structure of relationships influencing the adults and other children in the family. The interactions of all members and subsequent communication create what Adler termed the *family atmosphere.*

Family atmosphere is unique to each family system. The relationship between the parents and a child, or the parents and their children, is often the clearest signal of what factors constitute the family system. Parents are the natural role models, and children often use them as the basis for gender-specific behaviors and interaction styles with each other and outsiders. A child may experience parents as loving, angry, frightening, strict, joyful, easygoing, involved, protective, nurturing, respectful, or many other things. That subjective experience can determine which attributes will be incorporated into the child's set of values. Prevailing values play a significant role in the subsequent development of both the family and the child. Family members take a position relative to the family's values. Common areas in which family values develop include money, education, religion, and what is right and wrong. In the majority of families, the atmosphere is the social setting in which a child's growth and development occur and becomes the model for what is expected out of life.

An Adlerian counselor views a person's description of the family atmosphere as an indicator of development in the family system (Milliren et al., 2007). A counselor may observe and understand the family dynamics by asking family members how they subjectively experience the atmosphere. For example, a counselor might ask parents to provide a description of each child in the family, which may reveal the effects of a child's birth order and how the child has adapted to engage or challenge the family system. The counselor also may ask for the child's descriptions of family members, which can be useful for revealing important indicators of a child's self in the family relationships. Thus, a set of characteristics might be developed from descriptions of each family member's subjective relationships to other members (Adler, 1927/1946). In this way, descriptors provided by a child reveal the child's sense of belonging and knowledge of the relationship that the child has with family members.

Birth Order and Family Constellation

Adler (1927/1946, 1964) used the term *family constellation* as a structure to describe each member's niche within the family system. He noted that the family constellation consisted of parents, children, and any extended family members. Adler emphasized that birth order in this constellation influences a person's lifestyle choices. Within the constellation, a child defines his or her self in relation to other children and how the self is different from or the same as others in the family. For example, the parent a child aligns with affects the child's interpretation of his or her position in the family constellation. The child's position in the family also can be defined by how the child addresses family values; what techniques are used to negotiate dynamics within the constellation; how the members of the constellation handle the impact of culture, age, and gender differences; and how the demands of school and society are handled within the system.

Birth order for children and each of the siblings, the gender of siblings, and age differences between siblings are all variables of the family constellation (Ansbacher & Ansbacher, 1959). The family atmosphere is therefore a commonly shared experience for a child as well as others in the family environment. It is where a child learns how to interact with others. Behavior in other parts of a child's world often reflects that child's position and reactions within the family. Because most behaviors are carried from the home into the community environment, understanding the role of the family in a person's life is important.

The impact of birth order on development is not a rigid schema but rather a subjective interpretation of a person's family position. A counselor needs to understand a person's subjective thoughts and feelings about his or her birth position in the family. Adler (1927/1946) described five basic birth order positions: the only child, the oldest child, the second of only two children, the middle child, and the youngest child. As a child is added to the family, the total family system changes in its behaviors as birth order positions shift (see Sidebar 5.1).

Only Children

Parents have a strong influence on only children's early development. Adler (1927/1946) believed that because only children never have to share attention or feel replaced by another sibling, they may not learn how to cooperate with others. During the majority of their development they are surrounded by adults, so they easily identify with adults and soon learn adult language. Only children are more inclined to be high achievers and conscientious. They are very interested in perpetuating family values and are more likely to be pampered by parents. However, if parents are demanding and abusive, only children have to bear the abuse alone.

When parents are very capable, an only child may feel unable to compete at the parents' level, and the child may become discouraged. When parents are doting and provide for every need and want, the child may become helpless and unable to provide for himself or herself as an adult. As an example, Susan, an only child, was worshiped by her parents and grandparents. At the age of 35, Susan still lived alternately with her mother or grandparents. She did not have a job. Although

Sidebar 5.1. Self-Awareness

1. What birth order position are you?
   a. Are there gender differences between you and your siblings?
   b. How many years separate you from your siblings?
   c. How would you describe your relationship with your parents?
   d. How would you describe your relationship with your siblings?
2. In what ways might your birth order influence the therapeutic relationship with the following clients:
   a. Children
   b. Clients of a similar age/background
   c. A couple that is one or two generations older

Susan had attempted twice to find a job, she felt that others did not understand her needs.

Oldest Children

Both the only and the oldest child have all of their parents' attention. The first child is, in essence, an only child receiving all of the attention. According to Ansbacher and Ansbacher (1959), Adler believed that the oldest or firstborn child would be loved and nurtured in a certain pattern of behavior by the parents until the second child arrived. Adler found that the oldest may be more likely to become a problem child because of changes in the family. If there are three or more children in the family, the oldest may act precociously, conservatively, or introverted, at least more so than other siblings. The oldest may also feel sensitive toward and very responsible for younger siblings. As a result, the firstborn can suffer from neuroticism or substance abuse problems. The oldest also can be sensitive, be dependable, and seek adult approval. Like the only child, the oldest may tend to be perfectionistic, hardworking, and conscientious.

For example, John was the firstborn in his family. After the birth of his siblings he battled for his perceived loss of the center of attention. Even though he was the oldest, John felt that his siblings got all of the attention, and at times he would act like the baby. At other times, he was disobedient and would withdraw when he was told to care for his siblings. As John grew older, he became very responsible and acted as a parent at times. As an adolescent, John got a part-time job and quit school to contribute to family. John developed into an extremely hard worker, and he had very few friends and a meager social life (see Sidebar 5.2).

Second-Born Children

The second child is subjected to a very different set of circumstances from the first child (Ellenberger, 1970). Adler believed that the second child may react in a competitive way, seeing the first child as a pacesetter (Sulloway, 1995). At times, the second child is successful in the competition, but many second children act as if the competition is never done. This constant competition affects each child's lifestyle. Whereas the first child has a period of time when the parents' attention is not shared with another child, the second will always have to share the attention. A second child of only two children is extremely focused on the older sibling. In fact, the older child can have more influence on the second child than the parents. In the majority of families, the second child of only two may work at being the opposite

Sidebar 5.2. Case Study

Christopher is the oldest child in a single-parent family raised by his mother. He has two younger siblings, and all three children were born within a span of 4 years. Christopher excelled in sports and academics during high school and received a scholarship for college. The summer before Christopher left for college, his mother remarried. During his first year at college, Christopher's grades fell and he was put on academic probation. When Christopher came home, he would argue with his siblings and act immaturely.

1. How did Christopher's family atmosphere change?
2. In what ways might this change in family atmosphere influence Christopher?

of whatever he or she perceives the first to be. If the older child is more successful, the second child may be discouraged and may react very differently to lessen the discouragement that might come with competition.

An example of this is Beth, a second child who always felt that even if she was smart, there was no way she could be as smart as Keith, her older brother. Even though Beth excelled in school, she chose to focus all of her efforts on sports. She was involved in basketball, baseball, and gymnastics and played tennis with her parents. At 22, Beth began to have medical problems as a result of pushing herself in sports. She turned to the use of prescription drugs. When asked about some of the choices she was making, such as not taking care of herself and using drugs, Beth replied by saying, "I have to stay on the top of things. My parents expect that of me."

Middle Children

When a third child arrives in the family, a second child becomes the middle child (Ansbacher & Ansbacher, 1959). A middle child learns that he or she is caught between an oldest child, who appears to be the focus, and the youngest child, who seems to be able to get attention for doing nothing. To a middle child, life appears unfair, and he or she believes that the oldest and youngest align together and against him or her. Such situations can leave the middle child as the focus of problems, or the first and third children simply leave the middle child out of everything. The middle child becomes sensitive to criticism and is easily angered. The middle child's alliance may go to a peer group, and he or she may rebel against family expectations and traditions. This comparison of self to others becomes a constant in life.

Another characteristic of middle children is developing a poor-me attitude (Ansbacher & Ansbacher, 1959). Or, in families characterized by conflict, the middle child may become the peacemaker, trying to hold things together in the family. If there are four children in a family, the second child often feels like a middle child, and the third child will be more social and may align with the firstborn. Consequently, the middle child may rebel as a result of feeling squeezed out. As an example, Thomas was a middle child of three children who always felt squeezed out. He was very social, sometimes seeking out his peers because he felt left out in his own family. Thomas always felt he was never heard in his own family because he never measured up to his siblings.

Youngest Children

The youngest child is usually the most pampered and overindulged in a family. The position in the family as the baby will never change (Ansbacher & Ansbacher, 1959). The youngest is the second most likely to be a problem, after the first child. The youngest may feel incredibly inferior because everyone in the family is older and seen as superior. Because of the limited expectations of the youngest, he or she may go off on his or her own, which leads to egocentric behaviors. Typically, the youngest tends to depend on the family, especially wanting parents to do things for him or her. An example is Kent, who was the youngest in his family. Both his siblings always looked out for Kent, and they succeeded at everything they did. Kent felt that because his siblings succeeded, he did not need to succeed and at times he would rather not try. Although youngest children can be like Kent, they can also be good observers in families and use their observations to develop in ways siblings will not. At times, this can lead to the youngest surpassing siblings, becoming the most successful in the family. The youngest often concludes that he or she is either special or unwanted. The pampered youngest child is spoiled and overindulged, whereas the unwanted child feels neglected and ignored.

Many variables can affect the family constellation, influencing how the position of oldest, second, middle, youngest, or only child may be interpreted in the family constellation (Ansbacher & Ansbacher, 1959). One variable may be the number of years between the births of the children. Families with children born 2 years apart may have different dynamics than families in which children are born 3 or more years apart. Other factors, such as gender or differences in numbers of each sex in the family, can also make a difference in how the family constellation is affected (Adler, 1931). Another impact would be if a child had major illnesses. This can change the constellation. Single parents or blended families can cause variations in the meanings found in a family constellation. As with everything in Adler's system, birth order should be understood and viewed in the context of a person's own family, community, and universe. The five birth order positions discussed here and the potential patterns represent the point of view from which the child sees the world. A child's subjective interpretation regarding birth order, not the position itself, is what really matters, because birth position is uniquely defined by the person.

Early Recollections

Adler (1931, 1964) proposed that early recollections are important indicators for understanding a person's development. He regarded memories as a key phenomenon, considering the time and effort a person uses to store and recollect memories. Recollections in and of themselves are not as important as which memories are retrieved and how a person's perception is reflected in the choice of recollections. Any childhood experiences and remembrances of those experiences may have an impact on lifestyle development, but only the person can verify the significance through the retrieving and reporting of those memories from childhood. The subjective interpretation of those memories can be used to indicate how a person views self and others. Remembrances provide a view into a person's subjective perceptions of his or her lifestyle. Early recollections provide hints and clues that are valuable when attempting to find direction in a person's striving for social interest. They are helpful in revealing what is valued and what is dangerous in life. In the counseling setting, a client's early remembrances can provide important information about the client's thoughts, feelings, and behaviors within the social world. Exploring early recollections can be an intervention to identify a client's creative ways of belonging. Early recollections also can be used as metaphors that can be applied to current life scenarios to promote client understanding (Shifron, 2010).

MAJOR CONSTRUCTS

Adler's theory is comprehensive and addresses both normal and abnormal development using simple and understandable constructs. Adler disliked statistics and tended to use case studies and anecdotal information as the source of his theory synthesis rather than statistical tools or hypothesis testing (Uytman, 1967). Although his approach was not empirical, its soundness and intuitiveness made his material credible. Although he never presented individual psychology in a systematic manner (Milliren et al., 2007), it was accepted by professionals and laypeople because of its commonsense interrelatedness and integration of constructs.

Adler viewed a person as a complete being who creates his or her self rather than having the self generated by levels of consciousness outside of his or her control, as Freud proposed. The self consists of social aspects that begin with inferiority feelings compensated for and fueled by the "creative power to interpret experiences, both internal and external, influenced by both heredity and environment, in an individualist, subjective manner," a striving to belong (Milliren et al., 2007, p. 132). A person is understood as a complete and integrated individual with the creative power to interpret experiences and manifest a *lifestyle.* Adler emphasized positive growth, believing that where a person is going is more important than where he or she has come from.

Adler (1927/1946) stressed the importance of choice and responsibility in life as well as how a person strives for success and perfection. From birth onward, a person is *socially embedded,* which reinforces the responsibilities of society. The combination of self-direction and social connectedness led Adler to the following conclusion central to individual psychology: How a person is in the world results from social creation as much as genetic design. Adler said that this social influence is so strong that almost nothing is more important than a person's social world. A person operates from a unique *private logic* according to which he or she evaluates self and others and cooperates with others (Stein, 2008). Problems are created socially and occur as a result of the conflicts that arise as an individual performs the three life tasks of work, community, and love.

Adler (1927/1946, 1924/1959; see also Ansbacher & Ansbacher, 1959; Way, 1950) introduced the idea that inferiority feelings are normal and can be used as a source of striving to overcome such feelings. He felt that inferiority feelings, or *minus situations,* are normal reactions to a person being aware that he or she is not able to function in a way that he or she wishes. These experiences motivate the person to strive toward a *plus situation,* or mastery, superiority, and completion. Adler proposed that the direction of motivation is to the future rather than an attempt to escape past conditions. Working toward goals and purpose in life creates the momentum for continual striving.

Overall, a person is viewed as a social being within society who has the capacity to interpret and influence events (Way, 1950). An individual is proactive and can choose and act in a way that will lead to a goal. The world is viewed uniquely from a subjective frame of reference. Subjective reality is then defined as a person's feelings, beliefs, values, and understanding of the world. An individual's interpretation of the world, what is in it, and how experiences are viewed are important in determining how social problems are met. A person who is connected to others and equipped to meet the three life tasks of work, community, and love will have a healthy view of life and will contribute to social interest, whereas a person who is ill equipped will struggle with challenges in life and will have a negative view of others and the world.

Adler did not view individuals as specific types because of his belief in the unique, creative power of the person. However, for instructive purposes, he suggested four basic types: (a) dominant or ruling, (b) getting or dependent, (c) avoidant, and (d) socially useful. The first three types describe people who are at least partly unprepared to meet life's demands. At various levels, these types do not cooperate with others, do not contribute to society, and are in some way maladjusted. Individuals of these types may experience addictions, neurosis, psychosis, or other issues. The ruling type attempts to dominate others, the dependent type assumes that everyone will take care of him or her, and the avoidant type avoids problems. Each of these types creates dysfunction in the family and society. The fourth type, socially useful, cooperates, contributes, and is active in society with meaningfulness and connectedness to self, others, and the world. Adler conceptualized these personality types as active to passive, with the most effective being active toward social interest. Adler thought that early recollections were a way to assess a person's approach to being active or passive when dealing with life's challenges. Passive clients are safeguarding as a means of protecting themselves from feeling inferior. Similarly, clients who are overly active but in a misdirected, maladaptive direction are not aligned socially. Exploring clients' tendency toward either activity or passivity through early recollections along with striving toward social interest can lead to insight (Clark & Butler, 2012; see Sidebar 5.3).

Adler's Human Personality Theory

Adler believed that a person attributes meaning to life experiences, which makes his approach teleological. According to Milliren et al. (2007), over three distinct phases during his life, Adler developed and refined the premises of his theory: (a) explanation of inferiority feeling, (b) understanding of inferiority, and (c) social interest.

Phase 1

During the first phase, from 1907 to 1912, Adler's work focused on *organ inferiority* as he developed basic concepts to build his theory. Adler viewed a person as having a weak part of the self as well as a strong part. In his early work, he found that an individual responds to organic inferiorities with a compensatory action, making up for a deficiency in some way with another physical attribute (Way, 1950). The organ that is inferior can be strengthened, or other organs can be overdeveloped to compensate for the inferior organ. Applying this idea to a psychological viewpoint, Adler believed that a person can compensate for inferiorities by developing certain skills or personality traits that can be the source of the individual's striving. A person's development and the incentive from society push him or her toward overcoming the expressions of inferiority. Some people can handle these challenges of life, whereas others cannot.

Sidebar 5.3. Four Basic Types of Individuals

1. *Dominant or ruling:* These individuals seek domination over others.
2. *Getting or dependent:* These individuals assume that others will take care of them.
3. *Avoidant:* These individuals seek to avoid problems.
4. *Socially useful:* These individuals cooperate, are socially useful, and contribute to the active world.

The first three types of individuals are unprepared to meet life's demands. They may experience addictions, neurosis, psychosis, or other issues. The socially useful individual finds meaningfulness within society and is socially connected to others.

Adler viewed a person as a *holistic* system and also as a piece of the larger system, developing from birth to living in a family, to culture, community, and the world. Goals are set within the context of the subjective meaning of experiences. A person thinks, feels, and acts in relation to goals and works toward meeting certain life tasks with an aggressive drive that serves "as the superordinate force . . . for the confluence of drives" (Milliren et al., 2007, p. 135). That drive is a person's reaction to other basic drives, such as the drive for food or love. The need for love is present from childhood and is related to family as well as social and cultural relationships. If a person's drive and needs are met, he or she focuses on the subjective interconnected and holistic view of others and the world (Ansbacher & Ansbacher, 1959). If denied, the person will seek attention and may turn inward in a narcissistic way. In cases of posttraumatic stress disorder and trauma that result in symptoms such as nightmares, Hjertaas (2013) applied the idea of holism further as representing various components that work together to form the whole "and that dysfunction in one of these components can therefore affect the whole and cause a reshifting of its operation" (p. 193).

Adler believed that a *goal orientation* includes lifestyle goals as well as immediate goals. Emotions stir the drive to reach a goal. He viewed emotions as two types: conjunctive and disjunctive. Conjunctive emotions allow a person to stay connected through love, empathy, or joy. Disjunctive emotions create problems of anger, hate, or fear. Unity of lifestyle allows a person to choose emotions and achieve immediate or lifestyle goals. Goals are influenced by hereditary and social factors as well as one's creative power and subjective perspectives. Milliren et al. (2007) said, "Emotions are not something that control the individual; rather, the individual learns to use emotions to pursue goals" (pp. 141–142).

Phase 2

During the second phase, from 1912 to 1916, Adler developed a framework for understanding inferiority feelings and how to interpret those feelings as generators of striving toward the future. This was the time when Hans Vaihinger's *The Philosophy of "As If"* (cited in Ansbacher & Ansbacher, 1959) was published, which greatly influenced Adler's concept of *fictional goal.* Vaihinger believed that a fictional goal was the ultimate truth that was always beyond a person's interpretation; therefore, partial or biased truths needed to be created as fictions used in life. A person reacts *as if* understanding the world and *as if* everything seen and experienced in the world influences his or her reactions and behaviors in the present. Fictions direct a person in the present to overcome inferiority feelings and motivate him or her toward the future. Inferiority feelings do not have to restrict a person but rather can assist the person in understanding how they affect his or her decision making, such as career choices. When a person is aware of his or her guiding fictions, he or she can use them to help construct his or her career (Del Corso, Rehfuss, & Galvin, 2011). An example of a person's fiction might be that life is fair and work settings will reflect that fairness. This idea contradicts reality because not everything in life is fair, and bad things happen even at work; yet this fiction has value in everyday life.

In 1912, Adler published *The Neurotic Constitution* (Adler, 1912/1926), which included a shift in his theory (Ansbacher & Ansbacher, 1959). Based on Vaihinger's definition of fictions as unconscious ideas that have no counterpart in reality, Adler believed that people develop fictions as a protection to handle the social world. Fictions allow for a future-oriented momentum toward the goal of perfection rather than past-oriented responses to deficiencies. Creative power allows a person to choose how to react and interpret a situation in light of a subjective final goal or fictional goal. Coping with inferiority and striving for superiority are unique to a person (Ansbacher & Ansbacher, 1959). Adler viewed the unity of a person in terms of the fictional finalism. A person recognizes vulnerabilities and experiences inferiority when striving for superiority. Mistaken subjective interpretations result in flawed thoughts and behaviors. Through these experiences, a person's unique lifestyle is developed.

Phase 3

The third phase began in 1916 and lasted until Adler's death in 1937. He introduced the German term *Gemeinschaftsgefühl,* referring to social interest or community feeling, which became a central idea of Adler's theory (Ansbacher & Ansbacher, 1959). *Gemeinschaftsgefühl,* or social interest, is the term Adler used to define the goal of belonging to a social group and describes the innate drive of a person to cooperate and contribute with others for the common good (Adler, 1927/1946, 1964). According to Adler (1927/1946), a person strives to overcome inferiority feelings through self-improvement, self-completion, and contribution to others and society. Thus, a person is inextricably interconnected with others and the universe.

Social interest is linked to empathy with others and is an innate potential that allows cooperation and contribution in society (Ansbacher & Ansbacher, 1959). Adler believed that social interest is the essential gauge of mental health that involves a striving toward a healthy and socially active participation in life (Way, 1950). As social interest builds, inferiority feelings lessen. The three main *life tasks* of work, community, and love create the ties to society. Thus, an individual's uniqueness and how he or she exists in society are influenced by relationships. A person develops social interest in the absence of self-centeredness and neurosis.

Neurosis is a person's disheartened perspective about life in which he or she does not contribute to others (Adler, 1927/1946). A person who lacks community feeling becomes disconnected from society and the world. As a result, many of the problems experienced relate to anxiety and fear of rejection from society. Adler proposed that failures in life create neurosis, psychosis, and addictions as characterized by intense inferiority feelings that keep an individual unable to cope with life. Adler believed that a person is responsible for his or her own behaviors, thoughts, and feelings and that a person "can change" (Stein, 2008, p. 4).

Social Interest

A person is a social decision maker who acts in a manner consistent with the subjective meaning of his or her lifestyle (Ansbacher & Ansbacher, 1959; Way, 1950). In a person's lifestyle, the goal is to belong to a social group or culture. Shifron (2010) stressed that belonging is "the primary variable in clients' mental health" (p. 12). Cross-cultural considerations are inherent in Adler's theory, as demonstrated in his term *Gemeinschaftsgefühl.* Adler was ahead of his time in recognizing the destructive influence of some social-cultural interactions. He saw a person's culture as derived from the person's subjective view of life. Culture, then, is the person's interpretation of his or her social setting and is a strong indicator of how the person views self, lifestyle, and a community. From a cultural perspective, social interest includes factors such as helping, participating, cooperating, empathizing, and contributing. Culture "becomes a mediating factor that provides for the reconciliation of the individual's internal, personal, subjective environment or frame of reference with the demands of the person's external, common, objective environment or surroundings" (Milliren et al., 2007, p. 137). A balance exists with these factors in which a person can achieve goals in ways that also improve the welfare of others (see Sidebar 5.4).

Milliren et al. (2007) explained Adler's social interest "in terms of three different aspects: of its being an aptitude or innate potentiality; of its being a set of abilities; and of its being a generalized attitude" (p. 137). Innate aptitude influences the striving toward social interest and must be developed into abilities, especially cooperating and contributing to others so that a person can interconnect with others. Parents, guardians, and teachers should cultivate social interest in children from an early age by giving tasks that help them learn how to cooperate and contribute in society. In addition to teaching children, Adler suggested that parents and teachers role model how to be useful so that children can generalize their experiences to develop social interest and a sense of community with others. Adler believed that if social interest is supported and developed at the cognitive level, a person will acknowledge the necessary interdependence with others and recognize that the welfare of all is important (Way, 1950). At the affective level, a person will be empathic and have a deep belonging to others, and at the behavioral level, thoughts and feelings will be acted on, resulting in striving toward self-development as well as cooperating and contributing to others, resulting in a person's contribution to society.

The core of Adler's theory envisioned a person as capable of profound cooperation within society and striving for self-improvement and self-completion. Thus, the concept of social interest is both personally fulfilling and beneficial to others (Ansbacher & Ansbacher, 1959). At the same time, social interest denotes a recognition and acceptance of the interconnectedness of all people in positive ways. Greater personal development increases the ability to connect positively with others, learn from others, and develop the self. Social interest is a sense of community, a key to good mental health. If a child learns the importance of social interest, then he or she is more likely to continue to be mentally healthy throughout life. With a healthy foundation, a child is able to handle the life tasks of work and community. A discouraging family and unhealthy social setting create inferiority feelings, resulting in discouragement and an egocentric child.

Sidebar 5.4. Case Study

Bonita is a 30-year-old female who is married with no children. Her parents were both born in India and then moved to the United States, where they started their family. Bonita's parents arranged her marriage, which Bonita describes as lonely. She is employed full time and often spends her weekends visiting her parents, who live 3 hours away, while her husband remains at home.

1. What cross-cultural considerations are present?
2. How would you use social interest in your work with Bonita?

Adler also held strong beliefs about the importance of social equity and contributed to understanding of the marginalization of certain groups (Ferguson, 2001, 2003; Watts & Pietrzak, 2000). Adlerian theory had a role in inspiring individuals involved with the civil rights movement for racial equality. Adler regarded equality between groups as necessary for developing social interest in a community for *all* members to feel a sense of belonging (Ferguson, 2010). He believed in the importance of belonging in human existence and the impact of culture on the person. All of a person's interactions are calculated to connect the individual to the community. Adler's theory also included many concepts that can be applied to social justice issues in counseling. The emphasis on a person's subjective view of the world supports respect for an individual's values and culture. Adler believed in equality, civil rights, mutual respect, advancement of social values, and the importance of nurturing feelings of belonging in everyone.

APPLICATIONS

Overview

Overall, the Adlerian counseling process is designed to assist a client with growth. Adler proposed three phases of counseling: "(1) understanding the client; (2) explaining the client's behavior to him or her in a way that makes sense; and (3) strengthening social interest" (Milliren et al., 2007, p. 142). Dreikurs added a fourth phase in the first position of the four phases of building a relationship, resulting in four phases: relationship, investigation, interpretation, and reorientation (Abramson, 2007; Milliren et al., 2007, p. 142). Adlerian counselors' process of counseling varies widely based on Adler's basic assumption that each client is unique (see Sidebar 5.5).

According to Milliren et al. (2007), Adler's work was demonstrated in his case conceptualizations in two important works: *The Neurotic Constitution* (Adler, 1912/1926) and *The Practice and Theory of Individual Psychology* (Adler, 1924/1959). Actual examples of counseling interventions of Adler's therapeutic style are limited. Adler did not propose specific interventions because he believed that each client was unique. Counselor creativity and intuitiveness is imperative, and the array of intervention strategies is Adler's hallmark. Because of the client's uniqueness and Adler's creative approach, counselors need to read many of Adler's cases to familiarize themselves with the many applications from an experiential learning approach rather than explicit descrip-

Sidebar 5.5. Four Stages of the Counseling Process

The overall counseling process is designed to assist a client with growth.

1. *Relationship:* The focus is on building the therapeutic relationship.
2. *Investigation:* The therapist's focus is on understanding the client.
3. *Interpretation:* The therapist's focus is on explaining client behavior in a way that makes sense to the client.
4. *Reorientation:* The therapist's focus is on strengthening client social interest.

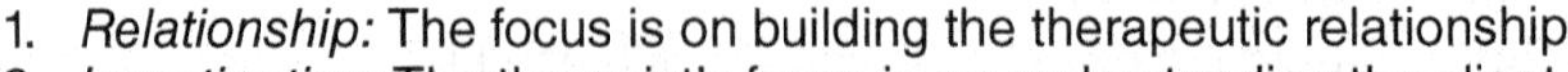

Adler did not propose specific interventions because of the uniqueness of each client. Instead, he emphasized counselor intuition and creativity.

tions of the process. An example of Adler's "indirect method of treatment" with a client with melancholia is presented below (adapted from Adler, 1964, pp. 25–26):

Adler: Only do what is agreeable to you.
Client: Nothing is agreeable.
Adler: (Later) Do not exert yourself to do what is disagreeable.
Client: (Finds Adler's response unusual and interesting, thus complies for a while.)
Adler: (Later he attempts a second rule.) It is much more difficult and I do not know if you can follow it. (He looks doubtfully at the client.)
Adler: If you could follow this second rule you would be cured in 14 days. It is to consider from time to time how you can give another person pleasure. It would soon enable you to sleep and would chase away all your sad thoughts. You would feel yourself to be useful and worthwhile.
Client: How can I give pleasure to others when I have none myself?
Adler: Perhaps you better train yourself a little thus: do not actually do anything to please anyone else, but just think out how you could do it.
Client: Oh, that is quite easy, it is what I have always done.
Adler: (Points out that this type of client is "dispensing favors to get the upper hand on others.")
Adler: Remember all the ideas you have in the night, and give me pleasure by telling them to me.
Client: I slept all night.

Goals of Counseling and Psychotherapy

The adaptability of Adler's theory is seen as one of its greatest strengths, and the emphasis on specific goal types can be beneficial when helping clients. Although the overall goal of counseling is encouraging social interest, clients may begin with wanting instant relief or possibly continuing what they are doing without feeling so uncomfortable. The goal of therapy is not necessarily fulfilling these expectations; rather, a counselor assists a client by distinguishing between life goals that account for the client's unique lifestyle and more immediate goals that account for everyday behaviors. The central aim of counseling is to help a client identify and understand mistaken beliefs about self, others, and life; make changes in those beliefs; and thus participate more fully in a social world.

The beginning process of goal setting assists a client in developing behaviors and beliefs characterized by actions that contribute to social interest (Abramson, 2007). A counselor works with a client toward being useful in life and developing a sense of belonging to society in terms of the client's perceptions of self and others and his or her lifestyle. A person who feels like a part of a community will have fewer inferiority feelings (Ferguson, 2003). In the beginning, a counselor helps a client develop a plan of what is wanted, how to plan to get what is wanted, what is stopping the attainment of goals, how mistaken beliefs and behaviors can be changed into constructive thoughts and actions, and how the use of strengths can help to achieve a synchronization of goals and provide for a healthy relationship between the client and counselor.

The Process of Change

Early in the counseling process, the counselor develops a relationship through empathy and encouragement. Encouragement is the most powerful intervention a counselor can provide for helping a client to transform beliefs and inspire courage to grow (Watts & Pietrzak, 2000). A client grows by gaining insight and using that insight to take steps that result in healthy relationships. Growth is not possible unless the client is willing to change his or her mistaken beliefs. A technique used to help a client recognize mistaken beliefs is *spitting in the client's soup,* which requires a counselor to point out certain unattractive behaviors of the client. Through the use of deliberate questions used by the counselor, the client makes a connection between the answer to the question and the problem. Once understanding occurs and a behavior is seen as unattractive, it is less likely to recur. Spitting in a client's soup, figuratively, helps the client to evaluate motivations for behaviors and any inferiority feelings as a result of the behaviors. A client may continue to behave in the same manner; however, the behavior becomes less attractive, making the client aware that he or she has the power to change behavior. Thus, Adlerian counseling rests in the counselor–client collaborative relationship of mutual respect to identify, explore, and evaluate mistaken beliefs and faulty assumptions within the client's lifestyle (Ferguson, 2003).

Adler saw confrontation as an important part of encouragement. Milliren et al. (2007) stated that "confrontation is frequently used as a way of holding the mistaken goals and beliefs up in front of the client, as with a mirror. Confrontation presents an opportunity . . . to make immediate change in beliefs, behaviors, or mood" (p. 145). It is followed by a reorientation of the client toward what will work. The main aim of counseling is to develop the client's sense of belonging and to empower the client to change behaviors and beliefs by increasing the client's self-awareness and modification of his or her life goals to accomplish change. Adler believed that assisting a discouraged client to function more effectively is an important part of the counseling process (Ferguson, 2003). Rather than focusing on major problems and mistakes, the counselor focuses on strengths while still addressing mistaken beliefs and behaviors.

The use of an Adlerian approach is also applicable to promoting change and growth in the context of counseling supervision. Bornsheuer-Boswell, Polonyi, and Watts (2013) proposed that supervisors use encouragement and "catching oneself" with counseling supervisees (p. 336). The authors viewed the encouragement of supervisees as a top priority in initial supervision sessions to facilitate an egalitarian and collaborative supervisory relationship, and the intervention of catching oneself helps supervisees monitor their behaviors that are not productive in a counseling relationship (e.g., countertransference), which can allow for more effective counseling.

Traditional Intervention Strategies

Lifestyle Analysis

A key function of the counselor is to make a comprehensive analysis of the client's lifestyle, which requires mutual trust and respect. The counselor gathers information through the use of questions about the client's lifestyle. Milliren et al. (2007) suggested the use of formal and informal assessment methods. In formal methods, information about the client's family, life goals, and beliefs is assessed. Assessment includes an exploration of the client's subjective perceptions of his or her family, including when the client was young. Informal analysis occurs throughout the counseling process. The counselor is able to get a perspective of the client's major areas of successes and failures and of the influences that have had a bearing on the client's family and social world. The following components are used in an analysis.

Family Constellation

The family constellation represents the client's understanding of the family and his or her ordinal place in the family (Adler, 1927/1946). Factors such as the number of siblings, nature of interpersonal family relationships, and cultural and familial values are all influenced by a client's observations of the interactional patterns within the family (see Sidebar 5.6).

Family Atmosphere and Values

The family atmosphere is the coming together of everyone in the family and subsequent patterns of communication within the family. Because the family is an interactive system, a key to assessing the family is asking each member what the family climate is like. The family values chosen depend on the unique family atmosphere, and parents are the role models for the values. Values play a significant role in a person's life. A client's values may be assessed by asking, "What did your parents believe was important in the family?"

Gender Roles in a Family

The family constellation and the relationships within the family affect gender-role expectations. Parents and siblings are role models for a child and affect how the child experiences and communicates in the world through his or her gender. Assessing gender roles includes exploring a client's evaluation of the conditions within the family related to birth order, the gender of siblings, and parental relationships. Family dynamics, including parenting styles and position in the family based on a child's gender, are several ways in which a counselor can view the role of a child in the family, but according to Milliren et al. (2007), "All of these are lifestyle patterns adopted by children to cope with the family situation" (p. 147).

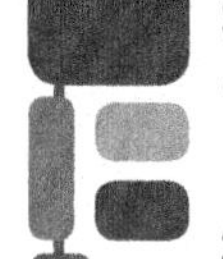

Sidebar 5.6. Intervention Strategies

1. *Lifestyle analysis:* What successes, failures, beliefs, and life goals does the client have?
2. *Family constellation:* How does the client describe his or her family? How does the client describe his or her relationship with parents and siblings?
3. *Family atmosphere and values:* What values and cultural experiences did the client experience in the family?
4. *Gender roles in a family:* What gender roles were modeled to the client by parents or siblings? How did gender influence family relationships?
5. *Early developmental experiences:* How do early developmental experiences affect the client's experience of life goals, lifestyle, and inferiority feelings?
6. *Encouragement:* What inferiority feelings does the client have, and in what ways can the therapist encourage the client to increase client social interest?

Early developmental Experiences

In addition to roles practiced in the family, early experiences are critical to a person's development and beliefs about his or her family and social settings, such as school or work. Early memories embody a client's beliefs about himself or herself and his or her social world that contain recollections of the client's inferiority feelings, life goals, and lifestyle.

Encouragement

Encouragement is one of the most powerful methods available for changing a client's beliefs and stimulating courage. It is central to all processes of Adlerian counseling (Watts & Pietrzak, 2000). The counselor must encourage the client by awakening his or her social interest. A counselor considers the relationship to be one between equals that is based on cooperation, trust, and respect. Encouragement helps to build rapport and maximizes the counselor–client relationship. It is used to assist a client in understanding dysfunctional behaviors and overcoming inferiority by generating alternatives and using strengths and resources. "Encouragement is often mistaken as praise, but praise is external control. Praise focuses on outcomes (doing well) . . . and is conditional. Encouragement focuses on effort or improvement rather than results" (Milliren et al., 2007, p. 149). By developing a relationship based on encouragement with the client, a counselor provides the basic form of social interest, which the client can then transfer to other relationships. Encouragement also can be found in Adler's approach to conceptualizing client problems: Clients do not need help with their problems; they seek help with how they are attempting to resolve their problems (Rasmussen & Johnson-Migalski, 2014).

Brief Intervention Strategies and Current Practices

The creative freedom inherent in Adlerian counseling demands a variety of strategies that suit the uniqueness of each client and capture the therapeutic opportunities the client presents with. When this freedom is limited via managed care or other restrictions, the Adlerian model can be flexible (Seligman, 2004). Specific techniques used at any one time depend on the counseling direction that is beneficial for a client. According to King and Shelley (2007), Adlerian therapy can be effective in the short term and long term. Though it is based on theory and philosophy, its methods can be understood and applied to prevention and growth. Recent approaches have applied a traditional Adlerian framework to trauma based in a holistic biopsychosocial view inclusive of "social embeddedness, holism, purposive behavior, and subjectivity and creativity" (Millar, 2013, p. 247). Henning (2013) reviewed Millar's (2013) Adlerian approach to trauma from a stage orientation framework. Other approaches use Adlerian theory when addressing posttraumatic stress disorder symptoms through a client's social connectedness and his or her lifestyle (Hjertaas, 2013).

Three examples of strategies founded in the original Adlerian theory and methods used by contemporary Adlerian practitioners include (a) Socratic questioning, (b) missing developmental experiences, and (c) play therapy with trauma. Socratic questioning leads a client to insight through a series of questions (Stein, 2008). It embodies the relationship of equals using an encouraging style. A counselor uses questions to gather information, clarify meaning, and verify feelings. More penetrating, leading questions uncover the deeper understanding of a client's private logic and goals. A counselor also explores both the short- and long-term consequences of a client's thinking, feeling, and acting. New ideas are generated, examined, and evaluated to help the client take steps toward a new direction. The results of this exploration are constantly reviewed and used to evaluate the impact of the client's new direction. The client is responsible for change. The role of the counselor is that of an assistant, not a superior expert.

Brief techniques can also be used as a strategy to assist clients with missed developmental experiences that are affecting their lives as adults. Some clients need additional, specific interventions to access or change thoughts and feelings. Stein (2008) suggested that guided and eidetic imagery, used in an Adlerian way, can lead to emotional breakthroughs with the client. Guided imagery can be used to access vivid symbolic mental pictures of significant situations involving chronic feelings of guilt and fear. This assists a client in meeting the needs of missed experiences from childhood and enables the client to work toward connecting with others.

The last strategy suggested by Morrison (2009) is the use of Adlerian play therapy, which can be used with traumatized children and family members. She noted that counselors can assist children who have been traumatized by disasters, abuse, or violence to investigate mistaken beliefs and establish a sense of social belonging. In addition to trauma counseling, Adlerian play therapy is one of the most practical and effective approaches to use when working with elementary school-age children (Taylor & Bratton, 2014) and can reduce disruptive behaviors in children of this age (Meany-Walen, Bratton, & Kottman, 2014).

Based on Adler's view of people, counselors should work with clients within clients' perceptions of their social and culture world. As noted by the American Counseling Association (ACA) and the Association for Multicultural Counseling and Development (AMCD), counselors should be culturally skilled in recognizing how culture colors counselors' views as well as clients' attitudes and beliefs about their world, including the many social aspects within a community based on social oppression, racism, elitism, and sexism. Counselors must also develop intervention strategies and techniques appropriate to each client's needs and his or her culture. As suggested by the ACA and AMCD as well as Lee's (2007) book *Counseling for Social Justice,* counselors should work toward understanding a client's unique subjective perceptions of the world based on the possibility of social exclusion, a process by which certain individuals and groups (i.e., individuals with disabilities; gays, lesbians, bisexuals, and transgender persons; women; certain ethnic and racial groups) are unable to access the social resources (e.g., housing, employment, health care, social engagement) that are available to others. These exclusions are unnecessarily and inappropriately imposed on people and limit a person from fully participating in society.

Clients With Serious Mental Health Issues

With the changes that have occurred in the 21st century, including the impact of managed care, the field of counseling has moved to include working from the medical model perspective (Seligman, 2004) along with its primary identification with the wellness model. A social constructionist viewpoint such as Adler's theory is one method counselors can use to incorporate the medical model with clients. Adler (1927/1946, 1924/1959) preferred the term *discour-*

aged as opposed to *pathological, mentally sick,* or the label *sickness* when referring to a person. He believed that disturbances or neuroses occur because of an exaggerated inferiority feeling or an insufficient feeling of community. Under these circumstances, a person may experience failure in situations that seem unattainable and become discouraged. When a person is discouraged, he or she first resorts to fictional means to mask—rather than overcome—inferiority feelings, attempting to bolster feelings of self. Eventually, views clash with reality and create difficulties in the person's social settings, which may lead to psychological disturbances. Symptoms such as anxiety, phobias, or depression were not Adler's main focus in understanding difficulties, but he did believe that a person's symptoms were important.

From an Adlerian viewpoint, three factors distinguish mild psychological disorders from severe disorders: (a) the depth of inferiority feelings, (b) a lack of feeling of community, and (c) the height of the final goal (Way, 1950). Adler preferred the perspective that the role of the counselor is not primarily to treat mental diseases but rather to discover the fictions in a client's lifestyle and thus lead a client to greater social interest. Even though Adler was not a proponent of diagnosis, today's managed care requires most counselors to use diagnoses and the *Diagnostic and Statistical Manual of Mental Disorders, Fifth Edition* (American Psychiatric Association, 2013). Seligman (2004) stated that individual psychology "seems most appropriate for people who are experiencing long-standing emotional difficulties and who are having difficulty developing self-confidence, mobilizing themselves, and finding a rewarding direction" (p. 196). Diagnoses that might suit individual psychology include behavior and relationship disorders of childhood and adolescence, adult depression or anxiety, and adult occupational problems. Seligman also noted that, with the push by managed care, counselors need to be flexible in using counseling skills and aligning techniques with a client's diagnosis as well as using a multidisciplinary focus to benefit clients. Seligman shared Adler's viewpoint that clients are unique in their social–cultural worlds, necessitating a match between counseling techniques and individual clients. As noted throughout this chapter, many would agree that Adler's theory is well matched with social justice issues such as the mental health concerns of marginalized or diverse individuals or groups of individuals. Adlerian counselors should seek to develop an awareness of social equality for all humans, with the sense that everyone has an equal right to be valued and respected. With the rise of social justice issues, cultural awareness, and sensitivity in counseling, the ACA and AMCD require that counselors move beyond the traditional theory orientation, as suggested by Adler, and also focus on education, prevention, and advocacy.

EVALUATION

Overview

The supporting research for Adler's theory and the limitations of assessing Adlerian concepts and techniques are described in this section. There are two major areas of limitations noted. A summary chart is provided. Finally, a case study is offered using Adlerian therapy.

Supporting Research

Adler's theory is one of the most simplistic and application-oriented theories available. As suggested by Adler (1964), the practical evidence of his theory is based on his case studies; many of his writings included excerpts from his studies. Milliren et al. (2007) noted that a limited number of empirical studies in the past were based on Adler's case studies or studies of individual psychology that were conducted by researchers who were not Adlerian practitioners. Empirical research on Adlerian theory began to evolve in the 1970s, as described in a 1983 summary report by Watkins (cited in Milliren et al., 2007) of 75 research studies published between 1970 to 1981 and Watkins's follow-up study in 1992 on 103 studies completed from 1982 to 1990. Watkins noted, during both of these periods, an increase in empirical research on Adler's theory; however, clinical trials were still very limited. In a recent narrative study, Mansager (2014) examined 15 individuals who completed an Adlerian certification program. He referred to a core foundation of Adler's theory when he said that participants' Adlerian "artistic ability" comes from "profound self-knowledge, creative spontaneity, rhetorical persuasiveness, and the courage to guess expansively" (p. 329).

Although there has been an increase in research on Adler's theory, there are still various viewpoints of the effectiveness of that research, specifically, criticism on how it was conducted or the many confounding variables present in the studies (Milliren et al., 2007). Extensive literature reviews have examined Adler's work on birth order, such as a review by Ernst and Angst (1983) on research published between 1946 and 1980, as well as Sulloway's (1995) meta-analytic review. More recent studies include Beck, Burnet, and Vosper (2006) on birth order and extraversion and Laird and Shelton (2008) on birth order and binge drinking. In addition, several assessment instruments have been developed, including Crandall's Social Interest Scale, Eckstein's Lifestyle Self-Assessment and Rule's Early Recollections Questionnaire. Also, various national and international organizations promote Adler's research—one such one is the Adler University (www.adler.edu).

Limitations

Although Adlerian counseling is viewed as a basic approach geared toward the layperson as well as the practitioner, some researchers and practitioners frequently criticize his theory for its lack of depth (Milliren et al., 2007). His theory has been considered as lacking a foundation that fully deals with the vast array of psychological issues that clients bring to counseling. Its assumptions have been seen as placing undue weight on concepts (such as birth order and early recollections) that are not always specific to human development. Some of the more general limitations of Adler's theory include the overwhelming number of concepts, the difficulty defining concepts, and the sole focus on the individual as the change agent. One of the most cited limitations of his theory is the lack of empirical evidence and comparative analysis. Managed care providers require counselors to use techniques with measurable outcomes, but few concepts in Adler's theory have been measured, or undergoing an experimental assessment of physical or behavioral variables that operate in terms of cause and effect. Adler's concepts are far from physical and behavioral, with inferiority feelings or social interest as examples of unquantifiable phenomena.

Summary Chart: Adlerian Theory

Human Nature

Individual psychology has a simplicity that lends to the theory's accessibility and comprehension. Adler viewed humans as possessing attributes that are purposeful, social, subjective, and interpretive in their approach to life. Adler considered personality, or lifestyle, to be established early in life. Birth order, family constellation, and early recollections are subjective interpretations in terms of lifestyle. A person's development is formed by lifestyle and is unique to the individual; thus, lifestyle is in agreement with thoughts, feelings, and actions.

Major Constructs

Individual psychology includes three central principles:

- *A goal orientation:* A central characteristic of Adlerian theory is striving toward a goal of superiority or success. Adler viewed people as imbued with an innate dynamic force, a striving that is intrinsic and involves a creative power.
- *Social interest:* A person is a unique individual and is part of the larger social system with an innate potential for coping with society, termed *social interest.* Unlike an instinct, social interest must be evoked and developed by a person. It is important to lifestyle, it is the criterion of mental health, and it influences the direction of the striving.
- *Holism:* A person is not internally divided or developed with conflicting forces; rather, Adler viewed the person as a whole organism in which all parts (thoughts, feelings, and behaviors) function cooperatively, even when different within a family, culture, community, and the world.

Goals

In a lifetime, a person will need to meet the three tasks of life: work, community, and love. A key goal in counseling is to assist clients with challenges when dealing with life tasks and cooperating and contributing to others and the world.

Change Process

Overall, Adlerian counseling focuses on helping a client identify and address mistaken thoughts and beliefs. There are four phases in which this process occurs: relationship, investigation, interpretation, and reorientation.

Interventions

Several traditional intervention strategies used by Adlerian counselors address a client's lifestyle through an analysis of birth order, family constellation, and lifestyle. Core interventions include lifestyle analysis, encouragement, and helping clients have the courage to deal with life and use their strengths to make changes in life.

Limitations

Although most would agree that Adlerian therapy is a simple approach and easily understood, many researchers criticize this theory because it is not empirically based.

THE CASE OF MARIA: AN ADLERIAN APPROACH

The three principles discussed in the beginning of this chapter—a goal orientation, social interest, and holism—are used to conceptualize this case and framed in the four phases of the counseling process: relationship, investigation, interpretation, and reorientation. During the first phase of Adlerian therapy, the counselor should establish an empathic, collaborative, and encouraging counselor–client relationship with Maria. Encouragement is one of the most important techniques the counselor will use to empower Maria to have the courage to make changes.

The investigation phase of the counseling process involves the counselor exploring Maria's subjective perceptions of her relationships, family, and lifestyle. A lifestyle analysis will assist in this process. The counselor will use open-ended questions to generate responses from Maria. In the initial analysis, Maria reports that she is a 32-year-old, Hispanic, single parent of two children and employed as a teacher. Although she excelled academically in college, has been a good teacher and mother, and has been involved in her family and community, Maria states that she is depressed, having crying spells and nightmares, not sleeping, having difficulty concentrating, having thoughts of suicide, and feeling lonely and frightened. She reports that her relationship with her family has become distant, and she is distancing herself from her friends and work relationships. This situation has left Maria feeling disconnected and socially isolated. When asked about her childhood, she states that her family was very close; however, as the oldest child in her family, she had many responsibilities within her Hispanic culture and was seen as a role model for her siblings while her parents ran the family business. As the oldest child, Maria reports being very dependable, hard working, and conscientious, which fits with Adler's characteristics of an oldest child. As a result of her childhood development, she is sensitive to her most recent challenges with her relationships and divorce.

Maria may have developed a discouraged lifestyle and may feel that she is not as competent as her family expects. The felt responsibilities of her role in her family are the roots of her inferiority feelings. Looking back on her childhood, Maria believes that her parents' requirement that she take care of her siblings was an indication of how much they loved her. Maria remembers an incident when she wanted to participate in a school activity but was told she needed to care for her siblings and was not able to attend the activity. After that experience, Maria always was responsible so her parents would love her. That thought continued into adulthood; however, when she married, she chose someone outside of her own culture, which resulted in divorce.

Based on information available in this case and consistent with other elements of Maria's story, Maria is discouraged and despondent about her lack of connectedness in her relationships with family and friends in her present lifestyle. Although her unconscious goal is to be free of all of the responsibilities she had in the past as a child, as well as the responsibilities she sees in her present life, Maria also needs to be connected to her family and friends. Maria reports of dreaming of "boxes and crates" that turn into "figures." Her dreams are a reflection of the challenges she is experiencing. As Adler suggested, dreams are expressions of one's lifestyle and thus are reflections of Maria's daytime feelings and the problems she is facing. The objects in her dreams represent all of the people in her life needing something from Maria and her feelings of being overwhelmed, lonely, and unable to connect socially. Just as Maria escaped to college and disobeyed her parents, she currently wants to escape again from all of her responsibilities.

In the interpretation phase, Maria appears to believe that others in her Hispanic culture need more than she is able to give. Her mistaken belief might be that she must be responsible for everyone or she will not be loved. This seems to be one theme that runs consistently through Maria's life, making her sensitive to her parents' and siblings' demands as well as her ex-husband's demeaning remarks about her profession, culture, and religion. As Adler would reflect in this situation, Maria's solution to her situation is to be depressed, fearful, overwhelmed, and unable to cope. Rather than setting limits with others when she should, Maria chooses to be depressed. Maria's private logic dictates that, in her family culture, ,she should be responsible for "everyone and everything." Her scheme of apperception sharply divides the need to be responsible from her need to take care of herself. Characteristics of the oldest child can be seen in Maria's relationships; she feels responsible for everyone. Maria's feeling of being overwhelmed is based on the responsibilities she mistakenly believes she must carry out to avoid losing the love of her parents and others. Maria's striving for superiority and lifestyle is expressed in her being a responsible daughter, mother, and teacher so that her parents and others will love her.

Through the use of Socratic questioning by her counselor, Maria could become aware of her need to take care of everyone and everything. As suggested by Stein (2008), a counselor's use of guided and eidetic images may elicit Maria's first recollections of being responsible for others when she was a child. After experiencing a gradual series of missing developmental experiences through these techniques, Maria can become open to having relationships without always having to care for others. She may then be willing to redirect her striving for connectedness into social interest that involves cooperation, and it is not always she who must contribute. She could work toward her goal of having more sharing and healthy relationships with family and friends.

During the reorientation phase, counseling with Maria will involve a lot of encouragement as well as confrontation based on a collaborative relationship. The counselor will reflect to Maria that she has a great deal of social interest as indicated by her history. Spitting in Maria's soup will be used to illuminate her mistaken belief that she is responsible for everyone. Maria will need to examine her own lifestyle through discussion and personal evaluation of clues embedded in her earliest recollections. In addition, the counselor will educate Maria that inferiority feelings are normal feelings that can be used as fuel for making changes in her life. The counselor will work with Maria to improve her self-confidence, self-esteem, and feelings of self-worth, at the same time encouraging Maria to have healthy boundaries in her lifestyle. Once she has been empowered to be aware of the choices she has made, Maria can then be empowered to make different choices. Her strengths include her strong family and cultural ties as well as her education and the ability to work and support herself and her children. Gradually, Maria can learn how much her "responsibility crusade" drove her life and what she missed, as a child and as an adult—warm, friendly contact with others without unlimited responsibility.

REFERENCES

Abramson, Z. (2007). Adlerian family and couples therapy. *Journal of Individual Psychology, 63*, 371–385.

Adler, A. (1917). *Study of organ inferiority and its psychical compensation* (S. E. Jelliffe, Trans.). New York, NY: Nervous and Mental Disease Publishing. (Original work published 1907)

Adler, A. (1926). *The neurotic constitution* (B. Glueck & J. Lind, Trans.). New York, NY: Dodd Mead. (Original work published 1912)

Adler, A. (1931). *What life could mean to you* (C. Brett, Trans.). Center City, MN: Hazelden.

Adler, A. (1946). *Understanding human nature* (W. B. Wolfe, Trans.). New York, NY: Greenberg. (Original work published 1927)

Adler, A. (1959). *The practice and theory of individual psychology* (P. Radin, Trans.). Patterson, NJ: Littlefield, Adams. (Original work published 1924)

Adler, A. (1964). *Problems of neurosis: A book of case histories* (P. Mairet, Ed.). New York, NY: Harper Torchbooks.

Adler, A., & Furtmüller, C. (1914). *Healing and education: Medical-educational papers of the Society for Individual Psychology.* Munich, Germany: Reinhart.

American Psychiatric Association. (2013). *Diagnostic and statistical manual of mental disorders* (5th ed.). Arlington, VA: Author.

Ansbacher, H. L., & Ansbacher, R. R. (1959). *The individual psychology of Alfred Adler: A systematic presentation in selections from his writings.* New York, NY: Basic Books.

Beck, E., Burnet, K. L., & Vosper, J. (2006). Birth-order effects of extraversion. *Personality and Individual Differences, 40*, 953–959.

Bornsheuer-Boswell, J. N., Polonyi, M. M., & Watts, R. E. (2013). Integrating Adlerian and integrated developmental model approaches to supervision of counseling trainees. *Journal of Individual Psychology, 69*(4), 328–343.

Clark, A. J., & Butler, C. M. (2012). Degree of activity: Relationship to early recollections and safeguarding tendencies. *Journal of Individual Psychology, 68*(2), 137–147.

Del Corso, J., Rehfuss, M. C., & Galvin, K. (2011). Striving to adapt: Addressing Adler's work task in the 21st century. *Journal of Individual Psychology, 67*(2), 88–106.

Ellenberger, H. (1970). *The discovery of the unconscious: The history and evolution of dynamic psychiatry.* New York, NY: Basic Books.

Ernst, C., & Angst, J. (1983). *Birth order: Its influence on personality.* Berlin, Germany: Springer.

Ferguson, E. D. (2001). Adler and Dreikurs: Cognitive–social dynamic innovators. *Journal of Individual Psychology, 57*, 324–341.

Ferguson, E. D. (2003). Social processes, personal goals, and their intertwining: Their importance in Adlerian theory and practice. *Journal of Individual Psychology, 49*, 136–144.

Ferguson, E. D. (2010). Adler's innovative contributions regarding the need to belong. *Journal of Individual Psychology, 66*(1), 1–7.

Henning, J. (2013). Working with survivors of traumatic life events: A response to Millar on the Adlerian approach. *Journal of Individual Psychology, 69*(3), 262–273.

Hjertaas, T. (2013). Toward an Adlerian perspective on trauma. *Journal of Individual Psychology, 69*(3), 186–200.

Hoffman, E. (1996). *The drive for self: Alfred Adler and the founding of individual psychology.* New York, NY: Addison-Wesley.

King, R. A., & Shelley, C. A. (2007). Community feeling and social interest: Adlerian parallels, synergy and differences with the field of community psychology. *Journal of Community and Applied Social Psychology, 18,* 96–107.

Laird, T. G., & Shelton, A. J. (2008). From an Adlerian perspective: Birth order, dependency, and binge drinking on a historically Black university campus. *Journal of Individual Psychology, 62,* 18–35.

Lee, C. (Ed.). (2007). *Counseling for social justice* (2nd ed.). Alexandria, VA: American Counseling Association.

Mansager, E. (2014). A narrative survey of classical Adlerian depth psychotherapist. *Journal of Individual Psychology, 70*(4), 323–331.

Meany-Walen, K. K., Bratton, S. C., & Kottman, T. (2014). Effects of Adlerian play therapy on reducing students' disruptive behaviors. *Journal of Counseling & Development, 92,* 47–56. doi:10.1002/j.1556-6676.2014.00129.x

Millar, A. (2013). Trauma therapy: An Adlerian perspective. *Journal of Individual Psychology, 69*(3), 245–261.

Milliren, A. P., Evans, T. D., & Newbauer, J. F. (2007). Adlerian theory. In D. Capuzzi & D. R. Gross (Eds.), *Counseling and psychotherapy: Theories and interventions* (4th ed., pp. 120–163). Upper Saddle River, NJ: Pearson.

Morrison, M. O. (2009). Adlerian play therapy with a traumatized boy. *Journal of Individual Psychology, 65,* 57–68.

Rasmussen, P. R., & Johnson-Migalski, L. (2014). Swimming upstream: Identifying and overcoming therapeutic challenges—Part 1. *Journal of Individual Psychology, 70*(3), 251–268.

Seligman, L. (2004). *Diagnosis and treatment planning in counseling* (3rd ed.). New York, NY: Kluwer Academic.

Shifron, R. (2010). Adler's need to belong as the key for mental health. *Journal of Individual Psychology, 66,* 10–29.

Stein, H. T. (2008). Adler's legacy: Past, present, and future. *Journal of Individual Psychology, 64,* 4–20.

Sulloway, F. J. (1995). Birth order and evolutionary psychology: A meta-analytic overview. *Psychological Inquiry, 6,* 75–80.

Taylor, D. D., & Bratton, S. C. (2014). Developmentally appropriate practice: Adlerian play therapy with preschool children. *Journal of Individual Psychology, 70*(3), 205–219.

Uytman, J. D. (1967). Alfred Adler. In P. Edwards (Ed.), *The encyclopedia of philosophy* (Vols. 1 & 2). New York, NY: Macmillan.

Watts, R. E., & Pietrzak, D. (2000). Adlerian "encouragement" and the therapeutic process of solution-focused brief therapy. *Journal of Counseling & Development, 78,* 442–448.

Way, L. (1950). *Adler's place in psychology.* London, England: Allen & Unwin.

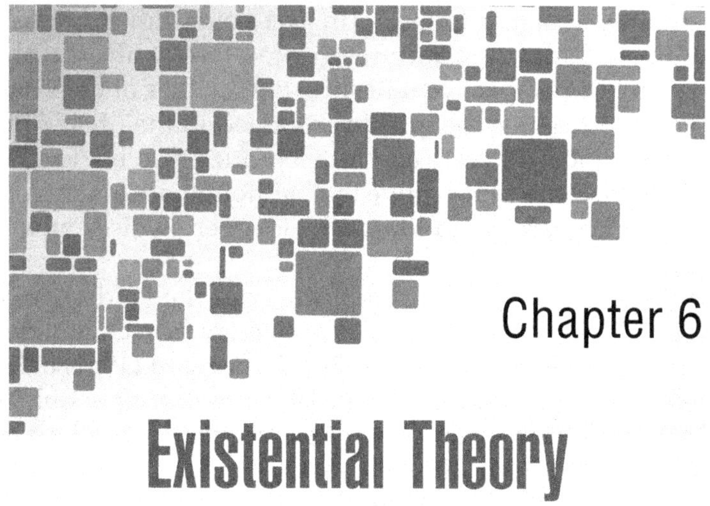

Chapter 6

Existential Theory

Mary Lou Bryant Frank

Psychological theories are an intimate reflection of the values and biases of the people creating the theories, and existential theory is no exception. Behaviorists trust that science and logic are the organizing factors for understanding. With equal passion, existentialists know that science is complementary to meaning, relationships are just as important as or more important than science, the subjective and individual experiences are as important as the objective and factual accounts, the journey is as important as the destination, and the process is as important as the product.

Unlike traditional psychoanalytic, cognitive, and behaviorist counselors and therapists, existentialists focus on an individual's unique experiences—the phenomenological world. Phenomenology focuses totally on the individual's perspective, setting aside the psychotherapist's point of view. By setting judgment aside, counselors can help hear clients' true desires and understand their situations as well as empower them to change.

The purpose of this chapter is to outline the background of existentialism, explore the developmental nature of the quest for meaning, examine the major constructs of existential thought, describe applications of the theory, summarize the evaluation of the theory, and explore the theory's limitations. The theory is summarized by an applied case analysis. It is hoped that, in the process of understanding a theory about existence, the reader will gain a deeper sense of self, an appreciation for what it means to live in awareness, and a heightened respect for the human struggle.

BACKGROUND

Existential Philosophers: A Groundwork for Theory

With roots in the philosophy of Søren Kierkegaard, Friedrich Nietzsche, and Jean-Paul Sartre, existentialism gained an audience within the post–World War II

European community, where it found form and voice. Emerging from the atrocities of war, vanquished idealism, and fragmented family life, the philosophers of this period developed a perspective reflecting the realities of their harsh existence. In the midst of the destruction, people reverberated to the philosophical writings of Nietzsche (1889) almost 50 years earlier: God must also be dead. These experiences with mortality led to a perspective that, although not always optimistic, was based in reality. Kierkegaard's and Martin Heidegger's voices moved existentialism to the forefront.

Kierkegaard (1944) pursued scientific truth from the landscape of the human perspective. People's problems were not knowledge or technology but a lack of passion, love, and commitment (May, 1983). Kierkegaard (1951) believed that unless science is examined in a relational context, truth is not possible. A subject can never be truly separated from the process of being observed and the context of that observation (Kierkegaard, 1951). It is no small wonder that Kierkegaard was not favored among the more objective, cognitive, and behavioral theorists influenced by René Descartes.

According to Descartes, an objective, rational examination was crucial to the development of empirical science. In the midst of a Cartesian mindset, Martin Heidegger (1949) built on Kierkegaard and developed an alternative paradigm. Heidegger's concept was antimechanistic and antitheoretic in a Cartesian sense. To Heidegger (1962), theories and humans were imperfect, and an objective reality was not reality at all. Existence is only understood in terms of being in the world (Binswanger, 1963) through subjective participation. Heidegger noted that, in striving for exactness, the Cartesian system was missing reality. Heidegger (1962) indicated that "scientific research is neither the sole nor the most immediate kind of this being that is possible" (p. 10). Heidegger's (1962) book *Being and Time* influenced many of the early existential psychotherapists.

Heidegger's notions of choice also influenced the existential psychologists (Barnett, 2009). It was Heidegger's (1962) idea that each choice represents the loss of an alternative. The past becomes important in terms of lost opportunities. People have the freedom to choose but must balance this with the responsibility for their choices. By encountering these limitations, people may experience nothingness, loneliness, guilt, and anxiety. These core concerns reverberated among authors around the world.

Approaches to Existentialism

Early Existential Theorists: European Roots

The early existential psychotherapists grew out of Europe. Ludwig Binswanger was arguably the first existential psychiatrist. Building on Heidegger's (1949) concept of being, Binswanger (1956) indicated that the most important focus was on the individual's unique experience. A colleague of Sigmund Freud, Binswanger shed the notion that the psychoanalytic theory provides the standard for normality. Binswanger (1956) focused most on what it meant to be human, and it was this focus in a therapeutic context that served as the basis for future existential psychotherapists.

Boss (1963) further developed existential psychotherapy. Influenced heavily by Heidegger's notion of subjectivity, Boss (1977) developed a therapeutic approach focused on human existence and the importance of understanding the human condition, or "being there" (*dasein*). Although he was influenced by Freud and Carl Jung, he did not agree with the analytical approach and set aside the psychosexual development and the preoccupation on psychopathology and instead focused on the human element. It is important to note that Boss's (1963) theory was also influenced by Asian philosophy in that the "being there" was seen as a being that was open and existing in the world context.

Victor Frankl was a key individual in the development of existential psychoanalysis and solidified the theory as it developed internationally. Like Boss (1977), Frankl (2004) survived the concentration camp experience of World War II. Frankl's contributions to existentialism are significant (Shaughnessy, 2014). Drawing on his experiences, Frankl (2004) detailed the psychotherapeutic approach called *logotherapy. Logotherapy* is derived from *logos*, "which focuses on the meaning of human existence as well as on man's search for such a meaning" (Frankl, 2004, p. 120). Frankl emphasized the freedom of the human spirit and the desire that people have to find meaning to define their lives.

Frankl (1984) helped to define the field of existentialism. Through work, developing values, and knowing suffering, people can find meaning and potentially happiness (Frankl, 1984). In his studies, Frankl indicated that, without meaning, people are likely to live hollow lives, seeking pleasure and ultimately finding suffering, depression, and hopelessness. To Frankl, psychological disorders were seen as a manifestation of a loss of meaning in one's life (see Sidebar 6.1).

Spirituality was also a discussion point of these early existential theorists. Whether an overt part of development or a natural aspect that could not be separated from one's own humanness, the spiritual part of existence was essential. Binswanger (1956), Boss (1977), and Frankl (1984) all noted that the spirit is an inseparable part of the self. When exploring questions of meaning and death, it is not uncommon for the answers individuals discover to be religious in scope and spiritual in substance.

Contemporary Existential Thought

For as many ways as meaning can be gleaned from life, there are diverse avenues to describe the process of finding meaning. Some contemporary existentialists, such as May (1992), Bugental (1999), and Schneider (2013), are more humanistic, whereas others are dynamic in their orientation (Montgomery, 2014; Yalom, 1980).

Sidebar 6.1. Self-Awareness: The Impact of Trauma and Finding Meaning

Today, if individuals survive a harrowing experience that is life altering, one almost expects to find posttraumatic stress behaviors. However, two important early psychologists, Boss (1963, 1977) and Frankl (1984), experienced the devastation of concentration camps amid the resultant death, loss, and inhumanity. Not only did they survive but they also both emerged with a philosophy of meaning. Frankl (1984) especially developed his theory in response to his experience, and his healing influenced his work. How have you come through stressful, if not traumatic, experiences? How long does it take you to return to your previous level of functioning? Do you ever get back to where you were? What made a difference for your healing?

Some existentialists later in life moved from one orientation to embrace a transpersonal focus, such as Frankl (2012), Bugental (1999), and Maslow (1998). All existentialists have held a deep respect for the individual struggle to be (see Sidebar 6.2).

Existential Counseling Therapies

Humanistic Existentialism

North American psychologists initially reflected the focus on universal concerns through humanism. The third force arose as an answer to the limitations of the Freudian and behaviorist approaches. Although Ludwig Binswanger (1956) started the existential approach in Switzerland, Rollo May brought existentialism to the United States (Hoffman, 2009). With humanism as the initial paradigm, the humanistic existential focus is on one's being a part of the world (Heidegger, 1962), a deep respect for relationships, and freedom as well as responsibility for one's choices. Yalom (2015), a preeminent existentialist of today, moved from embracing a psychoanalytic/psychodynamic orientation to existentialism with a decidedly humanistic tone:

> The most important thing I, or any other therapist, can do is offer an authentic healing relationship from which patients can draw whatever they need. We delude ourselves if we think that some specified action, be it an interpretation, suggestion, relabeling, or reassurance, is *the* healing factor. (p. 209, italics in the original)

The Existential-Humanistic Institute (www.ehinstitute.org) serves as a repository for important resources and solidifies the connection between the existential and humanistic approaches. Likewise, the blog "Authentic Engagement" fosters an ongoing conversation regarding existential humanistic relationships (https://www.psychologytoday.com/blog/authentic-engagement). Humanistic and existential theories are forever connected by their phenomenological approach to relationships and being in the world.

Psychoanalytic/Psychodynamic Existentialism

The wedding of psychoanalytic/psychodynamic and existential thought is not as impossible as might be imagined. Psychoanalytic existentialists (Frankl, 1984; Montgomery, 2014; Yalom, 2009), like their Freudian predecessors, also focus attention on the resolution of inner conflict and anxiety. Existentialism bridged with psychoanalytic and psychodynamic psychology suggests that there always is a tension that can only be partially eased through healthy relationships. Still, current

Sidebar 6.2. Self-Awareness: Experiencing the Existential Theorists

When you are reading about these existential theorists, go to YouTube and watch a video of them. Many current therapists (e.g., Frankl, May, Yalom) have videos available of them talking about their theories and their journeys. Although the URLs may change, the content continues to be posted. How is it, listening to them versus reading about their work? How does their personality reflect their theory? Has your opinion ever changed when you have gotten to hear someone versus reading about them? That can be true in counseling, when you read a person's intake interview written by another counselor and then begin seeing the client yourself.

psychotherapists (Montgomery, 2014) see the increasing evolution of psychoanalysis into the relationship-focused therapy of existentialism. Other existentialists (Schneider, 2014a) believe that the spiritual element cannot be ignored.

Transpersonal Existentialism

For some individuals, meaning emerges from the struggle with life and death, destiny and freedom, isolation and connection. Anticipated by Frankl (1984), transpersonal psychology and the religiously based counseling approaches offer a haven for people finding meaning in the spiritual realm. Frankl's belief was that the spiritual element could not be separated from the person and that it had to be addressed. Schneider (2014a), a contemporary existentialist, embraces spirituality as part of the existential struggle. The transpersonal existential approach perceives that a confrontation with death is an opportunity for the individual to rise above the given circumstances, to gain a broadened spiritual perspective, and to understand existential anxiety as unresolved spiritual understanding (Schneider, 2014b). The existential philosophers Buber (1970), Tillich (1980, 1987), and Ventimiglia (2008), as well as the psychological theorists Frankl (2012), May (1983), Maslow (1998), Bugental (Krug, 2009), and Wilber (2000), believed that, from an existential quest, a spiritual awakening could unfold. For some people, hope emerges from despair.

Beginning from a philosophical approach to the world, existentialism has evolved to a therapeutic orientation focused on helping people cope with the uncertainty and complex pressures of their lives. Recognizing the individual nature of experience in the context of an objective, scientifically oriented society, existential counselors and therapists validate the anxiety people experience. Following the path of early existential theorists, existentialism is grounded in realism, attempting to acknowledge the authentic human experience, the importance of meaning, the power of relating, and the reality of change.

HUMAN NATURE: A DEVELOPMENTAL PERSPECTIVE

The universality of existential concerns is evident in children as well as adults. May (1995) was the first to propose an existential developmental model moving from a naïve stage of innocence to adolescent rebellion and struggle, to conventional ascribing to tradition, and then finally moving beyond the ego and self-actualizing. People grow as they become more mindful and reflective of their present condition (Adams, 2013), regardless of the developmental time frame. An existential approach provides a perspective by which death can be understood at each stage of development (DeRobertis, 2011). Although existentialists do not propose discrete stages, finding meaning has developmental markers and implications.

Infants and children are continually growing and developing a sense of self. Caston (2015) indicated that even infancy needs to be included in an existential developmental perspective: "exploration of the pre-verbal months of an infant might be better served by appealing to . . . a phenomenological approach equipped to take into account the intersubjective feel of an infant's world" (p. 94). It is their struggle to be and to live in a world of relationships and death that illustrates that children are also not immune from the struggle to be human.

The anxiety produced by an awareness of nonexistence is overwhelming to all, especially children. Most children cope with death by denying it. Parents and adults, wanting to protect their children and themselves, foster denial in the first phase of life through avoidance and hesitant confrontation. "An existential therapist can help the child use his will in order to navigate the world in a way that affords him a greater sense of agency, efficacy and, perhaps most important of all, hope" (Quinn, 2010, p. 47).

Adolescents likewise encounter existential issues. Adams (2013) indicated that this period of development may be when existential concerns become most real. Whether or not they have the cognitive abilities to fully explore the existential landscape, adolescents encounter death. More important, the multiple developmental changes and pressures on teenagers can be magnified by isolation and depression (Brassai, Piko, & Steger, 2012). As adolescents struggle to find meaning, suicide can become a plausible response (Centers for Disease Control and Prevention, 2015), which explains the rise in suicide attempts and suicidal ideation at this age (see Sidebar 6.3). The existential crisis during adolescence can bring individuals to deeper questions about their lives and their desire to be.

Despite the contemporary focus on superficial, commercial fulfillment, many people still search for existential meaning as they reach critical developmental stages. Weaver (2009) suggested that midlife, with all its complexities and transitions, is a time for meeting existential issues through finding meaning, making peace with personal expectations, and developing an integrated self. In a study of older adults, Edwards and Milton (2014) found that existential variables and an existential relationship were important to those who were retired. Likewise, it was important to acknowledge thoughts of suicide when talking about the realities of aging, which entail death, loss, meaninglessness, guilt, and responsibility.

Gaining understanding about the meaning of life and taking responsibility for one's life serve to influence and inspire one's development. The process of development, whether spiritual or secular, is characterized by anxiety, of which death is the primary cause (Adams, 2013). Existential concerns permeate human existence, and the existential relationship is a vehicle to promote developmental growth (Longhurst, 2015). Even the terrorism and bullying that occur across so many fronts today are seen as manifestations of the existential struggle (Schneider, 2013). By facing their mortality in the various stages of their existence, people can shed the anxieties and depressions that can define them. Counselors with a personal and relational awareness of what it means to be can help a person learn how to make peace with dying and finally live.

A Worldview

Existential counseling is a viable therapy internationally as well as an approach that honors the value of all of the other therapeutic approaches. Today, 128 institu-

Sidebar 6.3. Self-Awareness: When Are We Ready to Talk About Existential Issues?

Are children and adolescents really ready for an existential approach to therapy? If you had experienced a death in the family as a child, do you think you would have been able to talk about the loss? Would you even have wanted to talk about it? How about an adolescent? Can children or adolescents conceptualize making sense of their lives or of finding meaning? These are research questions for existential counselors and psychotherapists, but they are larger questions for all of us who want to help young people live and have healthier lives. These questions can also help us face our existential anxieties.

tions offer training in existential therapy in 48 countries (Correia, Cooper, & Berdondini, 2014). The interest in existentialism is growing, as it uniquely acknowledges the usefulness of all psychotherapies.

Unique among theorists, existentialists have conceptualized their philosophy in context, developing a worldview of the value of each counseling approach. In a discipline that struggles with unity of thought, it is unique in being able to identify the utility of other approaches (Bugental, 1979). According to Bugental (1979), there are six levels of helping goals extending from behavioral change to spiritual development. Corresponding to the six goals are six different types of helping, from the use of behavioral counseling to a transpersonal approach to therapy. Likewise, the main constructs of existentialism illustrate the elements experienced by the client and counselor on the journey.

MAJOR CONSTRUCTS

To better understand existential counseling and psychotherapy, it is important to know the major tenets of this approach as well as the corollaries—the other sides of the existential struggle (see Table 6.1). Yalom (1980) detailed an approach focusing on death, freedom, isolation, and meaning. Others have since added to these, expounding on the importance of authenticity and existential relationships (e.g., Buber, 1970; May & Yalom, 2010; Yalom, 2015) and hazards inherent in the existential journey (Bugental, 1978; Longhurst, 2015).

Death/Life

Death, the ultimate truth, both in myth and in reality, is ever present. "If we are to live in that state of pure being, something within us must die. It's like when a caterpillar transforms into a butterfly. The caterpillar does not become a flying caterpillar; it morphs into a butterfly" (Dass, 2013, p. 6). How a person accepts this mortal condition—or finds ways to ignore it—determines his or her psychological well-being. Death is encountered in all counseling experiences. Relationships end, people lose opportunities, and people recognize their own mortality. Existential issues reflect grief that needs to be addressed and also involve letting go of the unhealthy or dysfunctional parts of the self in relation to oneself, others, and a potentially meaningless world.

Death anxiety can cause a person to connect as well as cause feelings of isolation and despair. A confrontation with death signals the rebirth of a more aware, alive, honest, and authentic being. Yalom (2015) detailed the many ways that death can enter the therapeutic space. According to an existential approach, most people experience tragedy, but in equal proportion, they experience joy (Maslow, 1998). Through finding meaning, people can transcend any pain of existence (Frankl, 1984; Gabriel, 2013; Yalom, 2015).

Freedom/Responsibility

Freedom comes after one's confrontation with one's inaccurate representation of oneself. It emerges only after one realizes that the world is an arbitrary construction of one's awareness. Hence, people can make each moment the way they wish and make their future different from any moments in their past. Frankl (1984) described how people may have tragedies in life, but it is their ability to choose their reactions that gives them freedom. Yang (2009) wrote, "To be

Table 6.1

Table of the Existential Journey

Major Constructs	Fear	Risk/Opportunity	What Happens in Existential Counseling?	Risk to the Counselor or Psychotherapst
Death/life	Is this is all there is? What can we do with what we have?	Confronting mortality means we have to face death and, by doing so, make peace with the idea that there is nothing beyond this life. We may emerge with peace whether there is or is not something after this life.	We can confront death as it occurs in all events and relationships, especially through the counseling relationship.	Dealing with death issues all of the time makes the counselor confront their own issues each session.
Freedom/responsibility	Can I do anything? I will be responsible for what I do or don't do.	Learning that although we are free and responsible, the risk is not doing anything.	We will be faced with the fear of risk in being and doing as it unfolds in the decision to be in counseling or not.	Awareness that we can only control our actions, not the success of the counseling process.
Isolation/connection	I am alone. Any connection is transitory and ultimately a loss, so why try?	Awareness that it is worth the risk to experience to connect, trust, and care about another person.	We will face being with another person who is a fellow traveler (Yalom, 2002) and who respects and understands the journey of life.	Willingness to go where there is no path, without techniques to keep us from the honesty of really being with another person.
Meaninglessness/meaning	Why me? Why not me? What can I learn from this experience?	Finding that life may inherently have no meaning, but it does not mean that we can't make sense of it for ourselves.	We confront the "why's" of existence. "He who has a why can bear any how." (Frankl, 1984, p. 126)	Confronting the meaning and substance of our life and work, daily.
Authenticity/vulnerability	Being known is a risk. So is being hurt (again).	Consciousness that we are flawed and can be hurt and acknowledging that our brokenness can connect us.	We can choose to remove the masks we wear, we can be free of fear of being known.	Losing the safety of being the "wise counselor" who directs the counseling process for the transparent fellow traveler. (Yalom, 2002)

aware of responsibility is to be aware of creating one's own self, destiny, life predicament, feelings, and if such be the case, one's own suffering" (p. 184). Søren Kierkegaard (1944) called it *angst.* Still, one's freedom to be is silhouetted by responsibility for one's actions.

Isolation/Connection

Isolation is a separation from oneself as much as from others. Isolation from one's true self keeps a person from connecting and contributing to the larger social order in more productive ways. Yalom (2015) indicated that to combat isolation, existentialism's focus on relationships promotes healing. Out of people's own fears, they erect walls to prohibit the connections they most desire. Although people are ultimately alone, they have the potential to connect and find meaning that can occur in the vehicle of the therapeutic relationship.

Meaning/Meaninglessness

As a key figure in the development of existential counseling, Frankl's (1984) focal point for existential psychotherapy was that, without meaning, people's lives were empty and meaningless. He believed that it was by finding meaning that people had reason to live. Longhurst (2015) also focused on the meaning that can come from an existential process. People transcend—that is, find meaning in their world—by fully being aware of themselves. Truly being oneself involves being more integrated inwardly and outwardly.

It is paradoxical that, as people become more open to their true feelings, they are better able to join with others and be one with the world. Through transcendence, they also become more capable. People are more aware of the potentialities in their lives and within themselves. Meaning is implicit in discovering oneself and in one's awareness that one is not alone.

Authenticity/Vulnerability

Existential authenticity is the context for freedom and responsibility. The authentic individual is not needy in relationships but is able to connect and benefit from them. Likewise, existential counselors respect the challenge of being authentic and vulnerable while they honor the client's power to change. Because of, not in spite of, the risks involved in being known, both the counselor and client can benefit.

Existential Relationships

The existential helping relationship is one of the most important aspects of the counseling or psychotherapy process (Longhurst, 2015). The client and counselor are but two travelers in life, with the counselor having skills in empathy as well as knowledge of the journey. Although skilled, the counselor or therapist is present with the client in a very real and immediate existence.

However, these only describe the functions, not the substance, of the existential encounter. The diversity and substance of relationships were probably best described by Buber (1970), who noted that relationships may be experienced at several levels or at a combination of different levels. Buber described some levels of relationships as superficial (e.g., I to it, I to I, it to it), others as lacking any individuality or objectivity (e.g., we to we) or compassion (us to them), and yet others as objectified and distanced (e.g., I to you). Buber's greatest contribution is the description of profound meeting, the core of the existential connection, the I-to-Thou relationship (Ventimiglia, 2008). The most potent form of help involves being present in a respectful, honoring encounter.

I-to-Thou relationships provide hope for genuine understanding and healing. Here, the counselor or therapist is a guide and a traveler on the same road (Bugental, 1978). At the I-to-Thou level, the whole person is considered and honored. May (1983) indicated that, for healing to take place, the counselor must enter the world of the client. The risk is that both the counselor and the client are changed in the I-to-Thou relationship (see Sidebar 6.4). May and Yalom (2010) indicated that "existential therapy always sees the patient in the center of his or her own culture" (p. 399). In a culture, in a world, where people are often lonely, existentialism offers hope.

Sidebar 6.4. Self-Awareness: Can You Risk Being Known?

Spinelli (2014) asked:

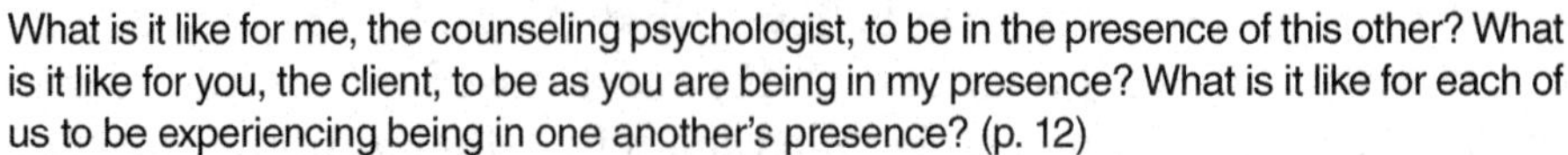

> What is it like for me, the counseling psychologist, to be in the presence of this other? What is it like for you, the client, to be as you are being in my presence? What is it like for each of us to be experiencing being in one another's presence? (p. 12)

How willing are you to be yourself in a counseling relationship? What are your vulnerabilities? What is behind your mask? What are you risking by being known?

In addition, connecting with others individually and within one's culture helps individuals to heal from their isolation (Henriksen, 2006; Maslow, 1954; Yalom, 2015). Accepting individuals means accepting, understanding, and respecting their culture (Gonzalez & Barden, 2014). It is the context of their world that concurrently shapes individuals' experiences of self and being. When studying Māori clients, Wilson (2013) found that using an existential cultural approach was an ethical and effective way to work with a non-Western or indigenous population. Culture becomes the vehicle by which an individual's sense of self and being are experienced. When people begin acknowledging and accepting their culture, they can start to reconnect with themselves and others.

Hazards on the Journey

The journey through the "dark night of the soul" can be difficult for counselors (Bugental, 1978, p. 77). They must protect themselves, their time, and their private lives. Making several such painful journeys with clients is bound to affect practitioners on a very personal level. "This journey was at times challenging and anxiety-provoking, but was also filled with warmth and humour despite meeting my own demons head-on, confronting my issues with helplessness, perfectionism, childhood difficulties and family dynamics" (Longhurst, 2015, p. 72).

Despite all of the concerns and warnings, it is valuable to take the risk to truly encounter another person. For the field, existentialism is an alternative and the only viewpoint with a coherent theory and approach that is sufficient in itself (Spinelli, 2014, p. 7) and that has a philosophical base (Tan & Wong, 2012). Life is a risk, death is inevitable, and people's experiences provide them with constant change. Existential therapy was developed to help clients and their counselors navigate this hazardous journey. When focusing on the impact of counseling, existentialism is uniquely successful in helping individuals find meaning (Vos, Craig, & Cooper, 2015).

APPLICATIONS

Overview

Although existential counseling or psychotherapy draws from a rich philosophical background, it continues to evolve to account for the changing world and context. Scholarship and research on existential psychotherapy shows continued development of goals, change, and techniques. The theoretical approach of existentialism has been adapted to the brief therapy mindset as well as to be applied to individuals with serious mental disorders. Existentialism remains a viable, popular, and international (Correia et al., 2014) model.

Goals of Counseling and Psychotherapy

As indicated by Frankl (1984), the existential goals of counseling or psychotherapy and change are "tragically optimistic" (p. 161). Frankl (1984) continued by indicating that existential counseling or psychotherapy has the following core principles: Suffering is a human achievement and accomplishment, guilt provides the opportunity to change oneself for the better, vulnerability motivates a person to become authentic, and life's unpredictability provides an individual with incentive to take responsible action. Rayner and Vitali's (2014) work focuses on the goals of existentialism, at the same time describing the existential therapeutic relationship that facilitates change and growth. Their research (Rayner & Vitali, 2014) provides a method by which change can be measured when using an existential paradigm.

The Process of Change

The notion of change and the counselor's ownership of creating change in the client has little meaning in existential counseling (Spinelli, 2014). Such relatedness-attuned existential views direct counseling toward an "uneasy form of therapeutic relationship that depends to a great extent upon the counseling psychologist's active willingness and ability to abdicate many of his or her most cherished assumptions; not least those of therapist-led and directed change" (Spinelli, 2014, p. 12). Although it is not directive, existential counseling still facilitates change.

Change is an important concept for the counselor and psychotherapist as well as for the person entering counseling. Change evolves from a client's willingness to participate in the interpersonal encounter by confronting loneliness, experiencing individuality, encountering true connection, and developing the inner strength to transcend the life situation (May, 1953). By reaching out to be with another person authentically, the client begins the process of transformation. Anxiety loses its power, and clients change as their fears melt into vital energy.

Through increased awareness of self and experience of the world, combined with their awareness of choice and responsibility, clients can experience their potential. Instead of a veiled existence, they are living consciously and responsibly; they are connecting with others as well as with aspects of themselves. Regardless, the catalyst for change is the relationship facilitating the development of awareness, acceptance, responsibility, vulnerability, and authenticity in the individual.

Traditional Intervention Strategies

Although supported by a fully developed theory and philosophy, techniques, when used, are complementary to the relationship and process. Existential theory is steeped in phenomenological awareness. Therefore, the following intervention strategies flow from a respectful understanding of the individual coming into counseling.

Telling the Story: Finding the Meaning of Myth

In his last work, May (1992) viewed myths as central to gaining existential meaning. "Myths represent the universality of the existential givens and the particularity of cultural responses to those givens" (Hoffman, 2009, p. 26). In the counseling or psychotherapy session, stories may help clients understand events in their lives. Clients also create their own stories as they detail their past and future. Only through sharing of the story can the healing begin, the meaning be understood, and the pain be honored and then released.

Presence

The existential relationship is the primary therapeutic intervention, and the client is an existential partner. Viewed with compassion, individuals are met with respect, and their uniqueness is valued (Nanda, 2013). The healing relationship is one of acceptance, openness, empathy, calmness, and mindfulness. As indicated by Landridge (2013), an existential counselor needs to be open minded and understand the individual's search to be.

Spillers (2007) stated that presence is also listening:

> Listening . . . focuses on the feeling tone beneath the words and invites response to the feeling tone rather than to surface content . . . the more clients feel understood and supported, the more fully they can participate in their own treatment. (p. 195)

For the psychotherapist, it is the skill in being there in the encounter with the client that is critical to the enterprise. The presence and the ability to be open to relate are central to every existential counseling experience.

Dream-Work

Counselors and therapists working in a variety of approaches have regarded dreams as the window to the unconscious. In existential counseling and therapy, dreams have an additional usefulness. Though unsettling, the existential experience of dreams moves the individual closer to authenticity. Dreams are like insight. They provide a reflection of people's inner feelings, hopes, and fears, and dreamers are compelled to discover their meaning.

Closure

Facing the end of the helping relationship is the final confrontation with reality. It is expected that additional issues will arise to delay the inevitable ending. The intervention of termination requires continued authenticity and willingness to be present. It is critical that the practitioner help the client by processing the ending of counseling or therapy and by creating a good parting, a "good" bye. The difficulty with and the honesty of this intervention is that it exposes the reality of ending that is present in all relationships (see Sidebar 6.5).

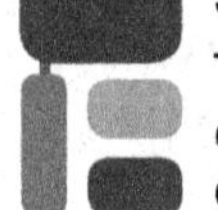

Sidebar 6.5. Self-Awareness: Dealing With Death in Therapy

The end of a counseling relationship affects both the client and the counselor. In an existential approach, the ending is even more significant because it signals the death of the counseling relationship. Death emerges another time for exploration. Epp (1998) indicated,

> When a counselor recognizes that he or she is as mortal as the client, all the faces of superficiality, superiority, and inequality . . . dissolve and counselor and client interact with equality and genuineness. When the counselor sees his or her own mortality in the client, I contend this is empathy. (p. 5)

How do you handle endings of relationships? A breakup? A death? How do you think your history and emotions might affect the ending of the counseling relationship?

Brief Intervention Strategies and Current Practices

Several authors have detailed approaches to existential issues within a brief counseling model (Bugental, 2008; Griffith & Gaby, 2014; Rayner & Vitali, 2014). In brief forms of existential psychotherapy, the limitations of the short-term approach may be beneficial (Lamont, 2012) and hasten the process by interjecting limited time together into the counseling space. Life does not always allow for long-term treatment of long-term problems, nor does it provide relationships without the possibility of death. Thus, brief existential approaches actually mirror the intense, transitory existence of life and the importance of the here and now in relationships.

Brief approaches to existential psychotherapy were detailed by Lamont (2012), Griffith and Gaby (2014), and Rayner and Vitali (2014). The benefit of the short-term model by Lamont is that it acknowledged that counseling, like life, is limited. Griffith and Gaby focused on hospitalized patients and showed how a brief, bedside existential approach can help individuals who have lost hope. A brief existential model and assessment system was developed and validated by Rayner and Vitali in the British Health Service. Although the process of finding meaning may not be completed, existentially focused brief counseling helps individuals find a map to begin the journey that mirrors reality. Existential counseling remains a viable model that conforms to the current health care approach and may even be improved by it (see Sidebar 6.6).

Current practices illustrate how existentialism is useful in numerous areas and with different populations. Existentialism is seen as a viable model from which to approach an understanding of sexuality (Milton, 2014). In health care (Gallien, Bian, Kim, & Tamanji, 2014), bioethics (Buffardi, 2013), and religion (Eick, 2014), existentialism is used because of its focus on meaning and death. Neuroscience (Griffith & Gaby, 2014) and the neuroscience of ethics (Frost & Lumia, 2012) expand on the usefulness of an existential approach in a medical setting. Existentialism is the focus of a number of international studies (Correia et al., 2014; Siew & Khong, 2013). Existential psychotherapy is also important in supervision (Spinelli, 2015) and with groups (Yalom, 2005). Strang, Henoch, Danielson, Browall, and Melin-Johansson's (2014) study illustrated that nurses working with dying patients were better able to talk about existential issues. Treatments including focusing on experiential and body work as well as terror management theory (Lewis, 2014) have benefitted from an existential framework. Existentialism has also been used in conjunction with other psychotherapy approaches: positive psychology (Bat-

Sidebar 6.6. Case Study: How to Proceed With Counseling?

Lonnie is a graduate student in counseling psychology. Although she is doing well in her program, she is starting to wonder whether she will be able to graduate. Her friends notice that she is no longer engaged with discussions and their activities. Lonnie decides to see an existential counselor. Because of the limitations of insurance, Lonnie has only 10 sessions. The first part of their counseling focuses on building the relationship and talking about what she needs to change. It becomes evident that Lonnie is worried and often overwhelmed about completing graduate school and getting an internship. What would be the first steps for the existential counselor? What could Lonnie expect in counseling? What would prove most challenging for you as the counselor? Have you ever had thoughts about being overwhelmed? What would help?

thyana, 2014), cognitive psychology (Gebler & Maercker, 2014; Hickes & Mirea, 2012), systems (Stolorow, 2013), and psychoanalytic/psychodynamic psychology (Montgomery, 2014). Although existentialism is not the primary theory adopted by many counselors and psychotherapists, it is having a considerable impact.

Clients With Serious Mental Health Issues

In *Diagnosis and Treatment Planning in Counseling* (Seligman, 2004), existential counseling was seen as more of a "treatment philosophy" (p. 212) than a model for treatment. The techniques listed were "life review and paradoxical intervention" (p. 212) focusing on helping people create meaning in their lives. It was described as a model for healthy, not seriously mentally ill, people.

In the years since Seligman's (2004) seminal book was published, existentialism has been applied to individuals with serious mental health concerns with some success. Still, at its heart, existential counseling remains focused on the relationship that facilitates an understanding of death, freedom, isolation, and meaninglessness (Yalom, 1980). However, the value of this attention has been seen as significant in treating individuals with numerous disorders. "The dilemmas, dysfunctions and disorders that individuals experience and bring to (existential) therapy are now to be considered as expressions and consequences of their grounding in relatedness" (Spinelli, 2014, pp. 8–9).

In Huguelet's (2014) review "The Contribution of Existential Phenomenology in the Recovery-Oriented Care of Patients With Severe Mental Disorders," an existential approach fits within "the recovery-oriented attitude . . . allowing patients to gain meaning and hope" (p. 346). The usefulness of existential psychotherapy with serious mental disorders is facilitated by "staying in a relational and interactive perspective, and by looking into patients' wishes instead of directing them into predetermined projects" (p. 364). Even with difficult-to-treat mental disorders, the existential therapeutic approach offers a perspective missing from other approaches and uniquely fits the newer wellness and recovery-oriented mindset.

In the book *A Concise Introduction to Existential Counselling*, Adams (2013) reviewed all of the mental illnesses that have benefitted from existential psychotherapy. The five main areas were anxiety, depression, addictions, trauma, and loss. In each case, symptoms were seen through an existential lens. Anxiety was seen as positive and normal because it is an indication of life and possibility. Addiction was viewed as only one option out of many that are available (Adams, 2013). Adams also noted that depression signals fears of one's own death and the finite time one has, just as trauma is a sign that life is uncertain. In the midst of psychological pain, existential counseling provides a trusting, honest, healing relationship.

Depression is a natural reaction to existential despair, and several studies reflect the fact that existential counseling not only addresses the life concerns but also provides an understanding of the symptoms. Gonzalez and Barden (2014) used a combination of culture and existential counseling to help survivors of breast cancer who had both anxiety and depression. The authors found that the existential interventions helped people cope and lessened depressive symptoms. Chen and Wang (2013) found that existential issues were predictive of depression in a student population. Morgan (2013) found the importance of using an existential approach to treat a depressed geriatric population. Varelius (2014) looked at how existential distress may be sufficient to consider assisted suicide in individuals who are dying. Hirsch, Webb, and Kaslow (2014) focused on suicide and the impact of religious and existential well-being and found that these factors were important when understanding suicidal thoughts and handling stress. Existential counseling can help individuals as they find meaning in life.

Another difficult-to-treat population that has responded successfully to an existential analytical approach is people with addictions (Kemp & Butler, 2014). "Addiction only serves to further alienate addicts from themselves and those around them. . . . So the addict seeks love, but finds hate" (pp. 257–258). It is through understanding addictions from an existential perspective (Kemp, 2013) that people can better understand the truth of the addiction as well as the honest relationships addicts seek.

EVALUATION

Overview

Unfortunately, existentialists tend to be congruent. The theory that focuses on existence over essence is more centered on theory, counseling or psychotherapy, and relationships than on generating testable hypotheses, developing succinct research designs, and advancing theories through scientific analysis (Landridge, 2013). Still, it is clear from the studies listed here that research and scale development continue to be important in the field of existential counseling.

Supporting Research

A number of studies have sought to understand the efficacy of existential psychotherapy. A meta-analysis (Vos, Cooper, Correia, & Craig, 2015) examined various forms of existential therapies for their ability to help clients address issues of meaning and anxiety about death. The research on meaning-based existential therapies was found to be the most impactful of the existential approaches. In another review of existential counseling, it was found that despite the small number of studies, "some clients may significantly benefit from certain types of existential therapy . . . particularly, clients in boundary situations in life-such as experiencing health crises" (Vos, Cooper, et al., 2015, p. 59).

Counseling outcome research continues to provide feedback on the existential model. In a recent study (Leibert & Dunne-Bryant, 2015), the main predictors of client change and positive outcomes of therapy were existential interventions of "client expectancy and the therapeutic alliance" (p. 233). Likewise, a lack of meaning in life has been found to be associated with more psychopathology (i.e., depression), and the parallel finding is that individuals find meaning with existential counseling (Volkert, Schulz, Brüutt, & Andreas, 2014). Existential concerns continue to be seen as key elements needed by individuals with depression and other disorders. Case studies of individuals with advanced cancer (Hall, Goddard, Martin, Opio, & Speck, 2013) found that dignity therapy, a combination of existential and psychosocial support, was helpful.

The need for increased research has led to the development of existential scales that can spawn more existential research. In "Systematic Review of Existential Anxiety Instruments" (Van Bruggen, Vos, Westerhof, Bohlmeijer, & Glas, 2015), it was found that 78 instruments have been developed, with five of them focused on existential anxiety. In this study, the Existential Anxiety Questionnaire assessed existential anxiety across the dimensions of "death, meaninglessness, and guilt" (p. 193). Although this scale was seen as the strongest and most researched, it does not measure all concerns (i.e., death, freedom, isolation, meaninglessness) and continues, like all existing scales, to need more work on content validity. The comprehensive review provides a good starting point for future research.

Several scales focus on assessing existential concepts. The Core Goal Attainment Form was used to illustrate how an assessment tool could be used in counseling as well as to validate goal attainment using an existential approach (Rayner & Vitali, 2014). In this research, individuals in counseling were able to meet their top two goals, validating the hope they had going into psychotherapy. Allan and Shearer (2012) developed the Scale for Existential Thinking, which was validated for construct validity on existential variables (i.e., meaning in life). The Life Orientation Scale was developed "to measure the meaning-mindset" in existential research (Wong, 2012, p. 1).

Addressing each research challenge, assessment must remain focused on the subjectively human person by using case study as well as qualitative and quantitative methodologies. It is a paradox. Existential research by definition needs a human focus. "Though research on effective psychotherapy continually shows that the most important factor determining outcome is the therapeutic relationship, the texture, the creation and the evolution of this relationship are rarely a focus of training in graduate programs" (Yalom, 2015, p. 205). Assessing existential counseling or psychotherapy can at first seem like trying to measure the counseling progress with a yardstick, knowing that the progress is neither linear nor unidimensional.

Limitations

Although existentialism may be used with a wide spectrum of concerns, it requires individuals to face their fears, anxieties, and responsibilities and to realize that change is a lifelong process. An existential approach also focuses on the interpersonal nature of counseling and psychotherapy and provides the client with insight through the therapeutic relationship. Individuals who avoid contact with others will find this approach intrusive. Nevertheless, not being provided with specific direction and solutions to their problems may be unsettling to those clients who want a more prescriptive, albeit dispassionate, approach.

Existentialists have been building research validating their approach, but the unscripted nature of the existential journey does not easily lend itself to the scientific process of measurement. In medicine, counseling, and related health care fields, existential concerns are being discussed and studied in outcome, developmental, meta-analysis, case study, and applied research. Existentialists would seem to be vulnerable in a battle of science but in actuality are becoming woven into the fabric of the healing process.

Summary Chart: Existential Theory

Human Nature

Existential theory is realistically optimistic about human nature. Humans can transcend their situation. In existential counseling, people have the freedom to choose and also have responsibility for their choices.

Major Constructs

Existentialism addresses several constructs within a culture and context: confronting fears of death, understanding isolation, confronting a meaningless existence, overcoming anxiety, accepting freedom of choice, knowing one's responsibility, and living authentically.

Goals

The goals of existential counseling and psychotherapy are to confront anxieties about the givens of existence; be authentic; and gain meaning from common, everyday endeavors and pain. Clients transform through courageous and subtle encounters with aspects of their humanness and through the interpersonal relationship with the counselor or therapist.

Change Process

Change evolves from a client's willingness to participate in the interpersonal encounter by confronting loneliness, experiencing individuality, encountering true connection, being responsible for choices, and developing the inner strength to transcend the life situation.

Interventions

Interventions in existential counseling and psychotherapy include understanding the client's world, sharing existence in the moment, fostering a centered awareness of being, encouraging self-responsibility, working with dreams, confronting existential anxiety, and learning from the counseling relationship.

Limitations

Existential theory uses a subjective lens through which to understand a world that has been focused on objectivity. Existential theory, which bases healing on the therapeutic encounter, may seem unfocused and lacking any specific techniques or plan. Growth occurring from this relationship may seem shallow and fleeting.

THE CASE OF MARIA: AN EXISTENTIAL APPROACH

Case Analysis

Maria's presenting concerns reflect an existential struggle with death, isolation, responsibility/freedom, and meaninglessness. From her early separation when attending college to her present situation as a single parent, Maria has been isolated from her culture and family. The more she wanted refuge in her family and culture, the more she was shamed by those she sought. Confronting a loss of identity, Maria experiences existential isolation. Her marriage never answered her search for self. She was forced to survive abuse, isolation, and shame. Other than her children, the focus of her reason for existence, Maria has lost her identity and sense of self in the world. Even the freedom to date and get back into "circulation" provides traumatic memories from her marriage and responsibility for the choices she has made. She was forced to survive abuse, isolation, and shame alone.

The potential loss of her role as a parent and her job teaching seems to have intensified the nightmares as well as her declining ability to maintain herself, her relationships, and her children. Maria coped in the past by creating meaning in and through others (e.g., a new family, teaching, and her children). However, her choices have brought her pain and abuse and have left her alone with responsibilities she feels unable to manage. Her brittle existence is crumbling with the fear of losing her independence. Maria's cultural ties have diminished as her family of origin has turned away from her. Organized religion referred her for help but did not save her. In facing her life without culture and with pressures to create a new meaning from her broken past, Maria, as in her dreams, has no escape, and that is terrifying.

Treatment/Intervention Plan

Maria's desire to work on these issues is paramount. Her current depression and hopelessness are paralyzing. A medication consult may be necessary if her depression does not abate and/or her suicidal ideation increases. Her current defense of withdrawal is not working, and she entered counseling expressing appreciation for an appointment and was early for it. She seems to be motivated to change.

The first phase of treatment is to develop a therapeutic relationship and understand Maria and her situation. Because Maria has been victimized by her culture and the majority culture, developing trust and groundwork for an honest I-to-Thou relationship is important. It is important to discuss her culture and the impact of any cultural or gender differences that exist between Maria and the counselor. A referral can be more easily made at this point. Next, it is important to hear her story of her current pain and help her reframe the paradigm for a cure. In the past, she sought to find herself through others, but now Maria will become instrumental in helping herself gain power in her life situation.

Her withdrawal has occurred over several years and has been a reaction to external pressures threatening her relationship with her children and her own integrity. Maria has developed a pattern of relating through others that was enforced by her culture. It became the only sanctuary in a world without meaning or direction.

By meeting her fears of loss (i.e., death) and engulfment and encountering the aspects of herself that are frightening (i.e., dreams), she will sense all that she has encountered and survived. Maria will also develop a stronger sense of herself and her responsibility for making her own choices. By continuing to flee or withdraw from anxiety-provoking situations (i.e., her teaching job), Maria avoids being and living.

The counselor is providing a context of relating to others that will help Maria to learn that her sanctuary (e.g., escaping through depression, living through others, and looking to others for her answers) only perpetuates her anxiety. Developing trust in the counselor and then trust in herself will help her in other relationships. At some point, group counseling will also help her understand that she is not alone in her struggle. By facing her insecurities, Maria will gain a sense of inner strength, awareness, and individuality. By taking responsibility, she can realize the freedom she has to be herself and the meaning in what is ahead for her life.

REFERENCES

Adams, M. (2013). *A concise introduction to existential counselling*. London, England: Sage.

Allan, B., & Shearer, C. B. (2012). The scale for existential thinking. *International Journal of Transpersonal Studies, 31*(1), 21–37.

Barnett, L. (2009). *When death enters the therapeutic space: Existential perspectives in psychotherapy and counseling*. New York, NY: Routledge.

Batthyana, A. (Ed.). (2014). *Meaning in positive and existential psychology.* New York, NY: Springer.

Binswanger, L. (1956). Existential analysis and psychotherapy. In E. Fromm-Reichmann & J. L. Moreno (Eds.), *Progress in psychotherapy* (pp. 144–168). New York, NY: Basic Books.

Binswanger, L. (1963). *Being in the world* (J. Needleyan, Trans.). New York, NY: Basic Books.

Boss, M. (1963). *Psychoanalysis and daseinsanalysis.* New York, NY: Basic Books.

Boss, M. (1977). *Existential foundations of medicine and psychology.* New York, NY: Aronson.

Brassai, L., Piko, B., & Steger, M. (2012). Existential attitudes and Eastern European adolescents' problem and health behaviors. *The Psychological Record, 62,* 719–734.

Buber, M. (1970). *I and thou* (W. Kaufmann, Trans.). New York, NY: Scribner's.

Buffardi, G. (2013). Bioethics in psychiatry: An existential contribution. *Existential Analysis, 24*(1), 19–36.

Bugental, J. (1978). *Psychotherapy and process: The fundamentals of an existential humanistic approach.* Reading, MA: Addison-Wesley.

Bugental, J. (1979). *The search for existential identity.* San Francisco, CA: Jossey-Bass.

Bugental, J. (1999). *Psychotherapy isn't what you think: Bringing the psychotherapeutic engagement into the living moment.* Phoenix, AZ: Aeig, Tucker & Theisen.

Bugental, J. (2008). Preliminary sketches for a short-term existential–humanistic therapy. In K. Schneider (Ed.), *Existential integrative therapy* (pp. 165–167). New York, NY: Routledge.

Caston, S. (2015). What does the existential phenomenological approach have to offer the current understanding of the pre-verbal months of an infant? *Existential Analysis, 26*(1), 94–102.

Centers for Disease Control and Prevention. (2015). *Suicide prevention: Youth suicide.* Retrieved from http://www.cdc.gov/violenceprevention/suicide/youth_suicide.html

Chen, J., & Wang, D. (2013). Relationship between existential anxiety and depression. *Chinese Journal of Clinical Psychology, 21,* 443–445.

Correia, E., Cooper, M., & Berdondini, L. (2014). The worldwide distribution and characteristics of existential counsellors and psychotherapists. *Existential Analysis, 25*(2), 321–337.

Dass, R. (2013). *Polishing the mirror.* Boulder, CO: Sounds True.

DeRobertis, E. (2011). Existential-humanistic and dynamic systems approaches to child development in mutual encounter. *The Humanistic Psychologist, 39,* 3–23.

Edwards, W., & Milton, M. (2014). Retirement therapy? Older people's experiences of existential therapy relating to their transition to retirement. *Counselling Psychology Review, 29*(2), 43–53.

Eick, C. (2014). Beginning the journey of informal counseling from a theistic existential approach. *Existential Analysis, 25*(2), 313–320.

Epp, L. (1998). The courage to be an existential counselor. *Journal of Mental Health Counseling, 20,* 1–12.

Frankl, V. (1984). *Man's search for meaning.* New York, NY: Washington Square Press.

Frankl, V. (2004). *On the theory and therapy of mental disorders: An introduction to logotherapy and existential analysis.* New York, NY: Brunner-Routledge.

Frankl, V. (2012). The unconditioned human. *Journal of Judaism & Civilization, 9,* 80–94.

Frost, C. J., & Lumia, A. R. (2012). The ethics of neuroscience and the neuroscience of ethics: A phenomenological-existential approach. *Science and Engineering Ethics, 18,* 457–474.

Gabriel, G. (2013). Roads of freedom: An existential phenomenological approach to psychotherapy journey. *Existential Analysis, 24*(1), 95–106.

Gallien, T., Bian, H., Kim, J., & Tamanji, E. (2014). Existential well-being and health. *Journal of Health Studies, 29*(4), 309–317.

Gebler, F., & Maercker, A. (2014). Effects of including an existential perspective in a cognitive-behavioral group program for chronic pain: A clinical trial with 6 months follow-up. *Humanistic Psychologist, 42,* 155–171.

Gonzalez, J., & Barden, S. (2014). Existential counseling as a vehicle to support Latina breast cancer survivors. *Counseling and Values, 59,* 49–64.

Griffith, J., & Gaby, L. (2014). *Brief psychotherapy at the bedside: Existential neuroscience to mobilize assertive coping.* Retrieved from http://www.psychiatrictimes.com/special-reports/brief-psychotherapy-bedside-existential-neuroscience-mobilize-assertive-coping

Hall, S., Goddard, C., Martin, P., Opio, D., & Speck, P. (2013). Exploring the impact of dignity therapy on distressed patients with advanced cancer: Three case studies. *Psycho-Oncology, 22,* 1748–1752.

Heidegger, M. (1949). *Existence and being.* South Bend, IN: Regnery.

Heidegger, M. (1962). *Being and time.* New York, NY: Harper & Row.

Henriksen, R. (2006). Multicultural counselor preparation: A transformational pedagogy. *Journal of Humanistic Counseling, Education and Development, 45,* 173–185.

Hickes, M., & Mirea, D. (2012). Cognitive behavioural therapy and existential-phenomenological psychotherapy: Rival paradigms or fertile ground for therapeutic synthesis. *Existential Analysis, 23*(1), 15–30.

Hirsch, J., Webb, J., & Kaslow, N. (2014). Daily hassles and suicide ideation in African-American female suicide attempters: Moderating effect of spiritual well-being. *Mental Health, Religion, and Culture, 17,* 529–541.

Hoffman, L. (2009). Introduction to existential psychology in a cross-cultural context: An East–West dialogue. In L. Hoffman, M. Yang, F. Kaklauskas, & A. Chan (Eds.), *Existential psychology East–West* (pp. 1–68). Colorado Springs, CO: University of the Rockies.

Huguelet, P. (2014). The contribution of existential phenomenology in the recovery-oriented care of patients with severe mental disorders. *Journal of Medicine and Philosophy, 39,* 346–367.

Kemp, R. (2013). Rock bottom as an event of truth. *Existential Analysis, 24*(1), 104–116.

Kemp, R., & Butler, A. (2014). Love, hate and the emergence of self in addiction recovery. *Existential Analysis, 25*(2), 257–268.

Kierkegaard, S. (1944). *The concept of dread* (W. Lowrie, Trans.). Princeton, NJ: Princeton University Press.

Kierkegaard, S. (1951). *A Kierkegaard anthology* (R. Bretall, Ed.). Princeton, NJ: Princeton University Press.

Krug, O. (2009). James Bugental and Irvin Yalom: Two masters of existential therapy cultivate presence in the therapeutic encounter. *Journal of Humanistic Psychology, 49,* 329–354.

Lamont, N. (2012). The end in sight: Engaging with an existential understanding of time when working in time-limited practice. *Existential Analysis, 23*(1), 89–100.

Landridge, D. (2013). *Existential counseling and psychotherapy.* London, England: Sage.

Leibert, T., & Dunne-Bryant, A. (2015). Do common factors account for counseling outcome? *Journal of Counseling & Development, 93,* 225–235.

Lewis, A. (2014). Terror management theory applied clinically: Implications for existential integrative psychotherapy. *Death Studies, 38,* 412–417.

Longhurst, L. (2015). A life worth living. *Counselling Psychology Review, 30*(1), 64–80.

Maslow, A. (1954). *Motivation and personality.* New York, NY: Harper & Row.

Maslow, A. (1998). *Toward a psychology of being* (3rd ed.). New York, NY: Wiley.

May, R. (1953). *Man's search for himself.* New York, NY: Dell.

May, R. (1983). *The discovery of being.* New York, NY: Norton.

May, R. (1992). *The cry for myth.* New York, NY: Delta.

May, R. (1995). *The courage to create.* New York, NY: Norton.

May, R., & Yalom, I. (2010). Existential psychotherapy. In R. Corsini & D. Wedding (Eds.), *Current psychotherapies* (4th ed., pp. 363–402). Itasca, IL: Peacock.

Milton, M. (2014). Sexuality: Where existential thought and counselling psychology practice come together. *Counselling Psychology Review, 29*(2), 15–24.

Montgomery, M. (2014). Love and hate: Existentialism and psychoanalysis. *Existential Analysis, 25*(2), 244–256.

Morgan, J. H. (2013). Late-life depression and the counseling agenda. *International Journal of Psychological Research, 6*(1), 94–101.

Nanda, J. (2013). Mindful relationships. *Sexual & Relationship Therapy, 28,* 120–131.

Nietzsche, F. (1889). *Twilight of the idols* (W. Kaufmann, Trans.). New York, NY: Viking.

Quinn, F. (2010). The right to choose: Existential-phenomenological psychotherapy with primary school-aged children. *Counselling Psychology Review, 25*(1), 41–48.

Rayner, M., & Vitali, D. (2014). CORE blimey! Existential therapy scores GOALS! *Existential Analysis, 25*(2), 296–312.

Schneider, K. J. (2013). *The polarized mind: Why it's killing us and what we can do about it.* Colorado Springs, CO: University Professor Press.

Schneider, K. J. (2014a). The case for existential (spiritual) psychotherapy. *Journal of Contemporary Psychotherapy, 45*(1), 21–24. doi:10.1007/s10879-014-9278-8

Schneider, K. J. (2014b). Enchanted agnosticism, awe, and existential-integrative therapy. *Spirituality in Clinical Practice, 1*(1), 71–73.

Seligman, L. (2004). *Diagnosis and treatment planning in counseling* (3rd ed.). New York, NY: Kluwer.

Shaughnessy, M. F. (2014). The holocaust, logotherapy, and Victor E. Frankl. *Journal of Social Sciences, 3*(1), 241–246.

Siew, B., & Khong, L. (2013). Being a therapist: Contributions of Heidegger's philosophy and the Buddha's teachings to psychotherapy. *The Humanistic Psychologist, 41,* 231–246.

Spillers, C. (2007). An existential framework for understanding counseling needs of clients. *American Journal of Speech-Language Pathology, 16,* 191–197.

Spinelli, E. (2014). An existential challenge to some dominant perspectives in the practice of contemporary counselling psychology. *Counseling Psychology Review, 29*(2), 7–14.

Spinelli, E. (2015). On existential supervision. *Existential Analysis, 26*(1), 168–178.

Stolorow, R. D. (2013). Intersubjective systems theory: A phenomenological-contextualist psychoanalytic perspective. *Psychoanalytic Dialogues, 23,* 383–389.

Strang, S., Henoch, I., Danielson, E., Browall, M., & Melin-Johansson, C. (2014). Communication about existential issues with patients close to death. *Psycho-Oncology, 23,* 562–568.

Tan, S., & Wong, T. (2012). Existential therapy: Empirical evidence and clinical applications from a Christian perspective. *Journal of Psychology & Christianity, 31*(3), 272–277.

Tillich, P. (1980). *The courage to be.* New Haven, CT: Yale University Press.

Tillich, P. (1987). *Paul Tillich: Theologian of the boundaries* (M. Taylor, Ed.). San Francisco, CA: Collins.

Van Bruggen, V., Vos, J., Westerhof, G., Bohlmeijer, E., & Glas, G. (2015). Systematic review of existential anxiety instruments. *Journal of Humanistic Psychology, 55*(2), 173–201.

Varelius, J. (2014). On the relevance of an argument as regards the role of existential suffering and the end-of-life context. *Journal of Medical Ethics, 40*(2), 114–116.

Ventimiglia, G. (2008). Martin Buber, God, and psychoanalysis. *Psychoanalytic Inquiry, 28,* 612–621.

Volkert, J., Schulz, H., Brüutt, A. L., & Andreas, S. (2014). Meaning in life: Relationship to clinical diagnosis and psychotherapy outcome. *Journal of Clinical Psychology, 70,* 528–535.

Vos, J., Cooper, M., Correia, E., & Craig, M. (2015). Existential therapies: A review of their scientific foundations and efficacy. *Journal of the Society for Existential Analysis, 26*(1), 49–69.

Vos, J., Craig, M., & Cooper, M. (2015). Existential therapies: A meta-analysis of their effects on psychological outcomes. *Journal of Consulting and Clinical Psychology, 83*(1), 115–128.

Weaver, Y. (2009). Mid-life: A time of crisis or new possibilities? *Existential Analysis, 20*(1), 69–78.

Wilber, K. (2000). *Integral psychology: Consciousness, spirit, psychology, therapy.* Boston, MA: Shambhala.

Wilson, P. (2013). Existential counseling and psychotherapy and Māori clients. *Asia Pacific Journal of Counseling and Psychotherapy,* 4(2), 137–146.

Wong, T. P. (2012). The meaning mindset: Measurement and implications. *International Journal of Psychology and Psychotherapy,* 4(1), 1–3.

Yalom, I. (1980). *Existential psychotherapy.* New York, NY: Basic Books.

Yalom, I. (2002). *The gift of therapy.* New York, NY: HarperCollins.

Yalom, I. (2005). *The theory and practice of group psychotherapy* (5th ed.). New York, NY: Basic Books.

Yalom, I. (2009). *Staring at the sun: Overcoming the terror of death.* San Francisco, CA: Jossey-Bass.

Yalom, I. (2015). *Creatures of a day: And other tales of psychotherapy.* New York, NY: Basic Books.

Yang, M. (2009). Existential themes in the parables of Jesus. In L. Hoffman, M. Yang, M. Kaklauskas, & A. Chan (Eds.), *Existential psychology East–West* (pp. 177–196). Colorado Springs, CO: University of the Rockies.

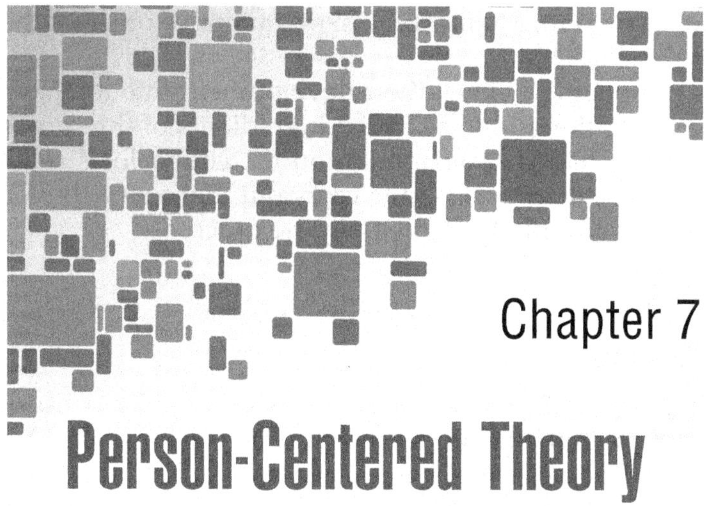

Chapter 7

Person-Centered Theory

Richard J. Hazler

The person-centered theory of Carl R. Rogers remains one of the most popular in the fields of psychology, counseling, and education. Rogers's perceptions of people and of how a supportive environment can assist in their development have had an immense impact on a wide variety of professions and on parenting. This approach was a major deviation from the psychoanalytic and behavioral models for working with people that were predominant in the early part of the 20th century.

Person-centered theory offered a new way of looking at people and their development, as well as how people can be helped to change. From this frame of reference, people were viewed as fully in charge of their lives and inherently motivated to improve themselves. The responsibility for personal behaviors and the choice to change them were seen as belonging fully to the individual. Here was a way to view and deal with human beings that did not rely on other people (counselors, psychologists, parents, teachers, etc.) as the primary directors of change. People could now control their own change if the right conditions were offered.

Rogers saw all individuals as having inherent qualities that made growth possible; attempting to change basic personality characteristics or behaviors was not necessary. He believed that people saw the world from their own unique perspective, which is referred to as a *phenomenological perspective.* It was further assumed that no matter what that phenomenological view of the world was, all people were continually attempting to actualize their best and most productive selves. This positive and optimistic view is often challenged by those who call attention to the unlimited opportunities to observe people as they think and act in ways that are harmful to themselves and others. However, Rogers believed that these thoughts and actions were primarily reflections of a distorted view of oneself and the world, distortions caused by trying to meet the expectations of others rather than trying to actualize one's own self.

The origins of Rogers's beliefs, their development into a major helping process, and an examination of the essential ingredients of that process serve as a foundation for this chapter. Information on the counselor's role in providing interventions and the methods used to carry out that role will then provide the practical base for beginning to implement the process.

BACKGROUND

Carl R. Rogers

Rogers was born in 1902 into a morally and religiously conservative family that was devoted to their children and committed to the concept of hard work. Dancing, watching movies, smoking, drinking, and anything that vaguely suggested sexual interest were clearly forbidden, although little was said about them. The family was able to convey its directions in subtle ways that were generally unspoken but nevertheless very clear to everyone.

Rogers had few friends and spent most of his time working, thinking, and reading. His early lifestyle caused him to pay close attention to his personalized experience of the world. In later years, this concept would become better known as a phenomenological approach to counseling.

Young Rogers's family moved to a farm, when he was 12, where he spent much of his time studying the varieties of insects and animals that were now available to him. This scientific approach to life, emphasizing work, scientific study, experimentation, and evaluation, would later set Rogers apart from other theorists: He was the first to intentionally and creatively subject therapeutic processes to rigorous scientific study. Those interested in his theories often overlook this aspect of his work, but it was a major contribution to the development of professionalism in counseling and psychotherapy (see Sidebar 7.1).

Sidebar 7.1. Rogers Struggles to Find Self-Worth

How does a person find self-worth as separate from parental directions?

The answer is that people struggle with their parents and with themselves. Carl Rogers was no different. He left home to study agriculture in college but later turned to religious studies and eventually to clinical psychology as he became more interested in people, beliefs, and values. His religious beliefs, like those of his parents, were strong. However, the more he studied and discussed the issues, the more his views diverged from his parents.' A 6-month trip to China as part of the World Student Christian Federation Conference encouraged his change to a more liberal viewpoint.

Explaining these changes to his parents was extremely difficult and often disappointing for all concerned, but Rogers reported great growth in his intellectual and emotional independence from these open confrontations. Later reflection on these times led Rogers to recognize that these were the times when he was learning to pay more attention to his own organismic valuing system and taking large steps toward overcoming the conditions of worth that had directed much of his life. The experience left him much more confident in himself as his belief and his ability to deal with difficult situations came more into congruence.

This idea that individuals can and must rely on themselves for direction and strength was to become another major emphasis in his theory as well as in his own life.

Theory Background

Rogers's first major work, *Counseling and Psychotherapy* (1942), came from his counseling with children and was a reaction to the highly diagnostic, probing, and analytic work that had gone unsupported by scientific research. He presented nondirective counseling along with a clear call for a more scientific approach to research on both his nondirective and other, more directive techniques. A decade of practice and research led to *Client-Centered Therapy* (Rogers, 1951), which expanded his concepts and renamed his approach. This new emphasis changed the role of the counselor from one who only reflected the content of client statements to one who also identified underlying emotions in client expressions. This revised helping relationship expanded the dimensions of accurate empathy.

Rogers's research efforts increased and broadened as he tested ideas on hospitalized schizophrenic patients rather than on the primarily normal population he had been serving. His research confirmed the view that the conditions present in the helping relationship did have a significant effect on both the progress of counseling and the outcomes for clients (Rogers, 1967). Work with client populations ranging from normal to extremely disturbed encouraged him to broaden the use of the person-centered concept to include all people.

During the 1970s and 1980s, Rogers focused more on groups than on individuals. He was a major promoter of personal growth groups, in which individuals worked together for the purpose of self-actualizing growth rather than toward a more limited goal of overcoming psychological illnesses (Rogers, 1970). Another group adaptation saw Rogers, in the last years of his life, using person-centered concepts in a group process format to deal with critical world conflicts. He traveled to areas with major social conflicts, such as Central America (Thayer, 1987), South Africa (Rogers & Sanford, 1987), Northern Ireland (Rogers, 1987b), and the Soviet Union (Rogers, 1987a), to run growth groups with leaders and nonleaders who had fought but never tried to understand each other. His accounts of these encounters make it clear that a person-centered orientation can be promoted in highly diverse individuals and cultures.

The enduring nature of Rogers's work can be seen in every current article or book that examines person-centered theory. The therapeutic conditions and related ways to implement them are emphasized early in virtually every counseling and counseling-related program (Kirschenbaum, 2009). Even as issues of managed care and medical treatment models have greatly increased the emphasis on diagnosis, symptom elimination, problem behavior reduction, and time-limited treatment, which are not conducive to a person-centered approach, all of these approaches begin with relationship development based on the importance of Rogers's core conditions (Miles & Mezzich, 2011).

Even such technique-driven counseling or therapy models as cognitive behavior therapy (Gilbert & Lehay, 2007), family counseling (Bott, 2001; Snyder, 2002), applied behavior analysis (Holburn & Vietze, 2000), and brief therapy (Presbury, Echterling, & McKee, 2002) are emphasizing the essential nature of these conditions for counseling success. Modern counselors may find few books with *person-centered counseling* in the title, but they will see the ideas deeply ingrained in virtually every modern approach to counseling.

HUMAN NATURE: A DEVELOPMENTAL PERSPECTIVE

The person-centered approach to counseling implies great confidence in each client. This confidence arises out of a belief that all people have an innate motivation to grow in positive ways and the ability to carry out such a growth process. This highly positive view of human nature varies widely from other theories that view human nature as evil, negative, or a nonissue. Such a positive view of human nature is essential for the person-centered practitioner because of the major responsibilities clients are given in the direction, style, and content of the helping relationship. The person-centered perception of people is based on five key beliefs: (a) People are trustworthy, (b) people innately move toward self-actualization and health, (c) people have the inner resources to move themselves in positive directions, (d) people respond to their uniquely perceived world (phenomenological world), and (e) there is an interaction of these key beliefs with external factors. The activation of these characteristics within a person's external environment brings about the most desirable aspects of development.

People Are Trustworthy

Person-centered counselors must treat their clients as trustworthy, or there will be no reason to allow them to take a leadership role in the helping relationship. From this point of view, words such as *good, constructive,* and *trustworthy* describe natural characteristics of human beings, although people also appear to take actions that demonstrate the opposite. These inappropriate actions are taken when the individual's ideal view of self does not match the real self. Individuals use defensive thoughts and actions to protect themselves from having to observe that they are not living the lives they believe they should. Such actions are not deceitful as much as they are direct actions based on conflicting perceptions of the person's world. All individuals are trying to improve and to act in the world as they see it in as honorable a manner as possible (see Sidebar 7.2).

Movement Toward Actualization

Human beings are viewed by the person-centered theorist as always striving to obtain the best of themselves. They seek any means to develop all of their abilities "in ways that maintain or enhance the organism" (Rogers, 1959, p. 196). This is the

Sidebar 7.2. Jessica Needs a Trusting Relationship

Jessica is a teenage girl who skips school and has been arrested for the fourth time for shoplifting. Many in society would judge her to be a bad person or one who cannot be trusted. She recognizes that lack of trust and consequently has little motivation to seek a productive relationship with key people in her life. Only when she is convinced of a meaningful relationship with a person who is genuine and trusting will she feel free to explore herself fully. That is the counselor's job.

A major part of that relationship will be a counselor who can convey genuine trust through words and actions. Anything less than this trusting relationship will simply confirm to Jessica that this is just another person who will not trust her and therefore is not to be trusted. The result will leave her with little motivation to work on her own potential for trustworthiness in a therapeutic relationship. Only when such trust can be established will the girl be able to accept the potential for an honest, respectful, and risk-taking relationship.

driving force in the positive development of the individual. It clearly moves the individual away from control by others based on conditions of worth and toward autonomy and self-control. This energy source is also seen as potentially more influential than environmental factors such as socioeconomic status, hunger, and danger, which also affect how the individual perceives or seeks self-actualization (see Sidebar 7.3).

Inner Resources

The actualizing tendency provides the motive for positive development in people, but do people have the capacity to carry out this motivation? Person-centered theory presumes that they do (Rogers, 1961). Holding the belief that people have the motivation to grow in positive directions does not automatically mean that counselors will also have confidence in a client's ability to follow through on that motivation. The person-centered approach emphasizes a belief that this ability to grow in positive directions is available to everyone.

The most heartwarming stories told throughout the ages have demonstrated how people can overcome tremendous odds to change and become people that others and they themselves like better. These same stories also cause people to question why it happens for some and not others. Person-centered theory emphasizes that these potential differences in degree of change and overcoming obstacles are not as important as people's beliefs that they can accomplish great things on the journey to improve. In many ways, it presumes two fairly well-accepted principles of human dynamics. The first principle states that people always have much more potential than they use most of the time. The second emphasizes that it is in the journey, more than a preconceived goal, where success is found. Person-centered counselors who can demonstrate confidence in these principles allow the necessary creative ideas and actions to emerge that can expand potential options and encourage growth in new directions.

An Individually Perceived World

The person-centered view recognizes that events will be perceived differently by different people (Rogers, 1961). Two countries go to war, two adults argue, two

Sidebar 7.3. Providing Jessica With Support for Gaining Self-Direction

Jessica's behaviors would likely be seen by many as inadequate self-control and little desire to overcome her problems. The result is that individuals and society would probably seek even more control over her and pressure her to change in ways deemed appropriate by others.

The person-centered counselor will take a very different approach with Jessica. This approach will recognize that Jessica is actually working toward making the most out of herself in the best ways she can and that she will continue to seek ways to gain control of her situation. Her actions are really reactions to people and a world that sees only her socially unacceptable behaviors and not the person trying to make the best of a situation that she cannot seem to control.

If the counselor provides a safe environment, Jessica can lower her defenses and antisocial behaviors without fear of being denounced for failures. When this occurs, she can be expected to continue pursuing self-actualization in productive and more socially viable ways.

cultures clash, and relationships often break down because each side perceives what is right to be different from the other side's perception. The person-centered view of these examples is that no two people perceive the world in exactly the same way and that this explains much of the variation seen in the preceding concepts. Cultural background and environmental factors play major parts in how individuals' perceptions and reactions can become very different (see Sidebar 7.4).

To effectively meet the American Counseling Association and the Association for Multicultural Counseling and Development's Multicultural Counseling Competencies, person-centered practitioners must pay particular attention to understanding themselves, be genuine in their interactions, continually work to better understand the world experienced by their clients, and apply active empathy in the broadest sense with clients.

Interaction With External Factors

A person-centered view of human development gives attention to external factors that affect psychological development in addition to critical internal forces. Even as infants, people make choices that induce growth and actualize potential. They reject experiences that are perceived as contrary to their well-being. However, these naturalistic ways of making choices become confused as the developing person recognizes that other individuals may provide or withhold love on the basis of how well the person assimilates values and behaviors set by others. This recognition can move individuals away from using their own best judgment to make personal choices and promote an alternative method that requires taking actions based on the presumed desires of others. The two theoretical concepts used to explain this aspect of development are unconditional positive regard and conditions of worth (Rogers, 1959).

Individuals who are given and can recognize unconditional positive regard feel permitted to continue trusting themselves as positive human beings. The belief is conveyed that although they will make errors of judgment and behavior, they will also strive to examine themselves continually and be able to take actions for their own improvement because they are good people. Recognizing unconditional positive regard helps individuals continue seeking their own development with the confidence that they will become increasingly effective human beings.

There are often strings attached to the regard and love offered by others. Children faced with this type of conditional love based only on what a significant other

Sidebar 7.4. The World Perceived by Jessica

Jessica does not perceive the world as the safe and kind place that another person who is successful in school, feels culturally accepted, and has a comfortable family life does. Neither will she perceive it as the rational world that the counselor is likely to perceive. Jessica may be stealing in part because of her different perceptions of the world.

Stealing is what Jessica sees as one of the very few options truly available to her that can help feed herself, her mother, and her infant sister. Jessica has no reason to believe the person or counselor who tries to tell her how it really is, because it is not that way for her at this time. The person-centered counselor must recognize these differently perceived worlds, work unendingly to understand Jessica's, and seek to help her grow through her personally perceived world rather than through the world as it is perceived by the counselor, parents, or other adults.

wants and in which differences or mistakes are unacceptable can come to believe that they are only good, loved, cared for, fed, or valued if they do just as others believe they should. These conditions of worth pressure developing persons to devalue their inherent potential for choice making and growth. They begin looking for directions and decisions that originate from external sources instead of trusting their more natural internal reactions to their environment. This process moves individuals away from confidence in their ability to run their own lives and toward seeking validation based on the lives and expectations of others.

MAJOR CONSTRUCTS

The core of person-centered theory is a set of beliefs about people and relationships rather than a series of programmable verbal and behavioral techniques. Counselors interested in implementing this theory must look first to themselves and their perceptions of others rather than to what specific behaviors ought to be performed. This is a challenging task, particularly for new practitioners seeking to know what they should do and to what extent they do things well. The following essential person-centered theory constructs must be perceived clearly before a practitioner can implement a person-centered approach effectively.

No Two People See the World Exactly Alike

Practitioners must recognize that whatever they personally believe reality to be will be different from the client's perspective and that each client will have a unique perspective. Therefore, asking the client to believe or act in a way that "everyone knows is right" becomes the counselor's opinion, based on his or her own phenomenological view rather than some ultimate fact. Because helping someone from a person-centered approach emphasizes this concept, it is imperative to understand the client's perspective as thoroughly as possible (see Sidebar 7.5).

Empathic Understanding Is Critical

Empathic understanding is critical to the person-centered approach because it refers to understanding the client's world from the client's point of view. This is no easy task, because it is hard for counselors to set aside their biased views of the world in an attempt to see things through the client's eyes. All other actions that counselors

Sidebar 7.5. The Abusive Husband's Perceived World

Consider the case of a physically abusive husband who is court ordered into counseling. One part of his reasoning for hitting his wife so hard and so often that she needed to be hospitalized is this: "I come home from work, there is no food on the table, there are dishes in the sink, and then she talks back to me. Of course I hit her. Anybody would!" No counseling degree is needed to realize that "No, anyone wouldn't hit her, and certainly not like you did."

Most people's perceived world makes it clear that this is not appropriate thinking or behaving. It is, however, an obvious sign that the client has a very different view of the world than the counselor and almost everyone else.

Person-centered counselors know that arguing with this person will not change him. What will help is gaining an accurate picture of his perceived world to better understand his perceptions and how they impede or assist change.

take will be inappropriate without empathy, because they would then be based on inaccurate perceptions of the client. This construct allows practitioners to respond effectively and assures clients that their confidence in the counselor is justified.

The role of empathy is continually gaining in importance as diversity and interactions between cultures increase (Comstock et al., 2008). The phenomenological perspective of person-centered counseling in many ways parallels the multicultural worldview concept. Both emphasize that people view the world differently, and thus counselors are required to learn about the client's world as fully as possible. It is through understanding the culture of clients and the multiple influences it has on them that counselors can make sense of the words, actions, and emotions that are seen and described by clients.

Self-exploration, genuineness, and active empathy implemented effectively allow for the implementation of cultural adaptations necessary for cross-cultural counseling to be successful (Sharf, 2015). These are the conditions that allow the traditional person-centered counselor to adapt counseling to cultures to counteract the potential for the stigmatization of minorities (Quinn, 2013) or to meet the unique needs of cultural entities within larger cultural groups (Sanders & Bradley, 2005). These are the conditions that encourage person-centered counselors to move beyond what is sometimes seen as a reflection-only model to the dynamic and evolving one it is meant to be.

Knowing the content of what a client says and knowing the feelings behind the words are the two essential elements of empathic understanding. The words and reasoning are important information that a counselor can interpret. The feelings, however, may come out in words, like *anger*, *frustration*, *love*, *fear*, *hope*, or in other ways, like a reddening of the face, facial expressions, posture, laughter, or tears. Empathic understanding combines all of these verbal and nonverbal clues to understand clients.

Practitioners must accomplish two important tasks to make empathic understanding a useful construct: (a) understanding and (b) accurately conveying that understanding. The most obvious of these is that counselors must set aside their own beliefs and enter the client's world so that they can understand, but understanding alone has minimal value as a counseling technique. The client must also be aware of exactly what the practitioner understands. Empathic understanding only improves the helping relationship when the client clearly recognizes what the counselor understands, so the counselor must effectively communicate that understanding back to the client in words and actions.

People Make Simple Mistakes in Judgment

People make simple mistakes in judgment all the time. They also make choices that appear to be right to them but that are ineffective because they are made to match the perceived world of others rather than the individual's own best judgment. People are attempting to act in response to how they believe others would have them act (conditions of worth) rather than trusting their own positive, growth-oriented nature and their tendency to actualize. Such decisions only increase clients' beliefs that they cannot make their own effective choices and must instead look to others for what is best to do or not do. They may find some limited social acceptance by choosing actions in this model, but they will not gain confidence to consistently implement them or gain confidence in their own ability to seek more productive changes as the need arises.

Place Confidence in the Client

Person-centered counselors place tremendous confidence in clients, even knowing that they will make mistakes in judgment along the way. This confidence is based on the belief that people are innately good and continually seeking a fully functioning experience in the world even as they make mistakes. People's tendency to actualize personal potential in positive ways is the force that the person-centered practitioner recognizes and seeks to free from self-induced constraints.

The person-centered counselor's task is to believe in clients' desire to do the right thing even though they are currently unable to perceive what that is or how to do it. This contrasts with other views of human nature that do not allow the practitioner to trust because client difficulties are seen as weaknesses or deficiencies standing in the way of personal progress unless the counselor corrects them. Person-centered clients are treated as effective human beings who are able to grow and succeed regardless of the nature of their difficulties.

The Perceived World of the Client May Not Approximate the World Sought

People come to counseling for help because of difficulties evolving from the fact that the world they perceive is not close to the world they would naturally seek for themselves. The natural, growth-oriented, self-trusting nature of these people has been pushed into conflict with their chosen world, where they continually look outside their true selves for decisions. They act based on perceptions of what others think is right, and the results of their actions are not personally fulfilling or effective. This conflict is termed *incongruence.*

It is a common occurrence, for example, to find that people who are abusive have also experienced an abusive environment. They have often struggled inside themselves, verbally and even physically, to reject the unnatural, hurtful, and untrusting aspects of the environment, but at some point they come to believe that this is just the way things are because others do it. They take actions based on the acceptance of this direction from others only to find it comes into conflict with the receiving and giving of love, caring, and self-trust they naturally desire. The result is increasing levels of incongruence both within themselves and in their relationships.

Congruent Individuals Trust Their Worldview

Congruent individuals are those who trust their view of the world, trust their ability to act on their basic positive nature, and generally gain the acceptance they expect. They feel confident about reacting in the present moment because of a belief in their ability to discriminate between appropriate and inappropriate behaviors. Those around them then generally verify this self-trust because congruent individuals' actions tend to be beneficial both personally and socially. When human fallibility causes errors in reactions, congruent individuals also have a view of the world that allows the reactions of others to be evaluated and appropriate adaptive responses taken for the immediate and distant future. More congruent people are not infallible, but they do have the ability to recognize and use mistakes to grow without devaluing themselves or others.

The congruence versus incongruence construct helps explain the concept of anxiety in person-centered theory. Low personal anxiety occurs when the perceived self is in line with actual experiences (congruence). Alternatively, the degree to which individuals' perceptions of themselves do not match the way they actually are (incongruence) is directly related to higher levels of anxiety. It is significant for the practitioner to recognize that, in person-centered theory, efforts are made to increase congruence in the client rather than directly reduce anxiety.

APPLICATIONS

Overview

The person-centered concept of a growth-oriented and competent individual in need of counseling presumes a scenario analogous to the growth of a simple garden bean. The bean seed has within itself all of the potential to grow but must be provided with the proper climate for it to achieve its full potential. It will develop as expected if placed in fertile ground where adequate warmth, sun, and water are available. Human hands do not need to touch it under the ground, nor should those hands help pull it out of the properly prepared ground. In fact, such human attempts to directly manipulate will almost surely doom the bean's development. The effective gardener knows that arranging the correct conditions and leaving the actual plant alone to seek its own growth is the best way to allow it to reach its greatest potential.

Fostering the natural growth of the bean is analogous to applying person-centered theory to counseling. The client has all of the necessary but, as yet, unfulfilled potential for attaining greater self-understanding, self-acceptance, self-growth, self-satisfaction, and self-actualization. The practitioner's task is to provide the essential growth conditions of a genuine human relationship in which acceptance, caring, and a deep understanding are developed and communicated effectively to the client. Providing these conditions involves using intervention strategies that allow clients to make changes in the direction of their greatest potential.

Goals of Counseling and Psychotherapy

Movement from incongruence to congruence is the cornerstone person-centered goal for people who are having psychological or sociological difficulties. These people are attempting to perceive more accurately their own positive nature and learn to use it more effectively in their everyday lives. As this occurs, they will better accept both their strengths and weaknesses as legitimate and evolving parts of their positive nature. This acceptance reduces distortions in their view of the world and leads to greater accuracy in the match between how they see themselves and their interactions with people, ideas, and things.

Reduced distortions and a greater trust in one's evolving positive nature lead to other specific outcomes that practitioners often identify as goals of counseling. Successful clients generally become more flexible and creative in their thoughts and actions as they free themselves from stereotypes and inappropriately imposed conditions of worth. They begin to see a wider range of potential for themselves, gain confidence in expressing their feelings, and are enthusiastic about the new aspects of their lives being opened. Newfound levels of freedom to trust the accuracy of feelings and thoughts allow the actions necessary to overcome senses of helplessness and powerlessness and the inability to make decisions about the present and future. This increased self-empowerment is perhaps the most noticeable outcome for everyone around an individual who has benefited from person-centered counseling.

The Process of Change

The process of change through the helping relationship is guided by the presence of three basic conditions: genuineness, acceptance and caring, and empathic understanding. Over the 6 decades since Rogers (1961) identified these conditions, their significance to the process of change has been integrated into virtually all schools of counseling (Joseph & Murphy, 2012; Kirschenbaum, 2009).

The first of these three conditions is the genuineness of the counselor. Clients must perceive that the counselor is a real person who has feelings, thoughts, and beliefs that are not hidden behind facades. This genuine nature allows clients to trust that whatever specifics of the relationship emerge, they can be recognized as both personal and honest. It also allows the client to see that being open and genuine, which includes revealing one's fallibility, is not a condition from which competent human beings must shrink. Most people's daily relationships are not highly genuine but instead controlled by facades and roles that cause people to doubt the information they receive from others.

The second condition is acceptance and caring provided by the counselor, which allows clients to be less anxious about their perceived weaknesses and the prospect of taking risks. People try to hide their weaknesses, which often results in limited success, various degrees of embarrassment, and an accompanying tendency to work even harder at hiding them. Acceptance and caring consistently felt by the client as unconditional positive regard reduces the degree of stress caused by these fears in the relationship. This, in turn, will increase the chance that the client can recognize, discuss, and work on these problem areas rather than hide from them.

The third condition for change is the counselor's empathic understanding of the client. This deep recognition of the client's internal frame of reference must be successfully communicated to the client in order to be effective. Neither counselor nor client can ever fully understand the client, but the degree to which they effectively explore the client's world together to arrive at common understandings will improve the client's abilities to understand and therefore take positive actions in his or her life.

Receiving attention and support from a genuine individual who can be trusted allows clients to explore themselves in areas and ways they cannot in less therapeutic situations. Having another person listen closely and consistently helps clients begin observing and listening to themselves better: "You're right, I am angry. And now that I say it out loud, I realize I've been angry for a long time." They begin to drop masks as they recognize aspects of themselves to be not quite as bad as they thought: "I do have the right to be angry even when someone else doesn't want me to be that way. I'm not comfortable with that idea, but it is there for now." Self-recognition and self-acceptance are key first steps in the growth process.

As individuals become open to their true experiences and more trusting of their own organism, they begin to see the blocks to growth that have burdened them. They also gain the confidence needed to both recognize and deal with their problems on their own. These new levels of self-confidence allow for the dropping of protective masks and for the acceptance of strengths and weaknesses as aspects that are both real and changeable over time. An internal locus of control develops as clients direct their lives rather than follow the direction of others.

A major part of the development process in clients is recognizing that they are fallible human beings who are always in a growth process. This is very different from the belief that one must be perfect to be good or loved. Accepting this position allows clients to view themselves as continuing to learn and grow throughout their lives and to see success as regular improvement rather than perfection.

Clients' confidence in their own ability to evaluate themselves, decide how to change, actually change, and accept their errors as learning steps thereby reduces anxiety and dependence on others for directing their lives. An accurate perception of the real world and their part in it will continue to give importance to the reactions and beliefs of others, but this information will now be seen as more equal in significance to the clients' own views. Consequently, clients will take more responsibility for their own existence and need less external intervention.

Traditional Intervention Strategies

The counselor looking for a specific list of things to say, actions to take, or diagnoses to make will not find them in this theory. Person-centered theory is much more related to who counselors are rather than what techniques they use. A practitioner's actions are focused around providing the conditions of genuineness, unconditional positive regard, and empathy in the relationship. How a practitioner genuinely shows unconditional positive regard or empathy is dictated to some degree by the type of person he or she is and the client's perceptions. This section offers suggestions and some specific behaviors that have consistently been identified with communication of the core conditions.

Active Listening

Demonstrating empathy for the client requires highly attentive and interactive listening skills. Counselors must first show that they are paying attention with physical steps such as facing clients, leaning toward them, and making good eye contact. Combining this with the use of facial and body expressions that relate to clients' comments will, at least initially, put practitioners and clients in physical contact. After putting themselves in the best possible position to listen, practitioners must then hear and see what is communicated by words and action to turn the bits and pieces into a holistic picture.

Acquiring information is only the first part of active listening. Practitioners must then reflect the content and feelings of clients back to them for their listening to have action value. Only in this way can practitioners and clients jointly discover understanding and misconceptions at one level and then move on to greater understanding.

It is expected that genuine counselors will never have a full understanding of the client's world and will make mistakes of various degrees trying to reflect it. The process of active listening helps both parties clarify the content and feelings of a situation and is a learning process for each participant. Practitioners who can treat their own mistakes and growth during this learning process in a genuine manner as a natural part of life also help clients accept their uncertainties and weaknesses.

Reflection of Content and Feelings

The first steps in the empathy exploration process tend to be the recognition and reflection of the actual words stated and the feelings that are most obvious. As client and counselor get to know each other better, an effective practitioner becomes better able to see behind these surface interactions to identify and convey feelings that the client does not even recognize that he or she is expressing. For example, a client may be distracted or become quieter periodically during the session. Initially, these reactions may appear to be related to the specific topic at hand. However, over time, the counselor may be able to tie these reactions to a theme that pulls what seemed to be very different discussion topics together in meaningful ways.

Describing to the client what has been recognized can be very valuable, even when it is as little as extended listening, observing, and reflecting of the client's world. At its most powerful, reflection can also bring together complex elements of the client's world that draw a much more accurate picture of the client as a whole than the individual elements provide separately. This process is similar to what you would experience in trying to describe your face and then looking in the mirror. The closer and longer you look in the mirror, the more detail you see to describe and the better you can describe the overall look of your face. Counselors who accurately reflect content and feelings act like a mirror by helping clients see what they are expressing so that clients can revise and expand perceptions of themselves based on counselor reflections.

Immediacy

Many of the most powerful interactions are those in which the content and feelings involved relate directly to the immediate situation between the client and the counselor; in other words, they depend on immediacy. The mirror analogy fits here because immediate feedback is provided, which is much more valuable than if the mirror only showed how you looked several hours or years earlier. Immediacy provides a here-and-now approach to the relationship in general and to feelings in particular. Those feelings that both client and counselor are currently experiencing are often the most therapeutic ones available. Statements that receive primary emphasis are ones like "Your words express calmness, but your hands are shaking as if you were nervous" and "Your statements make me feel. . . ." In contrast, nonimmediacy statements seen as less therapeutically useful might be "Why did you feel that way?" or "What did the other person think?"

A major reason for person-centered theory's emphasis on the here and now is that reactions between client and counselor can be verified, checked, and explored immediately by both participants. Statements or feelings from the past make use of only the client's perspective, thus reducing the practitioner's opportunity to be a vibrant part of the client's experience.

Genuineness and Self-Disclosure

To be genuine, counselors need to look closely at themselves before deciding how to be or what to do. People cannot be genuine and congruent by thinking, saying, or doing what someone else does. Knowing oneself and being comfortable with that knowledge is critical. Counselors must be more congruent than their clients, or they are likely to take more from the client than is given. One clear way to deal with these issues is for practitioners to seek quality helpful relationships, including counseling, for themselves and to work as hard on their own continued growth as they ask their clients to work.

Being genuine in counseling relationships requires counselors to explore and understand themselves before deciding how to be or what to do. Exploration of counselors' own values, beliefs, biases, and cultural norms and how they act on these is essential for the congruent communication necessary for clients to evaluate the counseling relationship as honest and trustworthy. Cross-cultural counseling requires even greater emphasis on such self-exploration, because when it is lacking, counselors will see clients' differences from themselves as being problems for correction rather than cultural differences in experiences, behaviors, and worldview. Only when person-centered counselors are continually examining and expanding understanding of their own values and biases will the genuineness they attempt to present in counseling be valuable and not counterproductive.

Being genuine does not mean sharing every thought, feeling, or story of the counselor's own experiences with the client. Such tactics would simply take the focus off the client and put it on the practitioner, which is unethical for any professional counselor. There are as many genuine statements or actions as there are people and situations. A useful one comes from a counselor being helpful, attentive, caring, and able to demonstrate genuine interest and involvement. The right statement matches who the counselor is and the counselor's experience with the unique client's situation at a given time in the counseling experience (see Sidebar 7.6).

Sidebar 7.6. Valencia's Mother's Death: Sharing Self as a Part of Being Genuine

Valencia expresses to her counselor her struggles with the recent loss of her mother. The counselor's task of being genuine through sharing some of his or her experience must balance meaningful information, connecting client and counselor with brevity so that the counselor's personalized understanding is made clear without reducing the focus on the client.

Not Helpful

Lacks counselor personalization. "I know how you feel, Valencia." We have all experienced an acquaintance saying something like this when we are hurting. We also know very well that the words coming from this person are nothing more than words. They are sympathy words but show nothing of personalized understanding. The receiver ignores, rejects, or can even get angry from such statements, and trust in the speaker's honesty and understanding is also diminished.

Detracts from client experience. "I understand how you feel, Valencia. I too struggled with my own mother's death. The way I dealt with it that helped me is. . . ." Telling stories of yourself and how you overcame something in an attempt to be genuine takes the emphasis off the client and puts it on the counselor. The more time taken by listening and understanding the counselor's experience, the further the counseling session gets away from understanding the client. Adding how the counselor dealt with the problem also suggests how the client could deal with the problem, thereby reducing the client's self-direction.

More Helpful

Briefly connecting feelings and experiences. "I hope you will tell me more of your experience. Our cultures are very different in how we relate to these tragic events, but if your experience is anything like the loss of my own mother, it must be both painful and complex." This statement communicates genuineness by recognizing the reality of the two different people rather than trying to indicate more understanding than is reasonable to believe. It keeps the emphasis on understanding the client while offering the counselor's genuineness through limited self-disclosure. The self-disclosure connects more to the client issues, "painful and complex," than through the specifics of the experience itself.

Appropriate self-disclosure allows clients to compare their views of the world with the view of another individual whom they have come to trust and value as a significant human being. Under nonthreatening circumstances, these highly personalized comparisons give clients the chance to review and revise their views based on information that might otherwise not have been available or that has been too threatening to accept.

Personalized Counselor Actions

The greatest misconception among new practitioners is that simplistic listening and reflecting is all the person-centered counselor does. This rigid reaction to his concept of an evolving and personalized theory was a major frustration to Rogers throughout his professional life. After one demonstration counseling session, a workshop participant confronted Rogers: "I noticed that you asked questions of the client. But just last night a lecturer told us that we must never do that." Rogers responded, "Well I'm in the fortunate position of not having to be a Rogerian" (Farber, Brink, & Raskin, 1996, p. 11). Rogers used his own thoughts and personality in many creative ways, just as all quality person-centered counselors do. These are the aspects of therapy that appear as metaphor, humor, confrontation, and at times even interpretation or directedness (Bowen, 1996).

Many counselors now use Rogers's relationship development model as the foundation on which to build other cognitive, behavioral, or emotional approaches (Hill, 2014). True person-centered approaches will have a consistent foundation, but the full range of the relationship must build on the unique aspects of the counselor, the client, and their personalized relationship. Although Rogers did not write about this in any exact fashion, he has been identified as generally supportive of this model, including being quoted as saying, "If a therapist has the attitudes we have come to request as essential, probably he or she can use a variety of techniques" (Wilkins, 2003, p. 92).

Non-Client-Centered Interventions

It is important to note the kind of techniques that will not be used as true parts of person-centered counseling. One key example is the specific diagnosis and detailed treatment planning that have become a major focus of the mental health field today. Insurance companies and government agencies increasingly require clear-cut statements of the client's so-called illness, its severity, and the estimated length of time it will take to be corrected. Because person-centered counselors do not view clients in an ill versus well context, they can have a great deal of trouble working with these issues. Person-centered theory is much better suited to helping people progress than it is to getting them over some designated level of a diagnosable condition.

One way that person-centered counselors have approached the assessment model is to deal with it as a joint task of understanding client needs in ways that allow client and counselor to determine how best to work together successfully (Sharf, 2015). Rather than assessment being viewed as something the counselor does to the client, it is viewed as the counselor and client's exploration of how they will work together and toward what goals. Counselors using this model see it as part of the counselors' congruence by being clear on how their roles and responsibilities will influence the relationship and potential success of counseling. This process is seen by those using it as similar to reaching agreement on many other ethical and practical conditions for their working relationship.

Many new counselors identify with a person-centered approach because it fits what they want to do and what has helped them grow in other positive relationships. However, when they attempt to use this approach, they often get caught up in many non-person-centered techniques, mostly for their own comfort. For example, there is little need for extensive questioning in the person-centered approach, because the task is to follow and interact with the client rather than to continually direct him or her toward issues to be explored. New practitioners are likely to begin seeking extensive information in clients' pasts rather than talking about current perceptions and interactions. The questions also tend to lead counselors into overanalyzing client comments and reactions to develop elaborate rationales for why clients do what they do. These reactions may come in part from the fact that student trainees have completed many years of education in which such tactics are highly effective methods for succeeding in academia. Now they are faced with doubts about their ability to use the new skills with real clients who can be hurt. This lack of confidence and experience often causes them to fall back on the questioning and directing tactics of the traditional academic community rather than the responding and following tactics of the person-centered approach. Just as clients need time and proper conditions to gain trust in their organism, it also takes time for new person-centered counselors to trust in their developing organisms.

Brief Intervention Strategies and Current Practices

Implementation of Core Conditions

Even the briefest counseling intervention techniques give importance to creating an environment that fosters client growth, development, and exploration in which the client is treated as trustworthy, resourceful, and capable of productive change (Cepeda & Davenport, 2006). The core conditions of person-centered counseling remain a part of counselor action-oriented brief interventions to achieve maximum effect.

Introduction of Constraints

Probably the most important action person-centered counselors take to meet brevity demands is to introduce the constraints that the counselor and client must work under as soon as possible. Doing so helps them evaluate how to best work together under the client's direction and the constraints on their relationship. Time available in a session, number of sessions allowed, and how progress will be evaluated are examples of important topics when brief time frames are involved. Gaining early goal clarity also becomes essential for the client to have a sense of where initial thoughts and efforts should be directed. Flexibility is essential because although person-centered counselors believe that clients can direct their own counseling, they also know that effective counseling creates learning that changes clients' perceptions of needs, goals, and directions.

Group Work

Many counselors choose person-centered group counseling as a means of giving additional time to more people. The better the counselor, the more clients seek their services. Group person-centered approaches have been found to be effective at providing the core conditions for group members as well as the counselor to produce positive therapeutic outcomes (Corey, 2011).

The Emergence of Neuroscience

Neuroscience is increasingly bringing new evidence to understanding and treating mental health and counseling. Certainly this will affect counseling in general and person-centered counseling in particular, but exactly how is not yet known. Motschnig-Pitrik and Lux (2008) explored relationships between person-centered theory and neuroscience theory regarding emotions, feelings, and thought. The results indicated a close correspondence of basic concepts and hypotheses, such as the actualizing tendency and the vital role of feelings in thought. It may well be that connections between neuroscience and mental health complement one another in producing a more complete and hence reliable image of human functioning.

Clients With Serious Mental Health Issues

Research confirms the success of person-centered counseling with a wide variety of serious mental health issues. A meta-analysis of studies on experiential therapies, the bulk of which were person centered, showed positive effects across a wide range of disorders (Greenberg, Elliott, & Lietaer, 1994). For example, adaptations of person-centered counseling have been found to be useful with diagnoses that have varied from the more common depressive disorders (Elliott, Greenberg, Watson, Timulak, & Freire, 2013) to those such as borderline personality disorder (Bohart, 1990), schizophrenia (Prouty, 1998), and dementia (Zeman, 1999). Seligman (2004) stated that mild disorders in the *Diagnostic and Statistical Manual of Mental Disorders*—such as adjustment disorders or common life experiences involving problems with issues like bereavement, religion or spirituality, identity, or acculturation—are particularly amenable to person-centered counseling.

Disorders that require clients to learn specific skills, such as those in sex therapy, call for much more counselor directness and behavioral techniques. Also, the client-directed nature of person-centered therapy requires a significant degree of client motivation, so those lacking such motivation become less viable candidates for person-centered counseling as the sole treatment model.

EVALUATION

Overview

The person-centered movement brought about innovations in research and training as well as a new approach to counseling. Emphasizing objectivity in the examination of client–practitioner relationships moved the profession forward in the evaluation of specific interaction variables in the process of counseling. This solid research background has not erased all concerns about the theory being considered simplistic when it is actually quite complex, requiring greater trust in the client than people often are able to offer and having few of the specific tactics for new counselors to fall back on that other theories provide.

Supporting Research

Rogers's perception of people and counseling as highly personal and individualized often gives newcomers to the field a sense that he and his theory deemphasize research over personal interaction. In fact, his early research has been recognized by some as "the birth of psychotherapy research" (Barrett-Lennard, 1998, p. 261).

Rogers was a major innovator in the development of research techniques, recognizing that for any theory or technique to remain credible and become more effective, solid research is essential (Sharf, 2015).

Rogers pioneered the use of taped transcripts (Cain, 1987) and other clinical measures to broaden the scope of psychological research (Hjelle & Ziegler, 1992). These techniques helped bring the more subjective aspects of people, counseling, and psychotherapy into respectability. Among his earliest significant publications were books on extensive research studies with standard mental health center populations (Rogers & Dymond, 1954) and more cases of people with schizophrenia (Rogers, 1967). All of this work demonstrated his commitment to research and established his basic concepts as valid and reliable sources of client progress.

Rogers's research and teaching tool that gets the most use today is the tape recording and transcribing of sessions with clients. Taking notes from memory was not satisfactory. He wanted to hear and see as much of the interaction as possible to judge both the client's reactions and his own work. This taping and evaluating of sessions has become common practice today.

Research on person-centered counseling as a total theory motivated many studies in its early years, but the momentum for such research has declined significantly over the past 40 years (Kirschenbaum, 2009). This appears to be due in part to the general acceptance of Rogers's basic concepts as necessary, if not sufficient, conditions for counseling success and the extensive research done on them in the 1950s and 1960s (Duncan & Miller, 2009). Most recent research has been on the core conditions, which are widely believed to be Rogers's common factors (See & Kamnetz, 2015).

A few researchers have questioned the methodological aspects of some studies. Concerns about sophistication and rigor have been raised (Prochaska & Norcross, 2009). These concerns may deserve particular attention when considered alongside the fact that less person-centered research is now being conducted at the same time that the core conditions are widely accepted.

Limitations

Person-centered theory may suffer most from the fact that it appears to be so simple to learn. The concepts are relatively few, there is not a long list of details to remember, and one does not need to recall a specific tactic for each diagnostic problem a client might have. The counselor can be lulled into a feeling of security by this apparent simplicity. For example, simple listening and reflecting of words and surface feelings are usually beneficial at the very beginning of a session. However, continued surface-level interactions that do not attend to the many dimensions of both the client and the practitioner quickly become seen as repetitive, nondirectional, and trite.

The few basic concepts in person-centered theory have a virtually unlimited complexity because counselors must be fully aware of both their clients' and their own changing phenomenological worlds. They must respond to the interactions between these worlds in ways that best fit the genuine natures of the client and themselves. This difficult task requires excellent understanding and continuing awareness of oneself and the client. New counselors in particular have a difficult time with this complexity. Feeling the pressure to remember and do a new thing or a right thing naturally makes it more difficult to be genuine and aware of all that is happening around and within themselves and others.

The supportive nature of person-centered theory is often misinterpreted to mean that one should not be confrontational with clients. Effectively functioning people confront themselves all of the time, and counselors must recognize that appropriate confrontation is a natural part of an effective helping relationship. Person-centered theory makes room for such confrontation, but it gives few specific guidelines as to where, when, and how it should occur.

A great deal of trust in the positive motivation and abilities of oneself and the client is required of the person-centered counselor. Such trust in people and a process is not easy to provide in all circumstances. Human beings have difficulty suspending their mistrust because of fears, previous experiences, and preconceived notions common to everyone. The more extreme one's negative experiences and reactions are, the more difficult it is to act fully on the person-centered belief system. The result is that most practitioners can place confidence in a bright, college-educated, law-abiding, depressed client but have more difficulty maintaining a similar confidence in a depressed rapist or murderer.

There are few techniques or activities to fall back on if the counselor does not have or cannot act on a great deal of personal knowledge, understanding, and awareness in the helping relationship. Many other theories provide more activities or tactics that allow the practitioner to give the process a boost when the relationship is not all it could be.

Summary Chart: Person-Centered Theory

Human Nature

The person-centered theory emphasizes a highly positive view of human nature in which people can be trusted to be continually seeking productive directions toward maximum self-actualization. Perceiving unconditional positive regard from their environment supports this development, whereas conditions of worth inhibit it and produce nonactualizing thoughts and behaviors.

Major Constructs

Clients have psychological and sociological difficulties to the degree that their phenomenological worlds do not match their true positive nature (incongruence) and its use in their everyday lives. Empathic understanding of clients' world is essential in helping clients find a more congruent match between their phenomenological world and their actions, feelings, thoughts, and responses from others.

Goals

Clients work to get in closer touch with essential positive elements of themselves that have been hidden or distorted. Less distortion and more congruence lead to greater trust that their organisms can be relied on for effective reactions to people and situations. This added trust results in reduced feelings of helplessness and powerlessness; fewer behaviors driven by stereotypes; and more productive, creative, and flexible decision making.

Change Process

The change process is stimulated when counselors provide the core conditions of genuineness, acceptance and caring, and empathic understanding. Change takes place as clients perceive these conditions and begin exploring and testing new thoughts and behaviors that are more in line with their positive, growth-oriented nature. This exploration, testing, and learning leads to increasing trust in their organism's ability to think and act in a wider variety of circumstances.

Interventions

This theory is marked by a minimum of specific intervention techniques, as counselors are asked to be genuine in a relationship rather than to perform a rigid set of actions. It is essential to interact in the immediacy of the situation and then evaluate the results with the use of active listening; reflection of content and feelings; appropriate self-disclosure; and other personally, professionally, and situationally responsive interactions.

Limitations

Success depends on counselors maintaining high trust in the feelings and actions of the client and themselves. Lack of trust often causes practitioners to fall back on safe, passive reflection responses. These are necessary early on but become increasingly inadequate as the need for a more comprehensive therapeutic relationship develops, one that includes directness that comes with additional culturally, situationally, and personally relevant feelings and interactions.

THE CASE OF MARIA: A PERSON-CENTERED APPROACH

The use of a client case study to view person-centered theory raises several problems. Person-centered theory places more emphasis on clients' perceptions of and feelings about their world than on the collecting of facts as seen by others. It disdains looking at work with clients as illness focused. In addition, the relationship with the counselor is much more critical to the success of therapy than the client's specific historical case development. Some person-centered practitioners might therefore choose to ignore the concept of a clinical case history (Seligman, 2004).

The fact is that the reason person-centered practitioners attend so closely to clients is precisely because they want to understand the client's perceived experiences and worldview as much as possible. The modified case study that follows examines potential phenomenological aspects of the client's situation as though the information had been acquired within the therapeutic relationship. It further emphasizes Maria's relationship with the counselor and suggests potential directions that her growth might take as a result of a positive therapeutic relationship.

Maria's Phenomenological World

Maria has a phenomenological view of the world that is incongruent with her true feelings, abilities, and potential, as would be expected with clients entering counseling. She has incorporated unattainable conditions of worth that come from a mixture of culture, religion, family, and personal relationships. In her currently perceived world, she will never be able to be a good enough daughter, mother, Catholic, teacher, or partner to satisfy those whose approval she desires. The harder she tries to please, the further she gets away from personal feelings of self-worth. She has lost trust in her own ability to feel, think, decide, and act in productive ways and is consequently trying to act in a world as others see it, which will not bring her feelings of success.

The fact that Maria's phenomenological world is frequently out of line with the world that actually affects her causes Maria great anxiety. She looks outside herself for ways to act, only to find that what others point to as the right way does not satisfy anyone—particularly her. She knows that who she is and what she does are not working, but she cannot identify other ways to view the situation.

Actualizing Tendencies

It should be obvious that Maria has never fully given into the conditions of worth that direct her in nonactualizing ways. She keeps experimenting and succeeding at new challenges, even as significant others disapprove of her actions. Attending the college of her choice rather than the one her parents wanted, marrying outside her religion, and eventually getting a divorce may or may not have been good decisions, but they do demonstrate an actualizing tendency that keeps Maria moving forward, even in the face of disapproval and rejection. The fact that she has come for counseling is further confirmation that she wants more out of herself and will take the necessary actions to make that happen.

Maria is a person who took on responsibilities as a teenager that should have been handled by adults, achieved academically, proved herself as a teacher, made it through an abusive marriage, and managed to care for two children on her own. Her actualizing abilities should be clear, even as her success is frustrated owing to distorted views and the absence of caring relationships in which she could be accepted for who she truly is and wants to be. This situation stops her from recognizing other alternative views of herself that could potentially lead to much greater self-actualization. The growth that Maria seeks demands that she take exploratory risks into uncharted waters that are frightening and not easily undertaken.

The Counselor's Role

A counselor valuable to Maria will empathically work with her situation, see her inner strength, trust in her willingness and ability to move in positive directions, and provide the core therapeutic conditions that will allow her actualizing tendencies to flower. These conditions will help Maria both clarify the intricacies of her own feelings and see the value in sharing her views accurately with another person. Maria also needs a counselor who is not burdened by false fronts so that she can trust the legitimacy of the human interaction (genuineness).

Unconditional positive regard for Maria can be conveyed in part by consistently showing confidence in her as a competent person who can think and act effectively. The counselor will not lead Maria to specific topics; suggest ways to act; identify her problems for her; or direct, reward, or punish her. Demonstrating attention, active listening, and a keen sense of empathic understanding without placing judgments on the information will help demonstrate this condition.

The counselor will listen and observe closely to grasp all verbal and emotional aspects of Maria. By regularly conveying back to Maria what the counselor sees, hears, understands, and feels, counselor and client will be able to check on the accuracy of their communications and correct misinterpretations. This is the learning process in which Maria presents ideas, the counselor tries to reflect them and possibly tie them into other previously recognized concepts, and both parties negotiate to reach mutual understandings. It is only from such struggle that accurate empathic understanding arises.

The counselor must create a relationship that is open and honest, in which what the counselor thinks, does, and says are consistent and in which taking on the role of counselor does not mean one cannot be a real person at the same time. Such consistency will allow Maria to trust the relationship as well as the ideas, skills, and behaviors that develop from it. As progress continues, Maria will recognize that because this is a real human relationship with genuine people, the ideas and actions can be transferred to her life outside counseling. The relationship therefore will be viewed as an immediate, natural, real, and dependable experience that can be duplicated in many respects outside the helping relationship.

The core conditions offer a great deal of challenge to the client. Maria will not always want to hear how the counselor is understanding and reacting to her, as these are aspects of herself she may find difficult to accept. Only the truly empathic counselor, who is also genuine, can successfully overcome such difficult issues. The many challenging times and confrontations in a person-centered approach are those that would be expected in any genuine human relationship.

Expectations for Progress

The person-centered counselor who adequately and consistently provides the necessary therapeutic conditions can expect Maria to progress in some general ways. It should be made clear, however, that Maria may not change in the ways that others deem to be best. Maria is seeking herself, and finding more of herself will likely reduce the control these others have over her. Such control will be replaced by increasing trust in her organism so that Maria will begin to realize her personal ability to control her own life while still considering the needs of others.

Maria becomes more open to talking and reacting honestly about difficult issues as her trust increases that the counselor will still think well of her, no matter how inappropriate certain aspects of her feelings, thoughts, and actions seem to be. Problems begin to appear as manageable and not nearly as terrible or insurmountable as Maria had believed. Her excitement about finding new ways to see the world will likely be followed by struggles to understand her new world and how to relate to it differently.

Maria will soon find a need to explore her new ways of viewing, feeling, and acting in the world outside of counseling. She will want to know how her children, family, boss, and dates might respond if she chooses to act differently. Such issues will be explored in the therapeutic relationship before she tries them out. Maria will want to understand both the good and bad results after they have been tried in real life. The new ideas, observations, and attempted behaviors involved in each new situation will expand Maria's view of the world and likely bring her back to the counselor for help in integrating the newfound information.

Pleasures, fears, successes, and disappointments will all be parts of Maria's development, but she will come to recognize that each experience provides learning that promotes confidence in her ability to self-direct and correct mistakes. Eventually, she will gain enough confidence in her immediate reactions to use a productive combination of her own ideas and those of others to develop positive outcomes. She will recognize that even when things do not work out as planned, she is effective enough to overcome mistakes and move forward.

REFERENCES

Barrett-Lennard, G. T. (1998). *Carl Rogers' helping system: Journey and substance.* Thousand Oaks, CA: Sage.

Bohart, A. C. (1990). A cognitive client-centered perspective on borderline personality development. In G. Lietaer, J. Rombauts, & R. Van Balen (Eds.), *Client-centered and experiential psychotherapy in the nineties* (pp. 599–622). Leuven, Belgium: Leuven University Press.

Bott, D. (2001). Client-centered therapy and family therapy: A review and commentary. *Journal of Family Therapy, 23,* 361–377.

Bowen, M. (1996). The myth of nondirectiveness: The case of Jill. In B. A. Farber, D. C. Brink, & P. M. Raskin (Eds.), *The psychotherapy of Carl Rogers: Cases and commentaries* (pp. 84–94). New York, NY: Guilford Press.

Cain, D. J. (1987). Carl R. Rogers: The man, his vision, his impact. *Person-Centered Review, 2,* 283–288.

Cepeda, L. M., & Davenport, D. S. (2006). Person-centered therapy and solution-focused brief therapy: An integration of present and future awareness. *Psychotherapy: Theory, Research, Practice, and Training, 43*(1), 1–12. doi:10.1037/0033-3204.43.1.1

Comstock, D. L., Hammer, T. R., Strentzsch, J., Cannon, K., Parsons, J., & Salazar, G., II. (2008). Relational–cultural theory: A framework for bridging relational, multicultural, and social justice competencies. *Journal of Counseling & Development, 86,* 279–287.

Corey, G. (2011). *Theory and practice of group counseling* (8th ed.). Belmont, CA: Brooks/Cole.

Duncan, B. L., & Miller, S. D. (2009). *The heart and soul of change: What works in therapy.* Washington, DC: American Psychological Association.

Elliott, R., Greenberg, L., Watson, J. C., Timulak, L., & Freire, E. (2013). Research on humanistic-experiential psychotherapies. In M. J. Lambert (Ed.), *Bergin and Garfield's handbook of psychotherapy and behavior change* (6th rev. ed., pp. 495–538). New York, NY: Wiley.

Farber, B. A., Brink, D. C., & Raskin, P. M. (Eds.). (1996). *The psychotherapy of Carl Rogers: Cases and commentary.* New York, NY: Guilford Press.

Gilbert, P., & Lehay, R. L. (2007). Introduction and overview: Basic issues in therapeutic relationship. In P. Gilbert & R. L. Lehay (Eds.), *The therapeutic relationship in the cognitive behavioral psychotherapies* (pp. 3–23). New York, NY: Routledge.

Greenberg, L. S., Elliott, R., & Lietaer, G. (1994). Research on humanistic and experiential psychotherapies. In A. Bergin & S. Garfield (Eds.), *Handbook of psychotherapy and behavior change* (4th ed., pp. 509–542). New York, NY: Wiley.

Hill, C. E. (2014). *Helping skills: Facilitating exploration, insight and action* (4th ed.). Washington, DC: American Psychological Association.

Hjelle, L. A., & Ziegler, D. J. (1992). *Personality theories.* New York, NY: McGraw-Hill.

Holburn, S., & Vietze, P. (2000). Person-centered planning and cultural inertia in applied behavior analysis. *Behavior and Social Issues, 10,* 39–70.

Joseph, S., & Murphy, D. (2012). Person-centered approach, positive psychology, and relational helping building bridges. *Journal of Humanistic Psychology, 53,* 26–51.

Kirschenbaum, H. (2009). *The life and work of Carl Rogers.* Alexandria, VA: American Counseling Association.

Miles, A., & Mezzich, J. (2011). The care of the patient and the soul of the clinic: Person-centered medicine as an emergent model of modern clinical practice. *The International Journal of Personal Centered Medicine, 1,* 207–222.

Motschnig-Pitrik, R., & Lux, M. (2008). The person-centered approach meets neuroscience: Mutual support for C. R. Rogers and A. Damasio's theories. *Journal of Humanistic Psychology, 48*(3), 287–319. doi:10.1177/0022167807306044

Presbury, J. H., Echterling, L. G., & McKee, J. E. (2002). *Ideas and tools for brief counseling.* Columbus, OH: Merrill Prentice Hall.

Prochaska, J. O., & Norcross, J. C. (2009). *Systems of psychotherapy: A transtheoretical analysis* (7th ed.). Pacific Grove, CA: Brooks/Cole.

Prouty, G. (1998). Pretherapy and pre-symbolic experiencing: Evolutions in person-centered/experiential approaches to psychotic experience. In L. S. Greenberg & J. C. Watson (Eds.), *Handbook of experiential psychotherapy* (pp. 388–409). New York, NY: Guilford Press.

Quinn, A. (2013). A person-centered approach to multicultural counseling competence. *Journal of Humanistic Psychology, 53,* 202–251.

Rogers, C. (1942). *Counseling and psychotherapy.* Boston, MA: Houghton Mifflin.

Rogers, C. (1951). *Client-centered therapy.* Boston, MA: Houghton Mifflin.

Rogers, C. (1959). A theory of therapy, personality, and interpersonal relationships, as developed in the client-centered framework. In S. Koch (Ed.), *Psychology: A study of a science* (Vol. 3, pp. 184–256). New York, NY: McGraw-Hill.

Rogers, C. (1961). *On becoming a person: A therapist's view of psychotherapy.* Boston, MA: Houghton Mifflin.

Rogers, C. (Ed.). (1967). *The therapeutic relationship and its impact: A study of psychotherapy with schizophrenics.* Madison: University of Wisconsin Press.

Rogers, C. (1970). *Carl Rogers on encounter groups.* New York, NY: Harper & Row.

Rogers, C. (1987a). Inside the world of the Soviet professional. *Counseling and Values, 32,* 47–66.

Rogers, C. (1987b). Steps toward peace, 1948–1986: Tension reduction in theory and practice. *Counseling and Values, 32,* 12–16.

Rogers, C., & Dymond, R. (1954). *Psychotherapy and personality change.* Chicago, IL: University of Chicago Press.

Rogers, C., & Sanford, R. (1987). Reflections on our South African experience. *Counseling and Values, 32,* 17–20.

Sanders, J. L., & Bradley, C. (2005). Multiple-lens paradigm: Evaluating African American girls and their development. *Journal of Counseling & Development, 83,* 299–304.

See, J., & Kamnetz, B. (2015). Person-centered counseling. In F. Chan, N. L. Berven, & K. R. Thomas (Eds.), *Counseling theories and techniques for rehabilitation and mental health professionals* (2nd ed., pp. 15–48). New York, NY: Springer.

Seligman, L. A. (2004). *Diagnosis and treatment planning in counseling* (3rd ed.). New York, NY: Springer.

Sharf, R. S. (2015). *Theories of psychotherapy and counseling: Concepts and cases* (6th ed.). Belmont, CA: Brooks/Cole.

Snyder, M. (2002). Applications of Carl Rogers' theory and practice to couple and family therapy: A response to Harlene Anderson and David Bott. *Journal of Family Therapy, 24,* 317–325.

Thayer, L. (1987). An interview with Carl R. Rogers: Toward peaceful solutions to human conflict: Part I. *Michigan Journal of Counseling and Development, 18,* 58–63.

Wilkins, P. (2003). *Person-centered therapy in focus.* Thousand Oaks, CA: Sage.

Zeman, S. (1999). Person-centered care for the patient with mid- and late-stage dementia. *American Journal of Alzheimer's Disease, 14*(5), 308–310.

Chapter 8

Gestalt Theory

Melinda Haley, Sarah H. Golden, and Rebecca D. Nate

Gestalt theory has a rich and varied background that has been historically controversial (Truscott, 2010). Although Fritz Perls is generally credited with being the foremost practitioner of Gestalt counseling and psychotherapy (Latner, 2013), with his wife, Laura Perls, often cited as the cofounder (Latner, 2013), his method was influenced by the Gestalt psychologists who preceded him, such as Max Wertheimer (Lyngzeidetson, 2011), Wolfgang Kohler, and Kurt Koffka (Wong, 2010). These psychologists laid the psychological groundwork for Perls's application of Gestaltism to counseling and psychotherapy (Wagemans et al., 2012). The difference between Gestalt psychology and Gestalt therapy is that the former is concerned with perception and cognition, whereas the latter focuses on personality, psychopathology, and psychotherapy (Sabar, 2013). In addition, awareness in the here and now is essential in self-regulation and thus in Gestalt therapy (Kalaitzi, 2012). Coined in 1890 by philosopher Christian von Ehrenfels (Rollinger & Lerna, 2015), the word *Gestalt* is a German term used to define a unique patterning in which the parts are integrated into a perceptual whole (Engelmann, 2008), such as a shape or form (Sabar, 2013; Wong, 2010). There are three parts to the definition of a *gestalt:* "a thing, its context or environment, and the relationship between them" (Kelly & Howie, 2007, p. 137), and the term represents the idea that the entire entity is composed of more than just its separate parts (Sabar, 2013). In addition, *gestalten* is a verb meaning "to bring order to (organize)" or "to transform" (Sabar, 2013). Gestalt qualities can be temporal or nontemporal, referring to processes over time, and shapes (Sabar, 2013).

BACKGROUND

This section reviews the background regarding the formation of Gestalt theory. A brief biography of each of the founders of Gestalt theory and counseling is provided, and some of the key founding concepts of Gestalt theory are explored. These concepts include phenomenology, existentialism, field theory, and dialogue and how these relate to Gestalt therapy.

Frederick (Fritz) Perls

Friedrich Salomon Perls was born in 1893, the middle child and only son of middle-class Jewish parents in Berlin (Latner, 2013). He later anglicized his name, becoming Frederick, although most people called him Fritz (Gregory, 2014). Perls received a medical degree in 1920 after a brief stint as a medical corpsman during World War I. He found his war experience brutal in military authoritarianism and racial prejudice. These experiences influenced his humanitarianism but also left him with a deep cynicism about human nature (Seligman & Reichenberg, 2013; Truscott, 2010). His early training in psychoanalysis took place in Austria and Germany (Latner, 2013), and he became associated with neurologist Kurt Goldstein (Latner, 2013). While working as Goldstein's assistant at Frankfurt's Institute for Brain Injured Soldiers in 1926 Perls became interested in the transforming of Gestalt psychology into Gestalt therapy (Perls, 1969b).

When Adolf Hitler came to power, Perls and his new wife Lore (Laura) relocated to Johannesburg, South Africa (Truscott, 2010), where they became the first psychologists in that area (Wheeler, 2004) and founded a psychoanalytic institute (Truscott, 2010). In 1946, Perls immigrated to the United States (Goodtherapy.org, 2015), and in 1951, he cowrote *Gestalt Therapy: Excitement and Growth in the Human Personality* (Perls, Hefferline, & Goodman, 1951). Following the favorable reception of this text, he established several Gestalt institutes throughout the country, the first in New York in 1952 (Truscott, 2010). Perls spent his remaining years training, conducting workshops, and establishing a legacy for Gestalt therapy through the founding of several more designated training facilities (Truscott, 2010). Among the institutions founded by Perls are the Cleveland Institute of Gestalt Therapy (1954), the Esalen Institute in California (1962), and another facility in Vancouver, British Colombia (1970), founded the same year of his death (Truscott, 2010). His work established him as a prominent practitioner of Gestalt counseling and psychotherapy (see Sidebar 8.1).

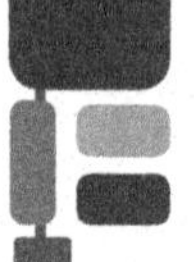

Sidebar 8.1. Six Factors Leading to Psychological Distress

According to the Transpersonal Psychology Pioneers website (www.atpweb.org/pioneers/pioneers.fritzperls.html), Perls described six factors that he found responsible for psychological distress:

- *A lack of contact:* no social support
- *Confluence:* the environment takes control
- *Unfinished business:* an inability to gain closure
- *Fragmentation:* a denied or fragmented self
- *Winner/loser:* conflict of values and expectations
- *Polarities:* never seeing gray, always black or white

Take a moment and review where you are on these six factors. For example, review your social support system. Is it adequate or is it lacking? How does your social support network contribute to your current mental health? If you find your social support network lacking, how could you facilitate the development of stronger social support? Think about your environment. Do you feel in control? How does that contribute to how you currently feel? Go through each of the six factors and evaluate where you fit on them. Do you agree with Perls that these six factors are responsible for psychological distress? Why or why not?

Lore (Laura) Perls

Fritz Perls's work was carried on after his death in 1970 by his wife, Laura. Lore (Laura) Perls, born in 1905, studied psychology and received a doctorate in science from Frankfurt University in Germany (Truscott, 2010). It has become increasingly clear since her own death in 1990 that Laura Posner Perls contributed significantly to Gestalt counseling and psychotherapy, having studied with Max Wertheimer and gained recognition as a Gestalt psychologist in her own right (Bandín, 2010; Gaffney, 2009). In collaboration with Fritz, Laura ran the Gestalt training institute in New York City for nearly 40 years (Goleman, 1990). Laura had four children, among them daughter Renate Perls and son Dr. Stephen R. Perls, a psychologist (Goleman, 1990). She continued her work long after her husband's death, becoming an influential force in Gestalt therapy and the training of Gestalt therapists until her own death stemming from complications with her thyroid in Pforzheim, West Germany (Goleman, 1990).

Paul Goodman

Another person who participated in the development of Gestalt therapy is Paul Goodman (Honeywell, 2011). When he met Perls in 1949, Goodman was already an accomplished classical scholar; wrote fiction and political criticism; and had been deeply influenced by his studies of Sigmund Freud, Otto Rank, and Wilhelm Reich (Honeywell, 2011). Goodman collaborated with Perls on *Gestalt Therapy: Excitement and Growth in the Human Personality* (Perls et al., 1951). Although Perls initially received the recognition for this work, many scholars have since come to credit Goodman with writing at least half of the manuscript, specifically the half dealing with the theory of Gestalt therapy (Kalaitzi, 2012; Stevenson, 2010). Goodman also is believed to have assisted in the second volume of *Gestalt Therapy: Excitement and Growth in the Human Personality* (Kalaitzi, 2012). Goodman also published *Growing Up Absurd* in 1960, a text about youth in society and the social movements of the time (Honeywell, 2011). Goodman's role is now seen as one of collaboration with Fritz and Laura Perls, and his own contribution to the development of the theory is acknowledged (Honeywell, 2011). It is interesting that after Fritz Perls's death, Goodman, along with Isadore From, conducted therapy with Laura and found themselves developing beliefs in opposition to those of Fritz Perls. It has been speculated that this change materialized from the resentment carried by Laura Perls that was evident during each therapist's sessions with Laura (Latner, 2013).

Phenomenology, Existentialism, Field Theory, Dialogue, and Gestalt Therapy

Gestalt psychology was not the only influence that inspired Gestalt therapy. Although the roots of Gestalt therapy can most certainly be found in phenomenology and field theory (Schulz, 2013), there exists within it the influential existentialist writings of Søren Kierkegaard, Friedrich Nietzsche, Martin Buber, Paul Tillich, and Martin Heidegger; the writings of Aristotle, William James, John Dewey, and Immanuel Kant; and the philosophies of Zen Buddhism and Taoism. In addition, there are also some added basic principles from psychoanalytic theory, humanistic theories (Schulz, 2013), and Reichian body therapy (Reilly & Jacobus, 2009). The coagulation of all of these perspectives placed the focus on improving clients' awareness of their subjective experience. Gestalt therapy does this by facilitating the client's ability to become authentic and make choices that lead to a meaningful life while setting in motion the natural process of growth that moves toward integration within self and between self and the environment (LaHood, 2014).

Phenomenology

Considered one of the theoretical pillars of Gestalt theory (Schulz, 2013), phenomenology, similar to *phenomenological field* (Sabar, 2013), is the study of human experience through attending to the subjective observations of individuals (Latner, 2013). Essentially, it is the examination of a phenomenon (Sabar, 2013). Inquiry into experience, or observing one's own experience, is inherently a subjective undertaking. The focus of inquiry may be internal (on the self) or external (on the environment), but the observations of the individual are considered to be relevant and meaningful. Phenomenology suggests a conscious awareness of the subject's own experience, life story, environmental factors, and self through self-observation (Yontef, 2010).

Existentialism

Existential thought came to the forefront during the 19th century (Schneider, 2011), when philosophers in Europe began contemplating the absolutism of such prior ideas as, What is truth and what is fact? and Was the whole person (gestalt) more than the sum of the parts? (LaHood, 2014). Existentialism is concerned with human existence as directly experienced. People seek to find meaning in their experience (Truscott, 2010). The popularity of existentialism increased significantly during the 20th century, namely, during the years around World War II (Schneider, 2011).

Field Theory

Another critical element of Gestalt theory is field theory (Schulz, 2013). *Field theory* is originally a physics term used to explain a phenomenon and how that phenomenon reacts to other fields. This way of thinking helps to interpret and assign meaning to events encountered (Schulz, 2013). Essentially it is the understanding and analyzing of causality (Sabar, 2013). Field theory focuses on the whole, in which all of the elements found within the field are in relationship to and influence one another. Thus, no individual part operates in isolation from any of the other parts in the field (Schulz, 2013)—this is known as *contextuality*, or the context in which an individual functions (Lyngzeidetson, 2011). The Gestalt therapy perspective relies heavily on field theory (Schulz, 2013).

Dialogue

The final pillar of Gestalt theory is dialogue (Schulz, 2013). The importance of dialogue in the counselor–client or therapist–client relationship has been recognized, and in recent years, this enhanced recognition has been thought to be the most important advance in Gestalt therapy (Reilly & Jacobus, 2009). The main objective of the dialogue component of Gestalt therapy is to facilitate rapport and relationship building with the client (Schulz, 2013). Listening and inquiring are important elements within the dialogue paradigm, though this process can be challenging with each new concept to be understood (Schulz, 2013).

The fundamental theory behind the dialogic approach is that people develop in relationship to others (Schulz, 2013). When a person is supported through a genuine and trusting relationship, that person can grow in a positive direction and can gain a positive sense of self. In contrast, when a person is not supported, he or she often experiences shame, and this can thwart the growth of a positive concept of self (Schulz,

2013). This is described as the interaction of an individual's existence and the environment (Kalaitzi, 2012). Therefore, empathic understanding through dialogue is seen as an important part of the change process.

HUMAN NATURE: A DEVELOPMENTAL PERSPECTIVE

Perhaps one of the most attractive features of Gestalt theory is its attention to the holistic nature of humankind (Lobb, 2012). As in existentialism and phenomenology, genuine knowledge is the expected outcome of what is apparent and evident in the experience of the perceiver (Lobb, 2012). Whereas the traditional Gestalt psychologists remained focused on cognition, perception, and motivation, Gestalt counselors and therapists engage the whole organism (person) and operate from the perspective that human beings have the capacity and strength to grow, to develop, and to become the persons they are meant to be (Lobb, 2012). A basic assumption is that individuals can cope with their life problems, especially if they are fully aware of what is happening in and around them. Centered in the present, the person in Gestalt counseling or psychotherapy is always in the process of being what he or she is, in the here and now (Sabar, 2013; Schulz, 2013). This concept has been referred to as the *developmental mind* (Lobb, 2012).

MAJOR CONSTRUCTS

This section discusses the major constructs associated with Gestalt theory and therapy. These include field theory, differentiation and contact, boundary disturbances, dichotomies and polarities, and foreground and background, to name just a few. There are many constructs associated with Gestalt therapy, and this section provides an overview of the major ones.

Field Theory: Organism and Environment

The scientific paradigm forming the basis of the Gestalt therapy perspective is field theory, with a view to the organism–environment as a field of activity (Schulz, 2013). In contrast to a reductionistic, unilinear, cause-and-effect model, field theory focuses on the whole, in which all of the elements found within the field are in relationship to and influence one another (LaHood, 2014). The environmental field includes physical and psychosocial interaction (Sabar, 2013). Field theory is based on the principle of interdependence (Peirson, Boydell, Ferguson, & Ferris, 2011).

Phenomenological Field

The phenomenological field is the field that is the focus of Gestalt therapy (Schulz, 2013). This field changes according to the individual's focused awareness (LaHood, 2014). At one moment, the focus may be entirely internal, attending to self and its interrelated parts. During the next moment, the phenomenological field may shift to a focus on the person in relationship to his or her external environment, which is made up of its own constituent and interacting parts. When the focus is internal, the field is represented by parts of the self, which may be broadly defined as mind and body.

Holism

Gestalt therapy is holistic rather than reductionistic; it is concerned with the differentiation and interrelationship of the parts that make up the whole rather than the parts in isolation from one another (Stevenson, 2010). In therapy, it means attending to the whole person (mind, body, spirit, environment, social world, organizations, and culture) rather than just one aspect of the client, such as the client's symptoms (Schulz, 2013). Attending to the holistic view of the mind–body problem is known as *isomorphism* (Sabar, 2013) Focusing on how the entire system works together, rather than as separate parts, will provide a more accurate conceptualization of the whole person (Schulz, 2013). *Molarism* is related to holism and is simply another way of saying "the whole is greater than the sum of its parts" (Lyngzeidetson, 2011, p. 4). Therefore, Gestalt therapy is a viable option for working from a cross-cultural framework, because it addresses the individual as a whole and all-encompassing approach while focusing on the present (Perera-Diltz, Laux, & Toman, 2012). Similarly, Gestalt theory also advocates that the individual cannot be understood in isolation but must be understood within his or her social and historical context and within the uniqueness of his or her field (Halbur & Halbur, 2011). This fits well with the basic tenets of cross-cultural counseling.

Differentiation and Contact

In Gestalt therapy, a healthy individual is one who can differentiate his or her self while also making contact with others. Contact involves the ability to be fully present, in the moment, and available (Lobb, 2012; Schulz, 2013). In fact, life is described as a constant process of contact and separation between a person and those with whom the person is in relationship, such as family members and loved ones, colleagues, and employers. Contact and differentiation, and connection and separation, define a goal of Gestalt therapy, which is to help clients become more integrated within themselves and in relationship to others—in other words, to help clients to create differentiated unity (Schulz, 2013). Differentiated unity for the client as a whole person means awareness of thoughts, feelings, and senses (i.e., taste, smell, hearing, touch, sight) or an integration of mind and body (LaHood, 2014; see Sidebar 8.2).

Sidebar 8.2. Mindfulness

As you have read, "Differentiated unity for the client as a whole person means awareness of thoughts, feelings, and senses (i.e., taste, smell, hearing, touch, sight) or an integration of mind and body." This is related to the concept of mindfulness. Take a moment from reading this chapter and engage in a mindfulness exercise to bring yourself fully into the here and now. Taking time to become centered in the here and now can also help you to destress. To begin, first sit quietly and focus on your own breathing. Try to breathe slowly in and out and pay attention as your chest rises and falls to how you feel as you breathe. Keep your attention and concentration focused on your breathing. If you find yourself starting to think about something else, bring your focus back to your breathing.

You can also practice being mindful in the here and now with others. Pick a person to engage in a conversation. As you talk to this person, really listen to what he or she is saying. Listen not only to the words but also to the tone of his or her voice, the inflection, the emotion behind the words. Being fully present means keeping your attention and focus on the person you are talking to rather than thinking about what you will say to him or her in return. It is both listening to the message and paying attention to the messenger. Again, if you notice your mind starting to wander or if you find yourself thinking about how you want to respond to what the person is saying, bring your mind back to focus on the individual with whom you are conversing.

Confluence

Confluence is the idea of viewing one's environment without boundaries (Lobb, 2012). When people cannot become differentiated, often what happens is confluence. This is the process whereby a person loses sight of himself or herself by incorporating too much of the environment or others into the self (Keenan, 2011). Being overly agreeable, or alternatively being on the fence to avoid conflict, is a form of confluence (Stevenson, 2010).

Boundaries

For survival, the organism—that is, the individual—must make contact with the environment (Lobb, 2012). The function of the individual's boundaries is to simultaneously be firm enough to differentiate self from others yet open or permeable enough to make contact with others (Schulz, 2013). This is sometimes called the *boundary,* or the contact boundary line that signifies an individual's field (Schulz, 2013). In this process, the individual assimilates nourishment from the environment and rejects or keeps out that which is not nourishing. Therefore, differentiated contact naturally leads to health and development (Schulz, 2013).

Boundary disturbances occur when boundaries between self and others are overly rigid, creating isolation, or are overly permeable, creating a merger in which differentiation of self is lost to confluence with the other (Sabar, 2013). An example of a boundary disturbance is *retroflection,* an internal split within the self in which elements of the self are rejected as not-self. In this situation, the individual does to self what is normally done to the environment—that is, differentiates between nourishing and toxic elements in the environment, assimilating the former and rejecting the latter (Lyngzeidetson, 2011; Stevenson, 2010). For example, an individual who strongly dislikes a person may punish himself or herself because he or she does not have the opportunity to punish the other person (Lyngzeidetson, 2011). The individual in this case disowns parts of his or her self. This undermines health and functioning.

Introjection occurs when material from the environment is taken in without discrimination concerning its nourishing or toxic qualities (Ginger, 2004). This can also be described as naivety, or failing to question things (Stevenson, 2010). Adopting values that are in contrast to the true self results in bad faith (Lyngzeidetson, 2011). Conversely, *projection* involves taking parts of the self and directing them outward onto others, also seen as blaming someone else (Stevenson, 2010), or imposing negative traits of the self onto others resulting in disassociating (Lyngzeidetson, 2011). Some people are unaware of disowned parts of themselves and routinely project them onto others. This interferes with achieving self-awareness, coming to terms with these disowned elements of the person, and accepting them.

Deflection is the avoidance of contact through diversion, or shifting the focus to someone or something else (Lyngzeidetson, 2011; Stevenson, 2010). That is, instead of being direct and genuine in a relationship, the individual may present a disingenuous, false image of himself or herself to others as a way of avoiding contact with the environment (Lyngzeidetson, 2011). A person exhibiting deflection might use sarcasm or cynicism (Lyngzeidetson, 2011). However, deflection also occurs when the individual fails to receive, attend to, or be aware of information coming from the environment, whereas *desensitization* is the act of dissociating one's self in order to feel no emotion or physical response to issues that are difficult to address (Stevenson, 2010).

Dichotomies and Polarities

In field theory, a distinction is made between dichotomies and polarities (Brownell, 2009). *Dichotomies* are unnatural splits in which a field is made up of separate, competing, either/or parts instead of integrated elements in relationship to one another that form a whole (Smith & Ledgerwood, 2010). However, *polarities* are a natural part of fields. Fields are differentiated into polarities—opposite parts that work in tandem or in contrast to one another to help clarify meaning (Stevenson, 2010).

When integration fails, splits occur. The parts of the person—those elements of mind and body that make the person what he or she is—are experienced as separate, not integrated (Sabar, 2013). Thus, a mother may dichotomize her capacity to be a caregiver from her ability to care for herself. However, health is found in integration, in which difference is accepted and various parts of the self work together.

Foreground and Background

Another principle of Gestalt therapy is that of the foreground and background in a phenomenological field (Yontef, 2010), also referred to as *selective attentiveness* (Lyngzeidetson, 2011). The goal is a well-formed figure standing in contrast to a broader, less well-defined background (Pack, 2009). The figure is in the forefront of the individual's awareness of the phenomenological field at any one time. This is to say that individuals have the ability to consciously ignore one element while bringing the other to the forefront (Lyngzeidetson, 2011). Problems occur when foreground and background are not well formed and clearly distinct from each other.

The concept of health according to Gestalt theory defines a situation in which awareness accurately represents and brings to the foreground the dominant need of the whole field (Kalaitzi, 2012; Lyngzeidetson, 2011). Gestalt therapy also abides by the law of *homeostasis* (or self-regulation), which is the organism's tendency to seek balance within itself and between itself and its environment, particularly psychologically (Kenofer, 2010; Lyngzeidetson, 2011). Thus, if the person needs food for energy, he or she becomes hungry, the need for food comes to the foreground, and the person eats. This returns the body to a state of homeostasis and equilibrium in which there is enough food to provide the energy needed for proper functioning (Lyngzeidetson, 2011). The natural human tendency is to seek out states of balance (Lyngzeidetson, 2011).

The Gestalt psychology principle of *prägnanz* (i.e., pithiness) is instructive in concluding the examination of the foreground–background dynamic (Schulz, 2013). In German, *prägnanz,* meaning "concise," "precise," or "simple" (Sabar, 2013), is the idea that the field will form itself into the best gestalt that global conditions will allow. That is, interacting elements in a field and their structure in relationship to one another tend to form themselves, creating foreground and background in the best possible way. Thus, there is an innate drive toward health and growth found in nature, of which humans are a part. In Gestalt therapy, achieving a high level of development in terms of perception, creation, thought, production, and clarity is referred to as "good Gestalt" (Sabar, 2013).

Transposabilty refers to the transfer of properties with the retention of the foundation of that property. For example, a musical melody can be recognized in many different keys while retaining its original form quality. In Gestalt therapy, this refers to the transposability of an individual's thoughts, feelings, and behaviors (Sabar, 2013).

An individual's extrasensory perception of the outside world and his or her internal experience of the outside world are known as *tertiary qualities*. These qualities are viewed as an almost heightened level of awareness that an individual reaches during which he or she has reached the gestalt, or whole, experience (Sabar, 2013).

Awareness

Awareness is the key to Gestalt therapy. In fact, a major goal of Gestalt therapy is awareness itself (Stevenson, 2010). Gestalt practitioners use the *cycle of awareness* as a method of problem solving (Latner, 2013). Through awareness, the organism/person naturally proceeds toward growth, integration, and differentiated unity, in which the parts of the field are separate from, and in contact with, one another. The premise is that the person has the capacity to be aware of his or her own needs and priorities (Lyngzeidetson, 2011). People can accurately know themselves and the environments of which they are a part and make decisions that are congruent with their growth. Being aware, knowing the environment, and being in touch with one's self means that the individual is responsible for self-knowledge, self-acceptance, the ability to make contact, and ultimately the ability to make choices (Lyngzeidetson, 2011; Truscott, 2010). Awareness develops as a result of addressing significant personal issues and through Gestalt-based experiments (Maher, Robertson, & Howie, 2011).

Awareness is a concept that one manages rather than a problem one solves (Stevenson, 2010). In Gestalt therapy, clients are directed to move from just talking about experience to directly experiencing what they are focusing on at any given moment in counseling and therapy. For instance, experiencing and expressing feelings is different as a process from talking about those very same feelings.

Often, people have more choices and are unconsciously making choices that constrict their lives and growth potential (Latner, 2011). Clearly, if the natural process of growth were going well, a client would be unlikely to come to therapy. Thus, it is helpful to understand the meaning of *impasse*. Typically clients reach an impasse—that is, become stuck—when they doubt their ability to be self-supporting and have relied too heavily on external support that is no longer available (Weisberg, 2015). It can be surmised that successful therapy would result in an individual developing the capability of making more deliberate choices (Latner, 2011; see Sidebar 8.3).

Responsibility

Clients are seen as responsible or response-able; they have the ability to respond to their environment appropriately and flexibly (LaHood, 2014). Although it can be important to distinguish between true limitations and real alternatives, ultimately the client has the responsibility to choose and value, to create a healthy balance between self and surroundings (Reilly & Jacobus, 2009). To accomplish this, the client must address *unfinished business*—those important needs, concerns, and issues that require the client's attention (Sabar, 2013). Through increased conscious aware-

Sidebar 8.3. The Cycle of Awareness

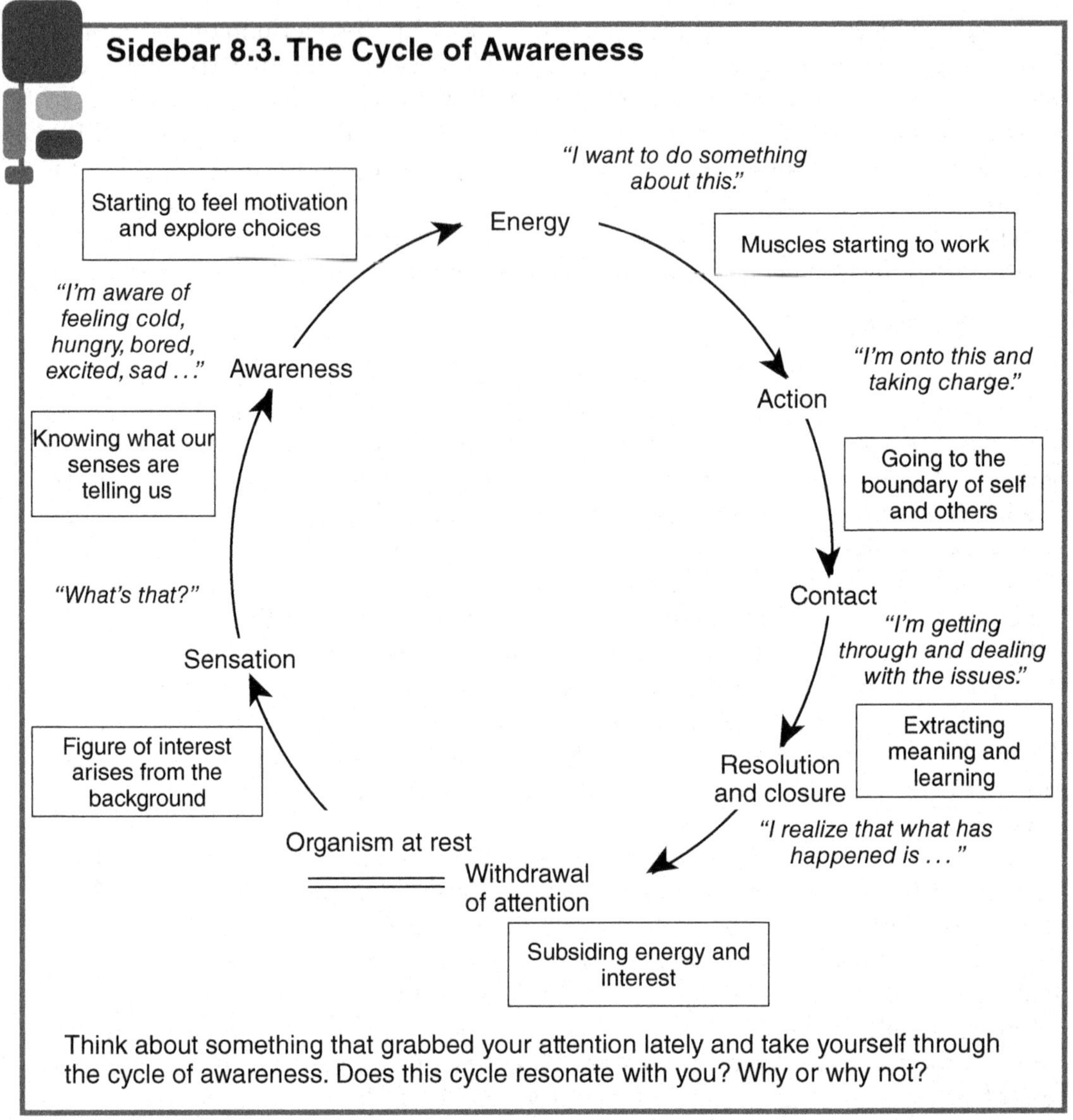

Think about something that grabbed your attention lately and take yourself through the cycle of awareness. Does this cycle resonate with you? Why or why not?

ness, clients also discover disowned parts of the self; this is sometimes called *self-rediscovery* or *existential regeneration* (Lyngzeidetson, 2011). These disowned parts of the self are raised into awareness, considered, and assimilated if congruent with the core of the client's true self or rejected if alien to the client's deepest sense of self. This process of reowning and taking responsibility facilitates integration. In this therapy model, both client and counselor or therapist are self-responsible. Counselors and therapists are responsible for the nature of their presence with the client, having both self-knowledge and knowledge of the client (Ivey, D'Andrea, & Ivey, 2011). They maintain nondefensiveness while keeping their awareness and contact processes clear and in tune with the client (Jones-Smith, 2014). A common method for resolving unfinished business is the empty chair, during which clients are instructed to imagine a person sitting in a chair, which serves as a reminder to consider other perspectives, prompting clients to examine aspects of the problem that may have initially been unexamined (Maurer, 2012).

Shoulds

Arbitrary regulation creates shoulds that can control the client's thoughts, feelings, actions, and relationships (Kenofer, 2010). Any counselor or therapist who has worked with clients has often seen the strong pull between clients' sense of what they should think, feel, or do and the emerging awareness of what they actually do think, feel, or want to do. It is apparent that Gestalt therapy places a high value on autonomy and self-determination (Kenofer, 2010). Although Gestalt therapy maintains a no-should ethic, there is one exception. The exception is the situation. Perls believed that when clients understand the situation they find themselves in and allow it to shape their actions, then they have begun to learn how to cope with life (Yontef & Jacobs, 2007). Otherwise, shoulds are categorized as a dysfunctional behavior (Kenofer, 2010; see Sidebar 8.4).

I-Thou, What and How, Here and Now

A shorthand for Gestalt therapy is reflected in the phrase "I-Thou, what and how, here and now," which was derived from the philosophical writing of Martin Buber (Horsley, 2012). The counselor or therapist and the client form an alliance based on self-responsibility and an agreement to strive to be present with each other during their time together; this is referred to as *the between* (Sabar, 2013). Furthermore, the focus of counseling and therapy is the what and how of a client's experience in the present, in the moments that the counselor or therapist and the client are together (Nevis, 2014). The client and the counselor or therapist explore together through experiments to gain insight and awareness that reveal what the client does and how it is done (Lyngzeidetson, 2011). According to Melnick, Nevis, and Shub (2005), the experiment is one method of teaching the client in which the client can learn. Experiments maintain a here-and-now focus, and the present reality, or principle of contemporaneity, involves a deep understanding of what is currently being experienced regarding the what and how of the client's internal and external processes (Latner, 2013; Schulz, 2013). The point of the experiment is to increase awareness, which is a necessity for growth (Wagemans et al., 2012).

The counselor or therapist is aware of the centrality of the client–counselor/therapist relationship and tends to it by being present, respectful of the client's capacity to heal and grow, and willing to be an authentic person in the therapeutic relationship (Rubenfeld, 2013). Rubenfeld (2013) viewed authenticity as one of the primary Gestalt-humanistic values. The client–counselor/therapist relationship is viewed as horizontal, not vertical. Thus, the two parties seek equality in relation to each other (Wagemans et al., 2012). In this process, when appropriate, the counselor or therapist may choose to share his or her own experience in the moment if it helps to facilitate the client's awareness (Lyngzeidetson, 2011).

Sidebar 8.4. Shoulds

Many of us have shoulds that direct our lives. Examples of some shoulds include "I should be getting straight As in school," "I should be a better friend," "I should feel grateful," "I should be able to stop drinking on my own," "I should be perfect." Reflect on your own set of shoulds. How do these influence your life? Did you recognize them before this exercise? If so, how do you try to control them? What if anything gets in your way?

Direct experience is the tool used to expand awareness, and the focus remains on the client's present experience. Awareness is made deeper and broader as counseling or therapy unfolds. Awareness is viewed as occurring in the right now, although prior events can be the object of present awareness (Lyngzeidetson, 2011). Even though an event took place in the past, the focus is on the awareness of it that is taking place in the now, such as the emotion experienced in that moment as the past is explored. Therefore, the present is understood as an ever-moving transition between past and future (Lyngzeidetson, 2011).

The Gestalt technique of focusing in the present moment and the here and now allows the counselor and client to connect based on the client's experience and current reality, therefore attending to heightened awareness to the impact of culture and the client's identity as it fits into his or her personal context (Novack, Park, & Friedman, 2013). Because of these features, Gestalt therapy may be effectual in work with a wide variety of age groups, including adolescents (Williams, 2010). Gestalt therapy may also be gender appropriate, thus effectual in working with both genders. Novack et al. (2013) suggested that Gestalt therapy may be appropriate for working with male populations, as it promotes the cognizance of choice and action while examining influential societal norms and the experiences of the individual.

APPLICATIONS

Overview

This section discusses the goals and desired outcomes of Gestalt counseling or therapy. An emphasis is on the process of change that leads to client growth. In addition, the specific strategies used in the change process are deliberated.

Goals of Counseling and Psychotherapy

According to Tillett (1991), "As creativity and spontaneity are central to Gestalt, and as there is intrinsic antipathy towards the concept of therapy as technique, it can be difficult to reach an acceptable definition of Gestalt therapy" (p. 290). However, practice may be illuminated by examining the goals of Gestalt therapy. According to Tillett, they include the following:

- Development and expansion of both physical and emotional awareness are emphasized. Intellectual insight and interpretation are limited.
- The relationship between client and therapist is existential and is central to the counseling or psychotherapy process.
- Conversations between client and counselor or psychotherapist are useful only to the extent that they support enactment and experimentation.
- Change should occur as the result of heightened awareness of the interactional process between client and counselor/psychotherapist or by activity and experimentation within the counseling or psychotherapy process. (p. 291)

Whereas Truscott (2010) echoed the primary goal of Gestalt therapy as awareness; Sabar (2013), as wholeness; Rubenfeld (2013), as authenticity; and Kalaitzi (2012), as self-regulation, Yontef (1995) suggested that Gestaltists are not concerned with a "preset end goal" (p. 273). However, Gestaltists do recommend the particular goal of phenomenological exploration rather than reconditioning of behavior or interpretation of the unconscious (Lyngzeidetson, 2011). This goal is valuable in that it places ownership and responsibility directly on the client and facilitates the client's engaging in an inherently natural process of growth. Burley and Freier (2004) suggested that the purpose of Gestalt therapy is the "process of interruption of the gestalt formation and resolution or destruction process" (p. 322). Burley (2012) also noted the importance of exploring every aspect of the gestalt formation and resolution trajectory.

Perls had a focus on further examining five elements of an individual in therapy: bad faith, phobia, stagnation, implosiveness, and explosiveness (Lyngzeidetson, 2011). Bad faith can be explained as a fake self, or an untrue version of the client, and helps evaluate authenticity. Phobia is the fear response to bad faith and, essentially, the process of shattering an individual's untrue self. Stagnation occurs when a client is stuck and unable to progress, also called being at an *impasse.* Implosiveness is achieved when one's true self is embraced, and explosiveness is the energy created in response to implosiveness. The process is known as *stratification* (Lyngzeidetson, 2011). In contrast to other forms of therapy, Gestalt therapy places a low level of importance on memory and the past (Lyngzeidetson, 2011).

The Process of Change

Understanding the process of change from a Gestalt perspective calls for an appreciation of Perls's goal for the process:

> The Gestalt approach attempts to understand the existence of any event through the way it comes about, which is to understand becoming by the how, and not the why; through the all-pervasive gestalt formation; through the tension of the unfinished situation (business). (Perls, as cited in Fagan & Shepherd, 1970, p. 361)

Specifically, the process of change in Gestalt counseling and psychotherapy consists of identifying and working through a variety of blocks or interferences that prevent the client from achieving a balance. Perls (1969a) described clients who block as follows: (a) those who cannot maintain eye contact, who are unaware of their own movements; (b) those who cannot openly express their needs; and (c) those who use repression, examples of which are insomnia and boredom (see Sidebar 8.5).

Another component to the theory of change in Gestalt therapy is the *paradoxical theory of change,* which is discussed in much of the current literature on Gestalt counseling and therapy. This theory posits that when individuals give up trying to become what they would like to become, when they stop struggling and just be what they are, change will occur (Fischer, 2012). The paradox is that change cannot occur until one first accepts things as they truly are (Fischer, 2012), or, as Yontef and Fuhr (2005) stated, "The more one tries to be what one is not, the more one stays the same" (p. 82).

Finally, the process of change in Gestalt counseling and psychotherapy contains a crucial feature that is both a valuable asset and a critical handicap: its open-endedness. Gestalt counselors and therapists rarely use techniques or tools that can be quantified from a proof of theory perspective. However, this open-endedness is the very quality that encourages creativity, inventiveness, response-ability, and spontaneous change and growth by the client.

Sidebar 8.5. Gestalt Therapy Elements

Yontef and Fuhr (2005) asserted that change in Gestalt therapy happens through three methodological elements: (a) field process thinking, (b) experiment in phenomenological awareness, and (c) existential dialogic contact and an ongoing relationship between counselor and client. According to Levitsky and Perls (1970), the process of change, which is aimed at helping clients become more aware of themselves in the here and now (Truscott, 2010), involves several precepts, including the following:

1. *A continuum of awareness:* Clients focus constantly on the how, what, and where in the body, in contrast to the why (Fischer, 2012).
2. *Statements rather than questions:* Many theorists and practitioners have found establishing response-ability to be more helpful and respectful than expecting answers to questions (Maher et al., 2011).
3. *Use of the first-person pronoun "I" rather than "it" or "they":* If a client says, for example, "People feel angry," the counselor or therapist asks the client to restate this sentence using, "I feel angry." Then the client owns his or her feelings instead of distancing himself or herself from them by saying, "I feel thus and so."
4. *The contact issue of addressing someone directly:* Clients are helped to express themselves and their feelings, thoughts, needs, and concerns as they occur in the moment directly to the counselor or therapist. Talking about or beating around the bush is discouraged (Lobb, 2012).

The process of change in Gestalt counseling and psychotherapy involves experience and activity (Wright, 2012). Yontef (1981) believed that all Gestalt techniques are a means of experimentation. He further stated that experimentation in the change process can be used to study any phenomenon that the client has experienced.

As Gestalt therapy continues to evolve, a greater emphasis is being placed on a dialogic approach as opposed to the traditional use of experimentation. This is not to say that the Gestalt counselor or therapist forgoes tried-and-true experiments to facilitate change, but it has been recognized that the contact between client and counselor or therapist in the therapeutic relationship is a key process to change (Cole, 2013). Therefore, this dialogic approach is used more today than it has been used traditionally in the past when experiments took center stage.

Traditional Intervention Strategies

Specific interventions are the concrete behaviors of experimentation that emerge from the cooperation that exists between the client and the practitioner (Yontef, 2010). They are labeled *experiments* because they are procedures aimed at discovery rather than exercises in the traditional sense (Pomerantz & Portillo, 2011). Experiments are not designed to control or initiate behavior change, though this was contradicted by Maher et al. (2011), who asserted that the new information gained as a result of the experiment facilitates change. Instead, experiments are conducted through counselor or therapist recommendations or suggestions for focusing awareness that clients can use to heighten intensity, power, flexibility, and creativity. The action in the experiment is seen as the natural completion of awareness (E. Polster & Polster, 2010).

Yontef (1995) provided the following purposes of experiments:

- "To clarify and sharpen what the client is already aware of and to make new linkages between elements already in awareness.

- To bring into focal awareness that which was previously known only peripherally.
- To bring into awareness that which is needed but systematically kept out of awareness.
- To bring into awareness the system of control, especially the mechanism of preventing thoughts or feelings from coming into focal awareness." (p. 280)

M. Polster (1990) saw experiments as a way of bringing out internal conflicts by making the struggle an actual process. She aimed to facilitate a client's ability to work through the stuck points in his or her life. The strategies of experimentation can take many forms, such as imagining a threatening encounter; setting up dialogue with a significant other; dramatizing the memory of a painful event; reliving a particularly profound past experience in the present through role playing; or exaggerating client gestures, posture, body language, or other signs of internal expression (Lyngzeidetson, 2011).

Perls believed that counseling and psychotherapy were means of enriching life (Dye & Hackney, 1975). From his perspective, it is clear that well people can get better. Intervention strategies suggested in this section are for clients who are fundamentally well but who need assistance in making it in a complex world. The aim of Gestalt counseling and psychotherapy is to take advantage of all dimensions of humanness by achieving integration. The goal is to enable a full experiencing of issues or events rather than just a cognitive understanding of them.

Given the goals of completeness, wholeness, integration, and fulfillment of the essentially healthy but needy individual (in the sense of an incomplete Gestalt), several intervention strategies may be used (see Table 8.1). Unfortunately, space restrictions do not allow for an in-depth discussion of all of the Gestalt experiments available to the practitioner. Therefore, Table 8.1 provides details—albeit brief ones—on several of these experiments. Readers are encouraged to continue exploring these experiments in more detail.

Brief Intervention Strategies and Current Practices

Generally, Gestalt therapy has not been known for its brevity, and it lacks dimensions usually associated with brief interventions, such as quantifiable behavioral goals (James & Gilliland, 2003). Within a managed care setting, it is difficult for administrators to accept the types of treatment goals set in Gestalt therapy because insight is neither concrete nor measurable, two criteria for treatment planning within the managed care setting (Haley & Carrier, 2010).

The process of change and perceived progress of a client is considered a function of the whole field, which includes the client's motivation, the therapeutic relationship, the clinical setting, and the client's social world (Clarkson & Cavicchia, 2013). Therefore, therapy can be a lengthy process and does not lend itself easily to a managed care setting. It should be reiterated here that Gestalt therapy is existential and phenomenological, and therefore the focus is not on facilitating behavioral changes within the client but rather helping the client to develop insight and interpersonal awareness. The purpose is for the client to discover, explore, and experience his or her own shape, pattern, and wholeness and to integrate all of his or her separate parts (Clarkson & Cavicchia, 2013). As a result of this insight and awareness, the client can achieve lifestyle changes (Burley & Freier, 2004).

Table 8.1

Gestalt Therapy Intervention Strategies

Experiment	Purpose	Technique
Location of Feelings	To encourage the client to directly experience sensations in the body that are connected to his or her current feelings.	Instead of asking the client, "What are you feeling?" the therapist tells the client, "Show me where you are feeling this anxiety, apprehension, or nervousness."
Confrontation and Enactment	To help the client to confront old behaviors, feelings, or expressions by acting out the various parts. This confrontation of self and then the enactment of disowned thoughts, feelings, sensations, or actions allow the client to discover and then reown neglected parts of the self.	The client is told to "be your hand," "be your sorrow," "be your hatred." This forces the client to own what has been disowned. By identifying with all of his or her parts, the client can become what he or she truly is and be able to take responsibility for the self.
Empty-Chair or Two-Chair Strategy; also called the "Hot Seat"	To help the client to achieve clarity. This is an extension of the confrontation and enactment intervention. It allows the client to become cognizant of how his or her behavior may be affecting others and to gain insight into all pieces of the problem or issue.	The client is asked to play one or more roles in addition to his or her own self. The client speaks to the part of each person connected to the problem by moving back and forth between the chairs. This technique can also be used for issues that are internal within the client by having the client move back and forth among opposing forces and play out all of the roles pertinent to the internal conflict. For example, in a conflict making a decision, the client can role-play both the pro and the con sides of the decision-making conflict.
Making the Rounds	To teach the client, through a group therapy technique, to be a group member and make some form of contact with other group members or practice new ways of being with each group member.	The client is asked to engage each member of the group. For example, this engagement may be soliciting feedback from each member or making a statement to each member.
Dream-Work	To help the client in the present to understand what may be going on in the here and now. Because images, fantasies, and dreams are the projections of the person, dreams can be seen as the metaphoric expressions of the content and can reveal certain aspects of the person. The dream is not interpreted or symbolized in Gestalt therapy. The dream is simply reenacted to bring awareness to the client regarding the different paths of self.	This technique asks the client to reenact the dream in the present and to play out the parts of the dream as if it were happening in the here and now. The client is told to animate the dream and give voice to all of the people and parts. This allows the counselor or therapist to help the client come into contact with, own, and accept responsibility for parts of the self that may not be well known or accepted, as every part of the dream represents some aspect of the self.
Unfinished Business	To resolve the unresolved feelings that have been left over from interpersonal relationships, most notably feelings of worry, resentment, grief, guilt, or rage. This exercise is designed to bring incomplete gestalts to closure.	The counselor or therapist helps the client to recognize his or her stuck points. The emphasis is on helping the client to recognize and accept what is rather than what could be.
Rehearsal	To help the client bring clarity out of confusion and enable the client to practice change. This intervention seeks to break the client from the habit of playing the prescribed role(s) he or she continues to play within society.	The client is asked to rehearse new sentences or actions that are different from his or her status quo.

(Continued on next page)

Table 8.1 *(Continued)*

Gestalt Therapy Intervention Strategies

Experiment	Purpose	Technique
Minimization	To eliminate the client's ability to minimize self-expression, such as with the conjunction *but*, as in, "I would like to do this, but . . ." or, "I am a good person, but . . ."; this prevents the client from disqualifying or taking away validity by adding ambiguity.	An example of minimization is when the counselor or therapist removes the client's use of the word *but* from his or her expressions by changing it to the word *and* (e.g., "I am a good person, but . . ." to "I am a good person, and . . .") This removes the ambiguity, which allows the client to be noncommittal.
Exaggeration	To help the client be more aware of feelings behind gestures of expression and eliminate his or her ability to minimize. The client is asked to exaggerate some aspect of feeling or expressive act (e.g., a gesture, posture, voice, inflection, or verbal statement). This also enables clients to become aware of subtle signals and cues they are sending through their body language.	The client is asked to exaggerate repetitively some element of his or her being, which includes, but is not limited to, a motion or speech pattern. Through the use of exaggeration, feelings that the client has but has not been aware of can become more apparent and the focus of attention. The client gains awareness of the inner meaning of his or her experience.
Reversal	To help the client bring out polarities that exist within the self, such as good girl vs. bad girl, the caring person vs. the selfish person, the puritanical person vs. the sexual person, top dog vs. underdog, and so on. The client is able to directly address parts of the self that have caused anxiety and therefore have been repressed.	The client is asked to reverse a statement or a way of being. If the client says, "I hate myself," he or she will reverse that statement to "I love myself." If the client is shy and inhibited, he or she would be asked to play the part of a gregarious exhibitionist. The truthfulness of this polarity is then explored for relevance, as overt behavior often represents latent impulses.
Exposing the Obvious	To bring out into the open the deep structures and processes going on within the client of which the client may be unaware.	The counselor or therapist pays close attention to the client in the here and now and exposes aspects of the client of which the client may be unaware. For example, "Are you aware that you are clenching and unclenching your hands?"
Explicitation or Translation	To encourage the client to give voice to a nonverbal expression—a bodily movement, visual image, physical symptom, and so on—which helps him or her to turn the explicit content into implicit reality. This enables the client to experience internally what has only been looked at externally.	The client is asked to verbalize or make explicit something affecting him or her. For example, "If your tears could talk, what would they say?" "If your body spoke words, what would they be?" "If the person who molested you as a child could really tell you his or her feelings, what would he or she say to you?"
Retroflection; also known as "Playing the Projection"	To help a client redirect his or her actions, thoughts, or energy, and regain lost power, energy, and self-support, by determining those aspects of the self that have been projected onto others and then facilitate bringing them back to the self. This enables the client to release his or her inhibitions, stop holding back impulses and choking off behavior, and stop projecting unwanted parts or disowned attributes of the self onto others.	The counselor or therapist has the client redirect to himself or herself what he or she has previously directed outward toward others. This splits the person into two: the giver and the receiver. When projecting, a person places onto someone else the traits, feelings, motives, and so on that he or she does not want to face within himself or herself. When a client makes a statement such as, "I don't trust you," the projection is retroflected or played with, and the client is asked to act out the role of the untrustworthy person.

(Continued on next page)

Table 8.1 *(Continued)*

Gestalt Therapy Intervention Strategies

Experiment	Purpose	Technique
Let the Little Child Talk	To enable the counselor or therapist to talk to the client's inner child. As part of the personality is formed in childhood, many aspects of that child are still found within the adult and influence the adult in all of us.	The counselor or therapist begins by asking the client's permission to speak to his or her inner child. The client is then encouraged to be a child and express feelings, thoughts, and behaviors that have been repressed by adulthood. This allows the adult to listen to the opinions and feelings of the child and let go of restraints and allow the self to be nurtured.
Say It Again; also called "The Repetition Game"	To disrupt a patterned habit of expression and to call attention to ways of perceiving. This technique disables the client's ability to get emotional distance from sensitive feelings by rote expression. This technique makes the client stop to experience the full impact of words and feelings.	The counselor or therapist instructs the client to keep repeating a sentence over and over. For example, a client says, "Nobody likes me." Through repetition, other messages come to the forefront. The end result is that the client may become aware that what he or she was really trying to express is that he or she has never felt loved.
"I Take Responsibility For . . ."	To help clients accept and recognize their feelings and actions and take responsibility for them instead of projecting them onto others.	The counselor or therapist facilitates this by making the statement, "I take responsibility for . . ." and then asks the client to fill in the blank. Typically, the client will make a statement such as, "I am uncomfortable in social situations and I take responsibility for my own feelings of dis-ease."
"I Have a Secret"	To explore feelings of guilt and shame and identify what attachments the client holds that keep him or her from resolving this conflict.	This is a group therapy technique in which group members are encouraged to think of a personal dark secret (but not disclose it to the group) and then imagine (project) how others would react to this secret if it were known.
Contact and Withdrawal	To help the client to understand the polar nature of existence and that it is okay for these polarities to exist. This helps the client to understand it is okay to withdraw from situations to preserve one's attention. For example, one must rest to have energy. This is a polarity, just as one must periodically withdraw from others to maintain closeness. Just as resting enhances energy, so too does temporary withdrawal enhance closeness.	The client is told that when he or she feels like withdrawing from a situation, he or she would close his or her eyes and fantasize about a place where he or she feels secure and safe. When the client feels this safety and security, the client then should open his or her eyes, having rested and enhanced energy, continue on, and reestablish contact.
Can You Stay With This Feeling?	To keep clients from running away from uncomfortable feelings or glossing them over without examination. It prevents the client from avoiding.	When the client expresses a feeling, mood, or state of mind that is unpleasant or uncomfortable and that he or she tries to discount, dispel, or minimize, the client is asked to elaborate on the what and how of his or her feelings.

However, given that Gestalt therapy is action oriented, it can in some ways be similar to cognitive behavior therapies, and therefore brief therapy benefits can be derived (Houston, 2003). There is no one way to conduct Gestalt therapy, and therefore it can be flexible to brief intervention (Brownell & Fleming, 2005). Gestalt therapy is interested in how a client does the things he or she does and in building self-awareness. This, in turn, can lead to the client making different choices in his or her life. As Houston (2003) stated it, "The aim of Gestalt Therapy is to awaken or mobilize people enough for them to get on better with their lives than they were managing before coming for help" (p. 3).

Houston (2003) advocated for brief Gestalt therapy, in which the client is active between sessions in applying the insight learned in session. Houston asserted that clients who are psychologically minded, insight oriented, motivated, and able to develop and sustain relationships are the best candidates for brief Gestalt therapy. In this manner, brief Gestalt therapy can be effective in as little as eight sessions.

Clients With Serious Mental Health Issues

The diagnosis of mental health disorders provides an increased insight into the impact of mental health issues while similarly guiding treatment plans contingent on diagnosis and presenting symptoms (American Psychiatric Association, 2013). It is difficult to have a discussion of Gestalt therapy in relation to clients with serious mental health issues because Gestalt therapy is holistic; it does not break a person down into separate pieces or variables, and therefore it is difficult to classify clients in the manner required by the *Diagnostic and Statistical Manual of Mental Disorders, Fifth Edition* (*DSM–5*).

Gestaltists do not believe in disease but rather in dis-ease, and the term *mental disorder* is inimical to the Gestalt approach. In its early development, Gestalt therapy was not commonly used in conjunction with psychosis and disordered issues (Arnfred, 2012). Gestaltists believe that disorders are holistic and organismic and that symptoms of dysfunction are not in an individual but rather in the reality of a person's experience (White, 2009). One of the goals of the therapeutic process is to induce the abilities of the individual to return to a restorative state in which he or she becomes more complete, balanced, and aligned (Clarkson & Cavicchia, 2013).

Gestalt theory relates the development of pathology to habitual self-interruption along the contact–withdrawal continuum. Contact–withdrawal is a concept that explains people's interactions with others (Bloom, 2009a, 2009b). People make contact with others from the outside boundary of themselves. Humans strive to be together with others in the world (Pack, 2009). When a person has a bad experience making contact with others, then he or she begins to withdraw to protect the self (Lobb, 2003). This self-protection prevents appropriate interaction with others, and interactions that could be classified as pathological result instead. The process of therapy then is interwoven with strategies that assist the client in the progression of self-discovery and cognition to a perception of the self as it fits into current reality and culture (Pfluger, 2014).

As a result of this hindered progress along the contact–withdrawal cycle, people's needs are not met and they become inhibited in their awareness and expression. As a consequence, they begin to internalize to meet their needs satisfaction. Part of the process of this internalization is that people begin to introject that which they cannot get from themselves and internalize messages given by others that they begin to see as truth. Believing they are bad encourages people's fear of abandonment by others, and they then begin to block their awareness, put up defenses, and retroflect (turn back on the self) to prevent themselves from expressing their wants or needs and to keep others from leaving them (Lobb & Lichtenberg, 2005). This is the Gestalt theory of pathology.

Conversely, normal, healthy behavior occurs when people act and react as total organisms—unfragmented, self-regulating, and able to converse along the contact–withdrawal continuum by not self-interrupting (Lobb & Lichtenberg, 2005). The healthy person concentrates on one need (the figure) at any present time, delegating other needs to the background. When the need is met, the gestalt closes and is completed, and no business is left unfinished. When the need is unmet, the gestalt remains open and the person accumulates unfinished business (Clarkson & Cavicchia, 2013).

Research supports that Gestalt therapy works best for overly socialized, restrained, and constricted individuals who intellectualize and have trouble clarifying their feelings (Seligman & Reichenberg, 2013). Gestalt therapy does not categorize clients according to the *DSM–5* criteria and has not been limited by the above constraints. Although not necessarily aligned with a specified context of diagnosis, Gestalt therapy is adaptable in the therapist's ability to work with various disorders, thus allowing the therapist flexibility, especially through experimentation (Van Baalen, 2010).

In fact, Gestalt therapy has been adapted to be used for a variety of modalities and issues. It has been used in group therapy and with issues related to self and divorce (Saadati & Lashani, 2013). It has also been utilized in the form of art therapy and sand therapy (Ferreira, Eloff, Kukard, & Kriegler, 2014), crisis counseling (Young & Lester, 2012), organizational consultation (Gestalt International Study Center, 2015; Stevenson, 2010), grief counseling (Bandín, 2012), and pastoral care and counseling (Hamilton, 2014) and with adolescent populations (Williams, 2010). Gestalt therapy has also been utilized in working with sex- and gender-related issues (Fallon, 2012) and masculinity-related issues (Novack et al., 2013) and has been foundational in many of the touch therapies (Zimmer & Dunning, 1998) as well as eye-movement desensitization and reprocessing therapy (Tobin, 2004).

Seligman and Reichenberg (2013) stated that Gestalt therapy can be used successfully with the following disorders: mood disorders, anxiety disorders, somatoform disorders, factitious disorders, adjustment disorders, and some personality disorders or personality traits (such as avoidant, dependent, narcissistic, histrionic, and obsessive-compulsive disorders). On reviewing various case studies and literature reviews, it is apparent that Gestalt therapy may be useful with a wide range of mental health issues, such as, but not limited to, depression (Ellison, Greenberg, Goldman, & Angus, 2009), posttraumatic stress disorder, substance abuse, anxiety (Sharf, 2012), bulimia nervosa (Pfluger, 2014), bipolar disorder (Van Baalen, 2010), borderline personality disorder and self-injury (Williams, 2010), schizophrenia (Arnfred, 2012), and dementia (Siampani, 2013).

It should be noted that caution has been mandated in the use of Gestalt experiments. Although these experiments may seem simple and easy to apply, many are not suitable for all clients, especially those clients who are emotionally fragile, because most of these techniques are very intense. The same cautions are espoused when counselors work with clients who are severely psychotic, severely disturbed, in crisis, or poorly motivated to change (Seligman & Reichenberg, 2013).

The skill of the Gestalt counselor or therapist is at issue when he or she is working with these types of clients. Improper methods or an inability to work with the client through the trauma, grief, rage, or other intense emotions brought up by these techniques can leave the client in a very vulnerable position. Individuals with more severe issues or disturbances will need long-term intensive counseling or psychotherapy. Although this can be done within the bounds of Gestalt therapy, it must be done with caution and skill.

Lobb (2003) advised that when counselors work with clients who are psychotic, paranoid, or schizoid, it is prudent to limit activities to those that strengthen the client's contact with reality. Gestalt therapy may also be contraindicated for some issues and populations. These might include those clients with a problem with impulse control, those who act out, or those who are delinquent. For these individuals, Gestalt therapy may reinforce those behaviors. In addition, Gestalt therapy may not be suited for use in all cultures, because its sometimes confrontational nature can make clients from some non-Western cultures uncomfortable (Seligman & Reichenberg, 2013).

EVALUATION

This section provides an overview of the unique contributions of Gestalt therapy to counseling and client health. Following that is a review of significant current research as to the efficacy of Gestalt therapy. This section concludes with a discussion of known limitations.

Overview

Several unique contributions have been made by the Gestalt counseling and psychotherapy model. The first is the emphasis on the client's inherent wholeness and capacity for self-awareness (Bowman & Nevis, 2005). The work of the counselor or therapist is to help clients use focused awareness on their own to free up energy for health and growth. A second contribution is the application of dialogue in the counseling or psychotherapy relationship. The counseling or psychotherapy dialogue provides contact between the client and the counselor or therapist. Dialogue is used to engage clients, not to manipulate or control them. The goal of the Gestalt therapist is to embody authenticity and responsibility in conversations with the client (Clarkson & Cavicchia, 2013).

A third contribution is the emphasis on the counseling or therapy process rather than sole reliance on techniques (Melnick et al., 2005). Beginning practitioners often depend on techniques more than process to help their client. In the application of Gestalt therapy, this creates difficulties because the process of counseling or psychotherapy must accommodate itself to the personalities and experiences of the counselor or therapist and the client. This often makes it difficult for the novice counselor or therapist to pinpoint an appropriate technique to apply to a particular problem. In Gestalt therapy, any activity that contributes to clients' awareness of self, others, and their experience of the larger world is seen as useful.

A fourth contribution of Gestalt counseling involves dream-work (Clarkson & Cavicchia, 2013). Confronting unfinished business through dream-work or other interventions allows the practitioner to challenge the client's past in a lively and provocative manner. The purpose of engaging the past is for the client to become aware of and work with concerns, even those from the past, that are a part of present experience and therefore undermine the client's current functioning.

A fifth contribution of Gestalt counseling and psychotherapy is its evolutionary shift from constructivism to social constructivism and the acknowledgment that organisms cocreate their own reality (Lobb & Lichtenberg, 2005). People are reactive and cocreate their own truth and reality. Gestalt counseling and therapy has helped the field of counseling evolve over time. Bowman and Nevis (2005) proclaimed that Gestalt therapy has increased a shared therapeutic worldview among practitioners, as there "has been movement (a) from deconstructive views of the world toward holistic models of existence; (b) from linear causality toward field theoretical paradigms; and (c) from an individualistic psychology toward a dialogical or relational perspective" (p. 5).

Finally, in this age of requirements for accountability to those who pay for services, such as third-party payers, the Gestalt approach lends itself well to treating certain diagnoses. According to Seligman and Reichenberg (2013), Gestalt therapy is appropriate for treating certain affective disorders, including anxiety, somatoform, and adjustment disorders, as well as occupational and interpersonal problems, and according to Houston (2003), Gestalt therapy can be effective as a brief therapy to fit the managed care environment.

Supporting Research

Gestalt therapy focuses on phenomenology and the subjective experience of the client. It is largely existential, experiential, and experimental in nature. There is not one direct path to conducting Gestalt therapy; therefore, the therapeutic approach is experimental and nondirective, allowing the client to develop cognitions to his or her own individual reality (Sharf, 2012). On the whole, Gestalt therapy has been commonly seen as lacking in conventional research and has also lacked transcription compared to other therapeutic approaches (Tønnesvang, Sommer, Hammink, & Sonne, 2010).

One of the attributes of this theoretical orientation includes the counselor's genuineness and authenticity individualized based on the client (Clarkson & Cavicchia, 2013). The evaluation of client outcomes in Gestalt therapy is idiographic—that is, assumed to be based on individual experiences unique to the subject of evaluation. Although individuals can be questioned about their unique experience of growth in Gestalt therapy, these reports do not lend themselves well to empirical research and the summation of findings via statistical analyses of group data. A comparison between Gestalt and other therapeutic approaches yielded the finding that Gestalt therapy may be similar to other approaches and therefore as effective as other therapeutic approaches (Tønnesvang et al., 2010).

Current research trends have suggested that Gestalt therapy is effective for working with a variety of disorders, populations, and context cases (Perera-Diltz et al., 2012; Williams, 2010). Based on a lack of research in areas of current Gestalt trends, there is an awareness among Gestalt practitioners of the need for continued research pertaining to evidence-based practices in Gestalt therapy as based on conference and association trends (Fischer, 2012). There is also a gap in research trends related to Gestalt therapy, as it has influenced specific fields within helping professions (Kelly & Howie, 2011). Kelly and Howie (2011) conducted a qualitative study examining the influence of Gestalt in the field of psychiatric nursing and concluded that this approach is complementary and useful to this field. Other recent research on Gestalt has examined the use of group Gestalt therapy for measuring self-efficacy in divorced women, concluding a positive increase in self-efficacy (Saadati & Lashani, 2013). Similarly, current trends in research have yielded studies on the impact of Gestalt in various fields as well as Gestalt applied to different situations. Overall research has demonstrated effectiveness compared to other therapeutic approaches and also to nontreatment groups (Sharf, 2012).

Limitations

One of the limitations related to Gestalt counseling and psychotherapy has little to do with the theory itself but with Perls (Reilly & Jacobus, 2009). The reliance on the workshop format developed during the 1960s seemed to lead to a reliance on Perls himself as a sort of guru who could answer any problem by demonstrating Gestaltism in a workshop (Stoehr, 2009). Although today's practitioners of Gestalt are gentler and less confrontational, the therapy is still largely associated with the antics of Perls himself (Yontef, 2007). In addition, Perls's work is sometimes seen as a potpourri of various theories—a little Freud, a little Carl Jung, and a lot of the Berlin school—yet Perls seldom credited them for their contributions. Consequently, in her later years and on reflection, Laura Perls noted that there were as many ways to do Gestalt therapy as there were Gestalt therapists, which further dilutes the practice of the theory (Brownell & Fleming, 2005).

Another limitation of Gestalt therapy is the temptation for novice counselors or therapists to use such Gestalt techniques (i.e., processes) as empty chair, top dog/underdog, figure–ground, and locating feelings without sufficient practitioner training. However, these processes alone can be of little value in helping the client. In addition, the intense emotional responses that some Gestalt experiments evoke can be harmful to the client if misused or abused by an inexperienced counselor or therapist (Melnick et al., 2005).

Other criticisms stem from counselors who use Gestalt therapy and integrate other techniques into a hybrid form of counseling that does not fit under the Gestalt theoretical umbrella. Sometimes these other techniques clash with Gestalt theory and are ineffectual (Brownell & Fleming, 2005). Some practitioners believe the client's cognitive process is important in counseling or psychotherapy work, yet many Gestaltists tend to deemphasize cognition, focusing more on feeling (Yontef, 1993). In addition, the holistic nature of Gestalt counseling and psychotherapy and its allowances for therapist creativity in developing treatments fly in the face of today's trend toward specialization in the medical field. Finally, Gestalt therapy does not lend itself well to diagnosis using the *DSM–5* (American Psychiatric Association, 2015) or behavioral contracting, which limits its applicability in managed care settings (James & Gilliland, 2003).

In addition, there may be some concerns regarding the use of Gestalt therapy for working cross-culturally with clients from minority populations. Gestalt therapy emphasizes individual responsibility for one's own happiness and advocates for the expression of emotion. Clients from cultures that are collectivist and emphasize collective responsibility, or clients who do not favor the expression of emotion, may find this therapy inapplicable, unhelpful, or even harmful (James & Gilliland, 2003).

Despite the limitations that may exist in Gestalt counseling and psychotherapy, its holistic nature is one of its most appealing features. Contrasted with more empirical scientific approaches, it offers a wide variety of opportunities to facilitate the client's journey toward greater health and development.

Summary Chart: Gestalt Theory

Human Nature

Rooted in existentialism and phenomenology, Gestalt counseling and psychotherapy focuses attention on the holistic nature of humankind. Gestalt counselors and therapists strive to encompass the whole organism and operate from the perspective that human beings have the capacity and strength to grow, to develop, and to become the persons they want to be. A basic assumption is that individuals can deal with their life problems if they are fully aware of what is happening in and around them.

Major Constructs

There are a number of major constructs connected with Gestalt counseling and psychotherapy: holism; the concept of unifying wholes, which includes mind and body, past and present, and individual and environment; field theory, or the idea that the individual in his or her environment produces a psychological field in which self-regulation can take place; figure–ground, or the idea that the client's unfinished business becomes figure or foreground during the therapeutic process and everything else temporarily recedes to ground or background; a here-and-now orientation, or an emphasis on the present rather than on the past or the future for the purpose of promoting the growth process; and boundaries and polarities, or the client's definition in relation to the environment and traits existing on the opposite ends of the same continuum (Yontef & Fuhr, 2005).

Goals

The goals of Gestalt counseling and psychotherapy are to identify themes that are central to the client's self-organization; conceptualize the issues and concerns of the client that will guide the sequence, timing, and methods used; establish and maintain a safe professional environment; and provide an atmosphere that invites contact between the client and the counselor or therapist.

Change Process

Change results from the identification and working through of a variety of blocks or interferences that prevent the client from achieving a holistic integration of all aspects of self and the capacity to achieve responsibility for self. Clients work through the cliché, phony, impasse, implosive, and exploding layers of neurosis during this process.

Interventions

Usually labeled as *experiments* because they are procedures aimed at discovery and not exercises in the traditional sense, interventions are designed to control or initiate behavior change (Melnick et al., 2005). Gestalt interventions may include locating feelings, enactment and confrontation, empty chair, dream-work, dialogue, making the rounds, unfinished business, playing the projection, rehearsal, and exaggeration.

Limitations

There are several limitations to and criticisms of Gestalt therapy. Gestalt theory is said to deemphasize the cognitive components of the counseling and psychotherapy process. It is often seen as a potpourri of theories and philosophies. The holistic approaches of Gestalt therapy can be incompatible with today's emphasis on time-limited, brief approaches. Another criticism is that the theory places too much emphasis on the here and now. Finally, Gestalt confrontation and emphasis on exploring emotion may not work well with cultures that emphasize collectivist responsibility or that do not advocate sharing emotional expression.

THE CASE OF MARIA: A GESTALT APPROACH

It should be understood that the goal of Gestalt therapy is not to facilitate direct change within the client through planned intervention but instead to facilitate the client's awareness and insight into himself or herself using creative experiments (Clarkson & Cavicchia, 2013). Specifically, from the existential perspective, the goal is to help the client become aware of his or her subjective experience as fully as possible. The desired outcome is that the client will become more authentic as a person. He or she will be able to shed his or her false self and the shoulds that make up his or her life. The client will then make better choices that lead to a better life situation; will develop the ability for growth; and will become more integrated within the self, with others, and between the self and the environment. Through this enhanced awareness of the self, the client will gain self-acceptance and be able to take responsibility for his or her choices and be in charge of his or her own destiny.

The objective of therapy for any client is to help the client become response-able and break through his or her stuck points. The therapy is not directive but is experiential and is conducted through a conduit of the here and now and through the client–therapist (I–Thou) relationship. The focus is on the process and not the content.

Case Conceptualization

Maria has experienced a series of disappointments and traumas in the past few years. She has survived an abusive relationship and the abandonment of herself and her children by her husband, she has endured estrangement and disapproval from her family of origin, and she is struggling to parent her children alone. She does not feel that she is receiving any support from her family or her employer, and it is clear that she feels alone and hopeless. In other words, she feels stuck and is at an impasse in her life.

Maria has also introjected and internalized toxic material from her environment through the negativity of her family and other important individuals in her life. Therefore, she has not been able to differentiate herself from significant others' views or goals for her. This has led to confluence, which has contributed to her problems. In addition, Maria is not currently experiencing any support through a genuine, trusting relationship, and thus her growth has been hindered and she has experienced a negative view of self. Consequently, she has become out of synch with herself, her culture, and her view of the world. She has also lost contact with important others and has withdrawn from her children, her friends, her family, and even herself.

Treatment Plan

Creative and spontaneous intervention is the method of the experienced Gestalt counselor or therapist. The major goal of Gestalt counseling or psychotherapy toward which interventions aim is autonomy and growth of the client through increased awareness. According to Yontef (1995), this can be *microawareness*—awareness of a particular content area and awareness of the awareness process. Through heightened awareness, clients can know what they are choosing to do and can ultimately accept responsibility for these actions. They can also discover available choices and alternatives they may not have recognized because of limited self-awareness.

To help facilitate client awareness and growth, the practitioner does the following:

- He or she identifies themes or presenting problems that are central to the client's self-organization.
- He or she conceptualizes the issues and concerns of the client that will guide the sequence, timing, and methods of the counseling or psychotherapy process.
- He or she establishes and maintains a safe and professional environment.
- He or she provides an atmosphere that invites contact between client and counselor or therapist and encourages interaction.

Specifically, in the case of Maria, it will be very important to establish contact with her through a genuine, trusting relationship in which she can feel safe and supported and can explore her emotion regarding the hurt and pain she carries within. When a person is supported through a genuine and trusting relationship, that person can grow in a positive direction and can gain a positive sense of self. Empathic understanding through the dialogue between counselor and client is seen as an important part of this change process.

One goal for Maria is to help her develop awareness of her emotions and her own needs, goals, and priorities as separate from those around her. Once Maria can accurately know herself and know her own wants and needs as separate from those of others, she can differentiate herself from her environment. She will become aware of how the choices she has made for herself have constricted her life and growth potential. This will enable her to make decisions for herself that will be healthy and contribute to her positive growth.

Toward this end, it is important to keep Maria present in the here-and-now exploration of her feelings, beliefs, and values as she relates her experiences to her therapist. Maria will need help in exploring the unfinished business of her divorce and family situation and in purging unexpressed emotions. In this manner, she will gain insight and can truly work through her unfinished business in a productive manner. This may help alleviate her bad dreams and provide better sleep for her.

It is also important for the counselor to view Maria as capable and response-able to empower her to help her learn to be self-directing and self-actualizing. One caveat here would be to proceed within the boundaries of Maria's culture, but it may be important to help her explore her culture and help her own it rather than have it be an introjected part of her environment. Maria has the response-ability to choose what she values and discover for herself which parts of her culture are congruent with her core, true self. This too will also help Maria become more integrated and differentiated, and she will gain valuable self-knowledge. One way of doing this is to help Maria explore the shoulds in her life to gain a deeper understanding of where these come from, which are helpful, and which contribute to her feelings of depression and sense of stuckness.

Experiments

In collaboration with the client, Gestalt counselors and therapists design experiments that will bring about greater self-knowledge and insight. This will allow the client to complete unfinished business by bringing the situation from the past and into the right now, whereby the client can use words, actions, or fantasy to complete the unfinished event (Melnick et al., 2005). Some of the experiments that could facilitate the goals outlined for Maria are listed here. Many experiments could be used in the case of Maria, but space prohibits us from discussing more than one or two here. We describe the following two techniques in an attempt to give the reader insight into how these experiments might be used and how they might enhance Maria's awareness.

Empty-Chair Technique

This technique can be used to help Maria express her feelings, understand her beliefs regarding her divorce, and help her deal with the unfinished business that continues to plague her surrounding this event. The counselor or therapist will ask Maria for her permission to proceed with the experiment. With her approval, the counselor or therapist will have Maria sit in one chair with another empty chair directly across from her. The counselor or therapist will then have Maria speak both her part and the part of her husband. This will allow Maria the opportunity not only to express her repressed and avoided feelings but also to express what Maria imagines her husband would say to her in response. This experiment will take Maria out of the safety zone of referring to her feelings in the past tense and bring her emotions into the present. The goal is to help Maria explore and work through her emotions in the here and now. Through the empty chair, Maria can speak directly to her husband and tell him of her anger and sense of betrayal and abandonment. In this way, Maria can complete her unfinished business with her husband and gain valuable insight into herself. This same technique can be used to work through her feelings of failure and rejection regarding other family members, her children, or her employer.

Unfinished Business

This is a powerful experiment that can help Maria greatly and should prove useful in alleviating her symptoms of depression and in diminishing her bad dreams. The purpose of exploring Maria's unfinished business is to resolve the unresolved feelings that have been left over from her interpersonal relationships, most notably feelings of worry, resentment, grief, guilt, or rage. This exercise is designed to bring Maria's incomplete gestalts to closure, which will help move these issues from her foreground to her background. The counselor or therapist can help Maria recognize her stuck points and help her move past them. The emphasis should be on helping Maria recognize and accept what is rather than what could be. The focus should be on helping Maria live in the right now rather than staying stuck in the past. She cannot change what happened, but she can change how she responds to what happens, and she can be instrumental in creating a more positive future for herself and her children.

REFERENCES

American Psychiatric Association. (2013). *Diagnostic and statistical manual of mental disorders* (5th ed.). Arlington, VA: Author.

American Psychiatric Association. (2015). *Understanding mental disorders: Your guide to DSM–5.* Retrieved from http://www.psychiatry.org/mental-health/understanding-mental-disorders

Arnfred, S. M. (2012). Gestalt therapy for patients with schizophrenia: A brief review. *Gestalt Review, 16*(1), 53–68.

Bandín, C. V. (2010). Reflections on process groups at the 11th international Gestalt therapy conference ("The Union of Differences"), Madrid, April 2009. *Gestalt Review, 14*(2), 196–203.

Bandín, C. V. (2012). "Espérame en el cielo": The process of grief according to Gestalt therapy. *Gestalt Review, 16*(2), 126–144.

Bloom, D. (2009a). Commentary I: The cycle of experience re-cycled: Then, now . . . next? *Gestalt Review, 13,* 24–36.

Bloom, D. (2009b). The phenomenological method of Gestalt therapy: Revisiting Husserl to discover the "essence" of Gestalt therapy. *Gestalt Review, 13*(3), 277–295.

Bowman, C. E., & Nevis, E. C. (2005). The history and development of Gestalt therapy. In A. L. Woldt & S. M. Toman (Eds.), *Gestalt therapy: History, theory, and practice* (pp. 3–20). Thousand Oaks, CA: Sage.

Brownell, P. (2009). Executive functions: A neuropsychological understanding of self-regulation. *Gestalt Review, 13,* 62–81.

Brownell, P., & Fleming, K. (2005). Gestalt therapy in community mental health. In A. L. Woldt & S. M. Toman (Eds.), *Gestalt therapy: History, theory, and practice* (pp. 257–277). Thousand Oaks, CA: Sage.

Burley, T. (2012). Holism in Gestalt theory: A response to Jacobs and McConville. *Gestalt Review, 16*(1), 44–52.

Burley, T., & Freier, M. C. (2004). Character structure: A Gestalt–cognitive theory. *Psychotherapy: Theory, Research, Practice, Training, 41,* 321–331.

Clarkson, P., & Cavicchia, S. (2013). *Gestalt counselling in action* (4th ed.). Thousand Oaks, CA: Sage.

Cole, P. (2013). In the shadow of the leader: Power, reflection, and dialogue in Gestalt group therapy. *Gestalt Review, 17*(2), 178–188.

Dye, A., & Hackney, H. (1975). *Gestalt approaches to counseling.* Boston, MA: Houghton Mifflin.

Ellison, J. A., Greenberg, L. S., Goldman, R. N., & Angus, L. (2009). Maintenance of gains following experiential therapies for depression. *Journal of Consulting and Clinical Psychology, 77,* 103–112.

Engelmann, A. (2008). Two important but almost never related beliefs. *Integrative Psychological and Behavioral Science, 42,* 87–91.

Fagan, J., & Shepherd, I. (Eds.). (1970). *Gestalt therapy now: Theory, techniques, and applications.* Palo Alto, CA: Science & Behavior Books.

Fallon, S. (2012). Sex, gender, and the theatre of self: Acting theory in (Gestalt) psychotherapy with a transsexual client. *Gestalt Review, 16*(2), 162–180.

Ferreira, R., Eloff, I., Kukard, C., & Kriegler, S. (2014). Using sandplay therapy to bridge a language barrier in emotionally supporting a young vulnerable child. *The Arts in Psychotherapy, 41*(1), 107–114.

Fischer, S. L. (2012). Editorial: Plus ça change, ça n'est plus la même chose: Change as "choiceful" learning and development. *Gestalt Review, 16*(2), 122–125.

Gaffney, S. (2009). The cycle of experience re-cycled: Then, now . . . next? *Gestalt Review, 13,* 7–23.

Gestalt International Study Center. (2015). *Edwin C. Nevis, PhD (1926-2011).* Retrieved from http://www.gisc.org/about/faculty/enevis.php

Ginger, S. (2004). Sandor Ferenczi, the grandfather of Gestalt therapy. *Gestalt Review, 8,* 358–368.

Goleman, D. (1990, July 18). *Laura Perls, 84, dies in Germany; founder of Gestalt psychotherapy.* Retrieved from the *New York Times* website: http://www.nytimes.com/1990/07/18/obituaries/laura-perls-84-dies-in-germany-founder-of-gestalt-psychotherapy.html

Goodtherapy.org. (2015). *Fritz Perls (1893-1970).* Retrieved from http://www.goodtherapy.org/famous-psychologists/fritz-perls.html

Gregory, S. (2014). An introduction to Gestalt therapy theory and practice. In C. Eigen (Ed.), *Inner dialogue in daily life: Contemporary approaches to personal and professional development in psychotherapy* (pp. 129–142). Philadelphia, PA: Jessica Kingsley.

Halbur, D. A., & Halbur, K. V. (2011). *Developing your theoretical orientation in counseling and psychotherapy* (2nd ed.). Boston, MA: Allyn & Bacon.

Haley, M., & Carrier, J. W. (2010). Psychotherapy groups. In D. Capuzzi, D. Gross, & M. Stauffer (Eds.), *Introduction to group work* (5th ed., pp. 295–320). Denver, CO: Love.

Hamilton, J. D. (2014). *Gestalt in pastoral care and counseling: A holistic approach.* New York, NY: Routledge.

Honeywell, C. (2011). Paul Goodman. *Journal for the Study of Radicalism, 5*(2), 1–33.

Horsley, J. (2012). Design, dialogue, and difference (or "self and the city"). *Gestalt Journal of Australia and New Zealand, 8*(2), 79–91.

Houston, G. (2003). *Brief Gestalt therapy.* Thousand Oaks, CA: Sage.

Ivey, A., D'Andrea, M., & Ivey, M. (2011). *Theories of counseling and psychotherapy: A multicultural perspective.* Thousand Oaks, CA: Sage.

James, R. K., & Gilliland, B. E. (2003). *Theories and strategies in counseling and psychotherapy* (5th ed.). Boston, MA: Allyn & Bacon.

Jones-Smith, E. (2014). *Theories of counseling and psychotherapy: An integrative approach.* London, England: Sage.

Kalaitzi, E. (2012). Calling for a Gestalt developmental perspective. *Gestalt Review, 16*(3), 273–291.

Keenan, B. (2011). Community and confluence: Undoing the clinch of oppression (1990/1994/2002). *Gestalt Review, 15*(1), 46–58.

Kelly, T., & Howie, L. (2007). Working with stories in nursing research: Procedures used in narrative analysis. *International Journal of Mental Health Nursing, 16,* 136–144.

Kelly, T., & Howie, L. (2011). Exploring the influence of Gestalt therapy training on psychiatric nursing practice: Stories from the field. *International Journal of Mental Health Nursing, 20*(4), 296–304.

Kenofer, B. (2010). Developing the concept of organismic need. *Gestalt Review, 14*(1), 54–70.

LaHood, G. A. (2014). Toward the embodiment and enactment of phenomenology, field theory and dialogue in Gestalt group process: A literature review. *Gestalt Journal of Australia and New Zealand, 10*(2), 38–59.

Latner, J. (2011). Review of the emergent self: An existential-Gestalt approach. *Gestalt Review, 15*(2), 180–188.

Latner, J. (2013). Fritz Perls in Berlin and after: Apropos Fritz Perls in Berlin 1893-1933: Expressionism, psychoanalysis, Judaism (Bernd Bocian). *Gestalt Review, 17*(2), 189–199.

Levitsky, A., & Perls, F. S. (1970). The rules and games of Gestalt therapy. In J. Fagan & Shepherd (Eds.), *Gestalt therapy now: Theory, techniques, and applications* (pp. 140–149). Palo Alto, CA: Science & Behavior Books.

Lobb, M. S. (2003). Creative adjustment in madness: A Gestalt therapy model for seriously disturbed patients. In M. S. Lobb & N. Amendt-Lyon (Eds.), *Creative license: The art of Gestalt therapy* (pp. 261–277). New York, NY: Springer-Verlag Wien.

Lobb, M. S. (2012). Toward a developmental perspective in Gestalt therapy, theory, and practice: The polyphonic development of domains. *Gestalt Review, 16*(3), 222–244.

Lobb, M. S., & Lichtenberg, P. (2005). Classical Gestalt therapy theory. In A. L. Woldt & S. M. Toman (Eds.), *Gestalt therapy: History, theory, and practice* (pp. 21–39). Thousand Oaks, CA: Sage.

Lyngzeidetson, A. E. (2011). *Psychology: Counseling and psychotherapy* [Pamphlet]. Boca Raton, FL: BarCharts.

Maher, A., Robertson, R., & Howie, L. (2011). The experience and development of awareness in Gestalt therapy training groups: A phenomenological study. *Gestalt Journal of Australia and New Zealand, 8*(1), 36–56.

Maurer, R. (2012). Creating a shift: The power of the empty chair. *Journal for Quality and Participation, 35*(2), 10–11.

Melnick, J., Nevis, S. M., & Shub, N. (2005). Gestalt therapy methodology. In A. L. Woldt & S. M. Toman (Eds.), *Gestalt therapy: History, theory, and practice* (pp. 101–115). Thousand Oaks, CA: Sage.

Nevis, E. C. (Ed.). (2014). *Gestalt therapy: Perspectives and applications* (Kindle ed.). Boca Raton, FL: CRC Press.

Novack, J., Park, S. J., & Friedman, A. N. (2013). Integrated masculinity: Using Gestalt counseling with male clients. *Journal of Counseling & Development, 91*, 483–489.

Pack, M. (2009). Supervision as a liminal space: Towards a dialogic relationship. *Gestalt Journal of Australia and New Zealand, 5*(2), 60–78.

Peirson, L. J., Boydell, K. M., Ferguson, H. B., & Ferris, L. E. (2011). An ecological process model of systems change. *American Journal of Community Psychology, 47*(3/4), 307–321. doi:10.1007/s10464-010-9405-y

Perera-Diltz, D. M., Laux, J. M., & Toman, S. M. (2012). A cross-cultural exploration of posttraumatic stress disorder: Assessment, diagnosis, recommended (Gestalt) treatment. *Gestalt Review, 16*(1), 69–87.

Perls, F. (1969a). *Gestalt therapy verbatim.* Lafayette, CA: Real Person Press.

Perls, F. (1969b). *In and out of the garbage pail.* Lafayette, CA: Real Person Press.

Perls, F. S., Hefferline, R., & Goodman, P. (1951). *Gestalt therapy: Excitement and growth in the human personality.* New York, NY: Julian Press.

Pfluger, I. (2014). Gestalt approaches to working with clients presenting with bulimia. *Gestalt Journal of Australia and New Zealand, 10*(2), 60–69.

Polster, E., & Polster, M. (2010). From the radical center: The heart of Gestalt therapy. *Gestalt Review, 14*(1), 8–23.

Polster, M. (1990). *Every person's life is a novel.* New York, NY: Norton.

Pomerantz, J. R., & Portillo, M. C. (2011). Grouping and emergent features in vision: Toward a theory of basic Gestalts. *Journal of Experimental Psychology: Human Perception and Performance, 37*, 1331–1349. doi:10.1037/a0024330

Reilly, J., & Jacobus, V. (2009). Gestalt therapy: Student perceptions of Fritz Perls in the *Three Approaches to Psychotherapy. Australian Journal of Guidance and Counselling, 19*(1), 14–24.

Rollinger, R., & Lerna, C. (2015). *Christian von Ehrenfels.* Retrieved from http://plato.stanford.edu/entries/ehrenfels/

Rubenfeld, F. (2013). Authenticity and the pursuit of happiness. *Gestalt Review, 17*(1), 107–108.

Saadati, H., & Lashani, L. (2013). Effectiveness of Gestalt therapy on self-efficacy of divorced women. *Procedia-Social and Behavioral Sciences, 84*, 1171–1174.

Sabar, S. (2013). What's a Gestalt? *Gestalt Review, 17*(1), 6–34.

Schneider, K. J. (2011). Existential-humanistic psychotherapies. In S. B. Messer & A. S. Gurman (Eds.), *Essential psychotherapies: Theory and practice* (3rd ed., pp. 261–294). New York, NY: Guilford Press.

Schulz, F. (2013). Roots and shoots of Gestalt therapy field theory: Historical and theoretical developments. *Gestalt Journal of Australia and New Zealand, 10*(1), 24–47.

Seligman, L., & Reichenberg, L. W. (2013). *Theories of counseling and psychotherapy: Systems, strategies, and skills* (4th ed.). Upper Saddle River, NJ: Prentice Hall.

Sharf, R. S. (2012). *Theories of psychotherapy and counseling: Concepts and cases.* Belmont, CA: Brooks/Cole.

Siampani, K. (2013). Incorporating sandplay therapy into Gestalt therapy in the treatment of dementia. *Gestalt Review, 17*(1), 35–58.

Smith, P. K., & Ledgerwood, A. (2010). Three problems with dual systems. *Psychological Inquiry, 21*(3), 242–249. doi:10.1080/1047840X.2010.502556

Stevenson, H. (2010). Paradox: A Gestalt theory of change for organizations. *Gestalt Review, 14*(2), 111–126.

Stoehr, T. (2009). Perls, Hefferline, and Goodman: Gestalt therapy—An afterword. *Gestalt Review, 13*, 82–95.

Tillett, R. (1991). Active and non-verbal therapeutic approaches. In J. Holmes (Ed.), *Textbook of psychotherapy in psychiatric practice* (pp. 290–297). Edinburgh, Scotland: Churchill Livingstone.

Tobin, S. (2004). The integration of relational Gestalt therapy and EMDR. *International Gestalt Journal, 27*, 55–82.

Tønnesvang, J., Sommer, U., Hammink, J., & Sonne, M. (2010). Gestalt therapy and cognitive therapy—Contrasts or complementarities. *Psychotherapy: Theory, Research, Practice, Training, 47*, 586–602.

Truscott, D. (2010). Gestalt. In *Becoming an effective psychotherapist: Adopting a theory of psychotherapy that's right for you and your client* (pp. 83–96). Washington, DC: American Psychological Association. doi:10.1037/12064-006

Van Baalen, D. (2010). Gestalt therapy and bipolar disorder. *Gestalt Review, 14*(1), 71–88.

Wagemans, J., Elder, J. H., Kubovy, M., Palmer, S. E., Peterson, M. A., Singh, M., & von der Heydt, R. (2012). A century of Gestalt psychology in visual perception: I. Perceptual grouping and figure-ground organization. *Psychological Bulletin, 138*, 1172–1217. doi:10.1037/a0029333

Weisberg, R. W. (2015). Toward an integrated theory of insight in problem solving. *Thinking and Reasoning, 21*(1), 5–39. doi:10.1080/13546783.2014.886625

Wheeler, G. (2004). Lineage and identity: Gestalt psychology and Gestalt therapy—A reply to Paul Shane. *International Gestalt Journal, 27,* 83–95.

White, G. (2009). Attending to the whole person. *Gestalt Journal of Australia and New Zealand, 5*(2), 84–87.

Williams, L. (2010). Making contact with the self-injurious adolescent: Borderline personality disorder, Gestalt therapy, and dialectical behavioral therapy interventions. *Gestalt Review, 14*(3), 250–274.

Wong, B. (2010). Gestalt principles (Part 1). *Nature Methods, 7*(11), 863–864. doi:10.1038/nmeth1110-863

Wright, N. (2012). Just do it—A case study in Gestalt experimental coaching. *Industrial and Commercial Training, 44*(2), 67–74.

Yontef, G. (1981, August). *Gestalt therapy: Past, present, and future.* Paper presented at the meeting of the International Council of Psychologists, London, England.

Yontef, G. (1993). *Awareness, dialogue, and process: Essays on Gestalt therapy.* Highland, NY: Gestalt Journal Press.

Yontef, G. (1995). Gestalt therapy. In A. Gurman & S. Messer (Eds.), *Essential psychotherapies: Theories and practice* (pp. 261–303). New York, NY: Guilford Press.

Yontef, G. (2007). The power of the immediate moment in Gestalt therapy. *Journal of Contemporary Psychotherapy, 37,* 17–22.

Yontef, G. (2010). Prologue from the radical center: The heart of Gestalt therapy (Erving and Miriam Polster). *Gestalt Review, 14*(1), 29–36.

Yontef, G. M., & Fuhr, R. (2005). Gestalt therapy theory of change. In A. L. Woldt & S. M. Toman (Eds.), *Gestalt therapy: History, theory, and practice* (pp. 81–100). Thousand Oaks, CA: Sage.

Yontef, G., & Jacobs, L. (2007). Gestalt therapy. In R. J. Corsini & D. Wedding (Eds.), *Current psychotherapies* (8th ed., pp. 328–367). Belmont, CA: Thomson Brooks/Cole.

Young, L., & Lester, D. (2012). Gestalt therapy approaches to crisis intervention with suicidal clients. In D. Lester & J. R. Rogers (Eds.), *Crisis intervention and counseling by telephone and the Internet* (3rd ed., pp. 120–134). Springfield, IL: Charles C Thomas.

Zimmer, E., & Dunning, T. (1998). Change agents. *Village Voice, 43*(24), 76–82.

Chapter 9

Cognitive Behavior Theories

Yurandol O. Powers and Cynthia R. Kalodner

Cognitive behavior theories (CBTs) are best conceptualized as a general category of theories, or a set of related theories, that have evolved from the theoretical writings, clinical experiences, and empirical studies of behavioral and cognitively oriented psychologists and other mental health workers. The hyphenated term *cognitive–behavioral* reflects the importance of both behavioral and cognitive approaches to understanding and helping human beings. The hyphen brings together behavioral and cognitive theoretical views, each with its own theoretical assumptions and intervention strategies. *Cognitive–behavioral* refers to the hybrid of behavioral strategies and cognitive processes, with the goal of achieving behavioral and cognitive change (Dobson & Dozois, 2001).

Throughout this chapter, the blending of aspects of behavioral and cognitive approaches into cognitive–behavioral counseling and psychotherapy can be seen. There is no single definition of CBT because there are so many different cognitive–behavioral theories. All cognitive–behavioral theorists value the role that cognitions play in the development and maintenance of psychological problems (Dobson, 2001). In order for a therapy to be a cognitive–behavioral one, it must be based on the idea that cognitions mediate (lead to) behavior change. Therapists using this model use treatment strategies that target cognitions in the service of changes in behavior and whose outcomes are based on cognitive, behavioral, and emotional changes (Dobson, 2001).

Cognitive behavior therapies have been used with clients from a variety of cultural and ethnic backgrounds, especially in the past decade. As understanding of the needs of diverse clients develops, adaptations of standardized CBT treatments have been developed and studied. Cultural adaptations are essential, as failure to consider the role of culture may alienate persons who are already disadvantaged and stigmatized. This chapter provides an overview of the highlights of cognitive–behavioral approaches to helping people.

BACKGROUND

To understand CBT, it is necessary to study the history of the development of behavior theory, various cognitive models, and the union of these approaches into CBT.

Watson and the Beginnings of Behavior Theory

Early behaviorism was based on learning theory; the development of clearly defined techniques; and systematic, well-designed research. The behavioral history of CBT began with the behavioral approaches developed by John B. Watson, who is usually recognized as the most influential person in the development of behaviorism (Craighead, Craighead, & Ilardi, 1995). *Behaviorism* was formed as a reaction against the Freudian emphasis on the unconscious as the subject matter of psychology and introspection as the method of its investigation. J. B. Watson (1930) claimed that behavior should be the sole subject matter of psychology and that it should be studied through observation. Furthermore, according to Watson, conscious processes (e.g., thinking) were outside the realm of scientific inquiry.

Using Ivan Pavlov's principles of classical conditioning, in which an unconditioned stimulus (loud bell) paired with a conditioned stimulus (white rat) leads to a conditioned response (startle), Watson trained Little Albert, a young boy, to fear a white rat, White Cotton, and even Watson's white hair! Though this experiment has come under scrutiny for research ethics, this demonstration was important because it highlighted that human emotions can be learned and modified using learning principles (Digdon, Powell, & Harris, 2014). Several other well-known conditioning model behaviorists, including Hans Eysenck, Stanley Rachman, and Joseph Wolpe, developed treatments such as systematic desensitization and flooding based on classical conditioning and counterconditioning. The relationship between stimulus and response is essential to these classical behavioral paradigms.

A critical contribution Watson brought to psychology was the methodology for conducting research. Methodological behaviorism is concerned with procedures for scientific inquiry and data collection (Moore, 2013). It has the following characteristics: an assumption of determinism, an emphasis on observation of behavior and environmental stimuli, the use of specific operational definitions of independent and dependent variables such that measurement is reliable, the necessity of being able to falsify hypotheses through research, the use of controlled experimentation, and replication of research findings to allow for generalization to other subjects or situations. Methodological behaviorism continues to have a strong influence on cognitive–behavioral research.

Skinner and Operant Conditioning

The work of B. F. Skinner on the principles of reinforcement and operant conditioning further developed the school of behaviorism. Skinner is the best known and most controversial figure in the field of behaviorism (Craighead et al., 1995; Goddard, 2014). Despite the fact that, until his death in 1991, Skinner maintained an adamant denial of the importance of cognitions and affect in understanding human behavior, his work has been tremendously influential in the field of counseling and psychotherapy. Skinner developed applied behavior analysis, which is based on operant conditioning. In *operant conditioning,* reinforcers shape behavior by being contingent on the response. Skinner's (1969) schedules of reinforcement defined how different amounts of reinforcement can be delivered to continue to support behavior changes. Key interventions in applied behavior analysis include reinforcement, punishment, extinction, and stimulus control, each of which involves a search for environmental variables that will lead to changes in behavior.

In operant conditioning, reinforcement is used to increase behavior. Examples of positive reinforcement include praise and money. Negative reinforcement, which also increases behavior, involves the removal of a negative stimulus, such as an electric shock or a ringing bell. An example of negative reinforcement is turning off a loud bell after a rat presses a bar. Punishment and extinction decrease behavior through the addition of an aversive stimulus or the removal of a positive reinforcer. An example of punishment involves following cigarette smoking with electric shock. In extinction, a behavior to be decreased is ignored; for example, a person who has the habit of interrupting conversation is ignored by friends when he or she interrupts, but friends listen when the comment is made in conversation without interrupting.

Wolpe and Systematic Desensitization

Joseph Wolpe is another major contributor to the development of behavior therapy. *Systematic desensitization* is the most thoroughly investigated behavioral procedure to treat simple phobias (Emmelkamp, 2003). According to the theory of reciprocal inhibition, which underlies systematic desensitization, when a response incompatible with anxiety (e.g., relaxation) is paired with an anxiety-evoking stimulus (whatever the client reports is anxiety producing), then the association between the anxiety-producing stimulus and anxiety will be lessened (Triscari, Faraci, D'Angelo, Urso, & Catalisano, 2011; Wolpe, 1958). Through the use of systematic desensitization, clients are desensitized to their fears. Clients are first taught to use progressive relaxation to become completely relaxed. Using a hierarchy of stimuli arranged from least anxiety provoking to most anxiety provoking, the counselor or therapist asks the client to imagine each stimulus while remaining relaxed (see Sidebar 9.1).

A Brief History of Cognitive Therapy

The earliest cognitive behavior therapies emerged in the early 1960s, but it was not until the 1970s that major works on cognitive behavior therapy were written (Dobson & Dozois, 2001). The cognitive revolution brought forth by Aaron Beck and Albert

Sidebar 9.1. Using Systematic Desensitization

Systematic desensitization involves gradual exposure to a fear-provoking item or situation to reduce associated anxiety and panic attacks. However, the individual must first learn relaxation techniques that will be effective when he or she is faced with anxiety-provoking situations. After learning relaxation techniques, with the assistance of the counselor or therapist, the client will create an anxiety hierarchy to categorize situations in order from least to most distressing. The counselor will assist and support the client in proceeding through the anxiety hierarchy therapy, pairing each anxiety-provoking stimulus with relaxation techniques. As a gradual desensitization occurs, alarm will be replaced with relaxation.

Ellis and others began as clinicians found that the available systems of therapy were not satisfactory. Aaron Beck (1976) was dissatisfied with psychoanalysis and behavior therapy. Though trained as a psychoanalyst, Beck objected to the unconscious aspects of Sigmund Freud's theory (Rosner, 2012), asserting that people can be aware of factors that are responsible for emotional upsets and blurred thinking. At the same time, he found the radical behavioral explanation for human emotional disturbance to be too limited to adequately explain human emotional difficulties. For Beck (1976), psychological disturbances may have been the result of "faulty learning, making incorrect inferences on the basis of inadequate or incorrect information, and not distinguishing adequately between imagination and reality" (pp. 19–20). Beck's work in cognitive therapy has been extremely influential in the treatment of depression and has been expanded to other psychological problems. The basics of his theory is presented later in this chapter (see Sidebar 9.2).

HUMAN NATURE: A DEVELOPMENTAL PERSPECTIVE

One wonders what development is for behaviorists and cognitive–behaviorists. Early behavior theory, with its emphasis on learning, seems somewhat antithetical to developmentalism. Early behaviorists' view of the development of human nature was limited to the learning concepts of operant and classical conditioning. Individuals, born with a *tabula rasa* (blank slate), learn to associate stimuli and responses; development can be seen as the sum total of these associations.

CBTs are not developmental in the same sense as stage theories. There is a stated assumption that behavior is learned; this applies equally to the explanation of how problem behaviors and adaptive behaviors are developed. Behavior is assumed to be developed and maintained by external events or cues, by external reinforcers, or by internal processes such as cognition. Development is based on each individual's different learning history, the unique experiences provided by the environment, and the individual's cognitive understanding of the world.

A historical perspective in cognitive behavior therapy highlights the emphasis on the present in understanding the presenting problems of a client. Childhood learning experiences are not usually the variables that are functionally related to current behavior, and the functional relationship is critical to assessment and treatment. A study examining the cross-cultural use of CBT by Australian Aboriginals found that "the qualities of CBT that were perceived to be effective were its adaptability, pragmatic here-and-now approach, capacity for low-intensity interventions, safe containing structure, promotion of self-agency, and valuable techniques" (Bennett-Levy et al., 2014, p. 1). Except as they may relate to present problems, past problems are not attended to in the same way as they might be within other counseling and psychotherapy systems (Beck, Rush, Shaw, & Emery,

Sidebar 9.2. Association for Behavioral and Cognitive Therapies

The major professional organization dedicated to CBT is now called the Association for Behavioral and Cognitive Therapies (www.abct.org). The organization was formed in 1966 as the Association for Advancement of Behavioral Therapies and changed to its present name in 2005. The new name tells about the increasing focus on the role of cognition.

1979; Karch et al., 2013). Because current problems are influenced by individual social learning history, past problems are not ignored, though it is clear that there is a relative lack of importance of early childhood experiences.

MAJOR CONSTRUCTS

Because CBTs are an amalgamation of behavioral and cognitive approaches, the cognitive–behavioral theoretical constructs contain aspects of both behavior and cognitive theories. Considering the separate behavioral and cognitive roots may illustrate the key constructs in CBT. Kendall and Hollon (1979) considered the treatment target; treatment approach; and treatment evaluation for behavior, cognitive, and cognitive–behavioral theories (see Table 9.1). For behavioral interventions, purely behavioral terms such as *behavioral excesses or deficits, learning theory,* and *observed changes in behavior* are used. Likewise, the cognitive interventions are based on purely cognitive terms such as *cognitive excesses or deficits, semantic interventions (cognitive),* and *changes in cognitions.*

Cognitive–behavioral interventions are considered to encompass a range of approaches limited by the purer behavioral and cognitive interventions (Karch et al., 2013; Kendall & Hollon, 1979). Treatment targets range from behavioral excesses and deficits to cognitive excesses and deficits, and cognitive–behavioral interventions target both cognitive and behavioral excesses and deficits. The treatment interventions also range from an emphasis on behavioral interventions, to an emphasis on cognitive interventions with some behavioral strategies included, to a full integration of cognitive and behavioral strategies. The evaluation strategy associated with cognitive–behavioral counseling and psychotherapy interventions ranges from an emphasis on behavior changes to an emphasis on cognitive changes, and in the middle are observed changes in behavior and cognition with methodological rigor. What CBTs provide, given this amalgamation model, is greater

Table 9.1

General Characteristics of Cognitive–Behavioral Interventions

		Treatment Target	Treatment Approach	Treatment Evaluation
Behavioral		Behavioral excesses or deficits	Behavioral learning theory interventions, environmental manipulations (e.g., token economies, contingency management)	Observed changes in behavior with rigorous evaluation
Behavioral	Cognitive–Behavioral	Behavioral excesses or deficits	Behavioral interventions, skills training, information provision (e.g., modeling, role playing)	Observed changes in behavior with rigorous evaluation
	Cognitive–Behavioral	Behavioral and cognitive excesses or deficits	Broadly conceived behavioral and cognitive methods	Observed changes in behavior and cognition with methodological rigor
Cognitive	Cognitive–Behavioral	Cognitive excesses or deficits	Cognitive interventions with adjunctive behavioral procedures	Examination of cognitive and, to a lesser extent, of behavioral changes
Cognitive		Cognitive excesses or deficits	Semantic interventions	Changes in cognitions, integrative changes, often but not always nonempirically evaluated

Note. From "Cognitive–Behavioral Interventions: Theory and Procedure," by S. D. Hollon and P. C. Kendall, 1979. In P. C. Kendall & S. D. Hollon (Eds.), *Cognitive and Cognitive–Behavioral Interventions: Theory, Research, and Procedures.* Oxford, England, Elsevier Ltd. Copyright 1979 by Elsevier. Reprinted with permission.

flexibility in treatment targets and interventions, with an emphasis on rigorous standards in the measurement of change and research evaluation (Kendall & Hollon, 1979; Zivor, Salkovskis, & Oldfield, 2013).

The Importance of Cognitions

The unifying characteristic of cognitive–behavioral counseling and psychotherapy approaches is the fundamental emphasis on the importance of cognitive workings as mediators of behavior change (Craighead et al., 1995; Dobson & Dozois, 2001). All cognitive interventions attempt to produce change by influencing thinking, which is assumed to play a causal role in the development and maintenance of psychological problems (Dobson & Dozois, 2001). The relationship between thoughts and behavior is a major aspect of CBT and counseling and psychotherapy. Thus, all cognitive behavior therapies share these three fundamental propositions:

- Cognitive activity affects behavior.
- Cognitive activity may be monitored and altered.
- Desired behavior change may be affected through cognitive change. (Dobson & Dozois, 2001, p. 4)

The Importance of Learning

The cognitive–behavioral model of psychological disturbance asserts that abnormal behavior is learned and developed in the same way that normal behavior is learned and that cognitive–behavioral principles can be applied to change the behavior. The importance of this statement lies in the focus on learning as the way behavior is acquired, rather than through underlying intrapsychic conflicts. It rejects the psychodynamic and quasi-disease models of development, which assume that underlying intrapsychic conflicts cause maladaptive behavior.

The Importance of Operational Definitions and Functional Analysis

In cognitive–behavioral approaches, problems are viewed operationally. The definition of the presenting problem must be concrete and specific, and observable whenever possible. It is assumed that problems are functionally related to internal and external antecedents and consequences. This assumption means that in order to understand behavior, it is necessary to know the events that precede (antecedents) and follow (consequences) the behavior. These events may be external and observable behaviors or internal thoughts and feelings. The functional relationship conceptualization of problems necessitates a clear understanding of the internal and external antecedents that contribute to a problematic behavior as well as the internal and external consequences that maintain behavior. This also means that the causes and treatments of problems should be multidimensional. Causes might include behaviors, environmental circumstances, thoughts, beliefs, or attitudes. Treatments are addressed in the intervention section of this chapter. Because there is rarely a single cause for a problem, treatments are comprehensive and designed to address multiple issues.

The Importance of Therapeutic Empathy

Often when cognitive–behavioral counseling or psychotherapy is described, the techniques and theory are emphasized while the importance of the relationship between the client and the counselor or therapist is underemphasized. This is unfortunate. The use of therapy manuals, which is increasing both in psychotherapy research and in clinical practice, exacerbates this concern about an overemphasis on techniques (Connolly Gibbons, Crits-Cristoph, Levinson, & Barber, 2003). The use of therapy manuals may be seen as restricting the counselor's ability to respond to the client's needs in the moment; however, detailed analyses of transcripts of cognitive behavior therapy sessions show that therapists do vary in their responses to clients (Connolly Gibbons et al., 2003). Therapists cannot become so reliant on techniques that they forget that clients require a warm and supportive environment in the therapeutic process. Thus, it is important to be clear that although cognitive–behavioral treatment manuals focus on the specific treatment techniques, the helping relationship is also addressed.

A study of depressed clients seeking treatment from a therapist using either a cognitive behavior therapy approach or an emotionally focused approach based on client-centered and Gestalt techniques showed that there were no significant differences between the ratings of the different types of therapists on variables such as empathy, unconditional acceptance, and congruence (J. C. Watson & Geller, 2005). This shows that, as therapists treat clients, they are able to do so within a therapeutic relationship, regardless of the theory underlying their approach. Beck (1976) described the importance of the relationship and included strategies for developing a therapeutic relationship in manuals. Burns and Auerbach (1996) highlighted the necessity of a warm, empathic therapeutic relationship in cognitive therapy. They provided an empathy scale that patients can use to rate how warm, genuine, and empathic their counselors or therapists were during a recent session. The necessary and sufficient conditions for personality change developed by Carl Rogers are included in Beck's cognitive therapy as "necessary, but not sufficient" (Beck et al., 1979, p. 47). In other words, these factors form the basis for the relationship, but the techniques of cognitive therapy are viewed as necessary to produce therapeutic change. The efficacy of the intervention is dependent on a relationship that is characterized by counselor or therapist warmth, accurate empathy, and genuineness (Beck, Wright, Newman, & Liese, 1993).

APPLICATIONS

Overview

There is great variability in the interventions practiced in cognitive–behavioral counseling and psychotherapy. Cognitive–behavioral interventions include various combinations of cognitive and behavioral techniques and are aimed at changing either cognitions, behavior, or both (Kendall & Hollon, 1979; see Table 9.1). Cognitive–behavioral interventions are directive, structured, goal-directed, and time-limited treatment, and most types involve the client in a collaborative relationship with the counselor or therapist. The use of homework assignments and skills practice is common, along with a focus on problem-solving ability.

Cognitive–behavioral interventions can be applied to counseling the culturally diverse. Providing culturally responsive cognitive behavior therapy includes accepting the client's core cultural values and belief systems, validating potential experiences of disparity and oppression, understanding the client's cultural context, and highlighting culturally related strengths and supports. For example, a Chinese client may expect a more directive counselor. Lin (2002) noted that Chinese clients have a tendency to seek information and advice as well as direct ways to solve problems. Therapists using cognitive behavior therapy may be able to connect with these needs by using problem-solving strategies and solution-focused approaches. However, other cultural issues, such as the influence of the family, may not fit as well with the internal locus of control and individual focus found in Western culture. It is clear that counselors who want to use cognitive behavior therapy with the Chinese are advised to read about Chinese culture and seek appropriate supervision (Lin, 2002).

Goals of Counseling and Psychotherapy: Case Conceptualization

Before selecting a goal for counseling or psychotherapy or conducting any intervention with a client, a counselor or therapist using a CBT orientation begins with developing a conceptualization, or understanding, of the case. Cognitive behavior therapy case formulation has five components: problem list, diagnosis, working hypothesis, strengths and assets, and treatment plan (Persons & Davidson, 2001). These are illustrated in the case presented at the end of this chapter. The problem list is a comprehensive list of the difficulties stated in concrete behavioral terms. Usually five to eight problems are identified in a variety of areas, such as psychological symptoms, interpersonal relationships, occupational problems, financial difficulties, medical diagnoses, lack of adequate housing, or legal issues (Persons & Davidson, 2001). Relationships between the problems may become clear when all of the issues are listed in this way. It is also useful to see a list of all of the issues so that a prioritization of issues can be used when preparing the treatment plan.

A comprehensive problem list requires a detailed assessment, and making one involves asking clients about areas that they may not have initially discussed. An important issue that clients may not report is substance abuse. It is for this reason that a global assessment is recommended. The counselor or therapist can use information derived from a standardized, structured interview along with the initial description of the presenting problem to develop an accurate picture of the problem. This usually begins by asking the client to describe the problem. However, clients do not always describe the most important problem in initial sessions. Sometimes they may not be ready to reveal the true problem until they have developed trust and confidence in the practitioner.

Another component in the case formulation plan is diagnosis, which refers to the *Diagnostic and Statistical Manual of Mental Disorders, Fifth Edition* (American Psychiatric Association, 2013), method of presenting information along five axes. Diagnosis is not always included in CBT conceptualizations, but it is important because it provides a link to the type of treatment that may be selected. (It is beyond the scope of this chapter to describe diagnosis in detail.)

The working hypothesis section is considered the most critical part of the case conceptualization. It is a way to present the connections between the issues on the problem list. There are subsections, including schemata, precipitating or activating situations, and origins. The *schemata* section concerns the core beliefs held by the client. *Core beliefs* refers to those thoughts that are central to the problem, and these beliefs may cause or maintain the problems. Usually, they are clients' negative thoughts about themselves, the world, others, or the future. *Precipitating or activating situations* refers to the specific external events that produce the symptoms or problems. They are things that may have happened just before the problem began. *Origins* refers to early history that might be related to the problems. Origins might explain how the client learned the schemata that maintain the current situation. Examples include modeling from family: Having a family with poor communication skills may explain why a client might have problems expressing himself or herself.

Strengths and assets refers to the positive aspects of a person's current situation. For example, a client may have good social skills, the ability to work collaboratively, a sense of humor, a good job, financial resources, a good support network, a regular exercise routine, intelligence, personal attractiveness, and/or a stable lifestyle (Persons & Davidson, 2001). It is always useful to know what is not a problem in a client's life. These strengths can be used when developing the treatment plan.

The treatment plan is the outcome of the case conceptualization. It must be related to the problem list and working hypothesis. The treatment plan tells about the goals for counseling or psychotherapy. Treatment plans are also complex and require attention to goals and obstacles as well as modality, frequency, interventions, and adjunct therapies. The goals of treatment must be reviewed with the client, and both counselor or therapist and client must agree on these goals. It is also important to know how progress in counseling or psychotherapy can be measured and monitored. Because cognitive–behaviorally oriented counselors or therapists are often focused on measuring outcomes, it is important to know how changes will be noted. For example, perhaps the counselor or therapist will ask the client to keep a diary of maladaptive thoughts or a count of binge eating episodes. *Obstacles* refers to the potential difficulties that may arise during treatment. An awareness of the obstacles may assist the counselor or therapist and client in coping more effectively with them. *Modality* refers to the type of counseling or psychotherapy that will be used—in this case, cognitive behavior therapy. *Frequency* refers to the number of sessions a week; most often, CBT is offered once a week. *Initial interventions* refers to the specific strategies that will be used in sessions. An example of initial interventions appears in the case study. Finally, *adjunct therapies* refers to additional therapy that might be used. An example of an adjunct therapy is pharmacotherapy.

The Process of Change

The process of change is concerned with understanding how a theory explains the mechanisms for therapeutic change. This is particularly important in the cognitive–behavioral arena because there are many different theories and many different interventions.

Self-Efficacy

The self-efficacy theory of Albert Bandura (1977, 1986) has been used to provide a cognitive–behavioral theoretical explanation for how people change. It has been proposed as a common pathway to explain how people change despite using different therapeutic techniques. Self-efficacy theory asserts that individuals develop expectations for their success in performing specific behaviors and that these expectations influence their decision to try new behaviors and maintain behavior changes (Bandura, 1977, 1986). Self-efficacy may be thought of as a sense of personal competence or feelings of mastery. The degree to which a person feels efficacious influences the amount of effort that he or she will apply in given situations. Thus, cognitive behavior therapy may work through increasing the self-efficacy of clients.

Bandura (1986) described four mechanisms through which self-efficacy can be developed: enactive attainments, vicarious experiences, verbal persuasion, and recognition of physiological states. *Enactive attainments,* the most powerful contributors to self-efficacy development, refers to an individual's own experience with achieving a goal. *Vicarious experiences* refers to observing others as they succeed or fail. Through the process of observing, individuals are provided with a basis for making comparisons to their own competence to perform the task. *Verbal persuasion* is a less powerful way to influence self-efficacy. The final source of self-efficacy, *physiological states,* refers to the emotional arousal or degree of apprehension one feels. Feelings of fear may lead to decreased performance, whereas a moderate amount of anxiety may be helpful when performing a new task.

These sources of self-efficacy can be applied to teach clients assertiveness skills. When clients are taught assertiveness skills, they practice making appropriate assertive comments. Enactive attainments are experiences of success that lead clients to feel able to repeat the assertive behavior. In assertiveness training groups, clients watch one another perform new behaviors; this is an example of vicarious experiences. Verbal persuasion is the source of self-efficacy based on telling clients, "You can do it"; like encouragement, it might increase self-efficacy, but other sources are more powerful. The physiological states mechanism can be used in assertiveness training to inform clients that a moderate amount of anxiety may be helpful as they attempt to make changes in their behavior.

It is important to recognize that all four sources of self-efficacy are involved in how cognitive therapy and other cognitive–behavioral interventions work. In the process of learning that cognitions contribute to behavior and affective difficulties, enactive attainments, vicarious experiences, verbal persuasion, and physiological states play major roles.

Does Changing Beliefs Lead to a Change in Behavior?

Addressing the question of how people change, Beck (1976) asserted that behavior and affective change are hypothesized to occur through the change in cognitions. The assumption is clearly that changing beliefs is the key to helping people. Research has demonstrated that cognitive therapy does indeed change thoughts and that there are reductions in psychological disturbances.

Traditional Intervention Strategies

Cognitive–behavioral interventions include aspects of both behavioral and cognitive interventions, and this section provides a few examples of some commonly used intervention strategies. The separation of behavioral, cognitive, and cognitive–behavioral techniques is rather artificial, as most cognitive procedures include behavioral components and some behavioral interventions also contain cognitive elements (Emmelkamp, 2003). However, in spite of this, a sample of some techniques most often associated with behavioral approaches follows. In addition, cognitive interventions are described briefly. The greatest attention is devoted to providing details of several CBTs of counseling and psychotherapy.

Behavioral Interventions

Behavioral interventions focus primarily on changing specific behaviors. Examples of purely behavioral interventions include reinforcement, extinction, shaping, stimulus control, and aversive control.

Reinforcement is a well-known behavioral strategy. *Positive reinforcement* is a procedure in which some behavior is increased by following it with something rewarding; for example, children who clean their room are given praise and attention, a gold star, or a new toy. Most important about reinforcement is that the receiver views the reinforcer as positive. *Negative reinforcement* is the removal of something aversive to increase behavior. The buzz most cars make when the key is put in the ignition is a negative reinforcer designed to increase seatbelt use. Both positive and negative reinforcement increase behavior and can be applied when clients want to increase a behavior.

Extinction is a behavioral intervention designed to decrease a problematic behavior. In this case, a reinforcer that followed the behavior in the past is removed, and the problem behavior decreases. For example, think about a child who repeatedly gets out of his or her seat in a classroom. When the teacher notices and asks the child to sit down, the child may return to the seat. However, the attention of the teacher is reinforcing, and the problem of out-of-seat behavior usually continues. Extinction is the procedure in which the teacher ignores the behavior until it stops. Extinction is characterized by *response burst,* which is a phenomenon in which the child may get out of the seat and wander around and continue to engage in negative behavior in an increasing manner, still trying to get the attention of the teacher. If the teacher gives in and attends to the behavior now, negative behavior is actually being reinforced! Response burst is to be expected and usually subsides when the individual learns that no amount of negative behavior will get the attention that has been reinforcing.

Shaping is a behavioral intervention used to gradually increase the quality of a behavior. Often used to teach a new skill, shaping works by reinforcing the behavior as it gets closer to the final goal. Shaping is used when there is a clearly identified behavior to be changed and when differential reinforcement (reinforcing the behavior that gets closer and closer to the target while ignoring the other behavior) can be applied to successive approximations of the behavior.

In *stimulus control,* some event in the environment is used to cue behavior. When a stimulus leads to behavior that is desirable and will be reinforced, the cue is called a *discriminative stimulus.* For example, seeing exercise shoes in the living room may act as a cue to use an exercise tape to do aerobics. The exercise shoes are a discriminative stimulus for exercise.

One example of *aversive control* is *punishment,* which is defined as the addition of an unpleasant event following a negative behavior to decrease the occurrence of that behavior. Punishment is not used often by behaviorists, but it has been used to eliminate dangerous behaviors, such as head banging or other self-mutilative behaviors in severely emotionally disturbed children.

Cognitive Interventions

Cognitive interventions focus on the role of cognitions in the lives of clients. One excellent self-help book written by Burns (1999) can be especially useful for clients using a cognitive–behavioral approach to recover from depression. This book, *Feeling Good: The New Mood Therapy,* was strongly recommended in a national study of psychologists who rated self-help books (Norcross et al., 2003). The book is a source of information about the different types of *cognitive distortions* that can be identified and changed through the process of cognitive therapy. Some types of cognitive distortions include all-or-nothing thinking, disqualifying the positive, and catastrophizing (Burns, 1999). *All-or-nothing thinking* is characterized by assuming that things are either 100% perfect or absolutely terrible; there is no gray area. Because few things are perfect, all-or-nothing thinking usually leads to depression, as everything is viewed as terrible. *Disqualifying the positive* is defined as rejecting any positive experiences (i.e., compliments) and assuming that these positive events do not really count for some reason. The person using this type of distortion may say, "I only received an A because the test was so easy" or "She is only complimenting me because she wants a ride in my new car." *Catastrophizing* is exaggerating a negative event so that it has much more impact than it deserves. Making a mistake at work or receiving a B on a quiz may be catastrophized into losing the job or failing the course. (Note that other books by Burns also used cognitive–behavioral interventions for self-esteem and panic attacks; see www.feelinggood.com.)

Cognitive therapy works through using many kinds of procedures, including thought stopping and positive self-statements, to change these negative or maladaptive kinds of thoughts. *Thought stopping* is a cognitive self-control skill used to help the client cope with negative cognitions that cause distress, are untrue, or are counterproductive (Bakker, 2009). It is designed to interfere with thoughts that run through the mind of the client and make it difficult to change behavior. In this procedure, the client imagines the troublesome thought running through his or her mind and the counselor or therapist shouts "Stop!" Although the client may be a bit surprised, the shout does usually stop the thought. The client can then replace the thought with a more adaptive one like, "I can handle this situation." Third-generation CBT therapists would caution against the use of thought stopping and strong interventions with the mind, as it might create internal conflict. Many variations of thought stopping have emerged, such as flicking a rubber band on the wrist, scheduling times of the day to worry, pinching oneself on the hand, reciting a positive affirmation, and writing down negative thoughts. Clients can learn to do this procedure on their own and can stop their own thoughts and substitute more useful ones.

The use of *positive self-statements* can go along with thought stopping. Statements such as, "My opinion is important" or "I am an assertive person" can be practiced over and over. It is normal that these thoughts may not feel quite right at first. The important point is that what clients tell themselves influences their feelings and behavior. The counselor or therapist may use the self-statements as a way to cue assertive behavior by saying, "If it were true that your opinion were important, how might you behave?" The client might be encouraged to try acting as if the statements were true (see Sidebar 9.3).

Sidebar 9.3. Case Study: Attending to Maria's Distorted Cognitions

You are Maria's counselor, and she tells you that she regrets a lot of the choices that she has made in her life. She describes how her family blames her decisions for disrupting the family unity. She makes the following statements to you: "No one cares about me" and "I've ruined my life and the lives of two families, and I am currently hurting my children." You want her to gain insight into her negative thoughts and replace them with more adaptive ones. Think about how you might use thought stopping as an intervention to decrease Maria's distorted views of herself.

Brief Intervention Strategies and Current Practices

The essence of cognitive behavior therapies is the union of behavioral and cognitive strategies to help people. Often, cognitive–behavioral strategies are designed to be brief interventions that include the use of treatment manuals, or guidelines for the implementation of interventions. These manuals have clearly described psychotherapy strategies. An advantage of using treatment manuals is that it eases the facilitation of training for counselors and also makes replication of research easier. Manuals for cognitive–behavioral treatment are available for a variety of psychological problems, and this material grows continuously. Barlow's (2008) text on the treatment of psychological disorders, for example, contains chapters on cognitive–behavioral approaches to treating a variety of anxiety disorders (panic disorder and agoraphobia, posttraumatic stress disorder, social anxiety disorder, and obsessive-compulsive disorder); mood disorders (depression, bipolar disorder); and other disorders, including substance abuse, eating disorders, sexual dysfunction, and personality disorders. A good reference for treatment manuals that are based on research can be found at www.psychologicaltreatments.org.

Beck's Cognitive Therapy

The primary principle underlying cognitive theory is that affect and behavior are determined by the way in which individuals cognitively structure the world. First developed to treat depression, cognitive theory was later extended as a treatment for anxiety and is now being used to treat other psychological problems, such as panic disorder and agoraphobia, drug abuse, and eating disorders (see Sidebar 9.4). Beck and Emery (1985) identified the following 10 principles of cognitive theory:

1. It is based on the cognitive model of emotional disorders.
2. It is brief and time limited.
3. It is based on a sound therapeutic relationship, which is a necessary condition.
4. It is a collaborative effort between the client and the counselor or therapist.
5. It uses primarily the Socratic method.

Sidebar 9.4. Cognitive Therapy

Interested readers are referred to full descriptions of cognitive theory in *Cognitive Therapy of Depression* (Beck et al., 1979), *Anxiety Disorders and Phobias* (Beck & Emery, 1985), *Cognitive Therapy of Personality Disorders* (Beck, Freeman, Davis, & Associates, 2003), and *Cognitive Therapy of Substance Abuse* (Beck et al., 1993).

6. It is structured and directive.
7. It is problem oriented.
8. It is based on an educational model.
9. Its theory and techniques rely on the inductive model.
10. It uses homework as a central feature.

The cognitive model of disturbance asserts that cognitions play a central role in human emotional problems. In cognitive therapy, there is an emphasis on internal thoughts, feelings, and attitudes rather than on behavior, although behavioral techniques are used in conjunction with cognitive therapy to help clients test their maladaptive cognitions and assumptions. Cognitive restructuring is used to identify automatic thoughts, evaluate their content, test the hypothesis that is generated, and identify underlying assumptions.

Unlike some dynamic therapies, cognitive therapy is time limited; treatment of anxiety disorders may take from five to 20 sessions (Beck & Emery, 1985; Vittengl, Clark, Thase, & Jarrett, 2015), and treatment of moderate to severe depression may take 20 sessions over 15 weeks (Beck et al., 1979). The pace of intervention is rapid, and longer term therapy is viewed as unnecessary to facilitate change. Some guidelines useful for keeping the counseling and psychotherapy process brief include keeping treatment specific and concrete, stressing homework, and developing the expectation that the intervention will be brief for both the client and the counselor or therapist (Beck & Emery, 1985).

Third-Wave Behavior Therapy

More recently, there has been an evolution of psychotherapeutic methods characterized as third-wave psychotherapies to treat a wide variety of problems. Among this third-wave movement are dialectical behavior therapy, acceptance and commitment therapy, mindfulness-based cognitive therapy, and behavioral activation. Whereas traditional behavior therapy seeks to eliminate or reduce intrusive thoughts and replace them with more positive thoughts, most third-wave behavior therapies "propose alternatives for intervention for intrusive thoughts, painful memories, unpleasant daydreams, or ruminative depressive discourses" (Barraca, 2012, p. 109). Through the use of understanding and acceptance of intrusive thoughts and their content, the client is able to use mindfulness as the fundamental concept to facilitate change.

Dialectical Behavior Therapy

Dialectical behavior therapy was developed in 1993 by Professor Marsha Linehan, who wanted to make adaptations to cognitive behavior therapy after recognizing its shortcomings in the treatment of borderline personality disorder (Barraca, 2012). Dialectical behavior therapy integrates variations of cognitive behavior therapy interventions with mindfulness and acceptance to teach the client effective coping strategies. Clients are given the tools to help them be successful in changing negative coping strategies to positive ones as well as to improve their overall well-being. Dialectical behavior therapy has been shown to be useful for treating a wide variety of presenting issues, including depression, substance abuse, suicidal behaviors, and eating disorders. This is explored in more detail in Chapter 10.

Acceptance and Commitment Therapy

A form of mindfulness-based therapy, acceptance and commitment therapy, challenges clients to accept their thoughts and feelings and still commit to change. This contextual approach to treatment suggests that one must manage the internal experience (memories, thoughts, sensations, etc.) differently from that of external events. Zarling, Lawrence, and Marchman (2015) noted the six core processes that acceptance and commitment therapy uses to increase psychological flexibility: present–moment awareness, acceptance of the difficult emotions or thoughts, a decrease in the believability of (or attachment to) thoughts, perspective taking, identification of values, and committed action in service of values. The belief is that clients can attain a more fulfilled life by overcoming negative thoughts and feelings by consistently choosing to act according to their values, even in the presence of difficult or disruptive events (cognitive or psychological).

Mindfulness-Based Cognitive Therapy

Initially developed as a group therapy to prevent the relapse or recurrence of depressive symptoms, mindfulness-based cognitive therapy is used to teach skills that permit "individuals to disengage from habitual ('automatic') dysfunctional cognitive routines" (Williams, Russell, & Russell, 2008, p. 524). Grounded in the Buddhist Zen tradition, mindfulness-based cognitive therapy integrates the practice of mindfulness with cognitive therapy as a technique to manage intrusive thoughts, improve one's emotional regulation, and increase mood while reducing depressive symptoms, stress, and anxiety. Mindfulness is a state of self-regulation. It is not considered a state of doing but a state of being in which an individual is fully aware of the present moment and disengaged with the internal and external environment. In mindfulness-based cognitive therapy, clients are encouraged to become more aware of negative thoughts and feelings and respond to those thoughts in ways that decrease rumination.

Behavioral Activation

Behavioral activation is a therapeutic paradigm used to improve thoughts, mood, and overall well-being by helping individuals understand the context of environmental sources of their presenting symptoms (Dimaggio, Salvatore, Lysaker, Ottavi, & Popolo, 2015; Hopko, Robertson, Lejuez, 2006; Pagoto et al., 2008). This therapeutic approach involves engaging clients in structured events aimed to be positive reinforcers while simultaneously reducing the intensity and frequency of aversive events and negative emotional responses. Clients are taught to identify internal as well as environmental triggers of depressive symptoms and the ineffective coping strategies they have maintained. Once the client is able to recognize this pattern, the goal is to help the client develop healthy alternative coping strategies.

Clients With Serious Mental Health Issues

Cognitive behavior therapies have been developed and used with clients with a wide range of clinical problems. The website mentioned earlier (www.psychologicaltreatment.org) provides information on the use of cognitive behavior therapy with clients who have a variety of clinical problems. The work on empirically supported treatments is indicative of the efficacy of cognitive behavior therapy with people who have serious mental illnesses, including anxiety and mood disorders and the more serious schizophrenia and psychotic disorders.

The use of cognitive behavior therapy in inpatient settings for children and adolescents has been elucidated by Stone (2007) and studied by Veltro et al. (2008). The latter research team noted that the ward atmosphere was improved by the use of group-based cognitive behavior therapy interventions for patients hospitalized for schizophrenia, major depression, bipolar disorder, or a personality disorder. In addition, readmissions declined and patient satisfaction increased after a group cognitive behavior therapy was added to the inpatient treatment program.

As an additional research-based example, cognitive behavior therapy has been used to treat schizophrenia (Turkington, Kingdon, & Turner, 2002). In this study, a brief cognitive behavior therapy program was applied by psychiatric nurses to individuals with schizophrenia. Caregivers of the individuals with schizophrenia were also included in the treatment. Symptoms of schizophrenia were reduced in participants in this study. Many patients expressed satisfaction with the cognitive behavior therapy approach; nearly 57% stated that the overall program "helped me more than anything previously to understand my illness" (p. 525).

Cognitive behavior therapy has also been studied as a treatment for panic disorder (Addis et al., 2004). Patients who received cognitive behavior therapy–based panic therapy improved more than those who received a control therapy. Applications of cognitive behavior therapy to clients who abuse substances have also revealed that cognitive behavior therapy can be an effective treatment (Baker, Boggs, & Lewin, 2001; De Wildt et al., 2002). Baker et al. (2001) implemented a cognitive behavior therapy program with users of amphetamines and found that significantly more people in the cognitive behavior therapy group than a control group were abstinent from drug use at a 6-month follow-up.

As indicated earlier, cognitive behavior therapy is a therapeutic approach that is diverse enough to be applied to a wide variety of clinical problems. Therapy manuals and research protocols continue to be the focus of ongoing research to study the use of cognitive behavior therapy with people who face a variety of clinical disorders.

EVALUATION

Overview

As indicated previously, there is a tremendous amount of research literature on the effectiveness of various cognitive–behavioral interventions for different types of disorders. The most recent studies have focused on diverse groups. The whole continuously developing body of work on empirically supported treatments is indicative of research that demonstrates the efficacy of cognitive behavior therapy for a variety of problems.

The following review is limited to research on the work of Beck and his work on depression. Reviewing the research that supports cognitive behavior therapy requires a book of its own. It is simply not possible to review the vast research on this topic in a few pages. Readers interested in cognitive behavior therapy with other clinical issues are advised to look in the publications described here. Because research on cognitive–behavioral treatment is ongoing, readers may find interesting articles published in journals such as, for example, *Cognitive Behavior Therapy, Cognitive and Behavioral Practice, Behavioral and Cognitive Psychotherapy,* and the *Journal of Cognitive and Behavioral Therapies.*

Supporting Research

Beck's Cognitive Therapy for Depression

The treatment of depression has received a great deal of attention from cognitive–behavioral researchers. Beck's cognitive therapy, developed for the treatment of depression, has been the subject of numerous treatment outcome studies. It has been compared with favorable findings to waiting list controls, nondirective therapy, behavior therapy, and various antidepressant medications. In an older but often-cited study, Shaw (1977) compared Beck's cognitive therapy to behavior therapy treatment for depression developed to restore an adequate schedule of positive reinforcement (including activity scheduling, verbal contracts, and communication and social skill development), nondirective therapy, and a waiting list control. Those treated by cognitive therapy had the best outcomes on self-report measures of depression. In addition, ratings by clinicians unaware of the type of therapy received by individual clients also were more favorable for the cognitive therapy treatment group.

A meta-analysis of treatment studies comparing cognitive therapy to no-treatment controls yielded the finding that cognitive therapy clients had lower final depression scores than 99% of the no-treatment control subjects (Dobson & Shaw, 1988). It is clear that cognitive therapy is better than no treatment. The next test involved a comparison of the effects of cognitive therapy and antidepressant medication. DeRubeis, Siegle, and Hollon (2008) compared the efficacy of cognitive therapy with antidepressants in a randomized, placebo-controlled study. The clients were moderately to severely depressed individuals seeking treatment for depression. Clients were randomly assigned to cognitive therapy, antidepressant medications, or a placebo pill. Cognitive therapy was administered by experienced counselors over a 16-week period. Self-report depression ratings were obtained during Week 8. Because there was a significant outperformance of the cognitive therapy and the antidepressant medications over the placebo, the placebo was discontinued at Week 8. The cognitive therapy and antidepressant medication interventions led to a reduction in depression at the end of the 16 weeks but revealed no significant differences in short-term outcomes. The results indicated that cognitive therapy can be just as effective for treating depression as antidepressant medications.

Another study that also used medication and cognitive therapy to treat depression found that the use of drugs and cognitive therapy was no better than the use of cognitive therapy alone (Beck, Hollon, Young, Bedrosian, & Budenz, 1985). Cognitive therapy and drug treatment were better than drug treatment alone, leading the authors to conclude that if a client needs antidepressant medication, the individual should get cognitive therapy with the medication. DeRubeis, Gelfand, Tang, and Simons (1999) reanalyzed individual patient data from four studies of cognitive therapy treatment for depression and concluded that cognitive therapy is as effective as medication for the treatment of severely depressed patients. Conclusions from this research indicate that cognitive therapy is as effective as medication in the treatment of depression, even in cases of severe depression. Another analysis of different treatments for depression (Wampold, Minami, Baskin, & Tierney, 2002) reported that CBT is as effective as other bona fide treatments and more effective than non-bona fide treatments.

Limitations

The union of cognitive and behavioral counseling and therapy into cognitive behavior therapy has been able to overcome many of the limitations of either type of therapy alone. However, those individuals who are more inclined toward psychodynamic interpretations continue to object to the lack of attention to unconscious factors in determining behavior and to concepts such as ego strength and insight, which are not included in this approach. In addition, experiential counselors and therapists indicate that cognitive–behavioral strategies do not pay enough attention to feelings. Insight and an emphasis on the past are features of other types of counseling and therapy that do not fit within the purview of cognitive behavior therapy.

The behavior therapy roots of current cognitive behavior therapy may be criticized as lacking attention to the role of thoughts and feelings, ignoring the historical context of the present problems, and allowing the counselor or therapist too much power to manipulate the client. Because the origins of behavior theory emphasized operationally defined behaviors and functional analysis, these are features that define the approach. These are the things that make behavioral counseling behavioral. The idea that behavioral counselors and therapists are manipulative comes from the use of external reinforcers and stimulus control types of treatments. It seems that this notion is maintained by token economy systems. In individual practice, behavioral counselors or therapists use informed consent to make changes in the contingencies of behavior.

The cognitive therapy roots may be described as too difficult to study empirically and as paying too much attention to cognitive factors while minimizing affective ones. Cognitive therapies focus to a large extent on internal events (thoughts), which cannot be directly observed. Although radical behaviorists object to this, most other types of counseling or psychotherapy would also fit this criticism. Cognitive therapy researchers have continued to develop thought-listing and monitoring strategies to alleviate this criticism. In addition, the cognitive strategies have been challenged for a lack of sufficient attention to affective factors. It seems that the emphasis on cognitions may lead to an intellectual understanding of the problem but may not help change the feelings associated with the thoughts. This limitation is related to the fact that the mechanism for understanding how behavior, thoughts, and feelings change is still not understood.

Research has shown that individuals conceptualize differently as a result of culture; for example, they use different reasoning processes (Chen & Davenport, 2005; Kohn, Oden, Munoz, Robinson, & Leavitt, 2002; Nicolas, Arntz, Hirsch, & Schmiedigen, 2009). This has important implications for cognitive–behavior therapy, as the focus is on addressing the client's thoughts and thought processes. Likewise, cultural norms regarding what behavior is appropriate and inappropriate can have a major impact on the therapist's approach to treatment. The therapy is thus limited by the therapist's expertise in and understanding of the client's cultural norms.

Summary Chart: CBTs

Human Nature

CBTs are not developmental in the same sense as are stage theories. There is a stated assumption that behavior is learned that applies equally to the explanations of how problem behaviors and adaptive behaviors are developed. Behavior is assumed to be developed and maintained by external events or cues, by external reinforcers, or by internal processes such as cognition. Development is based on each individual's different learning history, experiences, and cognitive understanding of the world.

Major Constructs

The major constructs of CBT are an amalgamation of behavioral and cognitive approaches and include an emphasis on behavioral and cognitive excesses or deficits, learning theory, observed changes in behavior, semantic interventions, and changes in cognitions. Operational definitions, functional analysis, and therapeutic empathy also serve as major constructs.

Goals

The goals of CBT are best viewed in terms of understanding the nature of the presenting problem from behavioral, affective, cognitive, and social perspectives; how progress in counseling and psychotherapy can be measured and monitored; the environmental contingencies maintaining the behavior; and which interventions are more likely to be effective.

Change Process

Because many different theories and interventions make up the cognitive–behavioral arena, the process of change is best understood in terms of how the theory explains the mechanisms for change. For example, Bandura's self-efficacy theory asserts that individuals develop expectations for their success in performing specific behaviors and that these expectations influence their decisions to try new behaviors and maintain behavior changes, whereas Beck asserted that behavioral and affective change occur through the change in cognitions.

Interventions

The interventions used in CBT treatments are best viewed in terms of behavioral interventions (reinforcement, positive reinforcement, negative reinforcement, extinction, shaping, and stimulus control) and cognitive interventions (identifying cognitive distortions, thought stopping, the use of positive self-statements, cognitive restructuring, the use of the empathic therapeutic relationship, the Socratic method, disputing, reframing, role playing, modeling, humor, homework, risk-taking exercises, relaxation exercises, systematic desensitization, bibliotherapy, shame-attacking exercises, self-instructional training, stress inoculation training, progressive muscle relaxation, and relapse prevention; see Sidebar 9.5).

Limitations

According to the views of critics of CBT, the theories are limited because of their lack of attention to unconscious factors in determining behavior and to concepts such as ego strength and insight, which are not included in the approach. Expe-

Sidebar 9.5. Progressive Muscle Relaxation

Progressive muscle relaxation is used to create a deep, relaxed state of mind. This technique is best practiced lying down in a quiet place, but it can also be accomplished in a seated position. There are two steps in progressive muscle relaxation: (a) tensing muscle groups intentionally and (b) releasing the induced tension. During this alternating of tensing and relaxing the muscles, the client is instructed to focus on the difference between the tension and relaxation in the body as he or she moves from foot to head. Progressive muscle relaxation teaches the client to induce relaxation and release tension.

riential counselors and therapists indicate that cognitive–behavioral strategies do not pay enough attention to feelings. Insight and an emphasis on the past (often seen as important in other theories) do not fit within the purview of CBT.

THE CASE OF MARIA: A COGNITIVE–BEHAVIORAL APPROACH

A cognitive–behavioral counselor would begin with a thorough assessment of Maria and then implement one of the cognitive–behavioral intervention strategies. Using Persons and Davidson's (2001) case conceptualization model as the basis of this discussion, we begin with a problem list. The case study provides bits and pieces of the kind of information necessary to understand the problems faced by Maria. It would be best to have the client explain the problem, which she does not do in this case description, at least not directly.

Maria's Problem List

1. *Depression:* Depression is evidenced by difficulty sleeping, crying, weight loss, and suicidal ideation. A Beck Depression Inventory score would be a useful bit of information. Depression is evidenced by sad affect, sleep disturbances, and disturbing dreams. Maria's words, "I have nothing to live for. No one cares about me. I've ruined my life and the lives of two families, and I am currently hurting my children," are indicative of her depressed affect and sense of hopelessness.
2. *Interpersonal difficulties:* She has difficulties, especially with her children and other family members. She is also unable to sustain a relationship with potential future mates.
3. *Problems at work:* Problems include difficulty concentrating and more absences than are acceptable to her principal.
4. *Acculturation issues:* Maria is Hispanic and grew up in a culturally encapsulated neighborhood.

Working Hypothesis

Schemata

Maria's thoughts about self, others, the world, and the future are as follows:

1. I am inadequate, irresponsible, inferior, ashamed, and guilty.
2. Others are demanding and don't understand me.
3. The future is hopeless.

Precipitating and Activating Situations

Origins

The onset of the problems appears to be related to abuse Maria suffered at the hands of her ex-husband, the end of their marriage, and the lack of support from her own family when this occurred. Her coping mechanism, putting energy into work, led to problems arising with her children.

Summary of the Working Hypothesis

When Maria was challenged to take responsibility for herself and family, she began to feel "less than." This cognitive schema of inadequacy, irresponsibility, inferiority, shame, and guilt brought about depression, and the spiral of depression into poor self-care has made it difficult for Maria to see an end to this stressful and sad life.

Strengths and Assets

Maria is intelligent, well educated, resilient, and caring. She has both children and a family of origin who can be brought into treatment to provide additional support. She is part of a culture that values the family and social group.

Treatment Plan

Goals

1. Reduce depressive symptoms.
2. Increase self-esteem and confidence.
3. Increase social support through family or extrafamily support.

Modality

1. Individual cognitive behavior therapy that is culturally sensitive
2. Group-based cognitive behavior therapy with women who have been abused

Initial Intervention

1. Focus on the present by assessing current depression and suicidality using the Beck Depression Inventory and clinical interview.
2. Develop social support through a group treatment program.
3. Incorporate meditative relaxation.

Asking Maria to describe her problem would help the counselor or therapist identify the primary presenting problem and provide the basis for deciding on goals for counseling or psychotherapy. This is not clearly presented in the case description; Maria may not know what she might be able to get out of counseling or psychotherapy. A first step might be to help Maria describe how she wants her life to be different than it currently is. The goals can be expressed in cognitive, behavioral, or affective statements. For example, Maria might indicate that she wants to feel less depressed or have increased energy. What Maria wants is not clear from the case description provided.

How can progress in counseling or psychotherapy be measured and monitored? The counselor might select cognitions, behaviors, or feelings to monitor. Maria could complete thought diaries or record the kinds of maladaptive thoughts she has during the day. She might be asked to keep track of these thoughts or some other target behavior. She could record a rating of feelings, which would provide useful information about how behaviors and thoughts contribute to her negative affect. The counselor or therapist could also use a variety of self-report measures such as the Beck Depression Inventory to provide a record of depression.

What are the environmental contingencies maintaining the behavior? In this arena, it is important to study Maria's issues in the particular contexts of her daily life. What happens at work that contributes to her negative thoughts and feelings? It could be that she is telling herself that if she cannot teach perfectly, then she should stay home in bed all day. Likewise, what are her thoughts about her children? Does she think that they want to spend more time with her? Or does she believe that they wish she would leave them alone? We do not know the thinking that is underlying her depression.

Which interventions are likely to be effective? It seems that the cognitive–behavioral interventions described in this chapter would be valuable for working with Maria. We have selected Beck's cognitive therapy to demonstrate how a particular approach would be used. Establishing rapport is a critical part of Beck's approach. The counselor or therapist would have to take special steps to establish good rapport with Maria.

A cognitive–behavioral counselor or therapist would establish a plan to work with Maria that focused on developing an understanding of the role her thinking is having in her current situation. Maria would be challenged to identify the thoughts that go through her mind at work and at home, especially thoughts that are tied to depression. Patterns of thoughts might be classified into general categories of cognitive distortions, such as all-or-nothing thinking, overgeneralization, or disqualifying the positive. As Maria learns how to identify thoughts, she may also begin to talk about some feelings and see that the thoughts and feelings are related to her problems. It is the primary task of the counselor or therapist to demonstrate that the thoughts, feelings, and behaviors are interrelated and that the counseling or psychotherapy will work through changing the maladaptive thoughts.

Once there is an understanding of some of the thoughts that Maria may be having, the counselor begins the process of changing the thoughts. Questions like, "What's the evidence?" "What's another way of looking at the situation?" and "So what if it happens?" (Beck & Emery, 1985, p. 201) are useful. Hypothesis testing, generating alternative interpretations, and decatastrophizing are some cognitive strategies that might be used. Self-monitoring thoughts might be used as a homework assignment to help Maria focus on thoughts and how they affect her behavior and feelings. It seems that one of the ways in which Maria copes with depression is to withdraw from contact with people. Although the withdrawal behavior is a consequence of the depression, it ultimately increases the depressed feeling she has because it isolates her from making real connections with others.

There are certainly other factors of Maria's case study that a counselor would want to address, including her risk for suicide and her parental and family relationships. We have focused primarily on the depression because it seems that it is the primary problem and the one for which there is great motivation to seek solutions. As Maria learns the strategies on CBT, she may be better equipped to address the other problems in her life.

REFERENCES

Addis, M. E., Hatgis, C., Krasnow, A. D., Jacob, K., Bourne, L., & Mansfield, A. (2004). Effectiveness of cognitive-behavioral treatment for panic disorder versus treatment as usual in a managed care setting. *Journal of Consulting and Clinical Psychology, 72,* 635–663.

American Psychiatric Association. (2013). *Diagnostic and statistical manual of mental disorders* (5th ed.). Arlington, VA: Author.

Baker, A., Boggs, T. G., & Lewin, T. J. (2001). Randomized controlled trial of brief cognitive-behavioural interventions among regular users of amphetamine. *Addiction, 96,* 1279–1287.

Bakker, G. M. (2009). In defence of thought stopping. *Clinical Psychologist, 13*(2), 59–68. doi:10.1080/13284200902810452

Bandura, A. (1977). Self-efficacy: Toward a unifying theory of behavior change. *Psychological Review, 84,* 191–215.

Bandura, A. (1986). *Social foundations of thought and action.* Upper Saddle River, NJ: Prentice Hall.

Barlow, D. H. (2008). *Clinical handbook of psychological disorders.* New York, NY: Guilford Press.

Barraca, J. (2012). "Mental control" from a third-wave behavior therapy perspective. *International Journal of Clinical and Health Psychology, 12*(1), 109–121.

Beck, A. T. (1976). *Cognitive therapy and emotional disorders.* New York, NY: International Universities Press.

Beck, A. T., & Emery, G. (1985). *Anxiety disorders and phobias.* New York, NY: Basic Books.

Beck, A. T., Freeman, A., Davis, D. D., & Associates. (2003). *Cognitive therapy of personality disorders* (2nd ed.). New York, NY: Guilford Press.

Beck, A. T., Hollon, S. D., Young, J. E., Bedrosian, R. C., & Budenz, D. (1985). Treatment of depression with cognitive therapy and amitriptyline. *Archives of General Psychiatry, 42,* 142–148.

Beck, A. T., Rush, A. J., Shaw, B. F., & Emery, G. (1979). *Cognitive therapy of depression.* New York, NY: Guilford Press.

Beck, A. T., Wright, F. D., Newman, C. F., & Liese, B. S. (1993). *Cognitive therapy of substance abuse.* New York, NY: Guilford Press.

Bennett-Levy, J., Wilson, S., Nelson, J., Stirling, J., Ryan, K., Rotumah, D., . . . Beale, D. (2014). Can CBT be effective for Aboriginal Australians? Perspectives of Aboriginal practitioners trained in CBT. *Australian Psychologist, 49*(1), 1–7. doi:10.1111/ap.12025

Burns, D. D. (1999). *Feeling good: The new mood therapy* (Rev ed.). New York, NY: Avon Press.

Burns, D. D., & Auerbach, A. (1996). Therapeutic empathy in cognitive-behavioral therapy. In P. M. Salkovskis (Ed.), *Frontiers of cognitive therapy* (pp. 135–164). New York, NY: Guilford Press.

Chen, S. W., & Davenport, D. S. (2005). Cognitive-behavioral therapy with Chinese American clients: Cautions and modifications. *Psychotherapy: Theory, Research, Practice, and Training, 42,* 101–110.

Connolly Gibbons, M. B., Crits-Cristoph, P., Levinson, J., & Barber, J. (2003). Flexibility in manual-based psychotherapies: Predictors of therapist intervention in interpersonal and cognitive-behavioral therapy. *Psychotherapy Research, 13,* 169–185.

Craighead, W. E., Craighead, L. W., & Ilardi, S. S. (1995). Behavior therapies in hertorical perspective. In B. Bongar & L. E. Beutler (Eds.), *Comprehensive textbook of psychotherapy: Theory and practice* (pp. 64–83). New York, NY: Oxford University Press.

De Wildt, W. A. J. M., Schippers, G. M., Van Den Brink, W., Potgieter, A. S., Deckers, F., & Bets, D. (2002). Does psychological treatment enhance the efficacy of acamprosate in patients with alcohol problems? *Alcohol & Alcoholism, 37,* 375–382.

DeRubeis, R. J., Gelfand, L. A., Tang, T. Z., & Simons, A. (1999). Medications versus cognitive behavioral therapy for severely depressed outpatients: Mega-analysis of four randomized comparisons. *American Journal of Psychiatry, 156,* 1007–1013.

DeRubeis, R. J., Siegle, G. J., & Hollon, S. D. (2008). Cognitive therapy versus medication for depression: Treatment outcomes and neural mechanisms. *Nature Reviews Neuroscience, 9,* 788–796. doi:10.1038/nrn2345

Digdon, N., Powell, R. A., & Harris, B. (2014). Little Albert's alleged neurological impairment: Watson, Rayner, and historical revision. *History of Psychology, 17*(4), 312–324. doi:10.1037/a0037325

Dimaggio, G., Salvatore, G., Lysaker, P. H., Ottavi, P., & Popolo, R. (2015). Behavioral activation revisited as a key principle of change in personality disorders psychotherapy. *Journal of Psychotherapy Integration, 25*(1), 30–38. doi:10.1037/a0038769

Dobson, K. S. (Ed.). (2001). *Handbook of cognitive-behavioral therapies* (2nd ed.). New York, NY: Guilford Press.

Dobson, K. S., & Dozois, D. J. A. (2001). Hertorical and philosophical bases of the cognitive-behavioral therapies. In K. S. Dobson (Ed.), *Handbook of cognitive-behavioral therapies* (2nd ed., pp. 3–39). New York, NY: Guilford Press.

Dobson, K. S., & Shaw, B. F. (1988). The use of treatment manuals in cognitive therapy: Experience and issues. *Journal of Consulting and Clinical Psychology, 56,* 673–680.

Emmelkamp, P. M. (2003). Behavior therapy with adults. In M. J. Lambert (Ed.), *Bergin and Garfield's handbook of psychotherapy and behavior change* (5th ed., pp. 393–446). New York, NY: Wiley.

Goddard, M. J. (2014). Critical psychiatry, critical psychology, and the behaviorism of B. F. Skinner. *Review of General Psychology, 18*(3), 208–215. doi:10.1037/gpr0000012

Hollon, S. D., & Kendall, P. C. (1979). Cognitive–behavioral interventions: Theory and procedure. In P. C. Kendall & S. D. Hollon (Eds.), *Cognitive and cognitive–behavioral interventions: Theory, research, and procedures* (pp. 220–247). Oxford, England: Elsevier.

Hopko, D. R., Robertson, S. C., & Lejuez, C. W. (2006). Behavioral activation for anxiety disorders. *The Behavior Analyst Today, 7*(2), 212–232. doi:10.1037/h0100084

Karch, D., Albers, L., Renner, G., Lichtenauer, N., von Kries, R., & Roseveare, D. (2013). The efficacy of cognitive training programs in children and adolescents: A meta-analysis. *Deutsches Ärzteblatt International, 110,* 643–652.

Kendall, P. C., & Hollon, S. D. (1979). Cognitive-behavioral interventions: Overview and current status. In P. C. Kendall & S. D. Hollon (Eds.), *Cognitive-behavioral interventions: Theory, research, and procedures* (pp. 1–9). New York, NY: Academic Press.

Kohn, L. P., Oden, T., Munoz, R. F., Robinson, A., & Leavitt, D. (2002). Adapted cognitive behavioral group therapy for depressed low-income African American women. *Community Mental Health Journal, 38,* 497–504.

Lin, Y. (2002). The application of cognitive-behavioral therapy to counseling Chinese. *American Journal of Psychotherapy, 56,* 46–58.

Moore, J. (2013). Sketch: Three views of behaviorism. *The Psychological Record, 63,* 681–691. doi:10.11133/j.tpr.2013.63.3.020

Nicolas, G., Arntz, D. L., Hirsch, B., & Schmiedigen, A. (2009). Cultural adaptation of a group treatment for Haitian American Adolescents. *Professional Psychology: Research and Science, 40,* 378–384.

Norcross, J. C., Santrock, J. W., Campbell, L. F., Smith, T. P., Sommer, R., & Zuckerman, E. L. (2003). *Authoritative guide to self-help resources in mental health* (Rev. ed.). New York, NY: Guilford Press.

Pagoto, S., Bodenlos, J. S., Schneider, K. L., Olendzki, B., Spates, C. R., & Ma, Y. (2008). Initial investigation of behavioral activation therapy for co-morbid major depressive disorder and obesity. *Psychotherapy: Theory, Research, Practice, Training, 45,* 410–415. doi:10.1037/a0013313

Persons, J. B., & Davidson, J. (2001). Cognitive-behavioral case formulation. In K. S. Dobson (Ed.), *Handbook of cognitive-behavioral therapies* (2nd ed., pp. 86–110). New York, NY: Guilford Press.

Rosner, R. I. (2012). Aaron T. Beck's drawings and the psychoanalytic origin story of cognitive therapy. *History of Psychology, 15,* 1–18.

Shaw, B. F. (1977). Comparison of cognitive therapy and behavior therapy in the treatment of depression. *Journal of Consulting and Clinical Psychology, 45,* 543–551.

Skinner, B. F. (1969). *Contingencies of reinforcement: A theoretical analysis.* New York, NY: Appleton-Century-Crofts.

Stone, M. H. (2007). Cognitive-behavior therapy groups in inpatient settings. In R. W. Christner, J. Stewart, & A. Freeman (Eds.), *Handbook of cognitive-behavior group therapy with children and adolescents: Specific settings and presenting problems* (pp. 145–158). New York, NY: Routledge.

Triscari, M. T., Faraci, P., D'Angelo, V., Urso, V., & Catalisano, D. (2011). Two treatments for fear of flying compared: Cognitive behavioral therapy combined with systematic desensitization or eye movement desensitization and reprocessing (EMDR). *Aviation Psychology and Applied Human Factors, 1*(1), 9–14. doi:10.1027/2192-0923/a00003

Turkington, D., Kingdon, D., & Turner, T. (2002). Effectiveness of a brief cognitive-behavioural therapy. *British Journal of Psychiatry, 180,* 523–527.

Veltro, F., Vendittelli, N., Oricchio, I., Addona, F., Avino, C., Figliolia, G., & Morosini, F. (2008). Effectiveness and efficiency of cognitive-behavioral group therapy for inpatients: 4-year follow-up study. *Journal of Psychiatric Practice, 14,* 281–288.

Vittengl, J. R., Clark, L. A., Thase, M. E., & Jarrett, R. B. (2015). Predictors of longitudinal outcomes after unstable response to acute-phase cognitive therapy for major depressive disorder. *Psychotherapy, 52*(2), 268–277. doi:10.1037/pst0000021

Wampold, B. E., Minami, T., Baskin, T. W., & Tierney, S. C. (2002). A meta-(re)analysis of the effects of cognitive therapy versus "other therapies" for depression. *Journal of Affective Disturbances, 686,* 159–165.

Watson, J. B. (1930). *Behaviorism* (2nd ed.). Chicago, IL: University of Chicago Press.

Watson, J. C., & Geller, S. M. (2005). The relations among the relationship conditions, working alliance, and outcome in both process-experiential and cognitive-behavioral psychotherapy. *Psychotherapy Research, 15,* 25–33.

Williams, J. M. G., Russell, I., & Russell, D. (2008). Mindfulness-based cognitive therapy: Further issues in current evidence and future research. *Journal of Consulting and Clinical Psychology, 76,* 524–529.

Wolpe, J. (1958). *Psychotherapy by reciprocal inhibition.* Stanford, CA: Stanford University Press.

Zarling, A., Lawrence, E., & Marchman, J. (2015). A randomized controlled trial of acceptance and commitment therapy for aggressive behavior. *Journal of Consulting and Clinical Psychology, 83*(1), 199–212. doi:10.1037/a0037946

Zivor, M., Salkovskis, P. M., & Oldfield, V. B. (2013). If formulation is the heart of cognitive behavioural therapy, does this heart rule the head of CBT therapists? *The Cognitive Behaviour Therapist, 6,* e6. doi:10.1017/S1754470X1300010X

Chapter 10

Dialectical Behavior Theory

Laura R. Haddock

Dialectical behavior therapy (DBT) is a therapeutic methodology initially developed by Marsha M. Linehan in the late 1970s to treat individuals with borderline personality disorder (BPD). According to the *Diagnostic and Statistical Manual of Mental Disorders, Fifth Edition* (American Psychiatric Association [APA], 2013), those with personality disorders demonstrate behavior that is pervasive and inflexible over an extended duration. In addition, these behaviors must cause significant distress or impairment in functioning and must be demonstrated in at least two of the following areas: cognizance, affectivity, interpersonal functioning, or impulse control. The typical behaviors and patterns that this population demonstrates are repeated across settings, and individuals do not adjust their behavior in response to experiences. Traits, coping styles, and interpersonal engagement with others and the world at large are elements of personality, and these characteristics initially emerge in childhood and typically solidify by late adolescence and early adulthood. The majority of people have adaptable personalities and are responsive to social and societal demands. Those who have personality disorders are rigid in their interpersonal engagement and demonstrate a lack of self-awareness as well as inflexible and maladaptive patterns of relating to others. It is believed that approximately 9% of the U.S. population meets the criteria for one of the personality disorders (APA, 2013). Refer to Sidebar 10.1 for an overview of characteristics of BPD.

As its name suggests, DBT is grounded in a dialectical perspective of reality and experience. It is grounded in a theoretical base that suggests that the world is in continuous change and ever shifting and that individuals are constantly in transition. An individual's knowledge base and coping skills developed from life experience provide the frame of reference for reacting to challenges, and the consequences of those reactions affect knowledge of self, others, and the world. This ongoing cyclical relationship between what the individual knows and does is of-

Sidebar 10.1. Characteristics of BPD

- Poorly developed, unstable self-image
- Compromised ability to recognize others' feelings
- Feelings of emptiness
- Excessive self-criticism
- Instability in relationships due to mistrust, neediness, or threats of abandonment
- Marked impulsivity
- Interpersonal hypersensitivity
- History of self-harm

ten destructive and leads to ongoing dysfunctional relationships, difficulty coping with stressors, or chronic frustration. Much research has been conducted on the treatment of BPD, and outcomes suggest that BPD may be less responsive to treatment interventions than other types of personality disorders (Butcher, Mineka, & Hooley, 2010). One significant element that interferes with the measurement of treatment effectiveness for BPD is the high incidence of comorbidity among personality disorders (Zimmerman, Rothchild, & Chelminski, 2005). Women suffering from BPD often demonstrate an elevated occurrence of major depression, anxiety disorders, or eating disorders, whereas men routinely suffer from substance abuse disorders and antisocial personality disorder (National Institute of Mental Health, n.d.). In addition, childhood trauma and neurobiological factors may also contribute to the development of BPD (Brandelow et al., 2005) and can require complex treatment interventions. See Sidebar 10.2 for assessments commonly used to assist in the identification of BPD.

The scholarly evidence base supports psychotherapy as the intervention of choice for the treatment of BPD (APA, 2001; Goldman & Gregory, 2010; Kendall et al., 2009) as opposed to psychopharmacotherapy and other treatment approaches. DBT combines customary cognitive–behavioral techniques for emotional regulation and reality testing with concepts of mindful awareness, distress tolerance, and acceptance predominantly derived from Buddhist meditative practice (Linehan, 1993a). DBT may help address a range of mood and anxiety symptoms and

Sidebar 10.2. Assessment Instruments

- *Longitudinal Interview Follow-Up Evaluation Psychiatric Status Ratings:* This measure evaluates the presence and severity of psychiatric diagnoses over time.
- *International Personality Disorder Examination:* This is the most widely established measure of personality disorders currently available and is used by the World Health Organization.
- *Millon Clinical Multi-Axial Inventory III:* This instrument is designed to help assess a number of disorders in the *Diagnostic and Statistical Manual of Mental Disorders*.
- *Borderline Symptom Checklist-23:* The Borderline Symptom Checklist was initially developed as a self-rating instrument for the specific assessment of borderline-typical symptoms.
- *Difficulties in Emotion Regulation Scale:* This 36-item self-report measure assesses difficulties in emotional regulation among adults and adolescents.

decrease suicidal or self-harming behaviors (Davidson et al., 2008; Linehan et al., 2006; Verheul et al., 2003). Specifically, individuals with self-injurious behaviors such as cutting or suicidal thoughts, gestures, and even attempts have shown a positive response to this therapeutic intervention (McMain, Korman, & Dimeff, 2001). Research indicates that DBT is also effective for treating other mental health problems, such as depression, bipolar disorder, posttraumatic stress disorder (PTSD), anxiety, eating disorders, or alcohol and drug problems (Bedics, Atkins, Harned, & Linehan, 2015; Feigenbaum, 2007; Fischer & Peterson, 2014; Katz, Gunasekara, & Miller, 2002; Lynch, Chapman, Rosenthal, Kuo, & Linehan, 2006; Lynch & Cheavens, 2008; McMain et al., 2001; Perepletchikova & Goodman, 2014; Quinn, 2009; Swales, Heard, & Williams, 2000).

BACKGROUND

Marsha Linehan is an American psychologist and author, and her primary work has been with suicidal clients, clients with substance abuse problems, and clients with BPD. When Linehan began her work as a psychologist in the 1970s, she sought to develop a successful treatment for individuals who were actively suicidal (Van Nuys, 2007). During an interview about DBT, she stated,

> My real target and focus was the person who found life so painful and the anguish so insurmountable that they truly wanted to be dead. I went to work with this group of people and I thought that I could treat them with the existing, of-the-day cognitive behavior therapy. . . . I was out not only to save the world but quite confident I could do it. (Van Nuys, 2007)

Linehan (1993a) created DBT after her clinical work indicated that her persistently suicidal clients had a high incidence of being raised in invalidating environments, resulting in demands for a therapeutic environment of unconditional acceptance. Her work with clients who react abnormally to emotional stimulation revealed patterns of behavior, including levels of excitement going up much more quickly, peaking at a higher intensity, and taking more time to return to baseline. This explained why individuals with BPD demonstrate catastrophe-driven lives and rapid emotional shifts. Because of their past invalidation, clients do not have any methods for coping with these sudden, powerful surges of emotion. Linehan explained that her clients

> came in, and . . . these people had so many problems. They were such an ever changing set of problems, so that one day it was one thing and another day, another. If you worked on one problem, another problem was more intolerable. You try to work on that problem and the person says, "well, I'm going to kill myself, this is all hopeless." (Van Nuys, 2007)

As a result, Linehan recognized that successful treatment was related to clients' willingness to change. This willingness to change appeared to be affected by people's ability to cope with stressors and accept their level of emotional dysfunction. Linehan discovered a significant deficiency in standard cognitive and behavioral treatments, which focused almost entirely on helping clients modify their thoughts, feelings, and behaviors. A treatment solely focused on change tended to be unacceptable to these clients, who often felt inadequate and criticized and dropped out of treatment. Obviously, if clients do not attend treatment, they cannot benefit from treatment. Conversely, a treatment focused entirely on acceptance nullified the seriousness of the client's suffering and the urgent need to produce change. Thus, Linehan (1993a) built DBT around a philosophy that encourages the balance and fusion of both acceptance and change. Chronically depressed clients can potentially benefit from psychotropic medication and can potentially need a referral for medication management. However, within the therapeutic process, acceptance-based interventions, frequently referred to as *validation strategies*, communicate to clients both that they are acceptable as they are and that their behaviors, including those that are self-harming, make sense in some way. According to Linehan,

> Within every unwise act, there is some inherent wisdom. [Like] taking heroin, which is a long term, dysfunctional, destructive behavior in our culture. Within there, is the wisdom of, "you feel better immediately." So there is dysfunction and function always coexisting together. (Van Nuys, 2007)

Counselors learn to highlight for clients when clients' thoughts, feelings, and behaviors are normal, helping clients discover that they have sound judgment and are capable of learning how and when to trust themselves. The new emphasis on acceptance does not occur to the exclusion of change. Clients must also change if they want to create a life worth living. The focus on acceptance used in combination with change-based strategies enhances the effectiveness of both approaches. In the course of merging acceptance with change, Linehan noticed that a third set of strategies, dialectics, came into play. Dialectical strategies give the counselor a means of balancing acceptance and change when emotions run high, as they often do in the treatment of clients diagnosed with BPD. Dialectical strategies and a dialectical worldview with an emphasis on wholeness and synthesis enable the counselor to blend acceptance and change in a manner that results in progress, momentum, and flow in individual sessions and across the entire treatment intervention. This counters the tendency found in the treatment of clients diagnosed with BPD to become hindered by arguments and polarizing or extreme positions. These three sets of strategies, together with the theories on which they are based, come together to form the foundation of DBT.

Although DBT has expanded to treat populations other than those with BPD and has been adapted to treat a variety of ages and settings, all treatment approaches are highly structured and all are based on Linehan's original works. Thus, not only did she create this treatment approach, but her theory is threaded through every adaptation of this model. See Sidebar 10.3 for biographical information on Dr. Marsha Linehan.

Sidebar 10.3. Marsha Linehan

Born: May 5, 1943, in Tulsa, Oklahoma
Alma mater: Loyola University, Chicago, Illinois
Occupation: Creator of dialectical behavior theory, psychologist, professor, author
Website: http://blogs.uw.edu/linehan/

HUMAN NATURE: A DEVELOPMENTAL PERSPECTIVE

DBT is considered a principle- or theory-driven therapy. Three primary theories create the foundation of the treatment. At its center, DBT is guided by behavior theory. It is also guided by the biosocial theory of BPD and the theory of dialectics (Linehan, 1993a). As a therapy guided by behavior theory, it conceptualizes behavior according to the principles of classical and operant conditioning, observational learning, and the transfer of information. The principles of learning theory state that a behavior will continue or increase when reinforced, will reduce or extinguish when punished, and will slowly cease when previous reinforcement is removed. As a fundamentally behavior-based treatment, the DBT model emphasizes the identification of stimuli that trigger dysfunctional behaviors through previously learned associations and the outcomes that shape the development and maintenance of a behavior. The central premise of DBT is that individuals with DBT struggle to tolerate and regulate strong emotional states. The goal of DBT is to teach healthy coping skills to help clients manage intense emotions without the use of self-destructive behavior, with the ideal result being improved relationships (Haddock, 2014). Intrinsic motivation (such as feelings of relief or a reduction in anxiety) or extrinsic motivation (such as increased attention or praise) may be complex, and the function of behaviors will depend on the range and relative strengths of these benefits. DBT conceptualizes behavior broadly to comprehensively address thinking, feeling, and behavior. Emphasis is placed on the function of behavior and the context in which behavior occurs. The strength of DBT is its ability to explain the development of thought and experience over time.

A significant assumption in behavior theory is that the factors associated with the preservation of behavior may be different from the factors related to the initial development of behavior. This hypothesis is particularly important in the conceptualization of chronic, longstanding problems, such as those associated with childhood abuse or trauma. Although a behavior may have originated in the context of abuse, it may now be maintained by current triggers and contingencies not directly related to the trauma history. For example, a client may have developed a tendency to dissociate in response to childhood abuse, but ultimately the client may dissociate in response to any strong negative emotion. In this case, processing the past abuse would likely have little effect on reducing the dysfunctional behavior. Effective treatment would more likely focus on intervention related to current triggers and emphasize the regulation of strong negative emotions.

In DBT, behavior theory influences all aspects of the treatment, including the method in which problems are defined, the ways in which behaviors are assessed, case conceptualization, and the interventions that are used. In general, the behavioral conceptualization of BPD within DBT emphasizes capability deficits and motivational factors in the maintenance of problem behaviors. Specifically, behaviors are viewed as maintained by some combination of deficits in skills, cued responding, reinforcement, or thought processes (Linehan, 1993a). Primary behavioral interventions from this view include skills training, exposure, contingency management, and cognitive restructuring (Linehan, 1993b).

Linehan suggested that BPD develops when a child who is biologically susceptible to difficulties regulating emotions is placed in environments perceived as interpersonally lethal or invalidating. The child is more sensitive to emotional stimuli, has more intense emotional reactions, and returns slowly to baseline. An invalidating atmosphere constantly trivializes, blames, and assigns socially undesirable characteristics to an individual's cognitive, behavioral, and emotional responses, despite the fact that the responses make sense in the context of facts, circumstances, norms, or events (Katz et al., 2002).

Some environments, such as those that are physically or sexually abusive, are pervasively invalidating, whereas others are invalidating only when there is a poor fit between the family's and child's temperaments. Still other environments do not start out as invalidating but become so as a result of stresses arising out of interactions between the individual and others. The intense emotional reactions of the individual with BPD elicit invalidating behavior from caregivers, which then elicits further emotional dysregulation, and it becomes a vicious cycle. This transaction between an emotionally vulnerable individual and an invalidating rearing environment leads to dysregulation across the individual's emotional system, characterized broadly by difficulty in regulating physiological arousal as well as difficulty in turning attention away from emotional stimuli. As a result, individuals who have BPD often experience considerable disruption of their cognitive, emotional, and behavioral systems when emotionally aroused.

Anger and emotional dysfunction are central problems in individuals with BPD. The individuals struggle with fears of abandonment and chaotic relationships; confusion about identity, values, or feelings; and a chronic sense of emptiness. Cognitive dysregulation in the form of rigid thinking, irrational beliefs, paranoid ideation, and isolation may also occur. Finally, as an attempt to regulate emotions, behavioral dysregulation such as impulsivity or suicidality is common. See Figure 10.1 for a visual representation of the cycle of emotional dysregulation.

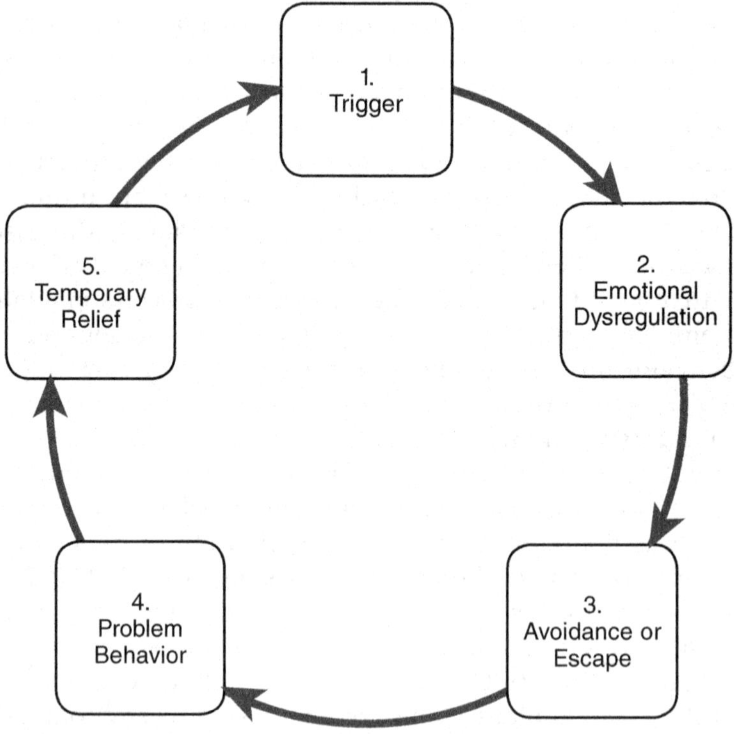

Figure 10.1. The Cycle of Dysregulation

Dialectics is the basis for understanding an individual's past experience and is the foundation of validation (Linehan, 1993a). DBT therefore expands on traditional behavior therapy by including interventions that attend to the role of invalidation in the development of BPD and emotional dysregulation in the maintenance of BPD, such as the provision of validation and teaching of behavioral skills.

MAJOR CONSTRUCTS

DBT is a comprehensive treatment that integrates cognitive behavior therapy with acceptance-based "Eastern psychological and spiritual practices" (Linehan, 1993b, p. 6). DBT is grounded in a support-oriented approach that emphasizes each individual's unique strengths so that clients may feel capable of accomplishing change. DBT is also a collaborative approach that incorporates consistent attention on the therapeutic relationship in an effort to facilitate trust and encourage client commitment to the therapeutic plan (Bedics et al., 2015). This approach requires commitment from clients, as homework assignments, role play, and practicing new ways of thinking and behaving are required elements of both individual and group therapy sessions. Clients must also learn and practice techniques for self-soothing and frustration tolerance. Counselors use mindfulness concepts and meditation, regulated breathing, and relaxation to teach clients to become more self-aware and attentive to situations. DBT promotes a balance between changing destructive behaviors and practicing acceptance of beliefs and behaviors (Haddock, 2014; McMain & Pos, 2007). It emphasizes the importance of the psychotherapeutic relationship, validation of the client, the impact of having been raised in an invalidating environment, and confrontation of resistance. DBT was developed from an approach that views BPD as a "combination of motivation problems and capability deficits" (Linehan, 1993b, p. 6). It is highly structured, particularly during the initial stage of treatment when the individual is lacking behavioral control and consequently engaging in dysfunctional and life-threatening behaviors. The main components of DBT are affect regulation, distress tolerance, improvement in interpersonal relationships, and mindfulness training. Ultimately, clients learn to restrain dysfunctional emotion-driven behaviors and to initiate behaviors that are free of current mood and contribute to the ability to meet long-term goals. Counselors of DBT do not approach helping clients through insightful discussions, although insight can be helpful at times. Learning new behaviors is critical in DBT and is a focus of every session, skills group, or phone call. Counselors considering training in DBT should be prepared to establish a therapeutic alliance rooted in a trusting, safe relationship. Chronic feelings of rejection, a history of abuse, and participation in self-destructive behaviors can leave individuals with BPD feeling stigmatized and shamed. See Sidebar 10.4 for additional counselor considerations.

Biosocial Theory

DBT's biosocial theory of BPD views the disorder as primarily one of pervasive emotional dysregulation, a result of both highly emotional vulnerability and deficits in the ability to regulate emotions. Biosocial theory helps a person to understand not only the etiology of BPD and its problem areas but also the maintenance of the disorder. Linehan (1993b) viewed dysfunctional behaviors in individuals with BPD either as an attempt by the individual to regulate intense affect or as

Sidebar 10.4. Implications of BPD for the Therapeutic Relationship

Individuals with BPD frequently grow to idolize their counselors and create an expectation that their counselors will save them. When counselors do not live up to these idealistic expectations, clients can quickly make them the enemy. Clients feeling frustrated or angry about a limit established by the counselor usually provoke this depreciation of the counselor.

Within a counseling session, it could play out something like this: The client notices that the counselor looks at her watch while listening to her story. She has an assumption or interpretation about what this watch check means. This might take the form of an automatic thought, something like this: "This person is bored with me and is going to leave me."

It is important that counselors take an active approach to managing sessions and setting limits around the treatment process. If the client's transference behaviors threaten the treatment progress, counselors must be prepared to work through the issue with the client or consider changing the treatment approach.

an outcome of emotional dysregulation. Thus, for example, clients may deliberately harm themselves as a means of distracting attention away from emotionally salient stimuli and thereby reducing anguish, or they may be lashing out when feeling overwhelmed. The DBT theory views emotions as involving a full system response and not merely the individual's phenomenological experience of the emotions. Linehan's model also assumes that emotions are prompted by events and function to organize and motivate action. Emotions inform individuals about the personal significance of situations (McMain et al., 2001). The accurate identification of an emotional response is critical to the regulation of emotions.

The DBT model assumes that individuals with BPD lack key interpersonal and self-regulation skills and that personal and environmental factors may block the use of appropriate responses to stressors or reinforce maladaptive responses. Thus, DBT is designed to facilitate the learning of new skills and generalization of the new skills across contexts.

Emotional dysregulation in individuals with BPD is viewed as resulting from the perfect storm of biological anomalies combined with an invalidating environment (Linehan, 1993a). These biological irregularities in BPD are believed to be caused by biological or genetic factors or childhood events. These irregularities are thought to result in emotional vulnerability offering insight into the affective instability and impulsive, self-destructive, and aggressive behaviors characteristic of BPD (Siever & Davis, 1991). Linehan (1993a) believed that an invalidating environment communicates to individuals that their interpretations and perceptions of their experiences are fundamentally wrong. The person therefore does not learn to accurately label internal experience or to regulate emotional arousal. In addition, these individuals do not learn to trust their own thoughts and feelings as accurate and reasonable responses to internal and environmental events. Rather, they are taught to invalidate their own perceptions and to scan the environment for cues about how to react. The invalidating environment also conveys to individuals that their experiences are due to unacceptable and undesirable character traits. For example, "A child is 'bad' for feeling angry, 'lazy' for not getting over loss quickly, or 'weak' for feeling afraid" (McMain et al., 2001, p. 186). Because the child is routinely ignored or punished for his or her emotional responses, appropriate coping mechanisms for dealing with these emotions are not learned. In addition, because the system within the environment commonly responds to hysterical displays of emotions, the extreme behaviors are inadvertently reinforced, teaching that extreme displays are needed to garner a response from the environment. This combination of ignoring or punishing emotional responses and reinforcing the extreme emotional states results in teaching the child to shift between emotional inhibition and extreme emotional states.

Emotional Dysregulation and Validation

In addition to using the theoretical tenets of behavior theory, DBT uses behavioral techniques, including a form of exposure therapy in which the client learns to tolerate painful emotions without enacting self-destructive behaviors (Linehan, 1993b). Therapy does not focus on maintaining a stable, consistent environment but rather aims to help clients become comfortable with change. In DBT, clients are asked to change. Clients track and record their problem behaviors with a weekly diary card. They also attend skills groups, complete homework assignments, and role-play new ways of interacting with people when in session with their counselor. In addition, clients work with their counselor to identify how they are rewarded for maladaptive behavior or punished for adaptive behavior. They expose themselves to feelings, thoughts, or situations that they feared and avoided, and they change self-destructive ways of thinking. The fundamental assumption is that clients are experiencing a dialectical conflict between themselves and their environment. DBT assumes that the potency, duration, and expression of the emotions trigger the resulting destructive behaviors. Counselors use DBT to help clients recognize how their attempts to reject, evade, and flee strong emotions paradoxically make those emotions more intense. By helping clients accept their emotions, facilitating the development of strategies for emotional recognition and regulation, and decreasing emotional avoidance, counselors help clients improve their ability to cope with stress and regulate their emotions.

As noted earlier, cognitive behavior therapy techniques were not enough to help clients who were suicidal and chronically self-harming in the context of BPD. It is not that the techniques were ineffective; it is just that, as stand-alone interventions, they caused distress. Clients found the pushing for change invalidating. It could be compared to asking someone with a back injury to carry bags of concrete to help the person's back get stronger. Telling the person just not to think about the pain even though every effort is painful is not effective. This was further complicated by routine feelings of depression.

Linehan (1993a) and her research team verified that when a counselor combined an emphasis on validation with an equal emphasis on change, clients were more likely to be cooperative and less likely to become disturbed and introverted. Validation for clients is not linear in nature. For instance, a counselor could understand that a client overeats to combat feelings of isolation and loneliness. Then, in response to self-loathing after bingeing, the client may make impulsive decisions that may lead to self-harm. The counselor could validate that the behavior makes sense as the only way the client has effectively decreased his or her anxiety. The counselor could validate that the binge eating makes sense given the client's history and worldview, yet the counselor does not have to agree that overeating is the best approach to solving the client's anxiety.

In DBT, there are several types and levels of validation. The most fundamental level is staying attentive to the other person. This means being respectful of thoughts, feelings, and behaviors. Other levels of validation involve helping the client regain confidence by assuming that the behavior makes sense and by treating the client with dignity and respect (Holmes, Georgescu, & Liles, 2006). In DBT, just as clients are taught to use cognitive–behavioral strategies, they are also taught and encouraged to use validation. In treatment and in life, it is important to learn to recognize what has potential for change and what about oneself one must accept as is.

DBT takes a contextual approach to the human experience. Rather than viewing thoughts or behaviors as if they were independent variables that can be changed or controlled, a contextual perspective suggests that personal experiences can only be understood meaningfully in the context in which they occur. From this perspective, the function rather than the content of thoughts is the primary focus of the therapeutic process. This perspective considers thoughts as dependent variables in need of explanation. For example, a student thinking about the concept of empathy when taking a counseling exam has a very different function or meaning than a person being preoccupied with this concept while attending a meeting at work about individualizing treatment goals.

The Four Skill Modules

As mentioned, DBT is highly structured with regard to the content of sessions and assignments for clients. Although treatment goals are individualized to meet each client's needs as appropriate for specific challenges and triggers, the therapeutic goals fall within four specific skill areas.

Mindfulness

Mindfulness is regarded as a core skill in DBT. Mindfulness involves increasing awareness of self and context through observation, explanation, involvement, and the capacity to control the focus of one's attention on the current moment. Essentially, it is the capacity to pay attention, nonjudgmentally, to the present moment. Mindfulness in DBT incorporates the ability to focus on one thing in the moment and to identify effective responses to distress. This approach assists individuals in finding a synthesis between emotional experience and logical thought. It is through the ability to mindfully attend to one's current emotional state and identify the associated, often obstructive thoughts and the reactions and behaviors of self and others that solutions can be generated and applied. Mindfulness is considered a basis for the other skills taught in DBT because it assists individuals to embrace and tolerate the potent emotions they may feel when attempting to change their routine or exposing themselves to distressing situations. The concept of mindfulness and the meditative exercises used to teach it originate from customary Buddhist practice, although the skills taught in DBT do not involve any religious or metaphysical concepts.

Interpersonal Effectiveness

Interpersonal response patterns taught in DBT skills training are comparable with those taught in many assertiveness or interpersonal problem-solving classes. They include efficient strategies for asking for what one needs, saying no, and coping with interpersonal conflict.

Individuals with BPD often have good interpersonal skills in a broad sense. The problems arise in the application of these skills to specific situations. An individual may be able to describe appropriate responses when discussing another person encountering a problematic situation but may be completely incapable of conceptualizing or applying an appropriate response when analyzing a personal situation.

The interpersonal effectiveness module focuses on situations in which the purpose is to modify something or to stand firm against changes someone else is trying to generate, thus resulting in goals such as learning to ask for what one needs or learning to say no. The skills taught are intended to maximize the likelihood that a person's goals in a specific situation will be met while at the same time not damaging either the relationship or the person's self-respect.

Emotional Regulation

Individuals with BPD and suicidal individuals are frequently emotionally intense and labile. They can be angry, intensely frustrated, depressed, or anxious. This suggests that these clients might benefit from help in learning to regulate their emotions. The DBT skills for emotional regulation include identifying and labeling emotions, identifying obstacles to changing emotions, reducing vulnerability, and increasing positive emotional events.

Distress Tolerance

Many contemporary approaches to mental health counseling focus on altering distressing events and circumstances. They have paid little attention to accepting, finding meaning for, and tolerating distress. This task has generally been addressed by psychodynamic, psychoanalytic, Gestalt, or narrative therapies along with religious and spiritual communities and leaders. DBT emphasizes learning to tolerate pain skillfully.

Distress tolerance skills represent a natural development from mindfulness skills. They have to do with the ability to accept, in a nonjudgmental fashion, both oneself and the current situation. The objective is to become skilled in calmly recognizing negative situations and their impact rather than becoming overwhelmed or hiding from them. This allows individuals to make prudent decisions about whether and how to take action rather than falling into the intense, desperate, and often destructive emotional reactions that are part of BPD.

Skills for acceptance include radical acceptance, turning the mind toward acceptance, and learning to distinguish between reacting skillfully from a realistic understanding of the present situation (willingness) and trying to impose one's will regardless of reality (willfulness). Clients also learn four crisis survival skills to help deal with immediate emotional responses that may seem overwhelming: distracting oneself, self-soothing, improving the moment, and thinking of pros and cons.

Dialectics

As a worldview, dialectical philosophy provides a foundation for DBT. Dialectics is a complex concept that has its roots in philosophy and science. Dialectical philosophy involves several assumptions about the nature of reality. It suggests that reality is made of interrelated parts that cannot be defined without reference to the system as a whole and that the whole must also recognize its parts. The system and its parts are in a constant state of change, and any change affects the system. It implies that reality, rather than being static and fixed, is constantly changing. It is always in flux and abounding with obvious contradictions. This approach suggests that on the one hand, one must be tolerant of inconsistencies, and on the other hand, one must be diligent in one's attempt to search for useful means of dealing with contradictions. Thus, clients learn that there is benefit to acceptance and to change. When a counselor addresses client dysfunction, this principle of interrelatedness and wholeness leads to a systemic conceptualization of behavior. A DBT counselor treats the whole individual rather than a diagnosed pathology. Similarly, the whole emotional system is addressed in counseling with the recognition that elements of the system are interconnected, influencing both the client's behavior and the environmental context external to the client.

DBT also involves specific dialectical strategies to help clients get unstuck from inflexible ways of thinking or viewing the world. For example, in response to a client's commitment to participate in the therapeutic process, the counselor might ask whether the client is sure he or she wants to do it because it is likely to be very hard work. This approach, called *devil's advocate,* causes the client to argue in favor of why and how he or she will complete the counseling and not drop out. The counselor guides the client in making strong and convincing arguments about participating in the counseling as opposed to being a cheerleader for the client to participate. This type of approach is intended to facilitate therapeutic movement so the focus does not become a battle of wills between the counselor and the client. The spotlight is on "teaching and modeling dialectical thinking as a replacement for dichotomous, either-or, black-and-white thinking" (Linehan, 1993b, p. 39). The group setting offers an environment to observe and participate in the process of change for both the group as a whole and each individual. The DBT model uses many techniques to assist in self-awareness, growth, and behavior modification (Linehan, 1993b). Figure 10.2 provides a visual map of examples of dialectical strategies.

To deal with demanding, narcissistic clients, counselors are required to be in either group or individual supervision. Supervision facilitates each counselor in setting rules and limits that are appropriate for that counselor without interpreting personal limits as representing a fear of intimacy or a need to be nurturing. Counselors are expected to make mistakes and to be accepting of their own mistakes. They are vulnerable to the pattern of comforting these demanding patients, then becoming angry and punitive, then feeling guilty and appeasing again. They must individualize the treatment to suit each client without undermining the ideology of DBT. Counselors must maintain a balance between nurturing and demanding change, giving clients needed help and guidance without doing for clients what clients can do for themselves. Counselors must maintain and communicate optimism that the counseling will help each client and take an individualized approach to treatment planning (Seligman, 2004). See Sidebar 10.5 for additional treatment planning considerations.

APPLICATIONS

Overview

DBT is a psychosocial treatment that targets maladaptive behaviors exhibited by some people that put them at risk for both psychological and physical harm. It is hy-

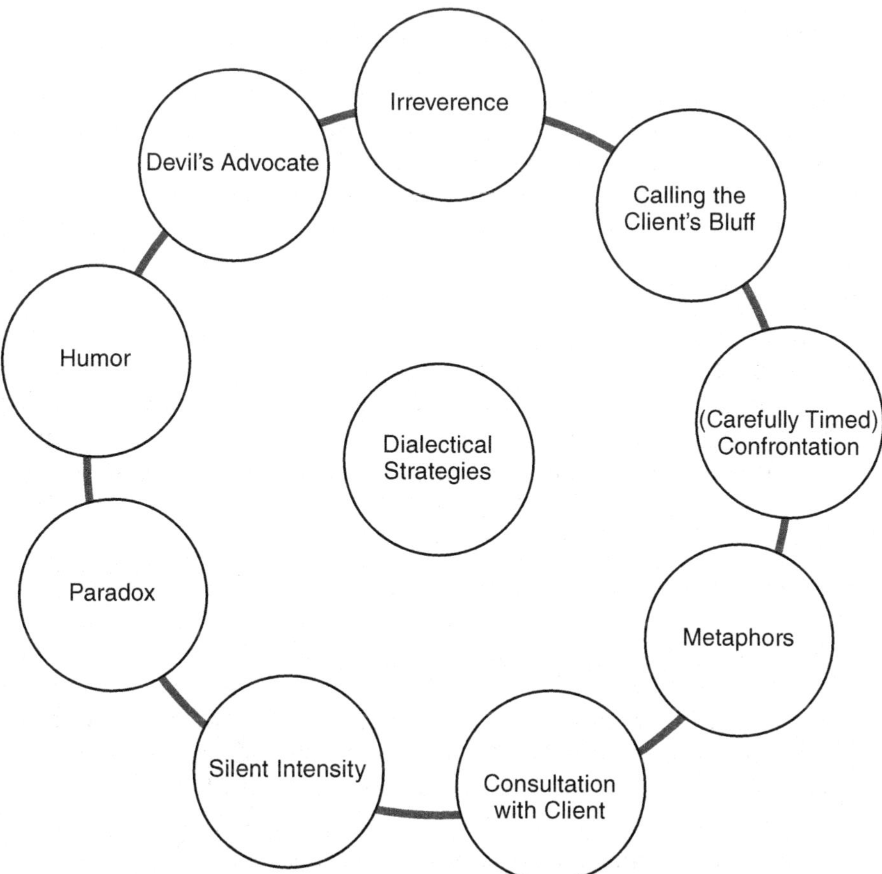

Figure 10.2. Dialectical Strategies

pothesized that such self-destructive behaviors occur as a result of intense emotional experiences. DBT applies a variety of cognitive and behavioral techniques, including problem solving, exposure training, contingency management, and behavior modification, to treat such maladaptive behavior. The treatment consists of three interconnected modes of counseling: individual counseling, group-based skills train-

Sidebar 10.5. Treatment Planning for Clients With BPD

With the use of DBT, it is especially important to establish a detailed treatment plan. Establishing clear boundaries is an important element of every treatment intervention with every client. The setting in which the counselor is working (e.g., private practice, hospital, community mental health agency) may also inform the counselor's expectations of the treatment protocol. For example, counselors will need to specify the following:

- The frequency of session scheduling
- A plan for managing between-session needs
- A plan for managing session tardiness
- A plan for what happens when the client misses a session
- Homework expectations
- The client's and the counselor's roles within the therapeutic process
- The counselor's between-session availability

ing, and telephone coaching. Each mode of counseling concurrently addresses skills relating to interpersonal effectiveness, emotional regulation, and distress tolerance. Teaching the art of mindfulness is also integrated into the model. The central goal of DBT is to improve quality of life, essentially assisting clients to create a life worth living despite the experience of intense emotion (Linehan, 1993a).

DBT is a long-term intervention that integrates individual and group therapies and typically requires clients to commit to 6 to 12 months of treatment. Since its first implementation, DBT has gained strong empirical support from randomized clinical trials (Geisser & Rizvi, 2014). Treatment teams should be utilized for treatment planning and collaborate frequently to track progress. Individual therapy typically occurs 1 hour per week and is focused on individual needs and the client's application of improved coping skills in relation to real-world events. The individual treatment is combined with 2 or more hours of weekly group therapy with a focus on learning and applying improved coping skills related to distress tolerance, interpersonal relationships, and the regulation of negative emotions. In addition to the individual and group therapy, DBT includes phone coaching between therapy sessions to dissuade against self-injurious or suicidal behaviors (Haddock, 2014).

Goals of Counseling and Psychotherapy

DBT organizes treatment into stages and targets and, with very few exceptions, adheres exactingly to the order in which problems are addressed (Linehan, 1993a, 1993b). The organization of the treatment into stages and targets prevents DBT from being a treatment that, week after week, addresses the crisis of the moment. In addition, it has a rational progression that addresses first behaviors that could lead to the client's death, then behaviors that could lead to premature termination of the counseling process, and finally behaviors that demolish the quality of life and the need for alternative skills. In other words, the first goal is to ensure that the client stays alive so that the second goal of staying in therapy results in meeting the third goal of building a better quality life. This is achieved partly through the acquisition of new skills and behaviors.

Before beginning the therapeutic process, the counselor explains to the client the treatment model, shares an understanding of the client's difficulties as identified from the assessment, and orients the client to the expectations of counseling. The client must commit to reducing self-injurious behaviors, to working on interpersonal challenges that may interfere with the process of counseling, and to working on developing new skills. The counselor adopts a dialectical position, highlighting both the need for change and the difficulties with change. This approach increases commitment and allows both the counselor and the client to identify obstacles that may need to be addressed.

After making a commitment to participate in counseling, clients participate in a structured therapeutic process organized into the following stages of counseling (see Figure 10.3). The targets of counseling are specific to each stage.

Stage 1: Moving from being out of control of one's behavior to being in control. The goal of this stage is for the client to move from behavioral dyscontrol to behavioral control so that there is a normal life expectancy.

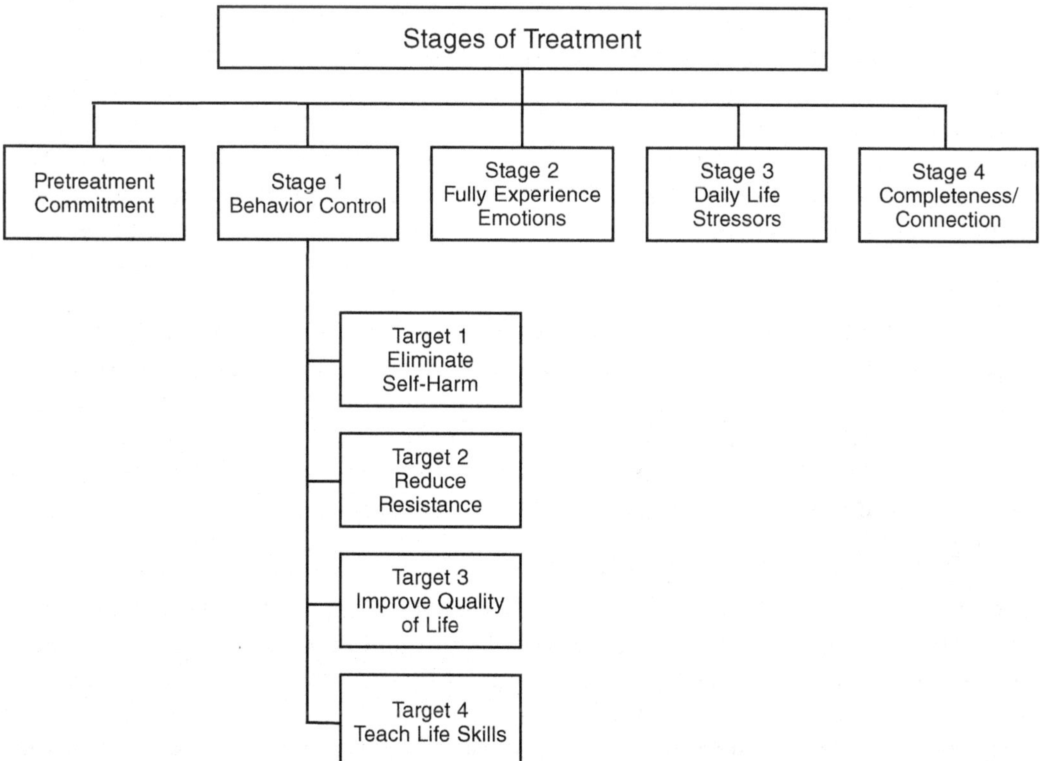

Figure 10.3. Stages of Treatment

Target 1: Reduce, then eliminate, life-threatening behaviors, such as suicide attempts, suicidal thinking, or intentional self-harm.

Target 2: Reduce, then eliminate, behaviors that interfere with the counseling process, such as behaviors that alienate helping professionals, intermittent completion of homework assignments, nonattendance of sessions, or noncollaboration with counselors. This target includes reducing and then eliminating the use of hospitalization as a way to handle crises.

Target 3: Decrease behaviors that destroy the quality of life, such as depression, phobias, eating disorders, nonattendance at work or school, disregard for medical problems, poor budgeting, inferior housing, or lack of friends. In addition, increase behaviors that make life worth living, such as going to school or having a rewarding job, having friends, effective budgeting, appropriate housing, or having minimal symptoms of depression or anxiety.

Target 4: Learn skills that help individuals do the following:

a. Control their concentration, so they stop obsessing about the future or worrying about the past. Also amplify self-awareness to assist with learning more about what contributes to feeling good or bad.
b. Initiate new relationships, improve existing relationships, or end unhealthy relationships.
c. Understand what emotions are, how they function, and how to experience them in a way that is not overwhelming.
d. Endure emotional pain without resorting to self-harm or self-destructive behaviors.

Stage 2: Moving from being emotionally shut down to experiencing emotions fully. In this stage, DBT addresses the client's repressed emotional functioning. The goal is to help the client move from a state of quiet desperation to one of full emotional experiencing. The main target of this stage is to help clients experience feelings without having to shut down by dissociating, avoiding life, or having symptoms of PTSD. Teaching clients to suffer in silence is not the goal of treatment. The counselor works with the client in this stage to treat PTSD symptoms and teaches the client to experience a full range of emotion without shutting the emotions down or allowing the emotions to become unmanageable.

Stage 3: Building an ordinary life and solving ordinary life problems. This stage focuses on problems in living, with the goal being that the client has a life of ordinary happiness and unhappiness. Clients work on common problems such as marital or partner conflict, job dissatisfaction, career goals, and so on. Some clients choose to continue with the same counselor to accomplish these goals. Some take a break from counseling and work on goals without a counselor. Still others take a break and then work with a different counselor in a different type of counseling.

Stage 4: Moving from incompleteness to completeness/connection. Linehan has promoted Stage 4 specifically for those clients for whom a life of ordinary happiness and unhappiness fails to result in spiritual fulfillment or a sense of connectedness to a greater whole. At the end of Stage 3, some individuals may have the lives they wanted but continue to feel somewhat empty or incomplete. In Stage 4, the goal of treatment is for the client to move from a sense of incompleteness toward a life that involves an ongoing capacity for experiences of joy and freedom.

Thus, DBT targets behaviors in a descending hierarchy:

- Decreasing high-risk suicidal behaviors
- Decreasing responses or behaviors by the counselor or client that interfere with the counseling process
- Decreasing behaviors that interfere with or reduce the quality of life
- Decreasing and dealing with posttraumatic stress responses
- Enhancing respect for self
- Acquiring the behavioral skills taught in group
- Including additional goals set by the client

The Process of Change

Linehan (1993a) hypothesized that a successful counseling intervention must meet the following five critical functions:

1. Improve and preserve the client's incentive to change. It is frequently the individual counselor who maintains the client's motivation for treatment because the counselor is the most significant individual for the client.
2. Boost the client's capabilities. Skills are acquired, strengthened, and generalized through the combination of skills groups, phone coaching, coaching, and homework assignments.
3. Ensure that the client's new capabilities are generalized to all relative environments.
4. Enhance the counselor's motivation to treat clients while also enhancing the counselor's skills. Counselors enhance capabilities and avoid burnout through weekly consultation meetings and supervision.

5. Structure the environment so that the treatment can take place. For example, the client and the counselor may meet with family members to ensure that the client is not being reinforced for maladaptive behaviors or punished for effective behaviors in the home.

Traditional Intervention Strategies

DBT consists of three parts (Linehan, 1993b). Individual counseling sessions are scheduled weekly during which a particular problematic behavior or incident from the past week is examined in detail, beginning with the series of events leading up to it, going through alternative solutions that might have been used, and exploring what kept the client from using more adaptive solutions to the problem. These individual sessions are 60 to 90 minutes, and the function is to relate skills learned to the specific goals and targets of the individual. The individual sessions have a clear structure and focus. Both between and during sessions, the counselor actively teaches and reinforces adaptive behaviors, especially as they occur within the therapeutic relationship. The emphasis is on teaching clients how to deal with emotional disturbance rather than reducing or taking them out of crisis. Telephone contact with the individual counselor between sessions is part of the DBT procedure. The purpose of these brief telephone consultations is to assist clients in identifying an appropriate skill to use and overcoming obstacles to using the skill effectively. A variety of techniques are used to generalize to the environment, such as flashcards, handouts, tapes of the skills, planned phone calls, and teaching skills to friends and family members.

In addition to individual counseling, weekly 2.5-hour group counseling sessions are conducted. This skills training group is intended to boost the capabilities of the client. The format is psychoeducational, structured expressly for the learning and rehearsal of new skills. These group sessions address specific modules, including interpersonal effectiveness, distress tolerance, reality acceptance skills, emotional regulation, and mindfulness skills. Group counselors are not available over the phone between sessions, and they refer clients in crisis to the individual counselor.

Neither component is used by itself. The individual component is considered necessary to keep suicidal urges or uncontrolled emotional issues from disrupting group sessions, whereas the group sessions teach the skills unique to DBT and also provide practice with regulating emotions and behavior in a social context. In addition to these two therapy components, counselors provide phone coaching between sessions to assist clients in overcoming challenges and consistently implementing appropriate responses. The hierarchy of goals within DBT is presented in Sidebar 10.6.

Sidebar 10.6. Goals of DBT

1. Decreasing suicidal and other self-injurious behaviors
2. Decreasing behaviors that interfere with therapy (e.g., lying to the counselor, missing sessions)
3. Decreasing behaviors that interfere with quality of life (e.g., substance abuse, eating disorder behaviors)
4. Increasing behavioral skills that can be used to regulate negative emotions, increase distress tolerance, and enhance interpersonal skills

The impact of culture on the treatment must also be considered in relation to the strategies used in DBT. For example, DBT places an emphasis on balancing irreverence with reciprocal communication. Any change in setting, treatment provider, or population may alter what is considered irreverent or reciprocal. Some counselors may be resistant to such strategies as potentially negative to the therapeutic relationship.

DBT uses the primary strategies of cognitive behavior therapy, including behavioral analysis, exposure, contingency management, and cognitive restructuring. However, a number of supplementary and distinctive strategies are included in the treatment to augment the value of treatment for individuals with BPD. Because the DBT model uses a workbook with handouts for clients, an obvious example of a need for cultural modifications is the language of the training manual. The handouts may need to be adapted not only to the culture in which they are being used but also to the specific populations using them, such as adolescents. In line with dialectical ideology, change strategies are combined with acceptance strategies. As a principle-driven therapy, DBT provides a framework in which the counselor selects and incorporates therapeutic techniques based on the target of the moment (Linehan, 1993b). Examples of some of these strategies follow.

Strategies to Increase Commitment to Therapy

Securing a commitment from the client to participate in the therapeutic process is critical. Treatment contracts, motivational strategies to adhere to goals, the use of dialectical strategies such as devil's advocate to engage clients in taking some ownership of the process, and the use of metaphors are often less threatening or confrontational for these clients, who require a great deal of validation.

Problem-Solving Strategies

The main problem-solving strategy in DBT is behavioral chain analysis, used to identify triggers that lead to dysfunctional behaviors. This strategy addresses the need for change. The client and counselor then generate and rehearse a solution, using existing skills and suggesting new skills. Obstacles are considered and resolved.

Validation Strategies

To balance asking for change, counselors use acceptance strategies. These strategies assist clients in learning to validate themselves, strengthen the therapeutic relationship, and act as a form of feedback.

Dialectical Strategies

While attempting to promote balance, counselors use dialectical strategies to facilitate comfort with movement between change and acceptance. This could include the counselor being nurturing yet challenging or moving between flexibility and stability.

Brief Intervention Strategies and Current Practices

As designed, DBT is not a brief intervention. In standard outpatient DBT, the client makes a commitment to 1 year of treatment consisting of a weekly psychoeducational skills training group, weekly sessions with an individual counselor to identify and reduce factors that interfere with the ability to use skills, and telephone contacts with the counselor on an as-needed basis when crises arise, thus facilitating generalization through this in vivo interaction. The counselor, in turn, agrees to provide 1 year of treatment during which the counselor will participate in a weekly consultation group for technical help and emotional support.

Evaluations of a year or less of treatment are important, as one must consider issues of cost-effectiveness and practicality in clinical settings where long-term treatments may not be possible. Miller, Rathus, Linehan, Wetzler, and Leigh (1997) adapted DBT for suicidal adolescent outpatients. They shortened the first phase of treatment from 1 year to 16 weeks. Pilot data suggest that these adaptations still result in promising treatments. However, the majority of studies conducted on the efficacy of DBT have involved a minimum of a year in treatment.

Those suffering from personality disorders routinely experience functional impairment across a variety of settings, and frequently their symptoms worsen under stress (Kress & Paylo, 2015). Counselors are charged with recognizing when clients may need care from a variety of treatment providers, which could include access to medication evaluation and management, individual and group therapy, and case management services. Clients also sometimes experience acute episodes of dysregulation that could require crisis stabilization or inpatient treatment when they are actively suicidal or homicidal. Intensive outpatient treatment provides a higher level of care than weekly outpatient treatment and allows clients to be at home and not in a hospital.

The stages of DBT provide the framework in which the treatment is conducted. The hierarchy of treatment informs the counselor what the goals of treatment need to be. Behavioral problem-solving strategies are the vehicle of change within DBT. Many appointments may be spent using specific problem-solving strategies to help the counselor and client identify and understand difficult behavior and then evaluate and incorporate a plan for more adaptive behaviors (Geisser & Rizvi, 2014).

Clients With Serious Mental Health Issues

Counselors treat a variety of disorders in a variety of settings (Seligman, 2004). Counselors should also consider that individuals who seek treatment for mental health issues such as depression or anxiety and are also diagnosed with personality disorders may not have as much therapeutic success as those who seek treatment and do not have a personality disorder (Crits-Christoph & Barber, 2007; Kress & Paylo, 2015). Dysfunctional personality characteristics may interrupt the therapeutic relationship, and clients may be less likely to engage in the work to make behavioral changes. Treatment providers have modified DBT for use in various settings, including inpatient programs (Barley et al., 1993; Bohus et al., 2000), day treatment programs, and residential programs. Adaptations have been developed for use with different forms of psychopathology, including substance abuse (Dimeff, Rizvi, Brown, & Linehan, 2000), eating disorders (Safer, Telch, & Agras, 2001), domestic violence (Fruzetti & Levensky, 2000), bipolar disorder (Van Dijk, 2009), and antisocial personality disorder (McCann, Ball, & Ivanoff, 2000). In addition, DBT has also been applied to various age groups, including adolescent inpatients (Katz et al., 2002), adolescent outpatients (Miller et al., 1997; Rathus & Miller, 2000), and geriatric populations (Lynch, 2000).

Although DBT is effective in the treatment of BPD and is showing value in the treatment of other chronic mental illnesses, there are several clinical concerns. The effectiveness for medication therapy is well documented for mental illnesses that include a physiological component, such as psychosis and mood disorders. Some techniques within DBT require a certain degree of cognitive functioning, which potentially limits its effectiveness with populations that have cognitive impairment. Finally, because applying the DBT model requires extensive and specific training, the lack of availability of trained clinicians may inhibit expansion of DBT as a treatment model.

Empirical evidence suggesting that DBT is efficacious as an outpatient treatment in urban settings is abundant (Lynch et al., 2006). However, one cannot assume that those results will generalize if the treatment is applied outside this context. Both cultural and systemic adaptations to the therapy may be required when the model is applied to populations beyond those with BPD. It is clear that new dialectics will emerge between the therapy and the population of choice. To progress from a state of static tension, both the therapy and the culture must adapt by reciprocally influencing each other. Because the model was designed in the United States and in response to one particular treatment population, care must be taken to consider needed adaptations in the therapy, the counselors, and the therapeutic system.

Finally, as the DBT model originated for the treatment of BPD, the stigma of this diagnosis cannot be overlooked. Some clinicians in the United States are hesitant to use a diagnosis of BPD out of concern for the potential negative impact of labeling. Cultures outside the United States may also hesitate to diagnose clients with BPD. As a model, DBT addresses these concerns and uses diagnostic labeling in a way that minimizes the negative impact and maximizes the positive. Within a behavioral approach to diagnosis, the therapist or counselor teaches clients about the diagnosis, allowing an opportunity to communicate to the clients that they are not alone in dealing with these issues. Informing clients that the treatment may help solve the problem communicates hope. Aligned with the concepts of DBT, acceptance balances change.

EVALUATION

Overview

DBT was designed by Marsha Linehan for the treatment of individuals with self-injurious behaviors, such as cutting or suicidal thoughts, urges, and attempts. Many clients with these behaviors are diagnosed with BPD. It is not unusual for individuals with BPD to also experience comorbidity with other emotional problems, such as depression, mood disorders, PTSD, anxiety, eating disorders, or substance abuse problems. DBT is a modification of cognitive behavior therapy that integrates individual counseling with concurrent skills training. Clients in standard DBT receive individual counseling, skills group counseling, and phone coaching. The therapy aims to assist clients in learning to control behavior, fully experiencing emotions, improving daily living skills, and achieving a sense of completeness. Skills used to reach these goals include mindfulness, interpersonal effectiveness, emotional regulation, and distress tolerance. This treatment is of particular interest because it focuses on intervening with a group of clients who are recognized as difficult to treat effectively. In addition, because this approach is incredibly specific and structured, there are challenges in adapting it to accommodate other treatment populations.

Supporting Research

Research to support the efficacy of DBT is rich (Valentine, Bankoff, Poulin, Reidler, & Pantalone, 2014). DBT is the most well-researched and efficacious therapeutic intervention for the treatment of BPD (Goldman & Gregory, 2010; Gunderson, 2011; Kliem, Kroger, & Kosfelder, 2010; Linehan et al., 2006). From the first randomized controlled trial of women with severe BPD and suicidal behavior (Linehan, Armstrong, Suarez, Allmon, & Heard, 1991), DBT clients have consistently shown a reduction in the frequency and severity of symptoms (Linehan, Heard, & Armstrong, 1993; Linehan & Tutek, 1994; Verheul et al., 2003). These improvements include a decrease in suicidal behaviors, a reduction in the number of inpatient bed days, and increased retention in treatment. Studies also indicate a reduction in suicidal ideation, anger expression, hopelessness, and depression. New studies are showing improvements among other populations, such as preadolescents (Perepletchikova & Goodman, 2014) and adolescents with eating disorders (Fischer & Peterson, 2014).

Limitations

Several concerns about this treatment model are related to the fact that BPD is a difficult disorder to treat, with a lengthy developmental history that is frequently slow to change. In addition, BPD is commonly comorbid with a range of serious mental health disorders, which thus potentially increases the complexity and length of treatment. In addition, neurobiological factors and childhood trauma have also been identified as elements that potentially contribute to the development of BPD (Brandelow et al., 2005) and can complicate treatment approaches. Furthermore, individuals with BPD have disordered attachment, which leads to difficulties with forming and ending relationships. To address these multiple complications, DBT is a staged therapy designed to continue for more than 1 year in most cases to allow for the Stage 2 targets. The effects of premature termination of treatment have not been fully explored. The DBT approach is also highly structured and specific with regard to interventions, and this model does not fit all populations (Wagner, Rizvi, & Harned, 2007).

Studies that have examined the efficacy of treatment have had limitations. For some studies, sample sizes were small and highly specific, thus limiting the generalizability of the results to standard clinical settings. In addition, the DBT groups were typically compared with treatment interventions that did not allow for the effects of motivated and enthusiastic clinicians, number of hours of treatment, counselor expertise, or supervision.

Finally, although thousands of treatment providers have been trained and are located all over the world, "there are not enough people trained," according to Linehan (Van Nuys, 2007). Thus, access to this specialized therapy continues to be somewhat limited.

Summary Chart: Dialectical Behavior Theory

Human Nature

DBT was developed to treat clients with BPD. It maintains that certain individuals who are exposed to invalidating environments during childhood in combination with biological factors react abnormally to emotional stimulation. DBT conceptualizes behavior broadly, to comprehensively address thinking, feeling, and behavior. Emphasis is placed on the function of behavior and the context in which behavior occurs. The strength of this approach is its ability to explain the development of thought and experience over time.

Major Constructs

DBT is a comprehensive treatment that merges cognitive behavior therapy with mindfulness-based practices of Buddhism. It balances the concept of learning behavioral change with the corresponding concept of learning acceptance. The DBT model emphasizes the identification of stimuli that trigger dysfunctional behaviors through previously learned associations and the outcomes that shape the development and maintenance of a behavior. It emphasizes the importance of the psychotherapeutic relationship, validation of the client, the impact of having been raised in an invalidating environment, and confrontation of resistance. It is highly structured, particularly during the initial stage of treatment when the client is lacking behavioral control and consequently engaging in dysfunctional and life-threatening behaviors. The main components of DBT are emotional regulation, distress tolerance, interpersonal effectiveness, and mindfulness training. Clients receive three main modes of treatment: individual counseling, skills group, and phone coaching. This model aims to reduce self-injurious and suicidal behaviors, behaviors that interfere with the therapeutic process, and behaviors that diminish the client's quality of life.

Goals

DBT targets behaviors in a descending hierarchy. Prior to the initiation of counseling, a commitment for participation is secured from the client. In the first stage of treatment, once treatment is initiated, the emphasis is on decreasing high-risk suicidal behaviors and moving from being out of control of one's behavior to being in control. The second stage of treatment helps clients move from being emotionally shut down to experiencing emotions fully by addressing any resistance that has the potential to interfere with the therapeutic process. The third stage of treatment works with clients on daily stressors and assists with solving behaviors that interfere with or reduce the quality of life. During this stage, the model also targets decreasing and dealing with PTSD responses. The final stage of counseling promotes moving from incompleteness to completeness through enhancing respect for self and promoting the acquisition of behavioral skills for coping with distress.

Change Process

The DBT model proposes that successful counseling intervention meets five critical functions: (a) improve and preserve the client's incentive to change, (b) boost the client's capabilities, (c) ensure that the client's new capabilities are generalized to all relative environments, (d) enhance the counselor's motivation to treat clients while also enhancing the counselor's skills, and (e) structure the environment so that the treatment can take place.

Interventions

DBT uses the primary strategies of cognitive behavior therapy. A number of supplementary and distinctive strategies are included in the treatment to augment the value of treatment. In line with dialectical ideology change, strategies are combined with acceptance strategies, including strategies to increase commitment to therapy, problem-solving strategies, validation strategies, and dialectical strategies.

Clinical experience would suggest that counselors with a variety of qualifications can become DBT counselors, although those with a behavioral background require less time. It seems likely that specific qualifications will not prove as predictive of success in the use of DBT as specific counselor characteristics, such as being nondefensive or being able to think conceptually and quickly. The various tasks and modalities of the model may also require a variety of counselor skills and characteristics. Thus, different members of a team could fulfill different roles according to their own strengths.

Another area of consideration is the duration and frequency of treatment. In the original model, clients attended concurrent individual counseling and group skills training for 1 year. However, as practitioners have attempted to use this approach with other populations, this extended time frame has been prohibitive in some settings and more time has been needed in other settings. Counselors must not overlook how adjusting the time frame of treatment will affect the efficacy while also considering how the intensity of treatment will affect the client. Current adjustments include a 16-week regimen for suicidal adolescents and a 2-year program for chronically mentally ill persons who have been in the mental health system for 10 to 15 years (Van Nuys, 2007).

Limitations

Concerns about this treatment model are related to the fact that BPD is a difficult disorder to treat, with a lengthy developmental history that is frequently slow to change. In addition, BPD is commonly comorbid with a range of serious mental health disorders, which thus potentially increases the complexity and length of treatment. Women are diagnosed with BPD at an estimated gender ratio of 3 to 1. Research indicates that BPD may be missed in men or may be diagnosed as antisocial or narcissistic personality disorders (Kress & Paylo, 2015). Men should be just as carefully assessed for BPD as women, as more recent epidemiological studies of non-help-seeking community samples have suggested a more equal gender ratio than the documented prevalence research suggests (e.g., Lynam & Widiger, 2007). Symptoms similar to BPD are seen across cultures and can be misidentified in individuals experiencing issues such as identity crises, substance abuse, sexual orientation conflicts, and pressure to determine a career path (APA, 2013). To address these multiple complications, DBT is a structured therapy designed to continue for more than 1 year in most cases to allow for the Stage 2 targets. This model does not fit all populations (Wagner et al., 2007). In addition, if this treatment approach were to be used within a managed care setting, third-party reimbursement could limit the number of contacts between a client and the counselor that are payable under the client's benefits. This could certainly decrease the feasibility of this treatment approach.

In determining the efficacy of the treatment, the treatment provider is of obvious importance. DBT is a complex treatment that requires the counselor to master a number of strategies and skills in addition to standard cognitive behavior therapy techniques. It requires, therefore, much intensive and extensive training and supervision. Newly graduated counselors should not attempt this approach until they have undergone considerable supervised practice under someone very experienced in the use of DBT.

THE CASE OF MARIA: A DIALECTICAL APPROACH

Presenting Problem

Maria presents with both serious affective impairment and personality dysfunction. Her symptoms include depression with suicidal ideation, interpersonal difficulties, and a trauma history related to suffering emotional and physical abuse. She displays impairment in her social and occupational functioning. She experiences feelings of self-doubt and concern that there is something wrong with her. She often feels scared and angry about the way she was treated by her husband and the rejection by her family. She is currently experiencing persistent emotional crisis and fears being perceived by others as inadequate and unacceptable.

Maria uses work as a way to feel good about herself but feels little relief from her depression from this coping method. In fact, she is currently impaired to such a degree that her employer is recommending a leave of absence, which only serves to further elevate her anxiety. She worries about how she will take care of her children. She feels lonely, depressed, suicidal, and unlovable and tends to perceive others as untrustworthy and against her. She has developed a pattern of behavior that involves avoiding interpersonal relationships, particularly of an intimate nature. It seems Maria would prefer to miss an opportunity for a close relationship than to risk the possible consequence of abuse or rejection.

Course of Treatment

Maria's daily symptoms of depression are debilitating and have resulted in frequent crying spells, sleep and appetite disturbance, and reduced effectiveness with parenting and at work. A careful and thorough medical exam should be conducted to help rule out physiological causes for symptoms, and she should be assessed for medication and may be prescribed antidepressants by a physician to assist in the management of daily symptoms.

The first four sessions of DBT are intended to obtain a comprehensive history and familiarize the client with treatment. By the fourth session, Maria and her counselor should mutually determine treatment goals, including increasing her ability to make decisions despite not knowing whether the right solution has been chosen; decreasing fear and avoidance in relationships; increasing her ability to tolerate criticism from her family; and developing a lasting, intimate relationship. Reducing suicidal ideation would also be a target. Diary cards would be introduced to track targets on a daily basis (Linehan, 1993b).

It is projected that in the early stages of treatment, Maria will demonstrate an overall willingness and ability to articulate goals for counseling. However, she may remain ambivalent about her own efforts and pessimistic about the possibility of change. An important part of treatment will include what is called *informal behavioral exposure* in standard DBT. Informal exposure is designed to help Maria learn new responses to a classically conditioned fear of being hurt or abandoned. Because DBT involves frequent feedback from the counselor, it will be explained to Maria that there will be many opportunities for informal exposure practice during the sessions themselves. After explaining the rationale behind the need to practice receiving feedback/criticism, because Maria's difficulty in doing so interferes with relationship development, the counselor will look for times during sessions when his or her comments are experienced as criticism/attack by Maria and use those moments to practice behaviors different from Maria's urge to escape or avoid. Thus, the counselor will have to be watchful for changes in Maria's affect during sessions and be willing to shift briefly to exposure practice before going back to the topic at hand.

The steps of the exposure technique for Maria might look something like this: The counselor notices a change in Maria's emotional presentation and interrupts the conversation using immediacy and asking if she feels as if she is being criticized.

- Maria will be asked to try and identify what resulted in this emotional reaction.
- Maria will be asked to identify her emotion and consider what she needs to experience the emotion rather than avoid the emotion.
- Maria will be asked to verbalize her automatic thoughts, such as, "She thinks I am stupid."
- Maria will be asked to continue to focus on the sensations associated with the emotion until it starts to recede.

Each informal exposure lasts from 1 to 5 minutes and ideally starts and ends with a rating of Maria's distress on a scale of 1 to 100. In addition, it is important for the counselor to support Maria's willingness to participate and validate the possibility of change.

Once the skills associated with in-session informal exposure are learned, homework assignments will be given to help facilitate growth in all relevant contexts. Examples may include practicing confiding in others, increasing social behaviors, or noticing criticisms of others and letting them go.

The primary goal of treatment is to help Maria get her behavior under control, including reducing her suicidal ideation. Other treatment targets include addressing behaviors that compromise her quality of life, such as withdrawal from interpersonal relationships. Flexibility in blending acceptance and confrontation to change is needed. The counselor may alternate between validation and pushing Maria toward change by offering critical feedback. At the same time, the counselor will improve Maria's capacity to change by teaching her skills to tolerate painful feelings.

A warm communication style and use of validation will balance the focus on change-oriented strategies. In accordance with the DBT model, the counselor may occasionally use an unorthodox communication style in an effort to move toward change. Irreverent communication or an offbeat style may be used to shift Maria from her extreme affective responses. The counselor may also use the strategy of playing the devil's advocate to help Maria gain a sense of control and to help her see a different point of view.

The dilemma for the counselor is that a focus on changing Maria's behavior may be experienced as invalidating. Likewise, an overemphasis on therapeutic warmth and validation may leave Maria feeling that there is no escape from her misery. The counselor must seek to validate Maria's efforts to change, the difficulty in making change, and the pain stemming from believing that others are critical of her efforts. At the same time, the counselor will push Maria to do more. The counselor will use praise to support her efforts to change behavior and balance this by confronting Maria about ongoing dysfunctional behavior. The counselor will offer insight into Maria's behavior in an effort to help her notice patterns in her behavior. The counselor will also focus on finding solutions to problematic behaviors, such as challenges to her dysfunctional belief that others are constantly rejecting her. The counselor will work to help Maria refrain from acting impulsively by encouraging her to act in a manner that is consistent with her personal goals.

A fundamental premise of the DBT approach is that problems in regulating affect represent the core dysfunction. Strategies are oriented toward addressing emotional dysregulation. Interventions in DBT focus on the various elements of the emotion response system, including emotions, cognitions, expressive-motor behavior, and action tendencies. The primary goal of the first stage of DBT is to treat out-of-control behaviors that threaten the individual's life, treatment, and quality of life and more generally to help achieve balance in behaviors and emotional experiencing. A number of secondary, complex patterns of behavior have the potential to interfere with treatment and may need to be addressed. Core behavioral patterns include emotional vulnerability and self-invalidation. The DBT counselor uses a number of specific techniques to directly enhance emotional regulation. These include exposure-based procedures, emotional validation, and the enhancement of capabilities (such as paying attention to experience; shifting attention away from cues associated with negative emotion; and learning to observe, describe, and understand the function of emotions). Ultimately, all counselors must maintain an awareness that DBT is a complex treatment that requires mastery of a number of strategies and skills in addition to standard cognitive behavior therapy techniques. It requires, therefore, much intensive and extensive training and supervision.

REFERENCES

American Psychiatric Association. (2001). *Practice guideline for the treatment of patients with borderline personality disorder.* Retrieved from http://psychiatryonline.org/pb/assets/raw/sitewide/practice_guidelines/guidelines/bpd.pdf

American Psychiatric Association. (2013). *Diagnostic and statistical manual of mental disorders* (5th ed.). Arlington, VA: Author.

Barley, W. D., Buie, S. E., Peterson, E. W., Hollingsworth, A. S., Grivia, M., Hickerson, S. C., . . . Bailey, B. J. (1993). The development of an inpatient cognitive–behavioral treatment program for borderline personality disorder. *Journal of Personality Disorders, 7,* 232–240.

Bedics, J., Atkins, D., Harned, M., & Linehan, M. (2015). The therapeutic alliance as a predictor of outcome in dialectical behavior therapy versus nonbehavioral psychotherapy by experts for borderline personality disorder. *Psychotherapy, 51,* 67–77.

Bohus, M., Haaf, B., Stiglmayer, C., Pohl, U., Bohme, R., & Linehan, M. (2000). Evaluation of inpatient dialectical-behavioral therapy for borderline personality disorder. *Behaviour Research and Therapy, 38,* 875–887.

Brandelow, B., Krause, J., Wedekind, D., Broocks, A., Hajak, G., & Ruther, E. (2005). Early traumatic life events, parental attitudes, family history, and birth risk factors in patients with borderline personality disorder and healthy controls. *Psychiatry Research, 134*(2), 169–179.

Butcher, J. N., Mineka, S., & Hooley, J. M. (2010). *Abnormal psychology* (14th ed.). New York, NY: Allyn & Bacon.

Crits-Christoph, P., & Barber, J. P. (2007). Psychological treatments for personality disorders. In P. E. Nathan & J. M. Gorman (Eds.), *A guide to treatments that work* (pp. 641–658). New York, NY: Oxford University Press.

Davidson, K., Norrie, J., Tyere, P., Gurnley, A., Tata, P., Murray, H., . . . Palmer, S. (2008). The effectiveness of cognitive behavior therapy for borderline personality disorder: Results from the borderline personality disorder study of cognitive therapy trial. *Journal of Personality Disorders, 20,* 450–465. doi:10.1521/pedi.2006.20.5.450

Dimeff, L., Rizvi, S. L., Brown, M., & Linehan, M. (2000). Dialectical behavioral therapy with borderline personality disorder. *Cognitive and Behavioral Practice, 7,* 457–468.

Feigenbaum, J. (2007). Dialectical behaviour therapy: An increasing evidence base. *Journal of Mental Health, 16,* 51–68.

Fischer, S., & Peterson, C. (2014). Dialectical behavior therapy for adolescent binge eating, purging, suicidal behavior, and non-suicidal self-injury: A pilot study. *Psychotherapy, 52,* 78–92.

Fruzetti, A. E., & Levensky, E. R. (2000). Dialectical behavior therapy for domestic violence: Rational and procedures. *Cognitive and Behavioral Practice, 7,* 435–447.

Geisser, S., & Rizvi, S. (2014). The case of "Sonia" through the lens of dialectical behavior therapy. *Pragmatic Case Studies in Psychotherapy, 10,* 30–39.

Goldman, G., & Gregory, R. (2010). Relationships between techniques and outcomes for borderline personality disorder. *American Journal of Psychotherapy, 64,* 359–371.

Gunderson, J. G. (2011). Borderline personality disorder. *New England Journal of Medicine, 364,* 2037–2042. doi:10.1056/NEJMcp1007358

Haddock, L. R. (2014). *Borderline personality disorder* [Practice brief]. Retrieved from http://www.counseling.org/knowledge-center/center-for-counseling-practice-policy-and-research/practice-briefs

Holmes, P., Georgescu, S., & Liles, W. (2006). Further delineating the applicability of acceptance and change to private responses: The example of dialectical behavior therapy. *Behavior Analyst Today, 7,* 311–324.

Katz, L. Y., Gunasekara, S., & Miller, A. L. (2002). Dialectical behavior therapy for inpatient and outpatient parasuicidal adolescents. *Adolescent Psychiatry, 26,* 161–179.

Kendall, T., Pilling, S., Tyrer, P., Duggan, C., Burbeck, R., Meader, N., & Taylor, C. (2009). Borderline and antisocial personality disorders: Summary of NICE guidance. *British Medical Journal, 338,* b93. doi:10.1136/bmj.b93

Kliem, S., Kroger, C., & Kosfelder, J. (2010). Dialectical behavior therapy for borderline personality disorder: A meta-analysis using mixed-effects modeling. *Journal of Consulting and Clinical Psychology, 78,* 936–951.

Kress, V. E., & Paylo, M. J. (2015). *Treating those with mental disorders: A comprehensive approach to case conceptualization and treatment.* New York, NY: Pearson.

Linehan, M. M. (1993a). *Cognitive behavioral treatment of borderline personality disorder.* New York, NY: Guilford Press.

Linehan, M. M. (1993b). *Skills training manual for treating borderline personality disorder.* New York, NY: Guilford Press.

Linehan, M. M., Armstrong, H. E., Suarez, A., Allmon, D., & Heard, H. L. (1991). Cognitive behavioral treatment of chronically parasuicidal borderline patients. *Archives of General Psychiatry, 48,* 1060–1064.

Linehan, M. M., Comtois, K. A., Murray, A. M., Brown, M. Z., Gallop, R. J., Heard, H. L., . . . Lindenboim, N. (2006). Two-year randomized controlled trial and follow-up of dialectical behavior therapy vs. therapy by experts for suicidal behaviors and borderline personality disorder. *Archives of General Psychiatry, 63,* 757–766.

Linehan, M. M., Heard, H. L., & Armstrong, H. E. (1993). Naturalistic follow-up of a behavioral treatment for chronically parasuicidal borderline patients. *Archives of General Psychiatry, 50,* 971–974.

Linehan, M. M., & Tutek, D. A. (1994). Interpersonal outcome of cognitive behavioral treatment for chronically suicidal patients. *American Journal of Psychiatry, 151,* 1771–1777.

Lynam, D., & Widiger, T. (2007). Using a general model of personality to understand sex differences in the personality disorders. *Journal of Personality Disorders, 21*(6), 583–602. doi:10.1521/pedi.2007.21.6.583

Lynch, T. R. (2000). Treatment of depression with personality comorbidity using dialectical behavior therapy. *Cognitive and Behavioral Practice, 7,* 468–477.

Lynch, T. R., Chapman, A. L., Rosenthal, M. Z., Kuo, J. R., & Linehan, M. M. (2006). Mechanisms of change in dialectical behavior therapy: Theoretical and empirical observations. *Journal of Clinical Psychology, 62,* 459–480.

Lynch, T. R., & Cheavens, J. S. (2008). Dialectical behavior therapy for comorbid personality disorders. *Journal of Clinical Psychology in Session, 64,* 154–167.

McCann, R. A., Ball, E. M., & Ivanoff, A. (2000). DBT with an inpatient forensic population: The CMHP forensic model. *Cognitive and Behavioral Practice, 7,* 447–456.

McMain, S., Korman, L. M., & Dimeff, L. (2001). Dialectical behavior therapy and the treatment of emotional regulation. *Journal of Clinical Psychology, 57,* 183–198.

McMain, S., & Pos, A. (2007). Advances in psychotherapy of personality disorders: A research update. *Current Psychiatry Reports, 9*(1), 46–52.

Miller, A. L., Rathus, J. H., Linehan, M. M., Wetzler, S., & Leigh, E. (1997). Dialectical behaviour therapy adapted for suicidal adolescents. *Journal of Practical Psychiatry and Behavioural Health, 3,* 78–86.

National Institute of Mental Health. (n.d.). *Borderline personality disorder.* Retrieved from http://www.nimh.nih.gov/health/topics/borderline-personality-disorder/index.shtml

Perepletchikova, F., & Goodman, G. (2014). Two approaches to treating preadolescent children with severe emotional and behavioral problems: Dialectical behavior therapy adapted for children and mentalization-based child therapy. *Journal of Psychotherapy Integration, 23*(4), 298–312.

Quinn, C. R. (2009). Efficacy of dialectical behaviour therapy for adolescents. *Australian Journal of Psychology, 61,* 156–166.

Rathus, J. H., & Miller, A. L. (2000). DBT for adolescents: Dialectical dilemmas and secondary treatment targets. *Cognitive and Behavioral Practice, 7,* 425–434.

Safer, D. L., Telch, C. F., & Agras, W. S. (2001). Dialectical behavior therapy for bulimia nervosa. *American Journal of Psychiatry, 32,* 89–94.

Seligman, L. (2004). *Diagnosis and treatment planning in counseling* (3rd ed.). New York, NY: Kluwer.

Siever, L. J., & Davis, K. L. (1991). A psychobiological perspective on personality disorders. *American Journal of Psychiatry, 148,* 1647–1658.

Swales, M., Heard, H. L., & Williams, J. M. (2000). Linehan's dialectical behaviour therapy (DBT) for borderline personality disorder: Overview and adaptation. *Journal of Mental Health, 9,* 7–23.

Valentine, S., Bankoff, S., Poulin, R., Reidler, E., & Pantalone, D. (2014). The use of dialectical behavior therapy skills training as stand-alone treatment: A systematic review of the treatment outcome literature. *Journal of Clinical Psychology, 71*(1), 1–20.

Van Dijk, S. (2009). *The dialectical behavior therapy skills workbook for bipolar disorder: Using DBT to regain control of your emotions and your life.* Oakland, CA: New Harbinger.

Van Nuys, D. (2007). *Wise Counsel interview transcript: An interview with Marsha Linehan, Ph.D. on dialectical behavior therapy.* Retrieved from http://www.mhsso.org/poc/view_doc.php?type=doc&id=13825

Verheul, R., Van der Bosch, L. M., Koeter, M. W., de Ridder, M., Stijnen, T., & Van Den Brink, W. (2003). Dialectical behaviour therapy for women with borderline personality disorder. *British Journal of Psychiatry, 182,* 135–140.

Wagner, A. W., Rizvi, S. L., & Harned, M. S. (2007). Applications of dialectical behavior therapy to the treatment of complex trauma-related problems: When one case formulation does not fit all. *Journal of Traumatic Stress, 20,* 391–400.

Zimmerman, M., Rothchild, L., & Chelminski, I. (2005). The prevalence of *DSM–IV* personality disorders in psychiatric outpatients. *American Journal of Psychiatry, 162,* 1911–1918.

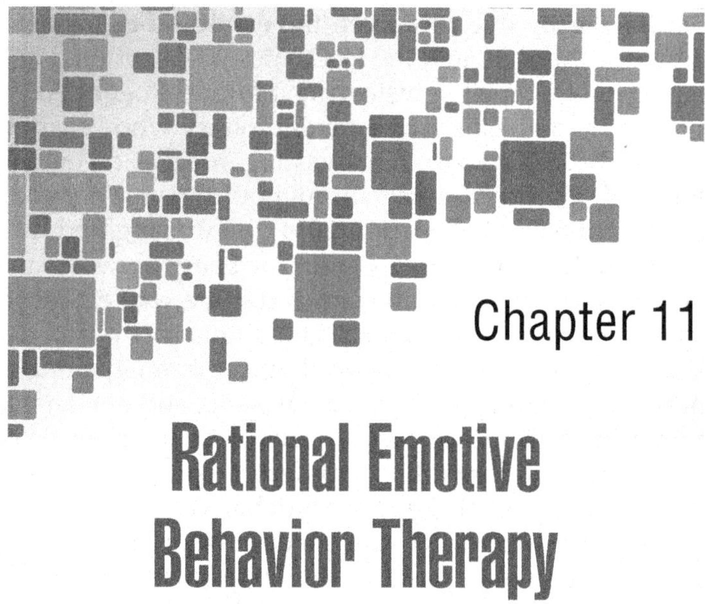

Chapter 11

Rational Emotive Behavior Therapy

Ann Vernon

Rational emotive behavior therapy (REBT) was the first cognitive behavior therapy to be introduced into clinical practice by Albert Ellis (1957/1975). Although thousands of counselors or therapists throughout the world have been trained in REBT, Ellis himself was one of the most significant promulgators of his theory. In its more than 60 years of existence, REBT has been applied successfully to individual, group, marital, and family therapy for a wide array of problems in numerous settings. REBT has a strong philosophical basis as well as commitment to the scientific method. The interconnectedness of thinking, feeling, and behaving is central to this theory, as is the notion that emotional distress results from dysfunctional thought processes. REBT is a global therapy that is implemented cross-culturally through training centers throughout the world affiliated with the Albert Ellis Institute (DiGiuseppe, Doyle, Dryden, & Backx, 2014). Ellis (2002b) often stressed that counselors and therapists must be multiculturally open minded, knowing as much as possible about the rules of other cultures. He also noted that REBT practitioners are "almost intrinsically multicultural" (p. 195) in that they accept all clients unconditionally, regardless of their cultural or religious practices.

BACKGROUND

Albert Ellis, who died of natural causes in 2007 at the age of 93, was the grandfather of cognitive behavior therapy and the founder of rational emotive therapy, currently known as *REBT.* In Michael Bernard's (2011) opinion, "Albert Ellis was a genius" (p. xvi), scoring in the 99th percentile on intelligence tests. Countless others throughout the world would attest to his intellect, given his tremendous understanding of emotional problems and his innovative approach to therapy. There is no doubt that his legacy lives on given the evolution of his theory, which he continuously tested on himself, and the fact that he is considered to be the second most influential psychotherapist in history next to Carl Rogers. As McMahon and Vernon (2010) noted, Albert Ellis was a revolutionary who "changed the face of psychotherapy worldwide" (p. xv). Ellis was regarded as a generous mentor by many counselors and psychotherapists throughout the world (Broder, 2001), and according to DiGiuseppe and colleagues (2014), he was a gifted theorist, teacher, and therapist. Although he had a reputation for being abrasive and abrupt and often seemed to delight in being flamboyant and somewhat eccentric, this was his public personality, and comments about his harsh manner reflect overgeneralizations. In fact, there was another side to Ellis that was often ignored, which was his ability to be compassionate, supportive, encouraging, and personable—characteristics to which numerous clients, colleagues, and personal friends could attest. His clients saw him as attentive, empathic, and dedicated to helping them overcome their problems (DiGiuseppe et al., 2014; see Sidebar 11.1).

Ellis was born in Pittsburgh in 1913 but spent most of his life in New York City. The oldest of three children, Ellis was frequently hospitalized when he was young for nephritis and also suffered from severe headaches (Ellis, 2004a). He was a very bright student who began writing stories, essays, and comic poems at the age of 12.

As a young man, Ellis was also very interested in romantic and sexual relationships, in part because he was anxious about dating. In fact, he had had a great deal of social phobia throughout his childhood and teen years (McMahon & Vernon, 2010). At age 19, to overcome his shyness toward women, he forced himself to talk to a hundred girls in the Bronx Botanical Gardens (Ellis, 2004a). His self-experiment was successful because he was married briefly to two different women in his younger years, sustained a relationship with Dr. Janet Wolfe for more than 30 years, and married Debbie Joffee when he was 90 years old. As a young man, he was often asked for advice about romance, and friends encouraged him to enroll in a clinical psychology doctoral program. After graduating from Columbia University, he started intensive psychoanalytic training. Although he had reservations about Sigmund Freud's theory of personality, he retained his belief in the efficacy of psychoanalytic techniques and spent 2 years in intense analysis. At the conclusion of his therapy, he worked under supervision with his own clients. However, he soon became disillusioned with this approach and began to question the validity of interpretation and insight as well as the effectiveness and efficiency of psychoanalysis (DiGiuseppe et al., 2014; McMahon & Vernon, 2010). In 1950, he began to experiment with different forms of therapy, including psychoanalytically oriented psychotherapy and eclectic-analytic therapy. Although he achieved better results with his clients, he still felt dissatisfied. He began putting his psychological and philosophical knowledge together in a different way and, between 1953 and 1955, reread philosophy and did a comprehensive study of all of the major therapy

Sidebar 11.1. What's the Difference?

As you read, Ellis is considered the grandfather of cognitive behavior therapy. Do you know that *cognitive behavior therapy* is an umbrella term that encompasses several different theories, including cognitive therapy and REBT? Do some research to learn more about the differences between cognitive therapy and REBT.

techniques. "As a result of this research, I came up with REBT by the end of 1954 and started practicing it in January 1955" (Ellis, 2002b, p. 14). It was first called *rational therapy* because of the emphasis on cognitions, then was called *rational emotive therapy* to demonstrate the importance of emotions, and now is known as *REBT* to stress the behavioral component of the theory (DiGiuseppe et al., 2014; see Sidebar 11.2).

As an innovator, Ellis was often criticized, but in an interview with Michael Broder in 2001, Ellis asserted that he probably received more criticism than most because he did original things. True to form, he did not let criticism stop him because he saw his motive as being effective and efficient. Therefore, he continued to change his ideas and revise his theory, striving to make it comprehensive and intensive so that "clients wouldn't just feel better, but they would also get better" (Broder, 2001, p. 78). As a therapist, Ellis saw his goal as solving personal and social problems, always trying to figure out better solutions. He maintained that the ability to solve problems is one of the keys to happiness (Bernard, 2011).

Ellis lived to work and spent most of his time doing therapy, writing about it, or giving workshops. Up until he was almost 90, Ellis worked from 9:30 a.m. until 10:30 p.m., 7 days a week, only interrupting his schedule for a brief afternoon nap in his office. In a given week, he saw as many as 80 clients, conducted at least five group therapy sessions, supervised trainees, and gave lectures and workshops throughout the world. Shortly before his 90th birthday he developed a severe infection, lost his large intestine, and almost died. After that he saw fewer clients, but for at least a year, he continued to do supervision with fellows in training and conduct his famous Friday night workshops. He also continued to do some writing, and at the time of his death, he had published more than 80 books and 1,200 articles, primarily on the theory and applications of REBT.

HUMAN NATURE: A DEVELOPMENTAL PERSPECTIVE

REBT is based on the assumption that humans have a biological tendency to think irrationally or dysfunctionally, as well as rationally or functionally (Dryden, DiGiuseppe, & Neenan, 2003). Therefore, even though they have an inborn propensity toward growth and actualization, human beings can readily sabotage their growth by their unrealistic, illogical, or other types of defeatist thinking (Dryden & Ellis, 2001; Ellis, 2001b, 2002b). Nevertheless, REBT theory clearly asserts that despite the tendency to think irrationally, humans have the ability to construct self-

Sidebar 11.2. Fun Facts About Albert Ellis

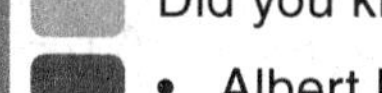

Did you know that . . .

- Albert Ellis lived on the sixth floor of the Albert Ellis Institute in a large brownstone near Central Park. He rarely left the building except for medical appointments, speaking engagements in the city, or training events throughout the world.
- Dr. Ellis was severely diabetic and regularly monitored his blood sugars, eating snacks throughout the day to keep himself healthy. He also exercised while listening to classical music.
- Prior to becoming a psychologist, he was an accountant while pursuing his interests in music, literature, politics, and philosophy.

enhancing thoughts, feelings, and behaviors and are strongly motivated to change things for the better (DiGiuseppe et al., 2014).

Fundamental to REBT is the notion that people's contradictory nature, along with their social upbringing, not only impels them to create happier and more fulfilling lives but also encourages them to elevate strong goals, desires, and preferences into absolutistic and unrealistic shoulds, oughts, and musts that lead to emotional and behavioral difficulties. Dryden et al. (2003) noted that these shoulds, oughts, and musts fall under three main categories: self-demandingness, other-demandingness, and world-demandingness. *Self-demandingness* refers to the idea that one must always perform well and win others' approval; if one does not, one is incompetent, is unworthy, and deserves to suffer. Self-hatred, anxiety, and depression often result from self-demandingness, along with procrastination, withdrawal, and obsessiveness. *Other-demandingness* implies that people with whom one associates must always treat one kindly, considerately, and fairly; if they do not, they are unworthy, bad, or rotten and deserve to be punished. Anger, rage, hurt, jealousy, vindictiveness, and violence develop as a result of other-demandingness. *World-demandingness* means that the conditions in which one lives must be enjoyable, hassle free, safe, and favorable; if they are not, it is awful, horrible, and unbearable. This form of demandingness often leads to anger, depression, self-pity, and low frustration tolerance, as well as withdrawal, procrastination, phobias, and addictions (Ellis, 1994).

MAJOR CONSTRUCTS

REBT has a strong philosophical basis (Dryden & Ellis, 2001; Ellis, 2002a, 2002b, 2004b). In fact, Ellis relied heavily on the teachings of Epictetus, a Stoic philosopher, who believed that "people are disturbed not by things, but by the view which they take of them" (Dryden, 2002c, p. 348). However, REBT is not a form of Stoicism, because the true Stoic attempts to develop an immunity to feelings, whereas REBT recognizes that rational thinking leads to the healthy expression of feelings. Contrary to what many people believe, emotions are a significant component of this theory.

In developing REBT, Ellis was also influenced by several psychologists, including Karen Horney and Alfred Adler (Ellis, 1994; Ellis & Dryden, 1997). Karen Horney's "tyranny of the shoulds" (Ellis & Dryden, 1997, p. 3) led to Ellis's emphasis on how absolutistic thinking creates and maintains emotional disturbance. Adler's work was important because he used active-directive teaching and emphasized people's goals, purposes, values, and meanings, concepts also inherent in REBT (Dryden & Ellis, 2001).

Developing a rational philosophy of life is a major construct of this theory. A rational philosophy is designed to help people increase their happiness and decrease emotional distress. DiGiuseppe and colleagues (2014) noted that the purpose of a rational philosophy is to identify beliefs that lead to survival, satisfaction with living, positive ways of relating to others, intimate involvement with a few others, and personally fulfilling endeavors. Furthermore, certain values promote emotional adjustment and mental health: self-acceptance, self-interest, social interest, self-direction, tolerance, flexibility, acceptance of uncertainty, commitment, risk taking, realistic expectations, high frustration tolerance, and self-responsibility.

The ultimate goal is to help clients adopt these values in order to maximize quality of life and minimize distress.

Commitment to the scientific method is also a central aspect of REBT. Applying the scientific method to one's personal life will help one give up dysfunctional beliefs that can lead to emotional disturbance and ineffectual behavior, according to Ellis (DiGiuseppe et al., 2014). Testing one's assumptions and examining the validity and functionality of beliefs are important, as is developing flexibility in adopting new beliefs to guide behavior. Ellis's theory includes some elements of constructivism, specifically in the sense that humans would be better off if they understood that they themselves create their images of how the world is or should be (Ellis, 2001b). However, whereas modern constructivists assert that people should be allowed to find their own reality and develop alternative beliefs on their own, REBT posits that some constructions—namely, rational beliefs—are more functional and lead to emotional adjustment. Therefore, REBT counselors or therapists focus on helping clients develop rational, as opposed to irrational, constructions (Dryden & Ellis, 2001).

Theoretical Assumptions

Ellis argued that REBT is more theoretical than most therapies and that the theory not only structures but also drives the entire therapeutic process (Trower & Jones, 2001). Like most generic cognitive behavior therapies, REBT ascribes to the notion that cognitions or beliefs cause emotions and behavior (Ellis, 2002a), and REBT theorists stress the interconnectedness of thinking, feeling, and behaving, suggesting that a change in one will affect changes in the other areas of functioning (DiGiuseppe et al., 2014).

According to this theory, irrational beliefs emanate from multiple environmental and genetic factors. Although these factors contribute to the acquisition of irrational beliefs, they are maintained because people rehearse them and continue to reindoctrinate themselves without reevaluating their thinking (DiGiuseppe et al., 2014). Thus, REBT theorists emphasize that irrational beliefs can be changed but acknowledge that this is often difficult and takes persistent practice.

Dryden and Ellis (2001) identified two major categories of psychological disturbance: ego disturbance and discomfort disturbance. Ego disturbance occurs when individuals make demands on themselves, others, and the world. If these demands are not met, people put themselves down by assigning a global negative rating to themselves and identifying themselves as bad or less worthy. This is in contrast to the concept of unconditional self-acceptance, which does not involve rating but acknowledges human fallibility.

Discomfort disturbance, or low frustration tolerance, occurs when individuals make demands on themselves, others, and the world in relation to comfort and life conditions. When these demands are not met, individuals begin to "awfulize" and develop an "I can't stand it" attitude (Dryden & Branch, 2008).

DiGiuseppe and colleagues (2014) identified seven principles of REBT theory:

1. Cognition is the most significant determinant of human emotions. As Ellis frequently stated, "We feel what we think" (p. 21), and although past or present events may contribute to how people feel, they do not cause emotions.

2. Irrational thinking is the major cause of emotional distress. Central to this theory is the idea that events and other people do not make a person feel bad or good (Dryden, 2003; Ellis, 2002b). Rather, emotional distress results from dysfunctional thought processes such as exaggeration, overgeneralization, oversimplification, illogic, faulty deductions, absolutistic rigid schema, and unvalidated assumptions. Therefore, the best way to reduce emotional distress is to change the way people think because irrational beliefs are "the core of psychological problems" (Dryden & Branch, 2008, p. 13).
3. The best way to change disturbed emotions is to change the way one thinks.
4. Multiple factors contribute to irrational thinking and psychopathology, and although social influences have some impact on humans' tendency to think irrationally, irrational beliefs also have a strong biological basis and are more related to mental health problems than are rational beliefs (Bernard, 2009). Furthermore, many of a person's self-destructive behaviors are not advocated by parents, educators, or the media, which strengthens the argument for a biological basis. For example, parents do not encourage their children to procrastinate or seek immediate gratification, yet that does not stop children from doing it. Furthermore, even though people give up irrationalities, they often develop new ones, and it is easy to revert to self-defeating behaviors even after working hard to change them. Unfortunately, it is sometimes easier to learn and practice self-defeating rather than self-enhancing behaviors. It is important to note that, although humans throughout the world think rationally as well as irrationally, culture affects the specific content of the irrational beliefs.
5. There are two types of emotions: helpful, functional, healthy, and adaptive versus unhelpful, dysfunctional, unhealthy, and maladaptive. This is an essential distinction because unhealthy emotions are directly related to irrational thinking and self-defeating behaviors, whereas healthy emotions result in rational thinking and constructive behavior.
6. REBT emphasizes present influences on emotions rather than past historical influences. Certainly, heredity and environment contribute to a person's pathology, but they are not the critical factors in maintaining dysfunction.
7. Irrational beliefs can be changed to rational beliefs by helping individuals recognize, challenge, and revise their thinking. Ellis maintained that while irrational beliefs create emotional and behavioral disturbance, they are also caused by the absence of rational beliefs. Therefore, the goal is not only to reduce irrational thinking but also to increase rational thinking.

APPLICATIONS

Overview

The following sections describe the goals of the counseling or therapy process and how change occurs, with specific emphasis on the therapeutic relationship and the A-B-C model that is a hallmark of this theory. A wide array of cognitive, emotive, and behavioral interventions that illustrate the multimodal nature of the theory are also presented.

Goals of Counseling and Psychotherapy

The goal of REBT is to help clients develop a rational philosophy of life that will reduce their emotional distress and self-defeating behavior and result in their ability to lead a happier and more fulfilling life (Dryden, 2002c; Ellis, 2001a). To achieve this goal, REBT counselors or therapists help clients identify how they prevent themselves from being happy by focusing on their irrational beliefs that lead to emotional and behavioral disturbance. They encourage clients to think more rationally (logically and flexibly), feel healthier, and act more efficiently to achieve their basic goals and purposes (Dryden, 2002c). Consequently, the counselor or therapist uses cognitive, emotive, and behavioral interventions that help clients feel better and get better.

A basic premise of this theory is that it is educative and preventive (Vernon, 2009c, 2009d). Therefore, another goal of the REBT counseling or psychotherapeutic process is to educate clients about how they disturb themselves and to actively teach them the A-B-C model (discussed later in "The A-B-C Model") so they can ultimately help themselves (Ellis, 2002a). Counselors or therapists using REBT encourage clients to read self-help books and listen to CDs. They share visual aids, worksheets, and articles that describe cognitive distortions and emotional disturbance. They may use hypothetical teaching examples or stories and metaphors. They do not hesitate to use themselves as models to teach the concept of self-acceptance by self-disclosing how they have made mistakes or learned to overcome low frustration tolerance, for example. With children and adolescents, REBT counselors and therapists use developmentally appropriate interventions that teach young clients the basic REBT concepts and how to help themselves overcome their problems (DiGiuseppe & Bernard, 2006; Vernon, 2006b, 2006c, 2009a, 2009c, 2009d).

The Process of Change

The REBT theory of change is basically optimistic in that it asserts that although humans have a biological tendency to think irrationally, they also have the ability to choose to change their irrational thinking and self-defeating emotions and behavior (Dryden & Ellis, 2001; Ellis, 2001a). According to this theory, there are several levels of change. The most long-lasting and elegant change involves philosophic restructuring of the irrational beliefs (Dryden & Ellis, 2001). At this level, change can be specific or general. According to Dryden and Ellis (2001), "Specific philosophic change means that individuals change their absolutistic demands ('musts,' 'shoulds') about given situations to rational relative preferences. General philosophic changes involve adopting a nondevout attitude toward life events in general" (p. 310).

DiGiuseppe and colleagues (2014) stressed that it is far better to help clients change their core irrational beliefs at the philosophic level rather than their automatic thoughts. Challenging automatic thoughts or inferences, reframing, and reattributions are considered inelegant solutions, and although they may be coping strategies for a particular event, they do not apply across a wide range of stimuli. As Dryden and Branch (2008) noted, "The more your clients acquire and implement a general rational philosophy, the more psychologically healthy they are deemed to be" (p. 33).

The REBT theory of change is quite simple. Specifically, if clients choose to overcome their emotional and behavior problems, first, they must acknowledge that they have a problem. They also need to realize that, to a large extent, they create their own disturbance. Second, they must identify any meta-emotional problems, which are secondary problems about primary problems (Dryden & Branch, 2008;

Dryden & Neenan, 2004). For example, clients often are depressed about being depressed or denigrate themselves for having a problem. Unless clients tackle these meta-emotional problems before they deal with the original issues, they will often fail to overcome the original disturbance. Third, they need to identify irrational beliefs and understand why the beliefs are illogical and irrational. Fourth, they must recognize why rational beliefs would be preferable and give them better results. Fifth, they need to learn how to challenge their irrational beliefs and replace them with rational alternatives. Finally, they need to keep working on their tendencies to think and act irrationally.

The Therapeutic Relationship

REBT counselors or therapists are active and involved as they educate clients and help them develop a rational perspective and effective problem-solving skills. For this reason, according to Velten (2002), "Rapport is more important in REBT than in most other types of therapy" (p. 76). O'Kelly (2010) concurred, pointing out that the REBT counselor or therapist is in jeopardy if he or she ignores the importance of the therapeutic alliance. In fact, the well-being of the client is at stake if he or she chooses not to continue in therapy because the counselor or therapist has neglected the development of a positive therapeutic relationship.

Ellis (2001b) noted that "we had better be in psychological contact with our clients; be congruent, genuine, integrated persons; experience accurate, empathic understanding of clients' awareness of their own therapeutic experience" (p. 122). He noted that although none of these traits are absolutely necessary, they are all highly desirable. Ellis himself preferred an active, directive therapeutic style with most clients (Dryden, 2002a; Dryden & Branch, 2008; Ellis, 2002b), but he did not insist that there is one specific type of relationship between client and counselor or therapist, stressing that the degree to which one is active-directive is a choice (Dryden & Ellis, 2001; Ellis, 2002b). DiGiuseppe and colleagues (2014) maintained that being active and directive is not incompatible with developing rapport and contended that because clients come to counseling or therapy for problems and want help, "one of the best ways to build rapport is to *do therapy* with the client" (p. 72, italics in the original). As the counselor or therapist work collaboratively on the problem, the bond will develop.

Dryden and Branch (2008) noted that the preferred counseling or therapy relationship is egalitarian in that the client and counselor or therapist are equal in their humanity. From another perspective, however, the relationship is unequal because the counselor or therapist has more expertise and skills and needs to help clients in their personal problem solving. This changes, however, as clients gain more insight and the counselor or therapist encourages them to assume more responsibility for change. Thus, as the counselor or therapist becomes less directive and clients become more effective problem solvers, the relationship becomes more egalitarian.

Dryden and Neenan (2004) emphasized that REBT counselors or therapists are encouraged to be flexible, and Dryden and Branch (2008) stressed the importance of varying the amount of structure as well as the degree of direction. According to Dryden and Ellis (2001), even though not all REBT practitioners agree with the active-directive style, it is possible to vary the style and at the same time adhere to the theoretical principles on which it is based. As Dryden (1999) stated, "Effective rational emotive behavioral counselors vary their therapeutic styles and can adopt a variety of therapeutic styles to fit with the therapeutic requirements of different clients" (p. 20). He and Branch also pointed out that research has shown that REBT counselors and therapists scored as high as those from other theories on the core conditions of empathy, genuineness, and unconditional acceptance.

Part of the rapport-building process involves coming to an agreement on the goals for change (Dryden, 2002b; O'Kelly, 2010) as well as being active and helping clients discover what they are doing to upset themselves. In this way, clients can leave the first session with some insight and hope, which, in turn, enhances the client–counselor/therapist relationship.

Dryden and Branch (2008) identified several therapist qualities that are desirable for change to occur. First is empathy. REBT distinguishes between affective empathy, which is communicating to the client that the therapist understands how the client feels, and philosophic empathy, which is communicating to the client that the therapist understands the rational and irrational beliefs that underscore the client's problem. Both types of empathy strengthen the therapeutic bond but are not seen as curative as in other theories.

Second is unconditional acceptance, which means that counselors or therapists accept the client as a fallible human being who has positive, negative, and neutral aspects. Furthermore, REBT counselors or therapists encourage their clients to accept themselves unconditionally but acknowledge that it is very difficult for most people to reach this unconditional level of acceptance because, according to Ellis, "a low level of self-acceptance is the universal condition" (Bernard, 2009, p. 67). Consequently, counselors or therapists must work diligently to teach clients unconditional self-acceptance and repeatedly reinforce their efforts to put it into practice. In addition, they also help clients develop unconditional acceptance of others.

Third is genuineness, which from an REBT perspective means that counselors or therapists do not hide behind a façade. They are genuine because they feel free to be themselves and at times self-disclose their own fallibilities. This genuineness has therapeutic purposes because it indicates to clients that counselors or therapists are humans too, and it also teaches clients what counselors or therapists did to overcome their own problems.

Fourth is humor. Ellis strongly believed that humor is a desirable therapist quality because, if modeled, it can help clients not take themselves and their life circumstances too seriously. Dryden and Branch (2008) noted that humorous interventions are directed at the clients' irrational beliefs, not the clients themselves, cautioning that the use of humor may not be appropriate with all clients, which is why it is so important to be flexible.

The A-B-C Model

Ellis developed a conceptual model to illustrate the major constructs of this theory as well as the process of change (DiGiuseppe et al., 2014; Dryden & Branch, 2008). In essence, the nature of emotional disturbance can be explained by recognizing that as people attempt to fulfill their goals, they encounter an activating event (A) that either blocks or helps them achieve these goals. Activating events may be positive or negative; may refer to real or perceived events; can be past, present, or future oriented; and can be an individual's own thoughts, memories, or emotions (Dryden & Branch, 2008). When individuals seek counseling or therapy, they strongly believe that the activating event has caused their negative emotional and behavioral consequences (C).

According to REBT theory, it is not the activating event (A) that creates the emotional and behavioral consequences (C) but rather the beliefs (B) people hold about these activating events. Although the activating event may certainly contribute to the consequence, two individuals can experience the same event and feel and react differently, which explains the relationship between A, B, and C. For example, consider two individuals who both applied for the same job and did not get it. Assume that one individual was devastated and the other was just disappointed. The difference in how they felt can be attributed to what they were thinking about the event. The devastated individual equated her failure to attain this job with her self-worth, thinking that this proved how incompetent she was. The disappointed individual wished that he would have gotten the job but realized that his failure to do so was not necessarily a reflection on his lack of skill.

Beliefs (B) are either rational or irrational. Rational beliefs are self-enhancing and help people achieve their goals; they are flexible, logical, and pragmatic (Dryden & Branch, 2008; Dryden et al., 2003). Rational beliefs are realistic preferences that typically result in constructive behavior patterns and moderate negative emotions (Dryden & Branch, 2008). Irrational beliefs are rigid, absolutistic, and illogical. They are inconsistent with reality and do not help people achieve their goals. They result in negative emotions such as depression, anger, anxiety, resentment, self-pity, worthlessness, and rage, as well as in maladaptive behaviors such as withdrawal, avoidance, violence, and procrastination (DiGiuseppe et al., 2014).

Originally, Ellis identified 13 irrational beliefs, but over the years they have been consolidated into five types of beliefs: demandingness, awfulizing, frustration intolerance, self-condemnation, and other-condemnation (DiGiuseppe et al., 2014). According to DiGiuseppe and colleagues, demandingness is an absolute expectation that people or events must be exactly the way an individual wants them to be. Awfulizing is when the negative consequences of something are exaggerated to an extreme. Frustration intolerance is the demand that life be easy and hassle free and that discomfort cannot be tolerated. Self- and other-condemnation stem from the concept of global evaluation of self or others, which implies that individuals can be rated and deemed worthless or unimportant.

As stated previously, irrational beliefs are illogical and are not validly inferred, whereas rational beliefs are logical and can be validly inferred from earlier premises. For instance, if a student wanted to get a good grade on his test, his rational and logical conclusion would be that studying and doing homework would help him achieve that goal. However, if he assumed that studying for tests and doing his homework meant that he absolutely must get a good grade and that the teacher could not give him anything except a top grade, he would be thinking irrationally because his conclusions are illogical.

Counselors or therapists can detect irrational beliefs in several ways: cognitively, emotionally, and behaviorally. Irrational beliefs can be identified cognitively by listening for "shoulds, oughts, and musts" as well as phrases such as "I can't stand it" or "That is horrible" (Nelson-Jones, 2000, p. 204). Irrational beliefs are present emotionally when there are extreme negative emotions such as panic, depression, or intense anger. When clients report feelings of depression, guilt, or extreme sadness, they are probably engaging in self-downing. When they are angry, counselors or therapists should look for musts and demandingness. Frustration and anxiety are often present with frustration intolerance. Behaviorally speaking, self-defeating actions signal the likelihood of irrational beliefs.

Once the emotional and behavioral consequences and the irrational beliefs have been identified, the next step in the A-B-C model is disputation (D), which is what REBT is probably best known for. Disputation is an active process that helps clients assess the rationality of their irrational beliefs (Dryden & Branch, 2008) and whether these irrational beliefs are helpful. The purpose of challenging these rigid and inflexible beliefs is to replace them with rational alternatives.

In an interview 2 years before Ellis's death, Ellis and Michael Bernard discussed the importance of not only disputing irrational beliefs but also "strengthening the conviction to which rational beliefs are held" (Bernard, 2009, p. 71). As Ellis stated at that time, "That's why I talk about helping clients prove to themselves the benefits of rational beliefs and to reinforce their conviction in rational beliefs" (p. 71). Ellis went on to say that it is particularly important to strengthen rational beliefs when working with children because children may not be able to learn disputing.

After disputing in various ways, the expanded A-B-C model places significant emphasis on the effective new rational belief. The effective new belief (EB) helps counterbalance the negative impact of the irrational belief and reinforces the rational way of thinking (DiGiuseppe et al., 2014). The EB can only be achieved after the irrational beliefs have been correctly identified and successfully disputed and when clients understand the BC connection, which means realizing that their emotions are caused by their beliefs. As a result of the disputation process and the identification of effective new beliefs, clients also experience more moderate, less disturbed feelings.

The Therapeutic Process

Dryden et al. (2003) identified 18 steps that counselors or therapists can use in each session to help them implement the A-B-C process to effect client change. They noted that these steps can be applied to all age groups, even though the techniques used at each step may differ. Monica O'Kelly, Dominic DiMattia, and Ann Vernon have adapted this model and have used it successfully in international training seminars. Their process is as follows.

The first step is to ask clients to identify the problem they would like to work on, which is considered the activating event (A). In the event that the client describes several different problems, the client and counselor must come to an agreement about which problem to work on first. The REBT counselor or therapist also typically asks for a specific example to help clarify the problem and generally does not encourage long, detailed elaboration of the activating event (A) but instead moves on rather quickly to ask about the emotional and behavioral consequence (C): how clients feel about the problem and how they behave in response to it. This is particularly helpful in that clients frequently minimize the degree of intensity of the feeling, and asking for the behavioral reaction is an effective way to more accurately identify the emotional consequence. After evaluating the emotional and behavioral consequence, the counselor or therapist evaluates secondary emotions by asking clients how they feel about feeling depressed, anxious, guilty, and so forth. As previously stated, it is important to deal with this secondary emotion first. In doing so, the counselor might ask something such as, "When you are so depressed, do you have any feelings about being depressed?" Clients may state that they feel angry about being depressed or depressed about it because it interferes with their life in so many ways. If a secondary emotion exists, the counselor or therapist helps the client identify and dispute the irrational beliefs associated with the secondary emotion.

After successfully dealing with any existing secondary emotions, the counselor or therapist then asks clients to identify their beliefs related to the identified emotional and behavioral consequence (B). This is a critical step and is often complicated by the fact that clients have difficulty identifying core beliefs but rather offer automatic thoughts or inferences. For example, if a client identified anger in response to her teenage children not picking up their rooms and leaving their things all over the house, to elicit beliefs, the counselor might ask, "So when you felt angry, what were you thinking?" The client might say, "Well, I wish they would learn to pick up after themselves without my having to remind them; I don't like the house to be such a mess." This response is actually quite rational because it expresses a wish instead of a demand, but because anger is a strong emotion that correlates with a demand, the counselor would then need to translate this into a core belief and help the client see the difference between her two beliefs by saying, "Well, if you were just wishing that they would pick things up without having to be reminded, you probably wouldn't feel so angry, so are you really thinking that your teens *shouldn't* leave things all over, that you *shouldn't* have to remind them to do it, and that you can't stand the mess?"

Once the beliefs have been elicited, the next step is to help the client see the connection between the beliefs and the emotions, which is the crux of this theory. Counselors and therapists want their clients to understand that it is not the event that creates their emotional and behavioral response, it is what they think about it. Therefore, the REBT counselor or therapist might ask the client if she always feels angry when her teenagers do not pick up the house or if she thinks that there may be some mothers throughout the world who would not feel angry. Then the counselor or therapist would ask her what she is thinking when she is not angry or what others might be thinking that would result in a different emotional response, helping her see that it is not the event but what she tells herself that results in the emotional disturbance. This step leads to goal setting: "So now that you see that your thinking influences your feelings, do you want to work on changing your thinking so that you feel less disturbed?"

Once there is an agreed-on goal, the counselor or therapist initiates disputing (D). Various types of disputations can be used mildly or vigorously (Ellis, 2002b). Disputing can be didactic, which is informational. In this process, the counselor or therapist explains the difference between rational beliefs (which are flexible and adaptive and help in goal attainment) and irrational beliefs (which are rigid and illogical and interfere with goal achievement; Dryden, 2002a). The Socratic questioning approach, another common form of disputation that is more preferable than the didactic dispute, involves the use of questioning that gives clients insight into the irrationality of their thinking (Dryden, 2002a; O'Kelly, 2010).

During the disputation process, several different types of cognitive disputes are used. In a functional or pragmatic dispute, the purpose is to question the practicality of the client's irrational beliefs. Because irrational beliefs result in self-defeating behaviors and unhealthy emotions, questions such as "How is what you are doing helping you?" or "What is this way of thinking doing for you?" are helpful (O'Kelly, 2010). Another type of dispute is the empirical dispute, which helps clients evaluate the factual aspects of their beliefs. Examples of empirical disputes include, "Where is the evidence that you are no good simply because you failed an exam?" and, "Where is the proof that life is not worth living if you do not get into graduate school?"

Another type of dispute is the logical dispute, which helps clients see how illogical it is to escalate their desires and preferences into demands (Dryden & Branch, 2008; O'Kelly, 2010). Typical questions could include, "Where is the logic that you must . . .?" or "How logical is it for you to think that just because you want a high-paying job that you should get one the first time you interview?" Philosophical disputing is the most elegant disputing approach that helps clients look at meaning and satisfaction in life. Because clients often focus on specific problems and lose perspective on other aspects of their life, a philosophical dispute such as the following will help them develop that perspective: "Despite the fact that there will be some difficult moments with this major life transition, do you think you can overcome the obstacles and still derive some satisfaction in your life?"

After the counselor or therapist has thoroughly disputed the irrational beliefs, the next step of the A-B-C model is to help the client develop and practice more effective beliefs (EB). These beliefs are generated after the irrational beliefs have been disputed; they counter and replace the irrational beliefs. For example, the counselor might say, "So instead of thinking that you are a total failure because you didn't perform perfectly in your piano recital, what could you think to yourself when you put yourself down for not being perfect?" After the client has verbalized several more effective beliefs, the counselor or therapist collaborates with the client in selecting meaningful homework assignments that help the client practice new learnings and maintain change. Homework assignments may include worksheets or various types of cognitive, emotive, or behavioral activities that are reviewed in the next session.

Maintaining Change

The REBT counselor or therapist recognizes that clients will backslide and therefore teaches them that it will take work and practice to maintain change (Dryden & Neenan, 2004). Throughout the counseling or therapy process, the counselor or therapist uses bibliotherapy, visual aids, homework assignments, role playing, and self-help materials to help clients develop skills to use inside and outside of counseling or therapy (Dryden et al., 2003; Vernon, 2009c). The counselor or therapist also helps clients review the A-B-C model to determine what caused them to fall back into their old patterns and then encourages them to practice disputing again and again until they can replace their irrational beliefs with rational alternatives (Nelson-Jones, 2000). Recording counseling or therapy sessions so that clients can listen to them again can also be very effective (Velten, 2002).

It is especially important to help clients develop a strong conviction in the rational alternative because intellectual insight is not sufficient to promote emotional and behavioral change. Therefore, counselors or therapists must persist in helping clients give up their irrational beliefs by continuing to use directive questions as well as other cognitive, emotive-evocative, imaginal, and behavioral techniques to help change irrational ideas. The ultimate goal is to help clients develop effective new beliefs and less disturbed emotions (see Sidebar 11.3).

Sidebar 11.3. The A-B-C Model

Do the A-B-C model on yourself. First identify a problem you have (A), then identify how you felt and behaved in relation to the problem (C). Then identify the irrational beliefs (B). Then write several examples of disputes (D) that would help you challenge the dysfunctional beliefs, and finally, identify several more effective beliefs (EB).

Traditional Intervention Strategies

Ellis (2002b) pointed out that REBT has a multimodal emphasis because REBT counselors or therapists use so many cognitive, emotive, and behavioral interventions to bring about change. Although REBT counselors or therapists use techniques from other schools of therapy, it is important to realize that REBT "is based on a clear-cut theory of emotional health and disturbance" (Dryden & Ellis, 2001, p. 325) and that the techniques are consistent with the theory.

Cognitive Interventions

The most common cognitive intervention is disputing irrational beliefs, which involves helping clients detect the beliefs, debating with them about whether their beliefs are true or logical, and helping them discriminate between rational and irrational beliefs (Dryden & Ellis, 2001). Although Socratic questioning is often used to encourage clients to think about how logical and functional their beliefs are, skillful counselors or therapists use a variety of disputing methods (Ellis, 2002b), including didactic explanations, humorous exaggeration, or the friendship dispute, to help clients see their own unreasonable self-standards (Dryden et al., 2003).

Other cognitive interventions include written homework forms, which help clients dispute their irrational beliefs between sessions (Dryden, 2002c; Dryden & Branch, 2008), and referenting, a type of cost-benefit analysis in which clients list positive and negative consequences of a particular behavior as well as long- and short-term consequences. This process helps them identify advantages and disadvantages of changing their irrational beliefs and behaviors (DiGiuseppe et al., 2014). Rational coping statements, which are factual and encouraging phrases such as, "Even if this is difficult I will give it my best shot" or, "I hope I do well on the test, but if I don't, it doesn't make me a failure as a person," can also be very effective, particularly if they are implemented after more forceful disputing has been done.

Semantic methods are also used, such as helping clients change "I can't" statements to "I won't," which helps clients see that they have a choice regarding how they think, feel, and behave. Other methods of introducing or reinforcing a rational philosophy include bibliotherapy, cinematherapy, or audiotherapy, in which clients are assigned books and materials to read, parts of movies to watch, or CDs to listen to (Dryden, 2002c; Ellis, 2002a, 2002b); using REBT with others to practice rational arguments (Dryden & Ellis, 2001); and using age-appropriate worksheets that help clients identify and dispute irrational beliefs (Vernon, 2002, 2006b, 2006c, 2009c).

Emotive Interventions

As DiGiuseppe and colleagues (2014) pointed out, a common misconception of REBT is that it is unemotional. On the contrary, a major outcome of REBT is to help clients experience healthy negative emotions as opposed to unhealthy emotions that result in self-defeating behaviors. In fact, numerous emotive techniques are routinely used by REBT counselors or therapists. For example, humor, in the form of exaggeration, is often used to help clients avoid taking themselves so seriously (Dryden, 2002c; Ellis, 2001a). Another popular use of humor is involves rational humorous songs (Ellis, 2002a) that Ellis and others have written to help clients understand the nature of irrational beliefs in exaggerated form.

Rational role playing is also an effective emotive intervention (Ellis, 2001a; Vernon, 2002, 2009c). Role playing can help clients express feelings and can help resolve various emotionally laden issues. Ellis cautioned that even though feelings are expressed through role playing, the relief may be temporary because clients have not explored the basic beliefs that resulted in the feelings. Therefore, it is important to do rational role playing that not only helps clients express feelings but also identifies the beliefs that created those feelings.

A variation of rational role playing is to do a reverse role play, in which the counselor or therapist takes the role of the client and the client assumes the role of the counselor or therapist. In this way, the client learns to dispute his or her own irrational ideas as played out by the counselor or therapist (see Sidebar 11.4).

Rational emotive imagery (REI) is one of the key REBT emotive interventions (DiGiuseppe et al., 2014; Dryden, 2002c). The purpose of REI is to help clients identify more rational and appropriate emotions in a particular problematic situation as well as to provide an opportunity for them to experientially identify self-statements and coping techniques that could work for them in stressful situations. In implementing this technique, the counselor or therapist invites the client to close his or her eyes and imagine a difficult situation that evoked strong negative emotions. After the client reconstructs this image and labels the upsetting feelings, the counselor or therapist asks the client to change the upsetting feelings to a more reasonable negative emotion. When the client signals that this has been accomplished, the counselor or therapist invites the client to return to the present and describe the healthy emotions, exploring how thoughts helped contribute to these less upsetting emotions. Clients are usually encouraged to practice REI for 30 days to help them learn how to change unhealthy negative emotions.

Experiential exercises are also used by many REBT counselors or therapists in individual counseling or therapy, as well as in classroom settings and small groups (Vernon, 1998a, 1998b, 1998c, 2006b, 2006c, 2009b, 2009c). These exercises help clients learn new skills and give them an opportunity to explore problematic areas. For example, Vernon (2002) discussed helping clients with procrastination by having them list things they typically put off doing and giving the list to the counselor or therapist. As the client lies on the floor, the counselor reads the items one by one. As each one is read, the counselor or therapist puts a stack of newspapers on the client's body. After the final item is read and the pile of newspapers is quite

Sidebar 11.4. Put It to Practice

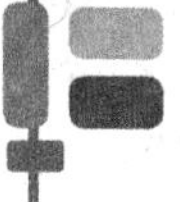

Find a partner and practice doing a reverse role play. You will play the role of the irrational client, and your partner will play the role of the counselor who helps dispute the irrational beliefs using logical, empirical, and functional techniques. If possible, record the session, and as you listen to it, note the different types of disputes.

high, the client is invited to talk about how he or she feels with everything all piled up and what steps to take to get out from under the pile of procrastination. Vernon also developed an experiential intervention to help clients let go of anxiety. After listing on separate strips of paper things the client is anxious about, the counselor or therapist helps the client dispute each situation, and when the client feels as if he or she is ready to let go of the beliefs associated with that anxiety, the client puts the strip of paper in a balloon, blows it up, and lets it go.

Behavioral Interventions

Behavioral interventions have always played an important role in helping clients change and are used to supplement and reinforce cognitive and emotive interventions. Oftentimes behavioral interventions are incorporated into homework assignments or are used in conjunction with other techniques. An example of a behavioral intervention would be to ask the client to respond to her friend's request to borrow her car in an assertive rather than nonassertive manner.

One of REBT's most unique behavioral interventions is the shame attack exercise (Ellis, 2004a, 2004b). Ellis (2004a) realized that shame is at the core of a significant number of people's emotional disturbance and that when people do something they consider shameful, they criticize their actions and think that they should never repeat them. Consequently, to help clients understand this concept, counselors encourage clients to do things in public that they regard as shameful or embarrassing, such as yelling out the stops on elevators (Nelson-Jones, 2000); approaching strangers in the subway and asking them what month it is, explaining that they have just gotten out of the mental hospital (Ellis, 2004a); or singing in the street (Ellis, 2001a). Shame attack exercises should not be illegal, harmful, immoral, or bothersome to others. Rather, they are "foolish, silly, and ridiculous" (Ellis, 2001a, p. 153) and are intended to help clients understand that although they may act bad or foolish, they are not bad persons. After doing shame attacks, clients often feel much less uncomfortable and anxious; at the same time, they realize that they can stand not having others' approval (see Sidebar 11.5).

Another behavioral intervention is skills training (DiGiuseppe et al., 2014; Dryden, 2002b). Although this is considered an inelegant solution if clients do not work on identifying and disputing irrational beliefs, many clients need practical skills to help them overcome deficits that can range from trade skills to interpersonal or social skills such as assertion (DiGiuseppe et al., 2014). Other behavioral interventions include rewards and penalties, in which counselors or therapists help clients arrange reinforcement for achieving a goal or penalties if they do not. Penalties often involve contributing money to a cause clients do not believe in as a forceful way to modify behavior (Ellis, 2001a, 2001c); rewards include things the client truly enjoys.

Sidebar 11.5. Shame Attack Exercise

Do you ever take yourself too seriously or think you must have everyone's approval? If so, try doing a shame attack exercise! Walk a banana down the street, wear your bathrobe and slippers to the supermarket, or stand beside a soda machine and ask for money to buy a drink—or anything else that would be embarrassing for you.

Brief Intervention Strategies and Current Practices

Ellis (2001b) stated that, "REBT was specifically designed from the start to be brief but effective for many (not all) clients" (p. 125). Although some clients are seriously disturbed and need more extensive therapy, Ellis (2001b) maintained that most individuals can be significantly helped in five to 12 sessions.

Beginning in the first session, REBT counselors or therapists teach clients the ABCs of emotional disturbance and show them not only how they construct and maintain their symptoms but also how to ameliorate them. This explanation contributes to significant improvement, which Ellis (2001b) maintained can occur in a few weeks.

Perhaps what distinguishes REBT theory from many others and also makes it briefer is that it is a self-help approach; clients are taught how to change their irrational thinking, so they can apply this technique to present as well as future problems. In addition, they learn to practice the skills and concepts between sessions by completing various homework assignments, using REI, or using rewards and penalties. All of these techniques, in addition to those previously described, are brief interventions.

There has always been the question of whether REBT would continue to thrive after Ellis's death, primarily because "his personality became synonymous with the theory" (DiGiuseppe et al., 2014, p. 6). That having been said, some felt that Ellis's persona may have hurt the theory and that his active-directive style and his foul language were offensive. In fact, although Ellis has been dead for several years, REBT is still alive and thriving, and the next generation has actively taken steps to ensure that the theory continues to occupy a prominent place in the field. Therefore, there is increased emphasis on the importance of the therapeutic alliance with greater attention paid to being sensitive and less flamboyant. There has also been some modification regarding awfulizing. Traditionally, Ellis would challenge clients by asking what was so awful or terrible about a particular event. However, if in fact the event had been traumatic, actively trying to persuade the client that it really was not that awful could come across as insensitive and jeopardize the therapeutic alliance. Therefore, it is now inappropriate to challenge catastrophic thinking when clients have experienced trauma or very negative events. Rather than trying to convince them that it really was not so awful, the sensitive approach would be to help them see that they can stand to live despite the trauma and to gently dispute their irrational belief that this should never have happened, as that is illogical. In essence, the current approach is much more empathic and effective.

There is also some discussion about the word *dispute*, as it may have a negative connotation in that it is synonymous with *argument* and *quarrel*. That certainly is not the intent of the disputation process, but until another term is found, counselors and therapists will continue to help clients dispute their irrational beliefs.

Clients With Serious Mental Health Issues

According to Seligman (2004), there has been an increase in the severity of disorders that counselors and therapists need to treat. Among the mental disorders included in Seligman's discussion, REBT has been applied to a wide variety, including the treatment of anxiety (Ellis, 2001b), social anxiety (Brown & Kocovski, 2014), depression (Feldman, Knouse, & Robinson, 2013), obsessive-compulsive disorder (OCD; Ellis, 1997), schizophrenia (Trower, 2003), borderline personality disorder (Ellis, 2001b), and substance abuse (Bishop, 2012). A brief description of REBT applications for these disorders follows.

Anxiety and Social Anxiety

From an REBT perspective, clients with generalized anxiety disorder are more likely to obsess about what might happen in the future rather than what happened in the past. Furthermore, these clients may have issues related to approval and self-worth: They fear rejection, or they fear criticism and worry about making mistakes and being a failure, which makes many life circumstances appear threatening. Their fears may be specific or vague.

DiGiuseppe and colleagues (2014) identified three cognitive phases to anxiety: first, the inference that something bad might happen; second, the irrational demand that it must not happen; and third, the irrational derivative that it would be awful, they would be worthless, and they could not stand it if something bad happened.

After assessing the irrational beliefs, REBT counselors or therapists would lead clients through the disputation process, paying special attention to their anxiety about being anxious ("I can't stand this, I shouldn't be anxious") and also noting the shame and self-downing that clients often experience about their worry and anxiety. They would help clients dispute their catastrophizing and awfulizing about their anxiety and teach them how to use distraction techniques by focusing on their breathing, tensing and relaxing muscles, and engaging in other forms of relaxation.

Although social anxiety disorder is a very common anxiety disorder, it can have a significant negative impact on individuals. Socially anxious people have high levels of perfectionism and ruminate after they have been in social situations (Brown & Kocovski, 2014). They are overly concerned about their mistakes and extremely sensitive to criticism, strongly maintaining that others expect them to be perfect. Counselors and therapists can use a variety of disputations as well as in vivo exposure and REI to help clients address their issues.

Depression

Ellis (2001b) maintained that REBT is an effective therapy with clients who are depressed because it specifically focuses on addressing irrational beliefs as opposed to correcting distorted negative inferences. For this reason, it may result in more pervasive and long-lasting change. Vernon (2006a) noted that depressive symptoms can be moderated by changing cognitions that are characterized by negative self-evaluations, catastrophizing, and selectively attending only to negative (as opposed to positive) aspects of situations. According to DiGiuseppe, Doyle, and Rose (2002), clinical depression results when individuals have one or more of the following beliefs: a negative view of themselves, a negative view of their environment, a bleak view of the future, the prediction that negative things will happen to them, a belief that they must do better and be approved of by significant others, and a belief that they should be treated better in life. DiGiuseppe and colleagues (2014) also noted that depression can be caused by self-blame, self-pity, and other-pity, which is focusing on bad things that have happened to others close to them.

The REBT counselor or therapist maintains that these irrational beliefs play a pivotal role in the development, progression, and alleviation of depression while at the same time acknowledging that depression may also be biological (Vernon,

2006a). When depression is primarily biological in origin, a combination of cognitive therapy and antidepressant medication is most likely needed (Wagner, 2004).

REBT counselors or therapists would use different intervention strategies to address the depression, including dealing with the secondary emotion of being depressed about being depressed. They would help clients see that although it may be difficult to overcome the depression, they can develop high frustration tolerance and persist in their efforts to get better. They would work with clients to dispute the irrational belief that they will never get better by asking, "Where's the evidence that you will always be depressed?" Encouraging clients to act as if they were not depressed is sometimes effective, as is a referenting list of the pros and cons of staying depressed.

OCD

Ellis (1997) indicated that the need for certainty contributes to individuals' tendency to develop rituals or obsessions but noted that OCD may be the result of biological deficiencies, in which case medication may be needed in combination with REBT procedures. Although techniques such as activity homework and in vivo desensitization are often used successfully with OCD clients, clients with severe OCD are so obsessed with their repetitive behaviors that they find it difficult to adhere to the behavioral, emotive, or cognitive techniques and fail to persist in changing their ritualizing.

Foa and Wilson (1991) identified several important considerations in treating OCD clients, including helping them recognize that the anxieties that underlie their OCD behaviors are unrealistic, illogical, and self-defeating. These authors also stressed the importance of helping clients develop high frustration tolerance so that they can work harder to overcome their repeated rituals. Ellis (1997) pointed out that these clients often put themselves down for having OCD and indicated that REBT counselors or therapists must help these clients accept themselves unconditionally with their OCD and use REBT techniques to help them dispute their anxiety, depression, and self-hatred about having this disorder.

Borderline Personality Disorder

According to Ellis (2001b), people with borderline personality disorder seem "to be born with innate tendencies that interact with their experience to produce several deficiencies" (p. 362). They have rigid and impulsive thinking styles, have inconsistent images of others, exaggerate the significance of things, and are demanding and self-downing and easily enraged, in addition to being overdependent and often alienated (Cloninger, cited in Ellis, 2001b). Ellis (2001b) maintained that individuals with borderline personality disorders have high levels of self-downing and low frustration tolerance. Although it is possible to help them minimize their disturbing themselves about their condition, the reality is that they can rarely be completely cured. However, Ellis (2001b) contended that improvement can be achieved by using REBT to teach clients how to accept themselves unconditionally, how to ameliorate the self-defeating nature of their low frustration tolerance, and how to challenge their dysfunctional cognitions.

Substance Abuse

According to Bishop (2012), REBT can be very effective in treating addictions in part because of the vast array of cognitive, emotive, and behavioral interventions that can be used to help clients reassess their lives and deal with their issues. Bishop stressed that a key component of the assessment process includes evaluating inferences, irrational beliefs, and distorted cognitions. Because the thinking of people with addictions is frequently characterized by awfulizing, low frustration tolerance, dichotomous thinking, and demandingness, the REBT counselor or therapist must help clients identify how their thinking impedes their recovery. Furthermore, because people with addictions tend to minimize the problem and the consequences, REBT counselors and therapists need to be prepared to deal with this denial and resistance, but not by shaming clients or being harshly confrontational. Rather, Bishop stressed that it is important to be nonargumentative and to use motivational interviewing techniques to motivate undermotivated clients who are often opposed to or ambivalent about treatment.

Not only does addiction affect the client seeking treatment, but it also significantly affects relationships. O'Farrell and Clements (2012) conducted numerous studies with impressive results using contracts. For example, the addicted partner would contract to begin each day by saying that he or she did not intend to drink that day, and the partner would simply thank him. The addicted partner could also request that the partner not bring up all of the bad things that had happened during periods of heavy abuse because it was not helpful in the recovery process.

REBT counselors or therapists need to be empathic, understanding how difficult it can be when a client relapses. They need to teach unconditional self-acceptance: The client is a worthy person regardless of his or her addiction. REBT counselors or therapists may engage clients in role playing related to drink-refusal situations; encourage them to keep a drinking log to increase their awareness of their dependence on substances; or use REI to help them deal with their shame, anxiety, and self-pity. They may also use the cost-benefit analysis procedure, which helps the client identify the good things about using and the not-so-good things, as well as the good things about stopping or moderating and the not-so-good things about it (see Sidebar 11.6).

EVALUATION

Overview

Ellis (1996) acknowledged that he was prejudiced, but he maintained that REBT is more likely to help people achieve "deeper and more lasting emotional and behavioral change than other methods of therapy" (p. 1). He noted that usually clients can improve significantly in 10 to 20 sessions, in individual as well as group therapy. In the following sections, supporting research and limitations are addressed.

Supporting Research

Because Ellis focused on theory and practice rather than research, REBT once had a reputation of having insufficient empirical support. However, in recent years,

Sidebar 11.6. A Case for REBT

Imagine that you are an REBT counselor or therapist who has just joined a practice with several other practitioners who were trained in psychoanalysis and client-centered therapy. If you wanted to persuade them to practice REBT, what arguments would you use? How would you explain the theory and the process of change to them?

under the direction of Daniel David, director of research with the Albert Ellis Institute, numerous studies have supported the efficacy of REBT.

David, Szentagotai, Lupu, and Cosman (2008) conducted research on the effectiveness of REBT, cognitive therapy, and medication in treating depression. Their findings indicated that REBT and cognitive therapy were more effective than medication 6 months after treatment and that effectively restructuring irrational beliefs also contributes to relapse prevention. Sciacchitano, Lindner, and McCracken (2009) found support for the REBT model in a study they conducted to investigate how secondary beliefs mediate the relationship between arthritis sufferers and their ability to cope. Hyland, Maguire, Shevlin, and Boduszek (2014) focused on the effectiveness of REBT with posttraumatic stress responses. The sample consisted of 210 men and 99 women ranging in age from 23 to 65 years. All participants had experienced at least one major trauma, such as being in a serious accident, being assaulted, or being in military combat. These researchers developed the REBT rational beliefs model of posttraumatic stress symptoms and used other standardized instruments. The results of this study, which contribute to the REBT literature as well as the trauma field, indicate that strengthening high frustration tolerance, preference, and acceptance beliefs helps to alleviate negative posttraumatic symptoms. Further research is needed to support the contention that REBT's theory of psychological health can be applied to other psychological disorders.

Ghirasim, Sandu, Raza, Miclutia, and Macrea (2013) found encouraging results in a pilot study using cognitive remediation therapy with schizophrenic patients in Romania. Although further research needs to be conducted, this study shows the promise of using cognitive methods with this population. REBT was also proven to be effective in reducing depression, anxiety, and stress in people with late-onset blindness (Jalali, Moussavi, Yazdi, & Fadardi, 2014). For additional information about supportive research, readers are directed to the *Journal of Rational-Emotive & Cognitive-Behavior Therapy.*

Limitations

In an interview with Michael Broder (2001), Ellis stated,

> My basic goals are to push REBT, and to improve it so as to help more people use it.. . . I want REBT to be successful in the world. . . . I think that REBT and Cognitive Behavior Therapy (CBT) are going to help more people more of the time in an efficient manner than other therapies. (p. 85)

Although Ellis acknowledged that considerable research needed to be done, he stood firmly behind two predictions he made at the American Psychological Association annual convention in 1956 (Ellis, 1994, p. 418): that "REBT . . . will prove more effective with more types of clients than any of the other kinds of psychotherapy that are now being widely employed" and that

> a considerable amount of . . . REBT will prove to be the most effective type of psychological treatment that helps to minimize the basic neuroses . . . of many clients, and particularly of many with whom other types of therapy have been shown to be relatively ineffective.

Perhaps one of the biggest limitations of REBT has been the negative influence of Ellis himself, as he acknowledged; in his opinion, professionals slighted or opposed REBT because, "I am a charismatic individual, with characteristics which many of them find distasteful" (Ellis, 2001c, p. 69). He admitted that his public manner and use of four-letter words were controversial and unconventional and that his use of the term *rational* may have been aversive to empirically minded psychologists. However, Ellis did not think it necessary to change his style. Professionals must recognize that they can adhere to the basic principles of this theory, which has been used very effectively with adults as well as with children, without emulating Ellis's style. In fact, this is being done as noted REBT professionals continue to practice and promulgate the theory.

Summary Chart: REBT

Human Nature

REBT theory clearly asserts that despite the tendency to think irrationally, humans have the ability to construct self-enhancing thought, feelings, and behaviors and are strongly motivated to change things for the better.

Major Constructs

REBT has a strong philosophical basis as well as commitment to the scientific method. The interconnectedness of thinking, feeling, and behaving is central to this theory, as is the notion that emotional distress results from dysfunctional thought processes.

Goals

The goal is to help clients develop a rational philosophy of life that will allow them to reduce their emotional distress and self-defeating behaviors.

Change Process

Change occurs as counselors or therapists help clients work through the A-B-C model of emotional disturbance, replacing irrational beliefs with rational alternatives that result in more moderate, healthy emotions and self-enhancing behaviors.

Interventions

A wide variety of cognitive, emotive, and behavioral interventions—including disputing, REI, rational role playing, bibliotherapy, shame attack exercises, experiential activities, and rational coping self-statements—are used.

Limitations

Limitations include the lack of outcome research, although this is changing. Another limitation is the overgeneralization that REBT is Albert Ellis. Although Ellis was the founder of the theory, numerous practitioners all over the world integrate the basic principles of this effective theory in their own style.

THE CASE OF MARIA: AN REBT APPROACH

Following the O'Kelly et al. model, the REBT counselor or therapist first asks Maria to describe the problem she would like to work on, using active listening skills and conveying genuine interest in her by asking pertinent questions to help focus the interview. Then the counselor or therapist asks Maria for a specific example to help clarify the target issue. During this time, the counselor or therapist is empathic, conveying interest in helping Maria resolve the issues that are troubling her.

Next, the counselor or therapist asks Maria to identify the emotional and behavioral consequences—how she felt in relation to the example she identified, if she experienced any bodily sensations associated with these emotions, and how she behaved in response. In this case, Maria indicates that she is depressed and anxious. She has also had some thoughts about suicide but feels so guilty because of her children and her religious beliefs that she stops herself from following through with this. In terms of a behavioral consequence, Maria also shares that she has difficulty concentrating, that she has been absent from work, and that her depression is negatively affecting her job performance.

After assessing emotional and behavioral consequences, the counselor or therapist will want to determine whether there are any relevant secondary emotions. At this point, the counselor or therapist may help Maria identify the irrational beliefs she has about being depressed and anxious. Based on Maria's disclosure that she should not feel this way, that she should be able to handle her problems, the counselor or therapist helps Maria dispute her irrational beliefs by asking how it helps her deal with her depression by feeling guilty and challenging her to think about what good it does to put herself down for feeling depressed and anxious. It is hoped that helping Maria see that she is human and that humans sometimes have strong negative reactions to upsetting life events will help her understand that it does no good to put herself down for feeling as she does and that if she can reduce her guilt, she will have more energy to deal with her depression and anxiety.

After the secondary emotions have been dealt with, the next step is to assess the client's irrational beliefs. The counselor or therapist can do this by asking Maria what thoughts she has when she feels so depressed, anxious, or guilty (it is helpful to take each emotion separately, first working on the one that is most troublesome to her). For example, if Maria identifies depression, she may be thinking that her life will never get better, that there is no use in living, and that she is a rotten person because she has created all of these problems for her children and family of origin. Next, the counselor or therapist will help Maria see that it is not the events themselves that create her negative feelings and behaviors. For example, the counselor or therapist can ask Maria whether she thinks every woman in her situation would feel depressed and anxious, and, if they would not, what might they feel? After dealing with this in some detail so that the counselor or therapist is certain that Maria understands the connection between what she is thinking and feeling/behaving, the counselor or therapist may ask Maria if she would like to work on changing her thoughts so that she can feel better. In this manner, the counselor or therapist and Maria establish the therapeutic goal.

Next, the REBT counselor or therapist may use a combination of logical, empirical, and functional disputes (D) to help Maria replace her irrational beliefs with rational alternatives. For example, the counselor or therapist may ask, "Where is the evidence that you have nothing to live for just because things have been difficult for you lately?" "How logical is it for you to assume that you alone have ruined the lives of two families just because you are divorced?" "How does it help you to think that you should have stayed with an abusive husband? Would that have made sense?" The counselor or therapist will also use philosophical disputes, such as, "Even though things are difficult for you at the present time, is it conceivable that you can overcome these problems and lead a satisfying life?" The best friend dispute might also be helpful in Maria's case. The counselor or therapist could ask, "If your best friend came to you and insisted that she stay with her abusive husband because she didn't want to ruin the lives of two families, would you advise her to stay with him or leave? If she stayed, what might the consequences be? Assuming you would not advise your friend to stay in this negative situation, why would you not apply this same advice to yourself?"

The counselor or therapist will continue to help Maria dispute her irrational beliefs but also strengthen the conviction of the new rational beliefs, with the goal of helping her adopt a more effective rational philosophy, which, in turn, will help her gain more emotional and behavioral control. This could be done through a reverse role play, in which the counselor or therapist plays the role of Maria, vocalizing her irrational beliefs, while Maria attempts to dispute them. Maria could also write her new rational beliefs on index cards and repeat them to herself on a daily basis to reinforce this new way of thinking. In addition to disputing, the REBT counselor or therapist can help Maria by using a combination of other techniques. For example, the counselor or therapist can teach her how to use rational coping self-statements to reduce her guilt. Bibliotherapy can help her learn more about self-forgiveness. The counselor or therapist can also work with Maria to establish a stress management plan that includes exercise and healthy eating.

The counselor or therapist can also help Maria deepen her conviction in rational thinking by having her describe how life could be different if she were to endorse these new beliefs. Maria can be encouraged to practice her new learnings by completing homework assignments, which will be checked each session.

Although REBT counselors or therapists will not deal with a lot of family-of-origin issues, the counselor will help Maria deal with her guilt and self-downing relative to her family's feelings about her decision to marry and her guilt over the divorce. Homework assignments such as writing letters to family members or learning how to communicate with them in a more assertive manner can be helpful.

The goal of counseling or therapy is to help Maria learn more effective ways of thinking, feeling, and behaving that will enable her to deal not only with present problems but also with future issues. The REBT counselor or therapist supports, challenges, educates, and empowers Maria by using a variety of cognitive, emotive, and behavioral strategies.

REFERENCES

Bernard, M. E. (2009). Dispute irrational beliefs and teach rational beliefs: An interview with Albert Ellis. *Journal of Rational-Emotive & Cognitive-Behavior Therapy, 27,* 66–76.

Bernard, M. E. (2011). *Rationality and the pursuit of happiness: The legacy of Albert Ellis.* West Sussex, England: Wiley-Blackwell.

Bishop, F. M. (2012). Helping couples deal with addictions. In A. Vernon (Ed.), *Cognitive and rational-emotive behavior therapy with couples* (pp. 169–190). New York, NY: Springer.

Broder, M. S. (2001). Dr. Albert Ellis—in his own words—on success. *Journal of Rational-Emotive & Cognitive-Behavior Therapy, 19,* 77–88.

Brown, J. R., & Kocovski, N. L. (2014). Perfectionism as a predictor of post-event rumination in a socially anxious sample. *Journal of Rational-Emotive & Cognitive-Behavior Therapy, 32*(2), 150–163.

David, D., Szentagotai, A., Lupu, V., & Cosman, D. (2008). Rational emotive behavior therapy, cognitive therapy, and medication in the treatment of major depressive disorder: A randomized clinical trial, posttreatment outcomes, and six-month follow-up. *Journal of Clinical Psychology, 64,* 728–746.

DiGiuseppe, R., & Bernard, M. (2006). REBT assessment and treatment with children. In A. Ellis & M. Bernard (Eds.), *Rational emotive behavioral approaches to childhood problems: Theory, practice, and research* (pp. 85–114). New York, NY: Springer.

DiGiuseppe, R., Doyle, K. A., Dryden, W., & Backx, W. (2014). *A practitioner's guide to rational emotive behavior therapy* (3rd ed.). New York, NY: Oxford University Press.

DiGiuseppe, R., Doyle, K., & Rose, R. E. (2002). Rational emotive behavior therapy for depression: Achieving unconditional self-acceptance. In M. A. Reinecke & M. R. Davison (Eds.), *Comparative treatments of depression* (pp. 220–248). New York, NY: Springer.

Dryden, W. (1999). *Rational emotive behavioural counselling in action* (2nd ed.). London, England: Sage.

Dryden, W. (2002a). *Fundamentals of rational emotive behaviour therapy: A training handbook.* London, England: Whurr.

Dryden, W. (2002b). Idiosyncratic REBT. In W. Dryden (Ed.), *Idiosyncratic rational emotive behaviour therapy* (pp. 2–14). Ross-on-Wye, England: PCCS Books.

Dryden, W. (2002c). Rational emotive behaviour therapy. In W. Dryden (Ed.), *Handbook of individual therapy* (4th ed., pp. 347–372). London, England: Sage.

Dryden, W. (Ed.). (2003). *Rational emotive behaviour therapy: Theoretical developments.* New York, NY: Brunner-Routledge.

Dryden, W., & Branch, R. (2008). *The fundamentals of rational emotive behaviour therapy* (2nd ed.). West Sussex, England: Wiley.

Dryden, W., DiGiuseppe, R., & Neenan, M. (2003). *A primer on rational emotive therapy* (2nd ed.). Champaign, IL: Research Press.

Dryden, W., & Ellis, A. E. (2001). Rational emotive behavior therapy. In K. S. Dobson (Ed.), *Handbook of cognitive behavioral therapies* (pp. 295–348). New York, NY: Guilford Press.

Dryden, W., & Neenan, M. (2004). *The rational emotive behavioural approach to therapeutic change.* London, England: Sage.

Ellis, A. E. (1975). *How to live with a neurotic: At home and at work* (Rev. ed.). Hollywood, CA: Wilshire Books. (Original work published 1957)

Ellis, A. E. (1994). *Reason and emotion in psychotherapy: A comprehensive method of treating human disturbances* (Rev. ed.). New York, NY: Carol.

Ellis, A. E. (1996). *Better, deeper, and more enduring brief therapy: The rational emotive behavior therapy approach.* New York, NY: Brunner/Mazel.

Ellis, A. E. (1997). REBT with obsessive-compulsive disorder. In J. Yankura & W. Dryden (Eds.), *Using REBT with common psychological problems: A therapist's casebook* (pp. 197–222). New York, NY: Springer.

Ellis, A. E. (2001a). *Feeling better, getting better, staying better.* Atascadero, CA: Impact.

Ellis, A. E. (2001b). *Overcoming destructive beliefs, feelings, and behaviors.* Amherst, NY: Prometheus Books.

Ellis, A. E. (2001c). Reasons why rational emotive behavior therapy is relatively neglected in the professional and scientific literature. *Journal of Rational-Emotive & Cognitive-Behavior Therapy, 19*, 67–74.

Ellis, A. E. (2002a). Idiosyncratic REBT. In W. Dryden (Ed.), *Idiosyncratic rational emotive behaviour therapy* (pp. 16–29). Ross-on-Wye, England: PCCS Books.

Ellis, A. E. (2002b). *Overcoming resistance: A rational emotive behavior therapy integrated approach.* New York, NY: Springer.

Ellis, A. E. (2004a). *Rational emotive behavior therapy: It works for me—it can work for you.* Amherst, NY: Prometheus Books.

Ellis, A. E. (2004b). *The road to tolerance: The philosophy of rational emotive behavior therapy.* Amherst, NY: Prometheus Books.

Ellis, A. E., & Dryden, W. (1997). *The practice of rational emotive behavior therapy* (2nd ed.). New York, NY: Springer.

Feldman, G., Knouse, L. E., & Robinson, A. (2013). Executive functioning difficulties and depression symptoms: Multidimensional assessment, incremental validity, and prospective associations. *Journal of Cognitive and Behavioral Psychotherapies, 33*(2), 259–274.

Foa, E. B., & Wilson, R. (1991). *Stop obsessing: How to overcome your obsessions and compulsions.* New York, NY: Bantam.

Ghirasim, N. I., Sandu, N., Raza, A., Miclutia, I. V., & Macrea, R. (2013). Cognitive remediation therapy in schizophrenia (CRT)—A pilot study on Romanian patients. *Journal of Cognitive and Behavioral Psychotherapies, 13*(2), 385–396.

Hyland, P., Maguire, R., Shevlin, M., & Boduszek, D. (2014). Rational beliefs as cognitive protective factors against posttraumatic stress symptoms. *Journal of Rational-Emotive & Cognitive-Behavior Therapy, 32*(4), 297–312.

Jalali, M. D., Moussavi, M. S., Yazdi, S. A., & Fadardi, J. S. (2014). Effectiveness of rational emotive behavior therapy on psychological well-being of people with late blindness. *Journal of Rational-Emotive & Cognitive-Behavior Therapy, 32*(4), 233–247.

McMahon, J., & Vernon, A. (Eds.). (2010). *Albert Ellis: Evolution of a revolution.* Ft. Lee, NJ: Barricade Books.

Nelson-Jones, R. (2000). *Six key approaches to counselling and therapy.* London, England: Continuum.

O'Farrell, T. J., & Clements, K. (2012). Review of outcome research on marital and family therapy in treatment for alcoholism. *Journal of Marital and Family Therapy, 38*, 122–144.

O'Kelly, M. (2010). *CBT in action: A practitioner's toolkit.* Melbourne, Australia: CBT Australia.

Sciacchitano, L., Lindner, H., & McCracken, J. (2009). Secondary beliefs: A mediator between illness representations and coping behavior in arthritis sufferers. *Journal of Rational-Emotive & Cognitive-Behavior Therapy, 27*, 23–50.

Seligman, L. (2004). *Diagnosis and treatment planning in counseling* (3rd ed.). New York, NY: Kluwer.

Trower, P. (2003). Theoretical developments in REBT as applied to schizophrenia. In W. Dryden (Ed.), *Rational emotive behaviour therapy: Theoretical developments* (pp. 228–246). New York, NY: Brunner-Routledge.

Trower, P., & Jones, J. (2001). How REBT can be less disturbing and remarkably more influential in Britain: A review of views of practitioners and researchers. *Journal of Rational-Emotive & Cognitive-Behavior Therapy, 19*, 21–30.

Velten, E. (2002). Idiosyncratic REBT. In W. Dryden (Ed.), *Idiosyncratic rational emotive behaviour therapy* (pp. 76–88). Ross-on-Wye, England: PCCS Books.
Vernon, A. (1998a). *The Passport Program: A journey through emotional, social, cognitive, and self-development* (Grades 1–5). Champaign, IL: Research Press.
Vernon, A. (1998b). *The Passport Program: A journey through emotional, social, cognitive, and self-development* (Grades 6–8). Champaign, IL: Research Press.
Vernon, A. (1998c). *The Passport Program: A journey through emotional, social, cognitive, and self-development* (Grades 9–12). Champaign, IL: Research Press.
Vernon, A. (2002). *What works when with children and adolescents: A handbook of individual counseling techniques.* Champaign, IL: Research Press.
Vernon, A. (2006a). Depression in children and adolescents: REBT approaches to assessment and treatment. In A. Ellis & M. Bernard (Eds.), *Rational emotive behavioral approaches to childhood disorders: Theory, practice, and research* (pp. 212–231). New York, NY: Springer.
Vernon, A. (2006b). *Thinking, feeling, behaving: An emotional education program* (Grades 1–6). Champaign, IL: Research Press.
Vernon, A. (2006c). *Thinking, feeling, behaving: An emotional education program* (Grades 7–12). Champaign, IL: Research Press.
Vernon, A. (2009a). Applications of rational emotive behavior therapy with children and adolescents. In A. Vernon (Ed.), *Counseling children and adolescents* (4th ed., pp. 140–157). Denver, CO: Love.
Vernon, A. (2009b). Applying rational emotive behavior therapy in schools. In R. Christner & R. Mennuti (Eds.), *School-based mental health: A practitioner's guide to comparative practices* (pp. 151–179). New York, NY: Routledge.
Vernon, A. (2009c). *More what works when with children and adolescents: A handbook of individual counseling techniques.* Champaign, IL: Research Press.
Vernon, A. (2009d). Rational emotive behavior therapy. In A. Vernon & T. Kottman (Eds.), *Counseling theories: Practical applications with children and adolescents in school settings* (pp. 153–184). Denver, CO: Love.
Wagner, K. D. (2004). Depressed adolescents: Medication or therapy. *Psychiatric Times, 5,* p. 20.

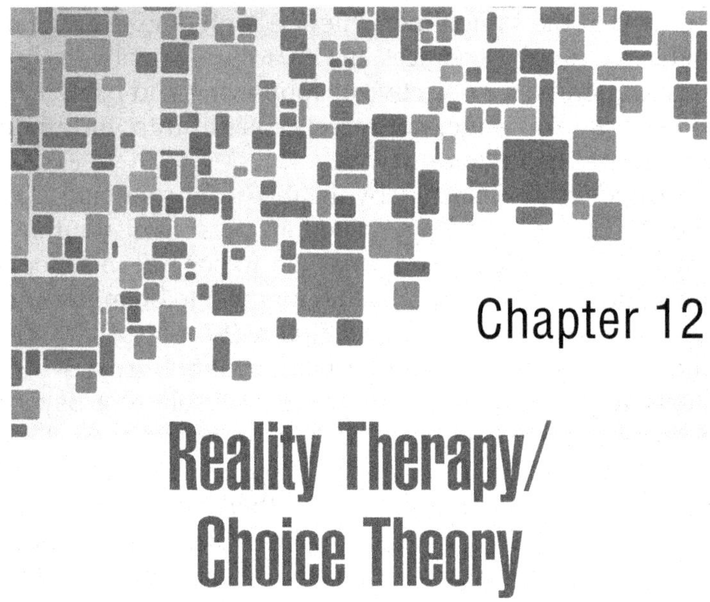

Chapter 12

Reality Therapy/ Choice Theory

Robert E. Wubbolding

Reality therapy, a practical method based on theory and research, aims to help people take better charge of their lives and fulfill their needs. Choice theory is the theoretical basis for reality therapy and is built on principles that emphasize current motivation for human choices and changes. To help clients make such changes, the counselor focuses on realistic choices, especially those touching on human relationships. The goals of reality therapy are twofold: process goals and outcome goals. The reality therapist helps clients examine their own behavior, evaluate it, and make plans for change. The outcome is more satisfying relationships, increased happiness, and a sense of inner control of their lives.

BACKGROUND

William Glasser (1925–2013), the originator of reality therapy, first began to develop this approach to counseling and psychotherapy while working in a correctional institution and a psychiatric hospital. A board-certified psychiatrist, Glasser had been trained in the traditional methods of psychiatry. He was taught to help clients gain insight so that after transference was worked through, they could achieve a higher degree of sanity. However, his experience had shown that even if these goals of the analytic approach were achieved, clients did not necessarily change their behavior, and many continued to have difficulty making productive decisions. With support and input from a sympathetic professor named G. L. Harrington, Glasser formulated the early principles of his new treatment modality.

The watershed year for reality therapy came in 1965, when William Glasser published *Reality Therapy*. In this then-controversial book, Glasser emphasized that people are responsible for their own behavior and that they cannot blame the past or outside forces and at the same time achieve a high degree of mental health. He asserted that behavior involves choices and that there are always options open to most people. Consequently, the objective of counseling and psychotherapy should be measurable behavioral change, not merely insight into and understanding of past events or current subconscious drives.

Though not greeted enthusiastically by the medical profession, Glasser's theory was well received by many, including corrections personnel, youth workers, counselors, therapists, and educators. He was asked to consult in schools to help students take more responsibility for their behaviors and to blame others less, and out of this work came his book *Schools Without Failure* (W. Glasser, 1968). In this work, he discussed how reality therapy can be used in large groups—what he called *class meetings.* Although not the same as group counseling or psychotherapy, the meetings have some of the same goals, such as increased self-esteem, feelings of success, and group members' sense of belonging and respect for one another.

At that time, many professionals saw reality therapy as a method rather than a theory. Then, in *The Identity Society* (1972), William Glasser formulated what might be called the theory's *sociological underpinnings.* He explained that three forces had contributed to the radical changes in Western civilization in the 1950s and 1960s: the passage of laws that guaranteed human rights, increased affluence that satisfied the basic need for survival for the majority of people, and the advent of instant communication via electronic media. These three gradual but important changes had facilitated the arrival of the *identity society*—a world in which people are more focused on their identity needs than on their survival needs. Most people want an opportunity to move beyond economic and political serfdom. Therefore, reality therapy found acceptance because it is a theory that facilitates personal empowerment by means of self-evaluation and positive planning for the future (see Sidebar 12.1).

Still, this pragmatic and culturally based method needed solid theoretical grounding. Such a foundation was provided by a relatively unknown theory of brain functioning. Powers (1973, 2009) described the brain as an input control system similar to a thermostat that controls the temperature of a room. W. Glasser (1984) extended Powers's control theory (or control system theory) by incorporating a system of needs to explain human motivation, and he then molded the theory to the clinical setting and the practice of counseling and psychotherapy. With the addition of these and many other ideas, it was no longer appropriate to call Glasser's theory *control theory,* and, consequently, the recognized name is now *choice theory* (W. Glasser, 1998, 2005, 2011).

Another major development in reality therapy has been the extended application described by Wubbolding (2000, 2011, 2014). The WDEP formulation (discussed

Sidebar 12.1. William Glasser's Final Words of Advice

Approximately 1 month before Dr. Glasser died in 2013, a young woman visiting him in his home asked for his advice about her son. The 4-year-old was beginning to act out in a way that was offensive to her. He paused for a long time and responded very clearly, "Always treat him as if he is good" and "Set up circumstances where he can only succeed." These two sentiments about parenting, delivered in his living room, constitute his last lecture and surely apply to parents of every social class and ethnic group around the world.

in "Utilize Procedures: The WDEP System") provides a pedagogical tool for learning and practicing the process of reality therapy. Wubbolding has also extended the theory to multicultural counseling based on his experience working in Asia, Europe, and the Middle East. In addition, he has provided credibility for the system by emphasizing research data and scientific validation. The system now is elevated beyond the work of one man and has reached the level of universal applicability.

In 2008, the European Association for Psychotherapy recognized reality therapy as a scientific and valid system after an 8-year effort by that association. This recognition is founded on two requirements: empirical validation and the existence of six national European reality therapy organizations (in Bosnia-Herzegovina, Croatia, Finland, Ireland, Slovenia, and the United Kingdom, and more recently Malta and Romania). Clearly, the European Association for Psychotherapy has accepted reality therapy as applying to clients from many cultures represented in the European Union.

HUMAN NATURE: A DEVELOPMENTAL PERSPECTIVE

Reality therapy provides a comprehensive explanation of human behavior as well as a methodology for addressing the vicissitudes of the human condition. Choice theory explains why and how human beings function and develop, and the WDEP system (Wubbolding, 1991, 2000, 2011, 2015a)—explained briefly in the following paragraph and in greater depth later in the chapter—provides a delivery system for helping oneself and others remediate deficiencies, make better choices, and become more fully self-actualized.

In the WDEP formulation, *W* implies that the counselor helps clients explore their wants. *D* means that clients describe the direction of their lives as well as what they are currently doing or how they spend their time. *E* indicates that the counselor or therapist helps in the clients' self-evaluation by asking such questions as, "Are your current actions effective?" Clients are then helped to make simple and attainable action plans, as implied by *P*. Thus, reality therapy is not a theory of developmental psychology per se. Still, as discussed in detail later, it contains ideas that harmonize with various stages of development.

Fundamental to reality therapy is the principle that human needs are the source of all human behavior. Infants as well as senior adults seek to control or mold the world around them to fulfill their inner drives, but here the commonality among people at various stages ends. As people grow, they develop specific wants unique to themselves. An infant, child, adolescent, young adult, middle-aged person, or senior adult has formulated a wide range of wants that are unique to that person yet similar to the wants experienced by others of the same age and culture. The commonality of general human needs is balanced by the diversity of specific wants.

Although the behavior of all human beings is designed to fulfill inner needs, it differs according to age and culture. Human behavior has an impact on the external world and, in a sense, shapes it as a sculptor molds clay. As a result, the input or perception that one gets from the world—a person's worldview (perception)—is dynamic, always changing, and unique to each person depending on age and culture. A developmental implication of the principles of choice theory is that the perceptual system or worldview is a storehouse of memories. Because human problems at many levels of development are rooted in relationships, Ford (1979) and Wubbolding (1988, 2011) emphasized the necessity of interpersonal quality time as a facilitative component of healthy development. When parent and child, friend and friend, spouse and spouse, or colleague and colleague spend quality time together, they build a storehouse of pleasant and healthy perceptions of each other. In order for quality time to serve as a solid support for effective growth and development, it must be characterized by effort and awareness of the other person; performed repetitively, without criticism; and satisfying to all involved. Quality time is a crucial component of human growth and development. Moreover, the activities labeled as *quality time* are determined by people's interests and levels of intellectual functioning as well as their age and degree of mental health.

MAJOR CONSTRUCTS

The underlying theory that justifies the methodology of reality therapy is called *choice theory*. Although choice theory (originally known as *control theory*) is separate from reality therapy and existed before reality therapy was developed, the terms *choice theory* and *reality therapy* are now sometimes used interchangeably. Norbert Wiener, a Harvard University mathematician, formulated many of the principles that have been subsumed under the name *control theory* (Becvar & Becvar, 2006; Wubbolding, 1994). Wiener described the importance of feedback to both engineering and biological systems (Wiener, 1948) as well as the sociological implications for human beings (Wiener, 1950). However, Wubbolding (2011) emphasized that the more proximate basis for the clinical applications was formulated by Powers (1973). Powers rejected the mechanism of behaviorism by emphasizing the internal origins of the human control system.

Most significant in the development of choice theory, however, was the work of William Glasser (1980a, 1984, 1998, 2001, 2005; W. Glasser & Glasser, 2008), who expanded Powers's work and adapted it to the clinical setting. Human beings, Glasser stated, act on the world around them for a purpose: to satisfy their needs and wants. He spoke of total behavior, which comprises actions, thinking, feelings, and physiology. All behaviors contain these four elements, although one element or another is more obvious at a given moment. Such behaviors, negative or positive, are the output generated from within a person to gain a sense of control or to satisfy needs.

Wubbolding (2000, 2008b, 2011, 2016) provided a summary of Glasser's choice theory as it applies to counseling and psychotherapy. First, human beings are born with five needs: belonging or love, power (inner control, competence, or achievement), fun or enjoyment, freedom or independence (autonomy), and survival or self-preservation. Preeminent among these general and universal human needs is that of belonging. Wubbolding (2005) stated, "No matter how dire one's circumstances, the human will and creativity are relentless in their pursuit of human closeness" (p. 43). Along with wants, which are specific and unique for each person, needs serve as the motivators or sources of all behavior (see Sidebar 12.2).

Second, the difference between what a person wants and what the person perceives he or she is getting (input) is the immediate source of specific behaviors at any given moment. Thus, reality therapy rests on the principle that human behavior springs from internal motivation, producing behavior from moment to moment (W. Glasser, 1998; Wubbolding, 2008b, 2011; Wubbolding & Brickell, 2015).

Sidebar 12.2. The Central Place of the Need for Fun

"The shortest distance between two people is a laugh." So spoke the universally loved comedian Victor Borge. If the relationship between counselor and client is central to effective counseling, clearly an effective counselor infuses humor into the counseling process. Many clients are unaware of how to have fun. As a result of encountering a skilled reality therapist they often learn the art of having fun without infringing on the rights or need satisfaction of other people or on their wants or actions chosen to satisfy their own needs. For example, persons engaging in a sport keep the rules because their opponents also have a legitimate right: to satisfy their own needs by playing the sport.

Third, all human behaviors are composed of doing (actions), thinking, feeling, and physiology. Behaviors are identified by the most obvious aspect of this total behavior. Thus, a student counseled for poor grades in school is seen as presenting an action problem. A person is labeled *psychotic* because the primary and most obvious aspect of his or her total behavior is dysfunctional thinking. Depression, anger, resentment, and fear are most obvious in some people, so their behavior is called a *feeling behavior.* For others, the most obvious component of behavior is the physiological element, such as heart disease or high blood pressure. Human choices are not aimless or random. They are all teleological; in other words, they serve a purpose: to close the gap between the perception of what a person is getting and what he or she wants at a given moment.

Fourth, because behavior originates from within, human beings are responsible for their behavior. In other words, everyone is capable of change. This change is brought about by choosing more effective behaviors, especially the action component, which is more easily controlled than the other components.

Fifth, human beings see the world through a perceptual system that functions as a set of lenses. At a low level of perception, the person simply recognizes the world, giving names to objects and events, but does not make judgments about them. At a high level of perception, the person puts a positive or negative value on the perception. Wubbolding and Brickell (2009) suggested that a middle-level filter exists whereby human beings see relationships among people, things, ideas, and so on as necessary prerequisites for placing a value on the perception. Exploring the various levels of perception and their helpfulness is part of the counseling or psychotherapy process.

In summary, choice theory is a psychology built on principles that emphasize current motivation for human choices. It stands in opposition to both psychological determinism and what William Glasser (1998, 2005) called *external control psychology.* Human beings are free to make choices; thus, although the past has propelled individuals to the present, it need not determine their future. Similarly, a person's external world limits his or her choices but does not remove them.

APPLICATIONS

Overview

Reality therapy is a practical method based on theory and research. It aims to help people take better charge of their lives. To help clients make such changes, the counselor focuses on realistic choices, especially those touching on human relationships. It is first necessary to establish a safe therapeutic environment similar to that espoused in most theories, although choice theory offers some unique ways to accomplish this. The WDEP system details the specific reality therapy procedures used to help accomplish these goals.

Goals of Counseling and Psychotherapy

The goal of reality therapy is to help clients fulfill their needs. Consequently, the counselor or therapist helps clients explore current behaviors and choices related to belonging, power, fun, and freedom. More specifically, the precise wants related to each need are examined so as to help clients fulfill their specific objectives or their wants. Therefore, assisting clients to make more effective and responsible choices related to their wants and needs is the aim of the counselor. These choices are seen as motivated by current needs and wants, not by past traumas, unresolved conflicts, peer pressure, or previous training.

The Process of Change

To understand how change can occur in a client's life, one needs to understand the following principles in the theory and practice of reality therapy.

Present Orientation

Choice theory, the theoretical basis for reality therapy, rests on the principle that the human brain functions like a control system—for example, like a thermostat—seeking to regulate its own behavior to shape its environment so that the environment matches what it wants. Therefore, human behavior springs from current inner motivation and is neither an attempt to resolve past conflicts nor a mere response to an external stimulus.

Emphasis on Choice

One of the goals of counseling and psychotherapy for the practitioner of reality therapy is to help clients make positive choices. Therefore, it is useful to see behavior as a result of one's choices, to treat it as such, and to talk to clients as if they had choices. Although no human being has total freedom to make better choices easily, it can still be helpful to see even severe emotional disturbance as a person's best choice for a given period of time. The work of the counselor is to reveal more choices to clients and to help clients see that better choices are possible.

Control of Action

To bring about change, one needs to recognize the component of one's total behavior over which a person has the most control. Therefore, choice is the action element. Although some people have an amazing amount of direct control over their physiology (some can choose to stop bleeding when they are cut), people seen in counseling and psychotherapy can rarely change their blood pressure, their ulcer condition, or their headaches through an act of will. People can rarely change their feelings of depression, guilt, anxiety, or worry merely by choosing to do so. Although they have some control over their thoughts, it is still not easy for them just to begin thinking differently from the way they have in the past.

Because people have the most control over the action element, helping them change their actions is more efficacious than helping them think differently or helping them feel better. It is more productive to help spouses choose to talk politely to each other than to help them feel better about each other. Increasing self-esteem is possible if a client chooses to act in ways that are different from ways in which he or she has acted previously.

The Importance of Relationship

The specific procedures of the WDEP system are based on the establishment of an empathic relationship. As is abundantly clear from research, the relationship between the client and the counselor is critical in effecting change. Reality therapy offers specific interventions aimed at helping clients make more effective choices, and these are most effective when a genuine relationship has been established. Counselors who use reality therapy effectively use many of the same skills and possess the same qualities as other counselors: empathy, congruence, and positive regard. Reality therapy offers specific ways, some unique to reality therapy and some incorporated from general practice, for establishing and maintaining a therapeutic relationship (Richardson & Wubbolding, 2001). Britzman (2009) stated, "Life-long relationships based on mutual respect, integrity and love are one of the strongest predictors of happiness" (p. 20).

Reality therapy developed out of a desire to see change happen in clients rather than have clients merely gain insight and awareness. Contributing to the efficacy of reality therapy is its emphasis on present orientation, choice, action, and the counseling relationship.

Traditional Intervention Strategies

Conventional counseling and therapy in the past often meant a long-term commitment for clients and counselors. Building rapport, obtaining and documenting a case history, and allowing for appropriate catharsis and insight constituted the focus of traditional counseling and therapy. Out of these dynamics, client change would gradually develop. Reality therapy is based on different premises. Clients are encouraged to take action in an effort to satisfy their five needs regardless of their history or insight or even whether they feel good about taking action. In fact, reality therapy had been criticized as *merely* a short-term problem-solving method. Although reality therapy can be used as a long-term method, the goal is to help clients improve rapidly.

Brief Intervention Strategies and Current Practices

The methodology used in reality therapy consists of establishing an appropriate environment or psychological atmosphere and then applying the procedures that lead to change: the WDEP system. Together, these constitute the *cycle of counseling* (see Figure 12.1). This cycle illustrates that the specific interventions summarized as WDEP are built on a trustful relationship. Trust-destroying and trust-building ideas (see "Tonics" and "Toxins") are listed in Figure 12.1. The process is described as a cycle because there is no single place to start when it is applied to clients. Counselors need to use their creativity to match the system to each client.

Create a Positive Environment

An atmosphere that provides for the possibility of change is characterized by specific guidelines and suggestions about what to do and what to avoid. These are designed for use by counselors, therapists, and case managers as well as supervisors and

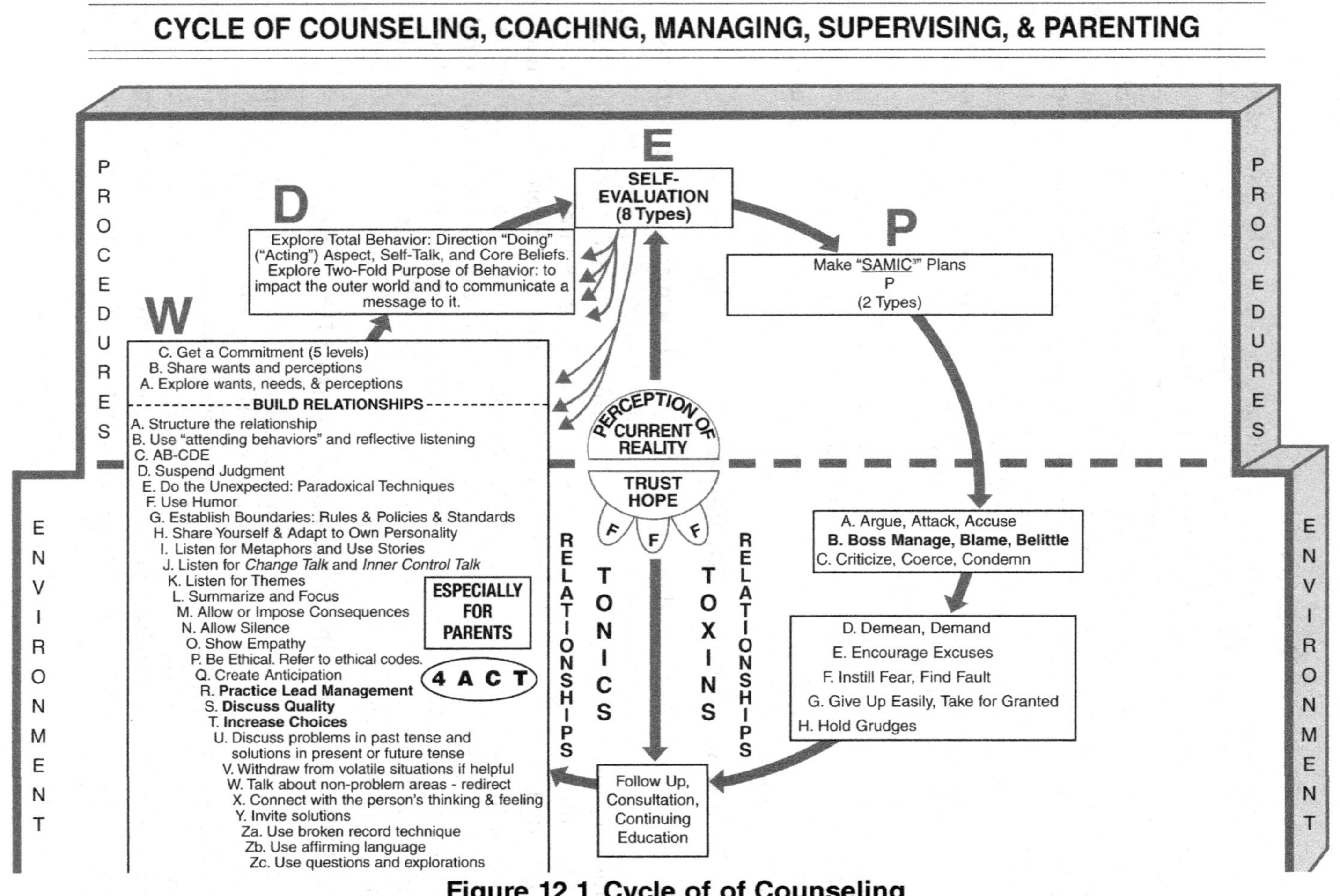

Figure 12.1. Cycle of of Counseling

Note. Developed by Robert E. Wubbolding, EdD, from the works of William Glasser, MD, founder of choice theory/reality therapy. Copyright 1986 by Robert E. Wubbolding, EdD (19th rev., 2015). Reprinted with permission.

SUMMARY DESCRIPTION OF THE "CYCLE OF COUNSELING, COACHING, MANAGING, SUPERVISING, & PARENTING"

The Cycle is explained in detail in books by Robert E. Wubbolding: *Reality Therapy for the 21st Century, 2000*
A Set of Directions for Putting and Keeping Yourself Together, 2001
Reality Therapy In APA's *Theories of Psychotherapy Series, 2011*

Introduction:

The Cycle consists of two general concepts: Environment conducive to change and Procedures more explicitly designed to facilitate change. This chart is intended to be a **brief** summary. The ideas are designed to be used with employees, students, clients as well as in other human relationships.

Relationship between Environment & Procedures:

1. As indicated in the chart, the Environment is the foundation upon which the effective use of Procedures is based.
2. Though it is **usually** necessary to establish a safe, friendly Environment before change can occur, the "Cycle" can be entered at any point. Thus, the use of the cycle does **not** occur in lockstep fashion.
3. Building a relationship implies establishing and maintaining a professional relationship. Methods for accomplishing this comprise some efforts on the part of the helper that are Environmental and others that are Procedural.

ENVIRONMENT:

Relationship Tonics: a close relationship is built on TRUST and HOPE through friendliness, firmness and fairness. **Cf. Caring Habits: Glasser**

A. Structure the relationship.
B. Using Attending Behaviors: Eye contact, posture, effective listening skills.
C. AB = "Always **B**e . . ." **C**onsistent, **C**ourteous & **C**alm, **D**etermined that there is hope for improvement, **E**nthusiastic (Think Positively).
D. Suspend Judgment: View behaviors from a low level of perception, i.e., acceptance is crucial.
E. Do the Unexpected: Use paradoxical techniques as appropriate; Reframing and Prescribing.
F. Use Humor: Help them fulfill need for fun within reasonable boundaries.
G. Establish boundaries: the relationship is professional.

4 A C T
- Affirm feelings
- Accept
- Show affection
- Action consequences
- Conversation (WDEP)
- Time together

H. Share Self: Self-disclosure within limits is helpful; adapt to own personal style.
I. Listen for Metaphors: Use their figures of speech and provide other ones. Use stories.
J. Listen for *Change Talk* and *Inner Control Talk.*
K. Listen to Themes: Listen for behaviors that have helped, value judgements, etc.
L. Summarize & Focus: Tie together what they say and focus on them rather than on "Real World."
M. Allow or Impose Consequences: Within reason, they should be responsible for their own behavior.
N. Allow Silence: This allows them to think, as well as to take responsibility.
O. Show Empathy: Perceive as does the person being helped.
P. Be Ethical: Study Codes of Ethics and their applications, e.g., how to handle suicide threats or violent tendencies.
Q. Create anticipation and communication hope. People should be taught that something good will happen if they are willing to work.
R. **Practice lead management, e.g., democracy in determining rules.**
S. **Discuss quality.**
T. **Increases choices.**
U. Discuss problems in the past tense, solutions in present or future tense.
V. Withdraw from volatile situations if helpful.
W. Talk about non-problem areas - redirect.
X. Connect with the person's thinking and feeling.
Y. Invite solutions.
Za. Use broken record technique.
Zb. Use affirming language.
Zc. Use questions and explorations.

Relationship Toxins: Cf. Deadly Habits: Glasser

Argue, **Boss Manage,** or Blame, Criticize or Coerce, Demean, Encourage Excuses, Instill Fear, or Give up easily, Hold Grudges.

Rather, stress what they **can** control, accept them as they are, and keep the confidence that they can develop more effective behaviors. Also, continue to us "WDEP" system without giving up.

Follow Up, Consult, and Continue Education:

Determine a way for them to report back, talk to another professional person when necessary, and maintain ongoing program of professional growth.

PROCEDURES: **WDEP**

Build Relationships:

A. Explore **W**ants, Needs & Perceptions: Discuss picture album or quality world, i.e., set goals, fulfilled & unfulfilled pictures, needs, viewpoints and "locus of control."
B. Share Wants & Perceptions: Tell what you want from them and how you view their situations, behaviors, wants, etc. This procedure is secondary to A above.
C. Get a Commitment: Help them solidify their desire to find more effective behaviors.

Explore Total Behavior:

Help them examine the **D**irection of their lives, as well as specifics of how they spend their time. Discuss core beliefs and ineffective & effective self-talk. Explore two-fold purpose of behavior: to impact the outer world and to communicate a message to it.

Evaluation – The Cornerstone of Procedures:

Help them evaluate their behavioral direction, specific behaviors as well as wants, perceptions and commitments. Evaluate own behavior through follow-up, consultation and continued education.

Make **P**lans: Help them change direction of their lives.

Effective plans are **S**imple, **A**ttainable, **M**easurable, **I**mmediate, **I**nvolved, **C**onsistent, **C**ontrolled by the planner, and **C**ommitted to. The helper is **P**ersistent. Plans can be linear or paradoxical.

Note: The "Cycle" describes specific guidelines & skills. Effective implementation requires the artful integration of the guidelines & skills contained under Environment & Procedures in a spontaneous & natural manner geared to the personality of the helper. This requires training, practices & supervision. Also, the word "client" is used for anyone receiving help: student, employee, family member, etc.

For more information contact:

Robert E. Wubbolding, EdD, Director

Center for Reality Therapy
5490 Windridge Court
Cincinnati, Ohio 45243

(513) 561-1911 • FAX (513) 561-3568
E-mail: wubsrt@fuse.net • www.realitytherapywub.com

The Center for Reality Therapy provides counseling, consultation, training and supervision including applications to schools, agencies, companies and other institutions. The Center is a provider for many organizations which award continuing education units.

Figure 12.1. Cycle of of Counseling *(Continued)*

Note. Developed by Robert E. Wubbolding, EdD, from the works of William Glasser, MD, founder of choice theory/reality therapy. Copyright 1986 by Robert E. Wubbolding, EdD (19th rev., 2015). Reprinted with permission.

managers in the workplace. They can also be taught to clients, parents, teachers, and others for use in improving their interactions with clients, students, employees, and children. The specific applications vary slightly, but the principles are quite consistent.

Among the behaviors that are toxic or deadly to human relationships are arguing, blaming, criticizing, demeaning, colluding with excuses, finding fault, and giving up on the relationship. The alternative to the quicksand of toxic or deadly behaviors is the effective use of the WDEP system. Asking about wants or goals quickly replaces endless and ineffective discussions. These procedures apply to persons from virtually any ethnic, religious, or cultural group. In speaking of this universal applicability, Jusoh and Ahmad (2009) stated, "The WDEP procedure can be used universally with the aspect of religion and culture. . . . WDEP in the counseling process [is] similar to Islamic concepts" (p. 3).

In the early stages of the development of the reality therapy delivery system, the advice was to never give up. A more realistic formulation is for a counselor to stay with the person past the time he or she expects to be abandoned. In other words, do not give up *easily*. Similarly, the counselor might be tempted to give up on the WDEP system if it fails to render the desired results immediately. Wubbolding (2011) emphasized that this is because the principles appear to be easy to practice, in view of the fact that the vocabulary is uncomplicated, yet proficient use of the skills requires repeated practice and supervision.

A positive environment, the basis for the WDEP system, not only is built on avoiding the uncongenial behaviors of arguing, criticizing, or giving up but also rests on tonic behaviors such as the global admonition to be friends in a professional manner. These efforts to establish an agreeable and harmonious atmosphere are sustained and nourished by the use of intervention strategies or tonic behaviors such as attending behaviors described by Ivey, D'Andrea, Bradford Ivey, and Simek-Morgan (2002). The acronym AB-CDEFG summarizes additional interventions: "Always be—courteous, determined, enthusiastic, firm, and genuine." Other tonic behaviors include the following.

Suspend Judgment

As stated earlier, all behavior is a person's best effort at a given time to fulfill his or her needs. Consequently, a counselor who keeps this principle in mind can more easily see quite harmful choices from a low level of perception, without approval or disapproval.

Do the Unexpected

Unpredictability is a quality that facilitates a helpful counseling or psychotherapy environment. Focusing on a strength, a success, or a time when the client felt good often generates the type of discussion that clients do not expect. Nevertheless, clients who are characterized by negative symptoms also, at least occasionally, choose positive symptoms (Wubbolding, 2008a, 2015a). Therefore, it is helpful to discuss in detail the circumstances when clients chose effectively, felt good, and remained in effective control of their lives. Wubbolding (1984, 2011, 2015b) described other ways for doing the unexpected and incorporated paradoxical techniques such as reframing, redefining, and relabeling into reality therapy. However, to be effective using these and other paradoxical techniques, one needs to invert one's thinking. Thus, causes are seen as effects; the objectionable is now a strength (Dowd & Milne, 1986; Fay, 1978; Seltzer, 1986; Weeks & L'Abate, 1982). Wubbolding (1993) stated that a depressed child can be seen as pensive, gentle, and thoughtful. An angry child can be outgoing with deep conviction. The bully is a leader and has ambition, whereas a submissive child is kind and cooperative.

Use Humor

A healthy and democratic sense of humor is a curative factor for the mental health specialist. Comedian and pianist Victor Borge once remarked that laughter is the shortest distance between two people.

Be Yourself

Although it is to be expected that students learning counseling skills will adopt the style of their teachers or that of the leaders in each theory, they also need to adapt the skills that fit their own personality and core beliefs.

Share Yourself

The creation and maintenance of a trusting relationship is facilitated by appropriate self-disclosure. According to a Swedish proverb, "A joy shared is twice a joy. A sorrow shared is half a sorrow." Although self-disclosure by a counselor can be helpful, it is best used in moderation.

Listen for Metaphors

Metaphors in this context are figures of speech, analogies, similes, and anecdotes that serve to quantify problems and thereby make them manageable. Their judicious and careful use by counselors can provide clients with more behavioral choices. Kopp (1995) warned, "As with all potentially powerful therapeutic interventions, these metaphor methods require sound clinical judgment" (p. 5). Also, stories and anecdotes can be humorous and thus help clients perceive their problems and decisions in a different light. Metaphors used by clients are often overlooked by counselors, or they are paraphrased. It is better, however, to use the metaphor, to extend it, and to return to it in subsequent sessions (Wubbolding & Brickell, 1998). The following metaphors might be stated by clients or initiated by counselors and therapists: "I feel like a floor mat" or "I feel like I'm on a merry-go-round." Using these metaphors, the counselor or therapist can offer clients specific choices, such as, "Would you like to get off the floor?" "Do you want to get off the merry-go-round?" and "What would you be doing today if you were on solid ground, away from the merry-go-round?" As with all such techniques used to enhance the counseling environment, metaphors do not constitute the essence of reality therapy. They do, however, serve to build trust between the client and the counselor.

Listen for Themes

Tying together the ideas, feelings, and actions of clients helps them to gain a sense of direction and control. The practitioner using reality therapy listens carefully for themes, such as previous attempts to solve problems, wants that are fulfilled, and what has helped and not helped the client. This technique is not exclusive to the practice of reality therapy, but in using it, the counselor listens for themes that are linked to the WDEP interventions (see "Utilize Procedures: The WDEP System").

Summarize and Focus

Similar to the identification of themes, this technique helps the counselor listen carefully and communicate to clients that they are being heard. Unlike summaries used in other theories, this one concentrates on components of the WDEP system. A counselor might summarize a client's statements by responding, "You've stated that you've tried to get a promotion at work and been unsuccessful, that you've approached your boss and described what you want, that you've put in extra hours. Nothing so far has gotten you what you want." The counselor has summarized what the client has done that has not worked and has omitted many other details.

Focusing means centering the conversation on the client rather than on outside forces over which neither involved party has control. Very little can be done to cause changes in other people. Nothing can be done to change the past. Thus, it is most helpful if the counselor gently and positively assists clients to discuss their own here-and-now wants, total behaviors, plans, hopes, frustrations, and perceptions.

Allow or Impose Consequences

Professional counselors have fewer opportunities to use this element of the environment than those who want to integrate reality therapy into their work. Probation and parole officers, halfway house workers, and others often function in a supervisory role and are required to impose consequences. It is assumed that the consequence is reasonable and not punitive and also that it is imposed to help rather than merely control the client.

Allow Silence

The use of silence in reality therapy, if timed properly, allows the client to conduct inner self-evaluation; reassess wants; think about what is controllable and, therefore, uncontrollable; and, in general, take responsibility for the direction of the session.

Be Ethical

The American Counseling Association's (2014) ethical principle concerning serious and foreseeable harm (Standard B.2.a.) is one of many that the practitioner of reality therapy practices. A trusting relationship and a professional atmosphere conducive to helping are built around solid ethical principles. Anyone using reality therapy properly knows, understands, and practices the ethical standards of various professional organizations. Professional disclosure is often required, as in Ohio (State of Ohio, 2009). Thus, counselors, therapists, and social workers must provide clients with a written description of their professional qualifications. Wubbolding (1986) and Wubbolding and Brickell (2005) emphasized that counselors and therapists should provide clients with information about the nature of reality therapy. These details help clarify the boundaries of the relationship as well as the advantages and limitations of the assistance that the practitioner can offer. Wubbolding (1990) also emphasized the importance of knowing how to assess suicidal threats and how this assessment is used in the practice of reality therapy. Informed consent, dual relationships, confidentiality, proper record keeping, and maintaining competence are among the many ethical issues impinging on the relationship between counselor and client. Remley and Herlihy (2010) stated, "Professionals individually determine the limits of their competence and practice accordingly" (p. 170).

Be Redundant or Repetitious

Often, the same questions are asked in various ways. When a client is defensive and offering excuses in the form of denial, the counselor or therapist sometimes repeats the same question in a different way. It becomes a theme aimed at helping clients evaluate their own behavior. "When you made that choice, did it help?" "Did it work for you?" "What impact did that action have on you and on others?" "Did it help you enough?" "Was the action the best you were capable of?" Such questions asked at various times become a haunting theme that gradually and supportively lessens denial and facilitates the clients' assumption of responsibility. However, like the overall art of counseling, the skill of being redundant is developed through practice and self-evaluation.

Create Suspense and Anticipation

In a counselor's effective use of reality therapy, there can be an element of drama. A counseling session should be a significant event in the lives of clients. An authentic buoyancy on the part of the counselor and a desire to reassure can elicit a feeling of curiosity and a sense of impending success. The ability to communicate a sense of optimism is an advanced skill and is developed with practice and training.

Establish Boundaries

There are limits within which a counselor operates, and these should be clarified. The ethical principle of dual relationships is clearly part of boundary classification (Herlihy & Corey, 2015). Furthermore, the client might want to shield certain areas from discussion. A useful question for counselors or therapists to ask is, "Is there any topic you would prefer we not discuss?" Such questioning empowers clients to choose what they want to work on. If clients have numerous topics that are forbidden territory (which is rarely the case), the counselor can ask them if it is helpful for them to conceal or mask potential topics. In any event, the wants of the client are paramount and are respected.

The aforementioned guidelines are designed to help the counselor using reality therapy to establish rapport, mutual trust, and a safe atmosphere in a brief and efficient manner. They also consist of swift and positive interventions that facilitate the client's expectation that the experience is worthwhile and significant. These environmental building blocks aimed at establishing and deepening the relationship provide a fundamental prerequisite for what is essentially the practice of reality therapy: the WDEP system (see Sidebar 12.3).

Utilize Procedures: The WDEP System

The specific interventions that are the essence of reality therapy are based on the trusting relationship described earlier as environment. The procedures or determinations (Wubbolding, 2011, 2016) are most appropriately formulated as the WDEP system as described in Figure 12.1 (C. Glasser, 1996a, 1996b; W. Glasser & Glasser, 2008; Wubbolding, 1989, 1991, 2000, 2011; Wubbolding & Brickell, 2005, 2015). They should not be seen as steps to be used sequentially or mechanically,

Sidebar 12.3. The Significance and Subtlety of Language

The effective use of reality therapy involves teaching clients about choice theory and the delivery system reality therapy, yet teaching need not be a direct explanation of concepts. Clients learn in a very indirect manner that they have more inner control than previously thought. A counselor states, "When you were upset about being rejected, you *felt* depressed. But you *are now* seeking help and are making plans that *are* propelling you to a more satisfying life and toward getting you what you *currently* want."

and although they are described in simple, jargon-free language, they can be difficult to implement. For instance, a counselor working with a student referred for a school discipline problem would probably not begin with a lengthy discussion of W (wants) but rather with an exploration of D (doing): In other words, what happened to bring about the referral? Thus, in conceptualizing the entire process, it is useful to see it as a cycle that can be entered into at any point.

W: Discussing Wants, Needs, and Perceptions

Because human beings are motivated to fulfill their wants and needs, it is important for the counselor or therapist to take the time to explore the specific wants of the client. The questions might include, "What do you want from your spouse? From your school? Your job? Your career? From your friends? Your parents? Your children? Your supervisor? From yourself? What do you want from me? From your religion?" Thus, there are at least 11 generic questions that can be asked. These are multiplied threefold if the counselor asks more precisely about each category: (a) "What do you want that you are getting?" (b) "What do you want that you are not getting?" (c) "What are you getting that you don't want?" The areas for exploration and clarification become almost endless when the counselor or therapist adds "How much do you want it?" "What would you need to give up to get what you want?" "What will you settle for?"

All wants are related to the five needs: belonging, power or achievement, fun or enjoyment, freedom or independence, and survival. Therefore, it is useful to help clients link their wants explicitly to their needs by asking, "If you had what you wanted, what would you have?" or "If your wants were met, what would that satisfy inside?" Such questioning of a parent often elicits the following: "I want my child to keep the curfew, get good grades, stay away from drugs, do the house chores, and be pleasant to the rest of the family. If I had that, I would have peace of mind. I would know that I am a good parent." The parent has specific wants and has identified the underlying need: achievement or power.

Discussing perceptions is also an important part of W. Questions about clients' perceptions are slightly different from those specifically relating to wants. Wubbolding and Brickell (2015) emphasized that helping clients, students, and institutions raise their awareness of and evaluate the contents of their perceived worlds plays a crucial role in assisting them to take better charge of their behavior, direction, and destiny. A parent might be asked, "What do you see when you look at your child?" Asking about perceptions is especially useful in groups and in family counseling, because arguments can be prevented. A counselor can intervene by reminding all present that they are discussing their viewpoints—what they see, not what is.

Part of the W of the WDEP system is eliciting a commitment to counseling. Change and growth will occur only if the client is committed to making changes in his or her actions. Thus, it is imperative that the counselor discuss the client's level of commitment to the process and its outcomes. The question, "How hard do you want to work at changing your situation?" gives the client an opportunity to look inward and reflect on the degree of responsibility he or she wants to assume.

Wubbolding (2000, 2011, 2015b) identified and developed five levels of commitment as described by clients:

1. *"I don't want to be here"*: This statement clearly illustrates that the client is at best reluctant and often resistant.
2. *"I want the outcome but not the effort"*: This level indicates that the client does want to change and is perhaps willing to gain effective control and take personal responsibility.
3. *"I'll try; I might:"*: Trying to make a change for the better constitutes the middle level of commitment to change. Still, trying to get out of bed early is not the same as doing it.
4. *"I will do my best"*: At this level, a person goes beyond trying and commits to specific action. However, such a commitment still allows for the possibility of failure.
5. *"I will do whatever it takes"*: The highest level of commitment represents an outcome centered on a no-excuses level of commitment.

The levels of commitment are developmental. The higher levels are more helpful than the lower ones, yet for some clients, "I'll try" is a major improvement. They should not be pushed too vigorously or too quickly to move to a higher level. Rather, the skillful counselor helps clients evaluate their level of commitment and gently leads them to the next level.

D: Discussing Behavioral Direction and Doing (Total Behavior)

The counselor helps the client review his or her overall direction with inquiries such as, "Where do you think you're going if you continue on the same path?" The exploration of the overall direction is only the embarkation point for further questioning about current total behavior. More time and effort are needed to help clients examine their specific actions. The counselor helps the client verbalize exactly what he or she did for a specific amount of time.

E: Helping Clients Conduct Evaluations

In the cycle of counseling and in the WDEP system of procedures, the element of evaluation occupies the central position (Wubbolding, 1990, 2015b; Wubbolding et al., 2004; see Figure 12.1). Like a keystone in an arch, its pivotal place supports the entire structure. If it is absent, the arch crumbles. The practice of reality therapy is firm and effective to the degree that the counselor assists clients in evaluating their own behavior, wants, perceptions, level of commitment, and plans. Wubbolding et al. (2004) stated, "Through skillful questioning clients ask themselves whether they are living as they want to live" (p. 225; see Sidebar 12.4).

Because of the prominent place of self-evaluation in the cycle of counseling, reality therapy is properly placed as a freestanding theory with other cognitive

Sidebar 12.4. Indirect Self-Evaluation

The customary self-evaluation "Is your current behavior helping you or hurting you?" can be supplemented in an indirect manner. Using an advanced reality therapy technique, a skilled counselor uses anecdotes and stories about individuals who have had issues similar to that of the client who reports an unceasing habit of repeatedly shouting at his 14-year-old son. The counselor relates a detailed and lengthy story that has a successful ending: "I know someone who had a similar problem with a teenager and decided to affirm his feelings as much as possible and to say very little about his negative actions."

theories. It is here, especially, at the cardinal point of self-evaluation, that cognitive restructuring takes place. Clients look inward and examine the effectiveness of their lifestyle and its specific aspects. Only now, when they have concluded that some part of their choice system (wants, behaviors, perceptions) is not helping them or is not as beneficial as it could be, do clients see that a change is necessary and that alternative and more effective choices are available. Because of the curative role of human relationships in reality therapy, many self-evaluation questions focus on the client in relation to others. The central questions focus on whose behavior can clients control and whether their lifestyle brings them closer to or further away from the people around them (W. Glasser, 2003, 2005).

More specifically, evaluation contains the following elements:

1. *Evaluation of behavioral direction:* After helping clients describe their overall life direction, the counselor asks them to judge whether their overall direction is in their best interest.
2. *Evaluation of specific actions:* The questions about specific actions are geared to the descriptions provided in clients' explanation of how a specific segment of their day was spent. Did their specific action choices help or hurt them or the people around them? Petersen (2005) stated, "The success of reality therapy lies in the client's ability to self-evaluate that present behaviors are not getting him/her closer to what s/he wants" (p. 13).
3. *Evaluation of wants as achievable:* The counselor assists clients in making judgments about their wants by asking such questions as, "Is what you want attainable or appropriate?"
4. *Evaluation of wants as appropriate:* Not all wants are beneficial to the client or others. Counselors help clients explore the merits, appropriateness, and helpfulness of their wants.
5. *Evaluation of perceptions or viewpoints:* Rarely are perceptions changed by a simple decision to view a person, a situation, or an event differently, yet they can be changed by altering behavior (W. Glasser, 1980a, 1998, 2011; Powers, 1973, 2009). However, because perceptions involve what people want, they occupy an important place in the evaluation process, so even though they are not directly changed, their desirability and appropriateness should be evaluated (Wubbolding & Brickell, 2015).
6. *Evaluation of level of commitment:* Clients are asked to decide whether their current level of commitment, such as "I'll try," is efficacious. Will it help them achieve their goals?
7. *Evaluation of new direction:* As new possibilities unfold for clients, it is useful to help them determine whether those possibilities are need satisfying. For instance, the rebellious student is asked, "How will cooperation at home benefit you and your family?" "What impact would this approach have on your friends and family?"
8. *Evaluation of plans:* From the beginning, even miniscule plan making was essential for the effectiveness of reality therapy. In working with a high school student, Wubbolding (1980) was able to help the student make a modest plan of action. This student had shut himself in his room on the weekends with the curtains and drapes closed. Although resistant at first, he eventually made plans to open the blinds and let the light in. He subsequently developed a

healthy social life by making rudimentary changes in his overall direction. Thus, the evaluation of plans is based not on whether they solve the basic problem but on whether they address the problem and aim toward the more effective fulfillment of belonging, power, fun, and freedom.

P: Planning

According to one saying, "To fail to plan is to plan to fail." W. Glasser (1980b) stated that plans vary: Some are detailed, whereas others are quite simple. However, he emphasized that "there must always be a plan. People who go through life without some sort of a long-term plan, usually divided into a series of small plans to reach larger goals, are like ships floundering without rudders" (p. 52).

The procedure of planning is often mistakenly viewed as the essence of the practice of reality therapy. Although it is important, it is effective only if based on a client's inner self-evaluation. Plans that are truly efficacious, or at least more likely to be carried out by the client, have at least eight qualities, which can be summarized by the acronym SAMI^{2}C^3 (Wubbolding, 2015b):

- S *Simple:* The plan is uncomplicated.
- A *Attainable:* The plan is realistically doable.
- M *Measurable:* The plan is precise and exact and answers the question "When will you do it?"
- I *Immediate:* The plan is carried out as soon as possible.
- I *Involved:* The helper is involved if such involvement is appropriate. The involvement is, of course, within the bounds of ethical standards and facilitates client independence rather than dependence.
- C *Controlled by the client:* The plan is not contingent on the actions of another person but is, as much as possible, within the control of the client.
- C *Committed to:* The client is firm about follow-through.
- C *Consistent:* The ideal plan is repetitious. A single plan can be a start, but the most effective plan is one that is repeated.

The common denominator to all planning is persistence on the part of the counselor. This coincides with the injunction "Don't give up."

In summary, the cycle of counseling or psychotherapy is a design for understanding reality therapy and an outline for knowing how to apply it. The environment consists of specific recommendations for building a firm but friendly atmosphere in which a client can feel safe and confident while realizing that the counselor or therapist actively seeks to be of help. The WDEP formulation is not a system that is intended to be followed in a mechanical manner but rather a system from which the proper intervention is selected at a given time because of its apparent appropriateness.

Once criticized as a short-term, problem-solving, symptom-focused method, reality therapy provides an effective tool for counselors working in the world of managed care and solution-focused counseling. The goals of the WDEP system include improvement in need satisfaction, especially human relationships; positive and productive living symbolized by employment and other signs; and learning the basics of reality therapy as a range of tools for further use and self-help (Wubbolding & Brickell, 2001). Users of reality therapy often aim to achieve measurable results in 10 or fewer sessions.

Clients With Serious Mental Health Issues

From the point of view of reality therapy, the diagnostic labels described in the *Diagnostic and Statistical Manual of Mental Disorders, Fifth Edition* (American Psychiatric Association, 2013), are not static conditions. They are negative symptoms (i.e., behaviors generated for a purpose—to fulfill wants and needs). As goal-directed behaviors, they can be replaced by more effective behaviors (i.e., positive symptoms). Seligman (2004) stated that reality therapy might be applied to disorders such as conduct disorder, oppositional defiant disorder, substance abuse, impulse control, and some personality disorders. The skilled reality counselor or therapist spends little time discussing diagnostic symptoms such as hallucinations, compulsions, psychoses, or depression (W. Glasser, 2003, 2005, 2011). Rather, the counselor and client search for specific solutions related to effective need and want satisfaction, especially directed toward a better sense of belonging and healthier relationships.

Consequently, in the application of reality therapy, medication can assist clients in making more effective choices. The theory began in a mental hospital and a correctional institution and is widely used in corrections. Though not describing diagnostic categories, Lojk (1986) demonstrated that reality therapy is still used successfully with correctional clients. B. Bratter, Bratter, Maxym, Radda, and Steiner (1993) successfully used reality therapy for delinquent youth whose diagnoses ranged from attention-deficit/hyperactivity disorder and conduct disorder to affective disorders, both depression and bipolar. In describing the success of the reality therapy program, T. Bratter, Esparat, Kaufman, and Sinsheimer (2008) stated that members of the 2008 class had been admitted to such universities as Brandeis, Oberlin, Sarah Lawrence, and the University of Chicago.

Casstevens (2013) researched the effects of choice theory/reality therapy focus groups in a wellness program conducted in a community-based clubhouse model serving adults with severe mental disorders. She concluded that the programs increased "the credibility of the overall approach to health and wellness program development in small non-profit organizations that serve adults with severe mental disorders" (p. 50).

The reality therapy counselor treats all behaviors as if some element of choice were present. In this way, clients feel both hope and empowerment. They realize that a better life is accessible and they are not irretrievably doomed to a life of mental illness.

Cross-Cultural Considerations

Reality therapy is an imminently cross-cultural method. Based on universal psychological principles, the method has been applied to cultures as diverse as Asian, Middle Eastern, South American, African, European, as well as those represented in North America. Instructors indigenous to various cultures have adapted the principles to their respective clients (Wubbolding et al., 2004). Practitioners using the principles of reality therapy are aware of their own beliefs and attitudes about their own culture and the cultures of their clients. Their application of the WDEP system is based on their knowledge of the particular group they are working with, and like any counselor, these practitioners need to be aware of their own biases as well as the strengths and cultural differences of the individual clients (Arrendondo et al., 1996).

EVALUATION

Overview

Although researchers continue to conduct studies validating the use of reality therapy, the widespread interest in the theory indicates that many practitioners have confidence in its efficacy. From 1975 to 2015, more than 8,500 persons worldwide completed the 18-month training program and were certified in reality therapy. Anecdotal evidence points toward the theory's usefulness with a wide variety of issues, such as eating disorders, child abuse, marriage, aging, elective mutism, career satisfaction, study habits, self-esteem, assertive behavior, and many others (N. Glasser, 1980, 1989; R.-I. Kim & Hwang, 2006; Olver, 2011).

Supporting Research

Practitioners of reality therapy represent virtually every helping profession: counselors, therapists, educators, managers, chemical dependency workers, corrections specialists, and many others. This overview of the research represents a sampling of some studies on reality therapy.

W. Glasser (1965) described the dramatic effect of a reality therapy program in a psychiatric hospital. The average stay in a ward of 210 men was 15 years. Within 2 years of the program, 75 men had been released, with only three returning. In a study of the effects of reality therapy in a rural elementary school, Bowers (1997) found improvements in relationships and self-concept but little change in school attendance. The author noted that school absenteeism was not a significant problem at this school.

Studying the effects of reality therapy in a therapeutic community in Ireland, Honeyman (1990) found significant changes in the residents' self-esteem, awareness of their inability to control their drinking, and insight into living in a more inner-controlled manner. Positive effects have also been shown when reality therapy has been used with teachers (Parish, 1988, 1991; Parish, Martin, & Khramtsova, 1992), undergraduate students (Peterson & Truscott, 1988), graduate students (Peterson, Chang, & Collins, 1997; Peterson, Woodward, & Kissko, 1991), foster parents (Corwin, 1987), negatively addicted inmates (Chance et al., 1990), and student athletes (Martin & Thompson, 1995). Y. S. Kim (2001) found a positive correlation between the use of group reality therapy with parents and self-esteem as well as parent–child relationships. Similarly, in a 1-year follow-up study of previous research, R.-I. Kim and Hwang (2001) found constant, positive, long-term effects on middle school students' sense of internal control.

In a study of the use of reality therapy among Malaysian mental health workers, Jusoh, Mahmud, and Mohd Ishak (2008) found reality therapy to be applicable in the Malaysian context when consideration is given to various beliefs and backgrounds of clients. "The eastern culture which emphasizes close relationships, authoritative orientation, large family structure, dependency on each other, loyal, collaborative, harmonious, emotional control, and conservatism is different from the individualistic western culture" (p. 11). The main adjustment lies in the process of self-evaluation that requires a balance between personal satisfaction and group harmony.

From 1986 through 2006, Professor Rose-Inza Kim, dean (retired) at Sogang University in Seoul, Korea, facilitated 250 studies. A meta-analysis of 43 studies (R.-I.

Kim & Hwang, 2006) addressing self-esteem and locus of control found that 28% of the members of experimental groups increased their self-esteem, whereas 23% of the members of control groups increased their self-esteem. The authors concluded that reality therapy group programs "are effective for improving self-esteem and internal locus of control" (p. 29). In 2015, Professor Kim stated that more than 500 studies have now been conducted in Korea on the effectiveness of reality therapy (personal correspondence). The first international conference of the William Glasser Institute International will be held in Seoul, Korea, in July 2016. More than 800 people from around the world are expected to attend (see Sidebar 12.5).

K.-H. Kim (2002) developed a responsible behavior choice program and tested it with 13 Korean elementary school children. Using a pretest–posttest design, she measured the effectiveness of eight sessions of group counseling in reality therapy. Compared with the control group, the experimental group showed a significant change in both locus of control and sense of personal responsibility. This research supports the effectiveness of short-term reality therapy. Adding further support to the use of brief reality therapy, Lawrence (2004) used reality therapy as a group counseling modality for persons with developmental disabilities. In six sessions, participants in the reality therapy experimental group showed significant changes in self-determination compared with the control group; their self-regulation, autonomy, psychological empowerment, and self-realization scores showed the impact of the short-term use of reality therapy. Application of choice theory/reality therapy resulted in significant increases in student achievement and student behavior and enhancement of the school as a place to work and learn. School improvement was exemplified by the decrease in student referrals to the Refocus Room by 59% in 1 year (McClung & Hoglund, 2013).

This brief selection of research studies illustrates the value of reality therapy as a reliable tool for counselors. However, many areas for possible study remain. Researchers could investigate further the effects of reality therapy on the areas already mentioned as well as on other issues dealt with by counselors.

Limitations

Reality therapy should be seen as an open system that will grow and change. It is not a narrow theory that is rigidly applied, yet as a freestanding cognitive behavior theory and practice of counseling and therapy, it has limitations. Some of these are inherent in the theory, and some reside in the skill of the practitioner.

Sidebar 12.5. Two Kinds of Research

For practicing counselors, there is scientific research and fire-in-the-belly research. Controlled studies and experimental research provide evidence that enhances counseling theory and methodology. Future research will add further credibility to reality therapy. Counselors gain a sense of personal confidence when they see the efficacy of reality therapy and when they observe clients changing behavior and living more productive lives. The obligation of professional counselors to justify their theoretical and practical orientation has become a cornerstone of care provided to the public. However, more convincing to counselors is their observation that clients, feeling oppressed by majority cultures, change their worldview from one of victimization to a sense of self-liberation and become masters of their choices.

Many clients believe that to make changes in their lives or to feel better, they need to gain insight into their past, resolve early conflicts, describe the negative aspects of their lives, or tell how they arrived at their present state. Many of these clients could be successfully encouraged to emphasize their present behavior, but some clients believe that no change can result without dealing specifically with past pain, and for them reality therapy will appear to avoid the real issues.

The concrete language of reality therapy may be another limitation. It contains little jargon or technical terminology, and the theory and practice use words like *belonging, power, fun, freedom, wants, plans, self-evaluation,* and *effective control.* Because the language of reality therapy is easily understood, it can appear to be easily implemented. Nevertheless, the effective use of reality therapy requires practice, supervision, and continuous learning.

Reality therapy is subject to the same criticisms that many counseling theories face. Because counseling theories and other psychological theories such as career development models are Euro-American in their origins, they are criticized as not applicable to non-Western individuals and ethnic minorities. This criticism is without substance. People from around the world study and use reality therapy. In fact, there are indigenous William Glasser Institute faculty on every continent except Antarctica. Still, as with any counseling system, the principles are applied differently in various cultures and adapted to the psychological and developmental levels presented by individuals.

Summary Chart: Reality Therapy/Choice Theory

Human Nature

Human beings, born with five basic needs, choose behaviors that are purposeful and designed to satisfy survival, belonging, power, freedom, and fun. The motivation originates from a here-and-now urge to satisfy one or more of these sources of behavior. The most important motivation is to establish relationships with other human beings.

Major Constructs

Emanating from the five basic motivators are specific wants or desires. When these are not fulfilled, people choose specific actions that are accompanied by cognition, feelings, and physiology. These four elements make up total human behavior. These behaviors are aimed at gaining input from the world around and are seen as choices. The input is called *perception.* People behave in order to have the perception that their wants are satisfied and their needs fulfilled. Human beings have control over only their own choices, not the behavior of others.

Goals

The goals of reality therapy are twofold: process goals and outcome goals. The reality therapist helps clients examine their own behavior, evaluate it, and make plans for change. The outcome is more satisfying relationships, increased happiness, and a sense of inner control over their lives. The plans are thus aimed at satisfying specific wants as well as the five motivators connected to their wants.

Change Process

Effective change occurs when clients feel connected to the counselor—that is, when there is a genuine therapeutic alliance. Experiencing an effective relationship with the counselor leads to change if the counselor is skilled in helping clients clarify their wants, evaluate their behavior, and make effective plans. Clients learn that no matter what difficulties they encounter, they always have choices.

Interventions

The WDEP formula summarizes the various interventions made by therapists. Therapists help clients identify and clarify their specific wants, including what they want from the counseling process. Therapists assist clients in describing each aspect of their total behavior and evaluating the attainability of their wants and the effectiveness of their actions. They then help clients formulate realistically do-able plans for fulfilling wants and satisfying needs.

Limitations

Reality therapy has been used with clients seeking help with decision making, facing developmental issues, dealing with crises, coerced into counseling, and with severe psychiatric diagnoses. The system is described in simple language that can lead to the misconception that the process is easy to implement. Another limitation is that reality therapy does not emphasize insight into problems. Consequently, clients seeking insight rather than change are less inclined to benefit from reality therapy.

THE CASE OF MARIA: A REALITY THERAPY APPROACH

In counseling Maria, the therapist or counselor may become enmeshed in her various and intense problems: a failed marriage, depression, out-of-control children, feelings of suicide, insecurity and distrust, work absences, expectations of family, lack of communication with parents, religious conflicts, no-exit nightmares, fear of sleeping, and losing weight. Although it is necessary to confront these daunting issues, the reality therapist can readily incorporate the Ericksonian principle: There is not a one-to-one correlation between the problem and the solution. As the counseling process develops, the therapist or counselor focuses on finding positive replacements for Maria's painful problems rather than encouraging endless heartrending discussions. This focus, however, does not exclude an effort to understand and empathize with her pain. In fact, the initial stage of relationship building could well include a thorough discussion of her feelings, her history, and her current worldview. In other words, the reality therapist establishes the relationship on the basis of Maria's current perceptions rather than on the therapist or counselor's perception of how Maria will eventually improve her need satisfaction (see Sidebar 12.6).

A skilled reality therapist establishes an empathic, ongoing, but time-limited relationship to help Maria especially satisfy her need for belonging with her chil-

Sidebar 12.6. A Cross-Cultural Application of Reality Therapy

Maya Angelou was fond of saying, "We are more alike than we are different." Applying reality therapy to Maria illustrates the universality of human nature. Problems, hurts, and disappointments characterize clients from virtually every culture. Consequently, reality therapy applies in ways that are similar but not identical for each person. You are invited to consider how reality therapy is universally applicable to clients who share the same needs and yet choose to satisfy them in diverse ways.

dren, family, and coworkers, resulting in an internal sense of control. A primary goal of such counseling or therapy is to help Maria abandon her negative symptoms and choose positive ones. Accomplishing this might involve systemic interventions, such as conferences with the school principal. The counselor would help Maria explore the impact of her religious commitments and how her spirituality can provide hope. The involvement of an understanding priest would possibly facilitate this process. Such efforts serve to make possible a viable support system.

Establishing the Environment

As in any counseling, a warm, caring relationship is the foundation for change. It is important to listen carefully to Maria, allowing her to tell her personal story and situation in her own words. Reflective listening and empathy are crucial at this stage. However, as the relationship progresses, the reality therapist does not listen passively but rather attempts to identify themes related to the procedures. For example, Maria's frustrations can be translated into wants. When she states that she feels lonely, the counselor can ask, "Would you like to have a meaningful relationship with a friend?" Because she is a verbal client, Maria will probably use metaphors to describe how she feels and other aspects of her current plight. Such metaphors might include, "I'm at the end of my rope," "I feel like I live in a dark woods," or "I feel like I'm sinking in quicksand; the more I struggle, the more I sink." These can be used later in the counseling to help her gain a sense of inner control.

In establishing the environment, the reality therapist intervenes directively and emphatically but does not encourage the venting of feelings in such a way as to indirectly communicate that merely talking will solve a problem. Feelings are always connected to actions. Such questions as "What did you do yesterday when you felt so depressed?" are very useful. The counselor also helps Maria describe problems in the past tense and solutions in the present or future tense. This results in addressing an immediate goal—communicating hope (i.e., Maria can improve her life and achieve some degree of happiness).

Following standard practice and ethical standards, the reality therapist assesses the seriousness of the suicidal ideation while eliciting from Maria the highest level of commitment (Level 5)—not to kill herself.

From the counselor's perspective, Maria is not hopeless. Rather, she is a strong and capable person characterized by determination and fortitude who has done her best to cope with offensive assaults from the world around her. After establishing a trusting atmosphere and communicating appreciation for both her plight and her possibilities, the counselor uses the WDEP system more explicitly.

Using the WDEP Procedures

The use of the WDEP system is not a step-by-step process. In fact, there is no absolute delineation between environment and procedures (see Figure 12.1). The counselor asks Maria what she wants to gain from the counseling process and what she wants to accomplish *today*—that is, what she wants to do differently when she leaves the counseling office (W). The reality therapist asks her, for instance, if she would like to seek a marriage annulment (W). If so, the referral to the appropriate priest could occur immediately. The counselor would ask her to evaluate (E) the impact of this choice on her relationship with her parents and how her return to the sacraments of the Church would satisfy her needs. Among the many explorations of her current behaviors (D), Maria describes her relationships in the context of how she talks to the people around her and how they talk to her (i.e., the use of tonics or toxins). She would be encouraged to evaluate the effectiveness (E) of three toxic behaviors: ABC—arguing, blaming, criticizing. Maria and the counselor would practice communication skills that replace what Glasser called *deadly habits.*

Ongoing assurances would accompany her descriptions of her wants, her current actions, and her evaluations. The counselor provides information, for instance, that Maria's nightmares are more than likely a temporary condition and that when she more effectively satisfies her five needs, especially her need for belonging, they will probably diminish. Examples of future plans for Maria might include developing friendships in her church, neighborhood, social groups, and so on. Strategies for satisfying her need for achievement or power could be exploring educational opportunities. Needs for freedom and fun could be met by developing an absorbing interest or hobby. Satisfying the needs for belonging and achievement would also be closely connected to satisfying the needs for freedom and fun.

This summary represents several interventions and goals of the counselor's work with Maria. Throughout the process, the reality therapist asks Maria how she feels *right now.* Maria will undoubtedly respond that she feels slightly better. The counselor emphasizes that even *talking* about solutions and taking initial positive steps is the road to symptom replacement. Rather than overcoming problems, Maria replaces them, leaves them behind, abandons them, and emerges from the quicksand. Before her lies the solid ground of a path bathed in the sunshine of effective choices.

It is clear that reality therapy deals with presenting problems, diagnostic issues, and embedded behaviors. However, the reality therapist believes that dealing with them is not always equivalent to analyzing them or engaging in repetitive introspective scrutiny. The path of ineffective behaviors with its external constraints and onslaughts is replaced by alternative choices.

Length of Treatment

Even though reality therapy began as a treatment modality for patients who needed long-term care in a hospital and a correctional institution, it has been more frequently applied in community agencies, schools, and addictions programs. In the past, it was sometimes viewed and criticized as merely a short-term method of counseling. At the present time its short-term process constitutes a strength. Maria's treatment and that of most clients is brief. The goal of reality therapy and the standard practice of counseling in general is improvement rather than cure. I would expect Maria's counseling to be terminated in eight to 12 sessions. Moreover, realistically the counseling relationship lasts as long as managed care allows, and so it is incumbent on the reality therapist to make each session action focused. As quickly as possible, the reality therapy counselor helps clients formulate plans related to their five needs: survival or physiological needs, involvement with other people, achievement or power, freedom or a variety of choices, and fun or enjoyment activities. The outcome is that clients live a more productive life with a map for success and require fewer mental health services.

REFERENCES

American Counseling Association. (2014). *ACA code of ethics.* Alexandria, VA: Author.

American Psychiatric Association. (2013). *Diagnostic and statistical manual of mental disorders* (5th ed.). Arlington, VA: Author.

Arredondo, P., Toporek, R., Brown, S., Jones, J., Locke, D. C., Sanchez, J., & Stadler, H. (1996). Operationalization of the Multicultural Counseling Competencies. *Journal of Multicultural Counseling and Development, 24,* 42–78.

Becvar, D., & Becvar, R. (2006). *Family therapy: A systemic integration.* New York, NY: Allyn & Bacon.

Bowers, E. (1997). The effects of CT/RT quality school programming on attendance, academic performance, student self-concept, and relationships in a rural elementary school. *Journal of Reality Therapy, 16*(2), 21–30.

Bratter, B., Bratter, T., Maxym, C., Radda, H., & Steiner, K. (1993). The John Dewey Academy: A residential quality school for self-destructive adolescents who have superior intellectual and intuitive potential. *Journal of Reality Therapy, 12*(2), 42–53.

Bratter, T., Esparat, D., Kaufman, A., & Sinsheimer, L. (2008). Confrontational psychotherapy: A compassionate and potent psychotherapeutic orientation for gifted adolescents who are self-destructive and engage in dangerous behavior. *International Journal of Reality Therapy, 27*(2), 13–25.

Britzman, M. (2009). *Pursuing the good life.* Brandon, SD: Unlimited.

Casstevens, W. (2013). Health and wellness at a clubhouse model program in North Carolina: A choice theory-based approach to program development and implementation. *International Journal of Choice Theory and Reality Therapy, 32*(2), 48–53.

Chance, E., Bibens, R., Cowley, J., Prouretedal, M., Dolese, P., & Virtue, D. (1990). Lifeline: A drug/alcohol treatment program for negatively addicted inmates. *Journal of Reality Therapy, 9*(2), 33–38.

Corwin, N. (1987). Social agency practice based on reality therapy/control theory. *Journal of Reality Therapy, 7*(1), 26–35.

Dowd, E., & Milne, C. (1986). Paradoxical interventions in counseling psychology. *Counseling Psychologist, 14,* 237–282.

Fay, A. (1978). *Making things better by making them worse.* New York, NY: Hawthorne.

Ford, E. (1979). *Permanent love.* Minneapolis, MN: Winston.

Glasser, C. (1996a). *My quality world workbook.* Chatsworth, CA: William Glasser Institute.

Glasser, C. (1996b). *The quality world activity set.* Chatsworth, CA: William Glasser Institute.

Glasser, N. (Ed.). (1980). *What are you doing?* New York, NY: Harper & Row.

Glasser, N. (Ed.). (1989). *Control theory in the practice of reality therapy.* New York, NY: Harper & Row.

Glasser, W. (1965). *Reality therapy.* New York, NY: Harper & Row.

Glasser, W. (1968). *Schools without failure.* New York, NY: Harper & Row.

Glasser, W. (1972). *The identity society.* New York, NY: Harper & Row.

Glasser, W. (1980a). Reality therapy. In N. Glasser (Ed.), *What are you doing?* (pp. 48–60). New York, NY: Harper & Row.

Glasser, W. (1980b). *Stations of the mind.* New York, NY: Harper & Row.

Glasser, W. (1984). *Control theory.* New York, NY: Harper & Row.

Glasser, W. (1998). *Choice theory.* New York, NY: HarperCollins.

Glasser, W. (2001). *Fibromyalgia: Hope from a completely new perspective.* Chatsworth, CA: William Glasser Institute.

Glasser, W. (2003). *Warning: Psychiatry can be hazardous to your mental health.* New York, NY: HarperCollins.

Glasser, W. (2005). *Treating mental health as a public health issue.* Chatsworth, CA: William Glasser Institute.

Glasser, W. (2011). *Take charge of your life.* Bloomington, IN: iUniverse.

Glasser, W., & Glasser, C. (2008, Summer). Procedures: The cornerstone of institute training. *The William Glasser Institute Newsletter,* p. 1.

Herlihy, B., & Corey, G. (2015). *ACA ethical standards casebook* (7th ed.). Alexandria VA: American Counseling Association.

Honeyman, A. (1990). Perceptual changes in addicts as a consequence of reality therapy based on group treatment. *Journal of Reality Therapy, 9*(2), 53–59.

Ivey, A., D'Andrea, M., Bradford Ivey, M., & Simek-Morgan, L. (2002). *Theories of counseling and psychotherapy: A multicultural approach.* New York, NY: Allyn & Bacon.

Jusoh, A. J., & Ahmad, R. (2009). The practice of reality therapy from the Islamic perspective in Malaysia and variety of custom in Asia. *International Journal of Reality Therapy, 28*(2), 3–8.

Jusoh, A. J., Mahmud, Z., & Mohd Ishak, N. (2008). The patterns of reality therapy usage among Malaysian counselors. *International Journal of Reality Therapy, 28*(1), 5–14.

Kim, K.-H. (2002). The effect of a reality therapy program on the responsibility for elementary school children in Korea. *International Journal of Reality Therapy, 22*(1), 30–33.

Kim, R.-I., & Hwang, M. (2001). The effects of internal control and achievement motivation in group counseling based on reality therapy. *International Journal of Reality Therapy, 20*(2), 12–15.

Kim, R.-I., & Hwang, M. (2006). A meta-analysis of reality therapy and choice theory group programs for self-esteem and locus of control in Korea. *International Journal of Choice Theory, 1*(1), 25–30.

Kim, Y. S. (2001). The development and effects of a reality therapy parent group counseling program. *International Journal of Reality Therapy, 20*(2), 4–7.

Kopp, R. (1995). *Metaphor therapy.* New York, NY: Brunner/Mazel.

Lawrence, D. (2004). The effects of reality therapy group counseling on the self-determination of persons with developmental disabilities. *International Journal of Reality Therapy, 23*(2), 9–15.

Lojk, L. (1986). My experiences using reality therapy. *Journal of Reality Therapy, 5*(2), 28–35.

Martin, S., & Thompson, D. (1995). Reality therapy and goal attainment scaling: A program for freshmen student athletes. *Journal of Reality Therapy, 14*(2), 45–54.

McClung, C., & Hoglund, R. (2013). A Glasser quality school leads to choosing excellence. *International Journal of Choice Theory and Reality Therapy, 32*(2), 54–64.

Olver, K. (2011). *Secrets of happy couples.* Chicago, IL: InsideOut Press.

Parish, T. (1988). Helping teachers take more effective control. *Journal of Reality Therapy, 8*(1), 41–43.

Parish, T. (1991). Helping students take control via an interactive voice communications system. *Journal of Reality Therapy, 11*(1), 38–40.
Parish, T., Martin, P., & Khramtsova, I. (1992). Enhancing convergence between our real world and ideal selves. *Journal of Reality Therapy, 11*(2), 37–40.
Petersen, S. (2005). Reality therapy and individual or Adlerian psychology: A comparison. *International Journal of Reality Therapy, 24*(2), 11–14.
Peterson, A., Chang, C., & Collins, P. (1997). The effects of reality therapy on locus of control among students in Asian universities. *Journal of Reality Therapy, 16*(2), 80–87.
Peterson, A., & Truscott, J. (1988). Pete's pathogram: Quantifying the genetic needs. *Journal of Reality Therapy, 8*(1), 22–32.
Peterson, A., Woodward, G., & Kissko, R. (1991). A comparison of basic week students and introduction to counseling graduate students on four basic need factors. *Journal of Reality Therapy, 9*(1), 31–37.
Powers, W. (1973). *Behavior: The control of perception.* New York, NY: Aldine.
Powers, W. (2009). *Living control systems III.* Bloomfield, NJ: Benchmark.
Remley, T., & Herlihy, B. (2010). *Ethical, legal, and professional issues in counseling* (3rd ed.). Upper Saddle River, NJ: Merrill.
Richardson, B., & Wubbolding, R. (2001). Five interrelated challenges for using reality therapy with challenging students. *International Journal of Reality Therapy, 20*(2), 35–39.
Seligman, L. (2004). *Diagnosis and treatment planning in counseling* (3rd ed.). New York, NY: Kluwer Academic.
Seltzer, L. (1986). *Paradoxical strategies in psychotherapy.* New York, NY: Wiley.
State of Ohio. (2009). *Ohio counselor, social worker and marriage and family therapist board laws and rules* (Chap. 4757, Rev. code). Columbus, OH: Author.
Weeks, G., & L'Abate, L. (1982). *Paradoxical psychotherapy.* New York, NY: Brunner/Mazel.
Wiener, N. (1948). *Cybernetics.* New York, NY: Wiley.
Wiener, N. (1950). *The human use of human beings: Cybernetics and society.* Boston, MA: Houghton Mifflin.
Wubbolding, R. (1980). Teenage loneliness. In N. Glasser (Ed.), *What are you doing?* (pp. 120–129). New York, NY: Harper & Row.
Wubbolding, R. (1984). Using paradox in reality therapy: Part I. *Journal of Reality Therapy, 4*(1), 3–9.
Wubbolding, R. (1986). Professional ethics: Informed consent and professional disclosure in reality therapy. *Journal of Reality Therapy, 6*(1), 30–35.
Wubbolding, R. (1988). *Using reality therapy.* New York, NY: Harper & Row.
Wubbolding, R. (1989). Radio station WDEP and other metaphors used in teaching reality therapy. *Journal of Reality Therapy, 8*(2), 74–79.
Wubbolding, R. (1990). Evaluation: The cornerstone in the practice of reality therapy. *Omar Psychological Series, 1*(2), 6–27.
Wubbolding, R. (1991). *Understanding reality therapy.* New York, NY: HarperCollins.
Wubbolding, R. (1993). Reality therapy. In T. Kratochwill (Ed.), *Handbook of psychotherapy with children* (pp. 288–319). Boston, MA: Allyn & Bacon.
Wubbolding, R. (1994). The early years of control theory: Forerunners Marcus Aurelius and Norbert Wiener. *Journal of Reality Therapy, 13*(2), 51–54.
Wubbolding, R. (2000). *Reality therapy for the 21st century.* Philadelphia, PA: Brunner Routledge.

Wubbolding, R. (2005). The power of belonging. *International Journal of Reality Therapy, 24*(2), 43–44.

Wubbolding, R. (2008a). More searching for mental health. *International Journal of Choice Theory, 2*(1), 6–9.

Wubbolding, R. (2008b). Reality therapy. In J. Frew & M. Spiegler (Eds.), *Contemporary psychotherapies for a diverse world* (pp. 360–396). Boston, MA: Houghton Mifflin.

Wubbolding, R. (2011). *Reality therapy: Theories of psychotherapy series.* Washington, DC: American Psychological Association.

Wubbolding, R. (2014). Reality therapy. In G. Vandenbos, E. Meidenbauer, & J. Frank-McNeil (Eds.), *Psychotherapy theories and techniques* (pp. 307–316). Washington, DC: American Psychological Association.

Wubbolding, R. (2015a). Reality therapy and school practice. In R. Witte & G. S. Mosley-Howard (Eds.), *Mental health practice in today's schools* (pp. 169–192). New York, NY: Springer.

Wubbolding, R. (2015b). *Reality therapy training manual* (16th rev.). Cincinnati, OH: Center for Reality Therapy.

Wubbolding, R. (2016). Reality therapy. In H. E. A. Tinsley, S. H. Lease, & N. S. G. Wiersma (Eds.), *Contemporary theory and practice in counseling and psychotherapy* (pp. 173–200). Thousand Oaks CA: Sage.

Wubbolding, R., & Brickell, J. (1998). Qualities of a reality therapist. *International Journal of Reality Therapy, 17*(2), 47–49.

Wubbolding, R., & Brickell, J. (2001). *A set of directions for putting and keeping yourself together.* Minneapolis, MN: Educational Media.

Wubbolding, R., & Brickell, J. (2005). Reality therapy in recovery. In *Directions in addiction treatment and prevention* (Vol. 9, Lesson 1, pp. 1–10). New York, NY: Hatherleigh.

Wubbolding, R., & Brickell, J. (2009). Perception: The orphaned component of choice theory. *International Journal of Reality Therapy, 28*(2), 50–54.

Wubbolding, R., & Brickell, J. (2015). *Counselling with reality therapy* (2nd ed.). Brackley, England: Speechmark.

Wubbolding, R., Brickell, J., Imhof, L., Kim, R.-I., Lojk, L., & Al-Rashidi, B. (2004). Reality therapy: A global perspective. *International Journal for the Advancement of Counselling, 26,* 219–228.

Chapter 13

Family Theory

Cass Dykeman

BACKGROUND

Why a Chapter on Family Theory?

Up to this point, the chapters in this book have focused on counseling and psychotherapy with individuals. Why care about the application of counseling to families? After all, the fathers and mothers of counseling did not seem to care about applying their ideas to whole families. In this chapter, I present reasons why you should care about the familial applications of counseling and psychotherapy. In addition, I define key terms, detail prominent theories, and discuss practical applications of these theories (see Sidebar 13.1).

So why should you care about family therapy? The following questions suggest possible reasons: What would family therapy theories add to your clinical reasoning? What would family therapy techniques add to your clinical tool bag? At the end of this chapter, I hope you can list many answers for both questions. Right now, let us start with the assertion that family therapy can enlarge the scope of your clinical reasoning and practice. Specifically, it can enlarge your scope from individuals to families and the larger sociocultural contexts that make up an individual's environment. Family therapy can help you look at the patterns of communication and relationship that connect people to one another and to their social and physical environments.

The scope of this chapter is counseling modalities whose prime focus is the family as a system (i.e., conjoint, strategic, structural, and transgenerational modalities). In the past decade, many individual counseling modalities have been successfully extended to a family setting (e.g., behavioral, cognitive, narrative, and solution-focused modalities). The theory and pragmatics of these modalities are addressed in the other chapters of this book.

Sidebar 13.1. Self-Awareness: Where Does Family Therapy Fit in Your Professional Skill Portfolio?

Write a brief paragraph about where you would like to be in 5 years as a professional counselor. Then answer the following questions:

1. To what extent do family therapy skills play a role in your professional goals?
2. Why did you choose this particular extent?
3. What role did your family-of-origin experience play in this choice?

Definitions

In elementary school education, there is a principle that in Grades 1 through 3, a child learns to read, and in Grades 4 through 6, a child reads to learn. In other words, literacy must precede the acquisition of ideas and their application. This principle is especially true when it comes to learning about family therapy. Family therapists have a maddening habit of both coining new terms and using common terms in unique ways. This habit can sometimes leave neophytes to family therapy in a daze. So to enhance your understanding of the theoretical and applied discussions in this chapter, I present the following family therapy terms:

- *Dyad:* This term denotes a two-person system (McGoldrick & Carter, 2001).
- *Family boundaries:* This term denotes the explicit and implicit rules within a family system that govern how family members are expected to relate to one another and to non-family members (Barker, 2003).
- *Family homeostasis:* This term is used to describe a family system's tendency to maintain predictable interactional processes. When such processes are operating, the family system is said to be in equilibrium (Sauber, L'Abate, Weeks, & Buchanan, 1993).
- *Family system:* A family system is a social system built by the repeated interaction of family members. These interactions establish patterns of how, when, and to whom family members relate (Sauber et al., 1993).
- *Family therapists:* Family therapy is practiced either as a specialty within a profession (e.g., counseling, clinical psychology) or as a stand-alone profession (e.g., marriage and family therapy). Persons who practice family therapy usually possess at least a master's degree.
- *Family therapy:* This is an umbrella term for therapeutic approaches for which the whole family is the unit of treatment. This term is theoretically neutral, as one can conduct family therapy using a variety of frameworks (Reber, 2002).
- *Family:* This term applies to two or more people who consider themselves family. These persons generally share a common residence and assume the obligations, functions, and responsibilities generally essential to healthy family life, such as economic support (Barker, 2003).
- *Triangulation:* This term describes the process of a third person or thing being added to a dyad to divert anxiety away from the relationship of the twosome (McGoldrick & Carter, 2001). See Sidebar 13.2 for a brief case example demonstrating triangulation.

The goal of this section was to add some new terms to your professional vocabulary. Now let us take a closer look at some major family theories and their clinical applications.

Sidebar 13.2. Case Study: Triangulation

Sara is a sixth-grade student at North Mercer Middle School. She is part of an intact family of five. Her sister Eve is an eighth grader at the same school. Eve has a very caustic and aggressive personality and finds herself in trouble at school with frequent detention. Although equally caustic and aggressive at home, Eve is rarely in trouble in the family setting because her parents, Donna and Joe, are unwilling to confront her behavior. Because Donna and Joe are concerned about Eve getting kicked out of school, they privately quiz Sara every evening about Eve's school behavior. Sara has reported to her school counselor her worry about Eve and the pressure she feels to make sure her sister does not get kicked out of school.

HUMAN NATURE: A DEVELOPMENTAL PERSPECTIVE

As with individual development, a family system can be seen as a developmental process that evolves over time. Developmental models of family life include the family life cycle and the family genogram.

The Family Life Cycle

Jay Haley (1993) offered the first detailed description of a family life cycle. He identified six developmental stages stretching from courtship to old age. Haley was interested in understanding the strengths families have and the challenges they face as they move through the life cycle. He hypothesized that symptoms and dysfunctions appeared when there was a dislocation or disruption in the anticipated natural unfolding of the life cycle: "The symptom is a signal that a family has difficulty in getting past a stage in the life cycle" (p. 42).

Over time, tension inevitably emerges in families because of the developmental changes they encounter (Smith & Schwebel, 1995). Family stress is most intense at those points when family members must negotiate a transition to the next stage of the family life cycle (Carter, Preto, & McGoldrick, 2016). On one level, this stress may be viewed as part of the family's response to the challenges and changes of life in its passage through time—for example, a couple may encounter tension while making the transition to parenthood with the birth of their first child. On another level, pressures may emerge from the multigenerational legacies that define the family's attitudes, taboos, expectations, labels, and loaded issues—for example, over several generations, a rule that men cannot be trusted to handle the money may impose stress when the female is absent. When stress occurs on both levels, the whole family may experience acute crisis.

Family therapists can find it difficult to determine the exact sources of stress on a family. Papp and Imber-Black (1996) presented an interesting vignette describing the power of illuminating a wide spectrum of stressors for a family. In this vignette, Papp and Imber-Black connected what was viewed as the developmental struggle between a mother and an adolescent son to a three-generation theme of footsteps. In this case, the adolescent's grades had plummeted, and he was both depressed and argumentative. Furthermore, he had engaged in some stealing activity. On the surface, these behaviors can be understood as either symptomatic of family life with an adolescent or symptomatic of life after the creation of a blended family. However, by teasing out a specific theme, Papp and Imber-Black discovered that the family's fears emerged as a story about the son following in the footsteps—in particular, the footsteps of a drug-dealing father and a larcenous grandfather. The therapists skillfully challenged three generations of the family to tell the family myth about their men who had chosen the wrong path. Sorting out the current stressors on the family through the lens of the family scripts encouraged the adolescent to leave behind the old stories to develop his own story. The process also helped his mother to realize how these historic scripts hid her son from her. This multigenerational storytelling intervention worked to free the young man from a catastrophic prophecy while bringing all members of the family into better communication (see Sidebar 13.3).

The Family Genogram

Genograms give family therapists another useful way to conceptualize family development. Typically, genograms are used to chart the progression of a particular family through the life cycle over at least three generations. They are like a family tree that includes information about birth order, family members, family members' communications, and issues of relationships. The work of Monica McGoldrick provides an excellent resource for clinicians unfamiliar with the use of genograms (see McGoldrick, Gerson, & Petry, 2008). Genograms often provide the basis for clinical hypotheses in family work and offer a culturally sensitive method for understanding individual or family clients. For example, Magnuson, Norem, and Skinner (1995) recommended mapping the relationship dynamics in the families of gay or lesbian clients. They pointed out the importance of mapping the relationship markers of gay or lesbian couples that are not recognized by general society. Gibson (2005) provided excellent guidance on the effective use of genograms in school counseling settings. A number of researchers have described the effective use of a genogram intervention with families of color (Lim & Nakamoto, 2008; McDowell, 2015b). The utility of genograms and eco-maps is such that they are increasingly being used in fields beyond family therapy, such as nursing, social work, and family medicine (Duhamel, Dupuis, Turcotte, Martinez, & Goudreau, 2015; Malan, Cooke, & Mash, 2015; Werner-Lin, 2015). A genogram is included as an organizing element in the case study presented later in this chapter.

MAJOR CONSTRUCTS

The present family systems theories emerged out of the ideas and debates in the social and physical sciences after World War II. First, I address two key theoretical antecedents to the major theories. Then, I describe each of the four major theories.

Sidebar 13.3. Self-Awareness: Your Place in the Family Life Cycle and Countertransference

First consider the following two questions:

1. What is the current family life cycle stage of your family of origin?
2. What is the present family life cycle stage of your present nuclear family?

Then consider the following question concerning both family states: What countertransferential reactions are possible when treating a family in a similar stage?

Theoretical Antecedents

Bateson

Gregory Bateson is acknowledged by many as the pioneer in applying cybernetic systems thinking to human interaction (Imber-Black, 2004). He saw that cybernetics provided a powerful alternative language for explaining behavior—specifically, a language that did not resort to instinct or descriptions of the internal workings of the mind (Segal, 1991). G. Bateson (1951) began to use these ideas to understand social interaction. For instance, he applied cybernetic principles to the study of families of schizophrenics (Haley, 1976). Bateson considered pattern, process, and communication as the fundamental elements of description and explanation. He believed that, by observing human systems, he could formulate the rules governing human interaction.

The Palo Alto Group

In 1952, while based in Palo Alto, California, Bateson received a grant from the Rockefeller Foundation to investigate the general nature of communication. He was joined on this project by Jay Haley, John Weakland, William Fry, and Don D. Jackson. This research team defined the family as a cybernetic, *homeostatic* system whose parts (i.e., family members) covary with one another to maintain equilibrium by means of error-activated negative feedback loops (Jackson, 1957). For example, whenever deviation-amplifying information is introduced (e.g., an argument between two family members or the challenge of a new stage in the family life cycle), a designated family member initiates a counterdeviation action (e.g., the family member exhibits symptomatic behavior) so that the family's existing equilibrium is restored (i.e., threatened changes are defeated). The emphasis on homeostasis prevailed in family therapy theory into the 1980s.

The recognition of the *symptomatic double bind* as a homeostatic maneuver regulating family patterns of relationship is considered the definitive contribution of the Palo Alto Group. The symptomatic double bind most often cited is Bateson's classic example of the interaction between a mother and her son who had "fairly well recovered from an acute schizophrenic episode" (G. Bateson, Jackson, Haley, & Weakland, 1956, pp. 258–259). Bateson described this interaction as follows:

> [The son] was glad to see her and impulsively put his arm around her shoulders, whereupon she stiffened. He withdrew his arm and she asked, "Don't you love me any more?" He then blushed, and she said, "Dear, you must not be so easily embarrassed and afraid of your feelings." The patient was able to stay with her only a few minutes more, and following her departure, he assaulted an aide and was put in the tubs. (G. Bateson et al., 1956, p. 259)

The Palo Alto Group noted both the incongruence of the mother's message and the fact that the son could not clearly and directly comment on it. They concluded that the son's craziness was his commentary on his mother's contradictory behavior. Bateson's work in the 1950s spawned the development of many family therapy models, including the strategic model of Haley (1991) and Madanes (1991). An examination of this model follows my discussion of the ideas of another Palo Altoan—Virginia Satir.

Major Theories

Conjoint Theory

Virginia Satir is among the best loved of all theorists in the field of family therapy—and, arguably, beyond. After leaving a career as a schoolteacher, she first practiced as a psychiatric social worker, then engaged in private practice work with families. In 1959, she joined the Mental Research Institute in Palo Alto. Satir gained international recognition with the publication of her first book, *Conjoint Family Therapy* (Satir, 1964/1983).

Satir acknowledged the impact of a diverse group of theorists on her life's work (Satir & Bitter, 1991). These included Fritz Perls (Gestalt therapy), Eric Berne (transactional analysis), J. J. Moreno (psychodrama), Ida Rolf (life-posturing reintegration), Alex Lowen (bioenergetics), and Milton Erickson (hypnosis). Her family therapy model reflects a growth perspective rather than a medical model for assessing and working with families. In her frame, illness is seen as an appropriate communicative response to a dysfunctional system or family context. Health, therefore, is developed when the system is changed so as to permit healthy communication and responses.

Like other communication theorists, such as Bateson, Satir defined *congruence* as the use of words that accurately match personal feelings. In other words, congruence is when direct communication and the meta-communication are the same. When using congruent communication, the person is alert, balanced, and responsive to any question or topic without needing to hold back. In contrast, *incongruence* is seen as communication wherein the nonverbal and verbal components do not match. Examples of incongruent communication include double messages, assumptions, ambiguous messages, and incomplete communication. Satir saw self-esteem as the basis for family emotional health. Her perspective was that there is a correlation between self-esteem and communication. Low self-esteem is associated with poor communication because low self-esteem affects behavior and interactions among the members of the system. She also held that maladaptive communication can be both learned and unlearned.

To demonstrate concretely to a family how incongruence occurs and is a source of pain and poor self-esteem, Satir would ask the family members to join in a game. The communication game would typically be used to work with two members. She observed that when a person delivers an incongruent or mixed message, there is little skin or eye contact. It is as though the sender is out of touch with the other person. In the communication game, Satir taught families to improve their communication through a series of interactions that concretely show people what happens when they do not look, touch, or speak congruently. Satir (1983) outlined these six steps as follows: (a) Two persons sit back to back and talk, (b) they turn around and "eyeball" each other without touching or talking, (c) they eyeball and touch without talking, (d) they are asked to touch with eyes closed and without talking, (e) they eyeball each other without touching, and (f) the two talk and touch and eyeball and try to argue with each other. By the last stage of the game, the couple usually finds it impossible to argue. The problem of delivering an incongruent message is clear to the family when one is touching, talking, and looking at the listener.

Besides the humor of this process, the provocative nature of this game encourages a deeper examination of the ways in which family members suffer and feel inadequate or devalued when engaged in incongruent communication patterns. These revelations are supported through steps toward increasing self-esteem and communication as the family moves from a closed to a more open system. Satir believed that a functional family is an *open system,* wherein there is a clear exchange of information and resources both within the system and with others outside the family. In contrast, a *closed system* is rigid and maladaptive.

Satir observed that family pain is symptomatic of dysfunction. She did not feel that the problems the family brought to her were the real difficulty. Rather, she saw that methods of coping within the family and rules for behavior that were fixed, arbitrary, and inconsistent decreased the family's ability to cope over time. Her approach involves the following five treatment stages: (a) Establish trust, (b) develop awareness through experience, (c) create new understanding of members and dynamics, (d) have family members express and apply their new understandings with one another, and (e) have family members use their new behaviors outside therapy. As the family members move through this cycle of change, they feel less anxious and more fully valued and valuing of one another (Satir & Bitter, 1991). In this way, self-esteem, communication, and caring are increased and pain is decreased.

Strategic Theory

Jay Haley left Palo Alto in 1966 and joined Salvador Minuchin in Philadelphia to pursue his growing interest in family hierarchy, power, and structure. In 1974, he established the Washington Institute of Family Therapy, where Cloe Madanes joined him. Their family therapy model has three roots: the strategic therapy of Milton Erickson, the theories of the Palo Alto Group, and the structural therapy of Minuchin.

Haley (1991) and Madanes (1981) asserted that a family's current problematic relational patterns were at some point useful because they organized family members in a concerted way to solve an existing problem. These patterns persisted because they protected the family from the threat of disintegration. Haley held that therapeutic change occurs when a family's dysfunctional protective patterns are interrupted. He noted that the role of family therapists, through the use of directives, is to provoke such interruptions. Haley offered therapist provocations such as the following: (a) A husband and wife with sexual problems may be required to have sexual relations only on the living room floor for a period of time. This task changes the context and so the struggle. (b) A man who is afraid to apply for a job may be asked to go for a job interview at a place where he would not take the job if he got it, thereby practicing in a safe way. For Haley (1990), therapist directives served three purposes: to facilitate change and make things happen; to keep the therapist's influence alive during the week; and to stimulate family reactions that give the therapist more information about family structure, rules, and system. Haley held that the goal of therapy was not client insight—in fact, the family need not understand the actual mechanisms of change. Furthermore, the therapist should act without trying to convince the family that the set of hypotheses guiding the therapy is valid. Haley (1990) commented, "The goal is not to teach the family about their malfunctioning system but to change the family sequences so that the presenting problems are resolved" (p. 135).

Haley's ideas have direct consequences for the family therapist wanting to practice a strategic approach. First, a strategic family therapist attends to what is defined by the family members experiencing the problem as the nature of the problem. Second, the therapist focuses on how the family is responding in attempting to resolve the problem. The assumption here is that it is often the very ways in which families are defining a problem and responding to it that may keep it going in a vicious problem–solution cycle (see Sidebar 13.4).

Structural Theory

Structural family therapists do not sit on the sidelines during therapy. Rather, they become involved with family members, pushing and being pushed. Minuchin put a strong emphasis on action in his own work as a family therapist. His justification for this emphasis was his belief that "if both I and the family take risks within the constraints of the therapeutic system, we will find alternatives for change" (Minuchin & Fishman, 1981, p. 7). He commented that observers of his structural family therapy work would notice (a) his concern with bringing the family transactions into the room, (b) his alternation between participation and observation as a way of unbalancing the system by supporting one family member against another, and (c) his many types of response to family members' intrusion into one another's psychological space (Minuchin & Fishman, 1981).

Minuchin's therapeutic maneuvers were based on his theoretical schema about family structure and family transformation. He carried out his vision by being uniquely himself. He stated,

Sidebar 13.4. Case Study: Changing the Problematic Interaction Patterns in a Client Family

First read pages 7–9 (Section 1.2.2) in the following Campbell collaboration full-text online protocol: www.campbellcollaboration.org/lib/project/209/ (Lindstrøm, Rasmussen, Kowalski, Filges, & Jørgensen, 2012).

You recently took into treatment the Garcia family. This intact nuclear family is composed of Tomás (age 40), Cathy (age 38), Sammi (age 16), and Nikki (age 14). The girls are a junior and freshman at Blaisdale High School in Claremont, California. Tomás is a gastroenterologist, and Cathy is a tax attorney. Sammi is a star athlete. She is an all-state second home lacrosse player who has drawn the scholarship interest of schools such as Stanford, Georgetown, and Virginia. Tomás and Cathy's lifelong nickname for Sammi has been "Star." Sammi has an outgoing and confident personality and gains friends and admirers of all ages with ease. Nikki is a quiet, shy girl who is a social isolate. Her main passion is reading. In fact, the family nickname for her is "Bookworm." Both students do well academically. Most of the family's activities focus on the out-of-town trips for Sammi's club lacrosse matches. The event that precipitated the Garcias coming into treatment was Sammi's second suspension from her high school lacrosse team. This time, the suspension was for intentionally slashing her lacrosse stick across a defender's left knee. This vicious slash broke the defender's patella. In the family intake interview, Sammi reported that she was simply trying to move the defender out of the way before she shot. Both Tomás and Cathy vigorously defended their daughter and raged at the injustice put on Sammi by the local league. During the intake interview, you watched the interaction between Sammi and Nikki. Nikki said nothing without a prompt from you and seemed afraid of Sammi. To check Sammi's unbridled aggressive behaviors, what might you do as a counselor to build a stronger parental position within the family's relational matrix?

> In families that are too close, I artificially create boundaries between members by gestures, body postures, movement of chairs, or seating changes. My challenging maneuvers frequently include a supportive statement: a kick and a stroke are delivered simultaneously. My metaphors are concrete: "You are sometimes sixteen and sometimes four"; "Your father stole your voice"; "You have two left hands and ten thumbs." I ask a child and a parent to stand and see who is taller, or I compare the combined weight of the parents with the child's weight. I rarely remain in my chair for a whole session. I move closer when I want intimacy, kneel to reduce my size with children, or spring to my feet when I want to challenge or show indignation. These operations occur spontaneously; they represent my psychological fingerprint. (Minuchin & Fishman, 1981, p. 7)

For Minuchin, family therapy techniques were uniquely integrated in the person of the counselor or therapist, who goes "beyond technique" to wisdom, specifically, wisdom concerning "knowledge of the larger interactive system—that system which, if disturbed, is likely to generate exponential curves of change" (M. C. Bateson, 1972, p. 439).

The work of José Szapocznik represents an updated manualized approach to structural family therapy (Szapocznik, Zarate, Duff, & Muir, 2013). Like Minuchin, Szapocznik's focus is on modifying maladaptive "patterns of interaction in the family influence the behavior of each family member" (Szapocznik, Hervis, & Schwartz, 2003, p. 1). More about the Szapocznik approach is addressed in "Evaluation".

Transgenerational Theory

Murray Bowen's (1978) approach to family therapy, like Haley's, had many roots. Specifically, Bowen merged concepts such as Sigmund Freud's unconscious id and Charles Darwin's theory of evolution with his own observations of schizophrenics at the Menninger Clinic and the National Institute of Mental Health. His core idea was the concept of the *differentiation* of self. It was through this concept that Bowen addressed "how people differ from one another in terms of their sensitivity to one another and their varying abilities to preserve a degree of autonomy in the face of pressures for togetherness" (Papero, 1990, p. 45).

Bowen also posited that there are two different systems of human functioning: an emotional and reactive system that humans share with lower forms of life and an intellectual and rational system that is a more recent evolutionary development. The degree to which these two systems are fused or undifferentiated is the degree to which the individual is vulnerable to the impulses of his or her emotional system and less attentive to his or her intellectual and rational system. For example, people are more likely to react emotionally rather than rationally when they are anxious. Bowen asserted that the extent to which persons have differentiated their thinking system from their emotional system will determine how able they are to maintain a sense of self in relationships with others, particularly members of their family.

Bowen believed that emotional illness was passed from one generation to another through the *family projection process.* Family projection process theory suggests that the ego differentiation achieved by children will generally approximate that of their parents. However, the family projection process often distributes the capacity for differentiation unevenly among family members. For example, one child may grow up with a high level of ego differentiation, whereas a sibling may grow up with a low level of differentiation. The hallmark of a high level of differentiation is a well-defined sense of self and low emotional reactivity, whereas a low level is characterized by a poorly defined sense of self and high emotional reactivity.

Low levels of ego differentiation occur when parents triangulate a child into their conflicts to dissipate the stresses of their relationship. Bowen (1978) held that triangles were the natural consequence of two poorly differentiated people who were overwhelmed by anxiety and seeking relief by involving a third party. Triangulation is how parents' low level of differentiation is passed on to the next generation. Recently, Klever (2005) presented empirical evidence supporting Bowen's theory of multigenerational transmission family unit functioning.

Bowen's work has influenced many present family therapy theorists. One of the best examples of the extension of Bowen's ideas is McGoldrick et al.'s (2008) work on genograms. This work was discussed earlier in the chapter.

The major constructs discussed in this section were developed by clinicians to understand how families function. As we have seen, family theorists conceptualized the communication patterns, structures, and relationship dynamics of their client families. The concepts they developed reflected their own therapeutic interventions. In this way, family theory is a rich resource for students and family practitioners.

APPLICATIONS

Overview

All counseling and psychotherapy approaches share a common goal of producing change in clients. In this section, I differentiate family therapy applications from the applications of the individualist approaches you have read about in the previous chapters. My goal is to help you find ways to add systems-level interventions to both your clinical reasoning and your counseling or therapy tool bag.

Goals of Counseling and Psychotherapy

Family therapy represented a watershed in the history of counseling or therapy. Before family therapy, the focus of counselors or therapists had been solely on the individual. The goal of counseling or therapy was always to change some cognitive, affective, or behavioral component of an individual. In contrast, family therapists aim to change systems within which individuals reside (Becvar & Becvar, 2013).

The Process of Change

Family therapists use cybernetics to understand change—specifically, the cybernetic control processes involving information and feedback. Information in the form of feedback precipitates shifts that either amplify or counteract the direction of change. Family therapists differentiate between *first-order change* and *second-order change.* Lyddon (1990) succinctly defined these different types of change as follows:

> First-order change is essentially "change without change"—or any change within a system that does not produce a change in the structure of the system. In contrast, second-order change is "change of change"—a type of change whose occurrence alters the fundamental structure of the system. (p. 122)

At any given moment, counselors or psychotherapists can only bring about one or the other type of change in their clients. Now, let us look at these change types more closely.

First-Order Change

First-order change occurs when a family modifies problem behaviors yet maintains its present structure. An example of a first-order change intervention is a family therapist instructing parents when they can fight with their son over bedtime. Through this intervention, the family therapist hopes to give the family relief from its problem behavior; radical change of the present family system is not a goal. Family therapists call the process of bringing about this type of change *negative feedback.*

Second-Order Change

In contrast to first-order change, *second-order change* refers to transformations in either the structure or the internal order of a system. Family therapists often seek to generate or amplify change processes that will alter the basic structure of a family system (Nichols, 2012). This goal embodies second-order change. An example of a second-order change intervention is a family therapist directing the more passive parent to take over bedtime compliance responsibility with the goal of changing the power dynamics in the marital dyad. Family therapists call the process of bringing about second-order change *positive feedback.*

Traditional Intervention Strategies

The case study for this chapter illustrates in detail one approach to family therapy. Besides the strategies presented in the case study, there are two additional points on family therapy applications to which I would like to draw your attention. The first is an understanding of the significance of nonspecific factors in family therapy outcomes. The second is how to structure the first session so that family therapy can get off to a good start.

Specific Versus Nonspecific Factors

A strong current trend in individual-focused counseling or therapy research is an examination of the specific and nonspecific factors involved in treatment outcomes. *Specific factors* are those counseling or therapy activities that are specific to a particular approach—for example, a strategic family therapist's use of a proscribing-the-symptom intervention. *Nonspecific factors* are those change-producing elements present in counseling or therapy regardless of theoretical orientation. Many nonspecific factors have been proposed, but few have withstood empirical testing. One exception is the working alliance. In fact, working alliance scores are the best known predictor of counseling or therapy outcomes (Horvath, 1994).

The modern transtheoretical definition of *working alliance* was promulgated by Edward Bordin (1994), who posited that there were three components of a working alliance: task, goal, and bond. He conceptualized these three components as follows:

1. *Task* refers to the in-therapy activities that form the substance of the therapeutic process. In a well-functioning relationship, both parties must perceive these tasks as relevant and effective. Furthermore, each must accept the responsibility to perform these acts.

2. *Goal* refers to the counselor or therapist and the client mutually endorsing and valuing the aims (outcomes) that are the target of the intervention.
3. *Bond* embraces the complex network of positive personal attachments between client and counselor or therapist, including issues such as mutual trust, acceptance, and confidence. (Horvath, 1994)

Overall, Bordin's working alliance model emphasized "the role of the client's collaboration with the therapist against the common foe of the client's pain and self-defeating behavior" (Horvath, 1994, p. 110).

Family therapy practitioners and educators have been slower to integrate nonspecific factors into treatment (Karam, Blow, Sprenkle, & Davis, 2015). There have been exceptions to this general torpor. One is William Pinsof of the Family Institute (Evanston, Illinois). In his research, Pinsof (1994) found a positive relationship between the working alliance and family therapy outcomes. Another exception has been J. Scott Fraser of Wright State University. His research team has produced a series of studies demonstrating the efficacy of a manualized approach that integrates nonspecific factors (Lee et al., 2015).

Given the effectiveness of the working alliance concerning treatment outcomes, persons practicing family therapy would be wise to attend carefully to such alliances. However, such attention would run counter to the preeminence family therapists give to technique. Coady (1992) noted that the emphasis in family systems theory on homeostasis has led to family therapists viewing family members as being dominated by the family system. He stated that family therapists "often expect families to exert an oppositional force against change efforts, and they feel compelled to manipulate the family into change" (p. 471). Unfortunately, such a perspective runs exactly counter to the formation of strong working alliances. I want to be careful to note that committing to building strong working alliances with your client families does not mean that you have to dismiss technique. Rather, it means acknowledging that techniques should not be separated from the interpersonal and cultural contexts in which they occur (Coady, 1992).

The Family Interview

From the start, Haley (1991) advocated brevity and clarity in counseling or therapy work with families. He stated, "If therapy is to end properly, it must begin properly—by negotiating a solvable problem and discovering the social situation that makes the problem necessary" (p. 8). To help family therapists start on a good note, Haley outlined a structured family interview for use during an initial session. The five stages of this structured family interview are as follows:

1. *Social:* The interviewer greets the family and helps family members feel comfortable.
2. *Problem:* The interviewer invites each person present to define the problem.
3. *Interaction:* The interviewer directs all members present to talk together about the problem while the interviewer watches and listens.
4. *Goal setting:* Family members are invited to speak about what changes everyone—including the problem person—wants from the therapy.
5. *Ending:* Directives (if any) are given and the next appointment is scheduled.

The information gained from the first interview helps the family therapist form hypotheses about the function of the problem within its relational context. Moreover, this information can help the family therapist generate directives to influence change. For Haley, "the first obligation of a therapist is to change the presenting problem offered. If that is not accomplished, the therapy is a failure" (p. 135).

Brief Intervention Strategies and Current Practices

No subfield in counseling can stand still and remain relevant. Family therapy is no exception. In the past decade, a number of factors have spurred innovation in family therapy. These factors include (a) the changing demographics of the nation, (b) the drive for greater health care cost containment, (c) increased knowledge concerning the active ingredients of counseling interventions, and (d) innovation in counseling research techniques. The end result of these factors has been brief manualized versions of integrative family therapy. Before I discuss these versions, the descriptor *integrative* needs definition. There exist a number of high-quality psychotherapy outcome studies that have pitted different approaches against one another (e.g., the National Institute of Mental Health's Comparative Depression Study, the National Institute on Alcohol Abuse and Alcoholism's Project MATCH). A consistent finding of these studies is that manualized versions of different psychotherapeutic approaches produce equivalent outcomes. Thus, psychotherapy research and practice has transitioned from a competitive era to an integrative era (Nuttall, 2008).

Prominent theorists in family therapy have developed and manualized integrated family therapy models. These models include J. Scott Fraser's *integrative family and systems treatment*, William Pinsof's *integrative problem-centered therapy*, and José Szapocznik's *brief strategic family therapy* (BSFT). All have been extensively researched. Szapocznik's manualized integration of systemic and structural modalities may be the most important going forward, given the extensive efficacy research done on this approach with clients of color.

Clients With Serious Mental Health Issues

Family therapy has been found to be applicable to persons with many of the mental disorders contained in the *Diagnostic and Statistical Manual of Mental Disorders* (American Psychiatric Association, 2013; Seligman, 2004). Multiple reviews have pointed to evidence that family therapy is more effective than therapy that does not involve a family member in treating the following issues: adolescent conduct disorders, adolescent suicidality, adult alcoholism and drug abuse, adult schizophrenia, aggression and noncompliance in attention-deficit/hyperactivity disorder, anorexia in young adolescent females, bulimia in young adolescent females, child and adolescent anxiety, childhood autism, childhood conduct disorders, childhood sexual abuse trauma, childhood sleep problems, dementia, depression in adults with chronic illnesses, obsessive-compulsive disorder, and poorly controlled asthma.

Overall, most counselors are likely to be more effective if they include relevant, available, and appropriate family members in treatment (Carr, 2014a, 2014b; Pinsof & Wynne, 2000). However, there exists little empirical guidance on the types of clients that counselors should *exclude* from family treatment (Johnson &

Thomas, 1999). Anecdotal evidence reported in the professional literature suggests excluding family members who possess one or more of the following characteristics: (a) a psychopathic personality, (b) a status as a perpetrator of abuse, (c) a psychosocial disorder incompatible with functional interpersonal communication, or (d) a chronological age inappropriate for the topic being discussed (Johnson & Thomas, 1999; Kokkvoll, Grimsgaard, Ødegaard, Flægstad, & Njølstad, 2013; Lund, Zimmerman, & Haddock, 2002; Prata, 2013).

EVALUATION

Overview

The emergence of managed care has radically altered the delivery of mental health services. Those who pay for treatment are increasingly demanding proof of efficacy. This demand for efficacy has extended to those professionals practicing family therapy (F. W. Kaslow, 2000). In this section, I review what is known about (a) supporting research and (b) limitations.

Supporting Research

Empirical research has not historically been a strong component of family therapy (Gladding, 2014). Lebow and Gurman (1995) noted,

> At one time, most research on couples and families was conducted with little or no connection to the outstanding clinical developments in the field. Alternative modes of investigation such as inductive reasoning, clinical observation, and deconstruction have dominated in the development of methods and treatment models. Some couple and family therapists have even been reluctant to acknowledge that empirical research has an important role. (p. 29)

Fortunately, this reluctance was overcome, and solid research evidence for the efficacy of family therapy for treating a dizzying array of issues now exists (Carr, 2014a, 2014b; Vilaça, & Relvas, 2014)—evidence that professionals practicing family therapy can use to defend their work in the world of managed care.

Based on the findings of Pinsof and Wynne (2000) and their strong recommendation regarding the inclusion of relevant and appropriate family members in effective treatment, it would seem obvious that counselors or therapists would rapidly adapt to this process. The truth, however, is that professional counselors or therapists have been slow to adopt this practice in their work. In fact, the latest study of the practice patterns of *family* therapists revealed that approximately half of therapists' client load was *individuals* (Doherty & Simmons, 1996).

Research on treatment outcome predictors is useful to family therapy practitioners. Unfortunately, little credible research has been conducted in the area. Two notable exceptions are efforts by Hampson and Beavers (1996) and by the Szapocznik research team (Horigian & Szapocznik, 2015).

Hampson and Beavers (1996) studied family and therapist characteristics in relation to treatment success. Their subjects were 434 families treated at an actual family therapy clinic in Dallas, Texas. Hampson and Beavers reported the following four predictors of successful treatment: (a) number of family therapy sessions attended, (b) third-party ratings of family competence, (c) self-ratings of family competence, and (d) therapists' ratings of the working alliance. Hampson and Beavers's measure of family competence included items on family affect, parental coalitions, problem-solving abilities, autonomy and individuality, optimistic versus pessimistic views, and acceptance of family members. The two reported that the six-session mark was the breakpoint in increasing the probability of good results. However, a sizable subset of families did well with fewer than six sessions. What distinguished this subset of families were their strong self-ratings of competence. Hampson and Beavers were careful to note that family size, family income, family structure (e.g., blended), family ethnicity, and counselor or therapist gender did not predict outcome.

In a related vein, José Szapocznik and his research team saw initial treatment engagement as critical to good outcomes in family therapy. They stated,

> The first step in BSFT then is to establish a therapeutic alliance with each family member and with the family as a whole. Challenging how the family functions prematurely, particularly challenging a powerful member in the family, can damage the therapeutic relationship with negative consequences such as one member's or the whole family's dropout, resistance to change, challenge to therapist's leadership, and lack of involvement in the therapeutic process. Indeed, research has shown that failure to maintain a balanced alliance with all family members can lead to early treatment dropout. (Briones, Robbins, & Szapocznik, 2008, p. 91)

Szapocznik et al. backed up their assertions about the importance of engagement with interesting research findings. In one study, they found that "93% of families that received the BSFT engagement were successfully engaged into treatment compared to 42% of families that received Engagement as Usual" (p. 87). They also reported that BSFT engagement led to dramatically better treatment retention (77%) than "Engagement as Usual" (25%; see Sidebar 13.5).

Sidebar 13.5. Case Study: Colluding With Repetitive Patterns of Maladaptive Interaction When Engaging Families in Treatment

First read pages 43–49 in the following family treatment manual: http://archives.drugabuse.gov/pdf/Manual5.pdf (Szapocznik et al., 2003).

Mr. John Jones works as counselor at the Smith County Mental Health Center in rural Oregon. The local school refers a Hmong family (the Xiongs) to him because of repeated discipline problems and suspected drug abuse by Fuechy Xiong (age 15). Mr. Jones calls Mrs. Xiong seeking to set up a time for a BSFT appointment, given the efficacy of this approach with substance-abusing youth of color. Mrs. Xiong says that she is happy to bring herself and Fuechy in for treatment, but that there is no way Fuechy's three older siblings or father will attend. Worried about Fuechy's behavior and substance abuse, Mr. Jones agrees to this structure. After seven sessions with Fuechy and Mrs. Xiong, no progress has been made. Thus, Mr. Jones comes to you for peer consultation. Given your understanding of the engagement principles of BSFT, what would you recommend to your colleague about what to do to get this family treatment on track?

Family is a culturally determined phenomenon. For example,

> the dominant American definition, reflecting white Anglo Saxon Protestant (WASP) values, focuses on the intact nuclear family unit. African Americans' definition of family refers to a wide network of kin and community. For many Italian Americans, family implies a strong, tightly knit three-or-four generation unit including godparents and old friends. The traditional Chinese definition of family includes ancestors and decedents. (N. J. Kaslow, Celano, & Dreelin, 1995, p. 622)

Thus, an effective family therapist must possess a high degree of cultural competence with diverse populations (McDowell, 2004). Otherwise, marginalization and colonization enter into and poison the family therapy process (McDowell, 2015a).

In a review of the literature on cultural competence and family interventions, Celano and Kaslow (2000) found family therapy to be the treatment of choice for culturally diverse clients. They noted that family therapists can be efficacious and culturally competent only when they do the following:

1. Recognize the effects of their own culture(s) on the therapy
2. Acknowledge that family therapies, theories, and techniques reflect the culture in which they were developed
3. Attend to the dynamic interplay of the cultural influences that affect the individual's and family's functioning
4. Devise and implement problem resolution strategies that are culturally acceptable (p. 217)

In another review, Falicov (2009) noted that there is wide conceptual and empirical support for the use of family therapy with Latinos if appropriate cultural adaptations are instituted. Beitin and Allen (2005) demonstrated the efficacy of a family systems approach with Arab American couples facing life in the post-9/11 world.

Limitations

One of the basic ethical principles in health care is the principle of nonmaleficence—that is, above all, do no harm. To carry out this ethical principle, you must make yourself aware of the limitations of each counseling or therapy approach contained in this book. To that end, I now present two important limitations of family therapy approaches.

First, the early language chosen for describing family systems was "combative and bellicose, often suggesting willful opposition: double bind, identified patient, family scapegoat, binder, victim, and so on" (Nichols, 1987, pp. 18–19). The choice of language emphasized the destructive power of families and contributed to an assault on the family by several pioneers in family therapy (Cooper, 1970). This assault has continued to the present because many family therapy educators and practitioners have overread this language and adopted a directive, manipulative approach to treatment. This overreading has led to unfortunate consequences. For instance, Green and Herget (1991) discovered that, at their family therapy clinic, many families found "paradoxical prescriptions as signs of therapist sarcasm or incompetence, that engender massive resistance, sometimes destroying all together the clients' faith and cooperative attitude in therapy" (p. 323). Also, Patterson and Forgatch (1985) uncovered, in their study of families in treatment, a direct relationship between client resistance and frequency of counselor or therapist directives.

Second, family therapists have ignored the different socialization processes operating for men and women. Thus, family therapists have not adequately considered how these socialization processes have disadvantaged women (Friedlander, Wildman, Heatherington, & Skowron, 1994). Walters, Carter, Papp, and Silverstein (1988) called for family therapists to review all family therapy concepts through the lens of gender socialization to eliminate the dominance of male assumptions. Their hope was that such a review would promote the "recognition of the basic principle that no intervention is gender-free and that every intervention will have a different and special meaning for each sex" (p. 29).

Summary Chart: Family Theory

Human Nature

Like models used to explain individual development across the life span, the creation and maintenance of a family system can be viewed as a developmental process that evolves over time. Developmental models of family life include the family life cycle, the family life spiral, and the family genogram.

Major Constructs

There are a variety of constructs associated with family theory, and each theory contributes discrete concepts. Conjoint theory, strategic theory, structural theory, and transgenerational theory were reviewed in this chapter as points of departure for some of the major constructs connected with counseling and psychotherapy with families.

Goals

The goals of individual counseling or therapy are usually aimed at changing cognitive, affective, or behavioral components of the individual. In contrast, family counselors and psychotherapists aim to change whole systems.

Change Process

For family theorists, change occurs as a result of shifting the interpersonal matrices that make up a family toward more functional processes.

Interventions

Strategies and interventions associated with systemic change in families are varied; many were first introduced in the context of a specific family theory. Because systemic change can be difficult to precipitate, family therapists must be well schooled and supervised in the application of interventions. In addition, practitioners must be able to set boundaries and limits with families and be powerful and strategic in their choices and development of treatment plans.

Limitations

The choice of language connected with family therapy often emphasizes the destructive power of families and contributes to an assault on the family. At times, practitioners forget that the proper use of interventions always involves consideration of cross-cultural variations that may limit applicability. Often, practitioners have ignored the different socialization processes operating for men and women and how these processes have disadvantaged women.

THE CASE OF MARIA: A FAMILY THERAPY APPROACH

The culture-specific interventions described in this case study were used, given the results of an ethnocultural assessment (i.e., acculturation level, socioeconomic status, educational status, spirituality, race and ethnicity) of this particular client family (Evans, Coon, & Crogan, 2007; Falicov, 2009; Ibrahim & Dykeman, 2011; Interian, Allen, Gara, & Escobar, 2008). Application of the interventions detailed in this case study, independent of such an assessment, would represent both a technical and an ethical error.

Background

Presenting Problem

Britney (age 8) was suspended by Roosevelt Elementary School for stealing money from her classmates. Britney was suspended along with two other classmates, both of whom had a long history of discipline problems despite their young age. This suspension was Britney's first. After the suspension, Roosevelt's school counselor, Jim Chen, held a conference with Britney's mother, Maria Jones (age 32). He reported to Maria that Britney had recently committed many disciplinary infractions—something they had not seen before in Britney. Maria acknowledged that she was having problems at home with both Britney and Mark Jr., Britney's brother. Mr. Chen noted that the kindergarten teacher was concerned that Mark Jr. (age 6) always seemed sullen and uncooperative.

In talking with Maria, Mr. Chen sensed that she was feeling overwhelmed with her children's behaviors. He asked whether she had considered counseling to gain support with these behaviors. Maria said that she had in fact consulted her physician and that this doctor had given her a referral to a respected child psychiatrist located downtown. However, Maria reported that she had not followed up on this referral because of the cost and downtown location. Also, she commented that her Catholic faith was very important to her and she was unsure whether a psychiatrist would respect her religious beliefs. Mr. Chen suggested to Maria that an alternative existed. He reminded her that because Maria was a school district employee, she could take advantage of the services offered by the school district's employee assistance program. Mr. Chen said that currently the employee assistance program allowed six counseling sessions per year per family member at no cost. Also, he noted that Catholic Social Services was one of the contracted providers. Maria went home and immediately called the Catholic Social Services office at her local parish, St. Gregory's. She scheduled an appointment for herself, Britney, and Mark Jr. for the next Tuesday.

Therapists

Mrs. Mesa and Sr. Benedict were the cotherapists assigned to work with Maria and her family. They were both staff therapists with the Tucson (Arizona) diocese's Catholic Social Services. Mrs. Mesa possessed a national certification in family therapy. Sr. Benedict held a national certification as an art therapist and had worked extensively with Latino families.

Family Demographics and History

Maria and her children lived in the Flowing Wells suburb of Tucson. Maria's former husband, Mark Jones (age 33), was a contract civil engineer working in Saudi Arabia. Maria and Mark had been divorced for 3 years. Maria worked as a middle school math and science teacher. Also living in Tucson were Maria's parents, Jose Flores (age 52) and Rosa Flores (age 51), and Mark's parents, Rob Jones (age 58) and Susan Jones (age 55). Both sets of grandparents interacted periodically with Maria and her children, but these relationships were very strained. Besides these grandparents, all of Maria's siblings lived in the Tucson metropolitan area. These were Juan (age 31), Enrique (age 29), Ernesto (age 28), and Bonita (age 25). Maria's relationships with her siblings were filled with tension. Especially painful to Maria was Bonita's refusal to talk to her. In contrast to the present, Maria and Bonita were close as children.

Maria's marriage outside her Catholic faith caused intense familial discord. This discord exposed subtle tensions and power alliances that existed in the Flores family. Only Ernesto attended Maria's wedding. Bonita blamed all current interpersonal conflicts in the Flores family on Maria and her "disloyalty" to the family. Following the lead of Maria's father, the Flores family maintained a strong covert adherence to a rule of not directly addressing personal problems such as family conflict (i.e., a no-talk rule). The one exception to this rule was the sacrament of confession with the parish priest. Besides this exception, the Flores family viewed the airing of personal problems as a sign of weakness, despite the Latino cultural approbation of *desahogo* (i.e., getting things off one's chest; Interian et al., 2008). Maria's genogram appears in Figure 13.1.

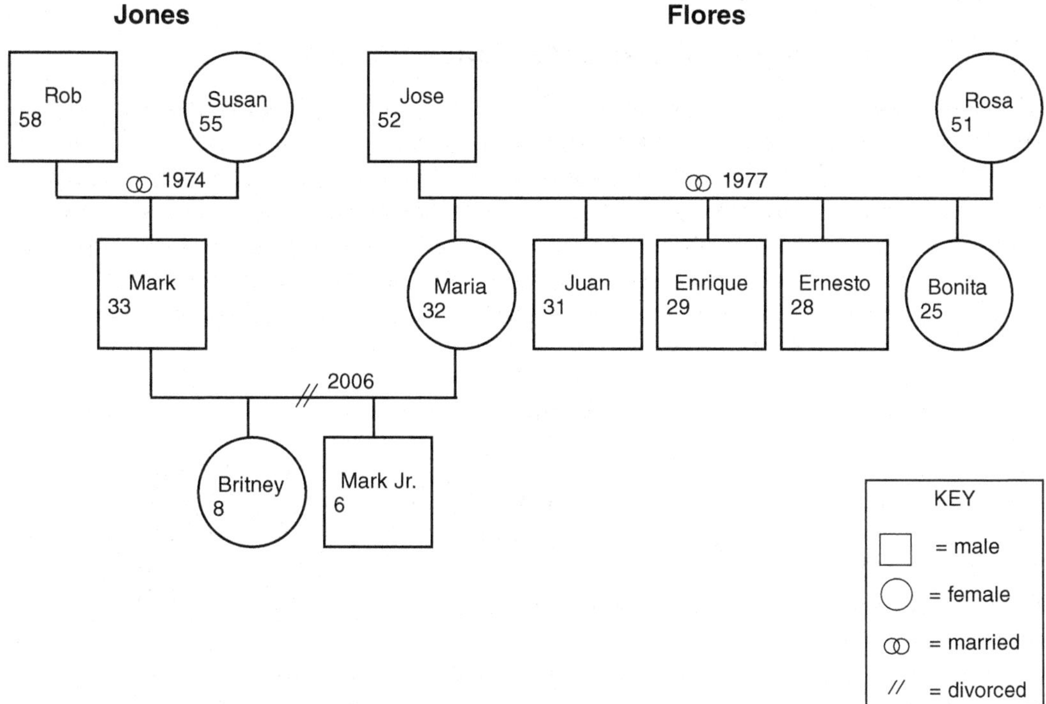

Figure 13.1. Maria's Genogram

Family Therapy Process: Opening Phase

Intake Session: Structure

Maria arrived 15 minutes early for her appointment and brought Britney and Mark Jr. as planned. Mark Jr. sucked his thumb during the interview. Britney was also quiet and appeared to believe that she was being punished. In the intake interview, Maria spoke of her financial fears, frustrations with parenting, and sense of alienation from her parish and family. The interview was scheduled for a longer period than is typically allotted for Euro-American client families. This additional time allowed the therapists to enact the cultural value of *personalismo* (i.e., a warm, empathetic social orientation), which can enhance treatment engagement (Evans et al., 2007; Falicov, 2009). To promote *personalismo*, the therapists took additional time to engage in *la platica* (i.e., small talk) with the family members at the start of each session (Interian & Diaz-Martinez, 2007).

Intake Session: Interview

Rather than initiate the therapeutic process with a long series of probing questions, Mrs. Mesa and Sr. Benedict decided to lead off with art making. They started the art-making process by introducing the material with a warmup drawing (i.e., individual free drawing). The second and third drawings focused specifically on the problems and resolutions identified by each family member. The assignments given for each of the tasks were as follows: (a) "Make an individual free drawing of anything that comes to mind," (b) "Make an individual drawing of why you think you are here," (c) "Make an individual drawing of how you would like the 'problem' to change," and (d) "At this time we will review the drawings you have made." Through these tasks and a few supplemental questions, Mrs. Mesa and Sr. Benedict were able to build the clinical background needed for effective case conceptualization and treatment planning.

Family Therapy Process: Case Conceptualization

Mrs. Mesa and Sr. Benedict diagnosed Maria as suffering from persistent depressive disorder (*Diagnostic and Statistical Manual of Mental Disorders, Fifth Edition*, 300.4; American Psychiatric Association, 2013). The therapists conceptualized this disorder as a posttraumatic symptom. The specific traumas in Maria's case were (a) the psychological and physical battering from Mark, (b) her family's rejection of her because of her out-of-faith marriage and subsequent divorce, and (c) her misperception that she could not fully participate in the sacramental life of her parish because she was divorced.

Family Therapy Process: Treatment Planning

The therapists felt that Britney's and Mark Jr.'s acting out was a symptom of the children's vicarious traumatization. This traumatization took place and was maintained by living in a family system with a parent who herself was a trauma victim. Mrs. Mesa and Sr. Benedict believed that if they could adequately address Maria's traumas, they could remediate the family structures that maintained Britney and Mark Jr.'s problematic behaviors.

To address Maria's alienation from her family of origin, the two therapists proposed that Maria bring her parents and siblings to the next session. Maria groaned and stated that she doubted whether they would all come because, "we don't talk about problems in the family." Sr. Benedict proposed that she call each family member and invite him or her to come to the next session. Maria thought that they might consider an invitation from Sr. Benedict, and she eagerly gave her permission. Sr. Benedict did call the family members, and after some persuading they all agreed to come. Mrs. Flores's sister agreed to babysit Britney and Mark Jr. during the sessions.

Trauma survivors such as Maria pose intense challenges for family therapists (Balcom, 1996). Unfortunately, most trauma treatment techniques are oriented toward individual or group work. However, art has been shown to be effective with both family dysfunctions and trauma resolution (Appleton, 1993; Dykeman, Nelson, & Appleton, 1995; Sobol, 1982). Haley (1990) held that metaphor was a basic means of family communication, and Sobol (1982) drew on this idea in designing her family therapy interventions. She chose art because its inherent metaphorical qualities can facilitate productive family communication—specifically, by permitting family members to express and represent problems in a less destructive way than with words or action.

Mrs. Mesa and Sr. Benedict decided that they would ask the members of the Flores family to participate in a series of drawing tasks and then use the information obtained through the art products to set goals and plan directives. They felt that art tasks could help restructure the Flores family system—specifically, by reconnecting family members via culturally powerful symbols. As in narrative therapy approaches, the metaphor that would emerge from the Flores family's art processes helped family members to rediscover their deep interconnectedness to one another (i.e., *familismo*).

Family Therapy Process

Session 1: Goal

The first session involved building a working relationship with the members of the Flores family and engaging them in a series of art tasks to help them begin to express themselves. The family members involved in the session included Jose, Rosa, Maria, Juan, Enrique, Ernesto, and Bonita.

Session 1: Method—Combining Strategic Family Therapy With Art

Both Mrs. Mesa and Sr. Benedict were worried about the Flores family's covert no-talk rule. The no-talk rule was the Flores family's particular operationalization of the Latino values of *respeto* (i.e., respect), *simpatia* (i.e., likeability) and *jeraquismo* (i.e., hierarchical social structure; Evans et al., 2007).

Sr. Benedict designed a series of five tasks to help the family members begin to express themselves. These tasks were as follows: (a) "Make an individual free drawing of anything that comes to mind," (b) "Make an individual drawing of why you think you are here," (c) "Make an individual drawing of how you would like the 'problem' to change," (d) "Now together, make a joint mural about your family," and (e) "At this time we will review the drawings you have made." He often used this series of tasks with families like Maria's that maintained structure by covert communication norms. The use of such tasks allowed him to do the following without running directly counter to *respeto, simpatia,* and *jeraquismo*: (a) elicit metaphorical information for planning future intervention, (b) provide drawing tasks that disrupt dysfunctional family communication patterns (e.g., a family's covert no-talk rule), and (c) help family members express themselves free of covert familial communication norms (Sobol, 1982). Given the tension present in the family system, each member of the Flores family welcomed Sr. Benedict's initial suggestion that they start out by working on their own drawing. The therapists had a wide array of drawing materials available for the family members to use, including oil and chalk pastels and felt-tip markers.

Session 1: Free Drawing Art Task

Maria's free drawing was a weeping, pregnant image of the Virgin. In high school, Maria and Bonita were members of their parish's Legion of Mary. They enjoyed belonging to this group because of a strong devotion to Our Lady rooted in Latino cultures (i.e., *Marianismo*). After 20 minutes, Mrs. Mesa had the family members stop their drawings and share them with the whole family. Maria showed her drawing of the Virgin. The family was moved to tears by Maria's expressive representation of the Virgin. Without words, they surrounded Maria. Bonita even took Maria by the hand. Sr. Benedict read these nonverbal behaviors as a sign that the family had moved to some new level of communication, a new level that contained acknowledgment of, and empathy for, Maria's suffering. To concretize this new connection to Maria, Sr. Benedict directed the other family members to add to Maria's drawing through the production of a joint mural.

Session 1: Family Mural Art Task

After the mural was completed, Mrs. Mesa asked each family member to discuss the feelings the mural evoked about the family. At this point, Britney asked her mom why her drawing of Our Lady was weeping. Maria hesitated and then began to sob quietly. Through the art task sequence, the family was moved from a distant to a closer physical proximity. At the end of the family art process, the therapists reviewed all of the drawings with the family.

When Rosa asked Maria why she drew a weeping Virgin Mary, Maria replied that the Virgin weeps for Maria because the Virgin understands the sorrow of pregnant, unmarried women. Then Maria walked over and knelt in front of her mother and began to weep uncontrollably herself. Rosa looked at her and softly said, "This is why you married Mark and left the family." Maria nodded yes, and Rosa kissed her on the forehead in reconciliation (see Sidebar 13.6).

Sessions 2–5: Goal

The next four sessions involved rebuilding family connectedness and trying on new styles of communication.

Sidebar 13.6. Self-Awareness: Organized Religion

In the case of Maria, organized religion plays a prominent role, as it does in many client families. Thus, consider the following questions:

1. What role did organized religion play in your experience of your family of origin?
2. What role does organized religion play in your experience of your present nuclear family?

Given your answers to these questions, what countertransferential reactions are possible when treating a family in which organized religion plays a prominent role?

Sessions 2–5: Methods

Again, Sr. Benedict used art tasks to facilitate culturally salient modes of communication. Despite this work, Maria's full reentry to her familial life remained blocked by her belief that as a divorced woman, she could not participate in the sacramental life of her parish. This left Maria feeling marginalized in the Flores family. Sr. Benedict corrected Maria's mistaken notion that divorced persons could not receive Communion. He also set up an appointment for Maria with a member of her own religious order who did marriage tribunal work. This sister would help Maria to receive a marriage annulment so that she would become free to remarry in the Church.

During one of these middle sessions, the art tasks served as a potent stimulus for self-discovery. Maria's chalk pastel drawing recounted her strong devotion to the Blessed Sacrament during her high school years. Maria shared how this devotion had helped her weather the typical turmoil of adolescence. Mrs. Mesa helped Maria negotiate with her parents to babysit Britney and Mark Jr. three times a week so she could spend an hour meditating in the Perpetual Adoration Chapel at St. Gregory's. Later, Maria reported to Mrs. Mesa that these hours were meaningful to her and gave her a sense of peace she had not felt in a long time.

Session 6: Termination

As Maria began to reenter full family and parish life, her dysthymia lifted and she began to have more energy for her work and her children. By the final session of family therapy, Maria reported that neither Britney nor Mark Jr. was having any disciplinary problems in school. Also, Maria's increased energy had begun to help her build a productive relationship with Rob and Susan Jones. Mrs. Mesa and Sr. Benedict worked with Maria to help her outline the boundaries she wanted to set in her relationship with the Joneses.

REFERENCES

American Psychiatric Association. (2013). *Diagnostic and statistical manual of mental disorders* (5th ed.). Arlington, VA: Author.

Appleton, V. (1993). An art therapy protocol for the medical trauma setting. *Art Therapy, 10,* 71–77. doi:10.1080/07421656.1993.10758985

Balcom, D. (1996). The interpersonal dynamics and treatment of dual trauma couples. *Journal of Marital and Family Therapy, 22,* 431–442. doi:10.1111/j.1752-0606.1996.tb00218.x

Barker, R. L. (2003). *The social work dictionary.* Washington, DC: National Association of Social Workers.

Bateson, G. (1951). The convergence of science and psychiatry. In J. Ruesch & G. Bateson (Eds.), *Communication: The social matrix of psychiatry* (pp. 257–272). New York, NY: Norton.

Bateson, G., Jackson, D. D., Haley, J., & Weakland, J. (1956). Toward a theory of schizophrenia. *Systems Research & Behavioral Science, 1,* 251–264. doi:10.1002/bs.3830010402

Bateson, M. C. (1972). *Our own metaphor.* New York, NY: Knopf.

Becvar, D. S., & Becvar, R. J. (2013). *Family therapy: A systemic integration.* Boston, MA: Allyn & Bacon.

Beitin, B. K., & Allen, K. R. (2005). Resilience in Arab American couples after September 11, 2001: A systems perspective. *Journal of Marital and Family Therapy, 31,* 251–267. doi:10.1111/j.1752-0606.2005.tb01567.x

Bordin, E. S. (1994). Theory and research on the therapeutic working alliance: New directions. In A. O. Horvath & L. S. Greenberg (Eds.), *The working alliance* (pp. 13–37). New York, NY: Wiley.

Bowen, M. (1978). *Family therapy in clinical practice.* New York, NY: Jason Aronson.

Briones, E., Robbins, M., & Szapocznik, J. (2008). Brief strategic family therapy: Engagement and treatment. *Alcoholism Treatment Quarterly, 26,* 81–103. doi:10.1300/J020v26n01_05

Carr, A. (2014a). The evidence base for couple therapy, family therapy and systemic interventions for adult-focused problems. *Journal of Family Therapy, 36*(2), 158–194. doi:10.1111/1467-6427.12033

Carr, A. (2014b). The evidence base for family therapy and systemic interventions for child-focused problems. *Journal of Family Therapy, 36*(2), 107–157. doi:10.1111/1467-6427.12032

Carter, B., Preto, N. A. G., & McGoldrick, M. (Eds.) (2016). Overview: The life cycle in its changing context: Individual, family and social perspectives. In *The expanding family life cycle: Individual, family, and social perspectives* (pp. 1–26). New York, NY: Pearson.

Celano, M. P., & Kaslow, N. J. (2000). Culturally competent family interventions: Review and case illustrations. *American Journal of Family Therapy, 28,* 217–228. doi:10.1080/01926180050081658

Coady, N. F. (1992). Rationale and directions for the increased emphasis on the therapeutic relationship in family therapy. *Contemporary Family Therapy, 14,* 467–479. doi:10.1007/BF00892195

Cooper, D. (1970). *The death of the family.* New York, NY: Pantheon.

Doherty, W. J., & Simmons, D. S. (1996). Clinical practice patterns of marriage and family therapists: A national survey of therapists and their clients. *Journal of Marital and Family Therapy, 22,* 9–25. doi:10.1111/j.1752-0606.1996.tb00183.x

Duhamel, F., Dupuis, F., Turcotte, A., Martinez, A. M., & Goudreau, J. (2015). Integrating the illness beliefs model in clinical practice A family systems nursing knowledge utilization model. *Journal of Family Nursing, 21,* 322–348. doi:10.1177/1074840715579404

Dykeman, C., Nelson, J. R., & Appleton, V. (1995). Building strong working alliances with American Indian families. *Children & Schools, 17*(3), 148–158. doi:10.1093/cs/17.3.148

Evans, B. C., Coon, D., & Crogan, N. L. (2007). Personalismo and breaking barriers: Accessing Hispanic populations for clinical services and research. *Geriatric Nursing, 28,* 289–296. doi:10.1016/j.gerinurse.2007.08.008

Falicov, C. (2009). Commentary: On the wisdom and challenges of culturally attuned treatments for Latinos. *Family Process, 48,* 292–309. doi:10.1111/j.1545-5300.2009.01282.x

Friedlander, M. L., Wildman, J., Heatherington, L., & Skowron, E. A. (1994). What we do and don't know about the process of family therapy. *Journal of Family Therapy, 8,* 390–416. doi:10.1037/0893-3200.8.4.390

Gibson, D. M. (2005). The use of genograms in career counseling with elementary, middle, and high school students. *The Career Development Quarterly, 53,* 353–362. doi:10.1002/j.2161-0045.2005.tb00666.x

Gladding, S. T. (2014). *Family therapy: History, theory, and practice.* Upper Saddle River, NJ: Merrill Prentice Hall.

Green, R., & Herget, M. (1991). Outcomes of systemic/strategic team consultation: III. The importance of therapist warmth and active structuring. *Family Process, 30,* 321–335. doi:10.1111/j.1545-5300.2004.00030.x

Haley, J. (1976). Development of a theory: A history of a research project. In C. E. Sluski & D. C. Ransom (Eds.), *Double bind: The foundation of the communicational approach to the family* (pp. 59–104). New York, NY: Grune & Stratton.

Haley, J. (1990). *Strategies of psychotherapy.* New York, NY: Norton.

Haley, J. (1991). *Problem-solving therapy.* San Francisco, CA: Jossey-Bass.

Haley, J. (1993). *Uncommon therapy.* New York, NY: Norton.

Hampson, R. B., & Beavers, W. R. (1996). Measuring family therapy outcome in a clinical setting: Families that do better or do worse in therapy. *Family Therapy, 35,* 347–361. doi:10.1111/j.1545-5300.1996.00347.x

Horigian, V. E., & Szapocznik, J. (2015). Brief strategic family therapy: Thirty-five years of interplay among theory, research, and practice in adolescent behavior problems. In L. M Scheier (Ed.), *Handbook of adolescent drug use prevention: Research, intervention strategies, and practice* (pp. 249–265). Washington, DC: American Psychological Association. doi:10.1037/14550-015

Horvath, A. O. (1994). Empirical validation of Bordin's pantheoretical model of the alliance: The Working Alliance Inventory perspective. In A. O. Horvath & L. S. Greenberg (Eds.), *The working alliance* (pp. 109–130). New York, NY: Wiley.

Ibrahim, F. A., & Dykeman, C. (2011). Counseling Muslim Americans: Cultural and spiritual assessments. *Journal of Counseling & Development, 89,* 387–396. doi:10.1002/j.1556-6676.2011.tb02835.x

Imber-Black, E. (2004). Meaningful voices, old and new. *Family Process, 43,* 411–412. doi:10.1111/j.1545-5300.2004.00030.x

Interian, A., Allen, L. A., Gara, M. A., & Escobar, J. I. (2008). A pilot study of culturally adapted cognitive behavior therapy for Hispanics with major depression. *Cognitive and Behavioral Practice, 15,* 67–75. doi:10.1016/j.cbpra.2006.12.002

Interian, A., & Diaz-Martinez, A. M. (2007). Considerations for culturally competent cognitive-behavioral therapy for depression with Hispanic patients. *Cognitive and Behavioral Practice, 14,* 84–97.

Jackson, D. D. (1957). The question of family homeostasis. *Psychiatric Quarterly Supplement, 31,* 79–90.

Johnson, L., & Thomas, V. (1999). Influences on the inclusion of children in family therapy: Brief report. *Journal of Marital and Family Therapy, 25,* 117–123. doi:10.1111/j.1752-0606.1999.tb01114.x

Karam, E. A., Blow, A. J., Sprenkle, D. H., & Davis, S. D. (2015). Strengthening the systemic ties that bind: Integrating common factors into marriage and family therapy curricula. *Journal of Marital and Family Therapy, 41,* 136–149. doi:10.1111/jmft.12096

Kaslow, F. W. (2000). Continued evolution of family therapy: The last twenty years. *Contemporary Family Therapy, 22,* 357–386. doi:10.1023/A:1007840732591

Kaslow, N. J., Celano, M., & Dreelin, E. D. (1995). A cultural perspective on family theory and therapy. *Psychiatric Clinics of North America, 18,* 621–633.

Klever, P. (2005). The multigenerational transmission of family unit functioning. *American Journal of Family Therapy, 33,* 253–264. doi:10.1080/01926180590952436

Kokkvoll, A., Grimsgaard, S., Ødegaard, R., Flægstad, T., & Njølstad, I. (2013). Single versus multiple-family intervention in childhood overweight—Finnmark Activity School: A randomised trial. *Archives of Disease in Childhood, 99*(3), 225–231. 10.1136/archdischild-2012-303571

Lebow, J. L., & Gurman, A. S. (1995). Research assessing couple and family therapy. *Annual Review of Psychology, 46,* 25–57. doi:10.1146/annurev.ps.46.020195.000331

Lee, M. Y., Hsu, K. S., Liu, C., Greene, G. J., Fraser, J. S., Grove, D., . . . Scott, P. (2015). Treatment efficacy of integrative family and systems treatment (I-FAST) with and without consultation: The role of model training in the sustainability of evidence-based family treatments. *Administration and Policy in Mental Health and Mental Health Services Research.* Advance online publication. doi:10.1007/s10488-015-0644-y

Lim, S., & Nakamoto, T. (2008). Genograms: Use in therapy with Asian families with diverse cultural heritages. *Contemporary Family Therapy, 30,* 199–219. doi:10.1007/s10591-008-9070-6

Lindstrøm, M., Rasmussen, P. S., Kowalski, K., Filges, T., & Jørgensen, A. K. (2012). *Brief strategic family therapy (BSFT) for young people in treatment for non-opioid drug use.* Retrieved from http://www.campbellcollaboration.org/lib/project/209

Lund, L. K., Zimmerman, T. S., & Haddock, S. A. (2002). The theory, structure, and techniques for the inclusion of children in family therapy: A literature review. *Journal of Marital and Family Therapy, 28,* 445–454. doi:10.1111/j.1752-0606.2002.tb00369.x

Lyddon, W. J. (1990). First- and second-order change: Implications for rationalist and constructivist cognitive therapies. *Journal of Counseling & Development, 69,* 122–127. doi:10.1002/j.1556-6676.1990.tb01472.x

Madanes, C. (1981). *Strategic family therapy.* San Francisco, CA: Jossey-Bass.

Madanes, C. (1991). Strategic family therapy. In A. S. Gurman & D. P. Kniskern (Eds.), *Handbook of family therapy* (Vol. 2, pp. 396–416). New York, NY: Brunner/Mazel.

Magnuson, S., Norem, K., & Skinner, C. H. (1995). Constructing genograms with lesbian clients. *The Family Journal: Counseling and Therapy for Couples and Families, 3,* 110–115. doi:10.1177/1066480795032005

Malan, Z., Cooke, R., & Mash, R. (2015). The self-reported learning needs of primary care doctors in South Africa: A descriptive survey. *South African Family Practice, 57*(1), 35–43. doi:10.1080/20786190.2014.1002677

McDowell, T. (2004). Exploring the racial experience of therapists in training: A critical race therapy perspective. *American Journal of Family Therapy, 32,* 305–324. doi:10.1080/01926180490454791

McDowell, T. (2015a). Critical decolonizing theories in family therapy. In T. McDowell (Ed.), *Applying critical social theories to family therapy practice* (pp. 1–12). New York, NY: Springer International. doi:10.1007/978-3-319-15633-0_1

McDowell, T. (2015b). Pace, place, and just practice. In T. McDowell (Ed.), *Applying critical social theories to family therapy practice* (pp. 53–66). New York, NY: Springer International. doi:10.1007/978-3-319-15633-0_6

McGoldrick, M., & Carter, B. (2001). Advances in coaching: Family therapy with one person. *Journal of Marital and Family Therapy, 27,* 281–300. doi:10.1111/j.1752-0606.2001.tb00325.x

McGoldrick, M., Gerson, R., & Petry, S. (2008). *Genograms: Assessment and intervention.* New York, NY: Norton.

Minuchin, S., & Fishman, C. (1981). *Family therapy techniques.* Cambridge, MA: Harvard University Press.

Nichols, M. P. (1987). *The self in the system: Expanding the limits of family therapy.* New York, NY: Brunner/Mazel.

Nichols, M. P. (2012). *Family therapy: Concepts and methods.* New York, NY: Pearson Higher Education.

Nuttall, J. (2008). The integrative attitude-a personal journey. *European Journal of Psychotherapy, Counselling & Health, 10,* 19–38. doi:10.1080/13642530701869326

Papero, D. V. (1990). *Bowen family systems theory.* Boston, MA: Allyn & Bacon.

Papp, P., & Imber-Black, E. (1996). Family themes: Transmission and transformation. *Family Process, 35,* 5–20. doi:10.1111/j.1545-5300.1996.00005.x

Patterson, G. R., & Forgatch, M. S. (1985). Therapist behavior as a determinant for client noncompliance: A paradox for the behavior modifier. *Journal of Consulting and Clinical Psychology, 53,* 846–851. doi:10.1037/0022-006X.53.6.846

Pinsof, W. M. (1994). An integrative systems perspective on the therapeutic alliance: Theoretical, clinical, and research implications. In A. O. Horvath & L. S. Greenberg (Eds.), *The working alliance* (pp. 173–198). New York, NY: Wiley.

Pinsof, W. M., & Wynne, L. C. (2000). Toward progress research: Closing the gap between family therapy practice and research. *Journal of Marital and Family Therapy, 26,* 1–8. doi:10.1111/j.1752-0606.2000.tb00270.x

Prata, G. (2013). *A systemic harpoon into family games: Preventive interventions in therapy.* New York, NY: Brunner/Mazel.

Reber, A. S. (2002). *Dictionary of psychology.* New York, NY: Penguin.

Satir, V. M. (1983). *Conjoint family therapy.* Palo Alto, CA: Science & Behavior Books. (Original work published 1964)

Satir, V. M., & Bitter, J. R. (1991). The therapist and family therapy: Process model. In A. M. Horne & J. L. Passmore (Eds.), *Family counseling and therapy* (pp. 13–45). Itasca, IL: Peacock.

Sauber, R. S., L'Abate, L., Weeks, G. R., & Buchanan, W. L. (1993). *The dictionary of family psychology and family therapy.* Newbury Park, CA: Sage.

Segal, L. (1991). Brief therapy: The MRI approach. In A. S. Gurman & D. P. Kniskern (Eds.), *Handbook of family therapy* (Vol. 2, pp. 171–199). New York, NY: Brunner/Mazel.

Seligman, L. (2004). *Diagnosis and treatment planning in counseling.* New York, NY: Springer Science & Business Media.

Smith, G. B., & Schwebel, A. I. (1995). Using a cognitive-behavioral family model in conjunction with systems and behavioral family therapy models. *American Journal of Family Therapy, 23,* 203–212. doi:10.1080/01926189508251351

Sobol, B. (1982). Art therapy and strategic family therapy. *American Journal of Art Therapy, 21,* 23–31.

Szapocznik, J., Hervis, O., & Schwartz, S. (2003). *Therapy manuals for drug addiction: Brief strategic family therapy for adolescent drug abuse.* Retrieved from http://archives.drugabuse.gov/pdf/Manual5.pdf

Szapocznik, J., Zarate, M., Duff, J., & Muir, J. (2013). Brief strategic family therapy: Engaging drug using/problem behavior adolescents and their families in treatment. *Social Work in Public Health, 28*(3–4), 206–223. doi:10.1080/19371918.2013.774666

Vilaça, M., & Relvas, A. P. (2014). The state of the art in family therapy research: What works? How it works? *International Journal of Social Science Studies,* 2(2), 10–19.

Walters, M., Carter, B., Papp, P., & Silverstein, P. (1988). *The invisible web: Gender patterns in family relationships.* New York, NY: Guilford Press.

Werner-Lin, A. (2015). Social work practice with families affected by hereditary cancer. In G. Christ, C. Messner, & L. Behar (Eds.), *Handbook of oncology social work: Psychosocial care for people with cancer* (pp. 231–237). New York, NY: Oxford University Press.

Chapter 14

Feminist Theory

Barbara Herlihy and Candace N. Park

The theory and practice of feminist counseling evolved from the feminist movement of the 1960s, which provided a forum for women to actively articulate their dissatisfaction with their second-class citizenship in a patriarchal social system. Feminism encompasses a range of belief systems based on the principle that women and members of other subordinate groups in society should have political, economic, and social rights equal to those of men and other dominant group members. Feminist theory is different from other, more traditional theories in that it includes an appeal for social justice and advocacy for social change (Worell & Remer, 2003).

BACKGROUND

Betty Freidan, one of the most vocal early feminists, put a face to feminism with her book *The Feminine Mystique* (1963). The National Organization for Women was instrumental in rallying the charge to reform social structure and traditional roles for women and was a strong voice for feminism during the 1960s and 1970s.

As the feminist movement grew, many women formed groups for the purpose of consciousness raising and to discuss their lack of a collective voice in politics, the workplace, economics, education, and other significant sociopolitical areas (Kaschak, 1992). Consciousness-raising groups began as loosely structured meetings of women who met to discuss their shared experiences of oppression and powerlessness but soon developed into sophisticated self-help groups that empowered women and challenged the social norms of the times (Evans, Kincade, Marbley, & Seem, 2005). Feminist counseling evolved from these consciousness-raising groups, which played important roles in educating, radicalizing, and mobilizing women in the early 1970s. Although these groups were instrumental in helping women gain personal insight, they were not as effective at producing political change. Thus, a need remained for broader change at a societal level.

As the therapeutic value of consciousness-raising groups became evident and the need for more structured groups grew, the 1970s marked the beginning of feminist counseling as a recognized approach to psychotherapy. Feminist counseling evolved without being founded by a specific person, theoretical position, or set of techniques (Enns, 2004; Evans et al., 2005). This early phase of feminist counseling was predicated on the assumptions that women had shared experiences of oppression and victimization and that only a proactive approach could be effective. Early feminist counselors helped name specific issues facing women and worked to adapt traditional therapies to meet the needs of women.

Feminist theory progressed through three distinct phases: radical, liberal, and moderate. Early feminist theory called for a radical form of counseling and psychotherapy, using techniques that were designed to help women see that a patriarchal society was at the center of many of their problems and that change would be virtually impossible until they were empowered to feel equal and act with equal voice. Radical feminist counselors vigorously communicated the goals and tenets of feminism, which included (a) encouraging financial independence, (b) viewing women's problems as being influenced by external factors, and (c) suggesting that the client become involved in social action (Enns, 2004). Radical feminist counseling encouraged active participation in social action groups and other social justice causes to ensure societal change that embraced gender equity. Walstedt (cited in Enns, 1993) emphasized the egalitarian nature of feminist counseling. The radical phase of feminist counseling theory lasted approximately 10 years and was the catalyst for the development of other grassroots counterinstitutions, such as rape crisis centers, that offered a wide range of services to women (Enns, 1993).

Not all feminists welcomed the new feminist counseling. Some feminists during this period implied that feminism and counseling were incompatible because counseling involved "one up/one down politics that encouraged women to focus on pleasing the therapist rather than assuming responsibility for themselves" (Enns, 1993, p. 8). Groups became the preferred method for feminist counselors because the balance of power between the counselor and clients was more equal, with both counselor and clients receiving and giving emotional support. Many more women could be reached through groups, thus effecting more sweeping social change (Kaschak, 1981).

The 1980s saw an infusion of feminist thought into other counseling theories in what has been termed the *mainstreaming era* (Dutton-Douglas & Walker, 1988). The idea was to put traditional theories to a political gender litmus test and remove those parts of the traditional approaches that promoted a dichotomous view of men and women (Elliott, 1999). Many early practitioners of feminist counseling promoted the goal of androgyny—integration of both traditional masculine and feminine characteristics as an ideal of mental health (Enns, 2004). Androgyny research (Bem, 1976, 1987) and behavioral skills training (Brown, 1986) became the standard for feminist counseling. Feminist counselors were encouraged to choose from all traditional intervention methods that did not support gender-biased outcomes (Enns, 1993).

Contrarily and simultaneously, during this same era, feminist counseling was being defined as a separate entity (Enns, 1993). Stages of feminist counseling were articulated, and skills for implementing feminist counseling were presented (Ballou & Gabalac, 1985; Fitzgerald & Nutt, 1986). Also, feminist personality theory was proposed to support and integrate feminist therapeutic practices (Enns, 1993). Feminist counseling became more liberal and less radical. Liberal feminists emphasize different goals than their radical counterparts. Liberal feminists view counseling as a process of gaining self-understanding and see the necessity for flexibility in helping the client solve problems (Enns, 2004). Since the late 1980s, there has been a movement within feminist theory that acknowledges feminine potential, focuses on equality, and acknowledges that many of the shared problems of women are created by a society that does not value them or allow them to exercise their free will. The tone of feminist counseling has become more moderate, adapting goals espoused by both radical and liberal feminists. During the 1980s, the demand for groups decreased, and individual counseling became the most frequently used form of feminist practice (Kaschak, 1981). Coinciding with the third wave of feminism that began in the early 1990s, feminist therapists began to incorporate tenets of the third wave into feminist pedagogy and counseling (Enns & Williams, 2013). Building on the contributions of second-wave feminism, third-wave feminists were interested in creating their own feminisms that addressed the perceived mistakes of the previous generation and allowed for differing views of feminism and activism. This third phase of feminist development in counseling is in continuous development and helps to further define and clarify the work of the feminist counselor (Enns, 2004; Walker, 1990).

Contemporary feminist therapists practice from a range of theoretical perspectives. Enns, Sinacore, Ancis, and Phillips (2004) identified four feminisms that have emerged and that focus on multiple discriminations in addition to gender. Postmodern feminists examine how reality is socially constructed and focus on the changing contexts in which oppression occurs. The perspectives of feminist women of color and lesbians, whose voices had been marginalized or overlooked at times by the second wave, have become more centralized in contemporary feminist psychology (Enns, 2012). *Womanists,* a term often preferred by feminists of color, consider the interactions of sexism, classism, and racism and work to eliminate all forms of oppression. Lesbian feminists believe that heterosexism is at the core of women's oppression. Although third-wave feminism has focused primarily on North American concerns (Enns & Williams, 2013), transnational and global feminists seek to link women's experiences throughout the world and to address the exploitation of women worldwide. Given the variety of perspectives, it is clear that there is no singular, unified feminist theory.

Like the feminist movement itself, feminist counseling has its critics and its supporters. Critics are often those who are unfamiliar with the precepts of the theories and those who harbor erroneous concepts that feminist therapy is anti-male just because it is pro-female. Although varied perspectives exist, Evans et al. (2005) described modern feminist counseling as an approach that incorporates the psychology of women, research on women's development, cognitive–behavioral techniques, multicultural awareness, and social activism into a coherent theoretical and therapeutic package.

HUMAN NATURE: A DEVELOPMENTAL PERSPECTIVE

The feminist perspective is grounded in the belief that traditional theories of human nature and human development, created by Western males in their own image, are not universally applicable. Rather, feminists believe it is essential to recognize that women and men are socialized differently and that gender-role expectations begin to influence human development from the moment a child is born. These expectations are strongly embedded in the fabric of society and have such a profound impact that they become deeply ingrained in the adult personality.

Gender-role socialization has been defined as a multifaceted process, occurring across the life span, of reinforcing specific beliefs and behaviors that a society considers appropriate based on biological sex (Remer, Rostosky, & Wright, 2001). This process has limiting effects on both women and men and has lifelong consequences:

- Men are encouraged to be intelligent, achieving, and assertive and to go after what they want. Women, by contrast, may have a kind of wisdom called *women's intuition* but are discouraged from being intellectually challenging or competitive. Behaviors that would be considered assertive in men are more likely to be labeled as *aggressive* when displayed by women.
- Men are encouraged to be independent; expression of dependency needs by men may be regarded as weak or effeminate. By contrast, women's dependency on others is less likely to be viewed in a negative light.
- Men are expected to be rational, logical, and stoic. Women, although they are expected to be emotional, may be labeled *hysterical* when they overtly express strong emotions. For men, anger may be the only emotion that can be expressed acceptably, and then primarily as a means of control, whereas it is more acceptable for women to cry or to ask for help.
- Experience is viewed as enhancing a man's sexual attractiveness, but Western culture sends mixed messages to young women: Women are expected to be sexually attractive, with their bodies on display, yet they are discouraged from making sexual choices and developing a healthy sexual identity (Elliott, 1999).

Feminist scholars have challenged the assumptions on which gender-role socialization and sex-role stereotyping are based. Notable among those who have reformulated the understanding of human development are Carol Gilligan, Jean Baker Miller, other women affiliated with the Stone Center in Massachusetts, Sandra Bem, and Ellyn Kaschak. Their contributions are discussed in the following sections.

A Different Voice

Carol Gilligan's work as a research assistant with Lawrence Kohlberg prompted her interest in women's moral development. After conducting and analyzing extensive interviews with women, she concluded that Kohlberg's model of moral development was less applicable to women than to men. She saw differences in the way women and men responded to moral dilemmas. Men generally reacted with a morality of justice that emphasized individual rights, whereas women tended to approach the dilemmas with a morality of care and responsibility that emphasized a concern that no one would be hurt. Noting that these concerns are embedded in a cultural context, Gilligan was concerned that traits such as compassion and caring are prized in women but at the same time are seen as a deficit in their moral development. In her book *In a Different Voice,* Gilligan (1982) asserted that concern for connectedness is central to women's development. Exploring developmental crises faced by girls at adolescence, she concluded that it is difficult for girls to maintain a strong sense of identity and voice when doing so would be to risk disconnection from a society that does not honor their needs and desires for relatedness and connectedness. Thus, it is necessary for women to recover and reclaim their lost voices so that they can move forward along the pathway to healthy growth and development.

A New Psychology of Women and Relational-Cultural Theory

Jean Baker Miller's (1976) pioneering work focused on gender inequality and the implications for personality development of membership in dominant and subordinate groups. In her view, because women are the subordinate group in society, they develop characteristics such as passivity and dependency to help them cope with this status. Focusing on relationships of dominance and subordination, Miller concluded that women differ from men in their orientation to power. Thus, the distinctive psychology of women arises from their position of inequality. She noted that women's sense of self is organized around being able to make and maintain affiliations and relationships. Miller conceptualized this difference as holding the potential for more cooperative, more affiliative ways of living. She called for a "new psychology of women that would recognize that women have a different starting place for their development that they stay with, build on, and develop in a context of attachment and affiliation with others" (p. 83). Relational-cultural theory, an approach to feminist therapy that grew out of Miller's work, emphasizes women's movement through connections, disconnections, and transformative new connections throughout their lives (Comstock et al., 2008).

Self-in-Relation

Jordan and Surrey's (1986) self-in-relation theory reflects a collaborative effort among women at the Stone Center in Massachusetts to reformulate women's development and psychology. Their work followed in the tradition of Miller and Gilligan, who argued for the development of new concepts, language, and theories to describe and understand female development. Jordan and Surrey paid particular attention to the positive, adaptive aspects of the mother–daughter relationship and offered a new model of female development that positively redefined the mother–daughter dyad and affirmed traditional female values of nurturance and connectedness. Their model challenged the traditional psychoanalytic tendencies to pathologize female development, particularly the mother–daughter relationship, and to engage in mother blaming as a way to explain adult psychological dysfunction. Postulating that mother–daughter sameness facilitates the development of empathy and the capacity for relatedness, they saw the core self of women as including an interest in and an ability to form emotional connections with others. According to self-in-relation theory, "women organize their sense of identity, find existential meaning, achieve a sense of coherence and continuity, and are motivated in the context of a relationship" (p. 142).

Gender Schema and Engendered Lives

Sandra Bem's gender schema theory provides another perspective on the powerful influence of gender-role expectations on identity development. *Schema* is a term used by cognitive psychologists to describe an organized set of mental associations used to interpret perceptions (Sharf, 2000). Bem (1981, 1993) argued that gender schema is one of the strongest perceptual sets people use when looking at society and their place in it. When children learn society's views of gender and apply them to themselves, stereotypes of masculinity and femininity are reinforced. Children learn very early that certain behaviors are desirable for girls to be considered feminine and boys to be seen as masculine. In adolescence, boys and girls tend to become highly gender focused as they become concerned with physical attractiveness and exploring their emerging sexuality. By adulthood, these gender schema are deeply ingrained and are limiting to both sexes. Ellyn Kaschak posited that gender is the organizing principle in people's lives. In *Engendered Lives* (1992), she focused on the societal impact of gender-role development. She argued that the masculine defines the feminine; that is, men determine the roles that women play (see Sidebar 14.1).

Conclusions

Feminist scholars, by positing different models of development for women and men, have provided a better understanding of relationships and a more comprehensive portrayal of human development over the life span. At the same time, they have been concerned that their work might be interpreted as dichotomizing the sexes. Although validating women's relational skills and recognizing their needs for connectedness and individuation are important contributions of feminist scholars, it is crucial to keep in mind that *all* people develop within the context of ongoing relationships and fail to thrive in the absence of human connectedness. A circular and reciprocal relationship exists between men and women, and an appreciation of the different filters through which they perceive and experience the world can broaden one's understanding of human nature and human growth and development.

MAJOR CONSTRUCTS

Although feminist counselors practice in various ways, depending on their approach, in general they share a commitment to a core set of principles (Enns, 2004). The first and most fundamental of these principles is that *the personal is political.* The basis for this belief is that the personal or individual problems that women and members of other subordinate groups bring to counseling originate in social and political oppression, subordination, and stereotyping. Thus, the goal of feminist counseling is not only individual change but also social transformation. Clients' responses are not viewed as dysfunctional or as having an intrapsychic origin but

Sidebar 14.1. Internalized Gender Messages

Feminist counselors believe that gender-role socialization is a powerful force that all people—including counselors—carry into adulthood, often at an unconscious level. Reflect on your own gender-role socialization as you were growing up. Make a list of the messages you received about what it means to be female or male (e.g., "Clothes don't look good on chubby girls. You need to lose some weight."). Reflect on how those messages you received and internalized might affect your perceptions of clients and their concerns.

are seen as ways of coping with an oppressive environment in which the clients have a subordinate status. Because the environment is a major source of pathology in the lives of women and other oppressed minorities, the toxic aspects of the environment must be changed if individual change is to occur.

A second principle, intertwined with the first, is that feminist counselors share a *commitment to social change*. Feminist counselors work to help clients not only to make internal, psychological changes but also to join with others in working toward social change that will liberate all members of society from subordination, oppression, and social role stereotyping. In feminist counseling, clients are encouraged to become active in furthering social change through such means as joining political action groups or confronting sexism and other -isms in their workplaces and their personal lives. Feminist counselors work with individual clients, couples, and families, but they also have an overarching commitment to broader social change. They are, themselves, involved in social change in their own communities and sometimes in larger spheres.

Third, feminist counselors are committed to the establishment of *egalitarian relationships* (Worell & Remer, 2003). One of the roots of women's problems is the unequal distribution of power between women and men and between other dominant and subordinate groups. Thus, it is important for feminist counselors to establish counseling relationships in which clients are viewed as equal partners in the therapeutic endeavor who have the capacity to change in directions that they themselves select and to decide on therapeutic goals and strategies. The counselor is viewed as another source of information rather than an expert in the relationship. Feminist counselors use a variety of means for sharing power with the client. Their twofold aim in building egalitarian therapeutic relationships is to empower the client and to model collaborative ways of being in relationship. It is important to feminist counselors that they do not replicate in the therapeutic relationship the power disparity that the client experiences in the larger social, economic, and political worlds (see Sidebar 14.2).

A fourth principle of feminist counseling is *to honor women's voices and ways of knowing*. A goal in feminist counseling is to help clients challenge the androcentric norms that compare women to men and that allow women to be defined by others. One of the ways that society has tended to devalue women's voices has been to prize the patriarchal norm of objective truth over subjective experience. Feminists call for an acceptance of feminist consciousness, which acknowledges diverse ways of knowing. The belief that underlies this tenet is that only women's unique experiences can provide a foundation of knowledge for understanding women. Forcing women's experiences into a traditional framework that ignores

Sidebar 14.2. Counseling Is . . .

Counselors of all theoretical orientations agree that clients should be provided with fully informed consent before entering into a counseling relationship. Most counselors provide a statement, usually both orally and in writing, that starts with a phrase like "I see counseling as a place where. . . ." In a brief paragraph, write out the words you would use to inform a client about how you see counseling. When you have finished, analyze your statement. In what ways do you think your statement is congruent—and incongruent—with what a feminist counselor would write or say?

their voice and status would devalue and distort both the experiences and the women themselves (Ballou & West, 2000). Instead, theories of feminist counseling evolve from and reflect the lived experiences of women that include a number of gender-based phenomena, such as sexual assault, domestic violence, eating disorders, and sexual harassment. Contemporary feminist therapists acknowledge that women's voices and experiences are diverse and are shaped by many other identities, such as race/ethnicity, generational status, sexual orientation, nationality, and ability status (Herlihy & Corey, 2016).

Fifth, feminist counselors *recognize all types of oppression*, not just those based on gender. Feminist counselors respect the inherent worth and dignity of every individual and recognize that societal and political inequities are oppressive and limiting to all people. Feminist principles have been expanded to encompass an awareness of the multiple interactions of gender with other variables that affect the lives of clients. Feminist counseling and multicultural counseling were historically mostly separate and disconnected movements (Reynolds & Constantine, 2004). Feminist therapy has been criticized for its lack of attention to sociocultural factors other than gender and for ignoring the contributions of "women of color who . . . have made important contributions to feminist understandings of psychotherapy that provide us with insights into our understanding of both gender and race/ethnic biases" (Espin, 1993, p. 104). In recent years, feminists have become more cognizant of the ways in which all people, depending on their position in a complex social matrix, are both oppressed and oppressor, both dominant and marginalized. When psychological distress is placed within a sociocultural context, it is apparent that experiences of oppression are interrelated in complex ways. Feminist counselors have called for cultural diversity to become a central and defining characteristic of therapy (Enns, 2004; Evans, Kincade, & Seem, 2011; Whalen et al., 2004; Williams & Barber, 2004) and for an integration of the feminist, multicultural, and social justice approaches to counseling (Crethar, Torres Rivera, & Nash, 2008; Evans et al., 2011). These three approaches share the goals of working toward social change and advocating for the empowerment of all clients by giving a voice to the unheard (Green, McCollum, & Hays, 2008).

APPLICATIONS

Overview

Although some feminist therapists practice counseling strictly from a feminist theoretical lens, many practice feminist therapy in conjunction with one or more other theoretical approaches (Worell & Remer, 2003). Worell and Remer (2003) encouraged combining at both the theoretical and applied levels when integrating more traditional theories with their empowerment feminist therapy. Integrating theoretical approaches is a deliberate approach, as opposed to drawing on a hodgepodge of techniques from multiple theoretical approaches based on the perceived needs of the client, which is often termed *technically eclectic* (Evans et al., 2011). Corey (2009) cautioned that using such an eclectic approach when integrating theory can lead to theoretical confusion and questionable practice.

Counselors practice multiple forms of feminist counseling today, basing their work on the unique combination of their feminist orientation and their counseling approach. Therefore, feminist counseling is highly personal for the counselor because it originates in the counselor's personal beliefs concerning the empowerment of women and the need to change social norms that inhibit self-direction. The goals of feminist counseling are basically twofold: to help clients understand that sociopolitical forces influence their lives and to understand how their problems can be interpreted as methods of surviving rather than as signs of dysfunction. The overall purpose of feminist counseling, however, is to help clients change by making choices based on their own personal experiences and strengths (Enns, 2004). The client is the expert member of the therapeutic dyad who is knowledgeable about his or her own distress and its social meaning (Brown, 1994). The process of change includes the development of self-help skills and tools that allow clients to problem-solve in the absence of the counselor. The feminist counselor helps the client explore how problems exist in both personal and social contexts (Enns, 2004), thus demonstrating that change must occur at both a personal level and a societal level.

Feminist counseling can be particularly effective with certain mental disorders that are commonly diagnosed among women in society. As is discussed later in the chapter, feminist counselors are reluctant to use the label *mental disorder* to describe symptoms of psychological distress that they view as communications about the experience of living in an unjust society. Instead, feminist counselors use a feminist analysis with alternative diagnostic systems (Kincade, Seem, & Evans, 1998). They consider the social meanings of diagnosis, broadening the focus to a more complex understanding of the client's experience and distress within a cultural context.

Feminist counselors operate from a complex knowledge base that includes the psychology of women; counseling and psychotherapy theory; perspectives on gender, race, class, and other societal positionalities; sociopolitical change strategies; and multicultural issues (Enns, 2004). This knowledge base is reflected in the goals, intervention strategies, and research agendas of feminist practitioners.

Goals of Counseling and Psychotherapy

Change often involves developing new attitudes toward the circumstances and realities of women's and men's lives, not just adjusting to those circumstances and realities. Feminist counselors help clients explore a full range of options available to them rather than concentrate solely on what is perceived to be the right course to take because of one's gender. This might take the form of self-analysis for the client, exposure to feminist literature, or participation in consciousness-raising groups or other support groups. At a societal level, uncovering emotional distress, anger, or outrage to promote social change and participating in social activism may benefit the client. Involvement in community action programs and social action activities can help the client gain both experience and confidence. Enns (2004) proposed five goals for feminist counseling: equality, independence/interdependence, empowerment, self-nurturance, and valuing diversity.

Equality as a goal of feminist counseling is designed to help the client gain freedom from traditional gender and other socially prescribed roles. An equal status in personal relationships, economic self-sufficiency, and work equity are all components of equality. It is the counselor's role to encourage the client to negotiate greater equality in intimate relationships, with friends, and with work colleagues.

This is done through exposing the client to information regarding the unequal status and power of women and men, and of dominant and nondominant groups, in Western society (Enns, 2004).

Balancing independence (personal attributes) and interdependence (relational skills) has proved to be one of the most difficult goals for feminist counselors to operationalize. Balancing personal attributes and relational skills moves feminist counseling away from the notion of androgyny as the model for mental health and focuses on the importance of valuing the relational skills of women. To accomplish this balance, the counselor helps the client to separate traits related to independence and interdependence from traditional perceptions about gender roles and what is considered masculine and feminine.

Empowerment is a major goal of feminist counseling in that it helps clients see that they have control over themselves and have the ability to actively advocate for others. Empowerment involves recognition that powerlessness is a learned behavior. Once clients become aware of gender-role socialization and how it relates to oppression, it is important for them to develop mechanisms to counteract the effects of sociopolitical forces that have limited their choices in life.

Self-nurturance is a pivotal goal in feminist counseling. A lack of self-care causes self-doubt, lack of self-esteem, an inability to develop trusting relationships, and difficulty in expressing needs (Enns, 2004). Developing self-nurturance involves becoming more self-aware—aware of personal needs, personal goals, desires, and self-identity. The aim of the counselor is to help the client to experience the sense of pleasure and mastery that comes with discovering self-value (see Sidebar 14.3).

Valuing diversity is a more recent goal of feminist counseling designed to create an inclusive feminist approach. This goal helps the counselor and client to recognize the many ways in which gender intersects with other factors in a multicultural society. Feminism and feminist counseling historically responded primarily to the concerns of middle-class White women. However, although women of color may experience oppressive -isms similar to those experienced by their White counterparts, they may also suffer from a lack of power and self-direction due to racism. Contemporary feminist counselors work to become educated about cultural plurality among the oppressed.

The Process of Change

Empowerment to change is the most essential aspect of feminist therapy. To change, the individual must understand and remove socialized conditioning that restricts decision making based on societal expectations of what is appropriate for men and women or for members of dominant and nondominant group members. A process of resocialization allows clients to value themselves and realize that their lived experiences are important. What was once considered pathology can be renamed as

Sidebar 14.3. Counselor Self-Care

Self-nurturance is an explicit goal in feminist counseling. Feminist counselors encourage self-nurturance in clients by modeling positive self-care in their own lives. In what ways do you practice self-nurturance? In what ways do you think your self-nurturance habits—and lack thereof—are evident to your clients, and what are the possible modeling effects on the clients?

a coping mechanism. The client then begins a process of relearning and practicing new behaviors that promote egalitarian relationships. An indicator of change is when clients actively advocate for themselves while participating in social action groups that promote societal change.

Traditional Intervention Strategies

Feminist counselors use many intervention strategies that they have adapted from the more traditional theories and approaches to counseling. All feminist counseling interventions seek to empower clients. The goal is to mobilize the client's resources to effect change at the personal, relational, and sociopolitical levels. Two important empowerment strategies are demystifying counseling and self-disclosure.

Feminist counselors strive to create an egalitarian relationship with their clients so that the inequities found in society are not replicated in the counseling relationship. For example, if the counselor calls the client by his or her first name, the counselor introduces himself or herself using his or her first name. A strategy for empowering clients is to demystify the counseling process at the outset of the relationship by paying careful attention to informed consent issues. It is important that clients participate in identifying and naming their problems; understand and agree to goals and procedures; realize that they are in charge of the direction, length, and choices of techniques to be implemented; and know their rights as consumers of counseling services. Feminist counselors provide their clients with information about their theoretical orientation, competencies, and alternatives to counseling so that the clients can make fully informed choices (Enns, 2004).

Feminist counselors engage in self-disclosure and state their values explicitly to emphasize the commonalities among women and decrease the client's sense of isolation, although they share with counselors of other theoretical orientations the commitment to ensuring that self-disclosures are in the client's best interests and are relevant to the client's needs. Brief and timely self-disclosures about the counselor's own struggles with issues serve the purposes of modeling coping responses to difficult issues and equalizing the therapeutic relationship (see Sidebar 14.4).

Reframing and relabeling are intervention strategies frequently used in feminist counseling. To reframe is to change the frame of reference for looking at an individual's behavior. When feminist counselors reframe a client's behavior, they consider the sociopolitical and cultural contributions to the client's issues, thus shifting the etiology of the problem from the individual to the environment. This change in perspective avoids blaming the victim for his or her problems. Negative labeling, such as defining a behavior as dysfunctional, is relabeled as a positive

Sidebar 14.4. Counselor Self-Disclosure

Counselor self-disclosure is a contentious issue in the literature, and the stance that counselors take toward self-disclosure is influenced to some extent by their theoretical orientations. Feminist counselors have articulated a rationale for self-disclosure that includes these potential benefits: (a) Self-disclosures can illuminate the commonalities among women and decrease the client's feelings of isolation, (b) self-disclosures can model ways to cope with problems, and (c) self-disclosing can help reduce the power differential between counselor and client. What is your own personal stance toward counselor self-disclosure? What do you see as the risks and benefits?

coping strategy. Feminine characteristics, such as sensitivity, compassion, or subjectivity, that may be devalued as weaknesses when viewed through an androcentric lens are revalued as strengths through the feminist lens. Thus, through reframing and relabeling, symptoms can be seen as coping mechanisms and weaknesses can be seen as strengths.

Bibliotherapy, although not unique to feminist counseling, is another strategy that feminists often find useful. Bibliotherapy involves reading and processing books or articles carefully chosen to help the client understand societal influences that affect his or her personal experiencing (Remer et al., 2001). This literature may address issues such as women's body image and appearance, sexual violence, relationships, and aspects of the life span. For example, a client concerned about her relationship with a significant other might be asked to read Lerner's (1989) *The Dance of Intimacy*. Such reading assignments serve to empower clients by increasing their expertise on topics of concern to them.

Another intervention strategy that has been associated with feminist counseling is assertiveness training. When women do not feel powerful, they may not act assertively and thus may give up some control over their lives. Feminist counselors teach clients assertiveness skills using direct teaching methods, bibliotherapy, and role play. Through assertiveness training, women learn to stand up for their rights without violating the rights of others. The aim of this training is to facilitate women's use of personal power to achieve personal change and effectively challenge their environments (Remer et al., 2001).

Although much of feminist counseling is conducted with individual clients, group work is often a preferred modality for some issues that women experience (Herlihy & Corey, 2016). For example, group approaches have been recommended for dealing with incest and sexual abuse, body image issues, battering, eating disorders, and sexual functioning (Enns, 2004). Feminist counselors may also encourage clients to participate in consciousness-raising groups. Although the popularity of consciousness-raising groups has waned in more recent decades, other types of groups, such as advocacy groups or political action groups, may be recommended to empower women and allow them to experience their connectedness with other women in a supportive environment.

Feminist Interventions

Some interventions used by feminist counselors are unique to the feminist approach. Gender-role analysis is an intervention strategy used to help clients learn about the impact of culturally prescribed gender-role expectations on women and how their lives are affected by them (Israeli & Santor, 2000). In a collaborative effort, the counselor and client examine the client's values and how these values are reflected in the client's role expectations for himself or herself and others. They identify the explicit and implicit sex-role messages the client has experienced and internalized. They then decide which of these messages the client wants to change.

According to Brown (1986), this analysis should include an exploration of (a) gender meanings in light of the client's family values, life stage, cultural background, and present conditions of living; (b) past and present rewards and penalties for gender-role conformity or noncompliance; (c) how the counselor–client relationship mirrors these issues or provides insight into them; and (d) the client's history in relation to victimization. During this process, clients learn that their methods of coping have been adaptive for living in an oppressive society rather than symptoms of pathology. They develop an empathic rather than self-blaming attitude toward themselves. Thus, gender-role analysis serves to help clients gain self-knowledge, increase their awareness of the sociocultural basis for distress, and identify areas for desired change. Following the analysis, a plan for implementing changes is developed that may draw on cognitive–behavioral or other strategies as appropriate to the client's needs.

Power analysis is an assessment and intervention strategy that aims to help women understand their devalued status in society and to help clients of both sexes become aware of the power difference between men and women. The counselor may begin by educating the client about various kinds of power and women's limited access to most kinds of power. Women are often uncomfortable with the term *power* because of their limited experience or exposure to only aggressive aspects of it. The counselor may help clients understand the differences among *power over* (which implies dominance or oppression), *power within* (which involves feeling that one has inner strength), and *power to* (which refers to goal-directed behavior that respects the rights of all involved; Gannon, 1982). Clients can then offer their own definition of power and consider how it fits for their ways of being in the world. Together, the counselor and client identify the client's usual means of exerting power and the effectiveness of those means. Next they identify ways in which the client's internalized gender-role messages affect his or her use of power, which synthesizes gender-role and power issues for the client (Remer et al., 2001). Finally, clients are encouraged to increase their repertoires of power strategies by experimenting in areas of their lives in which a lack of power previously prevented change. Power analysis empowers clients to challenge and change the oppressive environments in which they live (Worell & Remer, 2003; see Sidebar 14.5).

Over the past 10 to 15 years, feminist counselors have developed a more complex integrated analysis of oppression that recognizes that "gender cannot be separated from other ways in which a culture stratifies human difference, privileging some at the expense of others" (Hill & Ballou, 1998, p. 3). In an integrated analysis, procedures used in gender analysis and power analysis are expanded to consider the impact of other variables, such as race or ethnicity, class, sexual orientation, age, size, and religion. Because diversity is a central concern of the contemporary feminist approach, a multicultural, multidimensional analysis considers variables in addition to gender in examining personal, group, and institutional oppression in clients' lives.

Sidebar 14.5. Case Study: Date Rape

Alicia is a 19-year-old college sophomore who comes to the university counseling center. Alicia discloses that she has not been sleeping for the past week and has stopped attending classes. She reveals that a week ago she had an experience that "might have been date rape." She goes on to say that she had been drinking and may have "given him the wrong impression." She has not reported the incident, although she talked to her roommate, who suggested that she come see the counselor. How might a feminist counselor use power analysis and other feminist strategies to help Alicia?

Brief Intervention Strategies and Current Practices

As a general rule, feminist counselors have not embraced the general trend toward brief therapies for two reasons. First, the goals of feminist counseling are not compatible with a brief approach. Deeply ingrained gender biases are not easily brought into awareness, nor are they easily changed. Second, feminist counselors are cognizant that the push for brief (sometimes even single-session) therapy has been driven in large part by the managed care movement. Cost-saving measures that benefit the largely White-male-dominated health care corporations typically are not viewed by feminist counselors as an appropriate rationale for selecting therapeutic interventions. This is not to suggest that feminist counselors attempt to prolong the counseling relationship unnecessarily; clients often are encouraged to make the transition from individual counseling to a group format, such as joining a support group or political action group, as expeditiously as possible.

Clients With Serious Mental Health Issues

The feminist approach has called for a reformulated understanding of psychological distress. Feminist counselors reject the medical or disease model of psychopathology. The notion of psychological distress is reframed so that it is viewed as a communication about the experience of living in an unjust society. From this new perspective, psychic pain is not seen as a symptom of disease or deficit. Instead, it is defined as evidence of resistance and the will and skill to survive (Worell & Johnson, 1997). According to Brown (1994), *resistance* is a term that describes a person's ability to remain alive and strong in the face of oppression. Thus, a client's problems in living are not assumed to arise from within that individual but instead are assumed to derive from multiple sources within a complex social context.

Feminist counselors are concerned about problems inherent in the prevailing *Diagnostic and Statistical Manual of Mental Disorders, Fifth Edition* (*DSM–5*), medical model diagnostic system (American Psychiatric Association, 2013). Since Phyllis Chesler, in *Women and Madness* (1972), articulated the view that the *DSM* approach pathologizes any difference from the standards established by the dominant group in society, feminists have argued that it is important to assess not just symptoms and behaviors but also the context of women's lives (Brown, 1994; Santos de Barona & Dutton, 1997). Within this broader context, many symptoms can be understood as coping strategies rather than as evidence of pathology. Thus, feminist counselors use a broad, bio-psycho-socio-cultural-structural model of assessment and diagnosis (Ballou & West, 2000). Using this broader approach to assessment, feminist counselors familiarize themselves with the literature on gender and its relationship to clinical judgments of mental health and examine their own biases and expectations related to societal positionality. They actively inquire into the meaning of these positionalities for the client, assess the rewards and penalties of role compliance or noncompliance for the client, attend to the client's responses to the counselor's cultural characteristics and their own responses to the client's culture, and check their diagnoses to guard against inappropriately imposing stereotyped values of mental health. Arriving at a diagnosis is a shared process in which clients are the experts on their distress and its social meaning. Clients' understanding of the meaning of their behaviors is considered equally with the counselor's interpretations, and client strengths and resiliencies are identified (Evans et al., 2005). Some of the types of distress commonly experienced by women are discussed in the remainder of this section.

According to the *DSM–5* (APA, 2013), studies have demonstrated a higher prevalence of major depressive disorder in women than in men. From a feminist perspective, women have many more reasons than do men to experience depression. Women, who are taught to be helpless and dependent and to please others, may feel that they are not in control of their lives or their environments. Their subordinate position—along with their experiences of domestic violence, sexual or physical abuse, poverty, or harassment or sex discrimination in the workplace—can result in a sense of powerlessness that can manifest as symptoms of depression. Feminist counselors work to help clients reframe their understanding of the causes of their depression so that they can move away from blaming themselves for the problem and from believing that they must adjust to their circumstances. They help clients become aware of external forces that limit their freedom so clients can release self-blame and focus their energies on circumstances they can influence (Enns, 2004).

As a result of conflicting societal messages and multiple pressures and demands, women may experience symptoms of anxiety disorders. Rather than recommending an antianxiety medication, feminist counselors work with clients to help them develop concrete ways of challenging gender-role expectations, establish a self-nurturing program, join a support group for women who are experiencing role strain, develop relaxation skills, and identify and mobilize resources that are available (see Sidebar 14.6).

One specific anxiety disorder that has received considerable attention in the feminist literature is posttraumatic stress disorder. Feminist counselors have identified rape-trauma syndrome and battered-woman syndrome as women's typical responses to traumatic environmental events. They connect the personal to the political by stressing that violence influences the psychological self and that the symptoms are normal responses to abnormal events. They have proposed new diagnostic categories, such as complex posttraumatic stress disorder (Herman, 1992) and abuse and oppression artifact disorders (Brown, 1994), to describe reactions to a history of subjugation over a period of time. A feminist counselor, in working with clients who present with symptoms of posttraumatic stress disorder, addresses the connection between abuse and sexism and behavior patterns of learned helplessness, avoidance, and rescuing. The counselor listens respectfully

Sidebar 14.6. Case Study: Employee Assistance Program Counseling

Juanita is a 32-year-old account executive who has worked for a large advertising firm for 7 years and has received several promotions. She hopes to eventually be promoted to department manager. Lately, however, her work performance has not been up to her usual standards. She finds herself worrying that she will make a mistake or that she will offend her peers (most of whom are male) if she promotes her ideas too aggressively, so she has been holding back from offering her ideas during meetings and when interacting with her boss. She finds herself becoming increasingly anxious, so she makes an appointment with the firm's employee assistance program counselor. Assume that the counselor's theoretical orientation is feminist. How do you think the counselor will work with Juanita?

to the client and does not minimize the extent to which the client has been wounded (Chesler, 1990). In the therapeutic relationship, the counselor and client explore the ways in which emotions and cognitions have become constricted or distorted by fear or gender stereotyping, self-blame, or shame. The process involves naming the distress accurately, identifying the complex contextual factors that contribute to the client's problems, and transforming possibilities for oppression into opportunities for liberation and social change.

A feminist approach to working with clients with eating disorders focuses on messages conveyed by society, and by the mass media in particular, about women's bodies and androcentric standards for attractiveness. Feminist counselors use gender-role analysis to help clients examine the messages about body image that are conveyed by societal forces. They help clients challenge the media-driven ideal of a woman that is held up as the standard toward which they should strive. Power analysis may help women understand how they relinquish their personal power when they diet and dress to please others as well as how their preoccupation with weight, size, and shape contributes to a lack of power. Group work can be effective with women who suffer from anorexia, bulimia, and other eating disorders because groups provide a supportive environment for examining, challenging, and reframing body image.

Feminists have drawn attention to the high rate of sexual and physical abuse in the histories of women who have been diagnosed with borderline personality disorder (Brown & Ballou, 1992). Viewed from a feminist framework, borderline personality disorder is seen as a long-term chronic effect of posttraumatic stress. Feminist counselors, rather than focusing on a client's problematic behaviors, frame the symptoms as indicators of the client's strength as a survivor. The counseling process involves strategies such as establishing a contract that defines expectations for both counselor and client and sets limits in nonpunitive ways. Careful consideration is given to the client's level of readiness to explore past abuse to help the client strengthen her fragile sense of control over her inner and external worlds. Symptoms such as dissociation and mood swings are reframed as ways of coping. The counselor helps the client understand the needs behind behaviors that seem impulsive and self-defeating so that the client can find new ways to meet these needs. The feminist approach, built on a collaborative relationship and the coconstruction of diagnosis and treatment planning, provides a foundation for a more empowering and liberating helping process (Eriksen & Kress, 2008; Zalaquett, Fuerth, Stein, Ivey, & Ivey, 2008). Feminist counselors continue to propose new conceptualizations of reactions to abuse with the goal of changing the way the mental health professions deal with disorders that affect so many women (Enns, 2004).

Questionable practices in diagnosing are found with members of other nondominant groups, including children. Children are diagnosed with attention-deficit/hyperactivity disorder more often now than ever before, and the numbers continue to rise (Getahun et al., 2013). Racial disparities have also been noted among children diagnosed with attention-deficit/hyperactivity disorder, with White children being diagnosed at higher rates than racial/ethnic minority children despite displaying identical behavior, leading to concerns that many minority children are not being adequately treated (Morgan, Staff, Hillemeier, Farkas, & Maczuga, 2013). Although depression has been associated with abuse for decades, research indicates that adolescents who have been exposed to physical abuse are more likely than their nonabused counterparts to be diagnosed with major depressive disorder as well as conduct disorder (Kaplan et al., 1998).

EVALUATION

Overview

The feminist approach to counseling has not been researched extensively, although studies that have been conducted have generally shown positive results. Additional quantitative and qualitative research is needed to clearly establish the effectiveness of feminist counseling.

Feminist counseling has not been defined as clearly as some of the more traditional approaches. It is difficult to find adequate training programs. Mistaken perceptions continue to exist that feminist counseling is conducted only by women and for women.

Supporting Research

The theory and practice of feminist counseling have grown rapidly, outpacing their empirical support (Remer et al., 2001; Worell & Johnson, 2001). Therefore, validating the effectiveness of the feminist approach remains an ongoing challenge. Studies that have been conducted, however, have generally shown encouraging results.

In comparison studies, feminist counseling has been found to be a distinct modality (Worell & Remer, 2003) that is as effective as other, more traditional forms of counseling (Follingstad, Robinson, & Pugh, 1977; Johnson, 1976). Recently, controlled outcome studies have assessed whether feminist counseling is effective in meeting the goals it espouses. In a long-term follow-up study of feminist counseling outcomes, client self-ratings of improvement over time were assessed; results indicated that clients' resilience increased over time (Chandler, Worell, Johnson, Blount, & Lusk, 1999). Olson (2001) found evidence that feminist therapy using a narrative approach was helpful in treating clients with a history of anorexia.

Israeli and Santor (2000) evaluated existing research on several components of feminist counseling practice. They concluded that consciousness raising appeared to be the most studied feminist counseling intervention and that the research literature suggests that consciousness raising provides therapeutic benefit by allowing women to feel supported. Israeli and Santor recommended that future studies focus on evaluating the efficacy of other interventions and tenets of feminist counseling, such as gender-role analysis and social activism.

Further research is needed to assess the effectiveness of feminist counseling using not only traditional empirical methods but also qualitative techniques that are more synchronous with feminist principles (Evans et al., 2005). Qualitative studies, guided by the ethic of caring, offer perspectives and information that are not available when research is constrained by imperatives of objectivity, value neutrality, and emotional detachment (Blakely, 2007). A major challenge for the future of feminist counseling is to validate the efficacy of its applied practices with research that demonstrates client change (Worell & Johnson, 2001). This challenge is complicated by the fact that feminist counseling looks beyond individual change (Evans et al., 2005) and aims to achieve outcomes that are not easily quantifiable, such as improved self-esteem and quality of life, gender-role flexibility, involvement in social action, and awareness of socialization and oppression (Chandler, Worell, & Johnson, 2000; Moradi, Fischer, Hill, Jome, & Blum, 2000).

Limitations

One limitation of feminist counseling is that it is not as clearly defined as some of the more traditional theories. It has been argued that feminist counseling is not so much a theory as it is a philosophy or belief system about the importance of gender (Rampage, 1998) and that it is better defined as politics than as counseling. Because feminist counseling practitioners are diverse, reaching consensus on its scope and definition will be a challenging task.

It is difficult to obtain adequate training in feminist counseling. There are few feminist counseling training programs per se, although many counselor education programs have faculty members who contribute feminist principles and practices to the training of prospective counselors (Rave & Larsen, 1995). There is no official credentialing of feminist counselors.

The erroneous perception continues to exist that feminist counseling is conducted only by women and for women. This may discourage male clients from seeking counseling services from counselors who identify themselves as feminist practitioners. The historical association of feminism with some of the more radical elements of the women's movement may discourage some prospective clients, both female and male, from entering into counseling relationships with feminist counselors.

A major challenge will be to build alliances between feminist therapy, multicultural counseling, and social justice counseling, which have remained mostly separate and disconnected movements (Reynolds & Constantine, 2004). Feminist counseling has historically been criticized for its lack of attention to sociocultural factors other than gender. Over the past decade, feminist theorists have increasingly called for an integration of the feminist, multicultural, and social justice approaches to counseling (Crethar et al., 2008). Equally important to the future of feminist counseling will be the ability of its theorists, scholars, and practitioners to more clearly articulate its definition, make training more widely available, correct mistaken perceptions, and demonstrate its effectiveness through research.

Summary Chart: Feminist Theory

Human Nature

Gender-role expectations have a profound impact on human development. Because women and men are socialized differently, models of psychological development based on male development fail to recognize that women's identity develops in a context of connectedness and in relationship with others.

Major Constructs

The following are the five major tenets of feminist therapy: (a) The personal is political, (b) the ultimate aim is social change, (c) counseling relationships are egalitarian, (d) women's experiences and voices are honored, and (e) all types of oppression are recognized.

Goals

Based on the work of Enns (2004), the major goals of feminist counseling are change, equality, balancing independence and interdependence, empowerment, self-nurturance, and valuing diversity.

Change Process

External forces are recognized as the root of problems for women. Clients learn self-appreciation and self-value. They rename pathology as coping mechanisms. They learn to change their environments rather than adjust to them. They learn to advocate for social change and to develop egalitarian rather than hierarchical relationships.

Interventions

Although feminist counselors adapt interventions from a wide range of theoretical orientations, several strategies that have been developed specifically for feminist counseling are empowerment, gender-role analysis, power analysis, and integrated analysis of oppression. Other frequently used interventions are reframing and relabeling, bibliotherapy, assertiveness training, and group work. Group work has historically been used for consciousness raising and support.

Limitations

Feminist counseling is often incorrectly perceived as being conducted only by women or only for women. It is not as well grounded in research as some of the more traditional theories. It is difficult to find adequate training in feminist counseling.

THE CASE OF MARIA: A FEMINIST APPROACH

Maria's presenting issues include poor relationships with her immediate family, her in-laws, and her children; depression; sleep deprivation; loneliness; stressors related to an abusive marriage that ended in separation and divorce; an inability to develop a trusting relationship with the opposite sex; and issues related to cultural identity and values. A feminist counselor will describe to Maria the goals of feminist counseling and the counselor's personal philosophy concerning client empowerment and the need for an egalitarian client–counselor relationship. The counselor will help Maria see that her affiliations and actions may not be congruent with the cultural values of her Hispanic roots.

During counseling, Maria will be allowed to articulate, in her own words, her feelings of aloneness and the frustration she experiences when she is unable to receive support from her family or to develop other loving relationships. Expressing these feelings will allow Maria the opportunity to hear her own words and self-evaluate her position in an environment in which her feelings and opinions are validated. In addition, Maria will be able to more readily recognize the negative impact of self-deprecation and powerlessness.

Maria exhibits symptoms of poor self-esteem and a sense of powerlessness in trying to regain the support of her family members and proving to herself and others her value as a good mother and a good teacher. The counselor will guide Maria through some empowerment exercises based on the reality therapy approach so that she can understand the difference between what is in her personal control and what is not. The counselor will ask Maria such questions as, "What in yourself or your environment can you control or change?" After some probing by the counselor, Maria might say she has control over how she sees herself and her sleep environment.

To improve self-esteem, Maria can make a list of her positive attributes and positive things that other people have said about her. The counselor will encourage her to concentrate on these positive attributes by making verbal affirmations.

A cognitive approach can be used to help Maria make some personal changes. Maria might be instructed to name one thing that she would like to change about herself. The counselor and Maria will consider the change together to ensure that what Maria wants to change is in her control and that the result will be evident in a relatively short time. This will show Maria that she can effect change and that some things can be changed immediately. Small, immediate changes will encourage Maria and keep her from doubting herself.

To improve sleep, the counselor can remind Maria of the benefit of sleep in developing holistic wellness. Suggestions might include (a) referring Maria to a medical doctor to determine her physical fitness; (b) reserving the bed for sleep only, not for watching television, working, or worrying; (c) entering the bedroom only to go to bed; (d) developing bedtime rituals; (e) abstaining from napping; and (f) envisioning sleep as a pleasant, sought-after state of being. Dream analysis is also an appropriate technique to use to help Maria understand what her dreams mean and how they affect her interactions with people in her family and work environment. Paradoxical intention may be used to help Maria to redirect her thoughts and see sleep as the better alternative. For instance, Maria can get out of bed when she cannot sleep or when she has bad dreams. She can perform tasks that are necessary but unpleasant to do. An example would be for Maria to get up and clean all of the kitchen cupboards. This task may be so unpleasant that sleep becomes a much more appealing option.

Group support can help Maria deal with many of her issues, including loneliness, alienation, and family issues. Maria has problems in her important relationships. A homogeneous group composed of Hispanic women would be ideal to help Maria reconnect with her cultural peers and gain support from their shared experiences.

Maria feels incapable of reestablishing family relationships and developing new intimate relationships. It seems to be easier for her to totally withdraw than to try to change her behavior or the behavior of others. Feminist family counseling with Maria and her family can help them deal with family support, child-rearing practices, and extended family role issues. This will help Maria deal with her guilt concerning the responsibilities of motherhood while having the extended family play a larger role in helping with child care while Maria is working. When Maria improves her inner strength and is more confident in herself, her attitude toward approaching an intimate relationship may change. The counselor might work with Maria to clarify whether Maria wants to become involved in an intimate relationship and, if so, to visualize what that relationship would look like culturally and personally. The purpose of this exercise would be to see whether Maria's personal values and her cultural values are congruent.

It may be helpful for Maria to reconnect with her church and other advocacy networks for Hispanic women. Contact with advocacy groups can help Maria establish feelings of belonging. This reconnection with her cultural group also will help to improve her relationship with her family and provide a way for Maria to teach her children about her heritage. This may help Maria reconcile her departure from her family and the community. The counselor may suggest to Maria that she get involved with community groups that advocate for Hispanic women and other oppressed groups so that she can make a greater impact on society at large while improving her self-worth. For instance, if Maria were to get involved with an advocacy group that works to combat domestic violence against Hispanic women, her story may be an inspiration to other women and at the same time help Maria to feel that she is making a valuable contribution to her community.

The most important thing to consider about feminist counseling with Maria is the need for an egalitarian counseling relationship. Maria must feel that she has some important contributions to make to the counseling sessions. The counselor will consider Maria's culturally reinforced behavior and help her to reconnect with her cultural group. Maria's self-worth will improve when she understands that her behavior is not a symptom of pathology but, in fact, may be a part of the solution to some of her problems. Reconnections with family, church, and her community will nourish Maria's need for belonging, improve her self-worth, and provide her with a much-needed support system.

REFERENCES

American Psychiatric Association. (2013). *Diagnostic and statistical manual of mental disorders* (5th ed.). Arlington, VA: Author.

Ballou, M., & Gabalac, N. (1985). *A feminist position on mental health.* Springfield, IL: Charles C Thomas.

Ballou, M., & West, C. (2000). Feminist therapy approaches. In M. Biaggio & M. Herson (Eds.), *Issues in the psychology of women* (pp. 273–297). New York, NY: Kluwer Academic/Plenum.

Bem, S. L. (1976). Probing the promise of androgyny. In A. G. Kaplan & J. P. Bean (Eds.), *Beyond sex-role stereotypes: Readings toward a psychology of androgyny* (pp. 47–62). Boston, MA: Little, Brown.

Bem, S. L. (1981). Gender schema theory: A cognitive account of sex typing. *Psychological Review, 88,* 354–364.

Bem, S. L. (1987). Probing the promise of androgyny. In M. Walsh (Ed.), *The psychology of women: Ongoing debates* (pp. 206–225). New Haven, CT: Yale University Press.

Bem, S. L. (1993). *The lenses of gender.* New Haven, CT: Yale University Press.

Blakely, K. (2007). Reflections on the role of emotion in feminist research. *International Journal of Qualitative Methods, 6*(2), 1–7.

Brown, L. S. (1986). Gender role analysis: A neglected component of psychological assessment. *Psychotherapy: Theory, Research, and Practice, 23,* 243–248.

Brown, L. S. (1994). *Subversive dialogues: Theory in feminist therapy.* New York, NY: Basic Books.

Brown, L. S., & Ballou, M. (Eds.). (1992). *Personality and psychopathology: Feminist reappraisals.* New York, NY: Guilford Press.

Chandler, R., Worell, J., & Johnson, D. (2000, August). *Process and outcomes in psychotherapy with women. Joint task force final report.* Presentation at the Annual Convention of the American Psychological Association, Washington, DC.

Chandler, R., Worell, J., Johnson, D., Blount, A., & Lusk, M. (1999, August). *Measuring long-term outcomes of feminist counseling and psychotherapy.* Paper presented at the Annual Convention of the American Psychological Association, Boston, MA.

Chesler, P. (1972). *Women and madness.* New York, NY: Doubleday.

Chesler, P. (1990). Twenty years since *Women and Madness:* Toward a feminist institute of mental health and healing. *Journal of Mind and Behavior, 11,* 313–322.

Comstock, D. L., Hammer, T. R., Strentzsch, J., Cannon, K., Parsons, J., & Salazar, G. (2008). Relational-cultural theory: A framework for bridging relational, multicultural, and social justice competencies. *Journal of Counseling & Development, 86*, 279–287.

Corey, G. (2009). *Theory and practice of counseling and psychotherapy* (7th ed.). Belmont, CA: Brooks/Cole.

Crethar, H. C., Torres Rivera, E., & Nash, S. (2008). In search of common threads: Linking multicultural, feminist, and social justice paradigms. *Journal of Counseling & Development, 86*, 269–278.

Dutton-Douglas, M. A., & Walker, L. E. (Eds.). (1988). *Feminist psychotherapies: Integration of therapeutic and feminist systems.* Norwood, NJ: Ablex.

Elliott, J. M. (1999). Feminist theory. In D. Capuzzi & D. R. Gross (Eds.), *Counseling and psychotherapy: Theories and interventions* (pp. 203–229). Upper Saddle River, NJ: Merrill/Prentice Hall.

Enns, C. Z. (1993). Twenty years of feminist counseling and therapy: From naming biases to implementing multifaceted practice. *Counseling Psychologist, 21*, 3–87.

Enns, C. Z. (2004). *Feminist theories and feminist psychotherapies: Origins, themes, and variations* (2nd ed.). New York, NY: Haworth Press.

Enns, C. Z. (2012). Feminist approaches to counseling. In E. M. Altmaier & J. C. Hansen (Eds.), *The Oxford handbook of counseling psychology* (pp. 434–459). New York, NY: Oxford University Press.

Enns, C. Z., Sinacore, A. L., Ancis, J. R., & Phillips, J. (2004). Toward integrating feminist and multicultural pedagogies. *Journal of Multicultural Counseling and Development, 32*, 414–427.

Enns, C. Z., & Williams, E. N. (2013). *The Oxford handbook of feminist multicultural counseling psychology.* New York, NY: Oxford University Press.

Eriksen, K., & Kress, V. E. (2008). Gender and diagnosis: Struggles and suggestions for counselors. *Journal of Counseling & Development, 86*, 152–162.

Espin, O. M. (1993). Feminist therapy: Not for or by White women only. *Counseling Psychologist, 21*, 103–108.

Evans, K. M., Kincade, E. A., Marbley, A. F., & Seem, S. R. (2005). Feminism and feminist therapy: Lessons from the past and hopes for the future. *Journal of Counseling & Development, 83*, 269–277.

Evans, K. M., Kincade, E. A., & Seem, S. R. (2011). *Introduction to feminist therapy: Strategies for social and individual change.* Thousand Oaks, CA: Sage.

Fitzgerald, L. F., & Nutt, R. (1986). The Division 17 principles concerning the counseling/psychotherapy of women: Rationale and implementation. *Counseling Psychologist, 14*, 180–216.

Follingstad, D. R., Robinson, E. A., & Pugh, M. (1977). Effects of consciousness-raising groups on measures of feminism, self-esteem, and social desirability. *Journal of Counseling Psychology, 24*, 223–230.

Freidan, B. (1963). *The feminine mystique.* New York, NY: Dell.

Gannon, L. (1982). The role of power in psychotherapy. *Women and Therapy, 1*, 3–11.

Getahun, D., Jacobsen, S. J., Fassett, M. J., Chen, W., Demissie, K., & Rhoads, G. G. (2013). Recent trends in childhood attention-deficit/hyperactivity disorder. *JAMA Pediatrics, 167*(3), 282–288.

Gilligan, C. (1982). *In a different voice.* Cambridge, MA: Harvard University Press.

Green, E., McCollum, V., & Hays, D. (2008). Teaching advocacy counseling within a social justice framework: Implications for school counselors and educators. *Journal for Social Action in Counseling and Psychology, 1,* 14–30.

Herlihy, B., & Corey, G. (2016). Feminist therapy. In G. Corey (Ed.), *Theory and practice of counseling and psychotherapy* (9th ed., pp. 613–642). Pacific Grove, CA: Brooks/Cole.

Herman, J. L. (1992). *Trauma and recovery: The aftermath of violence.* New York, NY: Basic Books.

Hill, M., & Ballou, M. (1998). Making feminist therapy: A practice survey. *Women and Therapy, 21,* 1–16.

Israeli, A. L., & Santor, D. A. (2000). Reviewing effective components of feminist therapy. *Counseling Psychology Quarterly, 13,* 233–247.

Johnson, M. (1976). An approach to feminist therapy. *Psychotherapy: Theory, Research, and Practice, 13,* 72–76.

Jordan, J. V., & Surrey, J. L. (1986). The self-in-relation: Empathy and the mother–daughter relationship. In T. Bernay & D. W. Cantor (Eds.), *The psychology of today's woman: New psychoanalytic visions* (pp. 139–168). Hillsdale, NJ: Analytic Press.

Kaplan, S. J., Pelcovitz, D., Salzinger, S., Weiner, M., Mandel, F. S., Lesser, M. L., & Labruna, V. E. (1998). Adolescent physical abuse: Risk for adolescent psychiatric disorders. *American Journal of Psychiatry, 155,* 954–959.

Kaschak, E. (1981). Feminist psychotherapy: The first decade. In S. Cox (Ed.), *Female psychology: The emerging self* (pp. 387–400). New York, NY: St. Martin's Press.

Kaschak, E. (1992). *Engendered lives.* New York, NY: Basic Books.

Kincade, E. A., Seem, S., & Evans, K. M. (1998, March). *Feminist therapy theory and practice: A model for social and individual change.* Paper presented at the American Counseling Association World Conference, Indianapolis, IN.

Lerner, H. G. (1989). *The dance of intimacy.* New York, NY: Harper & Row.

Miller, J. B. (1976). *Toward a new psychology of women.* Boston, MA: Beacon Press.

Moradi, B., Fischer, A. R., Hill, M. S., Jome, L. M., & Blum, S. A. (2000). Does "feminist" plus "therapist" equals "feminist therapist"? An empirical investigation of the link between self-labeling and behaviors. *Psychology of Women Quarterly, 24,* 285–296.

Morgan, P. L., Staff, J., Hillemeier, M. M., Farkas, G., & Maczuga, S. (2013). Racial and ethnic disparities in ADHD diagnosis from kindergarten to eighth grade. *Pediatrics, 132*(1), 85–93.

Olson, M. E. (2001). Listening to the voices of anorexia: The researcher as an "outsider witness." *Journal of Feminist Family Therapy, 11,* 25–46.

Rampage, C. (1998). Feminist couple therapy. In F. M. Dattilio (Ed.), *Case studies in couple and family therapy: Systemic and cognitive perspectives* (pp. 353–370). New York, NY: Guilford Press.

Rave, E. J., & Larsen, C. C. (1995). *Ethical decision making in therapy: Feminist perspectives.* New York, NY: Guilford Press.

Remer, P., Rostosky, S., & Wright, M. (2001). Counseling women from a feminist perspective. In E. R. Welfel & R. E. Ingersoll (Eds.), *Mental health desk reference* (pp. 341–347). New York, NY: Wiley.

Reynolds, A. L., & Constantine, M. G. (2004). Feminism and multiculturalism: Parallels and intersections. *Journal of Multicultural Counseling and Development, 32,* 346–357.

Santos de Barona, M., & Dutton, M. A. (1997). Feminist perspectives on assessment. In J. Worell & N. G. Johnson (Eds.), *Shaping the future of feminist psychology: Education, research, and practice* (pp. 37–56). Washington, DC: American Psychological Association.

Sharf, R. S. (2000). *Theories of psychotherapy and counseling: Concepts and cases* (3rd ed.). Pacific Grove, CA: Brooks/Cole.

Walker, L. E. (1990). A feminist therapist views the case. In D. W. Cantor (Ed.), *Women as therapists: A multitheoretical casebook* (pp. 78–95). New York, NY: Springer.

Whalen, M., Fowler-Lese, K. P., Barber, J. S., Williams, E. N., Judge, A. B., Nilsson, J. E., & Shibazaki, K. (2004). Counseling practice with feminist-multicultural perspectives. *Journal of Multicultural Counseling and Development, 32,* 370–389.

Williams, E. N., & Barber, J. S. (2004). Power and responsibility in therapy: Integrating feminism and multiculturalism. *Journal of Multicultural Counseling and Development, 32,* 390–401.

Worell, J., & Johnson, D. (2001). Therapy with women: Feminist frameworks. In R. K. Unger (Ed.), *Handbook of the psychology of women and gender* (pp. 317–329). New York, NY: Wiley.

Worell, J., & Johnson, N. G. (Eds.). (1997). *Shaping the future of feminist psychology: Education, research, and practice.* Washington, DC: American Psychological Association.

Worell, J., & Remer, P. (2003). *Feminist perspectives in therapy: Empowering diverse women* (2nd ed.). Hoboken, NJ: Wiley.

Zalaquett, C. P., Fuerth, K. M., Stein, C., Ivey, A. E., & Ivey, M. B. (2008). Reframing the *DSM–IV–TR* from a multicultural/social justice perspective. *Journal of Counseling & Development, 86,* 364–371.

Chapter 15

Transpersonal Theory

Jonathan W. Carrier and Nathanael G. Mitchell

Transpersonalism is a developing and controversial field that includes a group of approaches made possible only in the late 20th century as ancient Eastern religious traditions became exposed to and eventually blended with modern psychotherapies in a historically unprecedented way (Sutherland, 2001). There is an acknowledgment by a number of theorists that the transpersonal area is perhaps the most challenging in counseling "due to its elusive content, wide ranging methodologies and fundamental philosophical issues" (Friedman & Hartelius, 2013, p. xxxi).

The term *transpersonal* has been seen to mean beyond (*trans*) the personal, ego, or self (Strohl, 1998). An effort has been made recently to further define transpersonalism by exploring the historical tenets of the field as well as current definitions (Friedman & Hartelius, 2013). There are three different meanings of the Latin word *trans*: beyond, pervading, and changing (Caplan, Hartelius, & Rardin, 2003; Tarnas, 2001). These three meanings, when applied to the term *transpersonal*, correspond to three overarching themes of the field: beyond ego, pervading personhood, and changing humanity (Hartelius, Caplan, & Rardin, 2007). Applied in this way, *transpersonal theory* can be defined as an approach to human nature and counseling that "1) studies phenomena beyond the ego as context for 2) an integrative/holistic psychology; this provides a framework for 3) understanding and cultivating human transformation" (Hartelius et al., 2007, p. 11). More recently, leading theorists in the field have proposed the following definition:

> The Transpersonal theory is a transformative approach of the whole person in intimate interrelationship with an interconnected and evolving world; it pays special attention to self-expansive states as well as spiritual, mystical, and other exceptional human experiences that gain meaning in such a context. (Hartelius, Rothe, & Roy, 2013, p. 14)

Based on these definitions, transpersonal theory stands at the interface of mental health practice and spirituality and is one of the few approaches to integrate psychological concepts, theories, and methods with the subject matter and practices of the spiritual disciplines (Davis, 2000). Transpersonal approaches have been called "the first of modern sciences to take human spirituality seriously" (Kelly, 1991, p. 430) and attempt a synthesis that rethinks both spirituality and the practice of counseling (see Sidebar 15.1).

Generally known in the literature as *transpersonal psychology*, transpersonal theory as it applies to mental health practice is concerned not only with the diagnosis and treatment of psychological problems associated with normal human development but also with difficulties associated with developmental stages beyond that of the adult ego (Grof, 2008). It is the idea "that there are stages of human growth beyond the ego (hence the term *transpersonal*) that sets these theories apart from other models of human development and psychopathology" (Kasprow & Scotton, 1999, p. 12). The practice of transpersonal theory can include discussions and interventions pertaining to spiritual experiences; mystical states of consciousness; mindfulness and meditative practices; shamanic states; ritual; the overlap of spiritual experiences with disturbed mental states such as psychosis, depression, and other psychopathologies; and the transpersonal dimensions of interpersonal relationships, service, and encounters with the natural world (Davis, 2000).

BACKGROUND

Although transpersonal approaches have only gained widespread acknowledgment and discussion within the past 15 years, William James first introduced the subjects of consciousness, spiritualism, and psychical research into the mental health fields more than 90 years ago (Grof, 2008; Leahey, 1994). Much is also owed to such well-known contributors as Carl Jung and Abraham Maslow (Davis, 2000; Grof, 2008; Vich, 1988). Jung (1912/1967) was the first clinician to attempt to legitimize a spiritual approach to counseling, and Maslow (1968), in addition to his central role in forming humanistic approaches, lent many of these ideas to the transpersonal movement. It was Maslow who labeled transpersonal theory the *fourth force* among major counseling theories. Maslow's conceptualization of self-actualization and peak experiences, during which an individual experiences a spontaneous, ecstatic, and unifying state of consciousness, became a catalyzing force to the budding transpersonal movement (Grof, 2008).

Sidebar 15.1. Integrating Spirituality and Mental Health Practice

The training of counselors most often focuses on the necessary tenets of diagnosis, treatment planning, counseling techniques, and special considerations for diverse populations. It is rare for a counselor education program to teach counselors to consider the spirituality of potential clients. Unfortunately, this approach may lead counselors to focus only on a client's problematic cognitions and behaviors and miss the spiritual aspects of the client's functioning. Transpersonal theory teaches counselors to consider the entire human being to improve life functioning, which includes a strong consideration of the client as spiritual being. Regardless of your preferred counseling theory or set of techniques, remember to consider the whole client, especially his or her spiritual functioning.

It was from these early humanistic tenets of self-actualization and the belief in tremendous human spiritual potential that transpersonalism was born. After the inception and acceptance of humanistic approaches, leaders of the field such as Maslow, Anthony Sutich, and Stanislav Grof expanded the concept of self-actualization to include the more spiritual, extraordinary, and transcendent capacities of humankind (Grof, 2008; Peterson & Nisenholz, 1995). Thus, transpersonal theories arose to explore the idea that the possibilities for greater mental health and human psychological experience may be incredibly further reaching than mainstream science or psychological practice could or would allow for.

Although the theoretical underpinnings of transpersonal theory can be credited to a number of individuals, theories, and philosophical approaches to mental health and spiritual experience, Ken Wilber (1977, 1980, 1981, 1983a, 1983b, 1984a, 1984b, 1995, 1997, 2000, 2007) has emerged as the primary leader of this burgeoning field. No serious discussion on transpersonal theory can take place without mention of Wilber and his wealth of knowledge and published material on the subject. Transpersonal theories have become somewhat varied throughout their evolution, and currently there are as many as five major approaches to the practice: transpersonal systems theory, altered states of consciousness, Grof's (2008, 2013) holotropic model, some types of Jungian theory, and Wilber's spectrum or integral approach (Bidwell, 1999; Birnbaum, Birnbaum, & Mayseless, 2008). Because Wilber is the primary founder of transpersonal theory as it exists today, and because his approach is arguably the most inclusive and transcendent of the major transpersonal theories, his conceptualization is largely used here as we delve into transpersonal theory and its views on human development, psychopathology, and counseling.

HUMAN NATURE: A DEVELOPMENTAL PERSPECTIVE

At its cornerstone, transpersonal theory has championed the idea that consciousness is ever evolving (R. S. Brown, 2013). Transpersonalism views the development of higher consciousness as being necessary for transforming people's lives, a belief universally reflected in all transpersonal theories of human development. Healthy development is marked by one's advancement from personal (pertaining to the self) to transpersonal (outside of the self) concerns. Wilber's (1997) transpersonal developmental model is one of the most accepted among transpersonal theorists for its explanation of the necessary transcendence to the transpersonal. It should be noted, however, that Wilber disidentified with the transpersonal label in the 1980s (Friedman & Hartelius, 2013), although his original early work remains a cornerstone of the field today. Wilber, Engler, and Brown's (1986) model essentially incorporates the accepted developmental stages of Sigmund Freud, Carl Jung, and Jean Piaget with the humanistic tenet of self-actualization and Eastern religious and philosophical thought. It has been noted that, for even major developmental theorists such as Piaget (1929), the development of the individual was considered to be connected with the growth of the felt experience of value and harmony of thought, leading to higher levels of self-awareness (Dale, 2013).

Wilber's (1997) model is hierarchical in nature, with reality and psyche being organized into distinct levels, with higher levels being superior to lower levels in a logical and developmental sense (Richards & Bergin, 2004). When an individual progresses to the next level of development, the problems of the previous stage are resolved, but new developmental challenges may appear. Thus, as each new level is attained, new psychological structures and abilities emerge, but so do the possibilities for new pathologies should development fail to continue (Kasprow & Scotton, 1999).

Wilber (2000) viewed an individual's life as being marked by the pseudoindependent progress of several developmental lines (stages) through all levels of life and consciousness. The self attempts to manage each of the lines, which are interdependent but advance at their own paces. These developmental lines are broadly arranged into three groups: the prepersonal, the personal, and the transpersonal. According to Kasprow and Scotton (1999),

- *Prepersonal functioning* occurs in the absence of full rational competence and a healthy, intact ego. It is instinctual and centers mainly on satisfying biological needs.
- *Personal functioning* is higher than the prepersonal and is controlled by and caters to the concerns of the ego. A sense of identity is created through thoughts and feelings about one's attachments, and behavior is regulated by this identity.
- *Transpersonal functioning* is the most ideal type of functioning and is associated with the diminishment of personal identification and the emergence of states of being and modes of knowing associated with levels of reality beyond personal identity.

Within the broad prepersonal, personal, and transpersonal states of functioning, a number of developmental lines, or stages, exist. These are composed of (a) *cognitive* stages, through which the individual develops greater intuitive, emotional, and interpersonal abilities; (b) the *vision logic* stage, characterized by the integration of mind and body, or thought and feeling; and (c) *psychic* stages, the heart of transpersonal development, through which the individual's consciousness extends beyond the ego and is able to merge with what is observed, attains the ability to access archetypes, and eventually learns to travel at will along all of the developmental lines (Bidwell, 1999; Kasprow & Scotton, 1999).

Wilber (1997) used the term *translation* to refer to this process of integrating, stabilizing, and equilibrating the different developmental lines on a horizontal level. In contrast, *transformation* is the process of transcending one consciousness (line or stage) and advancing vertically to the next. Development, then, occurs in the tension between these horizontal (translation) and vertical (transformation) dimensions or lines of human existence (Bidwell, 1999). Wilber (2000) held that defining this spiritual line is central to the development of the individual. Spiritual growth is thus measured by the individual's ability to transcend a subjective point of view and move on to higher earthly, spiritual, and even cosmic perspectives (Bidwell, 1999). This transcendence is the hallmark of the integrated self and stands at the center of Wilber's transpersonal model (Bidwell, 1999). Wilber (1995) stated that this is

> the cosmic evolutionary process, which is "self development through self transcendence," the same process at work in atoms and molecules and cells, a process that, in human domains, continues naturally into the superconscious, with precisely nothing occult or mysterious about it. (p. 258)

MAJOR CONSTRUCTS

Throughout its history, transpersonal theory has evolved into a number of similar but unique forms of practice and theory, making a discussion of the major constructs of the approach somewhat complicated. Lajoie and Shapiro (1992) sought to remedy this through an examination of the transpersonal literature to elucidate the root themes of the theory. Their research uncovered 30 distinct themes across the varied theories, of which five occurred most frequently: states of consciousness, highest or ultimate potential, beyond ego or personal self, transcendence, and spiritual. From this, Lajoie and Shapiro devised the following definition of transpersonal theory: "Transpersonal (theory) is concerned with the study of humanity's highest potential, and with the recognition, understanding, and realization of unitive, spiritual, and transcendent states of consciousness" (p. 91).

According to Davis (2000), the core concept of this definition and transpersonal theory is nonduality, or the fact that it is unitive: the recognition that each part (each person) is fundamentally and ultimately a part of the whole (the cosmos). Within this are two central tenets: (a) the intrinsic health and basic goodness of the whole and each of its parts; and (b) the validity of self-transcendence from the personal identity to a sense of identity that is deeper, broader, and more unified with the whole (Grof, 2013; Lajoie & Shapiro, 1992; Scotton, Chinen, & Battista, 1996; Walsh & Vaughan, 1993). It is important to understand, however, that in the process of fostering transcendence and unity, transpersonal counseling does not annihilate the individual but seeks to integrate psychological as well as spiritual development, the personal in addition to the transpersonal, and exceptional mental health and higher states of consciousness along with ordinary experience (Sperry & Shafranske, 2005).

It is perhaps as easy to describe transpersonalism by its differences from other theories of counseling and development than by its similarities. Transpersonalism's distinction from the major models of human functioning rests largely on its radically different philosophical worldview (Elkins, 2005). Transpersonal psychotherapies generally do not seek to challenge or supplant other models but instead consider an expanded view of human nature while incorporating elements of behaviorism, psychoanalysis, humanism, Jungian analysis, and Eastern philosophy (Strohl, 1998). However, it is in this very expanded view of human nature that transpersonalism diverges from the mainstream. According to Ajaya (1997), the major theories of counseling and development draw from four distinct philosophical paradigms:

- *Reductionistic:* Reductionism understands existence by breaking down a phenomenon, tenet, or behavior into its smallest parts. Reductionism views consciousness as the result of the interaction between these smallest parts.
- *Humanistic:* Humanism emphasizes the value and dignity of each individual and refutes the reductionistic premise that human experience can be broken down into its primitive component parts. The humanistic paradigm does not, however, allow for higher states of human consciousness.
- *Dualistic:* Dualism accepts that consciousness can transcend human experience. Dualism considers experience to be the result of a complementary interaction of the two primary principles of material phenomena and consciousness. It believes that a material-bound being can never comprehend the scope and transcendent nature of consciousness.

- *Monastic:* Monasticism sees all phenomena as creative, illusory expressions of a primary and unified field of consciousness. This pure consciousness is the fundamental source of all that exists, including human experience itself. Monasticism believes that human experience can attain an awakened state of consciousness in which the traditional concepts of space and time and cause and effect all lose their meaning.

Transpersonal theorists generally view mainstream mental health theory and practice as being largely reductionistic and generally oblivious to the greater scope of human experience and potential (Boggio Gilot, 2008; Dossey, 1999; Grof, 1985; Small, 2000; Weil, 1996). Humanistic theories, like reductionism, do not account for higher states of being but are more amenable to the transpersonal approach and serve as a bridge between reductionism and the tenets of dualism and monisticism (Strohl, 1998). Of the four paradigms, transpersonalism primarily encompasses both the dualistic and monistic approaches in an effort to reconcile the divine and human qualities of humankind (dualism) as well as uncover one's true source of being and the underlying unity of all existence (monasticism; Strohl, 1998).

According to Wilber (1997), although it differs fundamentally from most of reductionism and some aspects of humanism, transpersonalism acknowledges reductionistic (psychodynamic, behavioral, and cognitive–behavioral) and humanistic (humanism and person-centered) approaches as legitimate theories that emphasize important areas of human development and experience. In essence, according to transpersonalists, the theories of psychoanalysis, behaviorism, humanism, and all of their derivatives are effective niche approaches but do not account for the majority of human experience and existence. By contrast, transpersonal theory is viewed by its followers as truly eclectic and more encompassing because it incorporates many viewpoints from adjacent and even opposing theories while also focusing on expanded human qualities largely ignored by other theories (Daniels, 2013; Grof, 2008; Kasprow & Scotton, 1999; Strohl, 1998; see Sidebar 15.2).

APPLICATIONS

Overview

Ultimately, the goal of transpersonal counseling is not only to remove psychopathologies or resolve interpersonal difficulties but also to foster higher human

Sidebar 15.2. Transpersonal Counseling: From Eclectic to Transcendent

Transpersonal counselors recognize that clients will often benefit from commonly used reductionistic approaches such as cognitive, behavior, and psychodynamic therapies as well as humanistic counseling. However, although transpersonal counselors are very eclectic in that they will often use any technique they believe will help the client, they also believe that only using these techniques will miss the vast majority of the client's life experience and functioning. Consider that a transpersonal counselor is working with a client undergoing the very common experience of anxiety or depression. How might the transpersonal counselor utilize established reductionistic techniques along with transpersonal approaches to move the client beyond simple improvement to exceptional mental health and eventual transcendence?

development (Hartelius et al., 2007). Toward this end, transpersonal counselors seek to facilitate the development of a stable, cohesive ego and the exploration of the existential self (Strohl, 1998). However, according to transpersonal theory, these processes are only part of the development of a healthy self. Individuals will not be able to become whole until they awaken to the deepest levels of human existence (Hartelius et al., 2007). Transpersonal counselors deal with normal client problems and life difficulties, as do counselors from any other modality. What sets transpersonal counselors apart from the mainstream, however, is the added requisite of transcendent experience. In short, an individual is truly healthy not when he or she has achieved a satisfactory level of everyday functioning but when he or she has actually transcended the normal state of consciousness and everyday being to one that is unified with the highest levels and states of consciousness, being, and existence (Hartelius et al., 2007; Rama, Ballentine, & Ajaya, 1979; Williams, 1980; Wittine, 1993).

Goals of Counseling and Psychotherapy

Essentially, three dimensions apply to any approach to counseling and psychotherapy: content, process, and context (Vaughan, 1979). *Content* refers to the subject matter dealt with; *process* refers to the techniques and strategies used; and *context* refers to the counselor's view of counseling, suffering, healing, and mental health. Davis (2000) examined these dimensions as they pertain to transpersonal counseling:

- *Content:* The content of transpersonal counseling includes transpersonal and mystical experiences, peak experiences, and spiritual emergencies (Grof, 2008; Watson, 1994).
- *Process:* The processes of transpersonal counseling includes practices drawn from spiritual traditions such as meditation (Ferrer, 2008; Goleman & Ram, 1996), initiations and vision questing (Foster & Little, 1997), ritual, and shamanic inductions (Walsh, 1990).
- *Context:* The transpersonal context includes holding in view the client's intrinsic health, being mindful and present centered regardless of the particular content or processes, approaching counseling as both an act of service and an act of work on oneself, and recognizing nonduality in the counseling situation (Ferrer, 2002; Wittine, 1989).

The goals of transpersonal counseling are much the same as for any other type of counseling: to aid individuals with myriad mental health issues and life difficulties. However, transpersonal counselors are most concerned with fostering a deepening and integration of one's sense of connectedness, whether it be with self, community, nature, or the entire cosmos (Bidwell, 1999; Davis, 2000; Kasprow & Scotton, 1999). Regardless of the life difficulty or psychological problem at hand, transpersonal counseling will almost always seek to send the client inward (Bidwell, 1999):

> The more one can introspect and reflect on one's self, then the more detached from that self one can become, the more one can rise above that self's limited perspective, and so the less narcissistic or less egocentric one becomes (or the more de-centered one becomes). (Wilber, 1995, p. 256)

Transpersonal counselors generally accept that most people are unwilling, unable, or simply not ready to work at a transpersonal and transcendent level. Wilber (1997) stated that in the United States,

> a disproportionately large number of people who are drawn to transpersonal spirituality are often at a preconventional level of self development. This means that much of what American (spiritual) teachers (and counselors) have to do is actually engage in supportive psychotherapy, not transformative and transpersonal spirituality. (p. 227)

Thus, one of the primary goals of transpersonal counseling is to bring the client to a point at which he or she can begin to work on transpersonal issues. It is simply not enough in the transpersonal counselor's mind to bring a client to an acceptable or healthy level of mental health. If given the chance, the transpersonal counselor will always seek to go beyond this mark into the realm of transcendence, unity, and extraordinary mental health. As an example of this tenet, in a study on a transpersonal approach to healing following youth suicide, Kalischuk and Nixon (2009) identified self-reflection, self-care, and self-transcendence as overlapping healing patterns integral to families of youth who have completed a suicide attempt.

The Process of Change

It is often mistakenly thought that transpersonal counseling is oriented solely toward spiritual transcendence. Transpersonal leader Sylvia Boorstein (1996) warned against this, stating that zeal for work in the transpersonal realm should not come at the expense of overlooking relevant personal issues. Should a counselor gloss over the client's personal problems, without working through them and making them fully conscious, there will be no foundation from which spiritual work can begin (Small, 2000). In essence, it is impossible to transcend something that has never developed or become integrated (Small, 2000). Thus, the process of change in transpersonal counseling is marked by the overcoming of personal problems and life issues, which allows for primary work toward spiritual integration. As the client moves from normal functioning to transpersonal work, the process of unification and deepening the experience of connection usually engenders the highest human qualities, such as creativity, compassion, selflessness, and wisdom, all of which are indicative of psychological health and adjustment (Birnbaum et al., 2008; Kasprow & Scotton, 1999).

Traditional Intervention Strategies

Wilber (2000) called for an integrative therapy that takes a holistic approach—investigating and addressing each of the developmental lines or stages by using interventions that range from changing nutrition and exercise to cognitive restructuring or Jungian individuation to specific spiritual disciplines, depending on the client's developmental stage and pathologies. The transpersonal therapist must be ready to draw from all traditions, both Eastern and Western. "A truly integrative and encompassing psychology can and should make use of the complementary insights offered by each school of psychology" (Wilber, 1977, p. 15). According to Wilber (1997), the transpersonal counselor must be an expert in most forms of intervention, regardless of the theoretical modality. This extent of expertise is necessary because guiding clients through the maze of developmental possibilities is certain to require a wide range of interventions based on the client's personality, lifestyle, and personal experiences.

The core practice of transpersonal counseling includes meditation, mindfulness, intuition, yoga, biofeedback, breath training, contemplation, inward focusing, visualization, dream-work, guided imagery, and altered states of consciousness (Ajaya, 1997; Birnbaum et al., 2008; Boss, 1981; Davis, 2000; Hutton, 1994; see Sidebar 15.3). Other practices that are associated with transpersonal psychology, but not as commonly used as others, include shamanism, lucid dreaming, and psychedelic drugs (Davis, 2000; Walsh & Vaughan, 1993). It can be argued that of all of the interventions available to the transpersonal counselor, the most central is meditation. Comparing the role of meditation in transpersonal psychology with the role of dreams in psychoanalysis, Walsh and Vaughan (1993, p. 200) referred to meditation as "the royal road to the transpersonal." Meditation and related practices have a range of uses, including self-regulation, relaxation, and pain control, but are most commonly used in transpersonal counseling for self-exploration and self-liberation (MacDonald, Walsh, & Shapiro, 2013; Shapiro, 1994). Meditation allows the clients to disidentify from their masks or egos and realize their fundamental nonduality, leading to the liberation and transcendence of the self (Birnbaum, 2005; Goleman & Ram, 1996).

Another key aspect of transpersonal counseling, of which meditation is a part, is the exploration of human experiences known as *altered states of consciousness*. Metzner (1992) defined an *altered state of consciousness* as a change in thinking, feeling, and perception, in relation to one's ordinary, baseline consciousness, that has a beginning, duration, and ending. Delirium, hypnosis, deep meditation, and intoxication are all examples of altered states of consciousness (Walsh, 1994). Western theories have historically been slow to recognize the wide scope and enormity of altered states of consciousness as seen by the transpersonal theorist and have viewed many of these states, such as delirium and intoxication, as pathological (Bradford, 2012; Davis, 2000; Grof, 2008; Walsh, 1994; Wilber, 2000). According to Walsh (1994), one of the most dramatic examples of this Western resistance was that of the reaction to hypnosis and the Scottish physician James Esdaile. During his station as a medical doctor in India more than a century ago, Esdaile discovered the remarkable capacity of hypnosis to reduce pain and mortality in surgical patients. Esdaile's findings were so dramatic and foreign that Western medical journals refused to publish his reports. On his return to Britain, Esdaile arranged a demonstration before the British College of Physicians and Surgeons, during which he amputated a gangrenous leg while the patient, under hypnosis and without any anesthetic, lay smiling calmly. Instead of

Sidebar 15.3. Commonly Used Transpersonal Counseling Techniques

It is often mistakenly thought that transpersonal counseling is oriented solely toward spiritual transcendence. Although spiritual transcendence may be the ultimate goal of transpersonal counseling, counselors operating from this theory often use a set of techniques with the objective of symptom reduction as well as increased personal awareness. Commonly used transpersonal counseling techniques include meditation, mindfulness, intuition, yoga, biofeedback, breath training, contemplation, inward focusing, visualization, dream-work, guided imagery, and altered states of consciousness. These techniques are especially useful for clients suffering from anxiety and related disorders but may also be used in part for depression, as well as for grief and loss issues.

marveling at what could have been a revolutionary new find to modern psychological and medical practice, his colleagues concluded that Esdaile had paid a hardened rogue to pretend he felt no pain! Fortunately, over time, Western theory has become more accepting of alternate states of consciousness and has come to appreciate that many of these may be beneficial to counseling practice and the enrichment of human experience (Strohl, 1998).

When he or she deems the client ready, the transpersonal counselor is likely to attempt to aid the client in experiencing a range of altered states, through a variety of methods, after which they will examine and discuss together. Because many of these experiences can be quite varied, transpersonal counselors use a method known as *phenomenological mapping* to aid clients in organizing and understanding their experiences during the altered state (Wilber, 1997). The key point to phenomenological mapping is that it allows the client and counselor to map, compare, and differentiate states of consciousness on not one but multiple experiential dimensions and with greater precision than one could achieve by lumping them all together as one experience (Walsh, 1994). The result is that the individual can better appreciate the richness and variety of transpersonal states as well as clearly differentiate them from psychopathological states such as schizophrenia, with which they can be and have sometimes been confused (Walsh, 1990). Although some claim that all altered states are essentially the same, transpersonal theorists argue that different methods of attaining altered states lead to different altered states, requiring the need for differentiation and organization (Wilber, 2000). For example, Buddhist meditation, hypnosis, and intoxication may all lead to a different type of altered experience and must be discussed and examined separately to search for differences and commonalities (Wilber, 1997). Phenomenological mapping is absolutely necessary, according to Walsh (1994), because when key dimensions such as mental control, awareness of the environment, concentration, arousal, emotion, self-sense, and content of experience are compared, multiple differences between states come into view.

Wilber (1995) stated that once the altered states have been experienced and mapped, the individual must then undergo a process known as *deep structure analysis*. The purpose of deep structure analysis is to attempt to make coherent sense of the various alternate states of consciousness, identify possible commonalities among states, bring any developmental implications of the states into view, and reveal any hidden meanings among the states that may have an important impact on the individual's life (Walsh & Vaughan, 1993; Wilber, 2000). Deep structure analysis, according to Wilber (1997), allows the individual to cluster alternate consciousness states and experiences and identify a number of deep structures, which Wilber has classified into a number of hierarchical states. Although Wilber (1997) classified alternate consciousness experiences into a number of overarching deep structures, his three main deep structural states, according to Walsh (1994), are subtle states, causal states, and the ultimate condition:

- *Subtle states:* Once conscious mental activity has calmed, one may experience a range of altered consciousness states that fit into the category of subtle states. The experiences in these states can include experiences of light or sound; emotions such as love and joy; or visions of archetypes (which can vary by culture) such as shamanistic power animals, Christian angelic figures, and a range of others.

- *Causal states:* After subtle states have deepened and stabilized, then causal states devoid of any objects, images, or phenomena can arise. These states are the realm of pure consciousness and the transcendental source of all existential experience. These can be culturally described as the experience of Nirvana in Buddhism and the Tao of Taoism, among others.
- *The ultimate condition:* In this final state, objects and emotions from the subtle states reappear but are instantly recognized as expressions, projections, or modifications of consciousness. This is the final enlightenment and realization of consciousness in all things. It is connectedness with the entire universe and all things in it. This state is the highest goal and greatest good in all human existence. This experience can be culturally known as salvation, Zen's One Mind, or Hinduism's Brahman–Atman, among others.

It is important to note here that before advancing into alternative counseling methods such as altered states of consciousness, transpersonal counselors must gauge the readiness of their client carefully. For the unprepared individual, experiences of deep connectedness can fragment necessary ego boundaries and produce chaos, terror, and confusion (Kasprow & Scotton, 1999).

Brief Intervention Strategies and Current Practices

Most of what can be considered purely transpersonal interventions are not brief in nature. Even a lifetime may prove too short for most individuals to experience the highest states of connectedness. Although the complete transpersonal experience is by no means short term, transpersonal counselors can and do work with a variety of clients with problems that easily fit into the scope of normal life experience and require shorter term counseling. When faced with clients requiring brief interventions, transpersonal counselors are most likely to use established methods, such as cognitive–behavioral interventions, that are proven to work in time-sensitive counseling situations. A study by Hutton (1994) delineated transpersonal theory's liberal use of other interventions. In his study, transpersonal counselors reported using more approaches than practitioners of other therapies and were found to be more synthesizing in their approach than either psychoanalytic or cognitive–behavioral counselors. Hutton found transpersonal counselors to be similar to cognitive–behaviorists in their use of behaviorally focused visualization, biofeedback, and relaxation and similar to psychoanalysis in their use of intuition and dream-work.

Transpersonal counselors believe that attitudes, expectations, and beliefs create the reality that the client experiences (Strohl, 1998). An essential part of transpersonal counseling that is as effective in short-term counseling as in long-term counseling is the uncovering, examining, and addressing of the beliefs that govern the client's reality. The transpersonal counselor will attempt to aid the client in dismissing negative beliefs, thus cultivating positive and constructive thought patterns leading to productive behavioral habits (Strohl, 1998). It is transpersonal theory's practical yet existential approach to human experience that makes it an effective practice in both short- and long-term counseling situations (Lukoff, Turner, & Lu, 1992).

Transpersonal approaches have been reported in the recent research literature as being effective for use with sexual addictions recovery (Nixon & Theriault, 2011), substance use disorders (Nixon, 2012), bereavement (Hastings, 2012), juvenile offenders (Himelstein, 2011), gerontological development (Atchly, 2011; Wacks, 2011), understanding the motivations behind suicide (Neustadter, 2010), and families coping with the suicide of an adolescent child (Kalischuk & Nixon, 2009). The fact that transpersonal counseling has started to gain empirical support for use with a number of common life and developmental challenges, as well as mental health issues, speaks to the growing faction of transpersonal theorists who are calling for a more grounded, scientific approach to the field (Friedman, 2013; MacDonald, 2013), while others warn of the field becoming too scientific (Ferrer, 2014).

Clients With Serious Mental Health Issues

There are wide differences of opinion within the transpersonal community as to the appropriateness of doing transpersonal work with seriously mentally ill or psychotic individuals (Kasprow & Scotton, 1999). Jung (1960), Wilber (1984a), and Grof and Grof (1989) argued that transpersonal counseling is not appropriate for seriously mentally ill or psychotic individuals, whereas Lukoff (1996) suggested that transpersonal psychotherapy may be particularly appropriate for psychotic disorders, even serious ones. Building on the assertions of Lukoff (1996), a number of theorists within the field of transpersonal theory have recently advocated for alternative transpersonal conceptualizations of psychotic disorders (Phillips, Lukoff, & Stone, 2009) and have even discussed the positive functions of psychosis (Martens, 2010).

This issue is compounded by the resemblance of some altered states of consciousness (transpersonal experiences) to psychotic states such as in schizophrenia. Differentiating between altered states of consciousness and true psychotic states is of extreme importance to optimize counseling and prevent unnecessary or harmful treatment (Kasprow & Scotton, 1999). Several theorists (Agosin, 1992; Grof & Grof, 1989; Lukoff, 1985) have suggested guidelines for determining the difference. Lukoff (1985) suggested the following four criteria to establish the difference between altered states of consciousness and psychosis: Transpersonal experiences are more likely in clients with (a) good premorbid (pretranspersonal experience) functioning, (b) an acute onset of symptoms within a period of 3 months, (c) the presence of a stressful precursor that could account for the acute symptoms, and (d) a positive and exploratory attitude toward the experience. Building on this, Birnbaum et al. (2008) urged counselors to proceed with caution when choosing a transpersonal approach with clients exhibiting serious mental health issues (see Sidebar 15.4). Naturally, when the question arises as to whether the client is exhibiting psychotic symptoms or transpersonal experiences, the ethical counselor will always seek supervision or clinical consultation.

Another mental health issue transpersonal counselors must be aware of is that of spiritual emergencies. Spiritual emergencies, first documented by Grof and Grof (1989), are emergent trans-egoic experiences, or experiences, ideation, and behavior that appear to be pathological but are, in fact, part of the transpersonal developmental process that can occur as an individual crosses into a new stage of development (Cortright, 2000). As has been previously mentioned in this chapter, as an individual accesses a new line or stage of development, greater awareness and connectedness can occur, but so can the potential for greater pathologies. A spiritual emergency occurs when the crossing to another developmental line results in a negative experience or behavior. For example, a healthy or prepared individual who experiences Wilber's (1997) psychic level, which mediates a sense of connec-

Sidebar 15.4. Severe Mental Health Issues and Transpersonal Counseling

Empirically supported treatments or interventions are those that have been shown in the research literature to be effective with particular disorders or adjustment challenges. Counselors are ethically bound to use the empirically supported treatments available for their clients' problem behaviors, cognitions, or maladaptive functioning. In recent years, transpersonal therapies have been shown to have empirical support for use with sexual addictions recovery, substance use disorders, bereavement, juvenile offenders, gerontological development, and coping challenges. However, no studies to date have found stand-alone transpersonal counseling to be effective for the treatment of severe mental health issues such as schizophrenia, bipolar disorder, obsessive-compulsive disorder, or suicidality. Although supportive or ancillary transpersonal techniques can be used with any client issue, transpersonal counselors are ethically bound to primarily use established empirically supported counseling techniques when working with clients with severe mental health issues.

tion to something outside the ego boundary, may experience feelings of universal love and empathic understanding, whereas an individual unprepared for this loss of ego boundary may experience paranoid ideation and separation (Kasprow & Scotton, 1999). Transpersonal theorists believe that these spiritual emergencies can have powerfully transformative effects on a person's life when supported by the counselor and allowed to run their course to completion (Birnbaum et al., 2008; Grof & Grof, 1989; Lukoff, Lu, & Turner, 1998; Perry, 1976). Goretzki, Thalbourne, and Storm (2013) recently developed a spiritual emergency scale to help therapists to identify and measure up to 10 different types of spiritual emergencies.

Overall, the onus is on the transpersonal counselor to be aware of his or her own limits of practice as well as the limitations of transpersonal interventions with seriously mentally ill individuals. When faced with difficulties that may be beyond the scope of transpersonal interventions, it is the ethical responsibility of the counselor either to use a proven counseling method or refer the client to another mental health professional. Transpersonal counselors must also be prepared to deal with spiritual emergencies and the sometimes powerful aspects of clients experiencing new altered states of consciousness and deepening feelings of connectedness.

EVALUATION

Overview

Transpersonal theory is a fascinating and dynamic field that is fundamentally different from any other major theory of counseling and human development. It stands at the boundary of mental health practice and spirituality and is the lone approach in wide practice to integrate counseling concepts, theories, and methodology with the subject matter and practices of the spiritual disciplines (Davis, 2000; Grof, 2008; Kasprow & Scotton, 1999). However, transpersonalism's very uniqueness has made it difficult to examine in an ideal empirical setting, and for this reason, it draws criticism from researchers and practitioners unprepared to accept on faith what many continue to view as a fringe and radical theory (Grof, 2008). As experts progress further into the 21st century and explore and learn more about human experience and spirituality, transpersonal approaches will likely continue to gain more followers and greater acceptance from traditional theorists.

Supporting Research

When the various phenomena associated with transpersonal theory (connectedness, altered states of consciousness) are considered, the discourse can become excessively abstract, vague, or inaccessible to those unversed in its tenets and even more difficult to objectively examine (W. W. Adams, 1999). It is worth mentioning, however, that a large body of empirical evidence suggests links between spiritual and religious experiences and health (Koening, McCullough, & Larson, 2001; Miller, 1999; Pargament, 1997). In addition to this, many of the interventions used by transpersonal counselors are established methods well examined by researchers (such as cognitive–behavioral interventions), yet studies examining the techniques considered unique to transpersonal theory are aged and sparse at best. This, of course, is primarily because of the following question: How does one test enlightenment? Some older studies attempted to answer that very question with limited results. For instance, D. Brown, Porte, and Dysart (1984) examined advanced meditators who had reached at least the first of the four Buddhist stages of enlightenment and found that they exhibited enhanced perceptual processing speed and sensitivity. However, in another dated study (D. Brown & Engler, 1986), enlightened subjects given a Rorschach test were not found to be free of the normal psychological conflicts of dependency, sexuality, and aggression, as might be expected of an enlightened individual.

Hutton (1994) did not assess the efficacy of transpersonal counseling but did examine its similarities with, and differences from, cognitive–behavioral and psychodynamic approaches. He discovered that all three approaches shared the belief in a firm grounding in the traditional theories and practices of counseling, but he found that transpersonal theories were more accepting of other theories, whereas cognitive–behavioral and psychodynamic theories accepted mainly their own approaches and disregarded others. Hutton also found transpersonal theory to be far more accepting of clients' spiritual issues than either cognitive–behavioral or psychodynamic approaches.

Early in the history of the field, there was a significant dearth of empirical support for the practice of transpersonal counseling. During this time, transpersonal practitioners were quick to point out that many of its methods had been in use for hundreds, if not thousands, of years but did not easily lend themselves to modern empirical study. However, within the past 7 years, a burgeoning research literature has developed that empirically supports the specialized use of transpersonal counseling with sexual addictions recovery (Nixon & Theriault, 2011), substance use disorders (Nixon, 2012), bereavement (Hastings, 2012), juvenile offenders (Himelstein, 2011), gerontological development (Atchly, 2011; Wacks, 2011), understanding of the motivations behind suicide (Neustadter, 2010), and families coping with the suicide of an adolescent child (Kalischuk & Nixon, 2009).

It is important to remember that transpersonal theory is eclectic in nature and often draws from a wide range of empirically validated interventions. Although it is clearly difficult to assess many of its tenets, current research in the field of transpersonal theory has begun to center more on transpersonal counseling outcomes rather than the examination of such abstract concepts as enlightenment or altered states of consciousness.

Limitations

The primary criticism of transpersonal theory is that its methodology often delves into the highly abstract, the deeply spiritual, and what some might even consider the paranormal (a claim refuted by transpersonalists), making empirical study under controlled situations difficult at best (W. W. Adams, 1999). Secularists may perceive transpersonalism as unscientific nonsense, whereas Christian and other theistic writers may view its positions as the latest version of a spiritually misguided gnosticism that they hoped had been vanquished centuries ago (G. Adams, 2002). In addition to these views, there has also been some debate as to the ethicality and effectiveness of transpersonal interventions with serious mental health issues, with some practitioners calling transpersonalism in counseling downright dangerous (Ellis, 1962). For these reasons, transpersonal theory has attracted debate from such famous theorists as Albert Ellis, who spoke out against transpersonalism with articles titled "Dangers of Transpersonal Psychology" (1989) and "Fanaticism That May Lead to a Nuclear Holocaust" (1986) and held a spirited debate in the *Journal of Counseling & Development* in the late 1980s against Ken Wilber, who responded with the sarcastically titled article "Let's Nuke the Transpersonalists" (1989).

The limitations and criticisms of transpersonal theory have done little to halt its progress as a widely used counseling modality, however. The academic literature regarding transpersonal theory has continued to grow well into the 21st century and shows no signs of slowing down. Although followers of traditional theory may not be prepared to accept or understand some of the complicated spiritual tenets that lie at the core of transpersonal theory, more and more counselors and clients seeking counseling in a more deeply spiritual realm continue to be attracted to this burgeoning field.

Summary Chart: Transpersonal Theory

Human Nature

Transpersonalism views the development of higher consciousness as necessary for transforming people's lives. Healthy development is marked by one's advancement from personal to transpersonal concerns. Spiritual growth is measured by the individual's ability to transcend a subjective point of view and move on to higher earthly, spiritual, and cosmic perspectives. An individual's life is marked by the progress of developmental lines or stages, broadly arranged into prepersonal, personal, and transpersonal, through all levels of life and consciousness, which the self attempts to manage and navigate. Each stage carries with it new developmental hurdles and pathologies that must be dealt with. Successful navigation through these developmental stages eventually results in transcendence and connection or oneness with all things.

Major Constructs

Transpersonal theory is concerned with the study of humanity's highest potential and with the recognition, understanding, and realization of unitive, spiritual, and transcendent states of consciousness. Transpersonal theory is nondual. It is unitive and carries with it the recognition that each part (each person) is fundamentally and ultimately a part of the whole (the cosmos). It does not seek to replace other counseling models but instead considers an expanded view of human nature while incorporating elements of behaviorism, psychoanalysis, humanism, Jungian analysis, and Eastern philosophy. Proponents of transpersonal theory hold it to be the most eclectic counseling approach in use today, being inclusive of mainstream counseling approaches while focusing on expanded human qualities largely ignored by other theories.

Goals

The goals of transpersonal counseling are similar to those of other forms of counseling: to aid individuals with mental health issues and life difficulties. However, transpersonal counselors are additionally concerned with fostering a deepening integration of one's sense of connectedness, whether it be with self, community, nature, or the entire cosmos. A primary goal of transpersonal counseling is to bring clients to a point at which they can begin to work on transpersonal issues. Transpersonal counselors seek to bring a client beyond a healthy level of mental health and into the realm of transcendence, unity, and extraordinary mental health. The overarching goal is always transcendence and deepening of connectedness with the universe.

Change Process

The process of change in transpersonal counseling is marked by the overcoming of personal problems and life issues, allowing for primary work toward spiritual integration. As the client moves from normal functioning to transpersonal work, the process of unification and deepening the experience of connection engenders the highest human qualities of creativity, compassion, selflessness, and wisdom.

Interventions

The core practice of transpersonal counseling includes meditation, mindfulness, intuition, yoga, biofeedback, breath training, contemplation, inward focusing, visualization, dream-work, guided imagery, and altered states of consciousness. Practitioners are as eclectic as possible and are as likely to use traditional intervention strategies as those labeled *transpersonal,* particularly for shorter term counseling. Primary interventions of transpersonal counseling are meditation and altered states of consciousness. Counselors use these strategies to bring clients to the eventual goal of transcendence and enlightenment (see Sidebar 15.5).

Limitations

Transpersonal counseling has come under fire for not having enough empirical support in the literature (although support has increased significantly in recent years for a limited set of mental health and life challenges), causing some to question the ethicality of its use. There is also some question as to the effectiveness and safety of its use with clients with serious mental health issues. Furthermore, transpersonal theory may be too abstract and complex for a majority of Western philosophically oriented clients.

THE CASE OF MARIA: A TRANSPERSONAL APPROACH

The goal of transpersonal counseling is to assist the individual in achieving his or her highest potential. A careful examination of themes within Maria's personal history and dreams can help direct the transpersonal counselor toward goals and

Sidebar 15.5. Case Study: James, a Good Candidate for Transpersonal Counseling

James is a 43-year-old man who has been happily married to the same woman for 14 years. Together, James and his wife have a 14-year-old son and a 9-year-old daughter. James is comfortably employed as an electrical engineer and reports little to no financial stress. James is physically healthy and does not use drugs or alcohol. Overall, James reports that he has a "near perfect life." Nevertheless, James reports a "general feeling of uneasiness throughout most days" and "trouble falling asleep" most nights. Recently, James commented to his wife that he "wanted something more from life," which caused an argument. James reports that, "she just doesn't understand why I'm unhappy, but then again, neither do I."

Think about the focus that transpersonal counseling places on moving beyond normal mental health to exceptional life functioning and eventual transcendence. More accepted and established forms of counseling such as cognitive and behavioral approaches are most likely to focus on James's symptoms. Although a transpersonal counselor is also likely to help James with his feelings of uneasiness and sleep disturbances, what else might the transpersonal approach be able to do beyond this? How might the transpersonal counselor treat James as a whole person and integrate his life experience with greater meaning and spirituality? What techniques might the transpersonal counselor use to help James bring about greater self-awareness and self-acceptance?

techniques that will aid Maria in her process toward authenticity and potential. The first issue that needs to be addressed is Maria's willingness to be a client and her openness to transpersonal theory and techniques. Because Maria's family practitioner as well as her priest recommended counseling, her thoughts and feelings about these recommendations should be discussed openly and honestly.

In transpersonal counseling, terms such as *maladaptive, dysfunctional, irrational,* and other negative terms are avoided. Instead, the goal is to reframe Maria's current condition as a time of breakthrough: the birth of her authentic self. This reframing will facilitate Maria in moving through the helpless and hopeless state in which she currently finds herself. Instead of focusing on the bad decisions she has made, transpersonal counseling will seek to help Maria understand that her current discomfort may have been the impetus for her to move forward to authenticity and her highest potential.

Case Conceptualization

Throughout Maria's personal history and dreams is a pervasive theme of powerlessness and identification with the victim voice within. In her dreams, she is being chased by shadowy figures, and the room she is in has multiple exit signs with no readily available exit door. She is powerless to escape her pursuers, just as she felt powerless when she was demeaned and assaulted by her ex-husband and looked down on by her family. No matter how she wants to escape, in her dreams, she will soon be at the complete mercy of her pursuers. These shadowy pursuers can be seen as all of the things that Maria feels she has no control over. The multiple exit signs with no available exit indicate that Maria may be ready for change but does not know how to go about effecting it.

In her personal history, there are numerous examples of her identification with the victim. When she made an empowering personal decision to move away for college, she was accused of abandoning her family commitments. When she chose Mark as her husband, her family ostracized her until the birth of her first child. In almost every instance in which Maria made an empowering and adult decision, she was either looked down on or shunned by her family. Because Maria's culture places such a high value on family, her family's disapproval of the majority of her decisions has resulted in a great deal of psychological dissonance and loss of personal power. This theme of powerlessness extended into her marriage through the physical and emotional abuse she experienced from her ex-husband Mark.

Overall, Maria sees herself as being powerless to seek counseling on her own, powerless to make adequate adult decisions, powerless to effectively stand up to her family, powerless to stop the physical and emotional abuse she endured, powerless to stop depressive and suicidal thoughts, powerless to raise her children effectively, powerless to develop healthy relationships with men, and powerless to even obtain a healthy night's sleep. The issue is not that there is a victim voice within her; the issue is that it seems to be the only voice to which she is listening. There were times in her life when she may have been the victim and could do nothing about it. For example, she could not control (and is not responsible for) her parents' reaction to her life decisions. The victim voice was the most appropriate voice for this particular incident. The victim voice should be honored and understood to be an integral part of her journey but not placed on a pedestal above all others. Maria cannot reach her fullest potential if the victim is the only voice to which she listens.

Two other voices that Maria seems to be having difficulty understanding and accepting are her feminine and masculine voices. The feminine voice tends to be intuitive, nurturing, soft, and able to express emotions. The masculine voice tends to be strong, authoritative, and personally powerful. Maria has not been able to access either her feminine or masculine voice thus far. Expressing her feminine voice would allow Maria to come to terms with the fact that, although important to her culturally, her parents' and extended family's opinions are ultimately hers to choose whether to take or leave. Accessing her feminine voice would also allow Maria to reidentify with her role as a mother and as a woman. Finally, identifying with her feminine voice would allow Maria to understand that although she suffered physical and emotional abuse by a man, this does not mean that all men are not to be trusted.

Embracing her masculine voice would allow Maria to take more ownership of her life. Although she values her family's opinions, her masculine voice would allow her to choose to go her own way and feel confident in doing so. Her masculine voice would also aid her in presenting herself as the strong woman she is and would allow her to stand up to her former in-laws with regard to her child-rearing practices. Finally, identifying with the masculine voice would allow Maria to confront the powerlessness she feels in her dreams, her work, and her family and personal lives.

Maria has been uncomfortable with the feminine emotional, intuitive, nurturing side of herself, just as she has been reticent to honor the stronger, more in control masculine aspects of her person. Transpersonal theory holds that through the mutual respect and appreciation of the masculine and feminine divinity in each person, one's life comes into balance. Transpersonal theory further believes that all voices within each person should be honored to some extent. There is a time and a place for the victim voice, because things sometimes happen that are out of one's control. The victim voice allows the person to realize and accept this in order to move on both psychologically and emotionally.

Building on the idea of honoring all of the voices within, we can note that Maria is clearly in a great deal of emotional pain but has not yet chosen to honor the pain and work through it. It does not appear that Maria has successfully worked through the trauma of her abuse; the fact that she has been largely ostracized by her family; and the fact that she feels ineffective as a mother, a woman, and a professional. Instead of honoring and accepting the emotional pain that resulted from these things, she largely blames herself and identifies primarily with the victim voice. By refusing to effectively deal with and honor all of the voices present within her, Maria has inadvertently given all of the control to this voice, which therefore creates resentment between the victim and the other voices. This plays out in Maria's relationships with men. When she begins to date, she does not open herself to the possibility that she could trust and accept another man. She feels that because she has children and because she does not want to jump right into a sexual relationship, the men do not want to see her anymore. Rather than embracing the feminine voice within that could effectively communicate this to herself and the men she dates and accept the pain that comes naturally in developing relationships, she becomes withdrawn, blames the presence of her children, and strengthens her identification with the victim voice.

Maria may also be refusing to honor her other voices because of the nurturing qualities that may influence her to attempt to mend relationships with her family. She may be pulled by the voice of Western culture that idealizes the individual while simultaneously being pulled toward the voice of the more collectivist and group- and family-oriented Latino culture. A goal of transpersonal counseling is transcending beyond the self; however, Maria is unable to do this because she is not fully connected with all of the parts of herself. In an authentic person, the feminine voice, the masculine voice, the victim voice, and all other voices would have their proper place, work together, and be utilized to reach higher states of actualization. Maria's refusal to honor her feminine and masculine voices has caused an overidentification with the victim voice and led to a great deal of psychological and emotional distress.

Another issue to be examined is Maria's clear lack of unity with a power greater than herself. She reports a strong identification with her Catholic faith, but there is no further evidence that she accesses the spiritual voice within her. Transpersonal theory acknowledges the importance of a spiritual component in development, actualization, and human potential. Part of Maria's increasing depression, failed relationships with men, and loss of a sense of mother- and womanhood could be interpreted as an inadequate search for intimacy and personal strength that could be fulfilled in some part through spiritual development. Once Maria has learned to fully connect with herself, she can become more authentic and thus may be more open to using her Catholic background to have a spiritual connection with a power greater than herself.

Counseling Goals and Techniques

The first and primary goal for assisting Maria in reaching her highest potential would be to empower her to identify with more than the victim voice. Once this is accomplished, the second goal would be to help Maria to not focus on the chaos of all of the voices arguing but instead realize that each voice has its proper place in her life and should be honored. This would allow her to decide which voice or voices she would like to access at any given moment. The third goal would be to explore Maria's spiritual experiences and development.

To attain the first goal, empowering Maria to move beyond the victim voice, the transpersonal counselor could use several techniques. One such technique would be to examine her ancestry and culture. It is true that Latino culture identifies strongly with collectivist and family-oriented tenets, but this does not mean that Maria could not also be personally strong. Maria could study and get in touch with both the feminine and masculine voices that are present in her culture. In Latino culture, women are often respected as strong decision makers who often fill a role that is seen as masculine in Western culture. By bringing together and listening to the masculine and feminine voices, Maria would be less likely to break down, choosing instead to fight in the face of adversity. One way to get in touch with these voices would be through guided imagery. Maria could be taught to relax while the counselor could verbally guide her to mentally envision herself as a strong Latina woman. Through repeating this process, Maria could begin to identify with this cultural heritage and possess the shared masculine–feminine voice as her own. Another technique would be for Maria to give the victim character in her dreams a voice. What does it feel like to be powerless to find an exit? What does it feel like to be pursued by faceless people? These are just some of the questions that could allow Maria to give voice to the victim.

For Maria to be able to honor all of the voices within her and to discern which voices should be listened to at appropriate times, the counselor could encourage Maria to give credence to all of the voices in her life. Maria could give voices to the victim, pain, spirituality, masculine, feminine, mother, family, and professional. The transpersonal counselor would help Maria in identifying when it might be most appropriate to listen to one voice over another voice. Another good technique for this process toward unity of the self is bibliotherapy, which is well within the realm of transpersonal interventions.

Finally, the spiritual element of Maria's life needs to be addressed. An in-depth history of her spiritual development and experiences would be integral to this process. Once this is obtained, the counselor would have a good idea of how Maria values the spiritual and how it can be used to gain insight into her authentic self. Prayers, meditation, guided imagery, and Catholic spiritual traditions would be excellent tools to help Maria connect with something greater than herself. As she begins to continually unify herself with this power, her feelings of hopelessness and powerlessness will begin to dissipate.

Final Thoughts

It is important to note that these are just a few techniques that might be used with Maria. Transpersonal counseling and theory can be seen as an extension of or an umbrella over a wealth of other counseling theories. Techniques generally characterized from other theoretical orientations are embraced in transpersonal therapy. The overarching goal is to aid Maria in her process toward becoming an authentic self and achieving her highest potential, regardless of the intervention used (see Sidebar 15.6).

Sidebar 15.6. The Case of Maria: Transpersonal Counseling in Action

As you read through the transpersonal approach to the case of Maria, consider all of the tenets of transpersonal theory and counseling that we have covered in this chapter. Note the positive focus of the transpersonal approach. Maria is not sick; rather, she is on a journey to becoming her authentic self. Maria is not simply going to get better—she's going to become empowered to face future struggles with greater personal strength and confidence. Maria is also taught to honor all that she is, as well as her past. By helping her listen to all of her voices, transpersonal counseling does not cordon off parts of Maria's personality or life; instead, it helps Maria learn to take ownership of all that she was, is, and can become. Finally, transpersonal counseling does not ignore Maria's existing religious or spiritual beliefs, as may happen in more traditional forms of counseling. Her belief system and practices instead become a part of her whole and fully functional self. Regardless of your preferred theoretical approach to counseling, do not forget to consider how holistic and spiritual approaches, such as those found in transpersonal counseling, can help your clients in the way they are sure to help Maria.

REFERENCES

Adams, G. (2002). A theistic perspective on Ken Wilber's transpersonal psychology. *Journal of Contemporary Religion, 17,* 165–179.

Adams, W. W. (1999). The interpermeation of self and world: The empirical research, existential phenomenology, and transpersonal psychology. *Journal of Phenomenological Psychology, 30,* 39–66.

Agosin, T. (1992). Psychosis, dreams, and mysticism in the clinical domain. In F. Halligan & J. Shea (Eds.), *The fires of desire* (pp. 41–65). New York, NY: Crossroad.

Ajaya, S. (1997). *Psychology east and west: A unifying paradigm.* Honesdale, PA: Himalayan Institute.

Atchly, R. C. (2011). How spiritual experience and development interact with ageing. *Journal of Transpersonal Psychology, 43*(2), 156–165.

Bidwell, D. R. (1999). Ken Wilber's transpersonal psychology: An introduction and preliminary critique. *Pastoral Psychology, 48,* 81–90.

Birnbaum, L. (2005). Connecting to inner guidance: Mindfulness meditation and transformation of professional self-concept in social work students. *Critical Social Work, 6,* 111–121.

Birnbaum, L., Birnbaum, A., & Mayseless, O. (2008). The role of spirituality in mental health interventions: A developmental perspective. *International Journal of Transpersonal Studies, 27,* 65–73.

Boggio Gilot, L. (2008). Integral approach to mental suffering. *International Journal of Transpersonal Studies, 27,* 91–97.

Boorstein, S. (1996, Winter). Transpersonal context and interpretation. *ATP Newsletter,* pp. 5–8.

Boss, M. (1981). Transpersonal psychotherapy. In R. Walsh & F. Vaughan (Eds.), *Beyond ego: Transpersonal dimensions in psychology* (pp. 161–164). Los Angeles, CA: Tarcher.

Bradford, K. B. (2012). On the existential question of sanity: Buddhist and existential perspectives. *Journal of Transpersonal Psychology, 44*(2), 224–239.

Brown, D., & Engler, J. (1986). The stages of mindfulness meditation: A validation study: Part II. Discussion. In K. Wilber, J. Engler, & D. Brown (Eds.), *Transformations of consciousness: Conventional and contemplative perspectives on development* (pp. 191–218). Boston, MA: Shambhala.

Brown, D., Porte, M., & Dysart, M. (1984). Differences in visual sensitivity among mindfulness meditators and non-meditators. *Perceptual and Motor Skills, 58,* 727–733.

Brown, R. S. (2013). Beyond the evolutionary paradigm in consciousness studies. *Journal of Transpersonal Psychology, 45*(2), 159–171.

Caplan, M., Hartelius, G., & Rardin, M. A. (2003). Contemporary viewpoints on transpersonal psychology. *Journal of Transpersonal Psychology, 35,* 143–162.

Cortright, B. (2000). An integral approach to spiritual emergency. *Guidance and Counseling, 15,* 12–18.

Dale, E. J. (2013). Neo-Piagetian transpersonal psychology: A new perspective. *Journal of Transpersonal Psychology, 45,* 118–138.

Daniels, M. (2013). Traditional roots, history, and evolution of the transpersonal perspective. In H. L. Friedman & G. Hartelius (Eds.), *The Wiley-Blackwell handbook of transpersonal psychology* (pp. 23–43). Malden, MA: Wiley Blackwell.

Davis, J. (2000). We keep asking ourselves, what is transpersonal psychology? *Guidance and Counseling, 15,* 3–9.

Dossey, L. (1999). *Reinventing medicine.* New York, NY: HarperCollins.

Elkins, D. N. (2005). A humanistic approach to spirituality oriented psychotherapy. In L. Sperry & E. P. Shafranske (Eds.), *Spiritually oriented psychotherapy* (pp. 131–152). Washington, DC: American Psychological Association.

Ellis, A. (1962). *Reason and emotion in psychotherapy.* Secaucus, NJ: Citadel.

Ellis, A. (1986). Fanaticism that may lead to a nuclear holocaust: The contributions of scientific counseling and psychotherapy. *Journal of Counseling & Development, 65,* 146–150.

Ellis, A. (1989). Dangers of transpersonal psychology: A reply to Ken Wilber. *Journal of Counseling & Development, 67,* 336–337.

Ferrer, J. N. (2002). *Revisioning transpersonal theory: A participatory vision of human spirituality.* Albany: State University of New York Press.

Ferrer, J. N. (2008). What does it mean to live a fully embodied spiritual life? *International Journal of Transpersonal Studies, 27,* 1–11.

Ferrer, J. N. (2014). Transpersonal psychology, science, and the supernatural. *Journal of Transpersonal Psychology, 46*(2), 152–186.

Foster, S., & Little, M. (1997). *The roaring of the sacred river: The wilderness quest for vision and self-healing.* Big Pine, CA: Lost Borders Press.

Friedman, H. L. (2013). The role of science in transpersonal psychology: The advantages of a middle-range theory. In H. L. Friedman & G. Hartelius (Eds.), *The Wiley-Blackwell handbook of transpersonal psychology* (pp. 203–222). Malden, MA: Wiley Blackwell.

Friedman, H. L., & Hartelius, G. (Eds.). (2013). *The Wiley-Blackwell handbook of transpersonal psychology.* Malden, MA: Wiley Blackwell.

Goleman, D., & Ram, D. (1996). *The meditative mind: Varieties of meditative experience.* Los Angeles, CA: Tarcher.

Goretzki, M., Thalbourne, M. A., & Storm, L. (2013). Development of a spiritual emergency scale. *Journal of Transpersonal Psychology, 45*(2), 105–117.

Grof, S. (1985). *Beyond the brain.* Buffalo: State University of New York Press.

Grof, S. (2008). Brief history of transpersonal psychology. *International Journal of Transpersonal Studies, 27,* 46–54.

Grof, S. (2013). Revision and re-enchantment of psychology: Legacy of half a century of consciousness research. *Journal of Transpersonal Psychology, 44*(2), 137–163.

Grof, S., & Grof, C. (1989). *Spiritual emergency: When personal transformation becomes a crisis.* Los Angeles, CA: Tarcher.

Hartelius, G., Caplan, M., & Rardin, M. A. (2007). Transpersonal psychology: Defining the past, divining the future. *Humanistic Psychologist, 35,* 1–26.

Hartelius, G., Rothe, G., & Roy, P. J. (2013). A brand for the burning. In H. L. Friedman & G. Hartelius (Eds.), *The Wiley-Blackwell handbook of transpersonal psychology* (pp. 3–22). Malden, MA: Wiley Blackwell.

Hastings, A. (2012). Effects on bereavement using a restricted sensory environment (psychomanteum). *Journal of Transpersonal Psychology, 44*(1), 1–25.

Himelstein, S. (2011). Transpersonal psychotherapy with incarcerated adolescents. *Journal of Transpersonal Psychology, 43*(1), 35–49.

Hutton, M. S. (1994). How transpersonal psychotherapists differ from other practitioners: An empirical study. *Journal of Transpersonal Psychology, 26,* 139–174.

Jung, C. G. (1960). *The psychogenesis of mental disease.* Princeton, NJ: Princeton University Press.

Jung, C. G. (1967). Symbols of transformation. In *Collected works: Vol. 5* (pp. 121–131, R. F. C. Hull, Trans). Princeton, NJ: Princeton University Press. (Original work published 1912)

Kalischuk, R. G., & Nixon, G. (2009). A transpersonal theory of healing following youth suicide. *International Journal of Mental Health and Addiction, 7,* 389–402.

Kasprow, M. C., & Scotton, B. W. (1999). A review of transpersonal theory and its application to the practice of psychotherapy. *Journal of Psychotherapy Practice and Research, 8,* 12–23.

Kelly, S. M. (1991). The prodigal soul: Religious studies and the advent of transpersonal psychology. In K. K. Klostermaier & L. W. Hurtado (Eds.), *Religious studies: Issues, prospects and proposals* (pp. 429–441). Atlanta, GA: Scholars Press.

Koening, H. G., McCullough, M. E., & Larson, D. B. (2001). *Handbook of religion and health.* New York, NY: Oxford University Press.

Lajoie, D. H., & Shapiro, S. I. (1992). Definition of transpersonal psychology: The first 25 years. *Journal of Transpersonal Psychology, 24,* 79–98.

Leahey, T. H. (1994). *A history of modern psychology.* Philadelphia, PA: Temple University Press.

Lukoff, D. (1985). The diagnosis of mystical experiences with psychotic features. *Journal of Transpersonal Psychology, 17,* 155–181.

Lukoff, D. (1996). Transpersonal psychotherapy with psychotic disorders and spiritual emergencies with psychotic features. In B. W. Scotton, A. B. Chinen, & J. R. Battista (Eds.), *Textbook of transpersonal psychiatry and psychology* (pp. 271–281). New York, NY: Basic Books.

Lukoff, D., Lu, D., & Turner, R. (1998). From spiritual emergency to spiritual problem. *Journal of Humanistic Psychology, 38,* 157–186.

Lukoff, D., Turner, R., & Lu, D. (1992). Transpersonal psychology research reviews: Psychological dimensions of healing. *Journal of Transpersonal Psychology, 24,* 41–60.

MacDonald, D. A. (2013). Philosophical underpinnings of transpersonal psychology as a science. In H. L. Friedman & G. Hartelius (Eds.), *The Wiley-Blackwell handbook of transpersonal psychology* (pp. 312–329). Malden, MA: Wiley Blackwell.

MacDonald, D. A., Walsh, R., & Shapiro, S. L. (2013). Meditation: Empirical research and future directions. In H. L. Friedman & G. Hartelius (Eds.), *The Wiley-Blackwell handbook of transpersonal psychology* (pp. 433–458). Malden, MA: Wiley Blackwell.

Martens, W. H. J. (2010). Positive functions of psychosis. *Journal of Phenomenological Psychology, 41,* 216–233.

Maslow, A. (1968). *Toward a psychology of being* (2nd ed.). New York, NY: Van Nostrand/Reinhold.

Metzner, R. (1992). Therapeutic application of altered states of consciousness (ASC). In M. Schlichting & H. Leuner (Eds.), *Worlds of consciousness* (Vol. 5, pp. 185–193). Berlin, Germany: Verlag für Wissenschaft und Bildung.

Miller, W. R. (1999). *Integrating spirituality into treatment: Resources for practitioners.* Washington, DC: American Psychological Association.

Neustadter, S. B. (2010). Understanding the motivation for suicide from a transpersonal perspective: Research and clinical approaches. *Journal of Transpersonal Psychology, 42*(1), 61–88.

Nixon, G. (2012). Transforming the addicted person's counterfeit quest for wholeness through three stages of recovery: A Wilber transpersonal spectrum of development clinical perspective. *International Journal of Mental Health and Addiction, 10,* 407–427.

Nixon, G., & Theriault, B. (2011). Nondual psychotherapy and second stage sexual addictions recovery: Transforming "master of the universe" narcissism into nondual being. *International Journal of Mental Health and Addiction, 10,* 368–385.

Pargament, K. (1997). *The psychology of religion and coping: Theory, research, practice.* New York, NY: Guilford Press.

Perry, J. (1976). *Roots of renewal in myth and madness.* San Francisco, CA: Jossey-Bass.

Peterson, V. P., & Nisenholz, B. (1995). *Orientation to counseling* (3rd ed.). Needham Heights, MA: Allyn & Bacon.

Phillips, R. E., III, Lukoff, D., & Stone, M. K. (2009). Integrating the spirit within psychosis: Alternative conceptualizations of psychotic disorders. *Journal of Transpersonal Psychology, 41*(1), 61–80.

Piaget, J. (1929). Encore "immanence et transcendance." [Immanence and Transcendence] *Cahiers Protestants, 13,* 325–330.

Rama, S., Ballentine, R., & Ajaya, S. (1979). *Yoga and psychotherapy: The evolution of consciousness.* Honesdale, PA: Himalayan Institute.

Richards, P. S., & Bergin, A. E. (Eds.). (2004). *Religion and psychotherapy: A case book.* Washington, DC: American Psychological Association.

Scotton, B. W., Chinen, A. B., & Battista, J. R. (Eds.). (1996). *Textbook of transpersonal psychiatry and psychology.* New York, NY: Basic Books.

Shapiro, D. (1994). Examining the content and context of meditation. *Journal of Humanistic Psychology, 34,* 101–135.

Small, J. (2000). A psychospiritual approach to healing. *Guidance and Counseling, 15,* 9–12.

Sperry, L., & Shafranske, E. P. (Eds.). (2005). *Spiritually oriented psychotherapy.* Washington, DC: American Psychological Association.

Strohl, J. E. (1998). Transpersonalism: Ego meets soul. *Journal of Counseling & Development, 76,* 397–403.

Sutherland, M. (2001). Developing a transpersonal approach to pastoral counseling. *British Journal of Guidance and Counseling, 29,* 381–390.

Tarnas, R. (2001). A new birth in freedom: A preview of Jorge Ferrer's *Revisioning Transpersonal Theory: A Participatory Vision of Human Spirituality. Journal of Transpersonal Psychology, 33,* 64–71.

Vaughan, F. (1979). Transpersonal psychotherapy: Context, content, and process. *Journal of Transpersonal Psychology, 11,* 25–30.

Vich, M. A. (1988). Some historical sources for the term "transpersonal." *Journal of Transpersonal Psychology, 20,* 107–110.

Wacks, Q. V. (2011). The elder as sage, old age as spiritual path: Towards a transpersonal gerontology. *Journal of Transpersonal Psychology, 43*(2), 127–155.

Walsh, R. (1990). *The spirit of shamanism.* Los Angeles, CA: Tarcher.

Walsh, R. (1994). The transpersonal movement: A history and state of the art. *Journal of Transpersonal Psychology, 25,* 1–17.

Walsh, R., & Vaughan, F. (Eds.). (1993). *Paths beyond ego: The transpersonal vision.* New York, NY: Putnam.

Watson, K. (1994). Spiritual emergency: Concepts and implications for psychotherapy. *Journal of Humanistic Psychology, 34,* 22–35.

Weil, A. (1996). *Spontaneous healing.* New York, NY: Random House.

Wilber, K. (1977). *The spectrum of consciousness.* Wheaton, IL: Quest Books.

Wilber, K. (1980). *The Atman project: A transpersonal view of human development.* Wheaton, IL: Theosophical.

Wilber, K. (1981). *Up from Eden: A transpersonal view of human evolution.* Garden City, NY: Anchor Press/Doubleday.

Wilber, K. (1983a). *Eye to eye: The quest for the new paradigm.* Garden City, NY: Anchor Press/Doubleday.

Wilber, K. (1983b). *A sociable god: A brief introduction to a transpersonal sociology.* New York, NY: New Press.

Wilber, K. (1984a). The developmental spectrum and psychopathology: Treatment modalities. *Journal of Transpersonal Psychology, 16,* 137–166.

Wilber, K. (1984b). *Quantum questions: Mystical writings of the world's great physicists.* Boston, MA: Shambhala New Science Library.

Wilber, K. (1989). Let's nuke the transpersonalists: A response to Albert Ellis. *Journal of Counseling & Development, 67,* 332–335.

Wilber, K. (1995). *Sex, ecology, spirituality: The spirit of evolution.* Boston, MA: Shambhala.

Wilber, K. (1997). *The eye of the spirit: An integral vision for a world gone slightly mad.* Boston, MA: Shambhala.

Wilber, K. (2000). *Integral psychology: Consciousness, spirit, psychology, therapy.* Boston, MA: Shambhala.

Wilber, K. (2007). *The integral vision: A very short introduction to the revolutionary integral approach to life, God, the universe, and everything.* Boston, MA: Shambhala.

Wilber, K., Engler, J., & Brown, D. (Eds.). (1986). *Transformations of consciousness: Conventional and contemplative perspectives on development.* Boston, MA: Shambhala.

Williams, T. P. (1980). *Transpersonal psychology: An introductory guidebook.* Greeley, CO: Lutney.

Wittine, B. (1989). Assumptions of transpersonal psychotherapy. In R. Valle & S. Halling (Eds.), *Existential–phenomenological perspectives in psychology* (pp. 269–297). New York, NY: Plenum.

Wittine, B. (1993). Assumptions of transpersonal psychology. In R. Walsh & F. Vaughan (Eds.), *Paths beyond ego: The transpersonal vision* (pp. 165–171). Los Angeles, CA: Tarcher/Perigee.

Part 3

Constructivist Theories and Creative Approaches

CHAPTERS

16. Constructivist Theories:
    Solution-Focused and Narrative Therapies
17. Creative Approaches in Counseling and Psychotherapy

Constructivist theories are part of the fourth force of psychotherapy and counseling theories and relate to social constructivist philosophy. Social constructivism is an intellectual movement in the behavioral sciences that informs a social collaborative interpretation of reality. This reality incorporates a myriad of possible realities that, in turn, assist clients in choosing the reality that best fits their needs. Counselors using a constructivist perspective seek to facilitate change in how clients view their environment and explore the various meanings that could be used. Clients are encouraged to construct their world and to recreate how they see it with the counselor guiding them to aid in accomplishing their goals.

Although constructivist counseling has been paired with a variety of counseling theories, two specific theories are generally associated with constructivist counseling: solution-focused and narrative therapies. These two theories are introduced in

Chapter 16, "Constructivist Theories: Solution-Focused and Narrative Therapies," which addresses developmental perspectives, major constructs, applications, and the process of evaluation.

Just as sculptors, painters, architects, educators, engineers, and software developers use creativity to generate new ideas, paradigms, products, works of art, technology, and more, creativity is an equally critical human characteristic for counselors working in the mental health profession. **Chapter 17,** "Creative Approaches in Counseling and Psychotherapy," (a) addresses creativity as a theoretical construct used by counselors and other mental health professionals, (b) provides a historical context for the use of expressive therapies and the creative arts in counseling, (c) distinguishes creativity in counseling as an approach within the profession of counseling, (d) discusses the ethical parameters around using creative approaches in counseling practice, and (e) applies creativity in counseling as an approach to the case study of Maria.

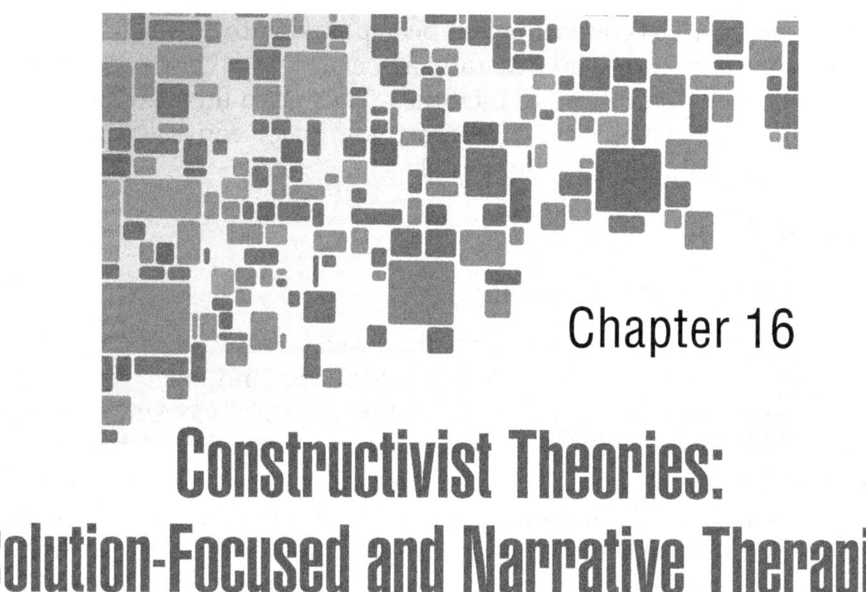

Chapter 16

Constructivist Theories: Solution-Focused and Narrative Therapies

Cirecie A. West-Olatunji and Marilyn Rush-Ossenbeck

Constructivist theories are part of the fourth force of psychotherapy and counseling theories and relate to social constructivist philosophy. Traditionally, whenever the idea of what is real is discussed, social constructivism is also not far behind. Cottone (2001) defined *social constructivism* as an intellectual movement in the behavioral sciences that informs a social collaborative interpretation of reality. This reality incorporates a myriad of possible realities that, in turn, assist clients in choosing the reality that best fits their needs. Social constructivist theorists assert that what is real evolves through interpersonal dialogue, interaction, and agreement regarding what is fact (Mahoney & Granvold, 2005). Within this framework, the role of the social constructivist therapist is to help clients interpret their subjective agreement with their beliefs regarding what is fact.

Social constructivist philosophy works to define the environment and its construction. Keaton and Bodie (2011) asserted that individuals often become confused regarding what is actually being socially constructed. Furthermore, it is dialogue that changes how individuals perceive their environment and the range of potential meanings possible. Counselors using a constructivist perspective seek to facilitate change in how clients view their environment and explore the various meanings that could be explored. Clients are encouraged to construct their world and to recreate how they see it with the counselor guiding them to aid in accomplishing their goals. It is important for the counselor to realize that what clients bring into session may not tell the whole story, so it is important to consider what is happening around them that may significantly influence their behaviors, thoughts, and attitudes.

Although constructivist counseling has been paired with a variety of counseling theories, two specific theories are generally associated with constructivist counseling: solution-focused and narrative therapies. These two theories are introduced in this chapter, and developmental perspectives, major constructs, applications, and the process of evaluation are discussed.

BACKGROUND

Solution-Focused Counseling

Solution-focused counseling stems from the brief therapy tradition (O'Connell, 2012) and was developed primarily by Steve de Shazer and Insoo Kim Berg in the 1970s at the Brief Family Therapy Center in Milwaukee, Wisconsin. This approach stresses two conditions: that the counselor is truly engaged and that the client is motivated toward key variances in the therapeutic process. These conditions differentiate solution-focused counseling from conventional frameworks in counseling and psychotherapy, and thus no emphasis is placed on the personality or past issues of the client.

Another key difference between solution-focused counseling and conventional theories is that the former approach functions according to the factors that have been found to cause change in clients: extratherapeutic factors, the client's view of the therapeutic relationship, therapeutic technique, and the client's expectations regarding hope (see Sidebar 16.1). Solution-focused therapy plays on the idea of social constructivism and encourages the client to look past the problem in the present and focus on how reality will look once the problem is solved (Murphy, 2015). This approach seeks to motivate the client both internally by kindling feelings of hope and will and externally by encouraging the client to use outside factors such as social support. As the name of the therapy suggests, the techniques focus on solutions, are goal directed, and are future oriented.

One final distinguishing feature of this approach is the unique position of the counselor during therapy. Insoo Kim Berg (De Jong & Berg, 2007) coined the term

Sidebar 16.1. Extratherapeutic Factors: Taking an Ecological Approach to Working With Clients

Before beginning to attend to environmental influences on clients' lives, counselors focused primarily on the intrapsychic factors, such as personality, that influence client concerns. Today, counselors are trained to consider the impact of various systems on clients' presenting as well as underlying problems. Systemic factors include clients' family dynamics, interactions at school or work, and social or historical influences. Thus, clients may be experiencing difficulties due to outside or extratherapeutic factors rather than to their own failings. Counselors are encouraged to inquire about clients' experiences at all levels of their interactions. Probes that can elicit more ecological information include the following:

- Please describe your relationships at home, at work, and in social settings.
- Based on what you have described today, I wonder what might explain the differential treatment you've experienced.
- Outside of your own strengths and weaknesses, what else might contribute to your current circumstances?

the *not-knowing position* in direct contrast to the *all-knowing position* that had previously been seen in the earlier forces, such as psychoanalytic and behavior therapies. This idea of working through clients' perspectives rather than their thoughts or behaviors is a different approach to resolving clients' issues. The counselor is no longer viewed as the expert in a hierarchical position but is horizontal with the client, working side by side. The solution-focused counselor maintains a relatively neutral position, and the true work occurs in the dialogue between the counselor and the client, not in the body of knowledge that the counselor may possess. Therefore, solution-focused counseling promotes the idea that the *process* of the counseling session is more beneficial to the client than the content.

Solution-focused counselors focus on the present and the future and empower their clients to avoid dwelling on their problem-laden past by utilizing a questioning process. This process helps clients to discover and invent what their future could look like by focusing on what is attainable (O'Connell, 2012). Counselors espousing this framework believe that many clients can become discouraged when they focus on goals that are not attainable or when it is not clear how to accomplish their goals. In addition, counselors avoid fixing areas in clients' lives that are not problematic. Instead, they draw on resources embedded in stories of success, coping, and resilience. To aid clients in navigating discouraging instances, the solution-focused counselor remains close during the questioning process and helps them to socially construct their own world.

Narrative Counseling

Having roots in family therapy and postmodernism, narrative counseling was originally created by Michael White and David Epson in the 1970s (M. White, 2011). The major purpose of narrative therapy is to interpret and alter the stories people create to make sense out of their lives. This principle can be interpreted through two other concepts: (a) People can only view the world based on their own experiences, and (b) people often compare and identify their lives based on the experiences of others (Jones-Smith, 2014).

When one takes a closer look at narrative therapy, the ideas of social constructivism come into sharper focus. Specifically, a narrative approach supposes that human beings' lives are woven by the stories they share and that these stories are socially constructed (Akinyela, 2014). Moreover, how stories are told as well as understood and the metaphors that define these stories are culturally mediated. Thus, clients exposed to narrative counseling will take their own personal and cultural point of view when retelling their life's story.

When considering the cultural interpretation of life experiences, it is important to note the reflexive questioning often displayed in this therapeutic approach (Kim, Prouty, & Roberson, 2012). Reflexive questions help to build bridges from behaviors and actions to beliefs or perceptions of reality. This is seen whenever a family is remembering an experience and several different stories emerge. Reflexive questions help to shape a client's true story, molding it in a way that is more beneficial. One way to develop reflexive questioning is to help clients identify their internal discourses, which are typically systems of words, actions, rules, beliefs, and institutions that share common values (Jones-Smith, 2014). Discourses can be related to social expectations, or the unwritten rules of society. This can be expressed with such words as *should* or *must* (see Sidebar 16.2).

Sidebar 16.2. A Reflexive Questioning Exercise: Building Bridges From Actions to Perceptions

When family members are asked to give an account of a situation, they are likely to have different versions of the same experience. Each one will narrate the story according to his or her own beliefs and perceptions of reality. Narrative counselors aid clients in uncovering the shoulds and musts in their environment. To gain a better understanding of this concept, try this exercise.

Gather three or more individuals together in a busy pedestrian intersection, such as a food court or lobby/reception area. Ask them to observe the happenings for about 10 to 15 minutes. Then reconvene the group in a quiet place to allow the individuals to journal about what they each observed. Finally, have them verbally share their journal observations with one another to compare their perceptions of the shared observation. Note the similarities and differences based on cultural, gendered, religious, and family values.

One key aspect of the narrative approach is that people construct their own meaning from their lives. They are also the experts on their own lives—not the therapist. Unlike in previous theories, which expressed the authoritative viewpoint of the counselor, in narrative counseling the counselor serves as a guide in the therapeutic process. In fact, narrative therapists are encouraged to go so far as to discard the idea that clients are bound by ideas, such as personality or psychopathology. Narrative theorists believe that the idea that clients are bound by such ideas creates a sense of arrogance in a counselor (M. White, 2011). The narrative counselor listens to the client during the session and looks for clues that might assist in helping the client resist problem-laden stories and influences from others. Once clients become aware of their problematic narrative and *restory* themselves, they often realize that they enjoy the new story and prefer it over the story that they came to the session to tell.

Though narrative therapy has been practiced for decades, new ways to apply the techniques continue to emerge. An example of this comes from Graham (2014), who applied these principles to clients suffering from video game addiction. Graham asserted that the techniques of narrative counseling are uniquely suited to this client population because video games are often structured around a story. By focusing on the talents inherent in being a successful gamer, clients can transfer those skills from online to offline and make significant changes in their lives. These skills could be transformed to better aid clients as they rewrite their life stories.

The emergence of these two approaches to constructivism in counseling helped to foster a transformation of the role of the counselor, from expert to facilitator. In addition, solution-focused and narrative counseling helped counselors to support clients in assuming a more empowering role during the therapeutic process and becoming agents of their own change. Although these two approaches typically predominate within the constructivist perspective, other applications of constructivist counseling have taken form as well that highlight the relationship between constructivism and human development over the life span.

HUMAN NATURE: A DEVELOPMENTAL PERSPECTIVE

In many ways, constructivism can be seen as a metatheory in counseling evident in a variety of theoretical approaches, including solution-focused, narrative, existentialist, cognitive behavior, and family systems counseling (see Sidebar 16.3). As a metatheory, this approach includes several essential elements, of which three are critical: activity, ordering, and reflexivity (Mahoney & Granvold, 2005). The idea of activity implies that human beings are not passive in the way in which they live their lives. Rather, they are actively and dynamically involved in the construction of their lives. Some theorists would say that individuals are audaciously involved in taking risks, choosing, and analyzing the results of their actions. Thus, human beings are reactive and responsive to life events.

The next aspect of constructivism articulates the need for human beings to have order. That is to say, human beings will automatically acquire a skill or respond to their environment and then create a pattern or a habit to create new patterns of thinking and feeling. In this manner, individuals are both proactive and generative simultaneously (Cottone, 2001). This dyadic process allows for stabilization and change to occur at an unconscious level, protecting and perpetuating integrity to people's choices.

Finally, constructivism consists of a self-organizing or self-regulating task. This reflexivity allows for self-reflection and self-awareness in an orderly fashion. Constructivist theorists posit that people's self-conceptualizations are constantly changing as they incorporate an understanding of their environment and reconceptualize themselves (Mahoney & Granvold, 2005). During the 1950s, George

Sidebar 16.3. Constructivist Counseling as a Metatheory: An Umbrella Concept

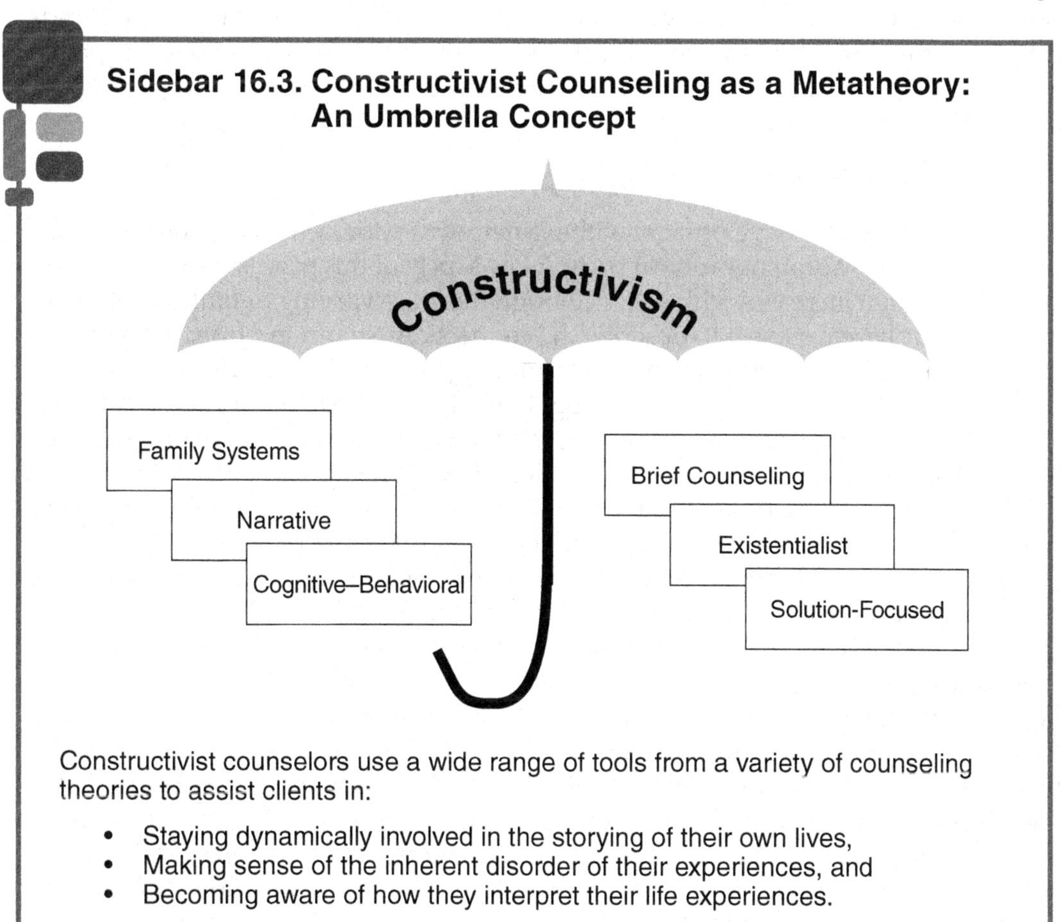

Constructivist counselors use a wide range of tools from a variety of counseling theories to assist clients in:

- Staying dynamically involved in the storying of their own lives,
- Making sense of the inherent disorder of their experiences, and
- Becoming aware of how they interpret their life experiences.

Kelly developed personal construct psychology. Kelly (1955) stated that individuals use personal constructs to predict their environment and that they investigate their hypotheses and conceptualizations in an ongoing manner so that they construct and reconstruct their lives on a daily basis.

The constructivist approach to counseling also emphasizes the developmental process across the life span. In this sense, normal waxing and waning through cycles of developmental changes can affect the ways in which human beings construct knowledge of self. Major stressors, such as complicated grief or trauma, can cause individuals to be susceptible to deviations in normal growth and development (Singer, 2004). As a result, human beings can resist developmental changes because these shifts may seem overwhelming. In addition, implicit in this viewpoint is the belief that diverse cultural perspectives are inherent in human beings' conceptualization of their experiences and meaning making. Thus, differences *between* as well as *within* groups are inherent in the process, as individuals are sharing expectations with others in their environment but also constructing their unique understanding of themselves and others (Esquivel, Oades-Sese, & Jarvis, 2010).

Constructivist theorists posit that life-span development is woven throughout the therapeutic process, given that self-definition, self-knowledge, and self-identity are continuous processes (Singer, 2004). Within the constructivist perspective, narrative therapy provides the clearest articulation of life-span development. In addition, within narrative counseling, scholars in the area of career counseling have advanced experts' understanding of the application of the narrative approach to career development across the life span.

Narrative Therapy and Development

The process of human development within a narrative approach focuses on coherence in an individual's autobiographical story. A key aspect of this process is identification stabilization that increases with age. Although there are varying definitions of *narrative coherence,* here we use it to describe the connections stemming from individuals' interactions with themselves or the environment (Klein & Bowles, 2010). Two forms of narrative coherence have been investigated: thematic and autobiographical. Thematic coherence suggests that, optimally, human beings achieve thematic coherence by developing themes that underlie events and behaviors. For example, as a result of losing a job, an individual might internalize this experience and exhibit depressed mood, irritability, and sleep dysfunction. These responses might be connected to prior vocational or developmental experiences. Autobiographical coherence connotes a shared expectation of how life is experienced by others.

Identification stabilization occurs when individuals narrate their experiences juxtaposed against their own identity (Westerhof & Bohlmeijer, 2012). In other words, how people relate their stories is connected to where they see themselves in relation to the story itself. Therefore, adults could recount a childhood story of falling off a bicycle in four ways: through identification, overidentification, underidentification, and shifting identification. They could (a) block the incident altogether from their memory, (b) continually tell the story as though it happened yesterday, (c) assume a victim position and fail to believe that they can resolve the situation, or (d) transform the story by restorying themselves as empowered and resourceful. In identification, proximity to and distance from the experiences are significant, as human beings tend to distance themselves from negative experiences, potentially causing blockage to the resolution of problems. Overidentification is characterized by a lack of distance between identity and experiences, often resulting in regressive, static narratives. Underidentification is seen as an inability to identify with personal experiences and is characterized by a lack of agency and a fragmented autobiographical narrative. Last, shifting identification connotes a balance between proximity and distance and the ability to construct new meanings or new stories. This restorying allows for the continuous construction of new identities (see Sidebar 16.4).

From a developmental perspective, human beings formulate their identity during adolescence and establish coherence to their life stories. Peer discourse and parent–child interactions play an important role in adolescents' ability to articulate their identity to themselves as well as to others (Singer, 2004; Thorne, 2000). As adolescents develop, this coherent story requires continuous redrafting for identity consolidation to occur. Failure to redraft may result in narrative foreclosure, in which an individual may halt the narrative.

Narrative Career Counseling

Two specific approaches to narrative career counseling are notable and help to clarify human development within a constructivist approach. The first is systems theory, which articulates the role of environmental influences on one's identity and the autobiographical narrative (Singer, 2004). The second is the theory of career construction (Del Corso & Rehfuss, 2011), which highlights the role of subjectivity in identity formation. The systems theory framework consists of several assumptions, including a focus on the individual, social, and environmental systems. However, for the purpose of clarifying the key aspects of this approach, we highlight here three additional aspects: (a) One's narrative changes over time, (b) chance plays an essential role, and (c) the process of identity formation is nonlinear (McIlveen & Patton, 2007). The concept of change over time within a systems approach suggests that career milestones are socially and environmentally created yet mediated by individuals' expectations about their experiences. Thus, individuals' career milestones are socially and environmentally constructed and yet mediated by their expectations about those experiences. The chaos reflecting the unpredictability of life is captured in this element of chance within one's life events and the need to dynamically and continuously create meaning and order. Finally, the reflexivity across past, present,

Sidebar 16.4. Case Study: Chloe Moves Out

Chloe is a 27-year-old college graduate and the youngest of three children. She has not been able to find a job to move out of her parents' home. Chloe has mood swings, such that some days she is depressed and despondent about her future. The counselor is able to schedule a family session in which Chloe's siblings counter her narrative, stating that they believe that, as a child, she received more attention from their parents. Chloe's overidentification with her life story may cause her to narrate her life experiences as a victim in believing that she received less attention from her parents than her siblings. When asked to share any exceptions to this narrative, Chloe is initially unable to do so. However, gradually she is able to construct new narratives about her identity. Eventually, Chloe is able to move out of her parents' home and live on her own.

and future and the interactions between individual, social, and environmental systems create a complex dynamic recursiveness of influences. From this perspective, the idea of linear causation of *event = choice* is rejected.

Savickas (2005) defined the *theory of career construction* as "the interpretative and interpersonal processes through which individuals impose meaning and direction on their vocational behavior" (p. 42). He articulated three aspects of this theory: vocational personality, career adaptability, and life themes. The concept of vocational personality extends trait and factor ideals to include these subjective experiences. In this manner, an individual is no longer passively assigned shared, public forms or traits. Rather, human beings engage in the process of name making in response to their vocational experiences. Career adaptability focuses on an individual's flexibility and responsiveness to vocational transitions and developmental tasks. From this perspective, the development of an individual's career becomes a psychosocial process in which identity and environment are synthesized to validate self-identity within socially constructed expectations. The last aspect of this theory provides a spectral view of human development within the concept of career construction. Life themes are an individual's narrative across time, place, and role. Thus, life stories weave a tale of continuity consisting of elements of vocational personality and adaptability.

In sum, human beings are constantly dialoguing with themselves and interacting with their environment to create a continuous pattern of stabilized identity and chaos. This process is crystalized during adolescence and restoried throughout one's lifetime to achieve newly transformed identities as a result of interacting with life experiences. However, individuals can get trapped in recycled, static narratives that lack agency and cause stagnation. Counselors wanting to adopt a constructivist approach to counseling are encouraged to seek advanced training to increase their knowledge of the major constructs within this approach and develop competence in transforming their role in the therapeutic process.

MAJOR CONSTRUCTS

Social constructivist theorists assert that anything that people know is bound by their sense of time and their perceptions of their culture (Mahoney & Granvold, 2005). The theories presented in this chapter expand on the belief that nothing can ever truly be known and nothing can ever truly be objective because the world is viewed through lenses made of people's past experiences, how they view the present, and what they think will occur in the future (Gladding, 2014).

Solution-focused counseling has roots in family systems therapy (Miller, Cardona, & Hardin, 2007). Because of this, there is an understanding that, even in an individual session, clients' systems (i.e., family, social, work, etc.) may influence how they deal with their issues and prevent them from identifying a clear solution. Clients often rely on problem-solving methods that do not work and are repetitive. This perspective draws from family systems theory's emphasis on the homeostasis of family patterns. Solution-focused counselors help clients to break away from these cycles of maladaptive behaviors and facilitate problem solving by encouraging clients to take new and different approaches (Murphy, 2015). Thus, solution-focused counselors do not spend a great deal of time dwelling on the problems. Rather, they focus on finding solutions in the present so that the future can be different and more beneficial.

To break these maladaptive cycles, counselors are to follow three rules: (a) If it is not broken, do not fix it; (b) once you know what works, do more of it; and (c) if something does not work, do not do it again—do something different (Gladding, 2014). Each of these rules indicates a clear path from which clients can explore their options as far as their own beliefs.

In solution-focused therapy, clients typically experience three sessions, and counselors are encouraged to terminate the process as soon as is possible for the growth and development of the client (O'Connell, 2012). However, solution-focused therapists believe that there is a difference between brief and short-term therapy: Short-term therapy connotes time-stamped constraints, whereas brief therapy focuses on resolving the problem without one session more than is necessary. Overall, solution-focused therapy strives for autonomy in the therapeutic relationship and relies on the idea that focusing unnecessarily on the problem can cause the therapy to be much longer than necessary.

Solution-focused therapy also incorporates specific concepts of change within the client. Within this perspective, the purpose of counseling is to change something: Either the client must change, or the client must change his or her environment; otherwise, counseling could have no purpose. The paradox is that clients often are resistant to change. To achieve this idea of change, solution-focused counseling subscribes to the belief that problems do not operate all the time and that they increase or decrease in their severity. The counselor may often seek to discover when the problem is not as intense or not a problem at all in order to build the client's confidence and encourage the posing of solutions. The counselor seeks to aid the client in constructing a reality in which this problem either does not occur at all or occurs very little (Jones-Smith, 2014).

Narrative therapy can also be used with families, not just individual clients. The narrative counselor works to externalize the problem that the family or individual client is experiencing (M. White, 2011). By externalizing the problem, clients are able to separate themselves from the problem. Often, when a family comes to counseling, family members may have already identified the single client and may have paired the problem with the identified client until the two have become blended. Therefore, when the client is able to separate the two, it becomes much easier to reauthor the solution and the reality. The counselor identifies two similar pathways of influence between the client and the problem. This influence is either the problem on the person or the person on the problem. Each of these viewpoints can produce varying degrees of problem-solving narratives from the client (Gladding, 2014).

A major difference between the narrative approach and other constructivist theories is that the narrative approach is nonsystemic (M. White, 2011). Most of the techniques focus on the use of language from both the client and the counselor. Other approaches, such as behaviorism and psychoanalysis, focus on the verbal and nonverbal behavior of the client, but narrative counseling is unique in that it focuses on the use and influence of language.

In narrative counseling, the story is the basic unit of experience through the shared language experience (Esquivel et al., 2010; Pennebaker & Chung, 2011). This approach differs from other therapies, such as behavior therapy, in which behavior is the basic unit of experience. The client determines what his or her life story means and how it will be told. The emphasis that this theory places on the power of the client's perception is motivating and empowering to the client, especially when the client discovers that he or she has the power to structure and synthesize his or her story in dynamic ways.

At any given time, clients can have multiple stories and multiple views of a certain event in their life. The stories that individuals tell dictate behavior; it is not behavior that dictates their stories. How individuals perceive the world around them determines the stories they tell, and the stories they have told in the past dictate the present and future stories they tell themselves (Westerhof & Bohlmeijer, 2012). Each narrative or story has different components. Each story has a setting, or what the area where the story took place looks like and when the story took place. The story incorporates characterizations in addition to the client's self-images and memorizations. Finally, each story has a plot with a beginning, middle, and end. Each story can, at different times, take on an alternative story or a preferred story. The alternative story helps clients to realize that their lives can take on different settings, characterizations, or plots and that no story is ever set in stone. A client's preferred story is only recognized once the client has recognized that the alternative stories are more beneficial than the original story (Jones-Smith, 2014).

The stories that clients share are always dynamic and sometimes differ greatly from the stories of the therapist. Multicultural narrative therapy offers insight into how to address the cultural needs of each client within the context of his or her life story and language and also juxtaposed with those of the counselor (Burke, Chauvin, & Miranti, 2004; Esquivel et al., 2010; Kim et al., 2012). An example of this is using narrative therapy with culturally diverse couples. One key component to consider is that the narrative counseling approach directs the counselor to attend to both the cultural stories of the counselor and those of both persons in the couple and respectfully extract the couple's experiences while paying careful attention to the influence of cultural messages on each partner's beliefs and values (Kim et al., 2012). Using this technique, both dominant and subordinate stories can be identified and acknowledged in an appropriate and culturally sensitive way for the benefit of the therapeutic relationship. In addition, narrative therapy can be used to help individuals from diverse backgrounds to deconstruct stereotypes or discriminatory stories with the counselor in order to find a new way of looking at each specific instance of cultural difference.

In summary, it is important to understand the role that family dynamics may play in clients' inability to restory themselves or their fear of restorying themselves. Thus, it may be necessary to explore family-of-origin structures and beliefs to elicit family-based stories embedded in clients' narratives. In addition, the process of counseling supersedes the content and radically changes the emphasis from behavior to language as salient aspects of the therapeutic process. How to execute these constructs in counseling sessions to promote resolution of clients' problems is also a key task of the constructivist counselor.

APPLICATIONS

Overview

Constructivist approaches in counseling highlight the need for client agency and a collaborative relationship between the client and the counselor. Traditional constructivist interventions have represented a wide range of theoretical perspectives, including family systems, feminist, cognitive–behavioral, solution-focused, and narrative approaches (Keaton & Bodie, 2011). These divergent interventions are connected to the idea that constructivism is more of a metatheory that serves as an umbrella philosophy. Recent applications of constructivism have given birth to the use of creative art therapy, multicultural tools, and social justice tools (Abrums, 2004; Esquivel et al., 2010; Pennebaker & Chung, 2011). Counselors should be aware that when they are working with clients with severe mental health issues, interventions based on clinical trials and intervention research can have the best outcomes.

The Process of Change

Counselors using a constructivist approach incorporate three important elements into their work with clients: (a) Clients are seen as agents of their own transformation, (b) counselors serve as facilitators of that change, and (c) the client and counselor are equals in the collaborative process of meaning making (Cottone, 2001; Mahoney & Granvold, 2005). Constructivism is unlike behavior therapy, in which the mechanism for change is behavior and people walk out of counseling with new behaviors; or cognitive therapy, in which the focus is on thoughts and clients leave counseling with new patterns and processes of thinking; or even existential therapy, in which one becomes more authentic through therapeutic engagement and meaning making. Here, the mechanism for change is *restorying,* so that clients walk out of counseling with energetic narratives that drive their lives and the way they see themselves. From a constructivist perspective, clients must first serve as active agents responsible for articulating and interpreting their experiences in order to restory themselves toward the resolution of stagnant narratives. This sense of agency enables clients to view themselves as directing their own lives and capable of shifting their identities to adapt to their environmental challenges. Clients are encouraged to construct a narrative about their events and behaviors and then articulate their role in this narrative as a form of self-identification. These narratives can be expressed in a variety of forms depending on the counselor's theoretical framework and the client's level of comfort and talents in expression. For instance, clients can be encouraged to write in a journal, write an essay, draw a picture, compose a song, or narrate a story. These activities can be directed within the session or used as homework between sessions.

In addition, counselors take on the role of facilitators of this empowerment process (Gladding, 2014; Miller et al., 2007). They assist in making meaning of the client's narrative to foster appropriate proximity to the experiences, allowing clients to articulate how they position themselves in relation to their environmental influences in a way that is neither too close nor too distant. As facilitators, counselors dialogue collaboratively with clients about their narratives to aid clients in developing insight into their identities. Counselors can pose questions to their clients to elicit a clearer understanding of the story, clients' vulnerabilities, and their sense of empowerment in the narrative. Clients who overidentify with their narrative may need assistance in gaining some distance to obtain a new perspective on the issues, as it may be difficult for them to see the problem from so close a vantage point (Akinyela, 2014; M. White, 2011). In this manner, use of the externalizing-the-problem exercise may be helpful. Alternatively, clients may underidentify with their narrative and exhibit signs of avoidance in which they distance themselves from their narrative, as it may represent negative experiences or evoke emotions that are uncomfortable. To address this underidentification, the counselor might utilize interventions that focus on identifying the emotions associated with the narrative and encouraging the client to push through these feelings to restory emotive responses to the original event (see Sidebar 16.5).

Last, the shared and collaborative meaning-making process between the client and the counselor occurs when each views the other as an equal in a horizontal relationship. Unlike traditional therapies, in which there is a *one-person counseling relationship* (T. White, 2007) between the client and counselor, constructivist counseling necessitates an egalitarian, collaborative two-person counseling experience in which client and counselor coconstruct meaning for the client's narratives (Jones-Smith, 2014). As clients transform their stories, counselors serve as a sounding board for the conceptualizations and reconceptualizations posed by clients. To foster this shared meaning making, counselors are encouraged to (a) relinquish their role as the person in power and authority to give way to the client voice and empowerment and (b) minimize the imposition of their own lived experiences on the client's narrative (Hoskins, 1995). The concept of client empowerment is critical in establishing a collaborative relationship between the client and the counselor. Thus, counselors using a constructivist approach should avoid using techniques such as educating and advice giving. Instead, counselors should focus on reflective statements that encourage clients to formulate their own conceptualizations of the problem and solutions. Furthermore, counselors may sometimes experience challenges of their own when facilitating client empowerment due to countertransference when they impose their self-narratives on the client. To minimize this effect, counselors are encouraged to seek peer or formal supervision and, when necessary, personal counseling.

Counselors also need to recognize cultural overlays to the interpretive experience and seek consultation when working with clients from nonmainstream or diverse backgrounds. More important, constructivist-oriented counselors are aware of their own solipsism and do not impose their own lived experiences on the client's narrative. Such countertransference issues can impede the collaborative meaning-making process. As an overarching theme, counselors are encouraged to reflect humanism in their interactions with clients. At the core, constructivist counseling approaches epitomize the idea that counselors believe in their clients'

Sidebar 16.5. Clients as Agents of Their Transformation: Three Tools for Joel

Joel (a musician) and his partner have been together for 6 years and are considering having children. However, Joel is anxious about parenthood because he had a difficult childhood and currently has a poor relationship with his parents. The counselor uses three interventions to assist Joel in resolving his ambivalence regarding this decision. He asks Joel to do the following:

1. Using colored pencils and an 8½ x 11" sheet of paper, draw a picture of his family of origin and then describe the nature and dynamics of his relationships with his family members
2. Compose two songs: one that communicates how he felt as a child growing up in his family and one that expresses how he wanted to feel
3. Identify three parent figures in real life or fiction that he believes personify ideal parenting and discuss what behaviors are appealing that can be adopted and integrated into his identity

abilities to resolve discrepancies in their life stories and transform their lives, now and in the future (Mahoney & Granvold, 2005).

Traditional Intervention Strategies

Depending on the theory applied through the lens of constructivism, counselors can use a host of interventions. From cognitive–behavioral to feminist applications, counselors have a wide variety of interventions from which to choose. Some of the more commonly used interventions include reminiscence and life review, storytelling, journaling, and externalizing the problem. Here, we explore several of these interventions to explain how they can be used to facilitate change from a constructivist perspective.

Reminiscence and *life review* refer to the recollection of memories. Both of these interventions are similar in nature and function, except that life review has an evaluation-of-meaning component, whereas reminiscence does not. During the mid-1950s, it was commonly believed that older adults naturally experienced reminiscence in preparation for the end of life. However, it is now known that (a) not all elderly individuals experience reminiscence; and (b) this process occurs throughout the life span, particularly during times of crisis and developmental angst (Pasupathi, Weeks, & Rice, 2006). Reminiscence serves several functions, such as preparation for death, problem solving, connection to others, and transmission of experiences and coping to others as a form of education (Webster, 2003). In preparing for death, individuals gather and organize their life stories in order to resolve the past. This gathering of life stories can be either a positive or negative experience based on how these narratives are remembered. Positive perspectives on one's life experiences can generate contentment, a sense of accomplishment, self-satisfaction, and an overall positive self-identity. Negative attitudes toward one's lived experiences can cause feelings of bitterness, resentment, discomfort, and shame and self-denigrating behaviors.

Recollecting life narratives can also aid in identifying coping mechanisms in times of crisis. When individuals encounter difficulties in life, there is a tendency to access prior memories of problem solving during challenges (Webster, 2003). If those memories do not reflect the effective resolution of problems, clients can become stuck in a negative cycle, reliving the original emotions stemming from the recollected event. However, if the recollections are helpful and positive, then they can reinforce agency, self-actualization, and resilience. Furthermore, such positive problem-solving responses can be shared with others to relive the experience as a way of validating others' coping abilities and exchanging recollections. This sharing of recollections helps to foster a sense of connection and identity at both the individual and group levels. Last, reminiscence and life review can function to educate others about how to cope with life's challenges. Thus, individuals can transmit their recollections to others in order to teach resiliency skills. This concept of the transmission of problem-solving skills is reflected in the concept of transgenerational resilience. In the aftermath of Hurricane Katrina, some New Orleans residents articulated their ability to cope with recovery after living through Hurricane Betsy 50 years prior (Frazier, West-Olatunji, St. Juste, & Goodman, 2009). These residents shared narratives of witnessing their parents rebuild their homes, neighborhoods, and businesses. In the process, their parents may have transmitted problem-solving ideation in the face of tremendous adversity. Disaster mental health counselors deployed to the Gulf Coast following Hurricane Katrina used numerous narrative group techniques to foster the sharing of recollections as a way of strengthening the bonds between residents. Such techniques included group work, brief essays about residents' successes, and photo journaling about their recovery. According to Cappeliez and Robitaille (2010), the purpose of reminiscence and life review techniques is to strengthen mastery, meaning, and goal management. When done well, individuals can benefit from reminiscence in that it can increase their sense of self-competence and self-confidence. The idea that, "If I've done it once, I can do it again" is at once empowering and liberating. Moreover, reminiscence can facilitate meaning making and order in clients' lives. Awareness and acknowledgment of one's self-constructed narrative helps to organize the chaos created in the daily dynamic interplay between one's environment and one's self, propelling individuals to make choices about who they are in relation to themselves, others, and the environment. In this manner, goals are perpetually established and managed for one's identity. Moreover, once action is taken and the consequences of those actions are evident, individuals interpret the meaning of those events in order to reset goals, stay on course, or stagnate.

Contemporary approaches to reminiscence and life review utilize a three-pronged method: reminiscence, life review, and life review therapy (Webster, 2003). Reminiscence focuses on recollecting positive memories with an emphasis on social interaction. Life review seeks to integrate positive and negative recollections to promote mastery, meaning, and goal management. Finally, life review therapy connects the therapeutic process to specific theoretical approaches, including cognitive–behavioral (journaling), creative (essay writing), and narrative counseling (externalizing the problem) approaches; these tools are discussed below. Journaling, within the framework of cognitive–behavioral counseling, highlights the need for clients to develop an emotionally coherent understanding of their identities over time. Thus, the purpose of constructing a journal is to organize one's experience of self and other in order to construct an identity. This is slightly different from the traditional application of cognitive–behavioral techniques that focus on the client's irrational thoughts and inner dialogue.

As a creative exercise, essay writing has been shown to have positive outcomes for physical and behavioral health. Essay writing has been associated with fewer physical health problems, such as lower physiological activation (e.g., lower cortisol levels) during trauma disclosures, fewer physician visits, and decreased use of health care services (Frisina, Borod, & Lepore, 2004). Studies investigating the relationship between essay writing and behavioral health have reported that (a) workers secured jobs more quickly than those in control groups, (b) employee absenteeism decreased, and (c) long-term improvements in mood were documented (Lumley & Provenzano, 2003). Counselors opting to use this method should be aware that several mediators can affect the outcomes of the intervention. Mediators include issues such as the disclosure topic (positive topics have shown better results), orientation to the topic (i.e., focusing on positive aspects or benefits), how long after the event the writing session is scheduled (immediately after is less productive), the duration of the writing session (less than 15 minutes has less of an impact), the time between sessions and length of the writing session program (longer time periods work better), the time between the writing session and the follow-up session (the longer the gap, the fewer the benefits), and individual differences (ethnicity, language, and gender, for example, have not been shown to be correlative; Pennebaker & Chung, 2011). In sum, essay writing can prove to be an appropriate constructivist intervention within the creative therapies when it is used appropriately based on existing research. Expressive writing has been theorized to be effective because (a) it allows individuals to disclose socially prohibitive experiences that may be shameful and (b) it gives clients permission to access their emotions in concert with their thoughts in relation to specific lived experiences.

A well-known intervention in narrative counseling is externalizing the problem. The goal of this technique is to separate the person from the problem in order to create distance between the client's identity and the narrative (M. White, 2011). This approach typically addresses overidentification with the story in order to foster critical reflection. This technique helps to minimize the severity of the issue, reduce client anxiety, and increase client agency. The counselor's role is to facilitate the client's active investigation in relation to the problem. Facilitating questions might include, "How is fear influencing your life?" and "How can you expose the secrets that fear is keeping hidden from you?" Thus, the counselor seeks to aid clients in gaining control over their narratives and ultimately their lives.

As discussed in Chapter 1, scaling and miracle questions along with problem-free talk are frequently used interventions in solution-focused and brief counseling. These interventions focus on changing clients' focus toward solutions or exceptions to the problem rather than maintaining an emphasis on the problems they are experiencing. These tools aid clients in being reflective and critical in analyzing their behaviors and identity in relation to the problem.

Brief Intervention Strategies and Current Practices

Most recently, scholars and practitioners have advanced contemporary approaches to constructivist counseling that reflect social justice and culturally informed perspectives. Specifically, interventions such as metaphors, critical reflection, proverbs (*dichos* in Spanish), folktales (*cuentos* in Spanish), and testifying have been investigated. Metaphors are useful in helping clients to transfer one concept to another and can serve as scaffolds to richer, more complex understandings of problems (Hoskins, 1995). To effectively use metaphors within a constructivist framework, counselors should ask descriptive questions to elicit thick description and detail with annotated feelings and thoughts as part of the narrative. Although this procedure may seem straightforward, counselors should anticipate the challenge of imprinting clients with their own narratives. Thus, counselors should establish proactive procedures to minimize this imposition on clients.

Critical reflection techniques begin with an exposition of the client's narrative, in which beliefs, values, and assumptions are laid out for dialogue and critical analysis (Beres, Bowles, & Fook, 2011). Once the story has unfolded, clients are encouraged to expand their comprehension of the problem in order to gain insight. This is followed by a period of deliberation about the action to be taken. During this process, counselors act as mirrors to the client's investigation. Finally, clients take action to restory themselves and integrate the experience into a new identity.

Another technique used to increase self-knowledge is using proverbs or *dichos* to think deeply and make connections between concepts. Proverbs are used by many cultures to express perspectives on situations found in the human condition (Burke et al., 2004; Esquivel et al., 2010). They are often used as guidelines for moral development and social behavior and are transmitted from adults to children (see Sidebar 16.6). For example, the African proverb "It takes a village to raise a child" connotes a belief in communalism, in which interdependence is valued within a family or community.

Other forms of storytelling include *cuentos* and the story circle. *Cuentos,* or folktales, have been shown to have positive outcomes for immigrant Latino students. Research has shown that *cuentos* are associated with reduced anxiety and increased coping among primary school Latino children and increased social competence (Esquivel et al., 2010). The story circle is a group technique borrowed from the literary community in which clients sit in a circle and share narratives that are linked thematically (Clay, Olatunji, & Cooley, 2001). This intervention promotes active listening skills as well as shared meaning making among group members.

Finally, scholars have discussed the role of testifying (i.e., telling one's story of adversity) as a form of resilience for African American women in particular. *Testifying,* as a coping mechanism, can be defined as asserting, affirming, and reclaiming one's own humanity and oneself as a whole while resisting oppression (Abrums, 2004). Testifying as resistance can be a powerful form of coping, because it allows individuals to name the oppressive processes, making them explicit in order to bear witness to pervasive acts and situations of inequality. Thus, testifying may be characterized as a social justice constructivist intervention that can be effective when working with individuals from socially and culturally marginalized groups. This form of storytelling integrates empowerment, voice, and agency to address systemic challenges within clients' environment.

A wide variety of contemporary interventions have been introduced that have some degree of research base to offer evidence-based practices. Note that counselors can use culturally informed tools, particularly (but not exclusively) when working with culturally diverse clients, to improve clinical outcomes, increase expediency, promote credibility, and enhance multicultural competence. Some issues, however, may be more severe than others and may require techniques that rely on clinical trials and intervention research for improving effectiveness.

Clients With Serious Mental Health Issues

Research investigating the use of constructivist approaches to address more severe mental health concerns has focused on narrative exposure therapy (NET) and cognitive–behavioral interventions. NET involves emotional exposure to the recollec-

Sidebar 16.6. It Takes a Village to Raise a Child: The Power of Proverbs

Stacy is a clinical mental health counselor who works with parents in an after-school program in a working-class neighborhood and has incorporated proverbs into the parenting skills psychoeducational groups. At the beginning of the session, Stacy gives each parent an individual proverb typed on a 3″ × 5″ index card and then asks each parent in turn to read the proverb given and explain its meaning to the group. The parents then dialogue about the meaning of the proverb and are encouraged to provide illustrative stories from their own experiences as parents (or children) that clarify the values embedded in the proverb. Parents take turns until the end of the session, and then one parent is asked to provide a summary of the entire meeting.

tion of traumatic events and, subsequently, the reorganization of those memories into a coherent, chronological story. This form of therapy has been primarily used to treat posttraumatic stress disorder (PTSD) among refugees and individuals who have survived war or other forms of organized violence or conflict (Robjant & Fazel, 2010). The goal is for the client to overcome avoidant strategies developed in response to the experience and explicate the story in detail. Then, the client is to repeat the story to reexperience the narrative in order to reconstruct the distorted memory. The final step is to restory the narrative to change the avoidant responses. Although NET has been shown to be effective with adult client populations, less is known about the usefulness of this approach with children. Young children in particular may not be developmentally mature enough to articulate a cogent story, especially if a significant amount of time has passed since the traumatic event occurred. Preliminary studies suggest that there have been positive outcomes with this client population, but insufficient evidence exists to support the use of NET with children (Schauer et al., 2004).

Cognitive behavior therapy is commonly used to treat severe mental illnesses, primarily because constructivism is seen as a philosophy rather than merely a technique. Thus, cognitive–behavioral interventions can be used in a congruent manner. Two interventions in particular have been successful with severely impaired clients: cognitive distancing/defusion and cognitive analytic therapy. The goal of cognitive distancing is to encourage clients to detect their thoughts in an objective way (Luoma & Hayes, in press). However, this task is merely a preparatory step and cannot by itself lead to change. The role of the counselor is to teach clients to analyze their negative thoughts. In this manner, the counselor facilitates clients' engagement in hypothesis testing to explore their own narratives. Cognitive defusion, borne out of cognitive distancing, is designed to enable clients to defuse thoughts and become aware of the dynamic process of meaning making and identity development (Garratt, Ingram, Rand, & Sawalani, 2007). Clients become aware that meaning-making thoughts are connected to social context.

The various applications of constructivism in counseling aid in clients' construction of self-identity. Traditional intervention strategies have given way to more contemporary interventions that include a focus on culturally informed tools for working with individuals from culturally marginalized groups. At present, more research has been presented that supports the use of constructivism-informed interventions borrowed from a host of theories, including narrative, cognitive behavior, and creative therapies. Clients with severe mental illnesses, such as PTSD, have benefitted from the use of NET, although applications with children have confounding outcomes. In addition, cognitive distancing and defusion have been shown to be effective with clients who have experienced extreme forms of trauma.

EVALUATION

Overview

Social constructivism in counseling is primarily represented in two major forms: solution-focused and narrative counseling. Each of these theories demonstrates the ideas that clients' worldviews are subjective and nothing can ever be written in stone. In this chapter, we have presented various techniques, constructs, and strategies for using these approaches with diverse types of clinical issues, settings, and clients. These strategies demonstrate effective and creative ways to empower clients to change their lives through their storytelling.

Solution-focused counseling focuses on the solution and not the problem and utilizes solution talk rather than problem talk. Clients learn to break away from circular patterns of problematic behavior in favor of new and innovative solutions to their issues. The counselor is encouraged to keep the counseling brief and to the point for the benefit of the client. Jones-Smith (2014) identified four goals that the solution-focused therapist should accomplish by the end of the sessions to determine whether the client can successfully terminate:

1. Find out what the client is hoping to achieve from counseling. Goals are framed in positive terms with expectancy for change.
2. Find out what the small, mundane, and everyday details of the client's life would be like if these hopes (the miracle) were accomplished.
3. Find out what the person is already doing or has done in the past that might help the client to realize his or her goals (the hoped-for situation).
4. Find out what might be different in the client's life if he or she made one very small step toward realizing his or her hopes (goals).

Each of these tasks helps the counselor not only to plan each session but also to keep treatment within the recommended three-session time frame in order to promote client autonomy.

Narrative counseling promotes the perspective that individuals are the only true experts on their lives (M. White, 2011). Related to this viewpoint is the idea that the story or narrative of the client is the basic unit of experience and the driving force behind his or her thoughts, beliefs, behaviors, and feelings. Past stories dictate the narratives that are used in the present and those that will be used in the future. Given that clients construct their own stories, one goal of the counselor is to aid in this reconstruction that takes place during the counseling process. The counselor helps the client identify alternative stories and transform them into his or her preferred stories. Narrative counseling is typically empowering to the client and is popularly used with individuals, families, and couples. This approach also takes a unique perspective on multicultural issues. The main focus of the counselor is identifying the client's story through the language that the client uses.

Supporting Research

Several studies have investigated the usefulness of solution-focused counseling, exploring spirituality, truancy in schools, academic skills, and substance abuse. In one study, Crockett and Prosek (2013) incorporated religious and spiritual rituals into therapy in order to create brief solutions rituals. They found that although solution-focused counseling often appears rigid, many aspects can be molded to benefit the client. Another area in which solution-focused counseling has been studied is schools. Enea and Dafinoiu (2009) found that applying solution-focused techniques in middle schools significantly reduced the amount of truancy. In addition, Fearrington, McCallum, and Skinner (2011) used solution-focused counseling with fifth graders who were failing mathematics and found that there was almost an immediate and sustained improvement among the majority of participants in terms of assignment completion.

Another population with which solution-focused counseling has been shown to be effective is clients who would qualify for a substance use diagnosis or drug rehabilitation treatment. Hayes, Curry, Freeman, and Kuch (2010) found that using this technique in conjunction with others helped to further educate alcohol-abusing college students about the dangers of their behaviors. Linton (2005) suggested using this approach with substance-abusing clients because of the client-centered nature of the techniques. Overall, solution-focused counseling has been applied to many different populations with promising results. It has been presented as a dynamic therapy and implies that there are many other areas in which it could be utilized in the future.

Narrative counseling has been explored for various clinical issues. For example, Alghamdi, Hunt, and Thomas (2015) utilized NET in order to reduce PTSD symptoms in traumatized firefighters in Saudi Arabia. They found that the therapy helped to greatly reduce those symptoms in the short term, but they also found that social support greatly affected those symptoms as well. Narrative therapy has also been investigated in relation to work with families. One study incorporated narrative counseling with families who had a family member who suffered from a traumatic brain injury and presented with several disabilities. Butera-Prinzi, Charles, and Story (2014) asserted that narrative therapy aided these families in feeling connected in the face of this tragedy and becoming validated. It also aided the families in realizing and applying some of their strengths.

In addition to families, narrative therapy has been found to aid children and adolescents with autism. Cashin, Browne, Bradbury, and Mulder (2013) used narrative therapy with students (10–16 years of age) who had been diagnosed with autism. They found that there were significant improvements in areas of psychological distress and measures of depression, anxiety, and other emotional problems. Despite these outcomes, very little is known about the effectiveness of narrative therapy with children and individuals with several developmental delays.

An additional form of narrative therapy is that of testifying. Testifying has been used in numerous capacities related to oppression and with those who experience inequality. Because a major component of narrative therapy is storytelling, testifying takes on a coping role among those who utilize it. Testifying has been described as a way of reclaiming a person's own identity as a human being through words in an effort to overcome oppression (Abrums, 2004). Testimony has been used in different contexts in which humans experience oppression on a daily and systematic basis. Park-Fuller (2000) explored the ways in which this form of narrative was beneficial for those who had experienced the Jewish Holocaust and found that testifying was beneficial for the individual. In addition, when engaging in group work, counselors can encourage testifiers to dialogue with one another to achieve greater support and clarification. Therefore, testifying is one aspect of narrative therapy that could be utilized both with individuals of a specific population that is at risk for oppression or with groups of that specific population.

Finally, Hedtke (2014) studied the uses of narrative counseling on grief and death. He found that by having the opportunity to create stories surrounding support and intervention rather than dwelling on loss and despair, families and children were able to become more hopeful and to find meaning in their current reality. This approach helped participants to have another option in their personal battle with cancer. Narrative counseling, like solution-focused counseling, promotes the ideals and plans of the client and seeks to help the client conceptualize as well as express them. This expression by the client is both empowering and effective in many different settings, as has been shown by prior research.

Limitations

Critics of constructivist counseling have suggested that this approach is too all encompassing without sufficient definition in that no reality is boundless. Constructivists counter by articulating that acknowledging multiple realities is not akin to acknowledging no reality at all and is more beneficial than imposing one static reality on everyone (McIlveen & Patton, 2007). Moreover, research has indicated that clients from a wide range of backgrounds, ethnicities, and belief systems can relate to constructivist approaches (Esquivel et al., 2010). These theories are often viewed as demonstrating cultural applicability because of the emphasis on the interpretation of the therapy session within the context of the client's language, culture, and worldviews.

However, several limitations have been highlighted in conjunction with solution-focused therapy. One is that this approach does not seem to focus on gender or power differentials, nor does it seem to provide any resources for clients who may be dealing with those kinds of issues. In addition, a larger criticism is that brief therapy focuses on the belief that the counselor does not need to know everything that led up to the creation of a problem. Thus, it may not be possible to resolve more severe mental health issues, such as trauma, neglect, abuse, and other chronic disorders, in three sessions or less using this approach (Jones-Smith, 2014).

Because of the length of counseling and the intense focus on solutions, this therapy is often criticized as being unsympathetic to the plight of the client, and the counselor may seem cold compared to counselors espousing other theories. One of the goals of solution-focused counseling is to limit problem talk, which many therapists of different theoretical orientations are said to focus on and which prolongs the problem. Because of this, the solution-focused counselor may appear to diminish the client's problems. The costs associated with this therapy may also be quite high compared to other therapies (Gladding, 2014).

Narrative counseling also has several limitations. One of the largest criticisms is that it is too closely related to social constructivism and that clients' issues are mainly found within themselves (McIlveen & Patton, 2007). Because narrative counseling takes the stance that clients' issues mainly have to do with how they view situations using their own logic, past experiences, or other environmental factors, it can completely disregard the fact that many clients may experience discrimination or prejudice from the outside environment. An additional criticism is that often this counseling approach produces so-called experts who espouse their own point of view, knowledge, and beliefs without sticking to the original therapy. Because this form of counseling promotes the idea that the therapist is not the expert, this can backfire, and the therapist could allow the client to dictate his or her own treatment or become an expert on the therapy (Jones-Smith, 2014).

Narrative counseling has also been criticized as being very intellectual. Thus, some clients may not respond well if they are undereducated or have mental challenges. This approach also promotes a focus on the here and now instead of clients' history of the issues or what brought the client into therapy (Gladding, 2014). Finally, little research of a qualitative nature has been conducted at this point in the therapy's development. Therefore, there is a need for more research that marries the heavy emphasis on language and the partnership between the client and the counselor.

Summary Chart: Constructivist Theories

Human Nature

Within a constructivist approach, counselors are encouraged to view reality as socially constructed wherein there is no belief in an absolute reality. Also, clients are to be viewed as capable and resilient in creating solutions to their own problems. Thus, the counselors' role is to facilitate clients' awareness of their own abilities, strengths, and potential.

Major Constructs

Solution-focused counseling is rooted in family systems therapy and is present oriented. The counseling sessions are intended to be brief, focusing on what works. Narrative theory is nonsystemic and relies heavily on the shared language experience. Clients are encouraged to externalize the problem. This approach has been shown to be effective with culturally diverse clients.

Goals

There are four major goals within the collectivist perspective. First, counselors must have faith that clients have the capacity to articulate their goals and identify the resources necessary to mediate their life challenges. Second, there is a focus on starting with small, concrete changes, as these can lead to larger changes. Third, it is important to consistently reflect an emphasis on goals with a future orientation. Fourth, counselors are to discuss solutions rather than talk about the client's problems.

Change Process

Within a solution-focused framework, clients are seen as agents of their own change, and counselors take on the role of facilitator. Counselors embracing this approach share meaning making with the client as a core element of the therapeutic process. Narrative counselors see clients as agents of their own change and also assume the role of facilitator within the counseling session. As with solution-focused counseling, shared and collaborative meaning making is a core element of change.

Interventions

Several intervention strategies are popularly used in solution-focused counseling. Of these, perhaps the miracle question, exception seeking, scaling, and problem-free talk are most common. Within narrative therapy, a major focus is on externalizing the problem through the use of essay writing, folktales (*cuentos*), proverbs (*dichos*), and testifying.

Limitations

Scholars have asserted that solution-focused counseling lacks a focus on power differentials, such as those affecting women and other socially marginalized individuals. In addition, the reduced emphasis on the past may limit the counselor's knowledge about the problem. Finally, problem-free talk may seem to diminish the client's problem. Critics of narrative therapy have suggested that counselors may appear to blame the client because of the emphasis on the intrapsychic process. Furthermore, the focus on the client as expert may discredit the counselor's expertise and training. Some experts view this approach as very intellectual and not as effective with less educated clients.

THE CASE OF MARIA: A CONSTRUCTIVIST APPROACH

Conceptualization

Maria may be affected by several environmental systems, including family, religious, cultural, and social systems. Within the family system, birth order dynamics suggest that being the oldest child and a daughter may have positioned Maria as the child with the most responsibilities in the family. She may have had child care and household responsibilities from an early age and could have internalized these responsibilities into her identity. From a cultural perspective, Latino parents often assign additional responsibilities to the oldest female child.

As a Catholic, Maria may be affected by religious values that relate to the definition of family, attitudes about women and their role in the family, and divorce. In addition, religious worldviews may also encourage feelings of guilt and shame for assuming nontraditional roles, such as caregiver or head of household, particularly for women.

Maria's cultural values may also play a significant role in her perspective on her presenting problem. As a Latina, Maria may have received messages from her family and community about the specific roles that women play in families and who are ideal partners. Issues of racial and cultural identity may also be salient to the factors that influence Maria's feelings of anxiety and depression. Having been educated in academic communities outside of her cultural frame of reference, Maria would likely have needed to resolve cross-cultural differences in social interactions that could have challenged her cultural belief and mores. Thus, issues of acculturation may need to be reviewed, discussed, and possibly deconstructed.

In addition, several social systems could play a role in Maria's current situation, including sexism, perspectives on divorce, lack of teacher empowerment, racism, and attitudes toward single parents. Thus, it would be important for the counselor to encourage Maria to reflect on the impact of external factors on her experiences and possible reactions to microaggressions to which she may have been exposed. Each of these social factors may play a part in her disposition and resilience on a daily basis.

An important aspect of Maria's presentation involves her identification stabilization. Maria may fail to believe that she can resolve her situation. This represents underidentification with her problem. She may need to transform her dream to restory herself as empowered and resourceful. This would help her to transform her story (shifting identification). Maria may be distancing herself from her narrative, as it could represent negative experiences or evil emotions that are uncomfortable. The counselor needs to help Maria to identify the emotions associated with the narrative and encourage her to push through these feelings in order to restory her emotive responses to the activating event or events. Based on this conceptualization of Maria, the following treatment plan is offered.

Treatment Plan

- *Session 1: Review the presenting problem and goals of the counseling experience.* Introduce the basic constructivist concepts that will be present in the sessions, focusing on a problem-free environment (e.g., "Most of the time, we will concentrate on the solutions rather than rehashing the problem"). Engage in facilitating questioning with Maria, such as, "How is fear influencing your life?" and "How can you expose the secrets that fear is keeping hidden from you?" Also, ask an exception question: "Are there times when you do not experience these problems?" Ask Maria to provide a summary of the session. For homework, direct Maria to locate a cuento (folktale) that she believes relates to her current experiences and bring it to the next counseling session. To prepare for the next session, locate cuentos online or at a bookstore to have available for discussion.
- *Session 2: Review the previous session.* Ask Maria to read the cuento that she has selected (if she has not brought one, you can share your collection of cuentos with her and ask that she select one to read in session). After Maria has read the cuento, engage in a dialogue about the symbolic meaning and moral of the folktale and how she thinks it relates to her problem. Present the miracle question to Maria: "Suppose that one night, while you were asleep, there was a miracle and this problem was solved. How would you know? What would be different?" Engage in a collaborative dialogue with Maria to allow her to imagine a solution to the problem without the constraints of her value-laden lived experiences. Direct Maria to provide a summary of the session. For homework, direct Maria to develop a lesson plan (such as one that she might create as a teacher) on overcoming fears that she could share with her own two children. Prepare for termination in the next session by reminding Maria of the brief nature of brief narrative counseling and the activities for the final session.
- *Session 3: Review the previous session.* Ask Maria to share her lesson plan on coping and resilience. Dialogue about what elements she has included in her conceptualizations of overcoming fear and how they might apply to her presenting problem. Review the counseling goals and discuss transformations. Ask Maria to articulate how she might apply these skills and this awareness to future situations.

REFERENCES

Abrums, M. (2004). Faith and feminism: How African American women from a storefront church resist oppression in healthcare. *Advances in Nursing Science, 27*, 187–201.

Akinyela, M. M. (2014). Narrative therapy and cultural democracy: A testimony view. *Australian and New Zealand Journal of Family Therapy, 35*(1), 46–49. doi:10.1002/anzf.1041

Alghamdi, M., Hunt, N., & Thomas, S. (2015). The effectiveness of narrative exposure therapy with traumatised firefighters in Saudi Arabia: A randomized controlled study. *Behaviour Research and Therapy, 66*, 64–71. doi:10.1016/j.brat.2015.01.008

Beres, L., Bowles, K., & Fook, J. (2011). Narrative therapy and critical reflection on practice: A conversation with Jan Fook. *Journal of Systemic Therapy, 30*(2), 81–97.

Burke, M. T., Chauvin, J. C., & Miranti, J. G. (2004). *Religious and spiritual issues in counseling*. New York, NY: Routledge.

Butera-Prinzi, F., Charles, N., & Story, K. (2014). Narrative family therapy and group work for families living with acquired brain injury. *Australian and New Zealand Journal of Family Therapy, 35*(1), 81–99. doi:10.1002/anzf.1046

Cappeliez, P., & Robitaille, A. (2010). Coping mediates the relationships between reminiscence and psychological well-being among older adults. *Aging and Mental Health, 14*, 807–818.

Cashin, A., Browne, G., Bradbury, J., & Mulder, A. (2013). The effectiveness of narrative therapy with young people with autism. *Journal of Child and Adolescent Psychiatric Nursing, 26*(1), 32–41. doi:10.1111/jcap.12020

Clay, L., Olatunji, C., & Cooley, S. (2001, March). *Keeping the story alive: Narrative in the African-American church and community*. Paper presented at the annual meeting of the American Counseling Association, San Antonio, TX. (ERIC Document Reproduction Service No. ED462666)

Cottone, R. (2001). A social construction model of ethical decision making in counseling. *Journal of Counseling & Development, 79*, 39–45.

Crockett, S. A., & Prosek, E. A. (2013). Promoting cognitive, emotional, and spiritual client change: The infusion of solution-focused counseling and ritual therapy. *Counseling and Values, 58*, 237–253. doi:10.1002/j.2161-007X.2013.00036.x

De Jong, P., & Berg, I. K. (2007). *Interviewing for solutions*. Boston, MA: Cengage Learning.

Del Corso, J., & Rehfuss, M. C. (2011). The role of narrative in career construction theory. *Journal of Vocational Behavior, 79*(2), 334–339. doi:10.1016/j.vb.2011.04.003

Enea, V., & Dafinoiu, I. (2009). Motivational/solution-focused intervention for reducing school truancy among adolescents. *Journal of Cognitive and Behavioral Psychotherapies, 9*(2), 185–198.

Esquivel, G. B., Oades-Sese, G. V., & Jarvis, M. L. (2010). *Culturally sensitive narrative interventions for immigrant children and adolescents*. Lanham, MD: University Press of America.

Fearrington, J. Y., McCallum, R. S., & Skinner, C. H. (2011). Increasing math assignment completion using solution-focused brief counseling. *Education & Treatment of Children, 34*(1), 61–80. doi:10.1353/etc.2011.0005

Frazier, K. N., West-Olatunji, C., St. Juste, S., & Goodman, R. (2009). Transgenerational trauma and child sexual abuse: Reconceptualizing cases involving young survivors of CSA. *Journal of Mental Health Counseling, 31*, 22–33.

Frisina, P. G., Borod, J. C., & Lepore, S. J. (2004). A meta-analysis of the effects of written emotional disclosure on the health outcomes of clinical populations. *Journal of Nervous and Mental Disease, 192*, 629–634.

Garratt, G., Ingram, R. E., Rand, K. L., & Sawalani, G. (2007). Cognitive processes in cognitive therapy: Evaluation of the mechanisms of change in the treatment of depression. *Clinical Psychology: Science and Practice, 14*(3), 220–239.

Gladding, S. T. (2014). *Counseling theories for human services practitioners: Essential concepts and applications (standards for excellence)*. New York, NY: Pearson.

Graham, J. J. (2014). Narrative therapy for treating video game addiction. *International Journal of Mental Health and Addiction, 12*, 701–707. doi:10.1007/s11469-014-9491-4

Hayes, B. G., Curry, J., Freeman, M. S., & Kuch, T. H. (2010). An alternative counseling model for alcohol abuse in college: A case study. *Journal of College Counseling, 13*(1), 87–96. doi:10.1002/j.2161-1882.2010.tb00050.x

Hedtke, L. (2014). Creating stories of hope: A narrative approach to illness, death and grief. *Australian and New Zealand Journal of Family Therapy, 35*(1), 4–19. doi:10.1002/anzf.1040

Hoskins, M. (1995). *Constructivist approaches for career counselors.* Retrieved from http://www.counseling.org/Resources/Library/ERIC%20Digests/95-062.pdf

Jones-Smith, E. (2014). *Theories of counseling and psychotherapy: An integrative approach* (2nd ed.). Thousand Oaks, CA: Sage.

Keaton, S. A., & Bodie, G. D. (2011). Explaining social constructivism. *Communication Teacher, 25*(4), 192–196. doi:10.1080/17404622.2011.601725

Kelly, G. A. (1955). *The psychology of personal constructs.* New York, NY: Norton.

Kim, H., Prouty, A. M., & Roberson, P. N. E. (2012). Narrative therapy with intercultural couples: A case study. *Journal of Family Psychotherapy, 23*(4), 273–286. doi:10.1080/08975353.2012.735591

Klein, K., & Bowles, A. (2010). Coherence and narrative structure in personal accounts of stressful experiences. *Journal of Social and Clinical Psychology, 29*(3), 256–280.

Linton, J. M. (2005). Mental health counselors and substance abuse treatment: Advantages, difficulties, and practical issues to solution-focused interventions. *Journal of Mental Health Counseling, 27*, 297–310.

Lumley, M. A., & Provenzano, K. M. (2003). Stress management through written emotional disclosure improved academic performance among college students with physical symptoms. *Journal of Educational Psychology, 95*, 641–649.

Luoma, J., & Hayes, S. C. (in press). Cognitive diffusion. In W. T. O'Donoghue, J. D. Fisher, & S. C. Hayes (Eds.), *Empirically supported techniques of cognitive behavior therapy: A step by step guide for clinicians.* New York, NY: Wiley.

Mahoney, M. J., & Granvold, D. K. (2005). Constructivism and psychotherapy. *World Psychiatry, 4*(2), 74–77.

McIlveen, P. F., & Patton, W. A. (2007). Narrative counseling: Theory and exemplars of practice. *Australian Psychologist, 42*(3), 226–235.

Miller, B. J., Cardona, J. R. P., & Hardin, M. (2007). The use of narrative therapy and internal family systems with survivors of child sexual abuse: Examining issues related to loss and oppression. *Journal of Feminist Family Therapy, 18*(4), 1–27.

Murphy, J. J. (2015). *Solution-focused counseling in schools* (3rd ed.). Alexandria, VA: American Counseling Association.

O'Connell, B. (2012). *Solution-focused therapy* (3rd ed.). London, England: Sage.

Park-Fuller, L. M. (2000). Performance absence: The staged personal narrative as testimony. *Text and Performance Quarterly, 20*(1), 20–42.

Pasupathi, M., Weeks, T., & Rice, C. (2006). Reflecting on life: Remembering as a major process in adult development. *Journal of Language and Social Psychology, 25*, 244–263.

Pennebaker, J. W., & Chung, C. K. (2011). Expressive writing and its links to physical and mental health. In H. S. Friedman (Ed.), *Oxford handbook of health psychology* (pp. 417–437). New York, NY: Oxford University Press.

Robjant, K., & Fazel, M. (2010). The emerging evidence for narrative exposure therapy: A review. *Clinical Psychology Review, 30*, 1030–1039.

Savickas, M. L. (2005). The theory and practice of career construction. In S. D. Brown & R. T. Lent (Eds.), *Career development and counseling: Putting theory and research to work* (pp. 42–70). Hoboken, NJ: Wiley.

Schauer, E., Neuer, F., Elbert, T., Ertl, V., Onyut, L. P., Odenwald, M., & Schauer, M. (2004). Narrative exposure therapy in children: A case study. *Intervention, 2*(1), 18–33.

Singer, J. A. (2004). Narrative identity and meaning making across the adult lifespan: An introduction. *Journal of Personality, 72*, 437–459.

Thorne, A. (2000). Personal memory telling and personality development. *Personality & Social Psychology Review, 4*, 46–56.

Webster, J. D. (2003). The reminiscence circumflex and autobiographical memory functions. *Memory, 11*, 203–215.

Westerhof, G. J., & Bohlmeijer, E. T. (2012). Life stories and mental health: The role of identification processes in theory and interventions. *Narrative Work: Issues, Investigations, & Interventions, 2*(1), 106–128.

White, M. (2011). *Narrative practice: Continuing the conversations.* New York, NY: Norton.

White, T. (2007). *Developing a two person psychology: A model for therapeutic change.* Retrieved from http://tony-white.com/wp-content/uploads/2013/12/Developing-a-two-person-psychology.pdf

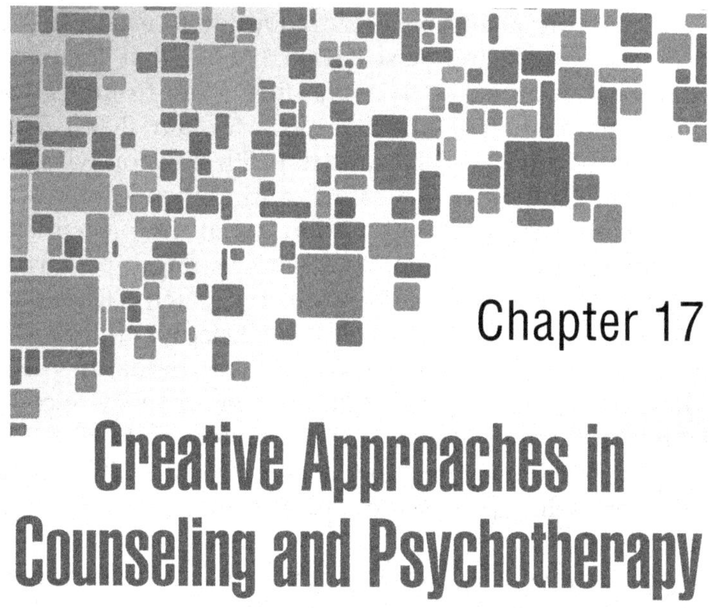

Chapter 17

Creative Approaches in Counseling and Psychotherapy

Thelma Duffey, Shane Haberstroh, and Heather Trepal

Creative approaches in counseling and psychotherapy are rich in history and universally available. Just as sculptors, painters, architects, educators, engineers, and software developers use creativity to generate new ideas, paradigms, products, works of art, technology, and more, creativity is an equally critical human characteristic for counselors working in the mental health profession (Duffey, 2014). Whether creativity emerges as a finger painting or a yoga pose, a novel concept or a paradigm shift in thought, people find opportunities to be creative in all areas of life, including the profession of counseling. This chapter (a) addresses creativity as a theoretical construct used by counselors and other mental health professionals, (b) provides a historical context for the use of expressive therapies and the creative arts in counseling, (c) distinguishes creativity in counseling (CIC) as an approach within the profession of counseling, (d) discusses the ethical parameters around using creative approaches in counseling practice, and (e) applies CIC as an approach in the case study of Maria.

BACKGROUND

In 1992, Samuel Gladding published *Counseling as an Art: The Creative Arts in Counseling.* This work provided an extensive history of the creative and expressive arts within counseling and promoted its value and place within the counseling profession. Gladding (2011) noted that, within the 20th century, "interest in the arts as an adjunct to traditional mental health practices thereby gained new recognition and acceptance" (p. 8). In light of this, several creative arts professions formed to establish their own credentialing and practice parameters (e.g., the American Dance Therapy Association, the American Music Therapy Association, and the American Art Therapy Association [AATA]; Gladding, 2016).

In 2004, an initiative organized by Thelma Duffey to establish a new division within the American Counseling Association (ACA) that focused on creative, diverse, and relational approaches to counseling grew from a grassroots initiative to a national organization (Duffey & Kerl-McClain, 2008). The Association for Creativity in Counseling (ACC) became the 19th division within the ACA and a home for counselors, counselor educators, and students interested in creative and relational processes in counseling. Grounded in the principles of creativity, diversity, and relational development, ACC and its flagship journal, the *Journal of Creativity in Mental Health*, became a forum by which CIC could be formally recognized, shared, and examined (Duffey, 2006). Deeply influenced by relational-cultural theory (RCT), ACC advocates using diverse modalities and creative interventions grounded in creativity and relational competency in counseling. ACC and the *Journal of Creativity in Mental Health* provide professional platforms for theory, research, and practice related to CIC. As a result, CIC joins the relational philosophy of the counseling profession with the innate creativity available to all people (see Sidebar 17.1).

Although *creativity in counseling* may be a relatively new term, the concept of CIC is not new. The use of creative and expressive arts has a long history in counseling and other helping professions (Gladding, 2016). *Creative and expressive therapy* is an umbrella term used to describe professions such as art therapy, music therapy, psychodrama, movement therapy, and poetry therapy, among others. These professions center on the use of various forms of media (e.g., art, music, poetry) to help clients understand and communicate their concerns. Creative and expressive arts therapies differ from CIC. The creative and expressive arts professions focus on specific creative media as distinct therapies rather than having a purposeful focus on creativity within the practice of professional counseling (Duffey, Haberstroh, & Trepal, 2009; Duffey & Kerl-McClain, 2008; Gladding, 2016). In addition, many creative and expressive arts practitioners begin as artists (e.g., musicians, poets, dancers) and are skilled at using these media prior to becoming trained as counselors (Gladding, 2016). Many of these professions promote professional certifications, codes of ethics, and standards of practice that demarcate and regulate the use of creative therapies. Art therapists seek the Registered Art Therapist credential, whereas music therapists may obtain either the Music Therapist Board Certified credential or the Registered

Sidebar 17.1. RCT: Healing Through Relationships

In her book *Toward a New Psychology of Women*, Jean Baker Miller (1986) brought to light the lack of psychological theories that considered how women grow and develop throughout their life span. This text subsequently laid the groundwork for RCT. Counselors who utilize RCT place great importance on the therapeutic relationship, including empowerment, mutual empathy, and genuineness (Duffey & Somody, 2011). The mutual empathy developed between client and counselor can serve as a platform on which the client realizes the potential to thrive (Duffey & Somody, 2011; Jordan, 2010). By promoting the importance of connections and relationships, RCT serves as an alternative to conventional therapeutic approaches that promote individuation over connection (Comstock et al., 2008; Duffey & Haberstroh, 2012). RCT counselors also concentrate on the strategies clients use to connect with and disconnect from others. RCT recognizes that disconnections are a natural part of life and that reconnections are important relational competencies (Duffey, 2006; Jordan, 2010).

Music Therapist credential, for example. Other creative arts therapies also maintain specific certification requirements respective to their practice. Professionals who seek these credentials must document training and supervised experience in each of the regulated creative arts therapies. Many of the organizations that credential creative arts therapists also register and approve supervisors. Interested counselors may consult Sidebar 17.2 for the websites of the national organizations associated with each creative arts therapy. Although many creative arts organizations define their approach as a unique profession, CIC was founded for counselors. It reflects and honors the synergy of creativity within the counseling relationship and supports the creative process within counselors and clients.

Ethical Considerations

Given that the counseling profession and other helping professions implement creativity in practice, each profession maintains codes of ethics and standards that guide its members' use of creativity and professional practices. Professional counselors follow the ACA Code of Ethics (ACA, 2014) and the ethics codes of their state licensing board. Likewise, individuals credentialed as creative arts therapists follow their respective professional ethics codes and standards. Professional counselors who are also credentialed creative arts therapists must negotiate the multiple standards of practice within which they operate.

With regard to professional counselors, the *ACA Code of Ethics* (ACA, 2014) maintains that "counselors practice only within the boundaries of their competence, based on their education, training, supervised experience, state and national professional credentials, and appropriate professional experience" (Standard C.2.a.). Kerl-McClain, Duffey, Haberstroh, and Trepal (2013) identified the following ethical recommendations surrounding the use of CIC: (a) Professional ethics are standards adopted by a professional community; (b) professional counselors subscribe to the *ACA Code of Ethics*, and other groups of professionals maintain their own ethics and practice codes; (c) individual state licensing boards also develop and maintain ethics codes; and (d) ethics codes demarcate professional boundaries.

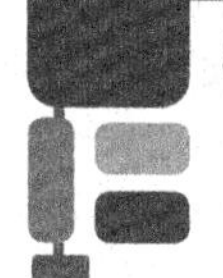

Sidebar 17.2. Websites of National Organizations of Creative Arts Therapies

Art Therapy

American Art Therapy Association, www.arttherapy.org
Art Therapy Without Borders, www.atwb.org

Dance/Movement Therapy

American Dance Therapy Association, www.adta.org

Music Therapy

American Music Therapy Association, www.musictherapy.org

Play Therapy

Association for Play Therapy, www.a4pt.org

Sandplay

Sandplay Therapists of America, www.sandplay.org
Association for Sandplay Therapy, http://sandplayassociation.com

ACC supports the position that trained professional counselors with an ethical foundation based on the *ACA Code of Ethics* (ACA, 2014) can use their creativity and the creativity of their clients. Thus, counselors can use music in their work with clients but not identify as music therapists or inform clients that they are participating in music therapy. The theory of CIC outlined in this chapter reflects this premise. Practitioners who understand CIC as an approach recognize that CIC is not a simple catchall or catalogue of activities void of theoretical and research underpinnings (Duffey et al., 2009; Gladding, 2016). This would be a simplistic view of the very dynamic depth of CIC, particularly as CIC is grounded in relational theory and embedded in the *ACA Code of Ethics* and ACA's 20/20 definition of counseling as a relationship (Kaplan, Tarvydas, & Gladding, 2014).

HUMAN NATURE: A DEVELOPMENTAL PERSPECTIVE

CIC, as an approach to working with clients in a mental health context, conceptualizes human growth as a byproduct of connecting with one's creativity in relationship with others. That is, barring medical or physiological concerns, each person has the potential for creative problem solving and expression, and this potential can be realized when there is freedom to be creative and a social and relational context in which to share one's creativity. In this respect, creativity is an innate quality that, when shared with others, is relational and mutually growth promoting. This quality, which promotes growth throughout the life span, is generally first seen in young children. For example, small children are often connected to their creativity. They play, many enjoy making art, and they sing along to their favorite songs. Many use humor, create games, and use their imaginations. Friends and family are often important to children as they share their creativity. Their creativity supports connection along a number of levels.

However, counselors using a CIC approach purport that, as important as it is to connect with one's creativity, this connection does not always progress easily throughout time and across a person's life span. As children grow and become socialized, many second-guess their creativity. They begin to question whether they are truly creative. They, in turn, become self-conscious and do not easily share their creative works or ideas. In these cases and over time, creativity as a human quality becomes misunderstood and relegated to those special people whose talent is exceptional (Duffey, 2006; Gladding, 2016). More and more, then, people become disconnected from their creativity—the life energy that motivates novel ideas, passion, or works of art—and from their resourcefulness.

MAJOR CONSTRUCTS

CIC is defined as a shared counseling process involving growth-promoting shifts that occur from an intentional focus on the therapeutic relationship and the inherent human creative capacity to affect change. Creativity is as fundamental to counseling practice as the therapeutic relationship. In the best sense, the therapeutic relationship ignites creative problem solving, understanding, flexibility, and adaptability. In turn, this shared creativity deepens the counseling relationship. Although there are any number of potential creative moments that naturally occur in counseling, media and creative interventions may be used to facilitate creative shifts in perspectives, thoughts, feelings, and behaviors. However, in all cases, the process must be intentionally relational rather than intervention driven.

CIC emerges from the shared connection, inspired dialogue, innovative ideas, new options, broader horizons, and feelings of freedom that can be generated through many kinds of interactions. CIC is based on the assumption that all people can be creative and, when actively fostered, draws on the creativity of the client and counselor to affect change. Counselors using a CIC approach to their work acknowledge the central role of the therapeutic relationship and a core set of beliefs and values.

These beliefs and values frame the major constructs of this approach. For example, counselors using CIC believe that cocreativity inspires action. Creativity involves openness, freedom, and new potential. Creativity is the very spirit of what counselors do. Creativity belongs to everyone and can be accessed by anyone (Duffey, 2006). Creativity, as an approach to counseling, centers on a client's ability to discover new possibilities through the shared creativity between client and counselor. In fact, counselors using this approach would say that clients' creativity, as well as their own, is among their greatest resources.

CIC Is Relational and Cocreative

Grounded in relational theories, counselors understand that relationships are fluid and that people grow as they navigate them (Jordan, 2010). In fact, CIC as an approach adopts ACA's 20/20: A Vision for the Future of Counseling relational definition of counseling (see ACA, 2015). It also suggests that integral to this relationship is the shared creativity that supports people facing times of transition and loss (Duffey, 2005b). In addition, creativity promotes problem solving, perspective shifting, creative imagination, and relational skill building. Counselors using this approach believe that shared creativity can support clients' belief in their potential, give them the courage to risk taking the steps to actualize it, and promote the kind of flexibility that helps them move out of an unproductive or disconnecting perspective to a more realistic and empowering one. Developmental growth, then, for counselors using this approach, occurs within a context of creativity and relationality. Inspired by the principles proposed by ACC, a division within the ACA, the major tenets of the CIC approach to practice purports the following:

- CIC is not simply an intrapersonal experience but rather is cocreated.
- Any shared activity creates possibilities for forming deepened connections and also poses risks for experiencing disconnection. Consistent with RCT, relationships undergo connections, disconnections, and reconnections.
- Counselors working from this approach explore the qualities and dynamics within a relationship that enhance connection with others and move through disconnections to reconnections. (Duffey, 2014; Duffey & Haberstroh, 2012, 2013)

CIC Is Respectful of Power and Context

Given the relational grounding of CIC, counselors working from a CIC approach consider context and power when conceptualizing client situations. By considering power dynamics, counselors and clients can better negotiate power in their relationship, which can serve as a template for negotiating the very real power dynamics that transpire in any relationship. Likewise, as counselors and clients take context into account, they can explore a larger perspective on a situation and approach the situation with more compassion for self and others (Duffey &

Haberstroh, 2013; see Sidebar 17.3). Based on a study reflecting the voices of ACC members on the relationship between creativity and relational competencies, CIC posits the following:

- Power used well supports the creativity and well-being of all people involved.
- Misused power exploits and diminishes people's creativity and opportunities to create possibilities.
- Creativity is a powerful force that can support a person's growth, particularly when it is shared. (Duffey et al., 2009)

CIC Is Expressed and Experienced in Diverse Ways

Creativity is a personally and relationally experienced construct that can be expressed in myriad ways. Whereas some people tap into their creativity in the confines of their rooms, sitting at a computer, writing or researching, or in sharing thoughts with others, other people experience creativity working with clay, reading a book, or painting a porch. CIC is an integrative theoretical approach that may utilize various media within traditional theoretical frameworks. Works of art, crafts, building projects, writing, and problem solving are some examples of how creativity can be expressed. Through such experiences as painting their house or planting their garden, people connect with that part of themselves that helps them tell their story and share. Although creativity can be experienced personally, in counseling it is expressed relationally.

CIC May Involve Creative Interventions or Other Media

When counselors use creative interventions, they may utilize a number of different media that innovatively characterize and communicate their theoretical approach. For example, counselors and clients may use books, literature, movies, music, technology, crafts, or photography in counseling. They may use poetry, journaling, puppets and other toys, and board games in session. These and other resources can support clients as they navigate personal, family, wellness, educational, or career goals. With theoretical intention and counseling skill, counselors use these interventions as thoughtful interventions to support client growth. CIC suggests the following:

- Creative interventions are purposeful and grounded in theory.
- A wide range of media can be used to support a person's growth.
- Media and creative interventions can help give voice to a situation in ways that talk therapy alone may not accomplish.

Sidebar 17.3. Case Study: The Importance of Considering Power Dynamics

Recently released from prison, Lisa is a Mexican American female referred to you by the criminal justice system. The court ordered Lisa to attend individual counseling as a condition of her probation. Lisa's felony charges relate to her addiction to heroin. Her primary goals for counseling are to regain custody of her children and maintain abstinence from drugs.

What are some of the social and institutional power situations that Lisa faced and will continue to face as (a) an ethnic minority, (b) a female, and (c) a convicted felon? What do you see the role of power playing in your relationship with Lisa? How will you use your power to support a productive outcome to Lisa's counseling?

CIC Promotes Shifts in Thoughts, Feelings, and Perspectives

One of the cornerstones of CIC is its role in helping clients move from limiting perspectives, thoughts, and feelings to more empowering and realistic ones. CIC acknowledges that people can become entrenched in perspectives that disconnect them from their core being and from others (Duffey & Haberstroh, 2013; Jordan, 2010). When people are entrenched, they can feel stuck in a situation, a bad relationship, or a distorted image of themselves or others. By expanding their perspectives to consider alternatives, clients have an opportunity to shift out of one perspective and into another. CIC purports the following:

- Their sense of being stuck in a situation, thought, or feeling can be a tremendous source of pain for clients.
- Creativity can be used by people to expand their perspectives and become more flexible in their thinking.
- Flexibility and openness offer opportunities for people to connect with possibilities within themselves and in relation to others.

APPLICATIONS

Overview

Counselors using CIC in their practice view counseling as relational and recognize the therapeutic relationship as core to their work. The counselors' and clients' creativity and any creative interventions they use are supported by the relationship. Creativity can involve intuition, spontaneity, flexibility of thought, and openness. It can involve the arts, books, movies and film, popular music, crafts, humor, and more. Creativity can promote new insights and ideas, problem-solving strategies, movement through challenges, productive relationships and reconnections, and a shift in perspective.

Goals of Counseling and Psychotherapy

The goals of the CIC approach in counseling are to help clients (a) connect with their innate resourcefulness, innovation, and creativity; (b) shift their perspective when appropriate to one that is more productive and realistic; (c) gain the freedom to connect with others more freely and comfortably because they are no longer blocked or stuck in a painful emotional place; (d) connect with their spontaneity, sense of fun, and levity; and (e) broaden their options for relating authentically and realistically.

The Process of Change

Focusing on Relationships

Counselors conceptualize the process of change in CIC as movement or therapeutic motion, which begins when clients and counselors connect in a counseling relationship that is based on the principles of RCT. Although many therapeutic interventions and schools of thought support the development of rapport and alliance, CIC only occurs in the context of the cocreation of a respectful, mutually empathic relationship. Change for clients begins when they experience compassion and engage in conversations with their counselors that are humanizing, honest, and respectful. From this relational foundation and place of healing and understanding, clients and counselors engage in the creative process. This process includes clients'

- Expression of divergent and innovative ways of thinking about problems, situations, and solutions
- Identification of hope for new possibilities
- Opportunities to try creative solutions
- Experience of relief, hope, and optimism for change
- Movement from feeling stuck into a creative way of being
- Movement out of chronic or situationally disturbing experiences, thoughts, and feelings to realistic and natural experiences of hope, freedom, and acceptance

Focusing on Context and Not Pathology

A focus on context rather than pathology liberates counselors to conceptualize the counseling process holistically and distances clients from stigma. Counselors communicate their commitment to understanding clients' concerns from a nonpathological frame. When clients move from perceiving themselves as being sick to understanding that they function within many contexts and within many relationships, they can gain the clarity and space to consider creative alternatives to their situations. This process reduces the shame and stigma associated with believing that one is sick or mentally ill. A contextual focus communicates that counselor creativity and creative interventions in counseling evolve from mere remedies for psychological afflictions to expressions of growth, change, and hope.

Accessing and Developing Shared Creativity

Counselors actively promote the potential for shared creativity in the counseling relationship. Clients begin to see themselves and their situations from new perspectives as they collaborate creatively with their counselor. Within this collaborative counseling relationship, counselors and clients access the media and resources available and meaningful for them. Creative interventions emerge from the relationship and from the experiences and knowledge of both clients and counselors. They can serve as catalysts for healing and for expanding clients' personal awareness. Creative interventions are not imposed by the counselor in a prescriptive format.

Experiencing New Perspectives, Self-Compassion, and Greater Creativity

Counselors working with CIC support their clients' growth through creative and relational means. For example, as clients experience creative moments in counseling, and as they connect with their counselors using creativity in its many forms, they develop their creative capacities while learning self-compassion and compassion for others. When clients expand their creative repertoire to include new methods for expression, thinking, and problem solving, these skills can transfer to their lives.

Traditional Intervention Strategies

The research body related to creative arts therapies in counseling and psychotherapy is growing (Boehm, Cramer, Staroszynski, & Ostermann, 2014; Pratt, 2004; Ray, Armstrong, Balkin, & Jayne, 2015; Rossiter, 2012). However, a number of authors have reported that methodological issues, the lack of standardized interventions, and small sample sizes historically limited the strength of evidence supporting these approaches (Pratt, 2004; Rossiter, 2012). Nonetheless, in recent years, researchers have noted that a number of studies have met the methodological rigor required for inclusion in meta-analytic studies (Boehm et al., 2014; Ray et al., 2015). Overall, creative arts therapies demonstrate moderate to strong treatment effects depending on the setting and populations studied (Boehm et al., 2014; Pratt, 2004; Ray et al., 2015; Rossiter, 2012). These effects correspond to those in research demonstrating the effectiveness of traditional talk therapies and suggest that creative media of expression are as effective as traditional approaches.

With regard to CIC, there are many traditional intervention strategies. Although they are too numerous to list, here we describe several common traditional creative arts therapies, including play therapy, art therapy, music therapy, and movement therapy.

Art Therapy

Art therapy is a distinct treatment modality that blends art and psychotherapeutic practice under the direction of a registered art therapist. These professionals work with clients via various methods of artistic expression, which can include painting, drawing, and sculpting, among others (AATA, 2013). There are many different theoretical approaches to art therapy, including person-centered, Adlerian, Gestalt, and cognitive approaches, among others (Rubin, 2001). Art therapy is utilized in many settings and with many populations, including children, adults, groups, and families (AATA, 2011).

The AATA maintains a database of outcome studies attesting to the effectiveness of art therapy (AATA, 2014), and a growing number of studies support art therapy for various conditions and issues (Slayton, D'Archer, & Kaplan, 2010). Metzl (2008) evaluated the scope of articles and research published in the AATA flagship journal *Art Therapy*. Metzl reported that although research was increasing, many of the sample sizes reported were smaller than standard expectations. Likewise, Maujean, Pepping, and Kendall (2014) conducted a systematic review of eight art therapy research studies published between 2008 and 2013. They found that art therapy was beneficial for adult populations, veterans, and adult prison inmates. Although the authors did not report on effect sizes or cumulative standardized effects across studies, they noted that art therapy produced significant differences in therapeutic outcomes in most of the studies they reviewed. Other large-scale reviews have focused on art therapy in trauma counseling (Eaton, Doherty, & Widrick, 2007) and in work with cancer survivors (Maujean et al., 2014). Eaton et al. (2007) concluded that a majority of the studies they reviewed were case studies, and only one study listed an effect size.

Dance/Movement Therapy

According to the American Dance Therapy Association (n.d.), dance/movement therapy is "the psychotherapeutic use of movement to promote emotional, social, cognitive, and physical integration of the individual." Dance/movement therapy covers a broad range of expressive modalities, including dance therapy, yoga, and organized sports, among others. Dance therapy may support mental health for people with various health concerns and physical diagnoses (Koch, Kunz, Lykou, & Cruz, 2014). In a review of 23 studies that included 1,028 participants, dance therapy increased the quality of life for many physically ill people (Koch et al., 2014). Moreover, Kiepe, Stöckigt, and Keil (2012) noted potential benefits of dance therapy for mental health and physical concerns in their review of 11 research studies. They suggested that future research focus on developing studies utilizing a priori sample size estimations, standardized interventions, and randomized research designs. Similarly, although dance therapy shows some promise in treating depression, a scarcity of controlled studies demonstrate its effectiveness for other issues (Mala, Karkou, & Meekums, 2012). Mala et al. (2012) called for standardized research to investigate the use of dance therapy, which echoes the methodological concerns in dance/movement therapy research and creative arts therapies research voiced by Ritter and Low (1996).

Music Therapy

Music therapy involves the use of music as an intervention in counseling. Certified music therapists plan interventions using music. Clients may listen to, compose, or reflect on various musical modalities (American Music Therapy Association, 2006). Music therapists work in a variety of mental health and rehabilitative settings (American Music Therapy Association, 2006). Music therapy helps individuals cope with chronic physical pain and other somatic and psychological concerns (Nickel, Hillecke, Argstatter, & Bolay, 2005). The use of music is effective in counseling with children and adolescents who suffer with autism (Whipple, 2004). Across several studies, these children and teens experienced increased social functioning, improved communication skills, decreases in anxiety, and increased focus and attention. The overall effects of music therapy as a therapeutic approach for working with children and adolescents with autism were strong. Whipple (2004) noted that the cumulative effect size was $d = .77$, which indicated a clear and large beneficial effect (Gold, 2004) of music therapy. Finally, music therapy may be helpful for people diagnosed with depression, but more systematic research is needed to firmly establish its effectiveness (Maratos, Gold, Wang, & Crawford, 2008).

Play Therapy

Play therapy is a distinct profession based on the idea that, developmentally speaking, children communicate primarily through play (Kottman, 2011). Play therapists work in many settings and usually counsel children ages 12 and younger; however, play therapists work with adults as well (Schaefer, 2003). Play therapists use various theoretical approaches in play therapy (e.g., cognitive–behavioral, child-centered, and Jungian approaches, among others) as well as directive and nondirective formats (Kottman, 2011). Play therapists use everyday objects associated with play to work with children. Sometimes children reenact a significant event with their play, and at other times, the play serves as a communication tool between the therapist and the child (Kottman, 2011).

Play therapy research studies indicate that play therapy is as effective as traditional counseling for both children and adults (Leblanc & Ritchie, 2001). Leblanc and Ritchie (2001) reported that 30 sessions of play therapy seemed to be the optimal duration of treatment for both children and adults. Focusing on children and play therapy, Lin and Bratton (2015) noted that child-centered play therapy facilitated growth and change in children, and effects across 52 studies revealed a moderate treatment effect. Similarly, Ray et al. (2015) reviewed 15 studies that investigated play therapy in the schools and found that play therapy was also moderately effective in schools. The most pronounced effect of play therapy was an increase in academic performance for students.

The Written Word: Expressive Writing and Bibliotherapy

Creative expression utilizing the written word can be a powerful tool in counseling practice. Researchers analyzed 23 studies and concluded that clients who suffer from depression benefit significantly from bibliotherapeutic interventions (Gregory, Canning, Lee, & Wise, 2004). Likewise, expressive writing increases physical and mental well-being for clients (Lowe, 2006). Researchers found that when clients wrote about emotions, they experienced a reduction in physical health problems and increases in psychological and physiological markers of good health (Pennebaker, 2004; Pennebaker & Evans, 2014). These studies attest to the power of the written word in giving clients alternative media of expression and space for reflection.

Animal/Pet-Assisted Therapy

The therapeutic use of animals dates back to the Middle Ages, and counselors increasingly recognize and utilize pets as a complementary form of treatment (Chandramouleeswaran & Russell, 2014). Animal/pet-assisted therapy can take several forms, including pet visitation, which focuses on establishing communication and a relationship between the person and the animal, and animal-assisted therapy, in which a certain type of animal serves specific goals in the person's treatment (Chandramouleeswaran & Russell, 2014). Popular examples of animals utilized in animal/pet-assisted therapy include dogs, cats, and horses. The use of horses in therapy is called equine-assisted psychotherapy.

Overall, it appears that use of the creative arts in counseling often facilitates growth and change for clients, and many creative arts therapies are empirically supported treatments for clients suffering from numerous physical and psychological diagnoses. Despite the various media for personal expression and therapeutic growth, creativity is the common process that defines work in the creative arts therapies. It can be argued that movement toward manualized and regulated creativity could stifle the dynamic and expansive process of creative growth for clients. Given that creativity is central to the work of many counselors who support these approaches (Duffey et al., 2009), we believe that creativity is common in effective counseling work.

Brief Intervention Strategies and Current Practices

Breaux (2011) contended that counselors combine traditional interventions and approaches with creative arts therapies. Likewise, CIC is inclusive and integrative in its scope, and counselors augment many other therapeutic strategies and approaches through the use of CIC. For example, the musical chronology and emerging life song (Duffey, 2005a) is an approach that incorporates narrative therapy, music, and cognitive therapy to restory a client's experiences and hopes.

The creation of a memory box is another example of a brief intervention appropriate for most settings. The first step is to ask the client if he or she is interested in pursuing the activity. Counselors using a CIC approach do not go forward with an intervention unless the client expresses interest. Next, the client and counselor collaborate on materials the client will bring to the next session. These materials may be used to decorate the box or become memorializing objects stored in the box. For example, the client might bring pictures, handwritten notes, e-mails, figurines, jewelry, and other significant personal objects (Imhoff, Vance, & Quackenbush, 2012). In the subsequent session or sessions, the client decorates the box and may choose to share his or her thoughts with the counselor as he or she does so. The activity produces several positive outcomes, including catharsis for the client (Denis & Makiwane, 2003) and strengthening of the therapeutic relationship.

Much like the musical chronology, counselors implementing the memory box intervention must assess for appropriateness and timing. Counselors practicing CIC believe that the implementation of any intimate intervention, such as the memory box, requires a therapeutic relationship based on trust and acceptance. This relationship creates an environment in which the client feels free to express the raw emotion often associated with grief.

Clients With Serious Mental Health Issues

Various expressive arts modalities have proven effective with clients who have serious mental health issues. For example, play therapy has been proven to be an effective treatment modality to use with children who display a range of problem behaviors (Bratton, Ray, Rhine, & Jones, 2005). Music therapy improved the mental state and social functioning of clients who suffered from schizophrenia (Mössler, Chen, Heldal, & Gold, 2011). Bibliotherapy done from a cognitive orientation has also proven effective in treating adult and adolescent clients with moderate depression in terms of reinforcing changes in thinking and shortening the total length of treatment (Gregory et al., 2004).

Studies investigating the role of mental health, psychopathology, and creativity have suggested that people suffering from serious forms of mental illness experience certain dimensions of heightened creativity; however, these individuals often struggle with problem solving and accessing their resourcefulness (Runco, 2004). Given that creativity encompasses many elements (e.g., divergent thinking, problem solving, inspirational moments), an increase in creativity across all domains is associated with experiences of well-being and mental health. Despite potential stereotypical associations of creativity with mental illness or madness, developing one's creativity is a worthwhile counseling goal and leads to increased functioning and emotional stability. In particular, individuals who suffer from mental illness can develop their cognitive creative abilities and problem-solving skills in counseling sessions (see Sidebar 17.4).

TECHNIQUES FOR IMPLEMENTING THE PROCESS OF CHANGE (TRADITIONAL)

According to Breaux (2011), there is significant overlap in the utilization of creative techniques. In addition, given the sheer number and scope of creative techniques

> **Sidebar 17.4. In Practice: CIC and Mental Health Diagnoses**
>
> Imagine you are a counselor working in a behavioral health care clinic. You are a member of a treatment team composed of doctors, psychiatrists, and other practitioners who utilize a medical model in their approach with patients. Your counseling approach is wellness oriented, strengths based, and firmly grounded in CIC. Your team meets once a week to staff client cases, in which you contribute information regarding your counseling efforts, client progress, and suggested next steps.
>
> How do you effectively navigate this system while preserving your identity as a counselor? How do you assimilate into this environment and maintain your relational focus? What challenges might arise as you attempt to advocate for your clients?

utilized by counselors, it would be difficult to adequately examine each individually. However, in the CIC approach, a basic assumption is that the process of change involves the counseling relationship.

EVALUATION

Overview

Each counseling relationship is unique in many ways. Counselors and clients enter into the counseling space with hopes, stories, life contexts, perceptions, and patterns of relating with others. These factors create the therapeutic narrative. When counselors engage intentionally and ethically, and when they are fully present in session and receptive to giving and providing feedback, clients benefit (Duncan, Miller, Wampold, & Hubble, 2010). The use of creative arts therapies in counseling adds additional dimensions to the counseling relationship and may open up new avenues for personal exploration and expression (Boehm et al., 2014; Pratt, 2004; Ray et al., 2015; Rossiter, 2012). How then do researchers distill the variables necessary for successful counseling, and how do creativity and creative approaches augment counseling outcomes? Some researchers purport that well-defined interventions delivered with specific target populations alleviate suffering for many common issues and disorders and that the interventions primarily drive outcomes (Baker & McFall, 2014). Creative therapies are a set of interventions that harness many media of personal expression, and a growing body of evidence supports their effectiveness (Boehm et al., 2014; Pratt, 2004; Ray et al., 2015; Rossiter, 2012).

Determining the effectiveness of a particular technique or intervention can be a daunting task, and many variables contribute to successful client outcomes (Duncan et al., 2010). Compounding these issues are calls from policymakers, insurers, and clients that ask counselors to demonstrate the effectiveness of their work. Counseling research is complex, and the quality of the therapeutic relationship may mediate the results from intervention studies. Nevertheless, empirical outcome research increasingly defines the evidence base for counseling practice. Although quantitative studies are similar in many respects, there are clear differences between empirically supported treatments and evidence-based practices (Laska, Gurman, & Wampold, 2014). Empirically supported treatments emerge from research studies that measure intervention procedures based on a clearly described disorder or feature of a disorder. Although one study may indicate the effectiveness of a particular intervention, many studies finding similar effects strengthen the evidence for specified interventions, and researchers can then use meta-analytic techniques to aggregate the overall effectiveness of outcome studies. Many research studies in the creative arts professions demonstrate the effectiveness of creative arts treatments with a wide range of individuals and issues. In this section, we present a review of the research on variables supporting CIC as a foundational professional practice.

Supporting Research

Creativity is a powerful human process that drives change within individuals, families communities, and the world. In fact, creativity is a core aspect of human performance and functioning (Scott, Leritz, & Mumford, 2004) and can be accessed and developed through training and interventions (Scott et al., 2004). CIC can emerge from and deepen a trusting counseling relationship and can be a space in which people learn to access and develop their creative skills. A review of 70 studies revealed that training in creativity significantly increased participants' divergent thinking, flexibility, attitudes, and cognitive complexity (Scott et al., 2004). CIC builds on the power of the creative process to open up new avenues for thinking, relating, and personal expression.

Context, Emotions, and Personality

Meta-analytic reports support the idea that increased creativity is most associated with feelings of well-being (Davis, 2009; Scott et al., 2004). When people are experiencing painful emotions, their creativity can be enhanced when their feelings and situation are acknowledged realistically (Baas, De Dreu, & Nijstad, 2008; Scott et al., 2004). The climate of organizations, families, and relational systems influences a person's ability to think and act creatively (Byron, Khazanchi, & Nazarian, 2010). Exploring the dynamics of creativity, Ma (2009) reviewed 111 quantitative studies that studied how the environment, social climate, and personality variables contributed to creativity. Creativity is fostered when environments are collaborative, relaxed, and flexible; allow for self-reflection; build on people's intrinsic motivation; and include reasonable expectations for performance (de Jesus, Rus, Lens, & Imaginário, 2013; Ma, 2009). Individuals who are open to new experiences, who can gain new information about their problems, and who can empathize with themselves and others seem to enjoy greater access to their creativity (Ma, 2009). These elements can all be fostered within an empowering counseling relationship.

CIC

People may struggle accessing their creativity when they feel that their circumstances are uncontrollable (Byron et al., 2010). The counseling relationship empowers individuals' growth across many domains (ACA, 2015), which promotes realistic growth and change. There is strong research evidence that creative thinking and problem solving are tied to feelings of well-being and are nurtured within supportive environments by individuals who lead in a transformational manner (Baas et al., 2008; Davis, 2009; Ma, 2009; Scott et al., 2004). Therefore, the counseling relationship is an ideal setting in which to foster clients' creativity. When people experience relief, connection, and happiness within a context like the counseling relationship, they can develop cognitive flexibility, increase self-expression, and generate new thoughts and solutions. Although counselors can use many media to facilitate CIC, creativity is a human capacity that people develop through training, facilitative interactions, and openness to the creative process.

Limitations

There are, however, barriers to counselors' understanding of creativity and its application in counseling. The first barrier is the enigmatic nature of creativity. A second complicating factor involves the many definitions of creativity. A third factor involves the socially constructed myths related to one's creativity. Creativity, then, remains a complex and multifaceted construct to conceptualize. As a result, not all counselors are aware of their own creativity, nor are they connected to the creative potential or power of their clients. In response, CIC as an approach debunks the myth that creativity is relegated to a special few and promotes the idea that a counselor's creativity is as therapeutic as effective listening, reflecting, or empathizing when it is bidirectional and shared (Duffey, 2006; see Sidebar 17.5).

Summary Chart: CIC

Human Nature

CIC is an approach that respects each client's capacity for creative problem solving and expression. Creativity is a developmental, relational, and mutually growth-promoting quality when shared with others.

Major Constructs

Major constructs of this theory include the following: CIC is relational and cocreative; CIC is respectful of power and context; CIC is expressed and experienced in diverse ways; CIC may involve creative interventions or other media; and CIC promotes shifts in thoughts, feelings, and perspectives.

Goals

The goals of the CIC approach in counseling are to help clients (a) connect with their innate resourcefulness, innovation, and creativity; (b) shift their perspective when appropriate to one that is more productive and realistic; (c) gain the freedom to connect with others more freely and comfortably because they are no longer blocked or stuck in a painful emotional place; (d) connect with their spontaneity, sense of fun, and levity; and (e) broaden their options for relating authentically and realistically.

Change Process

Counselors who use CIC support the ideas that (a) relationships are vehicles for change (including the relationship between the client and the counselor); (b) creativity is essential for human relationships and problem solving; and (c) the use of creativity allows for movement within the counseling session and the client's life, including the successful negotiation of complex situations and circumstances.

Sidebar 17.5. Yes, You *Are* Creative!

One of the myths associated with creativity is that only a select few possess the talent and skill necessary to be truly creative. The abilities to paint, act, and sing are valuable gifts and require a great deal of mastery, but they are not the only means of creative expression. "Creativity is for everyone and can be accessed by anyone!" (Duffey & Kerl-McClain, 2008, p. 70). Everyday, in every session, counselors utilize ingenuity and resourcefulness to help clients achieve their therapeutic goals. When we connect with the idea that creativity is the very spirit of what we do, amazing breakthroughs can result. Consider the following concepts as you consider your own unique abilities as a counselor *and* a human being:

- Recognize the value of creativity.
- Be open.
- Have fun as you explore new ideas.
- Develop your curiosity.
- Take risks.
- Brainstorm.
- Seek clarity.
- Practice shifting your perspective. (Duffey, 2014)

Interventions

This approach is not based on a specific intervention, although it may involve creative and innovative interventions using various media. CIC is based on the premise that allowing for the creativity of the client and the counselor presents a unique opportunity for change and movement.

Limitations

Creativity is a multifaceted and complex construct. Clients and counselors may not be connected to or value their creative potential.

THE CASE OF MARIA: CREATIVE APPROACHES

Counselors using a CIC conceptualization in the case of Maria would first recognize the context of Maria's experience and conceptualize her current stressors from a relational, multicultural, and strengths-based perspective. They would then use the power of their relationship and creativity to help her make sense of her experience, find compassion for herself through her connections, and gain clarity and balance while connecting to a more productive and realistic perspective of herself and her situation (Duffey & Haberstroh, 2013, 2014). These would be important goals for Maria as a woman navigating two worlds: the first, her beloved albeit personally conflicted familial and cultural histories; and the second, her contemporary lifestyle of choice, which is at odds with her long-held beliefs and the patterns of being of her family of origin.

Divorce can be experienced as a disenfranchised loss, according to CIC, and Maria's case is no exception. Members of her family did not want her to marry, so they are not sympathetic to her loss. In fact, they blame her marriage for the division in the family. Divorce often involves feelings of betrayal, rejection, and abandonment, and these natural feelings seem compounded for Maria in light of her family dynamics. Spousal abuse adds another powerful and confusing layer to her experience. Maria's circumstances set her up to second-guess and turn against herself.

A woman undergoing divorce, serving as a single parent, and negotiating conflict within her family, work life, and community would be challenged in the best of circumstances. Add to that the cultural dimension of negotiating traditional Hispanic values and the contemporary values she also carries (Duffey, Carns, Carns, & Garcia, 1998), and a woman in Maria's situation could reasonably be expected to feel disempowered and experience many of the symptoms she describes. Given Maria's history of being a leader in her community and a role model to her siblings, and given her current losses, challenges, and perceived failures, her feelings of shame and humiliation could understandably exacerbate her depressive symptoms and interfere with her sleep. These feelings, coupled with chronic disconnections and isolation (Jordan, 2010), could even lead to suicidal thoughts.

Thankfully, Maria's religion and some deep-rooted connection to life and others protect her from acting on her despair. They also provide enough support that she seeks out counseling and entrusts her story to a professional who can hopefully create a degree of safety. In the safety of the therapeutic relationship, Maria has an opportunity to represent herself authentically and reconnect with the resilient parts of her being. This is a goal for this approach. Moreover, rather than pathologizing Maria or attributing an issue with the self as a problem, counselors working with a CIC approach would normalize her experience. They would partner with her to work through those losses and disconnections using their relationship and their shared creativity.

Creative interventions, when used within a relational context, can be useful tools for supporting people facing grief and loss issues like Maria's. Grief and loss come in a variety of forms, and no two people experience them in exactly the same way. People facing losses such as divorce; disconnection from loved ones; feelings of failure; and a sense of overresponsibility, real or imagined, could understandably feel a wide range of emotions and display behaviors uncharacteristic of their norm (Duffey, 2014). These can be processed using creative interventions.

A Musical Chronology and the Emerging Life Song

One intervention involves using popular music from a person's life to tell his or her story. Songs that evoke memories can be helpful to clients working through grief, particularly when they feel stuck in their feelings and disconnected from others. If Maria enjoys music and if it carries memories for her, she could create a soundtrack of her life. Using the soundtrack as a backdrop, she could tell her story and process her experiences using songs that resonate with her life experiences as a catalyst. Music can serve as a point of connection to her experiences and to an engaged listener, her counselor. Music can also help her identify her counseling goals by designating a future song or a song she can live into (Duffey, 2005a; Duffey & Haberstroh, 2013).

The Process

- *Step 1:* Maria would reflect on and compile a song list chronologically.
- *Step 2:* The songs would provide context for her story, and she could process relevant experiences using her selected music to evoke deepened feelings and a fuller context to her memories. She would have an opportunity to revisit these memories and experiences with her counselor, who could guide her to expose feelings of self-contempt, judgment, or other unproductive attacks on the self.
- *Step 3:* Maria would identify a song or songs that reflect her current thoughts, feelings, and beliefs. This would serve as an emotional pulse or baseline.
- *Step 4:* Maria would select a song or songs that reflect her hopes for the future. This song would represent her counseling goals.

This process has been useful for women like Maria who carry unsympathetic perspectives of themselves and a sense of hopelessness—women who may be navigating two conflicting cultural worlds (Duffey et al., 1998). However, counselors using this intervention must be mindful of timing. The musical chronology is best used as a means of reminiscence and revisiting rather than an immediate or direct response to loss or crisis. In addition, sharing music can be a deeply personal experience, particularly when it evokes strong emotions, so it is best implemented when a relationship has been established. Finally, the musical chronology can provide a way for Maria to retell her story and to connect with a new perspective that supports her growth in relation to the people she loves (see Sidebar 17.6).

Sidebar 17.6. Self-Awareness: The Musical Chronology

The musical chronology intervention uses music to connect people with their life experiences and future goals. If you relate to music, which songs represent your significant past experiences? Which songs represent your current emotional state? Your hopes for the future?

As you consider the songs on your playlist, what thoughts and feelings arise? What would it be like to share these with a counselor or supervisor? What qualities would your counselor or supervisor need to have to make this experience comfortable and productive?

CIC acknowledges a shift in perspective as an important counseling goal for people struggling with issues of compassion, clarity, connection, and power. We next describe another CIC approach that can be used to help clients like Maria navigate painful experiences.

Developmental Relational Counseling (DRC)

Given the challenges and losses that Maria faces, she is vulnerable to perceiving herself unfavorably and unrealistically. DRC is a model designed to help people move from a connection to inaccurate and unproductive perspectives toward perspectives that are more compassionate and realistic (Duffey & Haberstroh, 2013, 2014). Based in RCT and influenced by the enneagram personality typology, cognitive theories, and narrative theories, DRC provides a framework by which people can assess their degree of accurate self- and other-awareness, their connection to a range of perspectives that influence how they see themselves and others, and their appropriate or inappropriate use of power.

As Maria reviews the DRC model, she is able to see how people can be connected to one of three perspectives depending on their circumstances. For example, people can connect to a self-denigrating perspective, which involves an inaccurate and disempowering self-perception of themselves or others. In contrast, people can connect to a self-aggrandizing perspective, which also involves an inaccurate, albeit self-promoting, self-perception. Either way, people connected to these dichotomous perspectives can become rigidly entrenched in their perceptions, disconnected from others, and ultimately disconnected from themselves. RCT would call this a form of condemned isolation (Jordan, 2010). Alternatively, people can connect to a clear and balanced perspective of themselves and others, which positions them to compassionately and accurately perceive themselves and others, ,regardless of the circumstances. Connecting to a clear and balanced perspective is a formidable goal, as can be seen in the case of Maria.

A look at Maria's situation shows an immensely competent woman who succeeded in many aspects of her life. She risked breaking the mold by venturing into uncharted areas and accomplished many successes along the way. She also traversed along a new cultural experience as a first-generation college student and wife to a man whose culture was different from her own. Some would say that Maria broke important ground. Unfortunately, she experienced chronic disconnections within her family and then suffered in an abusive marriage, which compromised her self-perception. After several years, she could no longer see herself through a compassionate or accurate lens. She was entrenched in a self-denigrating perspective.

Some counselors would expect Maria to reconsider her thinking and adopt a more productive perspective. Counselors working from a CIC approach would agree, but they would also recognize the inherent challenges involved in making the shift. Using a model like DRC could help Maria look at the facts of her life in context, explore her perspectives, examine the consequences of these perspectives, and see how she is currently connected to a self-denigrating perspective. Again, in looking at the model, she could connect with the feelings that this perspective promotes and recognize how her connection to the self-denigrating perspective intensifies her grief.

DRC provides a visual illustration of three perspectives and the thoughts and feelings that accompany them (see Figure 17.1). It offers a roadmap for people who identify in either extreme to move toward the center, or a clear and balanced perspective. DRC addresses issues of confidence, power, assertiveness, exploitation, shame, reactivity, and rigidity. It is based on the idea that feedback and receptivity to feedback are key elements in the change process (see Sidebar 17.7).

Counselors using CIC could also use dream-work to help Maria identify the intrapersonal and interpersonal dream figures and images that haunt her. Using guided imagery, they could help her neutralize those images and gain power in the situation. Together, they could use Gestalt principles to work with the dream and give voice to her fears. CIC via Jungian dream-work could help empower Maria by exploring the unacknowledged light within her that is reflected back to her in the shadow figures of her dream (Bogart, 2009). Like other interventions, dream-work is a creative approach that can help clients like Maria face the darkness of their feelings, give voice to their experiences, and potentially reframe a painful period into a meaningful and growth-promoting one.

In short, any number of creative interventions could be used with Maria. Bibliotherapy, the media, storytelling, and others, when grounded in the therapeutic relationship, can be important resources for clients as they navigate life stressors and complications. CIC provides counselors with opportunities to integrate any number of creative interventions and expand their cognitive flexibility and adaptability. This, in turn, invites their clients to participate in creative problem solving and movement into a richer relational and creative space.

Sidebar 17.7. Self-Awareness: The Three Perspectives of DRC

DRC outlines three possible perspectives individuals may adopt while reflecting on themselves and interacting with others. People coming from a self-denigrating point of view may underestimate their self-worth and become vulnerable to exploitation. In contrast, people who connect to a self-aggrandizing perspective display little regard for others and their feelings. When people are connected to a clear and balanced perspective of themselves and others, they relate from a place of compassion, direct communication, and responsible use of power.

- Recall a situation when you connected to a self-denigrating or self-aggrandizing perspective. Connect with that experience and reflect on what that experience was like for you.
- Think of the same situation and consider what connection to a clear and balanced perspective could look and feel like.
- What information will you share with your clients about connection and personal awareness based on your understanding of DRC?

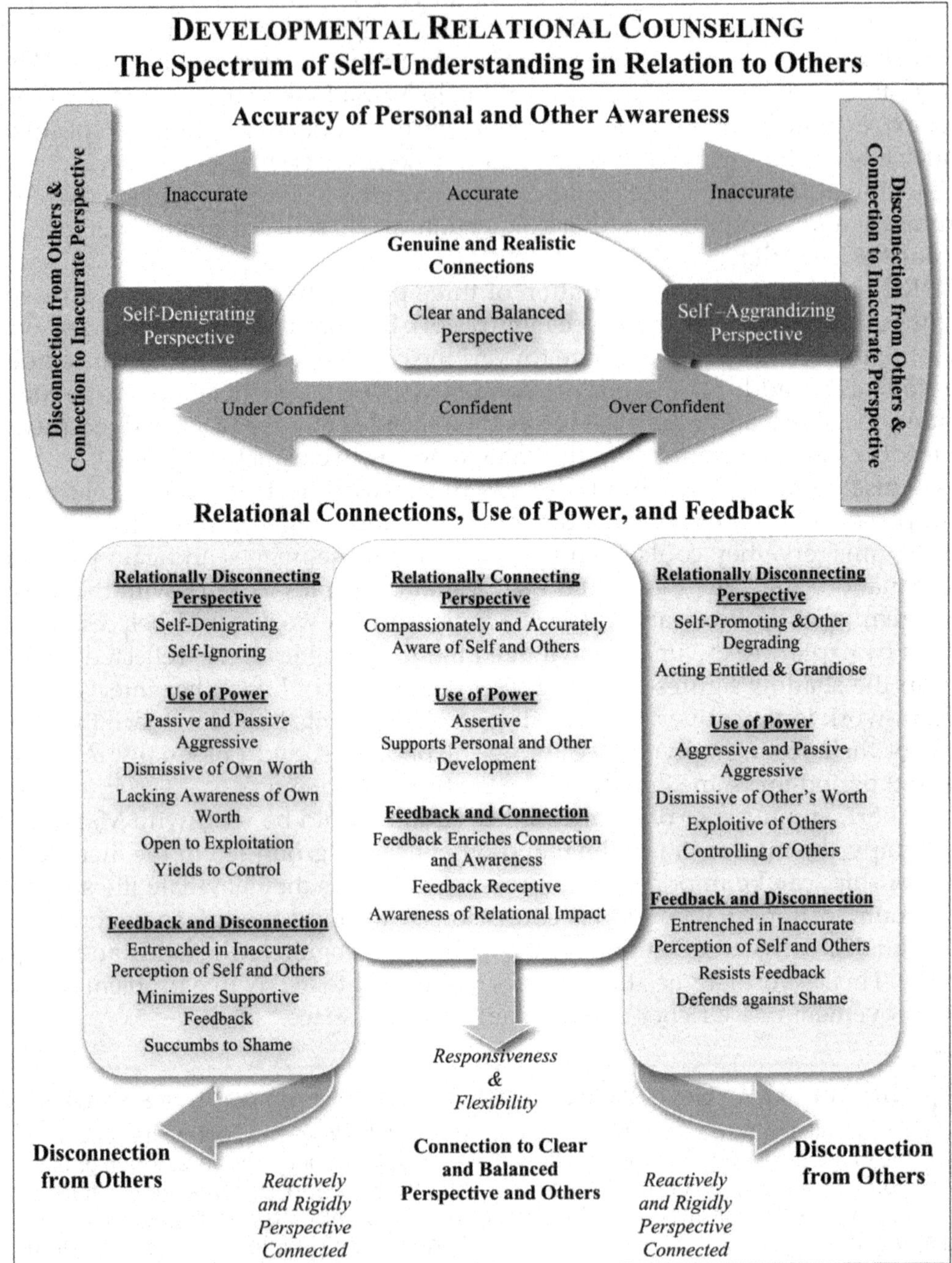

Figure 17.1. Developmental Relational Counseling Graphic

Note. Key concepts include the spectrum of self-understanding in relation to others, the continuum of awareness and perspectives, and the role of connections, use of power, and feedback. From "Developmental Relational Counseling: A Model for Self-Understanding in Relation to Others" by T. Duffey and S. Haberstroh, 2012, *Journal of Creativity in Mental Health, 7,* p. 265.

REFERENCES

American Art Therapy Association. (2011). *Art therapy supporting patient care in medical settings: Toolkit.* Retrieved from http://www.arttherapy.org/upload/toolkitmedicalsettings/medicalsettingstoolkit.pdf

American Art Therapy Association. (2013). *What is art therapy?* Retrieved from http://www.arttherapy.org/upload/whatisarttherapy.pdf

American Art Therapy Association. (2014). *American Art Therapy Association Research Committee art therapy outcome bibliography.* Retrieved from http://www.arttherapy.org/upload/outcomebibliographyresearchcmte.pdf

American Counseling Association. (2014). *ACA code of ethics.* Alexandria, VA: Author.

American Counseling Association. (2015). *20/20: A vision for the future of counseling.* Retrieved from http://www.counseling.org/knowledge-center/20-20-a-vision-for-the-future-of-counseling

American Dance Therapy Association. (n.d.). *About dance/movement therapy.* Retrieved from http://www.adta.org/About_DMT

American Music Therapy Association. (2006). *Definition and quotes about music therapy.* Retrieved from http://www.musictherapy.org/about/quotes/

Baas, M., De Dreu, C. K. W., & Nijstad, B. A. (2008). A meta-analysis of 25 years of mood-creativity research: Hedonic tone, activation, or regulatory focus? *Psychological Bulletin, 134,* 779–806. doi:10.1037/a0012815

Baker, T. B., & McFall, R. M. (2014). The promise of science-based training and application in psychological clinical science. *Psychotherapy, 51,* 482–486. doi:10.1037/a0036563

Boehm, K., Cramer, H., Staroszynski, T., & Ostermann, T. (2014). Arts therapies for anxiety, depression, and quality of life in breast cancer patients: A systematic review and meta-analysis. *Evidence-Based Complementary and Alternative Medicine, 2014,* 1–9. doi:10.1155/2014/103297

Bogart, G. C. (2009). *Dreamwork and self-healing: Unfolding the symbols of the unconscious.* London, England: Karnac Books.

Bratton, S. C., Ray, D., Rhine, T., & Jones, L. (2005). The efficacy of play therapy with children: A meta-analytic review of treatment outcomes. *Professional Psychology: Research and Practice, 36*(4), 376–390. doi:10.1037/0735-7028.36.4.376

Breaux, W. (2011). Integrative approaches: Expressive arts, narrative, and symbolism. In D. Capuzzi & D. R. Gross (Eds.), *Counseling and psychotherapy: Theories and interventions* (5th ed., pp. 357–377). Alexandria, VA: American Counseling Association.

Byron, K., Khazanchi, S., & Nazarian, D. (2010). The relationship between stressors and creativity: A meta-analysis examining competing theoretical models. *Journal of Applied Psychology, 95*(1), 201–212. doi:10.1037/a0017868

Chandramouleeswaran, S., & Russell, P. S. S. (2014). Complementary psychosocial interventions in child and adolescent psychiatry: Pet assisted therapy. *Indian Journal of Psychological Medicine, 36*(1), 4–8. doi:10.4103/0253-7176.127240

Comstock, D. L., Hammer, T. R., Strentzsch, J., Cannon, K., Parsons, J., & Salazar, G., II. (2008). Relational-cultural theory: A framework for bridging relational, multicultural, and social justice competencies. *Journal of Counseling & Development, 86,* 279–287. doi:10.1002/j.1556-6678.2008.tb00510.x

Davis, M. A. (2009). Understanding the relationship between mood and creativity: A meta-analysis. *Organizational Behavior and Human Decision Processes, 108*(1), 25–38. doi:10.1016/j.obhdp.2008.04.001

de Jesus, S. N., Rus, C. L., Lens, W., & Imaginário, S. (2013). Intrinsic motivation and creativity related to product: A meta-analysis of the studies published between 1990–2010. *Creativity Research Journal, 25*(1), 80–84. doi:10.1080/10400419.2013.752235

Denis, P., & Makiwane, N. (2003). Stories of love, pain, and courage: AIDS orphans and memory boxes. *Oral History, 31*(2), 66–74.

Duffey, T. (2005a). A musical chronology and the emerging life song. *Journal of Creativity in Mental Health, 1,* 141–147. doi:10.1300/J456v01n01_09

Duffey, T. (2005b). *Creative interventions in grief and loss therapy: When the music stops, a dream dies.* New York, NY: Haworth Press.

Duffey, T. (2006). Creativity, counseling, and mental health practice. Paradigm, 11(4), 7–8.

Duffey, T. (2014, September). *On being creative.* Keynote address presented at the Association for Research and Assessment in Counseling, Quad Cities, IL.

Duffey, T., Carns, M., Carns, A., & Garcia, J. (1998). The lifestyle of the middle-class Mexican American female. *Journal of Individual Psychology, 54,* 399–406.

Duffey, T., & Haberstroh, S. (2012). Developmental relational counseling: A model for self-understanding in relation to others. *Journal of Creativity in Mental Health, 7,* 263–271. doi:10.1080/15401383.2012.711709

Duffey, T. L., & Haberstroh, S. (2013). Deepening empathy with men using a musical chronology and the emerging life song. *Journal of Counseling & Development, 91,* 442–450. doi:10.1002/j.1556-6676.2013.00116.x

Duffey, T., & Haberstroh, S. (2014). Developmental relational counseling: Applications for counseling men. *Journal of Counseling & Development, 92,* 104–113. doi:10.1002/j.1556-6676.2014.00136.x

Duffey, T., Haberstroh, S., & Trepal, H. (2009). A grounded theory of relational competencies and creativity in counseling: Beginning the dialogue. *Journal of Creativity in Mental Health, 4,* 89–112. doi:10.1080/15401380902951911

Duffey, T., & Kerl-McClain, S. (2008). History of the Association for Creativity in Counseling: The evolution of a conference, division, and journal. *Journal of Creativity in Mental Health,* 2(3), 61–70. doi:10.1300/J456v02n03_06

Duffey, T., & Somody, C. (2011). The role of relational-cultural theory in mental health counseling. *Journal of Mental Health Counseling, 33*(3), 223–244.

Duncan, B. L., Miller, S. D., Wampold, B. E., & Hubble, M. A. (2010). *The heart and soul of change: Delivering what works in therapy.* Washington, DC: American Psychological Association. doi:10.1037/12075-000

Eaton, L. G., Doherty, K. L., & Widrick, R. M. (2007). A review of research and methods used to establish art therapy as an effective treatment method for traumatized children. *The Arts in Psychotherapy, 34*(3), 256–262. doi:10.1016/j.aip.2007.03.001

Gladding, S. (1992). *Counseling as an art: The creative arts in counseling.* Alexandria, VA: American Association for Counseling and Development.

Gladding, S. T. (2011). *The creative arts in counseling* (4th ed.). Alexandria, VA: American Counseling Association.

Gladding, S. T. (2016). *The creative arts in counseling* (5th ed.). Alexandria, VA: American Counseling Association.

Gold, C. (2004). The use of effect sizes in music therapy research. *Music Therapy Perspectives, 22*(2), 91–95. doi:10.1093/mtp/22.2.91

Gregory, R. J., Canning, S. S., Lee, T. W., & Wise, J. C. (2004). Cognitive bibliotherapy for depression: A meta-analysis. *Professional Psychology: Research and Practice, 35*(3), 275–280. doi:10.1037/0735-7028.35.3.275

Imhoff, B., Vance, K., & Quackenbush, A. (2012). *Helping bereaved children: 20 activities for processing grief.* Retrieved from http://iassw.org/documents/2015Conference/Session%2046%20Harden%20page%203.pdf

Jordan, J. V. (2010). *Relational-cultural therapy.* Washington, DC: American Psychological Association.

Kaplan, D. M., Tarvydas, V. M., & Gladding, S. T. (2014). 20/20: A vision for the future of counseling: The new consensus definition of counseling. *Journal of Counseling & Development, 92,* 366–372. doi:10.1002/j.1556-6676.2014.00164.x

Kerl-McClain, S. B., Duffey, T., Haberstroh, S., & Trepal, H. (2013, March). *Report from the Task Force for Ethics in Creativity in Counseling.* Presentation at the American Counseling Association convention, Cincinnati, OH.

Kiepe, M. S., Stöckigt, B., & Keil, T. (2012). Effects of dance therapy and ballroom dances on physical and mental illnesses: A systematic review. *The Arts in Psychotherapy, 39,* 404–411. doi:10.1016/j.aip.2012.06.001

Koch, S., Kunz, T., Lykou, S., & Cruz, R. (2014). Effects of dance movement therapy and dance on health-related psychological outcomes: A meta-analysis. *The Arts in Psychotherapy, 41*(1), 46–64. doi:10.1016/j.aip.2013.10.004

Kottman, T. (2011). *Play therapy: Basics and beyond* (2nd ed.). Alexandria, VA: American Counseling Association.

Laska, K., Gurman, A., & Wampold, B. (2014). Expanding the lens of evidence-based practice in psychotherapy: A common factors perspective. *Psychotherapy, 51,* 467–481. doi:10.1037/a0034332

Leblanc, M., & Ritchie, M. (2001). A meta-analysis of play therapy outcomes. *Counseling Psychology Quarterly, 14*(2), 149–163. doi:10.1080/09515070110059142

Lin, Y., & Bratton, S. C. (2015). A meta-analytic review of child-centered play therapy approaches. *Journal of Counseling & Development, 93,* 45–58. doi:10.1002/j.1556-6676.2015.00180.x

Lowe, G. (2006). Health-related effects of creative and expressive writing. *Health Education, 106*(1), 60–70. doi:10.1108/09654280610637201

Ma, H. (2009). The effect size of variables associated with creativity: A meta-analysis. *Creativity Research Journal, 21*(1), 30–42. doi:10.1080/10400410802633400

Mala, A., Karkou, V., & Meekums, B. (2012). Dance/movement therapy (D/MT) for depression: A scoping review. *The Arts in Psychotherapy, 39*(4), 287–295.

Maratos, A. S., Gold, C., Wang, X., & Crawford, M. J. (2008). Music therapy for depression. *The Cochrane Database of Systematic Reviews, 2008*(1), CD00451. doi:10.1002/14651858.CD004517.pub2

Maujean, A., Pepping, C. A., & Kendall, E. (2014). A systematic review of randomized controlled studies of art therapy. *Art Therapy, 31*(1), 37–44. doi:10.1080/07421656.2014.873696

Metzl, E. S. (2008). Systematic analysis of art therapy research published in art therapy: Journal of AATA between 1987 and 2004. *The Arts in Psychotherapy, 35*(1), 60–73. doi:10.1016/j.aip.2007.09.003

Miller, J. B. (1986). *Toward a new psychology of women.* Boston, MA: Beacon Press.

Mössler, K., Chen, X., Heldal, T. O., & Gold, C. (2011). Music therapy for people with schizophrenia and schizophrenia-like disorders. *The Cochrane Database of Systematic Reviews, 2011*(12), CD004025. doi:10.1002/14651858.CD004025.pub3

Nickel, A. K., Hillecke, T., Argstatter, H., & Bolay, H. V. (2005). Outcome research in music therapy: A step on the long road to an evidence-based treatment. *Annals of the New York Academy of Sciences, 1060*(1), 283–293. doi:10.1196/annals.1360.021

Pennebaker, J. W. (2004). *Writing to heal: A guided journal for recovering from trauma and emotional upheaval*. Oakland, CA: New Harbinger.

Pennebaker, J. W., & Evans, J. F. (2014). *Expressive writing: Words that heal.* Enumclaw, WA: Idyll Arbor.

Pratt, R. R. (2004). Art, dance, and music therapy. *Physical Medicine & Rehabilitation Clinics of North America, 15,* 827–841. doi:10.1016/j.pmr.2004.03.004

Ray, D. C., Armstrong, S. A., Balkin, R. S., & Jayne, K. M. (2015). Child-centered play therapy in the schools: Review and meta-analysis. *Psychology in the Schools, 52*(2), 107–123. doi:10.1002/pits.21798

Ritter, M., & Low, K. G. (1996). Effects of dance/movement therapy: A meta-analysis. *The Arts in Psychotherapy, 23*(3), 249–260. doi:10.1016/0197-4556(96)00027-5

Rossiter, C. (2012). Issues in creative arts therapy research: An interview with Lynn Kapitan, Ph.D., ATR-BC. *Journal of Poetry Therapy, 25*(1), 55–59. doi:10.1080/08893675.2012.654951

Rubin, J. A. (2001). *Approaches to art therapy: Theory and technique.* Philadelphia, PA: Brunner-Routledge.

Runco, M. A. (2004). Creativity. *Annual Review of Psychology, 55,* 657–687. doi:10.1146/annurev.psych.55.090902.1415

Schaefer, C. E. (2003). *Play therapy with adults.* Hoboken, NJ: Wiley.

Scott, G., Leritz, L. E., & Mumford, M. D. (2004). The effectiveness of creativity training: A quantitative review. *Creativity Research Journal, 16*(4), 361–388. doi:10.1080/10400410409534549

Slayton, S. C., D'Archer, J., & Kaplan, F. (2010). Outcome studies on the efficacy of art therapy: A review of findings. *Art Therapy, 27*(3), 108–118. doi:10.1080/07421656.2010.10129660

Whipple, J. (2004). Music in intervention for children and adolescents with autism: A meta-analysis. *Journal of Music Therapy, 41*(2), 90–106. doi:10.1093/jmt/41.2.90

Name Index

C

D

I

J

K

L

S

Y

Z

Subject Index

Figures and tables are indicated by f and t following page numbers.

A

B

C

D

G

H

K

L

M

N

O

P

Q

R

S

T

U

V

W

Y